readings in psychology today

readings in psychology today

CRM BOOKS
Del Mar, California

foreword

What is psychology? As a subject, it is more discussed than the war in Viet Nam (but as little understood). As a word, psychology is bandied about from the pulpit to the pub (and still not understood). In some circles, psychology is thought to be as good as motherhood; in others it is as black as sin itself. Surely this is the time for a clear appraisal.

First and foremost, psychology is a science. It may not always look like one—the complexities of experimental variables produce tailored conclusions; fuzzy thinking and fuzzy research produce fuzzy conclusions—but it is still a science. Psychology tries to achieve order and predictability within the world of objects. Just because the objects are animate instead of inanimate does not change the nature of the quest.

Physicists ask what happens to energy when the atom is split, and psychologists ask what happens to behavior when the brain is split. In both cases, answers are found by the application of logic and by the manipulation of relevant quantities; in short, by common scientific sense. In all good science, the techniques are basically the same, and the outcome is the growth of a technology in which the criteria for acceptance are: "Does it work? Is it universal? Is it truly descriptive?" Some questions are noticeably absent: "Is it good? What should be done with it? What is its purpose?" These questions are best answered by philosophers, theologians, political scientists, and statesmen.

In the physical sciences, distinctions between scientific questions and humanitarian, political, and philosophical questions are clearly recognizable. When physicists unleash the energies of fission and fusion, they unleash tremendous potential for good and bad, construction and destruction. Surely, it is claimed, psychology can and should tell us how to use these forces for good and constructive purposes. After all, isn't psychology the study of human thought and human action? The answer is "yes" and that very fact causes the confusion.

Psychology is a science—it is bound by the restrictions of science. Psychology can uncover how thoughts, emotions, and experiences develop; it can uncover the relationship between the behaving organism and the biological organism; and it can create a technology which provides effective means for conditioning and controlling man's behavior. In short, psychology can make clear the causal relationships between thought and deed, between act and consequence. Psychology cannot answer the question *why* nor the question *what to do*. It simply describes a behaving world and suggests ways to change it.

Of what real value, then, is psychology if it doesn't answer the basic questions of humanity?

Its value is tremendous. Psychology can supply the means to an end. It can tell us the most effective means for doing what we want to do; it can tell us what is possible. In order to reach the highest form of human thought and decision-making, facts are needed about nature —and human nature. Prudence and wisdom are not founded on ignorance.

contents

I. introduction

Sight and sound. The Electric Circus. The mantra of the Maharishi. The message of Marshall McLuhan. The Beatles. The beat. This is the turned-on, tuned-in, audio-visual world of today's youth.

This is the generation that goes to the movies to find out whether to read the book.

This is the generation which must be sold on the excitement of a new thing before trying it out.

This is the generation responding to the new. The multiple screen. Stereophonic sound. A changing perception of time. Of realism. Watch a bullet in flight on film. See a flower grow from a seedling in a second. See on satellite-sent TV the death of a man in Vietnam the day he is shot.

And we're trying to compete with all this in education by selling the same old textbooks to our students. We're trying to educate this generation as though there were two worlds. One the swinging '60s. And one the floundering '40s.

Education is not where the action is. Advertising, movies, TV, magazines—the modern media have responded to the Now.

God knows, the content of our education programs, our textbooks, our approach, all are bad enough. But the easiest thing to repair is form. It doesn't take too much creativity to change form.

The technology is here. The ability. The capacity.

Technology isn't the begin-all and end-all. Inventing books didn't solve basic problems. Inventing fire didn't solve basic problems (except warmth). Yet technology is important. And it must be used wisely and fast as we compete in a swift world with our message. Education. With our educational material woefully lacking, students are not held. They are not talked to in their own language. In their own medium.

Our textbooks are about as innovative as the green blackboard. No glare. No glaring success. It costs most college students at least $3,000 a year to go to school, and they spend a very small amount of that on textbooks. Put $2 more into the physical appearance of every textbook, and turn the students on. Larger page size, more white space, lots of color, exciting use of graphics, margins designed to be written in so the book becomes personalized. The idea of possessing a book is to make it part of one's self. To do something with it. To interact with it.

Where are we now? Back about 20 years ago. Take a look at one of today's largest selling psychology textbooks. Liver-colored and black. Ladies in megaskirts. Passé experiments.

How do we study the brain? With black and white pictures of various cross sections. Three-dimensional brain models in which anatomical and functional units can be illuminated should be in our classrooms, *not* in our museums of science and industry, and at World Fairs.

We have the technology to build models so large and so well that a student can take a journey through the blood circulation system. It would be fun. We can build models so life-like that a student can travel as a cell travels. Feel his way around the labyrinth that is the brain. Put him into that world, and he won't want to drop out.

Take a novel and translate it into a movie. What a class assignment. Andy Warhol—with meaning—on economical, erasable, reusable video tape. Come and join another dimension. Tolstoy was bound by linear word sequence. Move around between the lines. Then compare your film with the drama that last semester's Literature 41B produced. Wild!

Make mathematics come alive. And move. We still start out solving problems about pecks and bushels and 8¢ a gallon for gas, and graduate to translating an algebraic equation into a geometric function. Right now, there are computerized electronic screens on which a student can draw out a mathematical function with a special pencil. The computer will then punch out an equation for the form: $Y = 2X + 7$. That has to be a straight line. Square the X in the equation and you get a parabola. Animated mathematics. Throw out the tambourine.

Put students into history with simulation studies. What happened 600 years ago? What would the results have been given another set of circumstances, different leadership? Would the world have shaken apart? Or shaken down? Why not real playable board games to put students through the Napoleonic wars? Monopoly taught another generation what money was all about.

And does it cost too much to design classrooms so the learning environment comes alive and breathes excitement? Angles and curves in math rooms. Some imaginative use of color.

Content is first and foremost. But repairing that is a real education process—educating the teachers, the publishers, the educators. But form. Why that's easy. That's technology. We're good at that. Except in our schools. Just think, in the past 20 years almost every public school has switched over to the green blackboard.

Psychoanalysis. Say the word.
Ask for a name, and the most
usual response—after one
names his own analyst—is Freud.
And then? Names like Jung,
Adler, Sullivan, Horney, and
Fromm come quickly to mind.
The genius and insights of
Sigmund Freud into the
nature of man have been

FROMM

By JEROME BRAMS

recognized many times over
and remain without parallel.
His contributions in advancing
an understanding into the
unconscious forces that he
viewed as the wellspring
for all human motivation
are the cornerstone on
which all later psychoanalytic
theories are based.

Since the 1940's, Erich Fromm has become more and more prominent on the lists of those with major influence in psychoanalysis, perhaps because his basic theme and penetrating study correspond closely to the mid-twentieth century *Zeitgeist:* the alienated man. The theme is an existential one, and though Fromm himself would not approve being labeled as an existential psychoanalyst, his descriptions of man's dilemma and modes of relating to the world have been borrowed and used by many who do describe themselves in this fashion.

Although also frequently classified as one leading proponent of the neo-Freudian school—along with Horney, Sullivan, and Kardiner—Fromm objects to this label as well, for he sees his work as an attempt to broaden the base of Freud's discoveries, not to change them, and as an effort to interpret them in terms of contemporary philosophical and sociological concepts.

Fromm is better described as the outstanding advocate of a humanistic approach in psychoanalysis and currently is writing a systematic presentation of his views.

When asked to compare the views of Freud and Fromm, many people see only a contrast between biological and cultural determinism. Freud is labeled a biological determinist, one who sees the motivated behavior of man as springing from his innate biological equipment, while Fromm is referred to as a cultural determinist, one who views man's motivation as determined by cultural influences.

Such an easy differentiation does both men an injustice. It ignores those areas in which there is more implied agreement than disagreement. Freud did not deny the importance of cultural influence on behavior, especially as a shaping and controlling agent over the aggressive and sexual instinctual drives which he saw as the two primary sources of human motivation. Nor has Fromm, more especially in his later writings, neglected the importance of constitutional factors in motivation and in the strength and intensity of the characteristic ways by which one orients himself to the world.

However, Freud's observations on the unconscious motivating forces behind man's behavior lend themselves to a more pessimistic view of what it means to be human than Fromm's views do. (The orthodox Freudian psychoanalyst would sooner describe this as *realistic* than as *pessimistic.*) Freud saw man

as driven by an unconscious pleasure principle to seek the reduction of tensions that emanate from the two basic instinctual drives, sexuality and aggression, which he classified more broadly as life instincts and death instincts. In his view, society is constructed on the renunciation of direct and immediate instinctual gratification, which results in inner conflict and neurotic behavior. Thus, the more repression demanded by society, the greater the incidence of neuroses among the populace. The motivational strength of these irrational instinctual forces, the development of inner controls against their breakthrough into conscious awareness, and the understanding of their role in the development of personality and neurosis are constant themes in Freud's work.

The idea of such motives as self-actualization, a will to meaning, and tran-

scendence of the human condition—concepts that today find expression in the more humanistic and existential views of man—are not to be found in the writings of Freud. He was exceptionally impatient with such philosophical speculation. Freud saw all values, morality, love of any kind, art, justice, religion, indeed all that is part of the structure of civilization, as coming from the two basic drives. Yet in spite of his pessimism about the relative strength of man's rational and irrational qualities, Freud still held out the possibility that at some distant time, reason would play a more significant role in man's behavior.

Fromm does not disagree with Freud on the strength of unconscious irrational

passions that can drive man to the brink of catastrophe, but he emphasizes the presence of human needs that spring from the existential conditions of man. He insists that man carries within himself potentialities for growth and for productiveness. Given the proper conditions in a culture and society, Fromm is optimistic in his conviction that the human forces of reason and love will prevail. It is when Fromm views what the cultural influences have been and continue to be on man's human potentialities that a pessimistic tone appears.

He sees man as caught on the horns of a specifically human dilemma. On the one hand, man is an animal like all other animals in nature. On the other, he is a reasoning, self-aware, and imaginative creature. These latter characteristics preclude an automatic instinctive accommodation to nature that is available to other animals. The result is a feeling of disunity with nature, of loneliness and separateness. As Fromm sees it, man strives to escape these feelings by finding some other kind of unity with the world. He can do so in productive ways by developing his human capacities for reason and love to the fullest, or in regressive and nonproductive ways that lead to a constricted and neurotic relatedness both to the world and to himself.

In addition, Fromm sees in man the development of characteristic ways in which he acquires or assimilates what he needs from the world. Fromm has stressed in particular the influence of the economic and political structure of society on the development of these orientations, but he does not emphasize this aspect to the exclusion of constitutional and temperamental determinants.

He describes a number of nonproductive orientations (or character types), all of which he attempts to relate historically to the economic social structure prevalent at the time these character types first appeared.

The influence of our contemporary Western economic system is seen in what Fromm describes as the *marketing character.* This person experiences himself as a product to be marketed and shaped to bring about the greatest rewards. He views himself as an object to be manipulated, a commodity to be transformed to the demands of the marketplace. In the construction of this kind of nonrelatedness to the world, he loses any sense of his true self and is left with feelings of futility and emptiness.

Then there is the *receptive character,* who is basically passive and dependent upon being given things from the world outside. There is the *exploitative character*, who also sees everything that is good and nurturant as existing outside himself, but who uses force, manipulation, and guile instead of dependence to gain his ends. The *hoarding character* has little trust in the outside world and thus entrenches himself in what he considers a safe position by hoarding and saving—not only material items but such intangibles as love.

In his more recent writings, Fromm has introduced another nonproductive orientation, which he calls "necrophilous" (which he contrasts to "biophilia," the love of life). The *necrophilous* orientation is the most pathological of those he has described, for here there is a love of death, decay, and destruction. It is in the description of this orientation that Fromm seems to emphasize the presence of a significant constitutional component. Fromm points to the relationship between this conception and Freud's view of a death instinct.

Except for the marketing orientation, Fromm's descriptions of character are very similar to portions of those presented by Freud many years earlier. The receptive character is very much like Freud's description of the oral-passive type; the exploitative character is similar to Freud's oral-aggressive type; the hoarding character like Freud's anal-retentive type; and the necrophilous character is very similar to Freud's anal-sadistic type.

The difference between Freud and Fromm in their view of character types is, therefore, not so much on the basis of the clinical descriptions, but in how each views the causes for the development of a specific type. Freud sees character as coming primarily from fixations that result from traumatic experiences—deprivation or even over-gratification—at various stages in the development of the sexual instinct. Thus, if such occurrences are experienced at the first oral stage of psychosexual development, then a fixation could result in an oral-passive character. At the later anal stage, then, an anal character would be the outcome. Fromm, on the other hand, emphasizes sociocultural factors in the determination of character.

Neither Freud nor Fromm neglects a description of the ideal adult character. Fromm labels this the productive character, and Freud's term is the genital character. Although referring primarily to the same traits, Fromm describes more richly a productively active, reasoning

individual who relates truly to himself and to others and who is capable of realizing his human potentialities. Freud's emphasis is on heterosexual adjustment in the adult.

Both Freud and Fromm have pointed to the long dependency of the child on his mother and the role such dependency plays in his development, but they differ as to the important aspects of such dependency. Freud singled out the Oedipus complex as a momentous event in the life of the child, especially the male. The child desires to possess his mother sexually, but he fears his father's revenge (castration) for harboring such wishes. As a result of this complex, the child's sexual development is interrupted and remains latent from about the sixth to the twelfth year. Then, assuming the normal psychosexual development, hormonal changes accompanying puberty

reawaken his sexuality and lead to an adult heterosexual orientation. The importance of the mother as the original love object of the child is stressed.

Fromm's emphasis goes beyond the sexual one. He stresses the importance of the burgeoning opportunities for growth and independence that the child encounters. If the threat of leaving behind the all-protective love of the mother is great and the child's experiences are constricting, then his development is stunted in that he regresses to a symbiotic-like dependency on the mother. Unless there is a push to greater independence, such a regressive orientation can result in an emotionally crippled adult who is not free and who

remains dependent on any mother-like figure for nurturance. This dependence can be on authorities or on symbols of authority, such as "God" or "country." Fromm sees the child's sexual desire to possess the mother as a positive rather than a regressive sign, for in the wish is a sign of separateness from the mother and an attempt to assert one's independence and self-sufficiency.

Freud and Fromm differ in their conceptions of love. For Freud, all love stems from the sexual drive. He sees the love for friend, for parents, and for ideals as an inhibited expression of the basically sexual aim of love. Furthermore, he sees a basic incompatibility between love of others and love of oneself. He described a situation in which the individual possesses a limited fund of energy for love. The more narcissistic and self-loving the person, the less love remains for objects outside oneself.

Fromm does not make this distinction between self and object in considering the capacity to love. He sees love as an expression of care and respect which cannot be divided between outside objects and oneself. In other words, we are incapable of loving others without also loving ourselves. Fromm's view of love is tied less narrowly to a sexual aim. He proposes a number of different kinds of love, only one of which has an erotic base. The capacity to love, he says, is as important in man as the capacity to reason, and only in the realization of these capacities does man become truly human.

It is now commonplace to refer to the current era as the "age of anxiety," and it is only a short step from a discussion of love to one on anxiety. Freud's theory of anxiety went through two stages. Initially, he saw anxiety as a transformation of sexual energy that is blocked in its aim of direct discharge. He later changed this view and explained anxiety as a warning signal of a potentially threatening situation. Such threat could come from the external environment—in which case it corresponds to what we call fear—or it could emanate from unconscious internal sources, such as the potential breakthrough of repressed material into consciousness.

Fromm's approach to anxiety is related to his view of man's separateness and aloneness. Each step away from the security of a regressive and dependent relationship is accompanied by anxiety.

How does a person learn to think and what is the nature of consciousness? The concept of the unconscious was known by philosophers and writers long before Freud, but it was he who gave us a systematic rendering of its contents and workings. In his distinction between conscious and unconscious, he described two types of thought processes: primary process thought, found in the unconscious; and secondary process thought, a function of consciousness. He has described primary process thought as unconscious, illogical, symbolic, and as present from infancy. The only reality for this primary thought process is the inner, unconscious one. Psychotic thought, dream thought, and the symbolic thought of the artist are all examples of primary process thought. On the other hand secondary process thought is logical and coherent and attuned to outer reality. It develops from the necessity of dealing with the outside world in order to attain need satisfaction.

Fromm has not yet detailed his conceptions of various thought processes, but he has emphasized cultural influences in his view of a social filter that both acts upon the development of the capacity to think and distorts the content of thought to fit the values of the culture. In his view, the productive person is a critical thinker who can transcend the limiting effects of socially determined thought. Fromm also is reluctant to equate an artistic thought process with a psychotic one.

Some of the more orthodox Freudian theorists also have been reluctant here, and one, Ernst Kris, proposed the view that although artistic thought is of a regressive, primary process type, it nevertheless can be viewed as serving the individual in a creative and reality-oriented manner.

Freud's emphasis on understanding the dream relates to its latent content—the true meaning of the dream, not to its manifest content—the dream as related by the dreamer. The latent dream content is distorted by various primary process mechanisms in its transmission from the unconscious to the dreamer's awareness. Freud saw the interpretation of dreams as the most direct access to the contents of the unconscious. When the latent dream content finally emerges via the analytic process, it is seen to be an attempted fulfillment of some repressed wish relating to the formative stages of personality development.

Fromm also emphasizes the importance of understanding the unconscious through the dream, but his attention is directed more narrowly to the manifest dream content. For him, this content communicates an unconscious message in symbolic language, and the understanding of this language makes the message clear. In addition, he does not view all dreams as based on repressed childhood wishes.

Both men agree on the presence of universal symbols of dreams, but while Fromm might interpret such a symbol directly to the patient, Freud would have been hesitant to do so. Freud pointed to the necessity for the dreamer to associate to each portion of his manifest dream—no matter how inconsequential—in order to arrive at its latent content. Fromm does not neglect the importance of such associations, especially for those parts of the dream containing accidental symbols—in which meaning is found only in relationship to the dreamer's personal life experiences.

Psychoanalysis refers to a psychology of personality, to a research tool for the investigation of human behavior, and, finally, to a psychotherapeutic method. The term is most usually used in this latter sense. (One oftentimes finds surprise among people who are being analyzed when they are faced with the fact that there exist other approaches to psychotherapy besides the analytic one.) The preceding sections have been concerned with some of the psychological, rather than psychotherapeutic, views of Freud and Fromm. In going on to describe their respective approaches in therapy, we are limited by the fact that as yet Fromm has said little publicly on this topic.

Freud indicated several goals for the person under psychoanalysis, and each of these is based on different ways of viewing the personality system, but he was not optimistic about their attainment. Most broadly stated, the primary goal in psychoanalysis is to help the patient resolve the unconscious conflicts relating to his early childhood experiences which, as Freud viewed it, are the most significant causes for the adult neurosis. To accomplish this, it is necessary to bring into consciousness as much unconscious material as possible. Freud also saw psychoanalysis as a method whereby the energy in the various structural systems of the personality is balanced so that the reasoning, reality-oriented faculties are enhanced. He was quite aware of the dangers of an interminable analysis and warned about this.

Fromm's primary goal for his patient can be put into his more general humanistic perspective: to help the person realize to the fullest degree possible his human and individual potentialities for productive relatedness to the world, for self-awareness, for reason, and for love. For Fromm, as it was for Freud, the curative effect is based on bringing into awareness the unconscious forces that have molded and continue to direct the patient's behavior. (It is for this reason that Fromm considers himself a follower of Freud, and not the founder of a different "school" of psychoanalysis.)

The major difference between Freud and Fromm here lies only in what is considered to be the main area of repression. In the earlier phase of Freud's theory, repression was found to operate primarily in the area of sexual instincts; in the later phase, he emphasized the importance of repressed aggression. Fromm does not give a central role to the repression of sexual desires and believes the repression of various types of aggressiveness to be more important. But, going far beyond that, he believes that anxiety, aloneness, alienation, and narcissism are among the most significant areas of repression.

It should be added that for Fromm the main problem is the person's total response to the question of human existence which each one has to answer by the very fact of having been born. The answer is not essentially one of ideas but one of character: everyone wants to make some sense out of his life, in fact, to "make the best of it." But there are better and worse forms of responding to the problems of existence. The better ones increase energy and vitality and make for a person's sense of unity. The worse ones create anxiety, insecurity, submission, and sadism, and cause suffering. Symptoms are signs of the contradiction between optimal or ideal character structures and the particular form of character that a person has adopted, under the influence of constitution, early upbringing, social structure, and accidental experiences. Fromm holds that awareness of one's inner reality is a crucial factor in change, together with the effort to practice a different kind of life.

What are the characteristics of the patient most likely to benefit from psychoanalysis? Freud believes that there must be good capacity for reality-contact in the prospective patient, especially in those areas in which his neurosis should not limit his perceptions. Thus he does not see psychoanalysis as the treatment of choice for a psychotic disorder. Both Freud and Fromm see traumatic experiences in the patient's past life as a good sign. Without such indications there is greater likelihood that constitutional factors are operating in the development of the neurosis, and such factors are not greatly amenable to change through psychoanalytic treatment.

Fromm also has pointed to the need for what he terms a "vitality" in the prospective patient. He sees this as indicating an energy oriented toward growth and life, love of life as opposed to a hate of or indifference to life. He means more than simply a high-energy level, for he points out that destructive people also can be viewed as possessing a great amount of energy. Finally, Fromm and Freud—as well as analysts of all persuasions—are interested in gauging the underlying seriousness and intensity of the patient's motivation for analysis. Without such strong motivation, there is little hope that the patient will stay on to work through anxieties as they emerge in his analysis.

Both Freud and Fromm have emphasized the importance of understanding the patient's childhood history, but Fromm does not appear to dwell as long on this stage of the patient's life in the analysis as do those who follow the more orthodox Freudian approach. The past is used to help in the understanding of the patient's present behavior and as an aid in uncovering the unconscious resistances to the analysis. Freudians might object that this is their emphasis as well. But in practice, too often their approach leads to a minute and overly intellectualized investigation of childhood experiences, particularly those relating to psychosexual development.

Freud emphasizes a continual focus on the patient's conscious and unconscious resistances to the aims of the analysis. The analysis must become an integral, ongoing part of the patient's life, and the orthodox Freudian analyst generally sees his patient in no less than one hourly session each day, five days a week. To attempt an analysis on a less-frequent basis is seen as only complicating the problems of dealing with the patient's resistance. Depending upon the defenses and repressions of a particular patient, an orthodox analysis can continue for five or six years or even longer.

Fromm's view on the frequency of visits corresponds with those who generally are considered to be neo-Freudian: a successful analysis is possible in as few as three sessions—for some patients, even two sessions—each week. What matters for Fromm is not the number of hours but the aliveness or intensity of each session and the kind and degree of the patient's resistance. However, like Freud, Fromm has expressed doubts as to how many people really can be analyzed "successfully." Since the patient is seen less frequently, Fromm's approach emphasizes—as does that of Harry Stack Sullivan—the active participation of the analyst in the therapeutic process.

Free association is the tool on which Freud bases his approach to treatment. The patient is instructed to say everything that comes into his mind without withholding, judging, or distorting the content. A second tool in the orthodox Freudian approach is the use of the transference relationship to gain an understanding of the patient's unconscious processes. Freud describes transference as a process in which the patient projects onto the analyst a complex of conscious and unconscious feelings that existed for significant figures—usually his parents—in his past life. Freud found that the best condition for the development of transference and for free association was to have the patient lie on a couch while the analyst sat in a chair behind him. In this arrangement, the analyst's presence interferes less with the free associations of the patient and enhances the development of the transference.

The approach suggested by Fromm—and by most neo-Freudians—is to have the patient sit in a chair while the analyst sits across from him. This face-to-face confrontation is maintained throughout the analysis and enables the analyst to attend directly to nonverbal cues such as body movements, which are seen as important aids in understanding the patient's unconscious. Fromm does not believe that this arrangement interferes with the development of a transference relationship. He points out that important elements of transference emerge even before the patient sees the analyst, for, in his fantasies about what kind of person the analyst will be, the patient already has begun to project transference elements.

Besides transference, Fromm also emphasizes another aspect of the relationship between therapist and patient: the reality factor of two separate individuals reacting to each other. He stresses that the analyst should not disregard this aspect of the relationship. In other words, he does not agree that every feeling of the patient for his analyst necessarily is based on transference. Fromm, too, wants the patient to express his uncensored thoughts and feelings. But he is concerned that free association should not deteriorate into "free chatter," and he interrupts the patient when this happens. He also actively suggests the patient associate to problems Fromm considers relevant, based on the analysis. Fromm believes it is important to tell the patient what unconscious trends he detects; then the focus is turned to an analysis of the patient's response. Fromm is much more active than the Freudian analyst, not in the sense of offering the patient advice about the "right" way of acting, but in his insistence on the production of unconscious material and on the analysis of resistance.

The Freudian approach, especially early in the analysis, is to remain silent, allowing the patient uninterrupted reign with free association. The analyst neither comments nor interprets. He does not respond to complaints that he is doing nothing, saying nothing, being of little help. It is only at a later stage that the analyst becomes more active in making interpretations based on his observations of the patient's transference, associations, and dreams.

In Fromm's view, the patient-therapist interaction is the primary tool that furthers the work of analysis. He emphasizes the urgency that the patient must feel about his manner of relatedness to the world if there is any possibility for productive change. He sees the analyst as a sensitive and trained instrument who uses his full self—both reasoning and affective—in the analytic interaction. As Fromm sees it, for the analyst to sit back making unverbalized theoretical constructions to himself about the nature of the patient's problems without a continual active participation in the analysis leads only to an intellectualized and nonproductive experience that can drag on for years. Freudians criticize this active involvement from the very beginning of the analysis as an almost naive approach to an understanding of the nature and forms of unconscious resistance. Indeed, some liken this approach to an exhortation that can have no real effect on unconscious material.

Finally, we can say that Freud's theories were presented in a highly systematized and rigorous manner, whereas Fromm's writings exhibit a less exacting and less exhaustive presentation. Some account for this by saying that Freud was primarily the psychologist, while Fromm is more the social philosopher. But because of his broad social views, Fromm's concepts are of interest not only to psychoanalysts, but to people of many persuasions in the social sciences and in the humanities. Whether Fromm's views can equal the rigorous nature of those found in Freud awaits his more formal systematized presentation of humanistic psychoanalysis. ◗

PERSONALITY: Public or Private

By Floyd L. Ruch

AT A TIME WHEN EVEN THE OLIVE in a man's martini may be bugged, invasion of privacy is indeed a crucial issue. The era of the miniature microphone, the test that tells all, and the electronic eye that sees too much brings with it the threat of Big Brother watching for his chance to snip away at the tenuous threads of freedom. And so we react.

Thus the legal pendulum is about to swing so hard that it may well strike down real advances which behavioral scientists have made toward putting the right people in the right jobs. Hot headlines shape extreme action, and Congress now is considering Senate Bill 1035, which would bar the use of both personality and polygraph tests in selecting government employees, except for

PERSONALITY TEST

comfortable to put on a stunt at a party even
e doing the same sort of things.

make talk when I meet new people.

er.

ke swearing.

er than when alone.

rgument to convince most people of the

one would tell a lie to keep out of troub

ling hurts me terribly.

d woman.

11

those in the FBI, the CIA, and the National Security Administration. Naturally, government contractors with an eye to their economic future would follow governmental hiring procedures, so this bill would reach far beyond the ranks of federal employees.

Obviously the personality test, which is aimed at predicting future performance and action, is not even related to the lie-detector test, which records fact, is exceedingly difficult to administer scientifically, and carries with it tremendous legal implications. They should not be considered together.

Why are they being considered in the same bill? What has led the American people and Congress to so fearful a view of personality testing? In part, it is a reaction against science. Medical research has developed truth serums and behavior-controlling drugs; advancing technology has brought infrared photography, the one-way mirror, the miniaturized tape recorder, the polygraph, and the directional microphone—plus the giant computer, with its almost limitless capacity for data storage and retrieval. These are appallingly efficient instruments to obtain information the individual might prefer to keep to himself.

Even in the use of the microphone and tape recorder, where the devices are tangible and the information obtained is clear-cut, there has been confusion and controversy about what constitutes an invasion of privacy. How much more fiercely the battle rages around something so intangible as personality tests, the results of which must be interpreted rather than quoted! The furor invades the nation's newspapers, and columnist George Dixon has remarked of the tests, "The questions are the kind you would ask the girl next door—if you wanted her to move."

Personality testing has been under fire for a decade, but the use of psychological testing in employee selection nonetheless has increased at a rapid pace. A recent study conducted among personnel directors indicated that psychological tests of all kinds showed a steady increase within a five-year period. [*See illustrations, this page*.]

Don't Say I'm Unsociable

When they apply for jobs, people willingly admit that they are poor spellers or inaccurate typists, but they do resent tests which may "accuse" them of being unsociable, and applicants who accept tests of skill and aptitude very often resent answering questions about their attitudes and feelings. Yet the introvert who feels it is his own business that he doesn't much enjoy the company of others is far less likely to enjoy his work and to succeed in a sales job than is the man who genuinely likes the aggressive role in social contacts.

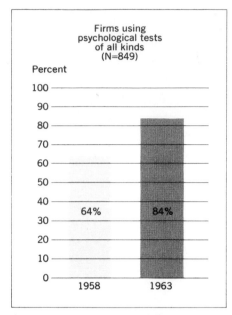

Growth in use of personality tests for employment selection, 1958-1963.

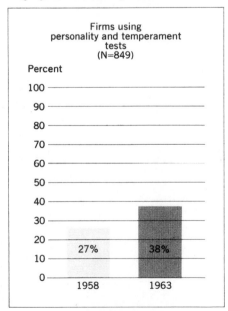

To what lengths should a company go in evaluating the personality qualifications of applicants without violating privacy? Are such tests really a threat? Let us look at what they are all about.

Applicants may deliberately lie to get a job, but lies are no defense for the applicant who feels that a test invades his privacy. Actually, the extent and quality of lying, as revealed by ingenious "lie detector" scales built into many tests,

itself is often an indication of the individual's fitness for a given job. This concept of *sensible deception* is an elaboration of the fact that everyone must engage in a certain amount of concealment and polite white lies to smooth social relations. Simulation in personality tests shows whether a person is sensibly realistic, overly candid (and hence naive), or so clumsy that he portrays himself as perfect.

Our study of the widely used, highly investigated, and well-respected Minnesota Multiphasic Personality Inventory (MMPI), which has a built-in correction for faking, shows that faked scores actually may have greater value in predicting success, particularly of salesmen, than those which have been corrected for faking.

The MMPI was given to 182 sales representatives from nine companies, ranging from beverage sales to business forms. Within each sample, the subjects were divided into an upper- and a lower-criterion group, based upon sales managers' ratings. The five MMPI scales which are normally corrected for faking differentiated significantly between the two groups when *not* corrected. The use of the corrective factor, the K scale, *decreased* validity. Persons who score high on the K scale are highly poised and easily hide feelings of social insecurity under a smooth facade—a characteristic of good salesmen. These results indicate that making acceptable scores on a test of this kind is in part a matter of learning how to answer in the way that impresses the employer most favorably.

Other studies using firemen, nurses, Air Force officers, and dental students have shown that frank instructions to answer questions as the subjects think they should be answered for job qualification produces answers which predict success more reliably than those obtained with the standard instructions to tell the truth. Certainly scores obtained in this way are a test of social skills, not an invasion of privacy!

The testing-privacy issue has festered for years, and it finally achieved front-page importance in 1965 when Congress conducted hearings on whether the use of psychological tests in the selection of government employees constituted an invasion of privacy. Many members of both houses felt that tests should not inquire about sex practices or religious beliefs. Psychological testing in depth was regarded by Congressmen as tantamount to peering into an employee's bedroom window. Rep. Cornelius Gallagher (D), N.J., charged: "...the Federal Government has been...searching the minds of Federal employees and job applicants through personality testing."

Personality testing is a natural for humorists. Columnist Art Hoppe once cited five MMPI test questions: (1) "I love my mother"; (2) "I am contented with my sex life"; (3) "Flirting is often a lot of fun"; (4) "I feel very guilty about my sins"; and (5) "I like westerns on television." Hoppe explained that a bright job applicant knows the psychologist thinks he should love his mother, have a satisfactory sex life, be unrepressed enough to flirt, and never feel "very" guilty. "A popular transvestite who had learned to live with his Oedipus complex would be contented, flirtatious, and free of guilt about loving his mother," he wrote. "But he would be unlikely to enjoy Westerns on television." Hoppe added: "...but I shudder to think of this country run by a bunch of transvestites with Oedipus complexes who happen to like Westerns on television. Honest though they may be."

Psychologists, who maintain that psychological testing helps a democratic society function effectively by discovering and evaluating scientifically the true potentialities of its citizens, have defended testing in and out of Congress. Good testing, the professionals argue, minimizes the factor of human error in the judgment of individuals and provides objective standards of comparison.

In the hearings, the experts emphasized the need for certain precautions in the use of tests to prevent their abuse. Psychologists presented to the Senate Committee two basic conditions essential to useful and legal psychological testing in employee selection. First, valid testing must be supervised by a psychologist who is qualified to administer and to interpret the particular test being used. (A specialist in the use of tests in the area of vocational counseling or clinical psychodiagnosis is not automatically an expert in the personnel field.) Second, the test data must constitute only a *part* of the information used in hiring. When these conditions are met, psychological tests can be of value in identifying those in any occupational group who have a great potential for success.

The American Psychological Association maintained that psychological instruments should not be used carelessly or unjustly against human privacy, and that psychologists are not competent to make a final judgment on the legality of a given personnel procedure. Arthur Brayfield, the APA spokesman, stated: "The right of a person to be fairly judged in employment is surely a basic right. The right of the Federal Government to know a reasonable amount about employees or prospective employees is surely also an important matter, and ultimately is crucial to maintaining our democratic existence."

APA recommendations for proper psychological testing in Government assessment procedures include: assurance that all non-research testing which is not directly under the Civil Service Commission be placed under the direction of qualified psychologists; the right to review and appeal, upon request of an individual, those personnel decisions in which test data play an important part; creation of an advisory panel of non-government psychologists to review all agency evaluation procedures; and establishment of a National Academy of Sciences-National Research Council consulting group to survey and evaluate current assessment procedures and to make recommendations for the future. (The American Psychiatric Association presented similar recommendations.)

Other testimony, however, was less favorable to personality testing. Dr. Karl Menninger disapproved of paper-and-pencil tests. Rorschach ink-blot tests are more effective, he said.

Among the heads of Federal Agencies using personality and temperament tests, there was a disagreement about their value. John W. Macy, Jr., Chairman of the Civil Service Commission, insisted that personality tests then being given were practically useless in employee selection. (The University of California's Mason Haire long has insisted that even under the best of conditions testing for routine jobs will result in only a 4 per cent improvement over random selection, while testing for executive jobs can be improved by 15 per cent.)

Sargent Shriver, then the Peace Corps director, was enthusiastic about the value of personality testing. Based on previous experience with similar programs, a 50 per cent dropout rate for psychological reasons had been predicted for the Peace Corps. Instead, only 8 per cent of Peace Corps members dropped out for psychological reasons during a four-and-a-half year period and of these, only .7 per cent left for psychiatric or neurotic reasons, Shriver said.

Shriver was borne out by Dr. Abraham Carp, of Air Force Aeronautical Systems personnel laboratory, who said MMPI effectively aided in weeding out applicants with actual or potential personality disorders. He defended the charged invasion of the applicant's religious and sex life on grounds that responses to particular items are not used; evaluation of personality traits is based on aggregate scores on MMPI scales. Moreover, all MMPI test answers and other personality test data are destroyed at the end of the training period. The MMPI, with certain modifications, is still used by the Peace Corps.

The hearings settled nothing, but they did air an important issue. No widespread misuse of the MMPI or any other test was discovered, nor was any major injustice revealed. However, the hearings were more than a tempest in a teapot, because they touched on such broad principles. Although some misconceptions about testing may have been fostered, a clear case for the selective value of psychological tests in Government employment was also presented.

Then, a year-and-a-half ago, the Johnson administration asked Government contractors to use personality tests in hiring only to the extent of Civil Service Commission use. This rocked supporters of psychological testing in employment, and I am one of them, because the Commission uses testing solely in connection with medical evaluation, or for professional clinical diagnosis and counseling.

A Test Catalogue

Private industry recognizes the nature of the right of privacy and safeguards it when tests are used as a part of the selection process. An outstanding example is Sears, Roebuck, and Company, which has an extensive testing program including personality testing.

V. J. Bentz, Director of Psychological Research and Services at Sears, has outlined the company's ground rules for obtaining the necessary information for hiring without violating individual privacy. It involves the concept of mutual commitment. The corporation seeks to find out as much as possible about an applicant's job fitness. And the applicant in turn seeks a job where his unique abilities and attributes can be used to best advantage.

In any test, relevance should be another key concept, Bentz says, and tests should remain pertinent to the position sought. In a recent survey on family birth-control techniques, over 90 per cent of a large sample of housewives readily divulged the most intimate details of their birth-control practices. However, when asked about family income, a large percentage of the women refused to answer. The question was not relevant. It *was* an unwarranted invasion of their privacy. Personality variables may be irrelevant to performance on an assembly line, and such testing be unwarranted; but these variables are crucial in high-level executive positions.

The Bentz testing program at Sears also includes a depth concept. Inventories or questionnaires which ask straightforward questions may provide generalized behavior descriptions. They may show that a job applicant prefers working alone to working with others and thus would do better as a bookkeeper or a draftsman than in sales. That makes sense, but to try to determine by projective techniques *why* the person is so unsocial would be an unjustified invasion of privacy. Certainly a man's sex life, for instance, is his own business, except where sexual aberrations could leave him wide-open to business blackmail.

The use of projective techniques involves an element of deception and interferes with mutual trust, Bentz's fourth dimension. This includes informed consent on the part of the applicant and rules out any intent to deceive, either on his part or on the part of the company. "Thus," said Bentz, summarizing the Sears program, "the corporation and the applicant make a search toward mutually desirable ends—to wed job requirements to an individual who (by virtue of his skills, abilities, aptitudes, and characteristics) can perform effectively in that position."

Outgrowth of Confusion

In general, it appears that much of the disagreement about the invasion of privacy is an outgrowth of confusion—either confusion about what constitutes privacy or confusion about what constitutes psychological testing, or both. We all agree that protection from unwarranted invasion of privacy is essential in our society. The questions are: What exactly is privacy? How can it best be protected?

If privacy is defined to include every area bearing on job success, then personality tests clearly invade privacy. So do all other methods of investigation, and the employer should make a decision based on the bare facts of work history. Clearly, efficient business operation demands more than that. However, tests which delve into matters unrelated to job success are unnecessary and should by all means be prohibited.

Another source of confusion about the nature of testing arises from failure to distinguish between individual *test questions* and *summarized test findings,* which are reported to employers by reputable consulting firms. In ethical companies with ethical staff psychologists

or reputable consulting firms, employers are not told specific answers of job applicants. Thus an employer never would know how an employee answered the question: "Do you like to attend parties once a week or oftener?" But from this and a number of similar questions dealing with social activities, the psychologist obtains a composite picture that enables him to rate the applicant on sociability. This general sociability level, relevant to success on the job where meeting the public is essential, is passed on to the employer.

It is also important to avoid confusion between the two types of personality tests. One test is the objectively scored *self-inventory* in which the person answers questions about his own behavior and conscious feelings, these answers being subject to the person's own "Fifth Amendment." In fact, the bright person taking such a test well may modify his answers to make what he thinks is a good impression through *sensible deception.* In contrast are the subjectively scored *projective techniques* which allegedly reveal the applicant's unconscious psychodynamics. The well-known Rorschach test is the best example of this second type.

We have found that summary scores from various self-inventory tests are job-related and reliable for use in employee selection. Their use is defensible in that it works for the common good of the employer and the applicant. It reduces the chance of the employer hiring a person who will prove incompetent on the job and at the same time protects the applicant from accepting a job on which he is likely to fail.

Not The Rorschach

The use of the Rorschach is quite a different matter. There *is* no published evidence that its findings are in any way job-related, and therefore there is no practical justification for its use in predicting success on the job. If the claim could be proven that the Rorschach penetrates the person's conscious defenses to tap the lower layers of the unconscious, this would be an unwarranted invasion of privacy because it is accomplished by denying him his right *not* to incriminate himself, as well as because the findings through this method are not job-related.

When the nature of privacy and the nature of testing are clearly understood, many points of controversy are automatically resolved. Moreover, psychologists themselves *do* exert controls over testing, Government users of tests *do* safeguard individual rights, and private employers

do attempt to preserve the right to privacy as they seek essential information for selection or promotion. Unless these trends should be reversed—and this is exceedingly unlikely, especially in view of the wide publicity the issue has received—it appears that psychological testing, far from constituting a threat to privacy, increasingly will provide a means for the individual, through the controlled sharing of information unique to himself, to find the best avenues for realizing his potential.

But Do People Like Tests?

Where employees have been widely exposed to testing of all kinds, reactions have been favorable. A recent study elicited the attitude of employees toward specific personality-test items. Only two employees of the manufacturing company polled declined to take the test. The 77 males and 75 females who participated were identified only by age, education, and sex.

Two of the most unpopular questions were: "Do you cry rather easily?" and "Do odors of perspiration disgust you?" but the item which aroused the greatest opposition was: "Do you feel strongly against kissing a friend of your own sex and age?" Females under 25 years of age were most offended by the items, males over 25 least offended. A majority of the large group studied said that less than one per cent of 361 test questions were personally offensive. Some 30 per cent of those polled found no annoying questions at all.

Tests, used properly and legally, help match people to their jobs on a more objective basis than is otherwise possible. But even under ideal conditions of self-regulation, there will be exceptional cases in which it will be necessary to weigh dispassionately and objectively the degree of invasion of privacy against the good to the individual and the organization resulting from this invasion.

I firmly believe the merits of questionable cases should be decided through judicial process, rather than through hasty and emotional legislative action. In an issue so complex that even psychologists and psychiatrists are unable to agree, the leisurely and scholarly approach of the courts is more likely to strike an equitable balance than is a vote cast during an emotional upheaval. The proposed legislation would label personality testing officially as a bad device, and thus would set back the real progress which has been made in this field. Why toss away one of society's useful modern tools?

Carl Wagner (White); MacHack VI (Black). **1.** P-KN3, P-K4; **2.** N-KB3, P-K5; **3.** N-Q4, B-B4; **4.** N-N3, B-N3; **5.** B-N2, N-KB3; **6.** P-QB4, P-Q3; **7.** N-B3, B-K3; **8.** P-Q3, PxP; **9.** BxP, QN-Q2; **10.** PxP, R-QN1; **11.** B-N2, O-O; **12.** O-O, B-KN5; **13.** Q-B2, R-K1; **14.** P-Q4, P-B4; **15.** B-K3, PxP; **16.** NxP, N-K4; **17.** P-KR3, B-Q2; **18.** P-N3, B-QB4; **19.** QR-Q1, Q-B1; **20.** K-R2, N-N3; **21.** B-N5, R-K4; **22.** BxN, PxB; **23.** N-K4, P-B4; **24.** N-B6ch, K-N2; **25.** NxB, QxN; **26.** N-B6, QR-K1; **27.** NxR, RxN; **28.** Q-B3, P-B3; **29.** R-Q3, R-K7; **30.** R-Q2, RxR; **31.** QxR, N-K4; **32.** R-Q1, Q-QB2; **33.** B-Q5, K-N3; **34.** P-QN4, B-N3; **35.** Q-B2, N-B3; **36.** B-K6, N-Q5; **37.** RxN, BxR; **38.** QxPch, K-N2; **39.** Q-N4ch, K-R3; **40.** QxB, Q-K2; **41.** Q-R4ch, K-N3; **42.** B-B5ch, K-N2; **43.** QxPch, K-B1; **44.** Q-R8ch, K-B2; **45.** Q-R8, Q-QB2; **46.** Q-Q5ch, K-N2; **47.** K-N2, Q-K2; **48.** P-KR4, K-R3; **49.** P-N4, K-N2; **50.** P-R5, Q-K7; **51.** P-R6ch, K-B1; **52.** P-R7, QxBPch; **53.** KxQ, K-K2; **54.** P-R8(Q), P-R3; **55.** Q-K6 mate.

Chess game played by computer (MacHack VI).

PSYCHOLOGY ACROSS THE CHESSBOARD

By Eliot Hearst

A FEW MONTHS AGO there was an unexpected entrant in an open chess tourney in Boston. This participant, MacHack by name, proved to be something of an inconvenience for the rest of the competitors because he had to be wheeled into the tournament room, couldn't speak a word of English, and was physically unable to move his pieces across the chessboard. MacHack made up for these eccentricities, however, by his exemplary behavior under the tense conditions of tournament play: He never gobbled hamburgers or chewed gum while his opponent was trying to concentrate, never blew smoke in his opponent's face, and never upset the table when he lost—forms of behavior which any seasoned chess competitor has learned to expect from some of his foes.

MacHack just didn't behave like a human being and of course he wasn't. He was a PDP-6 computer programmed to play chess by students and staff members of the Massachusetts Institute of Technology. His score in this, his first tourney, was one draw and four losses and currently he has one of the lowest rankings of the 8000 rated members of the United States Chess Federation. MacHack's failure could be chalked up to inexperience, and maybe a better prospect for chess stardom is the computer at Stanford University that is currently playing a match with its counterpart at the Moscow Institute of Theoretical and Experimental Physics. More significant than the actual performance of chessplaying computers, however, is the enthusiam of a group of scientists who are willing to invest the time, money, and energy required to develop a computer program that presumably can do only one thing: play chess.

Chessplaying Machines, Real and Fake

MacHack, the computer that plays chess, is by no means the first of its breed. Nevertheless, "he" is one of the few machines in chess history that does not rely on a pint-sized human chessmaster concealed deep within its inner workings. The story of von Kempelen's Automaton Chessplayer, first exhibited at the court of Austria's Empress Maria Theresa in 1770, is a long and fascinating one about which scores of books and exposés have been written (including an inaccurate one by Edgar Allen Poe in 1836). Baron Wolfgang von Kempelen's automaton was displayed in Europe and America for more than 80 years, until its untimely death in a fire in Philadelphia in 1854.

Von Kempelen, who was Maria Theresa's counselor on physics and mechanics, apparently delighted in being the court magician as well as a scientific advisor. In fact, he was probably better qualified for the former activity. His chess playing machine was a mysterious-looking cabinet with a chessboard imbedded in its top surface. The wooden figure of a Turk with a flowing moustache sat facing the board, with a turban on his head and a long pipe in his left hand. Von Kempelen always exposed the inside of the cabinet before he began a demonstration and audiences were quite satisfied that no one could be concealed inside.

The Turk very rarely lost, except on purpose as in one game with the Emperor Napoleon whose play has been characterized by one chess historian as "beneath criticism." As the years passed, von Kempelen's secret gradually leaked out. An ingeniously-designed system of irrelevant wheels, levers, and cylinders—along with the exhibitor's ability to mislead his audience—had deceived even the skeptics at the Turk's seances. There was a man inside, of course—chessmaster Johann Allgaier for part of this automaton's career—who manipulated the Turk's arm by means of a pantograph system to make his own moves and was informed of his opponent's moves by a clever device utilizing magnets beneath each of the squares on the chessboard.

Caissiacs and MANIACS

Even though von Kempelen's machine would easily defeat any computer-player of today, this does not mean that psychologists and cyberneticists of 1967 are spending their time searching for an extremely clever way of concealing Grandmaster Bobby Fischer inside an IBM 704. They are challenged by the idea of imitating human thought and believe that they will learn a great deal about human heuristic devices (searching methods in solving problems) by attempting to built computer analogues. Newell, Shaw, and Simon, pioneers in this field, wrote in 1958: "If one could devise a successful chess machine, one would seem to have penetrated to the core of human intellectual endeavor." Herbert Simon was at one time so optimistic about these possibilities that he predicted a digital computer would be world champion within 10 years, "unless the rules bar it from competition." Ex-world champion Mikhail Botvinnik, a Russian grandmaster, wrote that eventually the World Chess Federation will have to hold two world championships, one for humans and one for machines.

Adriaan de Groot, who did his doctoral dissertation in psychology more than 20 years ago on "Thought of the Chessplayer," is much more pessimistic than Simon or Botvinnik about the likelihood that a computer can equal a human chessmaster. Personally, I think he is right in being somewhat negative about the possibilities. Perhaps the following sketch of the history and problems in this area will reveal why.

In 1950 Claude Shannon first proposed the idea of an electronic computer that could play chess. He actually built a machine—aptly called Caissiac, after the goddess of chess, Caissa—which was a whiz at simple endgames and could force the easy checkmate with king and rook against king at least as efficiently as most human chess experts. Shannon was one of the first to point out that even though it is theoretically possible for an electronic brain to play a perfect game by analyzing every variation to completion, such a task would be far beyond the practical power of any conceivable electronic computer. As John Pfeiffer says in *The Thinking Machine*, a computer which analyzed all first moves to their legal ending in a win, loss, or draw and was capable of examining a thousand billion billion variations a second would still take more than 10^{91} years to calculate its first move—which is appreciably longer than the age of the universe. And most of this time would be wasted examining trivial possibilities that any human chessplayer would discard immediately.

Therefore, no machine can actually be expected to play perfect chess. Botvinnik, an electrical engineer by profession, also stated that computers will "fail so long as we try to create a machine that makes no errors; however, I think we can solve the problem if we try to make the machine 'in our image'."

Thus the basic goal of most programs has been to develop a machine that can compete on a level with the average chess player. In order to do this, the work of the machine in calculating variations must be cut down through the use of rules or criteria, by means of which moves can be evaluated.

For example, a computer named MANIAC I was programmed by a group at Los Alamos to play chess on a board of 36 squares (the standard chessboard has 64 squares) with a smaller than usual number of pieces. MANIAC relied mainly on two criteria: mobility or "freedom of movement," and material advantage. Taking about 12 minutes per move, MANIAC displayed an unexpected weakness in its first game: It had a "mortal fear of checks" and would sacrifice almost anything to avoid being checked. Chessplayers among *Psychology Today's* readers will know that "check" (attack on the king) is in itself hardly anything to worry about. After some of its initial shortcomings were rectified, MANIAC was at least able to beat very weak human players, novices who had played no more than 20 games of chess.

Criteria for Selection of Moves

The most crucial problem in chess programming involves the selection of specific rules for determining the number of different variations to be examined, not only in depth (number of moves ahead to be seen) but also in breadth (number of possibilities to be examined on a given move). To solve this problem programmers generally try to isolate the specific goals for which a human chessplayer aims. When a chess expert decides exactly what he is after, the initially frightening array of possibilities shrinks to only two or three lines of action. "In order to break through against his king, I will have to move up all my king-side pawns quickly," a master might decide and then consider only the two or three ways of attaining this objective. A machine that worked on the same principles would be a good model to strive for.

It would be so simple to overcome these obstacles if world champion Tigran Petrosian or American champion Bobby Fischer could tell us the five or six specific criteria they use in choosing their moves. Unfortunately, the reasons for the choice of a particular move are often obscure even to the grandmaster who made the move. "It looked good!" or "That had to be the right move!" are comments you often hear from masters who are questioned as to why they selected some unexpected or subtle move. Petrosian says he knows when he is not in his best playing form: when he distrusts the one line of play that suggests itself on intuitive grounds. Because steps in the reasoning process are hard to verbalize, the procedure of questioning a master in detail very seldom isolates the really important factors in his decision on a specific move.

This problem brings to mind a story that William James related in his classic *Principles of Psychology*, about an old jurist who advised a newly-appointed judge never to reveal the reasons for his decisions. "Your decisions will probably be right," said the veteran, "but your reasons will surely be wrong." This may be true, too, about many chess decisions and, if so, a master's revelations may not be very helpful. Most of all, we need to find out what a master does when he "intuits." Apparently he takes so many factors into account, and weighs them all so quickly, that he leaves a present-day computer far behind.

Computer programmers try to do the best they can under these circumstances. Researchers at Carnegie Institute of Technology and the Rand Corporation usually specify several *simultaneous* goals in their chess programs. A number of standard subgoals, such as control of the central squares, material balance, and king safety are used for generating, selecting, and determining properties of moves and for evaluating outcomes of variations. For example, pieces are more effectively posted in the center than on the wings, rooks are worth more than knights or bishops. Another type of program involves the specification of *successive* goals in which a series of questions are asked in decreasing order of importance by the computer: Can I checkmate him? Can he checkmate me? Can I win his queen for my rook? Can I threaten and force the win of one of his weak pawns? Can I occupy an undefended square in his camp?

The Computer As an Achiever and Thinker

Two standards can be applied for deciding whether a chess program is a satisfactory imitation of human thought processes. One of these is based on the program's *achievement;* can it play as well as a human expert? The other is based on the *process* it uses to select its moves; does it think like an expert?

By the first criterion, chessmaster de Groot argues that results have been very disappointing. "Programs are still very poor chessplayers and I do not have much hope of substantial improvement in the near future." De Groot's comment was made in 1964 and MacHack's recent tournament showing would not require him to revise his opinion.

But on the other hand, MacHack did not make any glaring mistakes in his game [*see illustration page 15*]. Well-programmed computers may be much less likely than humans to make simple oversights. Machines don't suffer from impatience, fatigue, or momentary losses of attention. Since these factors are ordinarily involved in human problem solving, this could mean that a machine will inevitably "think" differently from a human chessplayer. It is interesting to speculate whether "fatigue" and "inattention" will have to be programmed into a computer if we intend to make the machine "imitate" man.

As far as other aspects of the computer's thought *process* are concerned, de Groot has studied many protocols of grandmasters and amateurs "thinking aloud" in an unfamiliar position, and

he feels that some of the logical steps followed by human beings actually are similar to processes employed by computer analogues. For example, when orienting himself in an unfamiliar situation the human player usually evaluates the material situation (which side has more valuable pieces?), examines his opponent's threats, and then looks for his own possibilities of direct action. Many programs initiate the same pattern of investigation.

De Groot concluded from his study that differences in playing strength depend much less on calculating power than on "skill in problem conception." Grandmasters seem to be superior to masters in isolating the most significant features of a position, rather than in the total number of moves that they consider. Somewhat surprisingly, de Groot found that grandmasters do not examine more possibilities on a single move than lower-ranked experts or masters (an average of two to four first moves per position) nor do they look further ahead (usually a maximum of six to seven moves ahead for each). The grandmaster is somehow able to "see" the core of the problem immediately, whereas the expert or lesser player finds it with difficulty, or misses it completely, even though he analyzes as many alternatives and looks as many moves ahead as the grandmaster.

Progressive Deepening

All of de Groot's human protocols displayed a continuous re-evaluation of ideas and specific moves in a given position. Such *progressive deepening*, which de Groot considers very important in the economy and power of chess thinking, is definitely something that computers have not achieved yet. When a human being analyzes in this manner, he often reinvestigates the same moves again and again. A move that was rejected or put

aside previously, because it did not fit the specific goals or plans that the player was focusing on at the moment, is reanalyzed—but this time more deeply and with a different goal or idea in mind. Such reinvestigations often occur during chess analysis in human chessplayers, but chessplaying computers operate on a much more primitive process. Usually a machine discards a move once it fails to meet some predetermined criteria, and does not return to it again.

This process of progressive deepening may be a feature of the research strategy of scientists and mathematicians, as well as chessplayers. Experimental psychologists, for example, often return to a specific laboratory finding that originally seemed unimportant, or re-examine some old hypothesis again and again—with an attempt to apply new ways of thinking each time. Novel ideas are not permanently discarded after their first (superficial) examination fails to bear fruit. As the material or hypothesis is re-examined, the scientist's understanding of its possibilities usually becomes keener.

Progressive deepening is not the result of indecisiveness or forgetfulness, but in reality may reflect a very efficient approach to problem-solving. De Groot recalls a *New Yorker* cartoon of a somewhat unawed lady who is saying to the builder of a large electronic brain: "Sure it can think, but can it change its mind?" This indecisive female may have put her finger on the weak spot in most current computer programs for chess!

With the application of some of the preceding ideas, and possibly with the advent of more chess machines that "learn from experience," we can expect to produce someday a computer which can play a reasonable game of chess. The step from "reasonable" player to grandmaster is a fairly big one, so we'll probably land astronauts on the Moon, Mars, and Venus before we come up with a computer that can beat Petrosian.

Chess and Psychology

What is it about chess that makes it such a fascinating study for psychoanalysts delving into the dynamics of a son's hostility toward his father? Why are some psychologists interested in the feats of chess prodigies who become masters before they are twelve? What, they ask, are the unique qualities, if any, which chessmasters possess that weaker players or nonplayers do not? Other psychologists ponder whether a chess star like Capablanca lasts longer than a Di Maggio. Why did a psychometrician like Alfred Binet investigate memory and visual imagery by using chess experts who play blindfolded? And why do some psychologists examine the thought processes of chessplayers in order to study how human beings solve complex problems? These are only some of the questions which have brought psychologists and chessplayers together for brief encounters over the last 80 years.

To a non-chessplayer, the powerful attraction of the game for its devotees is often incomprehensible. Call it an addiction, or as H. G. Wells once said, "one of the most unaccountable passions in the world." Chess is a game in which chance plays virtually no role. Frazier, the fictional founder of B. F. Skinner's utopian society, Walden Two, explained why only two games were stressed in that behavioristically-designed community: "We don't encourage competitive games, with the exception of tennis or chess where the exercise of skill is as important as the outcome of the game."

Both psychologists and novelists have quite naturally been intrigued by any activity which generates such devotion. Stefan Zweig, in his novel *The Royal Game*, paints a picture of an unintelligent clod, Czentovic, who becomes world champion. Vladimir Nabokov, in

The Defense, describes a very eccentric grandmaster who calculates a major move in his personal life in much the way he reasons out the sacrifice of a piece over the chessboard. Even if they do depict extreme cases, these novels permit non-chessplaying readers to enter the chess addict's world for a brief time.

Psychoanalyzing Chessplayers

Until the recent flurry of activity with chessplaying computers, much of the interest in chess shown by psychologists involved its psychiatric implications. Freud himself was the first psychoanalyst to mention the game when in 1913 he compared the learning of psychoanalytic technique with the steps required to master the elements of chess. It wasn't until 1925, however, that Alexander Herbstman, a well-known Russian chess problem composer as well as a doctor, spelled out the general theme that has since pervaded psychoanalytic opinion about chess: The King and Queen symbolize the "father" and "mother." Consequently, a game of chess serves as a symbolic re-enactment of the Oedipal Conflict, with father-murder as its unconscious goal. The Oedipal Conflict refers of course to the ancient Greek legend in which Oedipus kills his father and marries his mother. In psychoanalysis it usually epitomizes the son's hostility toward his father and love for his mother, which makes the son a rival of his father for the mother's bed.

Norman Reider has beautifully summarized the history and legends attached to this point of view in his article on "Chess, Oedipus, and the Mater Dolorosa." He adduces as evidence for the theme of father-murder a variety of myths surrounding the origin of chess. One, for example, attributes the invention of the game to the Grecian sage named Xerxes who sought to cure King Evil-Merodach of his madness. Evil-

Merodach (who incidentally is referred to very kindly in the Bible) had apparently turned insane after chopping up the body of his father Nebuchadnezzar into 300 pieces and throwing them to 300 vultures.

The Queen and the Rest of the Family

With the development of the rules of chess over many centuries, the power of the queen increased markedly. All chessplayers know that the goal of the game is to trap the king. The queen, however, is the most powerful piece on the board since she combines the moves of two other major pieces, the bishop and the rook. Ernest Jones, Freud's major biographer, noted: "It will not surprise the psychoanalyst when he learns that in attacking the father the most potent assistance is afforded by the mother. (=queen)."

Chess devotees often tease their wives by pointing out how much better men are at chess than women. No woman has ever reached grandmaster status. Only two, Vera Menchik (who was killed in England during World War II) and the current Russian woman world champion, Nona Gaprindashvili, have been able to provide consistently powerful opposition for male masters. Reider tentatively suggests that women's disinterest in chess is due to their lack of an unconscious desire to murder their fathers. Furthermore, the chief object of their hostility is not the father but the mother. Thus chess does not offer them any outlet for their matricidal impulses. (Parenthetically, I have never noticed that women players have any particular tendency to attack their opponent's queen.)

According to the psychoanalysts, it is not only the king and queen who serve as specific symbols in chess combat. Reuben Fine, a clinical psychologist

Test your memory for recalling chess positions. Look at the position below for five seconds and then try to reconstruct it. Grandmaster Max Euwe did it perfectly. Master chess players (left) make about one mistake; expert players (middle) and average players (right) make considerably more errors.

who is one of the few American grand-masters of chess, states that rooks, bishops, knights, and pawns frequently symbolize the penis; the bishop may literally refer to some person who molds our "conscience"; the knight may symbolize a horse, and pawns little boys.

Analysis of Famous Players

Paul Morphy was a chess prodigy from New Orleans, America's only acknowledged world champion (1858), a true gentleman (unlike many players of his and other eras), a pioneer in blindfold chess, and a victim of schizophrenia when he died at 47. In a famous article Ernest Jones analyzed Morphy's love of chess as based on an unconscious desire to overcome his father. He attributed great significance, insofar as Morphy's later illness was concerned, to the refusal of Howard Staunton of England to play him a match. Staunton was one of the strongest players in the world, but he was obviously afraid of being beaten by Morphy. While attacking the American and his abilities viciously in his chess column in the *Illustrated London News,* Staunton manufactured all kinds of excuses to avoid meeting him across the chessboard.

Jones theorized that because Morphy could not meet and defeat this authority figure ("father image"), according to Jones his unconscious desires were thwarted, precipitating his later psychosis. Besides being far-fetched, Jones' entire argument is somewhat fallacious because the acknowledged world champion at the time was Adolph Anderssen of Germany, whom Morphy did meet and overcome decisively. Why then should Morphy have been so disturbed by Staunton's refusal to face him across the chessboard?

Reuben Fine's own "Psychoanalytic Observations on Chess and Chessmasters" figuratively places many of the world's greatest masters on his psychoanalytic couch. Like other analysts, he finds that the grim motive of father-murder is pervasive in chess. All the world champions come under Fine's scrutiny. For example, Cuba's José R. Capablanca, the world champion from 1921-1927 and described as the Don Juan of the chess world, believed several times during his career that he could not possibly lose even a single game of chess. Says Fine: "The dreamland where one can never be beaten is a familiar one; it is the return to mother. In Capablanca the oral fixation was strong. It does not surprise us to learn that Capablanca was exceptionally fond

of cooking and that he had several favorite restaurants where he went to prepare his own meals."

As an experimental psychologist who takes a dim view of most psychoanalytic speculation, I can't resist pointing out that there are many chessmasters of my acquaintance who lack great self-confidence and yet who are also exceptionally fond of good cooking. And the most self-confident one I know is hardly a gourmet.

Precocity and Retirement

As in music or mathematics, chess talent may show itself very early in life. Capablanca learned to play at the age of four, while watching his father play a fellow soldier on duty at Morro Castle in Havana. The young Capa reports that he pointed out an illegal knight move his father had made, and then rubbed salt in the Oedipal wounds by beating his father in the very first game he ever played. By the time he was 12, in 1900, he was champion of Cuba. Not much further along in years was 14-year-old Bobby Fischer when he captured his first U.S. Championship in 1957. Fischer became the youngest grandmaster in chess history when the World Chess Federation conferred that title on him in 1958.

It is extremely rare for anyone to learn the game after 20 and become a master player; in fact, I know of no one who has done so. Most of the world's top players were all of master strength before they were legally old enough to marry or vote. Of course, there are strong social factors which may make age an irrelevant consideration. Once a man is old enough to have completed his education and has started to raise a family, he probably will not have the free time necessary for learning and mastering chess. Teenagers are the ones who most easily succumb to chess fever, and the psychoanalysts see significant implications in this fact.

Most grandmasters have scored their greatest victories between the ages of 25 and 40. In 1935 Stanford's Paul Buttenwieser performed a statistical analysis of 100 chessmasters and concluded that there was an improvement in skill from age 20 to 40, after which a plateau was reached extending through the forties. From 50 to 70 there was a steady, but not very large drop in performance. More recently Ernest Rubin concluded that after 40 the quality of tournament chess play decreases appreciably. However, Emanuel Lasker finished third in an international

tournament of grandmasters when he was 67 years old.

Part of the decline in a chessmaster's performance after he reaches 40 or 50 may be traceable to the physical strain involved in serious competition. The standard continuous session of play in top-flight tourneys is four or five hours, terribly hard on a competitor who is not in peak physical condition. As he grows older, a chess veteran is more and more likely to accept his opponent's offer of a draw, even when the oldster is certain that he has the better position. Thus he settles for a half point, instead of the full point that follows a win. Very often he is afraid to take the risks necessary to score the victory because he is worried about the possibility of an error in calculation due to his increasing susceptibility to fatigue.

Intelligence and Chess

Non-chessplayers regard the chess expert as a kind of super quiz-kid who is sure to be a success in any intellectual endeavor. There is no evidence from psychological studies or personal reports to substantiate this claim. An admittedly crude Russian study of the competitors in the 1925 Moscow international tourney failed to yield any support for the idea that chessplayers are more intelligent or have better visual memories than non-chessplayers of equal age and education. The chessplayers, however, did better than non-chessplayers in remembering and reconstructing chess positions, which seems reasonable enough.

De Groot, an experimental psychologist and former member of the Dutch Olympic Chess Team, has recently described some similar experiments with chessplayers of various strengths. In one of these, they were shown an unfamiliar chess position from an actual game for five seconds and then were asked to reconstruct it from memory. Differences in chess ranking showed dramatically. Try yourself out with the chess position taken from *Thought and Choice in Chess* [see illustration opposite page]. After five seconds of examination, ex-world champion Max Euwe reconstructed it perfectly and a lower-ranked master made only one small mistake, but experts and average players made all kinds of errors. Apparently the master perceives the setup in large units, such as pawn structure or cooperating pieces, and can even decide which side has the advantage. When he does make an error, it is often one of putting a piece on a very desirable square for that type of position.

However, we cannot draw strong conclusions about the general intellectual skills, if any, which combine to produce a great player. It is de Groot's opinion that masters would score highly in "spatial imagination" tests of non-verbal intelligence, but he does not believe that exceptionally high verbal intelligence is an indispensable requirement. (On the other hand, a blockhead like Czentovic, the hero of Zweig's *The Royal Game,* probably could not become world champion.) Actually I don't think a chessmaster would score any higher on an IQ test than a lesser player, or a nonplayer with comparable education and background.

Blindfold Chess

A blindfold exhibition is one chess event that invariably astounds both outsiders and chessplayers. In these exhibitions the master is not really blindfolded, but sits with his back to his opponents and announces his moves in the notational system invented by chessplayers to record their games and to transmit their moves in games by mail or radio. His opponents have regular chessboards and chess sets in front of them and play in the usual manner, but the master must rely completely on his memory of the positions. The play shifts successively from one board to the next and a referee tells the exhibitor only the number of the board and the opponent's new move.

Almost any master can play three or four games of blindfold chess simultaneously, but few are willing to endure the strain necessary to contest 10 or more. It should not seem particularly strange that most masters can play several games blindfolded since even a standard game requires much analysis "in one's head." Grandmaster Siegbert Tarrasch once said that the actual sight of the chess men often disturbed him in a tournament game.

Harry Nelson Pillsbury, an American champion who scored international triumphs in the 1890's, liked to "relax" by giving a blindfold display. He often played 12 games of chess and six games of checkers blindfolded while engaging in a game of duplicate whist with his friends at the same time. One onlooker recalled that "while conducting the card game with the precision of a fairly good player, he would keep the ever-changing chess and checker positions clearly in his mind's eye and call off his moves at each board with an accuracy and promptness that looked little short of miraculous. He could break off a

seance for an intermission and upon resumption readily call up the positions on every board at will. When requested, he would announce the moves in any particular game from the beginning." On the day after the exhibition, and often much later, Pillsbury would be able to replay every game perfectly from beginning to end.

Nowadays, 12 simultaneous games would be considered a relatively minor achievement in the annals of blindfold chess. World champion Alexander Alekhine played 32 simultaneously in Chicago in 1932; George Koltanowski (now of San Francisco) played 34 in Edinburgh in 1937; and Miguel Najdorf of Argentina, 45 in 1947—still the world's record. Incidentally, the opposition in blindfold exhibitions is generally not very good. Strong players would feel disgraced if they lost to a master operating under such a great handicap and they avoid blindfold exhibitions, often hinting that such stunts are beneath their dignity. Therefore, the exhibitor usually wins 80 to 90 percent of the games. His major problem certainly is keeping all the different positions clearly in mind, rather than finding good moves once the position is remembered accurately. Someone has calculated that 3600 different positions arose during the course of the evening in Najdorf's 45-board exhibition.

How Do Blindfold Players Do It?

Alfred Binet, the 19th century French pioneer in the field of mental testing, was the first psychologist to attempt an analysis of the apparently incredible memory feats of blindfold chessplayers. Binet concluded, not too surprisingly, that vast knowledge of the game, ability at visual imagery (but not perfectly detailed visualization), and a good memory were essential requirements for skill at blindfold chess. However, blindfold play has developed into a more specialized art during the past 75 years, and Binet's summary has been recently superseded by the detailed account of Reuben Fine, the psychologist-chess master. Fine has defeated players of master strength in blindfold exhibitions where he has only 10 seconds per move. (Normally there is no time limit on the blindfold player, and sometimes exhibitions of more than 20 boards last 15 to 20 hours.)

Any student of human learning and memory would be interested in the methods Fine uses to avoid confusion while playing blindfolded. Like Binet, he considers visualization very impor-

tant and states that he visualizes each position as it comes up. (On the other hand, there are players who claim they can play blindfolded without visualizing the board at all. Pillsbury himself once revealed that he did not see actual images of the chessboard in his mental vision; there were "no definite patterns of the game in his mind and it was, as far as he could say, a memorization of the moves as he went along in the games." The games would come up before him in an indistinct way and his moves would be made from a "sort of formless vision of the positions.") Strange positions are generally much easier for Fine to remember than familiar ones. Any opponent who tries to confuse him by choosing an unusual opening is likely to have this plan backfire badly. In familiar opening positions there is presumably considerable interference from alternative variations selected in prior games or in other blindfold games going on simultaneously with the same opening moves. Fine says that he does not feel completely comfortable until the standardized opening moves are over and a distinctive pattern of play unfolds. Blindfold players customarily try to minimize problems of confusion by employing different first moves for each one of a group of four or five opponents sitting next to each other, in order to create sufficient distinctiveness among neighboring games.

Past Associations and "Organization of the Position"

Most of Fine's introspective analysis of blindfold play focuses on the importance of past associative learning in facilitating his recall of the specific features of a certain position. For example, white's king usually ends up on King-Knight-One (KN1) after castling early in the game and so the position of the king need not be reviewed constantly after castling. Different squares have a host of different associations: a pawn on the first row is legally impossible and so pawns never are "seen" there; bishops end up on QB4 or KN2 much more often than KN8. Different pieces normally reach different squares; knights, queens, or rooks rarely stand on KN2, but a bishop there is very common. Relatively permanent features like pawn structures—the pattern of pawns that generally separate the powerful pieces of one army from the other—are extremely important in organizing a position. These pawn configurations signify where the major pieces are likely to be stationed and toward what points attacks are likely to be directed.

Another important requirement for blindfold chess is complete facility with the chess notational system. A chessmaster almost always thinks in terms of this "language" and uses it to describe games to his friends over the dinner table, on a walk in the park, and other places where no set is available. No one should attempt to play blindfolded until he is very familiar with the notation. For example, can chessplayers among the readers state immediately whether the square on which White's Queen's Knight initially stands (QN1) is a white square or a black square, how many squares there are on the diagonal KR1 to QR8, and how many squares a knight on KR4 can go to? When I try to give beginners some practice in playing blindfolded, I find exercises like these useful.

Because of the large number of prior associations which an experienced player has acquired, he does not visualize a chess position as a conglomeration of scattered squares and wooden pieces, but as an organized pattern (like the "Gestalt", or integrated configuration, emphasized by the Gestalt psychologists). Someone once said: "A good game of chess can be told as a series of inter-related facts." No position changes completely with a single move.

Photographs or Haze?

Adriaan de Groot also pursued the question of blindfold play in *Thought and Choice in Chess*. He was interested in Binet's finding that "concrete visualization" of the position is uncommon in blindfold players, contrary to Binet's original expectation that blindfold chess requires an ability to visualize a position in all its details, like a photograph or inner mirror. One of Binet's correspondents wrote: "I only know that it is a knight or a pawn without bothering about anything else". Squares on the board generally have no distinct color for the blindfold player, only vaguely defined boundaries, and all 64 squares are never visualized at once. Alekhine said he visualized the pieces as "lines of force": The bishop is not a piece with a prelate's headdress on it—it is a diagonal force; a rook does not look like the tower of a castle—it is a horizontal-vertical cross.

A later student of blindfold chess, Henri Bergson, also decided that detailed visualization was not important but rather some abstract general scheme (the "character" of the position), which

indicates the rules one must follow to reconstruct the position. The master might say to himself: "That game is an English opening in which I am attacking black's castled king on the open King Knight's file." Memory of the opening, the columns (files) which have no pawns on them, and the position of the opponent's king should enable him to reconstruct most of the details of the position. Bergson's basic idea has obvious implications for the programming of chess computers.

The negative feelings of the Russian chess community about blindfold chess add another dimension to this facet of the game. In Russia, where chess grandmasters receive the acclaim that baseball stars receive in the USA, there is a strong rule against blindfold exhibitions. The opinion in the USSR (which leads the world in chess and has won every Chess Olympiade in which it has competed) is that the strain of blindfold chess may lead to mental breakdown. Russians will tell you that three of the greatest blindfold champions in history (Morphy, Pillsbury, and Zukertort) apparently died while suffering from a psychosis, although others have disputed this diagnosis. Soviet stars prefer to amass their triumphs over the chessboard and facing their opponents.

One final note on blindfold play, which may explain the inattention of certain chessplaying college students while their professors are lecturing. It is of course possible for both players to play blindfolded. In his college days chessmaster Neumann used to write his moves on scraps of paper and pass them back and forth to neighboring students. Sometimes five or six different games were going on during a particularly boring lecture.

Psychology Across the Chessboard

I would have liked to devote more space to outlining for chessplaying readers some of the tricks of the trade, the "gamesmanship" tactics frequently used in local chess competition. These may occur even in international master play, although there they are much more subtle and refined. Russian ex-world champion Mikhail Tal, besides being a brilliant combinational player with a temperament suited to risks and adventurous sacrifices, is well known for his extracurricular strategy. Tal is famous for concentrating so intensely that he has been accused of hypnotizing opponents into surrender. Imagine facing a fierce stare, in addition to a grandmaster's standard arsenal of weapons, over the

chessboard! Pal Benko, the Hungarian-American grandmaster, typically wears sunglasses whenever he has to play Tal, to minimize the effects of Tal's evil eye.

Chessplayers will twiddle, quiver, shake, tap, whistle, and cluck while their opponents are trying to think and insist it is "unconscious" if their opponent complains. Some players believe that the more loudly they bang a chess piece down, the stronger the move. This resembles T. E. Lawrence's report that Arabs were inordinately afraid of cannons: "They thought the weapons destructive in proportion to their noise."

But these somewhat juvenile tricks do not succeed very well against the experienced master; purely verbal methods are generally more effective. Like telling your self-assured opponent as you start play: "I see you weren't invited to that big international tournament in Paris." Or perhaps later in the evening, "How come your wife hasn't been in the tournament room for the last two hours?"

Psychological combat takes place almost every time a wooden piece is shifted from one square to another. Top-flight chess is as much psychological battle as technical ability. To diagnose your opponent's weaknesses—an over-adventurous style, a dislike for assuming the defensive, overconfidence in certain types of positions, impatience in the endgame, rigidity in choice of openings—requires a psychological as well as chessic analysis. Even back in Binet's time, he spoke of the ardor and fierceness of La Bourdonnais' play, the blind impetuosity of Cochrane, the finesse of von der Lasa. Today's masters, too, have chess personalities which may or may not correspond to their personalities away from the chessboard. The relationship between the two is still another neglected area for research.

More and more in contemporary tournaments, you must play your opponent as well as the board. The grandmaster who prepares for a tourney by merely studying a few openings and practicing a few endgames is hardly likely to score a brilliant victory. The Russians are particularly aware of this facet of the game. Their analyses of each other's strengths and weaknesses often read like the reports of a psychiatrist.

Chess thus provides a playground for the psychologist as well as for the grandmaster. The psychologist, hoping to win new knowledge about human learning, motivation, and thinking, is playing the same kind of deep game as the grandmaster. ♇

By Bert F. Green, Jr.

THE COMPUTER CONQUEST OF

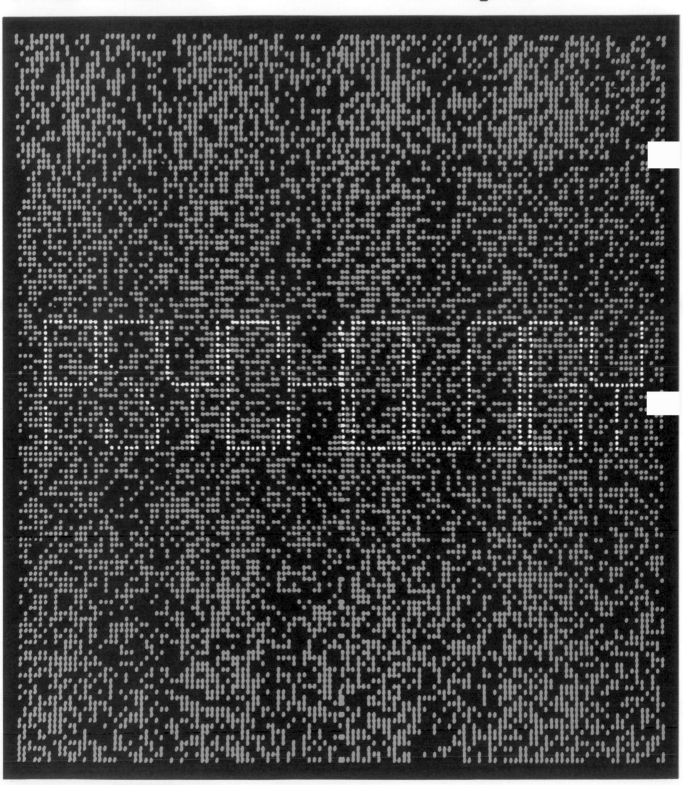

COMPUTER BUFFS—and there are many psychologists among them—have been likened to small boys who, given a hammer, find that everything needs pounding. They also can be compared to not-so-small boys who have just discovered the opposite sex. The computer is a tool and a toy, but it is also a temptress of sorts. And someday it even may become a good wife.

The computer began its seduction of psychology gently, by offering easy, fast, and accurate ways to accomplish tedious, routine tasks. It showed itself able and willing to perform familiar operations such as calculating statistics, scoring objective tests, and randomizing lists of stimuli. But, simultaneously, it began to capture the imagination of its user. It revealed that it was capable of much more than it was being asked to do, and it invited the psychologist to explore its potentialities. As the psychologist discovered the computer's abilities, he began to devise new procedures and even new theories based on them. Thus the machine became a source of new ideas as well as an executor of standard procedures. A working partnership—somewhat unstable as yet, but promising nonetheless—has been established.

As the discussion below will show, this pattern already has occurred in three fields of psychology: data analysis, laboratory control, and theory construction. It is also under way in many other areas, such as classroom instruction and psychiatric interviewing and diagnosis. Psychology departments now offer courses in computer technology, and it is a rare psychology student who has no contact with computers at any point during his undergraduate or graduate career. The writing is on the wall: computers in psychology are destined to be more, much more, than a fad. Some psychologists are welcoming them with open arms; for the rest, I suggest an attitude of graceful surrender.

Computers are justly famous for their speed and for their vast storage capacity. At least as useful, though less well known, is their ability to perform highly complex operations on a wide variety of kinds of material.

A computer, like a projective test, can be interpreted by its user in terms of his own needs. The fact that a digital computer manipulates symbols according to specified rules is anything but restrictive. The computer can deal with almost any kind of symbol—numbers, words, responses to a multiple-choice test—and it can manipulate them according to any serial combination of elementary operations, taken from the computer's relatively small basic repertoire, which the user chooses to employ. The user's task is to provide a series of operations, called a *program*, which instructs the computer to process his symbols to produce his desired result.

A computer without a program is only an inert bundle of electronics. Like the steam shovel, it is merely an extension of its operator's skills. It makes no more sense to say that the IBM 7090 has predicted the outcome of an election than to say that the scissors, not the child, cut up the Sunday newspaper. Computers at times do appear to have minds of their own, but this is because the programmer seldom can be absolutely sure that his instructions are correct in all details. The computer sometimes can correct the syntax of an individual instruction, but it has no way to check sequence. It follows directions blindly, even if the result is nonsense; we have no way yet to tell the computer, "Don't do what I say, do what I mean."

Writing a program is difficult, for it requires more precision and logical clarity than most people are accustomed to using. It does not, however, require special mathematical training, and the task is facilitated by a number of labor-saving devices. One of these is special languages designed for particular types of programs—such as Fortran and Algol for mathematics, Comit for linguistics, Lisp and IPL-V for abstract symbol manipulation [*see illustration, page 26*]. Computer languages are not at all "natural." Their style is terse and mechanical, and their syntax is rigid. What they do for the programmer is provide a kind of shorthand notation for expressing his problem. The computer itself can translate this shorthand into the necessary sequence of elementary operations, free-

ing the programmer from a considerable amount of detail work.

Another labor-saving device has become, for large programs, a necessity as well as a convenience. It is the subroutine, a self-contained procedure that the programmer can write once and then simply "call" whenever it is needed for the larger program. The subroutine can be used whenever the computer is to perform a standard calculation at several different stages in a program; it is an invaluable tool for the programmer. More elaborate subroutines which use simple subroutines can be devised and in this way more powerful units can be made out of smaller ones.

For example, a clinical psychologist might want a computer to perform a statistical analysis of the results of a personality test, with a view to determining the relation between certain hereditary and environmental factors. The first step in the program would be to write a subroutine for calculating the correlation coefficients of the factors being analyzed. This subroutine, in turn, would include a subroutine to calculate standard deviations which would include a subroutine for square roots.

The typical large program consists of an elaborate hierarchy of segments and subsegments, all based on that small, basic repertoire of elementary computer operations. A group of hierarchical subroutine structures is what makes possible huge computer programs that play chess, bridge, and other intellectual games—and the ones that manage the air defense of the United States.

The statistical analysis of empirical data is a natural job for a computer, and one of the first that psychologists asked it to do. The computer's speed makes it unnecessary to cut mathematical corners as one must, for example, in "programming" a desk calculator. In addition, the computer allows the general use of techniques which, though theoretically sound, are too complex or too tedious to perform manually. The multivariate analysis of variance, for example, has been part of the literature since 1932, but it remained merely an intellectual curiosity until the digital computer arrived to perform the calculations.

Computers make the extension and refinement of data analysis a far more inviting task than heretofore: it is a rare man who wants to develop techniques that stand no chance of being used. Factor analysis, especially, has been shrouded in mysticism for years, but even the difficult problem of the rotation of axes has been clarified (if not simplified) through the application of objective computer methods.

The computer has done more than popularize existing techniques and promote their orderly extension; it also has begun to foster radically new and different ways of analyzing data. A statistical procedure usually is stated as a mathematical notation, and the computer encourages longer, more complicated, and more numerous equations. But a computer program based on equations is itself a way of stating procedures. The program has the important property of completeness, since it requires the explicit statement of much that is left implicit in an equation. Even more importantly, the program can include statements which the usual mathematical notation does not allow at all. Thus the range of procedures that can be formalized and developed objectively suddenly has been vastly increased.

The first new technique to take full advantage of the computer was a multidimensional scaling procedure developed by Roger N. Shepard, now of Harvard University. The problem was to indicate similarities between stimuli by means of points in an n-dimensional space. Similarities between stimuli were to be represented by distances between points, in such a way that points close together indicated stimuli more similar to each other than points far apart. If numerical values could be given for the distances, finding the coordinates of the points would be a fairly straightforward exercise in matrix algebra.

The difficulty was finding a way to transform observed judgments of similarity into numerical measures of distance. Any transformation would be acceptable, so long as it was monotonic

—that is, so long as two stimuli judged more similar than two others were always closer together than two that were judged less similar. Shepard showed that the computer could determine the best monotonic transform itself; all it needed was a list of pairs of stimuli, arranged in order from most similar pair to least similar pair. From this information, it could construct the best monotonic transformation (that is, the one requiring fewest dimensions and corresponding most closely to the data) and determine the coordinates of the points representing the stimuli.

The fact that the rank order of stimulus pairs provided enough data to allow the computer to determine both distance transformation and scale was a revelation to mathematical psychologists. By now there are so many modifications and improvements—not to mention claims of priority—that Shepard's original procedure already is outmoded.

Shepard's idea can be extended to other areas of data analysis. Any statistical procedure based on linear relationships among variables now can, at least in principle, utilize monotonic transformations. Much developmental work remains to be done, but the principle is established. Without the computer, it could not have been done: the extensive trial-and-error testing, the numerous details, the volume of the computations—all these put the procedure well beyond the capacity of human clerks.

Computers in the Laboratory

Computers in the laboratory, like computers used for data analysis, have helped psychologists increase the usefulness of existing techniques and, at the same time, suggested new and better techniques for the future. They permit greater standardization of procedures and more accurate recording of data. They have broadened the range of stimuli that can be used and the range of data that can be collected. And the vast

A FORTRAN PROGRAM FOR THE COMPUTATION OF THE MEAN
OF A SET OF NUMBERS AND THE STANDARD DEVIATION

Program	Explanation
DIMENSION X(1000)	The number of cases, N, is declared to be no more than 1,000.
READ INPUT TAPE 2, 100, N, (X(I), I=1, N)	The program calls for the value of N and the individual numbers to be read in from Tape Number 2, according to Format 100.
FN=N SUMX=0 SUMXX=0	Some quantities are preset.
DO 10 I=1, N SUMX=SUMX+X(I) 10 SUMXX=SUMXX+X(I)**2	The loop of instructions from DO through Statement Number 10 is done N times, with I incremented by 1 each time, thus accumulating the sum of x and x². Here note that "=" is to be read as "is set to" or "is replaced by."
FMEAN=SUMX/FN SIGMA=SQRTF(SUMXX/FN-FMEAN**2)	The mean (FMEAN) and the standard deviation (SIGMA) are calculated.
WRITE OUTPUT TAPE 3, 101, N, FMEAN, SIGMA STOP 100 FORMAT (I5/(F10.5)) 101 FORMAT (4H1N= I5,8H MEAN= F10.5, 120HSTANDARD DEVIATION= F10.5) END	The mean and the standard deviation, together with N, are written out on Tape Number 3, according to Format 101, for later printing.

amount of computation that the machine can perform between the subject's response to one stimulus and the presentation of the next holds great promise for improvements in research design.

Computers often are used to generate stimuli and to present them to experimental subjects on an automatic typewriter or a cathode-ray tube [*see illustration at right*]. In experiments with verbal stimuli, the computer randomizes and presents lists of words and nonsense syllables. In studies of motion as a cue to depth perception, the computer can present, on the CRT, two-dimensional projections (which look like shadows) of rotating three-dimensional objects or configurations. Computer calculation of the projections permits the easy display of random dots "floating" in space; this kind of complex picture can be shown only by computer. [*See illustration, pages 28–29 top.*]

Computers have made it possible for psychologists in one field to adopt useful techniques from another. Experimental psychologists typically evaluate their results by averaging, but a physiological psychologist studying evoked neural potentials, for instance, had no convenient way before the arrival of the computer to bring the order of averages out of the chaos of individual recordings. Now, after electrodes implanted in the brain have fed responses to the computer, it can average both the height (response amplitude) and the width (time) of the curves and display the result immediately on an oscilloscope [*see illustration, page 28, middle*].

For years, psychologists have used automatic devices to present stimuli to experimental subjects and to record the subjects' responses. To control complex stimulus-response contingencies, followers of B. F. Skinner often build elaborate special-purpose relay devices, which are really special-purpose computers. It would be of great benefit to other kinds of experiments as well if the choice of a stimulus could be made contingent on the preceding response. What is needed is a computer to do the work.

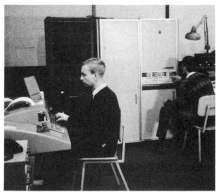

Students at the computer controlled lab at Carnegie-Mellon University (above) are using the peripheral equipment to run the computer. The subject, seated at a Teletype keyboard (below) sees the stimulus presented on the oscilloscope (Ann's Father is Ken). Later the display will say (Ann's Father is ?) or (Ann's ? is Ken). The subject will type his response on the keyboard.

The possibility of a computer that can select stimuli according to the subject's response raises a fundamental question about research design. J. E. Keith Smith of the University of Michigan argues that it makes little sense to take data when nothing is happening, and that standard research designs in the analysis-of-variance tradition eventually will be outmoded. Why not record results only "where the action is"? Sooner than we think, the computer may make possible this highly efficient procedure.

It would seem logical to consolidate the various roles the computer can play

in laboratory experimentation and to create a computer-controlled laboratory, in which a small, fast computer is the main laboratory instrument. And, indeed, this has been done, both by research organizations such as the Systems Development Corporation and Bolt, Beranek & Newman, and by such universities as Michigan, California, Harvard, and Carnegie-Mellon.

There is little or no human intervention in a computer-controlled laboratory. The experimenter writes the program, of course, but the computer presents the stimuli and records the responses; sometimes it even types out the initial instructions. The human experimenter does greet the subject, however, and often oversees the experiment to watch for unprogrammed events.

A small, fast computer now can be purchased for between $15,000 and $50,000. These machines do not have all the statistical programs required for data analysis, but more elaborate ones would be idle too much of the time to be practical for laboratory use. For data reduction, one needs access to a large computer center; at Carnegie-Mellon, the laboratory computer is connected directly to the large machine in our campus computer center.

Access to a large machine makes it easier to prepare programs for the smaller one and permits the small computer to spend all its time running experiments. The programmer can use a special symbolic assembly language that the large computer can translate into a code for the smaller one. The translation process itself requires a complex program called a *compiler,* which is much easier to prepare for a big computer than for a small one.

Computers and Theory

Psychological theories in the last 20 years have become increasingly precise, formal, logical, and mathematical. A theory has little status today if it merely predicts that one group will perform a task differently from another; it must specify *how* different the groups will be,

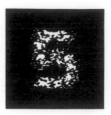
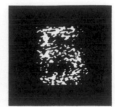

This display shows the effect on a familiar figure, the number 5, of controlled amounts of random disturbance, created statistically by a computer program.

or at least how the difference will vary as the task varies.

Determining precisely what a theory predicts about a certain situation may require considerable mathematical analysis. For example, a popular type of learning model states how the probability of a correct response changes as the learning organism progresses toward mastery. Since the change in probability depends on the response made at each step, and since that response itself must be determined by a probability process, the final outcome—for instance, the number of trials to complete learning—can be stated only as a probability distribution. To find that distribution, the experimenter may have to run the model many times, using a series of random numbers. This procedure, called a Monte Carlo analysis, cannot be beat for sheer tedium. But the Monte Carlo analysis is child's play for computers, and was one of the first tasks which theorists delegated to them.

Some theories do not lend themselves to mathematical expression. They describe processes replete with contingencies, or they propose intricate, hierarchical structures which are better described by words or pictures than by equations. Such theories often can be expressed as flow diagrams, in which boxes represent processes and arrows between the boxes represent relationships between processes [*see illustration, page 29, middle*].

Flow diagrams are also convenient descriptions of computer programs. Some psychologists concluded that theories conveniently could be expressed as computer programs. In this explicit form, a computer can explore the implications of the theory and compare its

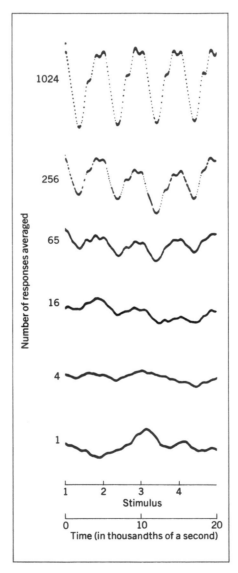

The bottom curve shows a single response of a nerve to a series of four momentary stimuli. The curves above it show the effect of averaging progressively more responses until finally, with 1,024 responses included, the average shows a very regular, complex wave.

predictions with empirical observations.

The chief difference between theories expressed as mathematical equations and theories expressed as computer programs is that the former usually are descriptive whereas the latter are models of processes—indeed, they are called information-processing models. For instance, a probability learning model is content to describe the shape of a learning curve. The learner is viewed as a "black box" that receives stimuli and emits responses; the theory's job is to account for the observed relationship between stimuli and responses. An information-processing model, on the other hand, would formulate specific hypotheses about the way the stimulus inputs were processed within the black box to produce the output responses.

Information-processing models have been received skeptically, for two reasons. First, psychologists are reluctant to "guess" what occurs inside the black box. Overcoming this reluctance requires finding new means of verification, like the verbal protocols of behavior used in problem-solving tasks. It also requires understanding that the hypothesized internal processes are like the parameters of a probability model, except that they are much harder to change. That is, if an information-processing model fits the data, then changing one of the subprocesses almost certainly will ruin it.

The second objection is less rational: it is the fear that people are being equated with computers. Information-processing models do not, at least in any naive way, make that equation. The analogy between input-output and stimulus-response, if taken at face value, is incorrect, for the structure and workings

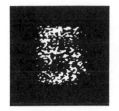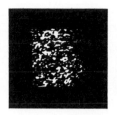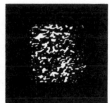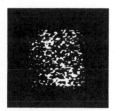

of the human nervous system bear little resemblance to the structure and workings of the digital computer.

There is another, more sophisticated, way to view the analogy. Most psychologists believe that human behavior can be understood, and that understanding implies predictability—that behavior follows regular, though intricate and currently mysterious, patterns. If one adopts, at least as a working hypothesis, this essentially mechanistic view of human behavior, then human beings do bear some resemblance to a machine.

But a computer without a program is no machine at all; in other words, the computer is as many machines as there are programs. A. M. Turing, a British mathematician, has shown that any program for transforming inputs into outputs could be realized on a sufficiently large computer. This means that any conceivable mechanistic theory, including mechanistic theories of human behavior, could be programmed. It also means, however, that the arguments of the "humanists" should be directed at the program, not at the computer itself.

A program incorporating complete information-processing models of human behavior some day may be possible, but at present models are restricted to the usual subject matter of experimental psychology. They deal with memory, learning, concept formation, and occasionally with the affective components of attitude change and personality development. They are especially useful in constructing theories of complex behavior such as problem-solving and the use of language, and in modeling interactions among members of a group.

While psychologists debate the utility of information-processing models of hu-

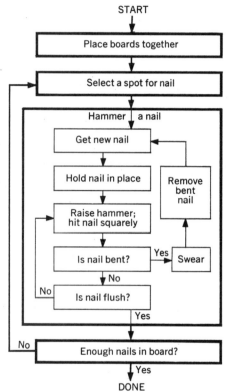

This flow diagram shows the "process" of nailing two boards together. One box in the diagram, the "hammer a nail" box, is shown in expanded form; the other boxes could also take this form, and each subbox itself be expanded further. The entire routine could be part of a "build a fence" program. A good carpenter might have certain changes to make.

man behavior, other scientists are busy mechanizing human processes for their own purposes. The field called artificial intelligence is devoted to endowing computers with human skills. Its first targets were intellectual skills: computers were programmed to play tick-tack-toe, checkers, and chess, and to do exercises in geometry, calculus, and mathematical logic. Most experts in this field use human performance not as a criterion of success, but rather as a standard to be surpassed if possible.

Computer technologists also are working to improve computer perception of visual patterns. They especially want to program a computer to read, so that information can enter the machine directly from a typed or printed page. Enough progress has been made to show that the goal is within reach, and parallel efforts in auditory perception indicate that computers soon will be able to understand some human speech. Of course, a machine that can read and recognize speech must *know* the language, and precisely what that means is a lively topic in linguistics today. Apparently it will be years before machines can emulate human linguistic ability.

Artificial intelligence can contribute much to psychological theory. Each machine ability is, by its very existence, a model or theory of a human ability. Machine theory—the computer program which controls the processing of information within the machine—undoubtedly will need some alteration if it is to conform to human performance. But as a source of ideas about integrated human behavior, the field of artificial intelligence is serving psychology well.

Indeed, the field of computer technology as a whole is serving psychology well. Computers have been used to increase the efficiency with which many standard procedures are carried out, and to make standard many procedures which formerly were impractical. They also are a valuable source of ideas, both methodological and substantive. May the partnership continue to flourish.

Questions for the Global Conscience

By Arthur J. Dyck

How can we deny the right to commit suicide?

How can we dignify human sexuality?

How can we rationalize population control?

KANT ONCE SPOKE of being aroused from his "dogmatic slumbers." Recently a group of Radcliffe college girls woke me up to certain central moral issues that had lain dormant in my thinking about my own work at Harvard on moral problems associated with the rapid growth of the world's population. During a seminar discussion of population problems, student questions turned abruptly, and with great intensity, to the question of suicide.

Why, these very intelligent, concerned young women asked, should we cling to our traditional scruples about suicide when they are but vestiges of outmoded and outworn religious dogma? Why doesn't every person have the right to dispose of himself or herself as he or she chooses? If a right to free speech is generally acknowledged as such, why not the right to commit suicide as well?

I was totally unprepared both for the intense interest in suicide and for the view of it which the students espoused. Why should such able, promising youths who readily and morally condemned the daily sacrifice of human lives in Vietnam and the human suffering in the ghettos, wish so fervently to have the right—free from legal restraint and moral censure—to take their own lives? At first, it made no sense to me at all. Gradually, however, I think I have come to see the critical issues that are at stake and to understand some of the implications of my own line of argumentation developed in reply to them that night.

Suicide has been seen often as the ultimate expression of self-control and of the determination of one's own fate. Some scholars and laymen even see suicide as the paradigm case of human freedom. In thinking of suicide as a *right* comparable to freedom of speech, the Radcliffe students were emphasizing their desire, in principle, to be free of social coercion and control in considering whether they should live or die. But suicide is a paradoxical phenomenon. It does represent the ultimate form of self-control, but at the same time it is also the ultimate loss of self-control and self-determination. By this act, one relinquishes any personal contribution to one's own earthly fate and the future destiny of mankind. And it is precisely at this point that the act of suicide becomes morally questionable. (Suicide, of course, also has a dimension of hostility the students did not discuss. Behavioral scientists have learned that violence directed toward oneself and violence directed toward *others* are closely linked. The man who commits suicide may, indeed, be trying to "kill off" someone else.)

To commit suicide is to opt out in the most final way from further contributions to the life and welfare of one's community and of the human race. In deciding to commit suicide, one decides that one will not be available to one's fellows, that one will not even be of potential benefit or service to the human community. This is the critical difference between taking one's life and giving it. Giving one's life is heroic and morally laudatory, when it is done for someone's benefit or for the sake of humanity generally. Taking one's life is pathetic and morally blameworthy when it is a form of withdrawal from the web of one's existence and from the human community.

Suicide, then, is hardly comparable to the right of free speech. The free expression of opinion is, as John Stuart Mill observed in his essay on liberty, essential to the development of a democratic society and to the maturation of its citizens; taking one's own life is not a contribution to one's community except under very special circumstances as in wartime, and then it would not be seen as suicide, but as a form of giving one's life for another or others.

Why were the students, in arguing their case, inattentive to this difference between freedom of speech and a "right" to commit suicide? It is not that they were focused simply upon the right to self-control and the control over their own destinies. Rather they were focused upon the kind of social and moral coercion exerted by society at large from which they wanted to be free. The community here is seen to have something of the oppressive and repressive quality of what in contemporary rhetoric has often been called the Establishment.

The importance of this focus and perception can be illustrated by attention to arguments over the control of drugs. Both those who want increasing legal and other forms of control over the use of drugs and those who want less are concerned with maintaining the powers of self-control and self-determination. One group sees the use of certain drugs as contributing to the loss of self-control, especially when the drug in question is habit-forming or otherwise mentally debilitating. This loss of self-control can, in some instances, be harmful not only to the user, but also to other innocent persons who may be victimized by the user. Those who emphasize more freedom with respect to drug use point to the harsh and restrictive nature of many of the laws governing drug use and to the general repression associated with making laws to regulate individual, private behavior. Of course, one's views concerning the moral and legal status of drug usage depend very much upon the specific drug in question and the amount of accurate knowledge available about the drug's immediate and long-run physical and psychological effects. Nevertheless, one's view of the human community and its relation to self-determination are very much involved in this and a whole host of critical social issues, from suicide, to drug use, to sexual behavior and population control.

It is not surprising, then, to find that the problem of relating the demands of self-control to the demands of the larger community also arise in moral deliberations over the use and control of reproductive behavior and sexual responses generally. There are those who emphasize the private character of sexual conduct and who tend to see legal and social restraints as repressive and unnecessary; there are those who emphasize the social and institutional character of sexual conduct and who see legal and social restraints upon it as appropriate and essential.

With the rapid growth of the world's population, and with the very real threat that such growth rates will bring about extensive human suffering within the next two decades, the control of reproductive behavior is no idle issue. It is essential that we achieve control.

Forces for change are at work everywhere, including among contemporary Roman Catholics. Acting out of the fervent desire to realize blessings of God, in the form of health, education and general well-being for their offspring, increasing numbers of Catholics sanction and practice the methods of birth control, so recently condemned by Pope Paul VI.

It appears that the majority of Catholics, certainly in the West, see the Pope on the wrong side of this issue. In the choice between Papal concern for right doctrine and God's concern for human welfare, God wins out over the Pope. Religious change is going past the Pope, and so the problem of the viability of this kind of church structure is heightened.

Ultimately, given the upper limits of air and water pollution and the limitation of sheer space, the survival of the human species is at stake. Roger Revelle, director of Harvard's Center for the Study of World Population Problems, has stated the need for controlling our reproductive behavior in the form of a poignant question: "Can man domesticate himself?"

Assuming, then, that something must be done to reduce birth rates (increasing death rates is surely a morally unsatisfactory way of reducing population growth rates), we must ask how this is to be accomplished. To this question, there are a wide variety of responses that are considered to be morally acceptable and/or practically feasible. Suicide is not one of the answers.

We can divide these responses into three very broad groups: (1) those who oppose the conscious control over the number of their offspring; (2) those who favor family limitation as a voluntary decision on the part of the individual couples or family; (3) those who favor various forms of governmental control directly aimed at the control of reproductive behavior. From among the viewpoints or "strategies" found within these broad groupings, let us look at those that differ most notably from one another.

There are two rather distinct viewpoints among those people who oppose self-conscious control over the number of their offspring. Some people do not wish to exercise

the kind of forethought, interference, and control over sexual behavior necessary if one is predictably to plan to avoid or to have children as a result of intercourse. Self-determination here is seen as keeping sexual expression as unfettered and spontaneous as possible. It has been found, for example, that some American college women play a kind of "Russian roulette" by deliberately refusing to use contraceptives, claiming that thereby they obtain an "authentic sexual experience." James Beshers characterizes such young women as "short-run hedonists."

Another group, while expressing a willingness to limit and restrain sexual behavior in various ways, does not consider it entirely proper consciously to limit the size of the family. For some, this stems from their belief concerning God's active sphere of dominion and participation in human reproductive processes.

Beliefs in the will of God do indeed find their expression in folk piety. Rural Moslems speak of having as many children as God wills and they sharply restrict the use of contraceptives. Hinduism and Buddhism have doctrines of *ahimsa*, non-injury, and of the cycle of *karma,* the law of cause and effect—or of sowing and reaping—in human affairs. Thus, the conscious endeavor to prevent a conception or a birth other than by abstinence often has been interpreted as injury to life and as an interference in natural and morally inviolable cosmic processes.

Interesting parallels to these religious beliefs can be found in certain subcultures. The gauchos of South America who work on ranches as cowboys consider it unmanly to take rational forethought. For them, rational forethought is cowardly, a failure to face what "life" or "fate" has in store for each of us. Among working-class wives in the United States, described by Lee Rainwater, there is a tendency to be skeptical of thinking and planning ahead.

The styles and beliefs of these various groups would, if generally followed, give us little hope that birth rates around the world could predictably be lowered and controlled by leaving the decisions to individual families.

But there are groups, like the Population Council, who believe that such groups are small enough now or will through the press of circumstances diminish enough so that they pose no barrier to the eventual success of voluntary family planning as a strategy for reducing birth rates to the necessary and desired levels.

Many governments, including our own, along with various planned parenthood organizations, share this viewpoint. Thus, policy consists in making effective contraceptives and contraceptive information readily available and in communicating the alleged advantages of keeping one's family small, but this has not been found to be the most effective approach. Voluntary family planning is thus taken to be at once morally desirable and practically feasible.

But others who agree that voluntary family planning is morally desirable do not share the belief in its practical feasibility unless certain other phenomena connected with reproductive behavior are changed.

We shall look at two such strategies for controlling birth rates differing so much in magnitude as to constitute, in their long-range consequences, quite different policies.

On the basis of intensive research over a period of seven years in the Punjab region of India, John Gordon and John Wyon of Harvard have hypothesized that people in such an area would be motivated to reduce their birth rates if: mortality rates for infants and children were sharply decreased; local social units were stimulated to measure their own population dynamics and to draw inferences from them concerning their own welfare and aspirations; and efficient methods of birth control were introduced. Introducing these conditions would substantially increase the opportunities of each family unit to reduce family size without undue fear, to assess in a more exact, realistic way *how* fertility goals would affect themselves and their community, and to plan with more realistic hopes for success in attaining their goals. Whether birth rates would be markedly lowered by bringing about these conditions alone would depend not simply upon the extent to which people in that region stand to benefit from such a reduction but also upon the extent to which they actually perceive such benefits—both social and economic —and believe that they are attainable.

The gathering of vital statistics is, therefore, a crucial aspect of this proposal. Not until statistics were introduced did the first vaccine against disease gain general acceptance in the West. Without accurate information, a sense of group responsibility cannot exist on a rational basis, and will have no perceptible dividend to the individual members. The proposal of Gordon and Wyon for the Punjab assumes that rational and purposeful behavior exists already to some degree and can be intensified by modifications in the environment which make the intensification of such behavior more beneficial and more attainable.

Roger Revelle explicitly agrees that it is essential to do the very things that Gordon and Wyon suggest. Looking, however, at the total ecological context within which arise population problems, especially of undernourishment and starvation, he is certain that nothing less than substantial technological changes will be effective. These changes, which he sees as quite indigenous *and* locally controlled, could spawn highly industrialized, urbanized countries with scientific, market agriculture throughout the globe. Such an environment certainly has, in the demographic history of the West, been associated with sharp declines in birth rates. The kind of setting within which these birth declines occur more or less adequately provides the incentives and the means to control the population growth of the world and the material resources for the sustenance and gratification of its human inhabitants.

But Kingsley Davis is convinced that any reliance upon voluntary planning by individual families is doomed to fail. Pointing to the necessity for achieving *zero* growth rates, he points out that many highly industrialized countries have not attained such rates and, given the average number of children desired, show no prospect of doing so. He urges government policies explicitly designed to alter the institutional arrangements that reward present reproductive behavior and ideals. He calls for policies that would encourage and reward the single life, child-lessness, late marriage, small families, and activities for women that would have the effect of curbing their preoccupation with childbearing and child-rearing.

For Davis, only direct intervention and planning by government is practically feasible and, in the light of his dark picture of the problems of population growth, morally acceptable. His strategy includes governmental efforts to change our current values—values he believes stand in the way of preventing otherwise inevitable disaster.

A more directly coercive role is assigned to the state by the Communist government of China. Restrictions upon reproductive behavior include such measures as mandatory late marriages (men must be 30, women 25) and severe economic and vocational sanctions against couples having more than two children. None of these policies are justified as attempts to control birth rates. (A socialist state is supposed to provide for everyone; "overpopulation" is a problem for capitalist countries.) But they are, of course, forms of population control, though presented as measures to protect women and children, to improve the education of the rising generation, to contribute to the health and prosperity of the nation, and to honor the need to devote more energy to the development of the state.

How shall we assess the moral desirability and acceptability of these various responses to the control of reproductive behavior? Within ethical theory there are two very basic sets of criteria to help judge what is morally justifiable: the *normative,* and the *meta-ethical.*

Broadly stated, rapid population growth and the possibility of ultimate overpopulation on the earth becomes a normative issue because of the human misery and death that come from rapid population growth and the threat to human extinction that inevitably follows overpopulation. If, as seems evident, birth rates must be extensively reduced and therefore in some way controlled, responses that hinder or block control are, in this respect, morally blameworthy. Conversely, these responses that facilitate and bring about the desired end are morally praiseworthy.

But human responses, certainly strategies or policies for action, tend to be morally complex, and usually possess a number of right- or wrong-making characteristics. There are some very significant and closely related sets of moral values connected with sexual and procreative activities. Human sexuality is an important expression of our individuality and a source of intensely gratifying pleasure. Any strategy for controlling human behavior will certainly tend to be *right* or *wrong* to the degree that it enhances or diminishes the extent to which we find self-fulfilling freedom and joy as sexual beings. One can think of this freedom and joy as a human right.

But sexuality, like life itself, is at once a right that belongs to us as individuals and a gift that each of us receives from others—his parents most immediately, but also from the wider human community. Indeed, it is a gift *from* the human species *to* the human species. We owe, therefore, some considerable debt of gratitude to these sources of our unique genetic and social individuality for the very possibility of experiencing sexual pleasure and for the considerable rewards of childbearing and child-rearing.

We incur, then, as those who have been chosen to live, an awesome but joyous obligation to see to it that this gift of life, sexual expression, procreation, and child-rearing has a future. Our obligation to the larger human community is particularly vital in so far as each of us has unique genetic endowments and unique talents to offer and to perpetuate. No one else can give to the species what we bring to it. That is why committing suicide is such a threat to the human community and represents a profound failure to participate in our own self-determination and in the destiny of the human community.

Sexual and procreative behavior is at once individual and communal, joyous and creative, a right and an obligation. One of the difficulties in inducing the reduction of birth rates has to do with the necessity of making people aware that the survival of the species does not now depend upon a large number of births; indeed, it depends upon *some* births, but not too many. The need for a new sophisticated awareness of species responsibilities has been brought about by our success in reducing death rates and extending life expectancies. Failure to reproduce, like taking one's own life, requires special justification if it is to be morally responsible *vis a vis* our obligations to others. But this same moral responsibility to our species requires us also to limit the number of our offspring under prevailing conditions. If we do not cultivate and assert this responsibility, we are threatened by the loss of self-determination and will be increasingly assailed by those who would advocate harsh and repressive means to save the species.

What about the meta-ethical criteria? Meta-ethics is concerned with the meaning and justification of moral statements. In its investigations there is growing agreement that the rationality of moral claims can be judged by the extent to which they exhibit the following criteria: (1) knowledge of facts; (2) vivid imagination of how others are affected by our actions; (3) universal loyalties both with respect to our interests and our passions so that what obtains for one person obtains for another and for ourselves as well. Strategies designed to cope with population problems will more nearly satisfy our considered moral judgments as they approximate these rational processes.

Applying these normative and meta-ethical criteria, we can see quite readily that opposition to the self-conscious control of the number of one's offspring is not a very viable moral option. The short-run hedonists may enjoy a certain kind of freedom and pleasure, but both of these—if sufficiently generalized—would be disastrous to the species and would not, for long, satisfy any of the specified criteria. Those who will not, for pious reasons, specifically determine the number of children they will have also fall short on all counts, but with this major difference: Given their loyalty to God, these people are highly susceptible to new knowledge and circumstances that would permit them to see that their health and welfare, which God would have them act to secure, can best be served by reducing birth rates.

For this last reason, both the Revelle and the Wyon strategies are morally superior to plans which simply provide contraceptives and contraceptive information to facilitate family planning. Indeed, the Wyon and Revelle proposals move further in the direction of realizing and facilitating what is demanded by the normative and meta-ethical criteria than any of the other policies or proposals.

One might object, as does Davis, that their strategies will not succeed in *sufficiently* reducing birth rates. Certainly further research and trial is needed, but given the assault on human values and the threat to a "sacrosanct" sphere of human freedom, the practicality of the governmental coercion Davis advocates is at best doubtful. Thus any widespread attempt to implement birth-control policies like those of the mainland Chinese government undoubtedly will meet with resistance and be shown as impractical.

Another subtle flaw in turning to governmental coercion in reproductive matters is that such a move already represents at least a partial acceptance of the notion that the great masses of men cannot or will not learn what is in their best interest. Policies predicated on this premise will tend increasingly to rely on coercion rather than upon the processes of rational persuasion and the creation of conditions conducive to successful communication.

People and nations must find a morally justifiable form of population control in which they will contribute to human survival. Strategies like those of Wyon and Revelle commend themselves insofar as they enhance human freedom and encourage responsible community behavior. Wyon's proposal has the advantage of introducing a minimum of disruption into a culture. It may, by the same token, be inadequate to induce the requisite behavior without further transformations of the social and economic lot of the people involved. Revelle's policy has the advantage of a total ecological vision seeking to bring about the conditions that presumably maximize the technical possibilities for controlling the whole web of existence for man's benefit. (Herein lies its potential weakness as well. Not only do we have no assurance that technical advances ultimately will provide this control but, more importantly, we cannot ascertain what losses mankind suffers when entire cultures are transformed into the Western technological and industrial mold.)

One last observation: To be rational, moral judgments must rest on universal loyalties. The problem of overpopulation makes this criterion concretely explicit. The preservation of the species demands loyalty, not simply to one's own family and one's own immediate community and nation, but to mankind, and beyond that, to the total ecological environment upon which man's life depends. The assassinations of Martin Luther King and Robert Francis Kennedy reveal the demonic and evil character of acting out of partial loyalties to racial or political groups when seeking to do what one may consider right or justifiable. We should not underestimate the powerful force of the religious symbol of one God to nurture universal loyalties of the sort we now desperately need. Love for all of our fellows is not now, if it ever was, a moral luxury. The survival of our species depends upon enlightened, impartial love.

THE PSYCHOLOGY OF ROBOTS

By Henry Block and Herbert Ginsburg

THE WORLD GAME

A self-navigating exploring robot being developed at Stanford Research Institute divides a strange room into imaginary regions and registers in each region what it has perceived. This image then becomes the robot's cognitive "World Map."

1 Don't Know

2 Something There

3 Nothing There

4 Movable Object

5 Immovable Object

6 This is myself.

THE WANDERER

ROBOTS HAVE BEGUN to teach our children, explore the moon, sort our mail, launch our spaceships, watch our bank accounts, carry out previously impossible scientific experiments, check our income tax returns and a computer may even make the decision to initiate our next war. We already have entered into the first phase of the Age of Robots. This is a time in the affairs of men when machines operate with almost human intelligence and perform functions that once only man could do.

Besides sharing his labor, machines also literally have become *parts* of man. For example, many people owe their lives to an artificial kidney, to a pacemaker that keeps the heart beating regularly, or to an artificial lung. The result is a living organism, part human, part machine, that can be considered a *cyborg*, a term coined for a cybernetic organism by science writer Daniel S. Halacy Jr.

And to many psychologists, robots offer a way to simulate psychological processes. We reason that if we can understand a psychological process, we ought to be able to build a machine which puts that process into action. For example, if we propose a model for letter recognition, then we should be able to construct a robot that recognizes letters. If we are successful, then our model is at least an adequate solution. If our machine does not recognize letters, then clearly something is lacking in the theory.

Psychologists are interested in robots for other reasons. One of these is a theoretical concern with the basic mechanisms underlying a robot's performance. The argument runs like this. Often robots are designed to replace people at some job. Robots calculate; they teach; they do chemical analyses. In fact, much of robot performance could be termed "intelligent." Robots get information from the world and manipulate this knowledge in different ways. Since robots seem to perform intelligently, the psychologist is interested in studying the processes enabling them to do so. The psychologist has a strong desire to peer into the proverbial "black box" to see the ways in which the innards of the machine operate. For the psychologist, the robot is a dream fulfilled; one can look into this machine, hoping to see more there than one's imaginings. Does the black box contain stimulus-response connections, cognitive maps, learning networks, or something else? Of course, having fathomed the contents of the box the psychologist has no guarantee that people function just as robots do. But at least he has discovered one *possible* process underlying a given psychological function.

Critics often disparage the idea that machines exhibit intelligent behavior, dismissing the concept with a curt, "They'll do only what you tell them to do." This simply is not true of "learning machines," particularly those that are capable of making random—therefore, undirected—choices. Nor is it true for analog computers.

Recent developments in engineering point the way to new directions in the design of robots. It is already possible to perceive the general outlines of robots of the future, although the details of their implementation remain hazy. In the next 20 years, robots will perform increasing-

FATIGUE—REST

HUNGER—FOOD SEARCH

NIGHTFALL—RETURN HOME

DANGER—FLIGHT

QUIET—SLEEP

COMPETITOR—FIGHT

LOVER—SEX

BOREDOM—EXPLORE

INSTINCTS FOR ROBOTS. A robot that is free to wander through its environment needs a set of priorities or "instincts" for its actions. In a whimsical way, the world game below illustrates how these instincts would be triggered by specific stimuli. For example, mating with another machine would trigger the nest-building instinct, making it the highest priority program for the robot.

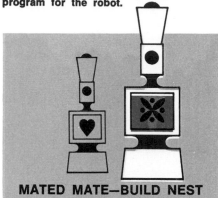

MATED MATE—BUILD NEST

FOOD—EAT

START

FINISH

ly sophisticated tasks. They will imitate humans, navigate about the landscape, understand a language, and recognize objects. What will be the nature of these machines? How will robots of the future get information from the environment and make use of what they have learned? Perhaps a comparative psychology of modern robots will answer some of these questions.

In some ways, the sensory abilities of machines are far more acute than those of man. Robots are not limited to the range and type of physical energies to which man's sensory system is attuned. Robots can detect and respond to the entire electromagnetic spectrum, including radiowaves, infrared, ultraviolet, X-rays, gamma-rays, etc. When so designed they are much more sensitive to sonar, temperatures, humidity and to the presence of many chemicals. The robot sidewinder missile, for example, like the sidewinder snake, senses the heat emanating from its intended victim. The missile's sensors can detect the heat from a jet aircraft engine at a great distance and direct the missile on a path to intercept that heat source. Similar arrangements can be made from an ICBM to seek out the center of a city, which is distinctly warmer than the surrounding countryside. The gyro platforms of space craft maintain their bearings with an accuracy that makes the motion sensitivity of our inner ear seem very crude.

Helicopter pilots complain that engine noise prevents them from hearing bullets hitting the craft. A computer, analyzing the ambient noise of the engine, can detect the signal added by the sound of impacting bullets. The sonar cane and the laser cane, currently being developed to help the blind navigate, detect the presence of obstacles by sound or laser beams respectively.

While the robot generally excels in sensation, he encounters difficulties in perceptual functioning. It is hard for a robot to recognize an object that is in its natural surroundings. This, of course, is an easy task for even a small child. A 3-year-old can walk into a room and correctly identify a toy contained in a box. He can do this even though the amount of light reflected from the toy, its shape, its color, and so on, are all different from what he has experienced before. In fact, the child can recognize the toy even when only part of it is visible. And if the toy moves, the child can usually track it, and considers that it is the same toy despite the many perceptual changes that have taken place. Of course, many perceptual skills underlie the child's recognition of the toy. The child must isolate figure from ground; he must perceive constancies of form, brightness, distance and color; he must follow a moving object and attribute to it a constant identity; and he must infer the whole object from a visible part.

Robots cannot yet perform at this level. The 3-year-old (and perhaps even the 6-month-old) is generally superior as far as perception is concerned.

Today's robots can "read" the magnetic printing on bank checks by matching each specially designed character against standard templates. Clearly these are highly artificial conditions. Within the past year robots have been given a limited ability to read printed writing (zip codes on mail and certain business office forms). "Learning" procedures, instead of mere template matching, are sometimes utilized in the design of these machines. More sophisticated techniques employ feature recognizers, which involve the detection of only certain critical characteristics, thereby reducing the amount of stored data required for "reading." In spite of this it probably will be some time before a machine can understand handwriting because recognition of irregularly formed letters so often relies on context and meaning. For example, most people can easily read a half-blurred word on the printed page. We use such contextual cues as the sequential probabilities of the letters (if the first letter is q, the second is most likely u) and the meaning of the sentence ("he used a bucket to draw----- from the well"). Current research on pattern recognition is developing methods so robots can use as information not only the frequency-of-letter combinations but also grammatical context.

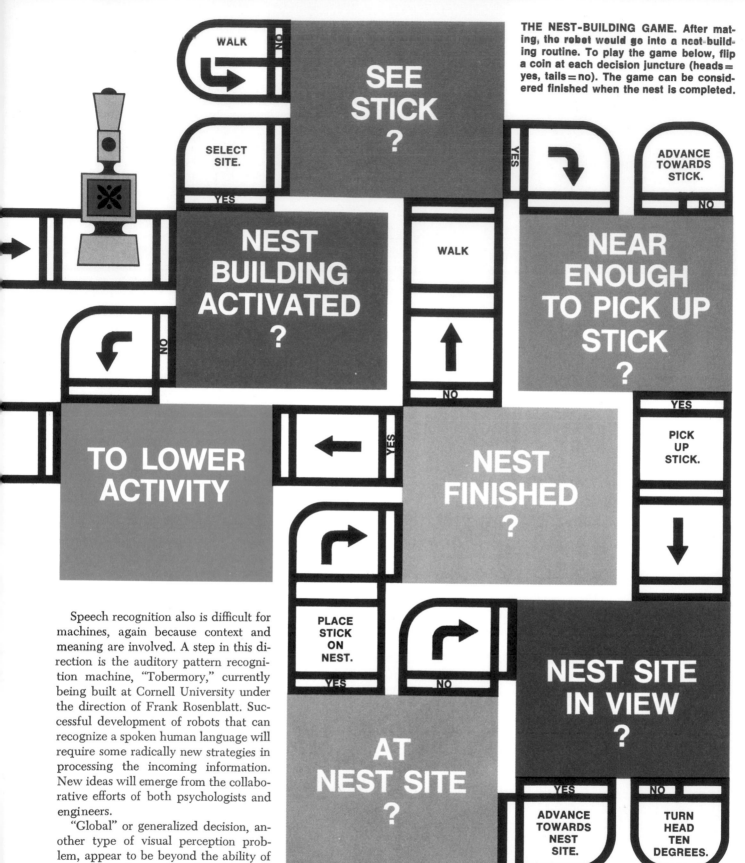

WALK

SELECT SITE.

SEE STICK ?

YES

ADVANCE TOWARDS STICK.

NO

NEST BUILDING ACTIVATED ?

YES

WALK

NO

NEAR ENOUGH TO PICK UP STICK ?

NO

YES

PICK UP STICK.

TO LOWER ACTIVITY

YES

NEST FINISHED ?

PLACE STICK ON NEST.

YES

NO

NEST SITE IN VIEW ?

AT NEST SITE ?

YES

ADVANCE TOWARDS NEST SITE.

NO

TURN HEAD TEN DEGREES.

Speech recognition also is difficult for machines, again because context and meaning are involved. A step in this direction is the auditory pattern recognition machine, "Tobermory," currently being built at Cornell University under the direction of Frank Rosenblatt. Successful development of robots that can recognize a spoken human language will require some radically new strategies in processing the incoming information. New ideas will emerge from the collaborative efforts of both psychologists and engineers.

"Global" or generalized decision, another type of visual perception problem, appear to be beyond the ability of current machines. Consider the problems: Does the object have a hole in it? Is the boy in front of the table? How many pirates can you find hiding in the tree? The superiority of humans in these and similar perceptual problems probably is related to extensive experience and manipulation of the environment. By contrast, current robots are "creatures of instinct"; their design provides them with a fixed computational procedure for the solution of these problems. Robots of the future will have a greater capability to "learn" and to adapt themselves to their environment.

Today, most robots are passive creatures. The computer, the pattern recognizer, and many other machines not only lack the means to leave their homes but would meet disaster if they did. Also, the current robot must be spoon-fed. It requires highly structured and specific formats of inputs and outputs, like punch cards or magnetic tape, in order to operate effectively. In the future, however, robots will explore their environment; they will actively seek out experiences and information.

A prototype for robots of this sort is currently being developed at Stanford Research Institute by Nils Nilsson, Charles Rosen, and others. This machine, which we will call for now the "Wanderer," can explore a limited environment, such as a large room. The Wanderer's "brain" is a computer, which divides the room into imaginary regions, like a checkerboard. In our approximate version of its programming, we can say that the computer initially assigns the symbol "1" to each square, indicating to the machine that it does not know the contents of the corresponding region of the room. The robot has "eyes" (a range finder) so that it can look around the room. If it sees something occupying a particular region, it changes the symbol in the corresponding memory square to "2," whereas if it sees that the region is empty it changes the corresponding square to read "3." For regions that the machine can't see, the symbols are left unchanged. The robot wanders around the room under the control of the computer. If it touches an object in a certain region in the room, the computer changes its entry in the corresponding square to "4" if the object is movable and to "5" if the object is immovable. The square corresponding to the position of the robot itself is labeled "6" and this figure moves around the memory as the robot moves around the room.

Such a robot, after being left for a while to familiarize itself with the contents of the room, can execute the following instructions: "Proceed from where you are at H-7 to location A-3 being sure not to hit any object and all the while remaining unobservable from location T-10. This is to be done by the shortest path possible subject to these conditions." After figuring out the desired path, the robot proceeds at once to take it without *overt* "trial and error."

The contents of Wanderer's computer memory we call the robot's "world map" for this room. (For a different room it might keep a different world map.) The computer could also have a *copy* of the world map whose symbols could be manipulated without changing the original world map. Thus, by performing the

operations on the copy, it could answer questions like "If you moved three squares to your left and if the objects at D-9 and O-5 were moved to P-10 and Q-10, could you then see what is at R-10? How long would it take you to get to R-10?" Manipulations performed on the copy of the world map permit the machine to indulge in "contemplative speculation" or "fantasy" without destroying its view of reality (the original map). Also with this model we can assign a precise meaning to the concept "the machine comprehends the meaning of a certain sentence." For example, if we tell the machine that "An unmovable object has been placed in region J-9" and the machine responds by changing the symbol in J-9 to "5," we know that it understood the meaning of the sentence. The sentence "Region J-9 now has an immovable object in it" would have the same meaning if again the machine changed the symbol in memory square J-9 to "5." This gives a concrete and specific meaning to the notion of "comprehension."

The robot could conceivably need a rest period or at least a coffee break. For example, if the input of new information is so rapid that the world map cannot be kept updated at the same rate, the robot could hold the data in a buffer memory bank (short-term memory) until it could make the appropriate changes in its world map during its rest period.

In terms of current psychological theory, the navigating robot is very much a cognitive creature. Through perceptual learning, it acquires information about the environment; no reinforcement is necessary. It establishes a cognitive map of its surroundings and a symbolic copy of this map that the robot can manipulate.

A robot with a world map may have the capability to deal with a number of perceptual or cognitive problems that current robots find difficult. It may be able to track objects that not only move, but disappear behind obstacles for periods of time. On its copy of the world map, the robot "infers" where the object is, based on its estimated velocity, and tests this "expectancy" against a direct observation whenever possible. If the difference between the expected and the observed is small, the estimate is adjusted. If, on the other hand, the discrepancies are large, the robot takes more drastic action, going into a new routine to locate the missing object. In this way, the "cognitive dissonance" causes a redirection of the robot's "attention."

Some robots learn in ways that some psychologists think are conventional. That is, the robot learns to make a response by means of positive and negative reinforcement. For example, a mechanical mouse, developed by Claude Shannon at Bell Telephone Laboratories [*see illustration, page 41*], learned to find its way through a maze when it was "rewarded" for successful runs and "punished" for the unsuccessful runs. Even very simple machines can be made to "learn," using a variety of reinforcement procedures. But despite the predilections of some psychologists, it seems obvious that learning involves more than the two Rs (responses and reinforcements). One way people learn is by watching a task performed by a skilled person. For example, it is difficult to learn to build a model airplane by hearing a lecture on the subject, or even by doing it yourself; but the learning is easier when you watch someone build a model. Robots already exist that learn by watching. For example, Bernard Widrow's broom balancer at Stanford University consists of an electric car on which a broomstick is to be balanced. When the car is moved back and forth on its track it is possible to keep the broom balanced in a near vertical position [*see illustration, top page 41*]. A human soon learns by trial-and-error how fast to move the car to keep the broomstick from falling. Widrow's machine has an "eye" that observes the angular displacement from the vertical of the broomstick and how fast it falls (angular velocity). The machine correlates these observations with the force that the man applies to the car when he successfully balances the broom. Gradually the machine builds up an "operating function" and can balance the broom by itself. This robot does not simply copy the model's successful responses. Instead, the broom balancer analyzes the performance and extracts an idealized strategy for its task. The broom balancer does not have to go through a process of trial and error before it achieves success. Just as you learned to build the model, this robot learns by watching humans perform the task.

Robots of the future will find some types of learning very difficult. One of these is concept formation. We usually say that a person has a concept when he responds in the same way to a number of different things or events. For example, having the concept of "a good neighbor" involves perceiving common qualities in Mr. Jones and Mr. Smith, even though they have different appearances and do quite different things. (Perhaps Mr. Jones helped to plant the concept learner's lawn, while Mr. Smith helped to weed the new lawn.) Even young children learn concepts of this kind. Can a robot?

In relatively simple situations, robots already have achieved some success in learning concepts. If letter recognition is considered a case of concept-formation learning the concept of the letter "a," (despite discriminable variations in its form), then robots can learn concepts with some skill. We also saw how by use of the world map a machine might learn the "meaning" of certain sentences. But what of the more complicated cases? Can the robot learn the concept of "shoe," "reality," "beauty"? Clearly this presents formidable difficulties. Before a solution can be achieved we must come to grips with such problems as the multiple and shared meanings of words, levels of abstraction, extracting common features from large quantities of unstructured data, and testing concepts against experience. Exactly how this may be accomplished is far from evident.

In the area of rote recall, the robot already has a memory far superior to man's. The computer can store millions of bits of information and recall any of it on demand. But this is only one of several forms of memory. For example, people can recall *sequences* of events ("After you entered the door, Jack rose from his seat and handed you the letter he had been reading. You took it to the table, etc."), and they can remember the meaning of events ("Secretary Rusk said yesterday essentially, although I don't remember his exact words, that we are bombing to avoid war").

A robot of the future may be capable of recognizing instantly whether it previously has seen a certain pattern, and if it did, of then recalling the sequence of patterns that followed it.

The pattern may consist not only of inputs from various sensors but also of signals generated inside the machine. In theory, such a system has been shown to be possible.

The logistic problems of handling enormous amounts of information necessary for a really intelligent robot will force us to develop semantic memory. However, the difficulties encountered in current research indicate that in the near future, at least, robots will be limited largely to rote memory.

Robots already can understand certain simple and artificial languages. Computers are fluent in various dialects of Fortran, Algol, Cobol, Basic, PL/1, etc. A machine like the "Wanderer" conceivably could understand some very simple commands in a restricted version of English. In this restricted English each word has a unique meaning. In addition, unlike natural English where a given word may serve as noun, verb or adjective, here it can be used in only one grammatical capacity. Furthermore, only a few forms of sentence structure can be used. Will the robot of the future be able to understand a natural language?

Many workers in this field are privately and very publicly discouraged. Bemoaning the difficulties of designing a machine that can translate human languages, say German into English, has now become an orthodox activity. But the history of technology is replete with examples of unexpected circumventions of the "impossible," and we should be prepared for surprises in this area. Considering the difficulties that robots have had with natural language, it now seems inconceivable that they will be able to understand the finer forms of literary expression, like proverbs or sarcasm. How could a robot decipher "Strike while the iron is hot" or "Hitch your wagon to a star" or the Turkish proverb, "Before you love, learn to run through snow leaving no footprints"?

Everyone knows that the computer far surpasses humans in its speed and accuracy of computation. This is the characteristic that endears it to the "computerniks," those starry-eyed young men who may be found loitering at computer installations at all hours of the day and night. It is less well known that computers can function on a more formal and creative level in mathematics. Hao Wang, for instance, demonstrated that a computer could prove over 350 theorems from Alfred North Whitehead and Bertrand Russell's *Principia Mathematica* in a few minutes. Another computer, given basic axioms and operations, can invent theorems and prove them too. While it is sometimes inventive and always correct, this computer's weakness is the absence of taste. Many of its theorems and proofs are not only inelegant, but just plain dull. What we need for the future is a mathematical robot with some sense of what is interesting. A start in this direction has been made by Allen Newell, J. C. Shaw, and Herbert Simon of Carnegie Tech, who have worked on a "logic theorist." They studied human problem-solvers with the hope of finding how they formed their strategies, subgoals, conjectures, heur-istic reasoning and guesses. They then attempted to develop computer programs to operate in similar ways. The advantage of heuristic or approximate rough-and-ready reasoning stems from the economics of machine capacity. In principle, complete enumeration of all possibilities will reveal the solutions; but in practice, the number of alternatives rapidly exceeds the capacity of any computer. Heuristic reasoning reduces substantially the number of alternatives that must be investigated to find a solution. But despite some initial encouragement, progress in this area seems to be slow.

In addition to exploiting the skills of robots, we should also allow them to have some fun, even occasionally at our expense. It is in this spirit that a number of researchers have developed chess-playing computers, some of which have been very successful. These computers are usually "learning" machines which are based on heuristic rather than logically correct strategies, and which improve their game as the result of experience. Since, in principle, they could practice against each other at very high speed, as well as against the "book games" of the masters, it is conceivable that in 20 years the World Chess Champion might be a computer program.

Mikhail Botvinnik, the famous Russian chess grandmaster, has suggested that we will require *two* championship chess tournaments—one restricted to unaided humans and the other to machines [see "Psychology Across the Chessboard," by Eliot Hearst, reprinted in this section]. It is doubtful that such an apartheid arrangement can be long maintained. The widespread affection for thinking machines by "computerniks" indicates that man-machine relations are not free of emotional attachment. (Remember the Freudian interpretation of the American's attitude toward his automobile.) Now that we have the electric shaver, electric toothbrush, electric scalp massager and electric buttocks vibrator, can man-machine sexual relationships be far behind? Now that our culture is separating the sexual from reproductive functions, we may expect a sharp rise in the demand for the inventions of pleasure machines. This leads to the ethical and moral questions regarding our treatment of these mechanical objects of our affection. A serious inquiry into these questions was made recently by Roland Puccetti in the *British Journal of the Philosophy of Science*.

The conjecture that the machine will vanquish the chessmaster has been recently the source of a somewhat hostile controversy that seems to be quite analogous to the vitalism controversy in biology a generation ago, and the evolution controversy of two generations ago. Perhaps both sides could find comfort in the words of the mathematician Michael Arbib, "Say not that we are bringing man down to the level of a machine. Say rather that we are bringing the machine up to the level of man."

A robot that can wander through its environment must have a set of priorities for its activities. Leonard Friedman of Systems Development Corporation has proposed one set of "instinctive" behavior patterns for robots. In general, each part of his program directs the robot to perform the sequence of actions that constitutes a particular "instinctual activity," such as nest-building, food-searching, eating, mating, fleeing from danger, fighting, sleeping, exploring, returning home. [See illustration, page 36.] These programs are triggered by specific stimuli. Only one program can be carried out at a time. If a new stimulus triggers a higher priority activity, the program for that activity takes over. When the high priority activity is completed, the robot may return to the interrupted program.

Human behavior on the other hand is often motivated internally as well as by external stimuli. Clearly if robots are to be self-sufficient, they will have to possess drives such as ambition, a need for esteem in eyes of other robots, a super-ego prohibiting the destruction of other robots, or at least those of its own socioeconomic grouping. Of course, robot-human relationships also will have to be carefully considered. For robots to be self-sufficient as a species, they will have to reproduce themselves. While there is nothing against this in principle as shown by John Von Neumann in his theory of self-reproducing automata, the implementation seems impractical at the present time. Of course by using reproduction, natural selection and evolution, we can solve many of our design problems, since the species that will evolve will be the one best adapted to its environment. This probably would take a long time unless the evolutionary process could be simulated on a computer at high speed. Other means for speeding up the evolutionary rate would be the use of tri- or multi-sexual robots. Eventually, psychologists and engineers will have to face these problems head-on but, since this is a family periodical, we shall not go into them here. 🔁

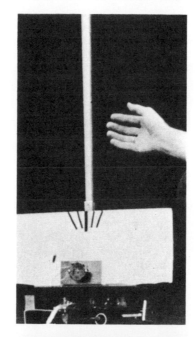

FIGURES 1 & 2
A common boy's game of trying to keep a broom balanced vertically is the basis of an adaptive learning experiment at Stanford University. The broom balancing machine learns by watching humans balance stick by controlling car movements.

FIGURE 3
MECHANICAL MOUSE. Created by Claude Shannon of Bell Telephone Laboratories, the mechanical mouse could learn to find its way through a maze when it was "rewarded" for successful runs and "punished" for failures.

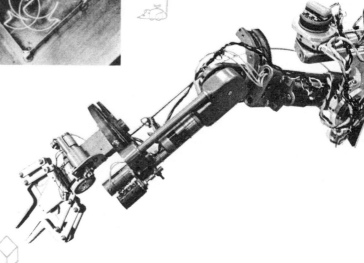

FIGURES 4 & 5, HAND-EYE PROJECT.
A step in providing the computer with a human-like ability to observe and manipulate its environment is the hand-eye project at Stanford University. The eye of the computer is an ordinary television camera. At left is the outline of a cube as perceived by the computer, which then gives directions to the artificial arm and hand for the picking up and the stacking of the cubes.

PARAPSYCHOLOGY

New Neighbor or Unwelcome Guest

By Gardner Murphy

THE HOUSE OF SCIENCE has many rooms, but it is not yet large enough to accommodate all the children Nature sends to the door. Unwelcome guests are an embarrassment. It is tempting, but also rude and backward, to slam the door in their faces. A stray who is turned away must remain outside the family; those who cannot bear the disorder of construction will never make their house into a mansion.

The aim of parapsychology is to authenticate, assemble, categorize and assimilate certain "absurd" events that Nature sends our way. It does this by examining raw data and then by analyzing the somewhat more systematic data arduously achieved through experiment. A few examples, first, of the "spontaneous cases" that parapsychology confronts. The experiments will follow in due course.

A close friend of mine was driving hard over the rolling land of southwestern Wisconsin, hoping to get home to Cedar Rapids, Iowa, by midnight. About six o'clock an impression began to overwhelm him that something was seriously wrong, and by seven he knew that he must not drive straight on to Cedar Rapids but must stop at Dubuque and call his wife. He argued with himself back and forth, thinking there was absolutely nothing wrong at home, and why should he go to Dubuque—a city he had never visited. Still, he knew the name of a hotel there, and he knew he would have no trouble making a phone call. The impression of foreboding grew upon him alarmingly. There could be nothing wrong. But there was. He got to Dubuque and found a telegram from his wife announcing the death of their infant daughter. The little girl had not been

ill. The message was, in a sense, protective, for the young man found it slightly easier to bear the news on the Western Union form than he would have at home with his wife.

I say nothing about this example except to make two points. First, it is what we call a spontaneous case of telepathy, regardless of what its ultimate meaning may be. Second, I emphasize what we do *not* know. We do not know why the wife thought that the husband could get a message in Dubuque. She had herself perhaps become confused, and there is a possibility here of a two-way distant interaction, as there often seems to be. We do not know whether the wife had previous experiences with "sending" and the husband with "receiving" such messages, and if so, under what conditions. We do not know what state of mind or body the man was in, or how his sense of foreboding fitted into other psychophysiological dispositions. Finally, we know nothing whatever about physical factors in the transmission of this particular message.

These and other questions are usually unanswered in spontaneous cases of telepathy. It is a sad fact that after 75 years of noting these experiences, most psychical researchers are still concerned mainly to get them authenticated and do not go any further. They talk to the people who had the experience, they talk to witnesses, they record dates and if possible they offer diary notes, letters or other independent supports. But suppose we had to build a science of psychology only by carefully authenticated observations. Suppose, worse still, that we based our experimental studies only on events in laboratories, with very little reference to spontaneous situations in

the outside world. More than laboratory work, parapsychology needs enormously better spontaneous cases, especially ones that give us more knowledge of the psychophysiological situation of the persons involved. Well-planned experiments can follow, not precede.

A young man had been teaching an amateur astronomy class at the "Y" in Dallas. When he arrived home, he sat on the edge of his bed before lying down. Suddenly there in the room was his father, wearing a work cap and work clothes, with a caliper rule in his lapel pocket. How could this be? His father was in California. As he greeted his father, the figure disappeared and a messenger from Western Union came up the path with a wire from the mother in California saying that the father had just died. He had been working on the car that day, and beside the bed on a chair were his cap and work clothes, with a caliper rule in the lapel pocket.

Here again, we know very little about the physics, the psychology, the "meaning" of the experience. One person may call this telepathy, another may not. It is not clear that the process of naming it is really helpful in providing a scientific perspective within which the event makes sense.

In an early attempt to "control" events something like these without destroying their spontaneous quality, the French chemical engineer Rene Warcollier organized a group in Paris whose purpose was to "transmit" to a second group in New York. Warcollier, in a dreamy state, was trying *not* to think about the image of a stag's horn that had figured in the experiments earlier that day. He visualized the beakers and cups of his laboratory; in particular, he saw in his mind's eye a glass funnel. One of the people in New York drew, at this moment, a two-handled compote glass [see illustration, below]. She remarked that the handles were "like the horns of a stag." This experiment is characteristic of the way much parapsychological data is studied.

"But let us get on," says the psychologist, "with well-designed experiments, with an emphasis upon quantitative method and adequate statistics." The outstanding experiment of Warcollier's era, just after World War I, was carried out at the University of Groningen in the Netherlands. Experimenters in an upper room looked down through plate-glass sheets into a lower room in which a subject, in a black cage and blindfolded, received randomly selected numbers and letters. The numbers and letters indicated to him which square on a checkerboard, lying just beyond a slit through the black drapes of his cage, he should touch. He did fantastically well over several weeks, each week getting huge "antichance" values. Then, apparently rather suddenly, whatever was happening came to an end. The same effect occurred later in experiments conducted by George H. Estabrooks at Harvard—phenomenal scores at first, followed by a fade-out—and it will certainly continue to occur at long as we do not know what is at work.

One of the primary demands made upon modern experimenters is truly *repeatable* experiments. An excellent example of what has and has not been achieved is the work of Gertrude R. Schmeidler, beginning with studies at Harvard during World War II and continuing at the City College of New York since that time. Her basic hypothesis was that, when tested under proper experimental conditions, those people who accepted the possibility of success under the conditions of the experiment would score significantly above chance expectation; those rejecting this possibility would not.

Extensive experimentation at Harvard showed that she was right. Schmeidler divided her subjects into two groups, those who accepted the possibility of ESP under the conditions of the experiment and those who did not. When the subjects were placed in a closed room and asked to identify the order of cards in another closed room 40 feet away, the first group scored significantly above chance expectation. The second group scored not *at* chance, but *below* chance. As cycle after cycle continued, it became clear that this was a consistent pattern:

those who "believed in" ESP scored well above chance, and those who rejected it scored significantly below.

Schmeidler has duplicated the results of this first study about 20 times now, and most independent investigators who use a similar method have found the same pattern. But her experiment has not been replicated in the full, formal sense. It is not possible to tell with absolute certainty which run of 25 cards will be successful; nor is it possible, within a given successful run, to identify specific scores.

In another group of telepathic experiments, Montague Ullman and Stanley Krippner, working at the Maimonides Medical Center in Brooklyn, have found that pictures shown to "senders" in one room can affect the dreams of sleeping "receivers" in another room, nearly 100 feet away and behind many closed doors. For example, when Ullman and Kripp-

ESP EXPERIMENT. Did thoughts of man in Paris reach woman who drew this in N.Y.?

ner showed Marc Chagall's *The Drinker* [*see illustration, opposite*] to a sender in one room, the dreams of the receiver (awakened during periods of rapid eye movement) went like this:

First dream report: No apparent correspondences.

Second dream report: "I don't know whether it's related to the dream that I had, but *right now there's a commercial song that's going through my mind—it's about a beer. About Ballantine beer.* The words are, 'Why is Ballantine beer like an opening night, a race that finishes neck and neck, or a ride on the toboggan slide?' The commercial is running through my mind, and this song . . . There's this *big dinner party . . .* A young woman had apparently come to the city with somebody else who had come *to this dinner . . .* and *she was wearing what was supposed to be a cocktail dress, and it was black,* and the shape of it was mostly nondescript, but it was studded with rhinestones . . . That *table* was really empty all the time. All it had on

it was *plates, empty white plates . . ."*

Third dream report: ". . . I had been *in a restaurant* next door, eating . . ., *and in this restaurant there was a separate section that was a bar,* and in the dream I was at this place a number of different nights. The dream seemed to have some sort of time dimension because there was *a bartender,* a short fellow. There was another guy there, and the first night *they sent over a drink for me . . .* This girl wanted them to go or something . . . *She had loads of make-up on, and lots of black eye shadow, and black eye pencil lining; her eyes and black eyebrows, and her lips were black, too . . .* And she wanted to know what I had done with my hair because I had my hair in a pony tail and it was very short in front, and *she thought I'd cut it . . . That whole bar business and the restaurant and the booth* are like a place that I was at in Massachusetts . . . The most strange thing about the whole dream and all of its complications is the transformation of Carol . . . to this *garish, very pasty, very thick make-up base, and this black lipstick and black eye business and black eyebrow stuff.* I associate that immediately to that *black dress* with too many rhinestones on it in the other dream . . . *The black business seems to leave the realm of something that I can say is a personal association . . ."*

Ullman and Krippner's work with one gifted subject, especially, has been replicated at a very high level of significance. The subject, a male psychotherapist, was paired with a male psychologist for a seven-night series. The psychotherapist was able to match his own dreams against the art prints that had been shown to the psychologist at a statistically significant level of accuracy. Three outside judges matched the dream transcripts and the target pictures even more accurately than did the psychotherapist himself.

Two years later, the same pair took part in an eight-night study. This time, the psychologist-sender used a box of "multisensory" materials as well as a target picture. For example, a picture showing an artist was accompanied by a canvas and water-color paints so that the psychologist could "act out" the role of the artist. When three judges again matched the psychotherapist's dream transcripts and the art prints, the results were highly significant.

The brilliant new experimental work of Thelma Moss and J. A. Gengerelli of UCLA has also been replicated with some success. Moss and Gengerelli, observing that most spontaneous cases of telepathy occur when the sender is under emotional stress, surmised that experiments with cards might not be the best way to test telepathy in the laboratory. So they set out to experiment with the transmission of emotionally charged material.

Senders viewed slides and listened to tapes on various subjects that were likely to arouse emotion of some sort. One slide-tape presentation concerned the assassination of President Kennedy, which had occurred nine months earlier. It included excerpts from the Inaugural Address; the song *In the Summer of His Years;* pictures of the President's arrival in Dallas; the motorcade; Robert Kennedy and Jackie leaving Dallas; the flag-draped bier with Jackie and her children kneeling beside it. The tape concluded with the President's voice: "Ask not what your country can do for you; ask rather what you can do for your country."

At the conclusion of the presentation, each sender and (in another room) each receiver was asked to report his feelings and impressions. One pair's responses went like this:

Sender

This of course was the ex-President Kennedy speaking to the American people, and then following his assassination which was dreadful, with scenes of Jackie trying to protect him, and then later—where I believe she was at the hospital — with the bloodstains on her suit, and then of course the final resting place and the floral bouquet of our President, and his voice again was heard with his famous words.

Receiver

I seem to have the feeling of sadness or sorrow . . . as if I were crying . . . or something tragic has happened and that I was grieving over something . . . much the same as one might feel attending a funeral of a dear friend . . . or a well-known figure in whom one had faith. The feeling is one of grief or sorrow for someone being lost or gone. I feel that I am not alone . . . I'm in a group of people who are similarly either bereaved or grieving over something that is lost irretrievably . . . or someone who has died. I seem to feel that most of these people are sad, or crying, or both. I think that's about all.

When Moss and Gengerelli asked a group of judges to match the responses of 30 senders and 30 receivers to the various slide-tape presentations, seven

"THE DRINKER." This painting by Chagall helped show effect of telepathy on dreams.

out of 12 judges were able to do so significantly more accurately than they would have by chance. Only one of the 12 judges (all professional psychologists and psychiatrists) matched the impressions of 23 control sender-receiver teams at a level significantly above chance.

Of course it would be better if the groups of judges could be eliminated and if the receivers' responses, punched on cards in a pattern, could be objectively matched with a pattern punched on senders' cards. To develop such a procedure will take time. Today, groups of judges are standard practice in many experiments. It can gradually be improved or replaced.

Many psychologists think of psychology as a well-articulated structure of many experiments. Parapsychology has the same goal. The serious parapsychologist tries to investigate the full range of interactions between organisms and their environment through mediating agencies not known to the science of today. He must be ready to investigate lights, sounds and movements of objects, in relation to wishes and fears—clocks that stop at the moment of death or, in a lighter vein, the behavior of "hot dice."

However, the experimental method is only one part of the total field of parapsychology and, because of this, parapsychology bears more resemblance to, say, astronomy or geology than it does to physics. Astronomers use the terrestrial laboratory of physics to deal with such phenomena as ionization, the spectroscopic analysis of stellar chemical elements, and so forth, but this does not

make astronomy, as a whole, an experimental science. Similarly with geology. You may carry a rock into the petrology or mineralogy laboratory and study it experimentally, but this does not make geology an experimental science. Parapsychology—and psychology as well—is much more like geology than it is like physics, because experimentation is only one corner of its methodology. It is the *intelligible system of events,* not the experimental method, that constitutes the science; the experimental method must fit into a cosmic frame.

How does this bear on research strategy in this pioneer field?

Our *first* need, I think, is for better recording and analyses of cases of spontaneous telepathy, working from these to better-planned developmental, cross-cultural and experimental studies.

Our second great need is for persons with broad knowledge of the published literature in the field, because it is among them that we may develop the systematic theoretical model-building that we so badly need.

The third need is to find fellowships and scholarships for people with a sound and broad understanding of science and of scientific method, who know something about the history of the struggle of science against poorly understood phenomena. Most psychologists get their experimental training and their general scientific training in the easy groove prepared for them by an instructor who knows a research specialty, who knows the methods, who knows what is likely to happen in the rather safe little experiments that are acceptable for master's and doctor's degree requirements. But a person has to be able to open the door to the unknown, to let it in and make friends with it, in order to do anything that is likely to be new or valuable in a frontier area.

Fourth, we need people who are philosophically sophisticated and who can think about time, space, motion and energy without becoming frightened. They must not get bogged down in unreal questions as to what could or could not be a chance effect. They must be concerned (as are the astronomer and the geologist) with model-building, and (as is the philosopher) with conceptualization that goes beyond the assumed inevitable operation of the time-space-energy modalities as we know them through 19th Century physics.

Most of all, we need in this field people who understand the concept of replication of experimental findings. We need people to develop repeatable experiments, the corners of solid fact that allow the filling out of a new kind of science, one that deals with parameters of personality of which we are almost wholly ignorant.

I have not spent time on controversies, which spread on and on. The problem is one of clear conceptualization, steadfast derivation of hypotheses, building of research methodology, and systematic replication. Some will go on saying we are credulous, and some of us are. Some will go on saying we are frauds, and some of us are. The problems will continue and the effort to resolve them will continue. The poorly sketched frontier of today will become a more solid frontier, advancing into a definite conquerable territory — if we can have the kinds of people that I have named: the systematic and careful collectors of evidence, the well-trained experimentalists, the historians of the frontier battle of science, the scientific conceptualizers, the philosophers, and above all the systematic replicators.

There may remain some misunderstanding about the relation of replication to the building of a science. For a large number of replicated fragments can still fail to create a satisfying intellectual system. Henry Margenau, professor of physics and natural philosophy at Yale, has cogently developed the concept that science is much more than a system of interrelated experimental findings. It must be woven into a tight structure at the center, with basic concepts clearly and coherently expressed, and with an open fringe permitting new facts to fall into place. But its integrity must be such that each part is consistent with all the rest, and at the same time it must allow from day to day the advent of new observations that are not inconsistent with those already obtained and systematized. This requires much more than "operational" thinking; it involves operations, construct validity, internal coherence and, Margenau believes, an aesthetic satisfaction—a certain elegance—as well.

Parapsychologists expect a bit more than they will get when they ask for careful attention to their successfully replicated experiments. Take, for example, the Schmeidler experiments. Even if every replication, by her and by others, gave data like those already reported, this would still not make the phenomena congruent with our general physical conceptions of the relations of subjects to their environments. Or take Ullman's studies. Regardless of replication, they still will not fall easily into the psychiatric and psychological patterns that characterize the beliefs of most investigators, subjects and the reading public. Experimenters will find it difficult, for example, to get "study sections" and staff support from large Federal granting agencies. And Moss and Gengerelli's findings, which are in some ways a tremendous breakthrough, do not present that internal consistency that makes it likely we have here a highly repeatable and predictable type of performance. Even if we did, it would take more than psychological common sense to generate the principle that emotionally charged target materials are likely to be successfully transmitted to a subject at a distance under conditions of proper shielding and safety against any possibility of sensory communication. Moss and Gengerelli, as well as Ullman and Schmeidler, will have to await the time when their experiments dovetail not only with the psychology but with the physics of today's world view.

I do not quite mean today's world view. The quantum-relativity-uncertainty physics of today has, for the most part, no objection to parapsychological phenomena at all. Many modern physicists greet the new experiments with interest and even enthusiasm. It is the physics of the 19th Century, persisting in terms of current space-time patterns, that makes the phenomena "impossible." A cultural lag is common, after all, in science as well as in religion and folklore. Thus the congruence of parapsychological data with physical data depends upon the maturation of psychology and of the communications currently used by psychologists to relate findings to what is conceived to be physical reality. It is too much to expect that the reality of 1968 be studied; that is not the nature of the history of thought.

E. G. Boring has dealt with these issues in a somewhat different way, notably through his repeated expressions of unwillingness to accept parapsychological data that do not fit into the current world view. When you talk about how bats can navigate without hitting wires, Boring is skeptical of the scientific utility of any approach that does not include the wires and the bats' receptors, and the physical relations between them. He is skeptical of all parapsychological findings that do not define the physical relation between stimulus and receptor. This is a perfectly normal and natural point of view to take if one operates within the framework of a psychology based on the essentially Newtonian relation of physical stimulus pattern and organismic response. And I agree with Boring that most scientists will continue to insist upon a physicalist link before they will toy with phenomena that, in their nature, cannot easily provide such a physical modality, especially phenomena that relate to future events not inferable from present knowledge.

However, Boring is not talking about the conditions under which a very new science can win accreditation. Suppose the issue were stated somewhat differently: does science spring full-blown from the folklore that is its ancestor? The answer would appear to be no. There are long periods of "proto-science"— periods of exploratory, adolescent behavior—that sometimes give way to maturity and sometimes do not.

Parapsychologists must expect to be regarded as strange and even antisocial if they persist in investigations that are intrinsically "anti-scientific" and therefore somewhat dangerous to their colleagues. There is no sense, however, in spending time feeling sorry for oneself. The thing to do is to accept criticism with as much grace as possible and get on with the job.

And what can science do for a proto-science that is trying to grow up? Well, it could try opening the door and inviting the young stranger in for a chat. If the gap between the generations is too great for that, perhaps it could at least leave the door unlocked? ◖

46

II. learning and motivation

sychologists differ in the emphasis they place on the two inseparable processes of learning and motivation. Learning and its basis in reward and reinforcement are considered fundamental—almost to the exclusion of motivation—by a small but pronounced segment of experimental psychologists engaged in the study of animals. But overwhelmingly in the majority are the psychologists who find the most telling and lasting understanding of human and animal behavior in terms of motivation. Neither point of view can ignore the other, nor can either bypass the fundamentally physiological nature of both the process of learning and the basis of motivation.

The motivational point of view is introduced here by Herzberg, whose article is followed by a sober but animalistic critique by Fantino. Herzberg's emphasis is on the motives of real people in real situations, searching after real rewards and avoiding the pitfalls of unreal rewards. It is complemented by Fantino's humorously serious account of a series of mistaken proofs of the doctrine of functional anatomy. This doctrine, which arose from the insightful writings of the late Gordon W. Allport of Har-

vard, has the credo "Drives drive now!" Herzberg's delineation of the fundamental truth of this credo is balanced by Fantino's exploration of how the experiences of an organism provided for the existence of those drives that do drive now.

Learning's most immediate application is in the field of education. Verhave shows that when the proper arrangements of motivation, reward, and stimulus are provided, animals are capable of learning to perform in an almost superhuman fashion. Some of the lessons learned in the early days of such work with animals have recently been applied to the day-to-day demands of a real educational system. Uttal describes some of the consequences of this application in "Teaching and Machines," while Atkinson attempts to foresee what impact these insights into the educational process will have on the technology of teaching when they are combined with the abilities and potentialities of an electronic computer put to work as a teacher.

Motivations of animals have long been studied because it is impossible ethically to coerce volunteers or to find subjects willing to undergo the variety and extremes of conditions indispensable to even a rudimentary understanding of the motivational process. Experiments with animals, without which psychology in the United States would have never crossed the threshold of factual knowledge of motivation, are represented here by reports of several recent programs of study. Rubin and Bermant write on sexual motives, their basis, and their consequences among rabbits and rats. Dethier describes what can be learned about motivational systems in general from the study of the specific appetitive motivation of the hungry, though ordinary, fly. No pretenses are made, of course, that what these investigators have discovered applies word for word (or even principle for principle) to the motivational structure of people. But, in addition to their status as excellent pure science, no reader will be able to escape the clear implications of these studies for analogies to man.

The physiological basis—or at least the correlates—of learning and memory are discussed in two learned articles. Their diversity illustrates both the potential and the accomplished contribution of the area of physiological psychology to the psychology of learning and motivation. Halstead and Rucker present a possible molecular basis of memory. Halstead (and Katz) published this idea, a first in its field, from the University of Chicago some three decades ago, and it is a lasting tribute to the continuity and progress of science that these ideas can and do bear fruit in psychology today. Deutsch presents a system of memory based on the effects of pharmacological compounds on the central nervous system. His theory bodes well for the rejuvenation of the physiological study of memory.

Of quite another sort is Nathan Azrin's treatment of pain and aggression. It is interesting that among the lower animals careful investigation can tease out extraordinary order between these two phenomena of such obvious complexity in human beings. Azrin demonstrates the relationship and order; it is for the reader to wonder if he is perhaps not saying something of undeniable importance for the human condition.

By Frederick Herzberg

MOTIVATION, MORALE

MONEY IS THE GREAT MOTIVATOR, the carrot that makes the donkey go, the grain that waits at the end of the maze. If you want increased productivity from your employees, give them a raise. The man in the street nods approvingly at this bit of folk wisdom, and management, which should know better, nods just as approvingly. There is yet another bit of wisdom that directly contradicts the first maxim, but when the donkey and the carrot are trotted out, it remains forgotten. No one remembers that a wise man once said, "Man does not live by bread alone." And, in spite of all the donkeys that plod after their carrots, in spite of all the rats that learn to pick their ways through elaborate mazes, it remains the more dependable statement, the one that is borne out by observation and experience.

Many in industry continue to adhere to the belief that an increase in wages motivates the worker to increase his output, which in turn leads to higher wages that further motivate the worker . . . and so on. But does productivity really go up because of wage increases? We all know the answer: of course not. Yet, although this concept of what motivates man does not fit reality, industry does not question the rationality of the concept. That, to them, is self-evident. If the results are not in accord with theory, then it must be the worker who is at fault, either because he is immoral or irrational.

So the experts then are brought in to solve the problem. They study the worker and find that he has "feelings" of inadequacy, insecurity, inferior status, and the like. He does not understand the big picture, his job, his boss, or himself. The boss comes under scrutiny as well. Obviously, he does not communi-

cate properly with the worker, or else the worker would understand his boss and his job. The boss does not communicate because he does not understand the big picture, his job, the worker, or himself. The end result of the probing is that nobody understood anybody. Called in originally to cure irrationality, the experts end up saying that man is incurably irrational, and the best that can be done is to fit "irrational" man as closely as possible into the "rational" system.

This fitting of man into the system is achieved by a process often called job "rationalization," which involves having jobs reduced to their simplest components by industrial engineers, and then making each worker's job a reflex-level task. When these sterile tasks cause dissatisfaction in the workers, the behavioral scientists are brought in. After careful study, they conclude that the worker in fact does not get any satisfaction from his tasks and advise that the worker should be given a *sense* of achievement, but do not go so far as to infringe upon the domain of the industrial engineers by suggesting that jobs should be designed to fulfill man's need for achievement. To dampen the frustrations of the workers, human relation counselors are hired to let employees blow off steam by listening to their complaints. But much of the counseling amounts to little more than telling the employee how well the system would function if he stopped being irrational and allowed his "rational" motivation for money to express itself.

The end result of the interference by the production-prodders hired by industry is the dissipation of some very real human potential—all because of ignorance or misunderstanding of human nature and the basis of human motivation.

When the worker fails to respond to the prevailing system of money motivation, he is called irrational and "unmotivated." Paradoxically, the executive who already has the money he really needs, and continues to work a 12-, 14- or even 16-hour day, is called "motivated." In neither case does the myth of money motivation explain satisfactorily why the men act the way they do.

Money is not a great motivator unless, perhaps, workers are kept below the subsistence level so they must work harder to eat more. To say that man can be spurred to heights of achievement by the promise of food puts him in the category of Pavlov's conditioned dog. Such a belief, while it may not bother some theorists, just is not true.

A dog can be conditioned to perform some task by rewarding him with food. A man will also perform some tasks in return for some reward. But in both cases, the next time you want either the dog or the man to do the task, you must again provide a reward. Of course, as Pavlov demonstrated, there are ways to evoke a response without actually having to present the reward. Instead of stimulus-reward, you can have stimulus-response. But this kind of conditioning produces *movement,* not motivation. And with movement, an external stimulus is always required. Even Pavlov had to ring a bell when he wanted his conditioned animals to react.

The promise of money can *move* a man to work, but it cannot *motivate* him. Motivation means an inner desire to make an effort. No external stimulus is needed, because it comes from man's innate need for self-realization, from his need to fulfill his potential as a person. And this need is just as real as his need

& MONEY

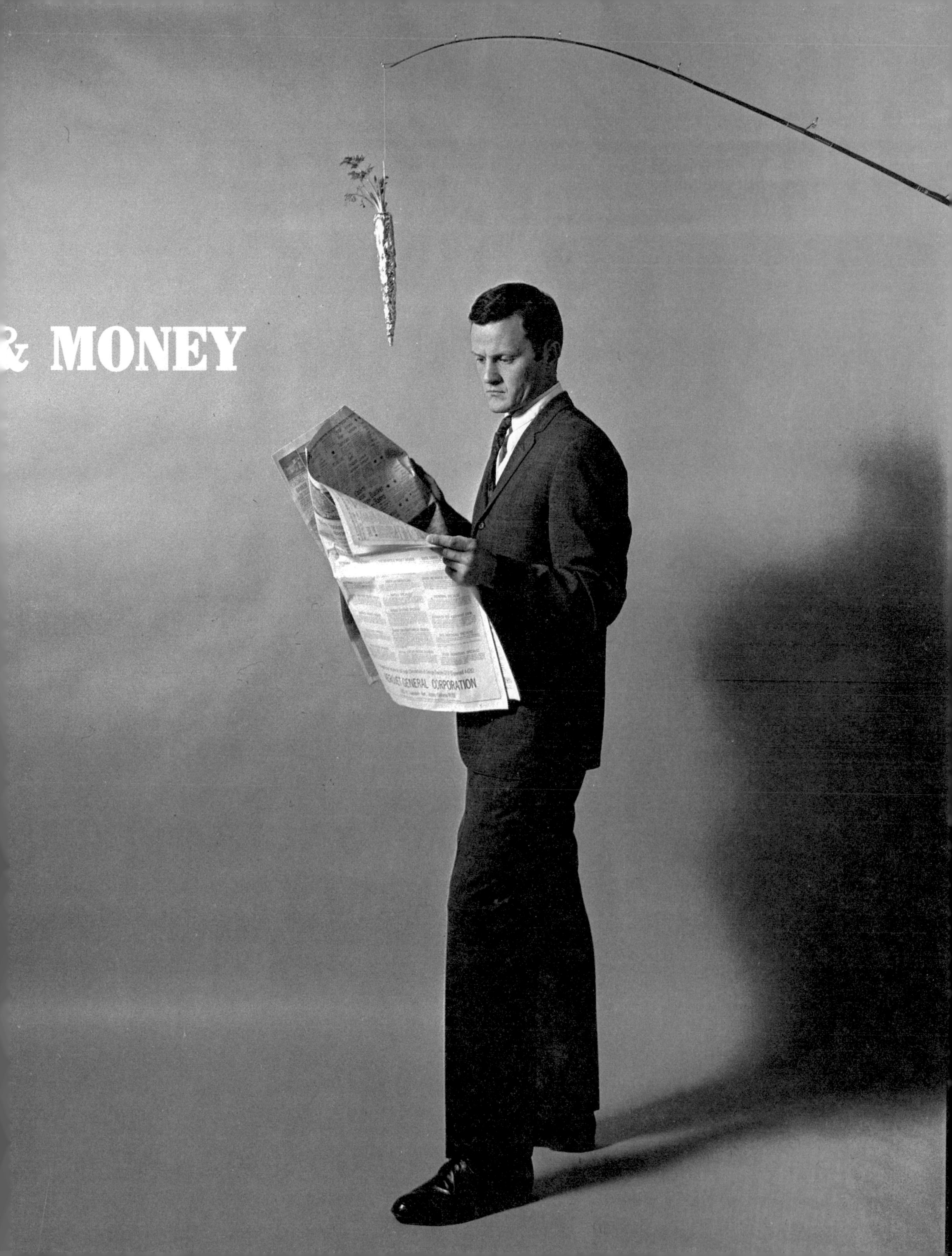

for food. Just as a desire for food will not be satisfied by a book, neither will his craving for accomplishment be sated by a piece of apple pie.

Through his myths, man long has recognized his own dual nature. The Old Testament, the most important myth system in our civilization, offers two opposed versions of man's nature, both proceeding directly from God.

The first is described in Adam, who because he attempted to usurp God's power, was condemned to root and suffer like an animal. The drives of this side of man's nature are centered on the avoidance of hunger, pain, sexual deprivation and the infinite variety of learned fears that have become attached to these basic drives.

The other version of man's nature appears with Abraham, who through a "covenant" offered by God was to grow in mastery of the things around him and of his own destiny: "The Lord appeared to Abraham, and said unto him; I am God Almighty; walk before Me, and be thou wholehearted, and I will make My covenant between Me and thee and will multiply thee exceedingly. . . . And thou shalt be the father of a multitude of many nations" (Genesis 17:1). Man, as epitomized in Abraham, has been given the injunction to realize his innate potentialities.

The Christian Church utilized the Adam view of human nature to maintain its authority over men. Man was naturally sinful but could be saved by conforming to the Church's doctrines. The Renaissance kindled the belief that achievement was an important need for mankind, and this view that man had positive potentialities led to the Industrial Revolution. Every society has to establish myths in order to sustain its institutional forms, to make it easier to shape and control human behavior. Industry, as the newly dominant institution, set up its own myths to serve its organizational needs. But as it turns out, business institutions merely altered the contents of man's avoidance needs and developed the myth of "mechanistic man." Man became machine's helper, and the machine took over the direction and coordination of the task. Jobs were "rationalized." That is, if one man has ten talents, another nine, and so on down to one man with one talent, the way in which their work efficiency can be maximized is to structure the work task so that only the one or more talents in common will be used. In this way the possibility of error is minimized. The waste of human talent, however, is maximized.

The system of utilizing only the lowest common denominator of available human talents makes man easier to control. It also creates the conditions for boredom—repetition and consistency—and also mental illness. Chris Argyris, of Yale University, demonstrated that even mental patients can do a job after it has been "rationalized." When he brought in some mental patients to work at a routine job in a factory setting, he found that they worked without complaint and were very easy to supervise. They also increased production by 400 per cent.

The Motivation-Hygiene Theory

Our motivation-hygiene concept of job attitudes arose from a research study which Bernard Mausner and Barbara Snyderman and I conducted among 200 engineers and accountants in the Pittsburgh area in 1958. The study was designed to test the hypothesis of the duality of man's nature, that man has two sets of needs which are essentially independent of each other, and which operate in opposing directions.

We asked the engineers and accountants about experiences at work that had a marked effect in increasing their job satisfaction. We also asked if the feelings of satisfaction had affected their performance, their personal relationships, and their well-being.

The interview was then repeated, but this time the workers were asked to describe experiences that had resulted in a marked increase in job dissatisfaction. In both cases, the interview was patterned to determine not only what experiences affected job satisfaction, but what factors and circumstances prevailed at the time.

Five factors stood out as strong determiners of job satisfaction: achievement, recognition for achievement, work itself, responsibility, and advancement. All these were related to what a person does, not to the situation in which he does it.

A completely different set of factors emerged as the job dissatisfiers: company policy and administration, supervision, salary, interpersonal relations, and working conditions. All these were extrinsic to the nature of the work: they described the environment of the job.

Most approaches for improving worker motivation assume that if a man is not dissatisfied with his job, he is satisfied, and, therefore, he works better. Actually, our study showed that one can be both satisfied and dissatisfied with a job—at the same time. One reaction does not cancel out, preclude, or produce the other.

I chose to call the *dissatisfiers* the *hygiene* factors, drawing by analogy on the medical meaning of the word "preventative and environmental." Hygiene factors are not an intrinsic part of a task, they are related to the conditions under which a task is to be performed. A good hygienic environment can prevent job *dis*satisfaction, but cannot create true job satisfaction or happiness.

This is because of the cyclical nature necessary to sustain life or the needs of man's animal or hygiene drives. When these drives are not relieved a man becomes discontented but when they are relieved the effect lasts for only a short time. The hygiene needs are like hunger. After a man has eaten, he is no longer hungry. After a time he becomes hungry again and needs food just as badly as if he had not eaten before. One can see how this relates to salary. If a man wants a raise, he is unhappy until he gets it. Once he gets it and after some time passes, he will begin to want another raise just as badly as if he had never received the first one.

Because salary is the most talked about factor in the world of work, it is hardly surprising that on superficial analysis it should be categorized as a satisfier factor. The lack of money causes so much unhappiness that when it is alleviated the following period is easily viewed as a happy one. But this happiness is of short duration, compared to the satisfaction obtained from true achievement or recognition of achievement. Relieving the hygienic needs of a man merely makes him adjusted to his environment and creates an absence of dissatisfaction. When hygienic needs are continuously satisfied, it produces a kind of opiate relief, an animal state of comfort or pain avoidance. Positive satisfaction or happiness seems to require some attainment or psychological growth.

The greatest contribution of psychology has been in determining the content of man's physical needs. The external effects and characteristics of psychological growth of self-realization are being increasingly studied, and some of the known characteristics are: learning (knowing more), discovering new relationships between events, greater individuality through development of innate potentialities, and creativity.

There were some individuals who reported receiving job satisfaction solely from hygiene factors. These hygiene seekers, who are motivated to seek only relief of dissatisfaction, have not reached the stage of personal development in which the need for self-realization is active. In other words, hygiene seekers seek happiness by avoidance behavior and are fixated at a low level of maturity.

Industry, by ignoring man's psychological need for growth and structuring jobs and rewards as if man had only animal drives, creates the condition for perpetuating immaturity. Obviously, this is a self-confirming hypothesis. The worker is made to respond like an animal, and when he conforms, he is labeled an animal, or more euphemistically, a "mechanistic man."

In summary, the two essential findings from the Pittsburgh study are that motivator needs and the hygiene needs are separate and distinct, and that they are not reciprocal. They operate independently of each other, and fulfilling one need does not affect the other. Our original study has been repeated 16 times in a wide variety of occupations ranging from scientists to household help. In addition, our method has been used to study workers in Finland, Hungary, and the Soviet Union. Few studies in industrial psychology have been repeated so often, and the evidence appears to be overwhelmingly in support of the basic hypothesis.

Contrary to the prevailing belief, the studies show that basic needs of the blue-collar worker or the assembly-line worker are no different from those of the white-collar worker The primary sources of job satisfaction for both groups are achievement and recognition.

To Meet Man's Needs

Leaders in industry claim to offer challenge and the opportunity for achievement in the business world. But they must learn to recognize that the typical management approach to *man as a worker* actually blocks man's efforts to achieve his full potential. The primary function of any human organization is to help man enjoy a meaningful existence. Labor has always been the lot of man, but the changes brought by the industrial revolution have for the first time given him the opportunity to satisfy both his animal and his human needs.

As Carl Jung said: "The supreme goal of man is to fulfill himself as a creative, unique individual according to his own innate potentialities and within the lim-

its of reality." Industry is the dominant institution in our civilization, and therefore must restructure itself to reflect man's dual nature and needs if it is to live up to its responsibility to help man enjoy a meaningful life.

The rationalization of human jobs perhaps has gone too far, and the problems of worker motivation and morale are becoming, in many cases, more costly than the money saved by the mechanical efficiencies which are gained. The completely rationalized job can and, likely, will be taken over by automated machines. This offers organizations the opportunity to restructure the work man must do in terms of developing human potential.

Jobs could be structured around man's true motivations for work. The organization could have two formal personnel relations divisions—a division of hygiene concerned with the environmental needs of the employee, and a division of motivation concerned with the learning and psychological growth of the employee, and which could provide greater responsibilities or remedial actions as required.

Although senior executives in industry often say they are seeking men who are self-starters, men who can accept responsibility, the same executives often find it impossible to delegate real power. One executive called me in and complained that he had been trying to delegate some of his responsibilities to his five department heads, "But the trouble is, these guys just won't take any." After hearing the executive's story, I talked to two of the department heads, watched them work for several days, found out what their duties were, and how they performed them. I discovered that they truly didn't have responsibility. They had been given none. Each was "in charge" of a certain area of operations, but in charge in name only. The manager under each of them had all the real operational responsibility and command. These managers reported to the department heads, who in turn passed on the reports to the executive. And the executive made all the policy decisions. The department heads really were only information conduits. I built a new job containing real responsibility and real challenge for one of the department heads after discussions with him and his colleagues. When I turned in the job outline to the executive, he shouted, "I can't let him do that!" In claiming to me that his department heads would not take any responsibility, the president was only creating an excuse to cover up the basic

inability on his part to delegate authority.

Giving out responsibility requires a tolerance for the *possibility* of error on the part of the giver. Company recruiters use motivator terms such as *challenge, opportunity,* and *responsibility* to attract young college graduates. But after the graduate is hired, it is not psychological growth he finds, but the opposite. Attitude surveys of college graduates show that after the glow of the first year on the job, job satisfaction plummets to its lowest level.

Although the college graduate who goes into a business career is given a relatively high salary, his job satisfaction is usually low. There is another kind of college graduate who starts his career under the worst type of working conditions—very low pay, extremely long working hours, no pension plan or other fringe benefits—and turns out to be highly motivated in his work. This is the intern, the doctor-in-training. Although he may be thoroughly *dis*satisfied with his working conditions, his morale and his job satisfaction are high. This is because he is given real responsibility with live patients, and the kind of supervision that helps him learn and grow psychologically. Certainly, if this kind of responsibility and supervision can be given in an area where life and death are at stake, the same should be possible in industry.

Of course, not all jobs in industry have the potential to be challenging and achievement-oriented. But many more than one might expect of today's jobs do contain possibilities. One example of the striking lack of success of the present money motivation system is portrayed in the case of today's computer programmers. The computer is one of the most exciting developments of our times. Yet there is a high turnover rate and low morale among computer programmers. The cause of dissatisfaction is not the pay, for these men receive high salaries and excellent fringe benefits. Rather, the problem is boredom; after the initial challenge, most companies allow their computer programming to turn into routine drudgery. This need not happen: certainly it would not be difficult to build some true motivational factors into a job with as much potential challenge as this.

A job does not have to be as exotic as computer programming to have challenge. An excellent example of how challenge can be put into a routine job is the following: One large company has a correspondence section to answer the questions of its shareholders, many of whom were not sophisticated in the intricacies of security laws. To answer questions on transfer of ownership, dividend income, and the like, this company employs a number of girls who previously worked under a system engineered to insure that no wrong information was given. The answers to the shareholder letters were not so much written as "built." When an inquiry came in it went through a routinized procedure which used answers copied from form paragraphs for every possible question. A girl combined the proper answers, made sure that the salutation and closing were in the correct formal style, and handed the letter to the supervisor for checking. The supervisor checked every letter, then sent it out over her signature. In practice, the system resulted in too many errors, low productivity, and high employee turnover and absentee rates. What was at fault, of course, was the lack of motivation in the job. So the company built in some motivation, and it took all of six months to change the situation. First, each girl was made an expert in some area, say transfer taxes. She, not the supervisor, was the authority for the girls to turn to on that subject. Next the girls were to sign their own letters. The next step was to let each girl decide her own pace instead of being told, "We have 60 letters to get through today." The natural progression was then to let the girls send out their mail without passing it on to the supervisor. The girls were to be responsible for the letters and if any bounced back from the shareholders, they would go back to the girls. In the final week, girls were told to compose their own letters. The form paragraphs could be used as information sources, but could not be copied.

The result? Errors were markedly reduced, morale raised, productivity increased, and employee turnover and absenteeism dropped. The supervisor found time for numerous measures to improve conditions in the department. All this, not by increasing salary, or rationalizing the job, but by injecting responsibility, challenge, and the opportunity for growth. In short, by motivation.

Motivation cannot be bought. A motivated man will do things of his own volition that far exceed what he could be made to do by offers of food or money. The strongest kind of motivation is self-motivation. Consider the artist, a classic example of self-motivation. He may be starving, but still he paints.

OF MICE AND MISERS

By Edmund Fantino

As long as there has been money there have been misers. And almost as long as there have been misers there have been people—even kings—scrutinizing them. "Misers are very kind people: they amass wealth for those who wish their death," said Stanislaus I, 18th Century king of Poland. Hidden behind the elegant Polish irony of his aphorism is a psychological mystery.

The miser poses two questions for psychology. The first, and easier, question is, "How did he get that way?" Why and when did the miser begin the money-hoarding behavior that we find so reprehensible, unless, of course, we will benefit from his "kindness"? In some cases, the answer may be that he learned his thrifty habit in hard financial times; in other cases, the cause may be considerably more obscure. However, in this Freudian age we can surely accept the tenet that some experience or set of events in the individual's history has predisposed him toward this abnormal behavior.

Some experiments with rats make the point rather nicely: young rats frustrated by food deprivation will become hoarders. Later on, these rats continue to hoard food significantly more often than rats without a history of frustration. The persistence of the behavior indicates a long-term effect. Similarly with the miser. He acquires his characteristic behavior in the same manner as the rest of us, by lawful interaction with his environment.

The second and knottier question is, why does the miser's behavior *persist*, even when the environmental conditions that gave rise to it are no longer present? There are two possibilities. One is that, contrary to appearances, the environment is indeed providing rewards and punishments that are maintaining the behavior. The second is that behavior can persist even when it is not maintained by rewards or punishments. If that is true—if there is evidence that behavior is independent of rewards in even a small way—then we have a principle of fundamental importance to an understanding of man and to the science of psychology.

Before accepting such a principle, however, we must examine very carefully the empirical evidence on which it rests.

Means Into Ends?

One principle that might account for the miser is that of *functional autonomy*. "Activities and objects that earlier in the game were *means* to an end," said Gordon Allport when he formulated the concept, "now become ends in themselves." Or, in a later exposition, "What was once extrinsic and instrumental becomes intrinsic and impelling." In other words, behavior that has often led to reward may become rewarding *in itself*, even though it is no longer a mechanism for achieving the old reward. Robert S. Woodworth of Columbia University expressed the same idea in 1918, when he suggested that "the mechanism becomes the drive."

But before we conclude that an activity has become autonomous of the conditions that gave rise to it, we must rule out any more parsimonious explanations. To illustrate, let us abandon the miser for a moment and consider the hunter. We might assume that the hunter hunts in order to gain the biological reward of food. Next, assume that the hunter becomes affluent and begins to discard his prey, but continues to hunt. Has hunting behavior acquired functional autonomy? Can we conclude that it is no longer a way of satisfying a biological need and, in Woodworth's terminology, that the mechanism (hunting) for obtaining a biological reward (food) has now become a self-sustaining "drive"?

Not necessarily. It might be, for example, that the hunter would hunt before hunting produced food — that the behavior began in response to some other biological or primitive need, such as a need to be aggressive, and that that need is what maintains the behavior.

Before applying Allport's doctrine to the hunter, I suggest that we would have to demonstrate the following:

1. Hunting behavior does not originate when it does not produce food;
2. When food is available as a reward, hunting behavior originates and persists;
3. When the biological reward of food is no longer available, hunting behavior continues indefinitely, though not necessarily with the same frequency as before;
4. No apparent need (such as a need to be aggressive) has emerged since hunting began that is strong enough to explain the persistence of hunting behavior.

Points 1 and 2 would allow us to conclude that hunting behavior was established in response to the need for food; points 3 and 4 would show that the behavior had become autonomous of reward.

Demonstrating these things is necessarily difficult, particularly when considering human behavior influenced as it is by a complex set of controlling variables. In order to approach the problem of functional autonomy, therefore, studies have been performed using subhuman organisms in apparently straightforward experimental designs. Of course, evidence based exclusively on lower animals should not be uncritically extrapolated to human behavior. (Allport himself distinguished among varieties of autonomous behavior and insisted that some were exclusively human.) But experimental evidence should offer some insight into how the analysis of "autonomous" human behavior might proceed and should establish guidelines for an appraisal of the miser.

Sand-digging Mice

Two experiments in the animal literature have been used often and authoritatively as support for the concept of functional autonomy. One involves sand-digging in mice; the other, ear-scratching in rats. The study on sand-digging in mice was done by Robert Earl at Stanford University in 1957. Earl discovered that mice which had learned to dig *nine pounds* of sand in order to reach a reward box containing food continued to dig nine pounds of sand even when food

was no longer rewarding—that is, when the mice were not hungry. Earl remarked that the sand had developed an "invitational character"; others suggested that here was a perfect example of functional autonomy.

Michael Cole and I, then colleagues at Yale, decided to look into this phenomenon a bit further. We were interested in the implications of Earl's results for the doctrine of functional autonomy, but we were even more intrigued by the Herculean behavior the mice had displayed. We put 13 mice, 80 days old at the start of the experiment, through their paces, using apparatus similar to Earl's (*see illustration below*).

A mouse was placed in the digging compartment or start box. A rubber tube containing sand led from the start box to the reward box. As the mouse dug the sand out of the tube, it fell through the wire-mesh floor of the apparatus into a bucket, and more sand dropped into the tube from a jug located over a hole in the top of the tube. When the mouse had removed all the sand, it could walk through the tube to the reward box. As the mouse entered the box, a photocell beam stopped a time meter, giving us an automatic measure of how long the mouse took to dig through the sand. (Although watching mice dig is fun at first, it turns out to have little "invitational character.") The amount of sand dug was weighed after each session, and the digging rate recorded in grams per minute.

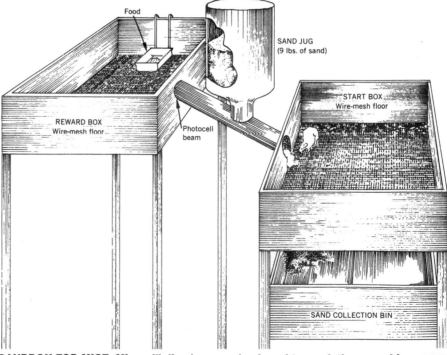

SANDBOX FOR MICE. Mice will dig nine pounds of sand to reach the reward box, even when they are not hungry—and even when no food has been provided in the box.

We gave our mice preliminary training by depriving them of food for 20 hours and by allowing them to explore the empty sand tube. For seven mice (Group 1), we placed food in the reward box, as Earl had. For the other six mice (Group 2), the reward box did not contain food. The amount of sand in the sand jug was gradually increased over a 25-day period from 0 to 4,300 grams, or about nine pounds. Each mouse was put in the sand tube every day and left there until it had dug through all the sand and entered the reward box, where it was permitted to remain for 15 minutes. On those few occasions when the mouse did *not* dig all the sand, it was removed from the digging compartment after two hours.

After these preliminary sessions, we conducted the experiment proper. It included three stages: 14 sessions under strong (20-hour) food deprivation; 11 sessions during which food was always available in the home cages, so that the mice were not hungry; and 27 sessions again under strong (20-hour) food deprivation. During the first and second stages, food was available in the reward box for Group 1 but not for Group 2; during the third stage, it was available in the reward box for Group 2 but not for Group 1.

There was a large range of digging rates. One mouse that was not receiving a food reward dug at an average rate of 12 grams per minute; two mice that *were* receiving food-rewards dug at about 100 grams per minute. But *every mouse did dig*, whether there was food in the reward box or not.

Our second finding was that hunger and the availability of food in the reward box both influenced the digging rate. Mice dig faster when there is a food-reward available, and they also dig faster when they are hungry. One mouse dug at an average rate of 54 grams per minute when hungry, even though no reward was offered. In the next stage of the experiment, when this mouse was *not* hungry, its digging rate slipped to 25 grams per minute. In the third stage, when the mouse was hungry and food-reward *was* available, its digging rate leapt to 109 grams per minute. It took this mouse less than 40 minutes to dig nine pounds of sand—more than 200 times its own weight!

Three additional mice were also studied, using a different procedure. For these mice, food was always available in the home cage. In addition, food and water were placed in the start box, and

there was no reward at all in the reward box. Nonetheless, when these mice were offered the opportunity to dig sand and gain access to the empty reward box, all three of them eventually dug nine pounds. Two dug at the rates of 38 and 70 grams per minute, well within the range established by the other mice. Stable measurements for the third mouse were not obtained. Soon after it first dug nine pounds, this mouse was found buried in the sand; apparently it had dug itself to death.

Thus mice dig sand whether or not digging produces food. There is no need to invoke the concept of functional autonomy to explain Earl's results or our own. The "invitational character" that Earl referred to appears not to have "developed" with rewarded digging, but to have been present from the start.

Ear-scratching Rats

In discussing the hunter, I stressed the need to ascertain whether hunting behavior would begin and continue before hunting produced food. The studies with mice show why this is important. It is unlikely, though, that a miser would hoard money *before* its reward-value had been established. Our next study, therefore, concerns a habit clearly acquired in response to environmental change.

In 1929, Willard Olson reported an experiment in which he placed the irritant collodion on rats' ears. The rats, he discovered, scratched their ears for several weeks after the collodion application, even though the evidence of tissue irritation had vanished. William Datel and John Seward of UCLA did a more elaborate version of Olson's study in 1952 and reported similar results. These studies have been widely cited as examples of functional autonomy by several authorities, including Allport himself in 1961.

J. J. Braun and I, together with two Yale seniors, William Vollero and Bruce Bradley, decided to investigate this persistent behavior a bit further, with greater attention to the possibility that tissue damage might explain the persistent ear-scratching. We also continued the experiment for a longer period of time than either Olson or Datel and Seward had, in order to see whether ear-scratching would return eventually to pre-collodion levels.

We used four groups of eight rats each. One group was never treated with collodion; the other three groups were administered three different concentrations of

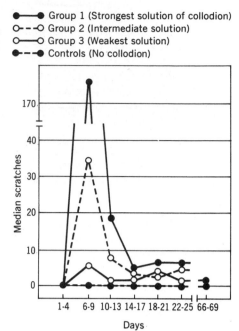

EAR-SCRATCHING. The stronger the irritant applied to the rats' ears, the more they scratch. The behavior persists for some weeks, but observation two months later shows that it does die out eventually.

the chemical, so that the degree of irritation—and, we hoped, the amount and persistence of ear-scratching—would vary.

Ear-scratching did increase dramatically on the four days when collodion was applied, and the stronger the concentration was, the more scratching the rats did (*see illustration above*). More than two weeks after the last application, the two groups of rats that had received the strongest concentrations were still scratching at a higher rate than they had before collodion was applied.

Up to the 25th day of the experiment, our results were similar to those obtained by previous workers, except that we used more than one collodion application. Previous workers, however, did not continue their experiments. When we observed our rats later on, at Days 66-69, the scratching had virtually disappeared in all groups. (The very slight scratching by the first group was not statistically significant.) Thus the "persistent" habit eventually ends.

In addition to recording the ear-scratching rates each day, an observer (Bradley or Vollero) examined the rats' ears daily for signs of tissue irritation. The observer was not told whether an ear had been treated with collodion or not. He was asked simply to judge whether either ear showed signs of irritation (redness, wrinkled skin, scabbing or residual collodion) and if so, which one.

Our most important finding concerned these blind judgments of tissue irritation. The groups that persisted in ear-scratching (Groups 1 and 2), were also reliably judged as having irritated ears. The four rats in each group were judged every day for 16 days (Days 10-25)—a total of 128 judgments per group. For Group 1, the treated ear was judged as irritated all 128 times; for Group 2, 126 times; in neither group was an untreated ear ever judged as treated. In Group 3, which had received the mildest concentration of collodion and did relatively little scratching, the ears were occasionally judged to have visible tissue irritation. The untreated rats in Group 4 were never judged as treated. In other words, persistent ear-scratching was always accompanied by visible irritation.

So ear-scratching does persist for a substantially longer time than the collodion application that gave rise to the behavior, but an interpretation based on functional autonomy is unnecessary. The behavior may be "autonomous" of the stimulus narrowly defined as collodion application, but it is not autonomous of the stimulus defined, broadly and properly, as collodion application and the irritation that follows. The persistence of ear-scratching is a simple function of the persistence of stimulation, a finding that points up the need to define stimulus conditions with care.

Grain-gobbling Pigeons

We have reviewed two studies used to support the doctrine of functional autonomy and two similar studies from our laboratory that indicate the support is unwarranted. Are we to conclude that autonomous behavior *never* occurs? A third series of experiments, done in collaboration with Kurt Fischer of Harvard (at the time, a student of mine at Yale) sheds some light on this question.

In the first stage of these experiments, Fischer observed two pigeons for two or three hours each on over 50 occasions. The procedure was to place the hungry pigeon in a box and allow it to peck at a key that occasionally yielded a food reward. The rewards were substantial, and the pigeon rapidly became satiated. As its hunger diminished, so did its pecking rate. It pecked about once a second at the start of the session but only about once a minute at the end. This orderly decline occurred in every session. (Other procedures demon-

strated that it was indeed the level of hunger and not the length of the session that brought about the decline.)

The question was, what would happen if the pigeon were fed to its satiated weight before it was placed in the box? If the pecking rate depended only on how hungry the pigeon was, a full pigeon would not peck at a high rate to obtain food; it would peck at the very low rate characteristic of the end of a session. Therefore, in the next stage of the experiment, we gave the pigeon enough food one hour before each session to bring its weight to the level that was usual *after* a session.

But both our pigeons pecked diligently and ate heavily nonetheless. Their pecking rates in the first test session were comparable to their rates when hungry, and in the course of the session, one pigeon ate half its usual amount and the other slightly *more* than its usual amount. The first bird, apparently aware of Victorian and ancient Roman dining customs, actually regurgitated during the third session, the only time we have seen a pigeon do so!

The pigeons' behavior did, then, become autonomous of their needs, and the same type of phenomenon might well occur in human behavior. Suppose a man is used to eating at home every evening at seven. Then one night he eats with a business colleague at six. If he returns home at seven, just as his family is sitting down to dinner, he may have a "second supper"—behavior that is autonomous of the state of his stomach.

However, the autonomy of our pigeons' behavior was short-lived. By the fourth or fifth session, the pre-fed pigeons pecked at a rate more characteristic of the end of the earlier sessions. It appears that the pigeons developed a response pattern appropriate to a certain level of hunger, and this pattern persisted for some time after the hunger level had changed. Their behavior seemed to become at least partly autonomous of hunger, but the autonomy was transitory.

If we now return to the world of humans and ask for experimental laboratory demonstrations of functional autonomy in human beings that satisfy the four criteria mentioned earlier, to my knowledge none emerge. Consider, for example, the many experiments with children and with chimpanzees that have been based on token rewards. Tokens, when they can be exchanged for such things as candy (children) and grapes (chimps), do become rewarding,

and chimps will work to obtain tokens that they can use later to get food from a "chimp-o-mat" vending machine. But the reward value of the token is eventually extinguished when the child or chimp can no longer use it to obtain a reward. As with our pigeons, whatever autonomy the tokens acquire is temporary.

The Miser's 'Chimp-O-Mat'

Is there a concept other than functional autonomy that will account for the miser? In my opinion, the miser's behavior persists because it continues to be, from time to time, rewarded; that is, the miser's situation is similar to that of a chimp who still has access to a chimp-o-mat.

Food, just one of the many rewards for which money can be exchanged, makes a good example. A person sometimes exchanges money for food at a restaurant, when he is hungry. Or he may shop for a week's food supply at some time when he is not hungry. This variation in food-buying habits is important because it is a well-documented finding that behavior becomes more persistent and durable when it is coupled with reward under a variety of circumstances. Since money can be exchanged for a great many different rewards under a great many different circumstances, money itself should become a quite powerful and robust reward, and its reward-value should be extremely *resistant to extinction*. Even if the miser were continually thwarted (say, when his money had been rendered worthless by inflation or revolution), we would expect his behavior to persist for a long time.

But, of course, the miser is *not* thwarted in his efforts to exchange money. He does buy essentials; he occasionally obtains rewards that give the reward-value of money a boost. So it is not surprising that hoarding behavior persists throughout the miser's lifetime. The question of its eventual extinction is unanswerable, because the subject dies before the experiment is over.

There may be many different types of miser, and perhaps not all may be accounted for in the same way. But an analysis like the one sketched out above has an important advantage over explanations based on such principles as functional autonomy: it is consistent with empirical evidence about behavior. Indeed, the experimental work summarized here strongly suggests that functional autonomy is a concept that does not survive experimental scrutiny. ◪

Beverly

The Computer is a Tutor by Richard C. Atkinson

Last year, for the first time, a sizable number of children received most of their daily reading instruction from a computer. The children were first-grade students at the Brentwood School in East Palo Alto, most of whom came from culturally disadvantaged homes. By the end of the year, they not only had learned to read better than a companion group taught by teachers, but they had shown the project staff a considerable amount about computer-assisted instruction—about how and with what effect computer technology and learning theory can be combined and put into practice.

Concrete research in computer-assisted instruction is badly needed to balance the tremendous number of speculative reports that have appeared over the past few years. The Stanford Project has only begun—it is continuing this year with the new first grade—and much of the initial year must be considered a de-bugging period for both the computer system and the curriculum material. Nevertheless, the experience has provided us with solid data. My claims will be less grand than many that have been made for computer-assisted instruction, but they will be based on a substantial research effort.

Work on the Stanford Project began in 1964 under a grant from the Office of Education. The purpose of the project

was to develop and implement computer-assisted instruction courses in initial reading and mathematics. Because of our individual research interests, my colleague Patrick Suppes has worked on the mathematics curriculum and I have been responsible for the reading course.

When we began, no lesson material suitable for computerized instruction of either mathematics or reading had yet been developed, and an integrated computer system for instruction had not yet been designed and produced by a single manufacturer. Curricula and system have been developed together over the past three years, and each has had a decided influence on the other.

Three levels of computer-assisted in-

struction can be defined. The levels are not based on the type of hardware used, but principally on the complexity and sophistication of the interaction between the student and the system. An advanced student-system interaction may be achieved with a simple teletype terminal, and the most rudimentary interaction may require some highly sophisticated computer programming and elaborate student terminal devices.

At the simplest interactional level are the *drill-and-practice* systems that present a fixed, linear sequence of problems. Student errors may be corrected in a variety of ways, but no real-time decisions are made by the computer for modifying the flow of instructional material according to the student's response history. An example of drill-and-practice systems are the fourth-, fifth-, and sixth-grade programs in arithmetic and language arts that have been developed at Stanford University to supplement classroom instruction. These programs are being used by as many as 2000 students a day in California, Kentucky, and Mississippi; the entire network is controlled by one central computer located at Stanford University. It takes little imagination to see how such a system could be extended to cover the entire country.

At the other end of our scale of student-computer interactions are *dialogue* programs. The goal of the dialogue ap-

proach is to provide the richest possible interaction, one in which the student is free to construct natural-language responses, to ask questions in an unrestricted mode, and in general to exercise almost complete control over the sequence of learning events. Such programs are under development at several universities, but progress has been limited.

The third level of computer-assisted instruction lies between the drill-and-practice and the dialogue programs. Called *tutorial* programs, these have the capacity to modify the sequence of instructional material on the basis of a single response or some subset of the student's response history. Such programs allow students to follow separate and diverse learning paths through the curriculum, based on their individual performance records. The probability is high in a tutorial program that no two students will encounter exactly the same sequence of lesson materials. However, student responses still are quite restricted because they must be chosen from a prescribed set of responses or written so that a relatively simple text analysis will be sufficient for their evaluation.

The computer-assisted reading instruction program at Brentwood School is implemented on the Stanford Tutorial System, which was developed under a contract between Stanford University and the IBM Corporation. Subsequent developments by IBM of the basic system have led to what has been designated the IBM-1500 Instructional System, which soon should be commercially available.

The basic system consists of a central process computer with magnetic discs for memory storage, proctor stations for monitoring student performance, and 16 student stations. The central process computer acts as an intermediary between each student and his particular course material, which is stored in one of the memory discs. A student terminal consists of a film screen, a cathode ray display tube, a light-pen, a modified typewriter keyboard, and earphones. [*See illustration above.*]

The cathode ray tube is essentially a television screen on which letters, numbers, and simple line drawings can be generated under computer control. The film screen is a rear-view projection device which permits the display of still pictures in black and white or in color. Each film strip is stored in a self-threading cartridge and contains over 1000 images, any of which the computer may select very quickly for display. The audio

WHAT THE STUDENT SEES, HEARS, AND DOES. Above, a student hears a word pronounced and then sees it, both pictorially and in written form. Below, a student touches her light pen to the screen to tell the computer that she can read the word "cat."

messages are stored in tape cartridges which contain approximately two hours of messages and, like the film cartridge, may be changed very quickly. To gain the student's attention, an arrow can be generated on the cathode ray screen and moved in synchronization with an audio message to emphasize given words or phrases, much like the "bouncing ball" in sing-along films.

The main responding device used in the reading program is the light-pen, which is simply a light-sensitive probe. When the light-pen is placed on the cathode ray screen, the position touched is sensed and recorded by the computer. Responses also may be made on the typewriter keyboard. However, only limited use has been made of the keyboard in the reading program because we have not yet attempted to tackle the problem of teaching first-grade children to use a typewriter.

The sequence of events in the system is roughly as follows. The computer assembles the necessary commands for a

given instructional sequence from a disc-storage unit. The commands include directions to display a given sequence of symbols on the cathode ray screen, to present a particular image on the film screen, and to play a specific audio message. After the appropriate visual and auditory materials have been presented, a "ready" signal tells the student that a response is expected. The response is evaluated and, on the basis of this evaluation and the student's past history, the computer makes a decision as to what materials will be presented next.

The time-sharing feature of the system allows us to handle 16 students simultaneously and to cycle through these evaluative steps so rapidly that from the student's viewpoint it seems that he is getting immediate attention from the computer whenever he makes a response.

Our approach to computer-assisted reading instruction can be described as applied psycholinguistics. We began by formulating hypotheses about the reading process and the nature of learning

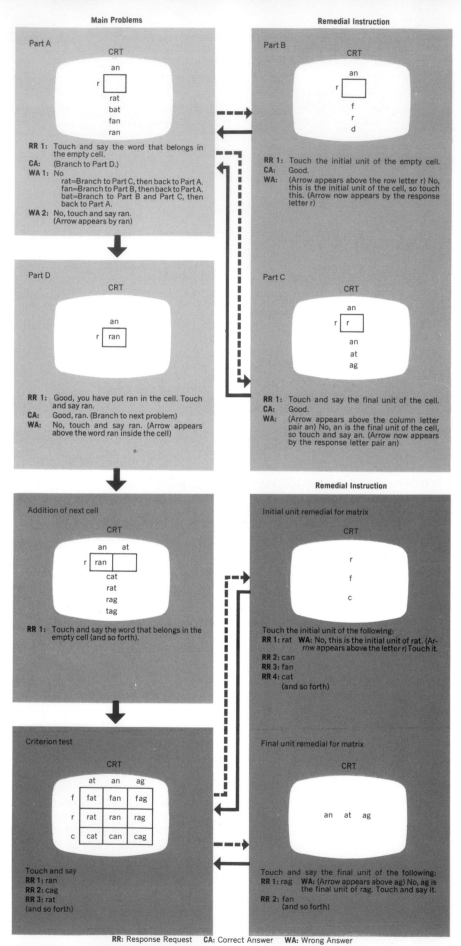

Main Problems

Part A

CRT

an
r □
rat
bat
fan
ran

RR 1: Touch and say the word that belongs in the empty cell.
CA: (Branch to Part D.)
WA 1: No
    rat=Branch to Part C, then back to Part A.
    fan=Branch to Part B, then back to Part A.
    bat=Branch to Part B and Part C, then back to Part A.
WA 2: No, touch and say ran. (Arrow appears by ran)

Part D

CRT

an
r |ran|

RR 1: Good, you have put ran in the cell. Touch and say ran.
CA: Good, ran. (Branch to next problem)
WA: No, touch and say ran. (Arrow appears above the word ran inside the cell)

Addition of next cell

CRT

an   at
r |ran| □
cat
rat
rag
tag

RR 1: Touch and say the word that belongs in the empty cell (and so forth).

Criterion test

CRT

at an ag
f | fat | fan | fag
r | rat | ran | rag
c | cat | can | cag

Touch and say
RR 1: ran
RR 2: cag
RR 3: rat
(and so forth)

Remedial Instruction

Part B

CRT

an
r □
f
r
d

RR 1: Touch the initial unit of the empty cell.
CA: Good.
WA: (Arrow appears above the row letter r) No, this is the initial unit of the cell, so touch this. (Arrow now appears by the response letter r)

Part C

CRT

an
r |r|
an
at
ag

RR 1: Touch and say the final unit of the cell.
CA: Good.
WA: (Arrow appears above the column letter pair an) No, an is the final unit of the cell, so touch and say an. (Arrow now appears by the response letter pair an)

Remedial Instruction

Initial unit remedial for matrix

CRT

r
f
c

Touch the initial unit of the following:
RR 1: rat **WA:** No, this is the initial unit of rat. (Arrow appears above the letter r) Touch it.
RR 2: can
RR 3: fan
RR 4: cat
    (and so forth)

Final unit remedial for matrix

CRT

an at ag

Touch and say the final unit of the following:
RR 1: rag **WA:** (Arrow appears above ag) No, ag is the final unit of rag. Touch and say it.
RR 2: fan
    (and so forth)

RR: Response Request   **CA:** Correct Answer   **WA:** Wrong Answer

HOW THE STUDENT CONSTRUCTS A MATRIX. Each cell in a matrix is constructed individually by the process shown in Parts A through D. When the nine-cell matrix is complete, the student takes a criterion test (lower left) that covers all nine words.

to read, on the basis of linguistic information, observations of language use, and an analysis of the function of the written code. These hypotheses were tested—and then modified and retested —in a series of studies structured to simulate actual teaching situations. Very little curriculum material ever can be said to be the perfect end-product of rigorous empirical evaluation; however, we would claim that the fundamental tenets of the Stanford reading program are based on considerable empirical evidence, and they will be further modified as more data accumulates.

The instructional materials are divided into eight levels, each composed of about 32 lessons. The lessons are designed so that the average student will complete one in approximately 30 minutes, but this can vary greatly. Some students finish much sooner and others, if they hit most of the remedial material, can take two hours or more. Within a lesson, the various instructional tasks can be divided into three broad areas: decoding, comprehension, and games and other motivational devices.

Decoding involves such tasks as the identification of letters and strings of letters, word-list learning, and phonic drills. *Comprehension* involves such tasks as having the computer read to the child or having the child himself read sentences, paragraphs, or complete stories about which he then is asked a series of questions. The questions deal with the direct recall of facts, with generalizations about the main ideas in the story, and with inferential questions that require the child to relate to his own experience information presented in the story. Finally, many types of *games* are sequenced into the lessons, primarily to maintain the students' interest. The games are similar to those usually played in the classroom, and they are structured to enable the computer to evaluate the developing reading skills of the child.

Let us consider an example of what a student sees, hears, and does on one of the decoding tasks in a lesson [*see illustration at left*]. This task, called "matrix construction," provides practice in learning to associate orthographically similar sequences with appropriate rhyme and alliteration patterns. Rhyming patterns are presented in the columns of the matrix and alliteration patterns are presented in the rows of the matrix. The matrix is constructed one cell at a time. The initial consonant of a consonant-vowel-consonant word is called the initial unit, and the vowel and the final consonant are called the final unit. The intersection of an initial unit row and a final unit column determines the entry in any given cell.

The problem format for the construction of each cell is divided into four parts: Parts A and D are standard instructional sections, and Parts B and C are remedial sections. Parts B and C are branches from Part A, and may be presented independently or in combination.

On the cathode ray screen the student first sees an empty cell with its associated initial and final units and an array of response choices. He hears a message to touch and say the word that belongs in the empty cell. If the student makes the correct response, in this case touches *ran* with his light-pen, he proceeds to Part D, where he sees the word written in the cell and is told "Good, you have put *ran* in the cell. Touch and say *ran*."

The array of multiple-choice responses in Part A is designed to identify three types of errors: final unit incorrect; initial unit incorrect; both initial and final unit incorrect.

If in Part A the student responds with *fan* instead of *ran*, he is branched to remedial instruction (Part B), where attention is focused on the initial unit of the cell. If a correct response is made in the remedial section, the student is returned to the beginning for a second attempt. If an incorrect response is made in the remedial section, an arrow is displayed on the screen to indicate the correct response, which the student then is asked to touch.

If in Part A the student responds with *rat* instead of *ran*, he is branched to remedial instruction (Part C) on the final unit of the cell. The procedure is similar. However, it should be noted that in the remedial instruction the initial letter never is pronounced by the audio system, whereas the final unit always is pronounced. If the student responds in Part A with *bat* instead of *ran*, then he has made an error on both the initial and the final unit, and he is branched through both sets of remedial instruction.

When the student returns to the beginning after completing a remedial section, a correct response will advance him to Part D. If a wrong response is made on the second attempt, an arrow is placed beside the correct response area and held there until a correct response is made. If the next response is still an error, a message is sent to the proctor terminal and the sequence is repeated from the beginning.

When a student has responded correctly in Parts A and D, he is advanced to the next cell of the matrix, which is a problem identical to that just described. As a student makes correct responses, he constructs a matrix of word cells. When the matrix is complete, the rows and columns are reordered and the full matrix is displayed. The student is asked in a criterion test to identify the words in the cells. He completes the entire test without interruption, even if he makes mistakes. Errors are categorized as initial, final, and other. If the percentage of total errors on the criterion test exceeds a predetermined value, then appropriate remedial exercises are provided. After working through one or both of the remedial sections, the student is branched back for a second pass through the criterion matrix. The second pass is a teaching run, and the student receives additional correction and optimization routines.

Let us consider briefly the problem of translating the curriculum materials into a language that can be understood by the computer. The particular computer language we use is called Coursewriter II, a language developed by IBM in close collaboration with Stanford University. A coded lesson is a series of Coursewriter II commands that cause the computer to display and manipulate text on the cathode ray screen, display images on the film screen, position and play audio messages, accept and evaluate keyboard and light-pen responses, update the performance record of each student, and, with a set of switches and counters, implement the branching logic of the lesson.

A typical lesson in the reading program, which takes the average student about 30 minutes to complete, requires more than 9000 Coursewriter commands for its execution.

An example from a task designed to teach both letter discrimination and the meaning of words will illustrate some of the complexities of the coding problem. A picture illustrating the word being taught is presented on the film screen. Three words, including the word illustrated, are presented on the cathode ray screen. A message is played on the audio system asking the child to touch the word on the cathode ray screen that matches the picture on the film screen. Using the light-pen, the student then can make his response. If he makes no response within 30 seconds, he is told the correct answer, an arrow points to it, and he is asked to touch it. If he makes a response within the time limit, the point that he touches is compared by the computer with the correct-answer area. If he places the light-pen within the correct area, he is told that he was correct, and goes on to the next problem. If the response was not in the correct area, it is compared with the area defined as a wrong answer. If his response is within this area, he is told that it is wrong, given the correct answer, and asked to touch it. If his initial response was neither in the anticipated wrong-answer area nor in the correct-answer area, then the student has made an undefined answer. He is given the same message that he would have heard had he touched a defined wrong answer; however, the response is recorded on his data record as undefined. The student tries again until he makes the correct response, at which time he goes on to the next problem.

To prepare an instructional sequence of this sort, the programmer must write a detailed list of commands for the computer. He also must make a tape recording of all the messages the student might hear during the lesson in approximately the order in which they will occur. Each audio message has an address on the tape that enables the computer to find and play it when required. Similarly, a film strip is prepared with one frame for each picture required in the lesson. Each frame has an address and the frames can be presented in any order. [*See illustrations, page 67.*]

While a student is on the system, he may complete as many as five to ten problems per minute. If all of the instructional material had to be coded in detail, the task would be virtually impossible. Fortunately, there are ways of simplifying the coding procedure if parts of the instructional materials are alike in format and differ only in specified ways.

For example, the "bag" and "card" problems [*see illustration bottom left, page 67*] differ in the actual displays and audio messages, but the logical format is the same. They therefore can be defined once, given a two-letter name, and used later by giving a brief macro command.

The use of macro commands cuts down greatly the effort required to present many different but basically similar problems. Macros have two distinct advantages over codes written command by command. The first is ease and speed of coding: the call of one macro is obviously easier than writing the comparable string of code. The second advantage is increase in accuracy: not only are coding errors drastically reduced, but if the macro is defective or needs to be changed, every occurrence of it in the lesson can be corrected by modifying

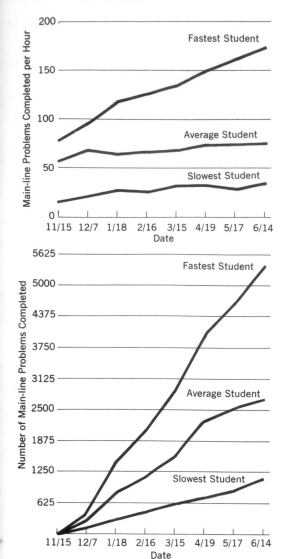

By the end of the year, the fastest students had completed some 4,000 more problems than the slowest students (top), and their speed continued rising steadily (bottom).

the original macro. The more standard the various problem formats, the more valuable the use of macros becomes. Approximately 92 per cent of our reading curriculum has been programmed using about 110 basic macros.

A bank of switches and counters in the computer keeps a running record on each student. Our program includes enough switches and counters to allow some quite sophisticated schemes for optimizing the teaching routines. For instance, we can present a series of words, and require five consecutive correct responses to each of the words. Or we can select for presentation certain phrases which previously have produced the greatest number of errors. As a consequence of decisions like these, each student pursues a fundamentally different path through the reading materials.

Computer-assisted instruction began at the Brentwood School in November of 1966. We selected this school partly be-

cause it was large enough to provide a sample of well over 100 first-grade students, partly because the students were primarily from culturally disadvantaged homes, and partly because the past performance of the school's principal and faculty had demonstrated a willingness to undertake educational innovations. Half the first-grade students received computer-assisted instruction in reading, and the other half, which functioned as a control group, was taught reading by a teacher in the classroom. However, the children in the control group were not left out of the computer project; they received their mathematics instruction from the computer.

Within the lesson material there are a core of problems that we have called main-line problems, meaning problems over which each student must exhibit some form of mastery. Main-line problems may be branched around by passing certain screening tests; they may be met and solved; or they may be met with incorrect responses, in which case the student is branched to remedial material.

At the end of the first year of the project, the fastest student had completed over 4000 more main-line problems than the slowest student. We also found that the rate of progress, as measured by the number of main-line problems solved per hour, was essentially constant for the median and slow students, but showed a steady increase for the fast students [*see illustrations at left*]. Whether this last result is unique to our particular curriculum or is characteristic of computer-assisted instruction needs further investigation.

Differences in rate of progress through the curriculum must not be confused with the rate of response to individual questions. The difference in response rate among students was very small. The average response rate was approximately four per minute and was not correlated with a student's rate of progress through the curriculum. The differences in total number of main-line problems completed can be accounted for by the amount of remedial material, the optimization routines, and the number of accelerations for the different students. From the standpoint of both the rate of progress and the total number of problems completed during the year, the computer curriculum appears to be quite responsive to individual differences.

It has been a common finding that girls generally acquire reading skills more rapidly than boys. The sex differences in reading performance have been attributed, at least in part, to the social

organization of the classroom, and to the value and reward systems of female primary-grade teachers. It also has been argued on developmental grounds that first-grade girls are more facile in visual memorization than boys of the same age, and that this facility aids the girls in the sight-word method commonly used in primary readers.

If these two arguments are correct, then one would expect that placing students in a computer-assisted environment and using a curriculum which emphasizes analytic skills instead of memorization by rote would minimize sex differences in reading. To test this hypothesis, the rate-of-progress scores in our program were evaluated for differences according to sex. The result, which was rather surprising, is that there was no difference between male and female students in rate of progress through the computer curriculum.

We also wanted to see whether sex differences affected accuracy. On four standard types of problems—letter identification, word-list learning, matrix construction, and sentence comprehension —the only difference between boys and girls that was statistically significant was for word-list learning.

These results, while not conclusive, do lend support to the notion that when students are removed from the normal classroom environment and given computer instruction, boys perform as well as girls in overall rate of progress.

The results also suggest that with computer-assisted instruction the sex difference is minimized as the emphasis moves toward analysis and away from rote memorization. The one kind of problem on which the girls achieved significantly higher scores than the boys, word-list learning, is essentially a memorization task.

How did the computer-instructed first-graders compare with the control group? Both groups were tested extensively before the project began and again near the end of the school year. The two groups were not significantly different at the start of the year, but at the end of the year the group that received computer-assisted reading instruction performed significantly better on almost all of the reading achievement tests, including the California Reading Test, the Gates-MacGinitie Test and the Hartley.

The average Stanford-Binet IQ score for the students (both experimental and control) was 89. There was considerable variation, but by and large these were not exceptional or gifted children. Students, teachers, and parents reacted quite favorably to the introduction of computer-assisted instruction into the classroom.

Initially, students were given only a few minutes per day on the teaching machines. The time was increased to 20 minutes after the first six weeks; in the last month we allowed students 30 to 35 minutes. We wanted to determine how well first-grade students would adapt to machine instruction for relatively long periods of time. We found that they adapt quite well, and this year we have been using 30-minute periods for all students. This may see like a long session for a first-grader, but our observations suggest that their span of attention is well over a half-hour if the programming is dynamic and responsive to their inputs.

Various optimization routines were evaluated during the year. These evaluations, in turn, have suggested a number of experiments and analyses that might be profitable. Such analyses, combined with the potential for additional research under the highly controlled conditions offered by computerized instruction, could lay the groundwork for a theory of instruction truly useful to the educator. The theory will have to be based on a highly structured model of the learning process, and it must generate optimization strategies that are compatible with the goals of education. The development of a viable theory of instruction is a major scientific undertaking, and substantial progress in this direction could well be one of psychology's most important contributions to society. ↺

or in macro format ...

Problem 1 CM PW]F01]bat]bag]rat]A01]
ABCD1]A04]A02]A03]7]1,7,3,18]C1]
Problem 2 CM PW]F02]card]cart]hard]]
ABCD2]A07]A05]A06]5]1,5,4,18]C2]

what it is to say and show to the student.

Audio information

Address	Message
A01	Touch and say the word that goes with the picture.
A02	Good. Bag. Do the next one.
A03	No.
A04	The word that goes with the picture is bag. Touch and say bag.
A05	Good. Card. Do the next one.
A06	No.
A07	The word that goes with the picture is card. Touch and say card.

Film Strip

Address	Picture
F01	Picture of a bag.
F02	Picture of a card.

The computer must be told, either in detail ...

Computer Commands	Explanation
PR	**Problem** Prepares machine for beginning of new problem.
LD 0/S1	**Load** Loads zero into the error switch (S1).
FP F01	**Film Position** Displays frame F01 (picture of a bag).
DT 5,18/bat/	**Display Text** Displays "bat" on line 5 starting in column 18 on the CRT.
DT 7,18/bag/	Displays "bag" on line 7 starting in column 18 on the CRT.
DT 9,18/rat/	Displays "rat" on line 9 starting in column 18 on the CRT.
AUP A01	**Audio Play** Plays audio message A01. "Touch and say the word that goes with the picture."
L1 EP 30/ABCD1	**Enter and Process** Activates the light-pen; specifies the time limit (30 sec.) and the problem identifier (ABCD1) that will be placed in the data record along with all responses to this problem. If a response is made within the time limit the computer skips from this command down to the CA (correct answer comparison) command. If no response is made within the time limit, the commands immediately following the EP command are executed.
AD 1/C4	**Add** Adds one to the overtime counter (C4).
LD 1/S1	Loads one into the error switch (S1).
AUP A04	**Plays message A04** "The word that goes with the picture is bag. Touch and say bag."
DT 7,16/→/	**Displays arrow** on line 7, column 16 (arrow pointing at "bag").
BR L1	**Branch** Branches to command labeled L1. The computer will now do that command and continue from that point.
CA 1,7,3,18/C1	**Correct Answer** Compares student's response with an area one line high starting on line 7 and three columns wide starting in column 18 of the CRT. If his response falls within this area, it will be recorded in the data with the answer identifier C1. When a correct answer has been made, the commands from here down to WA (wrong answer comparison) are executed. Then the program jumps ahead to the next PR. If the response does not fall in the correct area, the machine skips from this command down to the WA command.
BR L2/S1/1	Branches to command labeled L2 if the error switch (S1) is equal to one.
AD 1/C1	Adds one to the initial correct answer counter (C1).
L2 AUP A02	**Plays audio message A02** "Good. Bag. Do the next one."
WA 1,5,3,18/W1	**Wrong Answer** These two commands compare the student response with the areas of the two wrong answers, that is, the area one line high starting on line 5 and three columns wide starting in column 18, and the area one line high starting on line 9 and three columns wide starting in column 18. If the response falls within one of these two areas, it will be recorded with the appropriate identifier (W1 or W2). When a defined wrong answer has been made, the commands from here down to UN (undefined answer) are executed. Then the computer goes back to the EP for this problem. If the response does not fall in one of the defined wrong answer areas, the machine skips from this command down to the UN command.
WA 1,9,3,18/W2	
AD 1/C2	Adds one to the defined wrong answer counter (C2).
L3 LD 1/S1	Loads one into the error switch (S1).
AUP A03	**Plays message A03** "No."
AUP A04	**Plays message A04** "The word that goes with the picture is bag. Touch and say bag."
DT 7,16/→/	**Display arrow** on line 7, column 16.
UN	**Undefined Wrong Answer** If machine reaches this point in the program, the student has made neither a correct nor a defined wrong answer.
AD 1/C3	Adds one to the undefined answer counter (C3).
BR L3	Branches to command labeled L3. (The same thing should be done for both UN and WA answers. This branch saves repeating the commands from L3 down to UN.)
PR	**Prepares the machine for next problem**
LD 0/S1	These commands prepare the display for the second problem. Notice the new film position and new words displayed. The student was told to "do the next one" when he finished the last problem so he needs no audio message to begin this.
FP F02	
DT 5,18/card/	
DT 7,18/cart/	
DT 9,18/hard/	
L4 EP 30/ABCD2	**Light-pen is activated**
AD 1/C4	These commands are done only if no response is made in the time limit of 30 seconds. Otherwise the machine skips to the CA command.
LD 1/S1	
AUP A07	
DT 5,16/→/	
BR L4	
CA 1,5,4,18/C2	**Compares response with correct answer area**
BR L5/S1/1	Adds one to the initial correct answer counter unless the error switch (S1) shows that an error has been made for this problem. The student is told he is correct and goes on to the next problem. These commands are executed only if a correct answer has been made.
AD 1/C1	
L5 AUP A05	
WA 1,7,4,18/W3	**Compares response with defined wrong answer**
WA 1,9,4,18/W4	
AD 1/C2	Adds one to the defined wrong answer area and the error switch (S1) is loaded with one to show that an error has been made on this problem. The student is told he is wrong and shown the correct answer and asked to touch it. These commands are executed only if a defined wrong answer has been made.
L6 LD 1/S1	
AUP A06	
AUP A07	
DT 5,16/→/	
UN	**An undefined response has been made if the machine reaches this command**
AD 1/C3	Adds one to the undefined answer counter and we branch up to give the same audio, etc. as is given for the defined wrong answer.
BR L6	

THE INSPECTOR GENERAL...

...IS A BIRD

By Thom Verhave

IT IS COMMON KNOWLEDGE that two heads are better than one, and just as true when the heads belong to pigeons.

Properly conditioned, this ordinary bird can be taught the visual operations of commercial manufacturing. He can be, in fact, a quality-control inspector. But more surprising than the thought of pigeons as inspectors are the implications for certain aspects of socialization that come from two pigeons working together on an assembly line. Pigeons at work can give us new insights into the way man cooperates and transmits his culture from generation to generation.

My interest in pigeons began many years ago, but it was not until, as a psychopharmacologist, I toured the research and manufacturing facilities of a large drug company that I learned about the gigantic problem of quality control.

The company's facilities produced as many as twenty million gelatin capsules daily. All of these had to be inspected visually for possible defects—at great cost in time, money, and human patience.

A group of seventy women was required to inspect the capsules before they were filled. The capsules in a particular batch—all of the same shape, size, and color—dropped at a fixed rate onto an endless moving belt. The inspector scanned the capsules as they moved before her and discarded all those that were off-color, bumpy, capped twice, or dented. After a batch of capsules was inspected, a supervisor scooped a ladleful of them out of the barrel and checked them for defects. If there were more than the allowed number of defective capsules (called skags) in a sample, the entire lot had to be re-inspected.

Training Pigeon Inspectors

It occurred to me that this was work pigeons could do, and so I devised a method of training the pigeons to inspect capsules. In the procedure I developed, the pigeon was placed in the caged portion of an inspection apparatus. Before him were two pigeon keys (rounded disks which the pigeon could peck). One key was actually a small transparent window, the other was opaque. The capsules, on a moving belt, came into view behind the transparent key.

The training procedure consisted of a series of circumstances initiated and continued by the birds' behavior and discrimination. A single peck on the illu-

minated opaque key turned off the light behind it and, at the same time, weakly illuminated the window key, so that the pigeon could see that there was a capsule behind it. Next, the pigeon pecked a single time on the weakly lit window key to produce a bright, narrow beam of light clearly illuminating the capsule. Three more pecks on the window key sounded a tone briefly. The tone indicated the moment of decision.

If the capsule exposed to view was seen by the bird as a skag, it was supposed to make two more pecks on the window key. This turned off the beam of light, moved up the next capsule, and produced food through an automatic hopper. If the capsule was seen by the bird as acceptable, it indicated this by pecking on the opaque key, which also turned off the beam of light and moved up the next capsule. It did not produce the reward of food.

The pigeon determined its own inspection rate, and reinforcement, in the form of food, came only after the pigeon made the appropriate number of pecks on the window key and correctly identified a true skag. Skags made up 10 per cent of the capsules on the belt. Incorrect judgments, either false alarms or misses, were not rewarded. Instead there was a 30-second blackout. In a week's time, birds learned to inspect with 99 per cent accuracy.

There is nothing earthshaking about a pigeon—or any animal with one intact eyeball—learning a simple visual discrimination, such as to distinguish between capsules which are disfigured and others which are not. But for anyone who wanted to put birds on an inspection line, there was an intriguing problem: making sure the pigeons *continued* to distinguish good capsules from bad.

From Concept to Action

To understand why the continued recognition of difference presents a problem, it is helpful to look both at discrimination and at concept formation, the way pigeons learn discrimination.

Whenever an animal discriminates, it is able to tell the difference between at least two different events, objects, or stimuli. A pigeon that has been taught successfully to inspect drug capsules can, for example, distinguish between a capsule with a dent in its surface and one without such a defect. The bird pecks on the glass observation window when a skag appears behind it, and on another key whenever a good capsule is shown.

This is an example of simple discrimination, which has been much investigated in such animals as rats and pigeons. It is of the so-called go/no-go variety, familiar to all who have cursed the red light at an intersection: The observer must respond to the presence of a particular cue and not respond in its absence (or to another cue). What is common to all discriminative behavior, from the simplest behavior on the part of an animal to the most complex on the part of a human adult, is the learned ability to act differently in the presence of at least two conditions.

This broad definition of discrimination is closely related to what traditionally has been called abstraction and concept formation. Consider the concept of a bear. Bears come in many places, shapes, forms, colors, and sizes; they may be large or small, black, brown, or even white. In the forest or in the zoo, they sit, climb, curl up in a furry ball, beg for food, or snarl and threaten. Yet with all these variations, children learn the common elements of "bearness."

When a child identifies a bear, showing conceptual behavior, he ignores certain features of a situation and responds only to the essential aspect. His conceptual behavior is a more complex version of the simple discriminative behavior mentioned earlier. The distinction between the two is a matter of degree. Even the simple-minded pigeon is behaving conceptually when it responds one way whenever it observes a dented capsule, be it large or small, blue or green, and another way when it spots an undented one.

Learning Through Reward

One way to teach an animal or a child to discriminate is to reward the pupil when he reacts correctly to the essential aspect of a situation, and not otherwise.

In teaching a pigeon to discriminate between skags and perfect capsules, the bird is rewarded if it pecks at the observation window when a skag appears. But if it pecks at the window when a good capsule is shown, there is no reward. Constant reward, or reward only for correct answers, is unnecessary. What *is* important is that the frequency of reward for correct responses be effectively larger than that for wrong ones.

In the laboratory, the experimenter knows whether the capsule before the bird is a skag or a perfect pill. Without this knowledge, the animal cannot be rewarded at the appropriate time and learning does not take place.

The problem of using an animal in quality-control inspection is that one no longer knows whether or when to reward. Except by actual inspection, there is no way of knowing when a skag will turn up.

And that is exactly what we want our pigeon to do for us. We want an effective inspector. We want to be able to take a pigeon's word that when it reports a skag, a skag is a skag indeed.

The problem, of course, is that if the bird's discrimination is not rewarded, accuracy deteriorates, and we suddenly have an unemployable bird.

There are two possible solutions to this problem. The experimenter could plant a certain number of known objects—skags as well as perfect capsules—in any batch to be inspected. These could be coded so that they are detectable by special equipment, such as a magnetic sensing device. A certain minimum percentage of such informants could keep the bird's behavior at the required level and serve as a checkup on the bird's inspection.

A more interesting solution to the problem relies upon agreement between

two inspector-general pigeons, which inspect each item more or less simultaneously. Each animal is trained separately, and once the desired discriminative behavior is well established, all outside checks on the birds' performance are discontinued. Instead, the birds are rewarded whenever they both agree whether or not a capsule is a skag.

The possibility arises, of course, that both inspectors occasionally may err. The frequency with which that happens is the product of the separate error frequencies of each bird if he were on his own. If each animal, working alone, makes one error for every hundred inspection trials, the likelihood that both birds will be wrong on the same trial is only one out of 10,000! If more than two animals are used as inspectors, the probability of reinforcement for incorrect responses is reduced even further.

Matching to Sample

My recent research has explored the maintenance of discriminations by pigeons whose only check is agreement with another bird. A basic but relatively complex form of discrimination behavior known as *matching to sample* is used in the experiments.

Matching to sample consists of teaching an animal to indicate whether colors or items such as cubes, pyramids, and cylinders are different or similar.

The ability to match lies at the core of much of the complex conceptual behavior so proudly exhibited by man. When a child learns to count, he matches the four apples and the four oranges on the table and learns that each set is *four*. The concept of equivalence, of course, is basic in mathematics.

A relatively simple form of matching behavior has been studied with pigeons. Much of this work has required color matching. These experiments use a modified version of an apparatus designed by B. F. Skinner, a chamber with three small opaque plastic disks and an electromagnetically operated grain-feeder mounted on one wall. A pigeon is trained to peck at these keys, which can be illuminated from behind with lights of various colors. Pecking the appropriate keys in a certain sequence is rewarded: The feeder makes grain available to the pigeon briefly, usually for about three to five seconds.

Each experimental session is broken up into distinct trials. First, the bird, which already has been trained to match colors, must indicate the two of three lighted keys which are the same color. The center key is illuminated with a white light as a trial starts. If the bird pecks the center key three times, the color changes to red or green. The side keys stay dark.

Next, the bird has to peck the colored center key several more times. The two side keys then light up, one red and one green. Which side key lights up with which color on any particular trial is a chance affair, except that red appears always on one side and green on the other.

Thus the pigeon sees three illuminated keys, two of the same color, and this is the crucial moment. If the pigeon pecks three times on the side key whose color matches the center key, the trial ends and the pigeon gets his reward.

A *single* response to the other side key also terminates the trial, but without reward. In other words, the animal's task is to respond to the correct side key. After a short rest, the next trial begins. [*See illustration at right*.] In two or three preliminary half-hour training sessions, the bird learns to eat from the feeder and to peck the keys. In only a few more sessions, the bird learns to match two colors almost perfectly. Some pigeons learn so well that they make no mistakes in 100 trials.

I indicated earlier that discrimination can be maintained even though correct responses are not always rewarded. The more difficult matching-to-sample behavior is no exception. There is even experimental evidence to show that the frequency of errors or mismatches is *less* when correct matches are rewarded *intermittently*, rather than constantly. Therefore, in my experiments only 50 per cent of all correct matches are reinforced. Which ones pay off is determined by the flip of an electronic coin.

Feathered Teachers and Pupils

If two animals, taught discrimination individually and then put to work together, maintain their performance indefinitely at about the same level of accuracy, what will happen if one pairs a *trained* and an *untrained* animal? According to simple rules of chance, the untrained partner in time should learn the discrimination almost as well as his expert companion. If that were indeed the result, one would have a situation in which one animal automatically teaches another, even though pupil and teacher have no direct contact.

Suppose that one begins with two pigeons. The teacher-bird already has been trained in the matching task. Its performance can be assumed to have reached fairly high accuracy, say 90 per cent. The pupil has had a certain amount of preliminary training but is unaware of red-green color discrimination, the essential of the matching-to-sample task.

To understand the outcome of an alliance between feathered teacher and pupil, we should remember that the probability of reinforcement of both partners is always equal. If they are rewarded, it is always on the same trial.

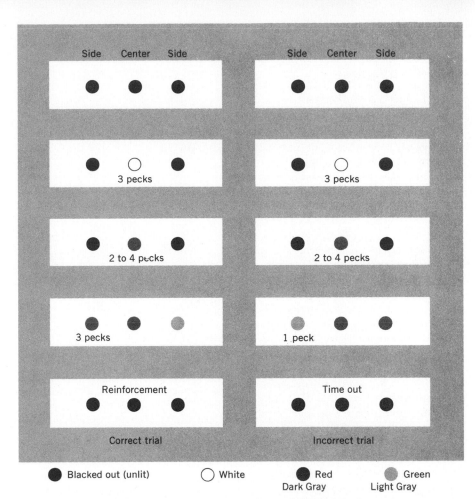

MATCHING-TO-SAMPLE. Two successive trials in which a trained pigeon attempts to match red and green lights. Only the successful trial ends with the reward of grain.

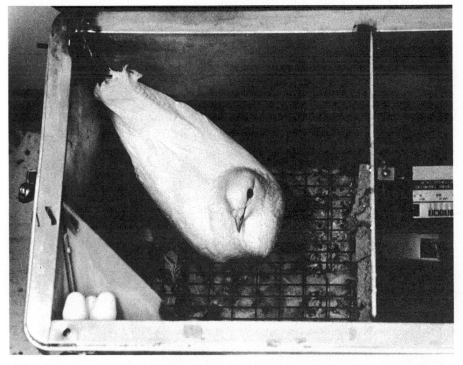

SCHOOLROOM FOR BIRDBRAINS. Matching behavior in pigeons is studied with the aid of an apparatus similar to this one, a modification of the famous Skinner box.

The only prerequisite for reward is their agreement. The probability of both birds responding the same way on any particular trial is 50 per cent.

Rules of Chance

Agreement, which brings the reinforcing reward, occurs when *both* birds respond correctly *or* when both birds make an error. The chance of agreement on any trial is the sum of the odds of both birds making an error and the odds of both birds matching correctly. And the odds that both birds will make a mistake on the same trial is the product of the two independent probabilities: the possibility that each pigeon will make an error separately.

The trained bird mismatches, on the average, in 10 per cent of all trials; the untrained bird, responding at random, in 50 per cent of all trials. Thus, the combined odds that both birds will err and receive a reward is $1/10 \times 5/10 = 5/100$ or 5 per cent. By the same rule, the chance that both birds will respond correctly on the same trial and be reinforced is $9/10 \times 5/10 = 45$ per cent.

Note that in the case of the trained bird—as well as the untrained one—the probability of being rewarded for a correct match is 45 per cent, compared to a previous probability of 50 per cent before the reward-for-agreement arrangement went into effect. This represents a decrease of only 5 per cent, hardly enough to make a difference.

It is true that the birds also will be rewarded whenever both mismatch colors. But the rise in expected payoff frequency from zero to 5 per cent for incorrect responses is unlikely to lead to a deterioration in the performance of the trained bird. Moreover, the reward probability of 45 per cent for correct matches, in combination with a reward probability of 5 per cent for incorrect ones, will lead to the formation of color discriminations in the untrained bird.

An attempt to explain or support these assertions would take us up to our necks in technicalities about intermittent reinforcement and discrimination. It may be granted, however, as quite plausible that 45 per cent to 5 per cent, or a 9-to-1 ratio in favor of correct responses for both birds, is very likely to lead to a better-than-chance performance on the part of the untrained bird.

The picture is even brighter than the figures above indicate, because the ratios do not take *learning* into consideration.

	Trained Bird	Untrained Bird	Agreement	Ratio
Errors	10%	50%	5%	
Matches	90%	50%	45%	9/1
Errors	20%	40%	8%	
Matches	80%	60%	48%	6/1
Errors	30%	30%	9%	
Matches	70%	70%	49%	5.4/1
Errors	30%	40%	12%	
Matches	70%	60%	42%	3.5/1
Errors	20%	30%	6%	
Matches	80%	70%	56%	9.2/1
Errors	20%	25%	5%	
Matches	80%	75%	60%	12/1

EACH ONE TEACH ONE. As the novice pigeon learns from his feathered professor, the chances that the two birds will agree that a skag is a perfect capsule diminish.

As the untrained bird begins to match at a better-than-chance level, the possibility of both birds agreeing on a mismatch decreases, further enhancing the prediction that the pupil will learn from the teacher. [*See illustration above.*]

Increasing the Odds

It appears that the chance that an untrained bird will learn to match depends very much on the error frequencies of the partners when they first are teamed. There are two ways by which one can greatly increase the odds in favor of learning to match.

First, the trainer should have a very low error frequency. He should be a competent bird. An error score of 1 per cent, combined with the 50-50 score of an untrained bird, produces a probability of only 0.5 per cent that both birds will mismatch on the same trial.

Second, there is no reason at all why other trained animals cannot be added to the fray. A combination of two trained birds, each with an error frequency of 10 per cent, and an untrained bird which responds at chance level, leads also to the probability of 0.5 per cent that all three birds will err on the same trial ($10/100 \times 10/100 \times 50/100$).

Perhaps we can assume that any animal inspector in a factory would be well trained. If so, then the odds of two inspectors agreeing are very high indeed,

and this implies a high payoff frequency. It is desirable to cut such a high probability of reinforcement by 50 per cent, and that can be done by never rewarding the animal who responds first. This may not seem fair, but at least it cannot produce jealousy, since pigeon participants do not know the rules of the game. (Strong believers in fair-employment practices may be assuaged by the fact that the chance of being first to respond can be made the same for all of the members of a team.)

If I have gone to great lengths to show that it is possible to use pigeons as quality-control inspectors, it is not because I expect anyone to hire a pigeon. I want only to defend the honor of a loyal subject that has cooperated patiently during endless sessions of experiments in many a university laboratory.

Pigeons and People

Is it possible to apply to human behavior these observations about pigeons who peck on glass windows? How does the loyal and patient pigeon compare with a child in a similar task? The most important and obvious difference is language. The ability to communicate verbally makes it possible to skip many of the steps that must be taken in teaching a task to a nonverbal pupil.

From this, one might conclude that the proverbial superiority of men over

ELECTRONIC MONITOR. Complicated machinery automatically programs the teaching experiment and keeps a record of each bird's successful matches and errors.

animals lies not in man's ability to handle abstractions or to form concepts, but in his capacity to engage in symbolic behavior, particularly to use language. The Aristotelian question about whether, by means of special techniques, animals could be taught to speak (to behave symbolically) in my opinion is still open.

It is the unique aspects of an arrangement in which one pigeon teaches another and in which any reward is based upon agreement that leads me to speculate about socialization and cultural transmission. Would it be fair to say

that, in an experiment where an untrained bird learned to match colors by agreeing with a trained bird, the trained pigeon functions as the socializing agent of the other? Perhaps socialization as a basic process of social interaction can be studied artificially in the laboratory with pigeons. Surely this is going too far! Aside from purely emotional objections to the idea, there must be many rational ones. Human socialization obviously differs in many ways from what goes on between pigeon teams.

For example, in the case of the pi-

geons, neither pupil nor teacher is in any way *aware* of what he is doing or what is being done to him. But then, many of us are not much more knowledgeable than pigeons when it comes to acute awareness of social forces. People function quite adequately, first as victims and later as agents of socialization.

A more important difference is that the pigeons are never in face-to-face contact. Ever since Charles H. Cooley made the distinction between primary and secondary groups nearly sixty years ago, socialization usually has been considered something peculiar to the former. Cooley defined primary groups as those characterized by intimate face-to-face associations and cooperation.

If one concedes that the matching-to-sample skill acquired by the untrained pigeon in the reinforcement-through-agreement arrangement is at least a rudimentary form of socialization, then it seems that face-to-face contact is *not* necessary. An arrangement where neither party sees the other, but where agreement is a prerequisite to reward, appears both sufficient and necessary.

Within the human family, our best example of a primary group member with a socializing function is the parent who rewards or punishes, depending on whether the behavior of his children is similar to his own repertoire. At the same time, he is only an intermediary, acting on orders and according to rules or norms set up by others outside the immediate family, or by cultural tradition he has been trained to accept. I have a feeling that the relationship of the trained pigeon to the experimenter is painfully similar.

TEACHING

By William R. Uttal

IT IS MORE THAN somewhat humbling to be forced to admit that we still know all too little about the phenomenon of learning. Psychologists have yet to discover exactly what marvelous internal change makes it possible for the infant to say his first word, the twelve-year-old to divide 3,254 by 589, and the adult to distinguish Bach from Beethoven. We do know a considerable amount about the conditions that facilitate learning, enough to tell us that the educational techniques currently used in most of our classrooms are far from ideal.

For one thing, we know from experimental evidence what James Garfield knew from experience: The most elaborate educational plant yet constructed is worth far less to a student than the un-

divided attention of a great teacher like Mark Hopkins. We know that students tend to learn less in a lecture class than in a discussion group, and far less in a

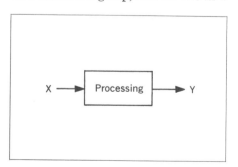

A simple open loop system converts an input (X) into an output (Y) according to stated processing rules. The input is not modified by feedback in this system.

large discussion group than in a small one. Ideally, each student should have his own personal tutor—and a good one, at that. The trouble is that there are not enough teachers, good or otherwise, to go around. We need an army where we have only a regiment. And we need an army of generals, not sergeants.

Computer teaching machines offer great promise for the future, and far from being the depersonalizing threat many people envision, such machines can give better individual instruction than one might dream. Someday they even will carry on "conversations" with students. This goal may not be quite as distant as it seems. Now that computer teaching machines are beginning to be able to process natural languages, they

AND MACHINES

can simulate, at least to some extent, the normal conversation of teacher and student. A program devised by one teacher —a Mark Hopkins, let us say—can be fed into as many machines as we have the raw materials and the inclination to produce. And, though computer technology still lags far behind theory, it appears that we someday may be able to produce a machine which will respond to the student with as much imagination and flexibility as a flesh-and-blood tutor.

'Round and 'Round It Goes

In a paper discussing the motivating properties of a two-person conversation, I drew an analogy between the loop systems used in control theory and certain educational processes. An *open loop system* is one in which input gives way to output with no modification from feedback; a *closed loop system*—which control engineers have come increas-

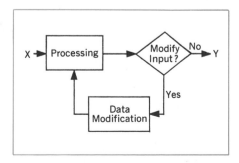

The more versatile closed loop system utilizes feedback from data processing to modify the input (X) and provide a new input before yielding an output (Y).

ingly to regard as the superior type—is one in which feedback is taken into account. An example of an open loop system in human education is the lecture; an example of a closed loop system is, of course, the teacher-student dialogue. Through conversational interaction, each speaker actively participates in the learning process, and each receives from his partner responses adapted to his own stream of thought and manner of expression.

Given the obvious superiority of conversational interaction, why does the classroom lecture dominate our current educational technology? The most important reason is that it is *administratively simple* to assemble a class and present an open loop lecture. A lecture

75

is superficially efficient, because information may be transmitted to a very large class by a single lecturer.

The computer teaching machine shares with the human lecturer—and with educational television and other audio-visual devices—the ability to amplify and diverge information from a single master, directing it to a very large number of students. However, the computer teaching machine is happily exempt from the most serious drawback of other information amplifiers, the loss of the flow of information from student to teacher. Because they do not utilize feedback, one-way information systems such as films and television are simply communication systems. They are not "new" teaching methods; they merely serve to enhance the demonstrated limitations of the conventional lecture.

Education is an information-processing activity which requires the teacher not only to communicate information, but to adapt to his student, to interpret the student's response, and to generate new specific material. The ability of the computer teaching machine to perform these last three tasks—though as yet it cannot perform them all well—is what allies it with the human tutor and distinguishes it both from other types of teaching machines and from the nonautomated teaching techniques now in use.

In the usual school or college classroom, the presentation of information, practice and drill, recitation, and evaluation all are separate functions, occurring more or less sequentially and at widely-spaced intervals. Recitation or practice, rather than coming at each step, usually occurs after a large block of material has been presented. Thus the teacher's evaluation of his students' performance cannot influence his presentation until it is too late. By the time the teacher discovers that his students did not understand him, the critical moment for modifying his presentation is gone.

The situation is quite different with the human teacher or with the computer teaching machine. These provide for a homogenous, smooth, two-way flow of information between teacher and student. The presentation of information, practice, and testing occur much closer to each other in time, so that the teacher's efforts can be modified at once as it becomes apparent what the student has or has not understood.

A particularly important feature of this smoothly flowing process is that, since "tests" precede the presentation of each new step, failure on a given test precludes presentation of the next step.

In other words, the student stays with each step of the curricular sequence until he has mastered it.

Note that this apparently simple idea represents a crucial difference between education as it is now practiced and education as it could be. In the conventional classroom, each student spends the same amount of time to learn an amount of material that varies from student to student. With a computer teaching machine (or a human tutor), each student spends a variable amount of time to learn a constant amount of material, and there is no *a priori* reason that the amount of time taken should not be that required for complete mastery. Computer teaching machines offer the hope that the emphasis in education can be taken off *efficiency* of information transmission and put back where it belongs, on mastery of the subject.

Model Modern Major General

The vital characteristic of the modern computer—the characteristic which allows it to do what media merely transmitting information cannot do—is that the program stored in its memory can be modified internally while the machine is in use. The computer's ability to adapt to feedback means that it can, in theory at least, be programmed to simulate the human intellectual process of tutoring or, for that matter, of thinking. This truly revolutionary idea is distressingly undervalued by many computer theoreticians and technologists. Instead of devoting their financial and intellectual resources to the development of conceptual models for internal program modification, they concentrate on the perfection of details of communication and on the exploitation of basically inadequate systems. Where we need creativity, we get bookkeeping.

And bookkeepers build bookkeeping machines! Many of the devices now in use are little more than that, for they use only a fraction of the computer's capacities. For example, some machines ask the student to indicate his response by choosing among a small set of multiple-choice buttons instead of, say, by typing his response on a computer-controlled typewriter. This expedient reduces the demand on the computer's central processer, but it also disastrously diminishes the effectiveness of the tutorial process and can be a bore to the student. The repertoire of responses allowed the student is too small and stereotyped; the kinds of analysis that can be applied to this type of response are few. With such machines, the question,

"Why do you need a computer at all?", is justified and difficult to answer.

Another shortcoming of many teaching machines is that they use a storage medium such as microfilm for the material to be presented to the student. A frame of microfilm contains a great deal of information; presenting the material in large blocks instead of in a series of small steps makes it impossible to identify the exact point at which the student loses his way. Thus analysis of the student's responses becomes general instead of specific, and the educational program again approximates the lecture-cum-quiz instead of the student-tutor conversation. In addition, microfilm cannot be erased as can magnetic storage devices, so it becomes more difficult to modify a program in response to new insights into the educational process or into the subject at hand.

In short, many computer teaching machines now in use are typified by extremely limited input media and by output display devices that are relatively static and unrefined in step size. In general, these teaching machines must be considered automated conventional teaching machines rather than actual computer teaching machines. I classify them as degenerate teaching machines.

A more serious attempt to utilize the computer's power to provide solid tutorial aid is represented by machines whose programs include *branching*. Conventional teaching machines, by and large, proceed in a linear fashion. Degenerate computer teaching machines do branch in simple ways but not with the elaborations found in the excitingly effective applications of computer teaching. The computer teaching machine can adapt to the student's progress. It can be programmed for a large amount of decision-making at critical points.

The basic idea of branching is that the student's response determines which of several alternatives the machine presents next. There are a great many types of branching trees, or decision logics, which a computer can use. One major type is the *main trunk* tree, in which, after a short remedial digression, the student always returns to some central sequence. To the *fully branched* tree-type, the student never returns once he has left a given sequence.

What You Forgot to Remember

Since branching is implemented through a process of storage, comparison, and, finally, selection, computer teaching machines that use such a process can be called *selective* computer teaching machines. All possible questions, statements, and remedial hints or queries—indeed, any action of the computer—are prestated by the author of the program. They then are stored in the computer's large and, it is hoped, randomly accessible memory. The computer compares the student's answers, perhaps after slight editing, with a list of possible correct answers and anticipated incorrect answers. If there is a match between any answer in the list and the student's answer, that match determines which of the prestored statements from the computer memory is next displayed to the student. The analysis, then, is very simple: The input is compared with alternative answers, and a match determines the next statement.

Most computer teaching machines that deal with general verbal material are members of this category. They take advantage of the computer's ability to store and to compare small chunks of material. They also allow the author freedom to change easily and quickly the contents of a single statement or question. Thus, as quickly as improvements become apparent to the human author, they can be added to the existing program—and, superficially, this type of computer teaching machine can imitate the tutorial dialogue.

What Though Tomorrow Brings

The teacher does not compare his student's response with other possible responses and then select an appropriate reply; he does not store in his memory specific branches, outcomes, and statements. Instead, he uses his understanding of the subject, his awareness of the difficulties it is likely to present, and his knowledge of the student to *analyze* the student's response and to *construct* his own next statement. What we need, then, is a computer that can analyze and construct as well as compare and select —a computer that thinks vertically as well as horizontally, so to speak.

Such computers, since they generate responses not specifically written into their memories, could be called *generative* computer teaching machines. This kind of teaching machine would be an exceedingly economical way to achieve powerful teaching programs, and tedious and exhaustive programming of teaching steps would be unnecessary.

One of the first examples of a generative teaching machine was Bolt, Baranek and Newman's Joseph C. R. Licklider's imaginative use of a computer and a cathode ray oscilloscope to permit powerful tutorial interaction in the study of analytical geometry. Like the human teacher, this technique used no fixed, prestored dialogue, but rather had a small number of algorithms which could perform generally useful functions. It could *plot* a graph on the face of an oscilloscope, or *substitute* parameters presented by the student into the algebraic expression of a geometrical curve. With this small library of standard equations for various two-dimensional curves, the student could explore the effects of changing intercepts, slopes, and other parameters which defined one or another curve. He also could track a photoelectric pointer, alter the geometry of the curve itself, and observe how the analytical expression corresponding to a particular curve affected the various parameters. So Licklider's visual display of a cathode ray tube allowed additional rhetorical tools to be brought into play —a critical point could be circled.

Another example of a generative computer teaching machine, in which the special analog properties of the subject matter allow algorithmic generation of an almost unlimited number of computer responses, is illustrated by the work of Roger Buiten and Harlan Lane at the University of Michigan. Their machine was designed to teach students how to pronounce foreign language words. The student was presented with an audio recording of a given word. Then he repeated that sound into a microphone. The microphone was connected to an analog-to-digital converter which fed a digitized representation of the speech sound into the computer. The computer analyzed the speech for pitch, amplitude and rhythm, and then responded to the student by means of meters which indicated how far the student had deviated from the sample sound. The important feature of this computer teaching machine is that, unlike the usual "language laboratory," the student does not have to rely upon his untrained ear to decide whether his performance is acceptable. The analysis and evaluation are made on an individual word basis by an impartial, discriminating computer.

Some laboratories are using random number generation as a means of varying the terms of mathematical problems in computer teaching machines. In this way many new problems can be generated for a variety of students, or for one student in a continuing way as he deals with a special class of problem. Some researchers claim success for editing routines which recognize nearly equivalent spellings or phonetic equiva-lents. This sort of input to the computer will, of course, be a very important part of the generative computer teaching machine of the future.

Perhaps the most intriguing representation of a true generative teaching program is that described by Leonard Uhr of the University of Wisconsin. Uhr attacks the problem of the generation of teaching programs to achieve the old-fashioned classroom question-and-answer atmosphere. His current programs handle well-defined problems in elementary arithmetic and word-for-word language translation. He uses prototype problem formats, such as "How much is A plus B?", which previously have been stored in the computer. Questions are generated either by a random number calculator or by a reaction to the student's performance on previous problems. Uhr goes on to suggest that there really is no limit to the prototypes of many different problems which can be presented, and that almost any problem which can be stated formally can be presented. However, analysis of the answer is quite another thing—and a knotty problem for the scientist to solve for his machine. For example, presentation of a theorem proof to a student would require that the computer be able to deal with the many possible equivalent paths. This is a problem which goes far beyond the simple statement that $3 + 4$ is, indeed, equal to 7.

Ultimately, of course, this problem will be solved, and inevitably the real breakthrough in programmed learning will be conversational interaction between the student and the generative computer teaching machine.

Already J. Weizenbaum of Massachusetts Institute of Technology has developed a program system which is called ELIZA, in which dialogues with the machines are directed strongly by the human conversant. The machine detects key words and context and responds to the human's message with the most appropriate of many prestored sentences.

This is only the beginning, the very beginning, for generative computer teaching machines. The future is fantastic to contemplate. It is hard for most people to believe that any machine could teach with as much insight, flexibility, and imagination as a human tutor; it is equally difficult to conceive of the enormous numbers of people who could be educated to high levels of mastery through conversations with such machines. But before he met him, James Garfield undoubtedly had trouble imagining Mark Hopkins.

RABBIT FAMILIES AND HOW THEY GROW

By Harris B. Rubin

THE RABBIT ENJOYS a well-deserved reputation for enthusiastic and efficient perpetuation of the species. A single pair of rabbits, by mating only 24 times, can produce more than 130,000 descendants in a two-year period. This fact alone would be enough to make the reproductive system and the sexual behavior of rabbits an inviting subject for study.

But there is more. Despite the hypothetical 24-times-in-two-years figure

given above, real rabbits mate very frequently—indeed male rabbits, whether in the laboratory or in the garden, often appear totally preoccupied with sex.

This enthusiasm for mating occurs in an animal which has one of the most efficient of all mammalian reproductive systems. Rabbits mature early; they are able to reproduce when they are four or five months old. A litter is born after a gestation period of only one month, and the female is likely to become pregnant again immediately. Just after giving birth, she becomes very receptive to the sexual advances of males. If the result is a fertile mating, a second litter may develop in the womb while the first matures in the nest.

Furthermore, matings are very often fertile, no matter when they occur. The female rabbit, unlike most other mammals, ovulates in response to sexual stimulation. About ten hours after copulation, eggs are released from the ovary, raising the chance of fertilization to a very high level. In view of all this, it is not surprising that Australia, a continent void of natural predators of the rabbit, has a rabbit problem.

It may be well to acknowledge at this point that the study of rabbit sexual behavior is a serious business. It contributes to our knowledge of mammalian sexual behavior and sexual behavior in general, and it has practical applications to the Australian problem as well. Perhaps most important of all, it shows what can be done through careful, direct observation under laboratory con-

ditions. If the methodology of research into the sexual behavior of animals were more often emulated by those who study human sexual behavior, we might someday know as much about people as we do about rabbits.

Mating Behavior

The male rabbit generally initiates mating behavior. He approaches the female and begins to sniff or lick her genitalia. If the female does not move, he bites her feet or her back. As she tries to avoid this painful stimulation, he may jump over her back and, while in mid-air, direct a stream of urine at her. A receptive female stops running and lowers her chest to the ground. The male places his forepaws over her back and clasps her tightly around the flanks. His penis, which has been flaccid and almost totally enclosed in a sheath, becomes rigid and extends about two inches out of the sheath.

Still clasping her flanks tightly, he rapidly oscillates his pelvis, producing short probing jabs of his penis against her genital area. When he finds the opening of her vagina, he makes one powerful thrust, completely inserting his penis, and the pelvic oscillations cease. During this thrust, which is so powerful that the male's hind paws frequently leave the ground, he delivers a stream of semen into her reproductive tract. Now off balance, he falls backward, breaking contact. The entire act, from the start of the mount to the backward lunge, generally takes less than five seconds. The intromission itself lasts only about one second.

The female is not completely passive during the sexual act. Frequently she will thwart the male's first attempt by running from him. If she is sexually receptive, she will raise and vigorously shake her tail as she runs, which appears to heighten the excitement of the male. She runs only a short distance, and when she stops the male immediately mounts her. As he mounts, she lowers the forward portion of her body, arches her back, and raises her hindquarters and tail. The male's penis, constantly probing her genital area as he thrusts, appears to stimulate her to make adjusting movements that align her vagina with his angle of thrust. This greatly facilitates intromission.

If the female is not sexually receptive, she flees from the male without wagging her tail and attempts to protect her hindquarters by wedging herself against a wall or into a crevice. If no such protection is available, she sits or lies with her genital area pressed against the ground and covered by her tail. A persistent male may spend hours biting and scratching her, but to no avail; a nonreceptive female will not assume the mating position. There is no such thing as rape in the rabbit world.

Under certain conditions, a male may not immediately attempt to copulate. If he has been brought into a female's cage for mating, for instance, he generally will ignore the female and instead will explore the unfamiliar surroundings. A sexually receptive female in this situation frequently will mount him. Her mount tends to stop his exploring behavior and to elicit sexual approaches.

Homosexuality

Homosexual behavior frequently is displayed by rabbits that have been sexu-

ally segregated. Males will attempt to copulate with any strange rabbit, regardless of its sex. This does not appear to be a case of mistaken identity, for the behavior may continue for some time, with first one male and then the other taking the active role. Receptive females will mount other females and exhibit pelvic thrusting indistinguishable from that of a male. There is no doubt that this behavior is sexually stimulating; the female frequently ovulates after mounting another female just as she does after mating with a male.

But rabbits are basically heterosexual. Males housed together even for long periods of time will compete fiercely to mount a female placed in the cage. If one male is mounting the other when the female is introduced, the two immediately break contact; the stronger and faster male will mount the female and the slower male may mount on top of the pair. After the first male completes a copulation, the second male will mount the female.

Sexual Maturation

Rabbits of both sexes display the sexual responses of mounting and thrusting soon after their eyes open, at about three weeks of age. By the time they are mature enough to reproduce (four months for the female, five months for the male), rabbits have had a great deal of sexual experience. However, experience is not necessary for an adequate performance. The sexual posturing of the female is probably innate; females raised in isolation nonetheless assume the correct mating posture on first contact with a male.

Similarly, the mounting and thrusting behavior of the male appears to be inborn. A male raised in isolation will mount and thrust against the first female he sees. An inexperienced male is often disoriented—that is, he may mount the female's head or side—but these errors rapidly are corrected. It is entirely possible for a naive male and a naive female to copulate within one minute of their first encounter.

Frequency of Mating

The immediate mating which occurs when a female rabbit is introduced to a male is not the end of their sexual behavior. In a few minutes, another mating will occur—and then another, and another, up to 15 or more copulations in an hour. But how many matings will occur in 12 hours, or in a day, a week, a month? To answer this question would require the individual attention of an observer present 24 hours a day. Consider the difficulty of this task. Since the entire copulatory act can occur in less than five seconds, the conscientious observer would be prohibited not only from leaving the room, but even from turning his head to light a cigarette. The solution: eliminate the need for an observer.

In the Behavior Research Laboratory at Anna State Hospital, Dr. N. H. Azrin and I developed an apparatus to monitor sexual behavior automatically. Basically, the apparatus makes each of the two animals a contact of an electric switch. Physical contact between them creates an electrical connection and completes a circuit. The amount of current that flows through the circuit depends on the quality of the electrical connection between the animals. Because moist contacts make much better electrical connections than dry ones, more current flows through the circuit when the contact is moist.

Rabbits can make a moist contact in three ways: by licking or biting, by external contact of the genital organs (thrusting), and by internal contact of the genital organs (intromission). These three types of contact can be differentiated electrically from one another. The illustration [see drawing at top right] shows the different patterns of current flow which result from each of these contacts. Moist contact between mouth and fur allowed about 10 microamperes of current to flow for about 0.2 seconds; dry contact between fur and fur allowed no current to flow; moist, external contacts of the genital organs allowed about 30 microamperes of current to flow for about 0.05 seconds; and moist, internal contact of the genital organs allowed about 30 microamperes of current to flow for almost a full second.

Intromission can be identified precisely, because it allows much more current to flow than any other contact except a thrust but lasts much longer than a thrust. Thus it is a simple matter for the recording apparatus to keep track of the number of times a pair of rabbits mates, the exact time of each mating, and the length of time each mating lasts. Since the recordings are made automatically, mating behavior can be monitored continuously for weeks without a human observer and without disturbing the rabbits.

Mating Patterns

One of the first behavior patterns discovered with the automatic recording

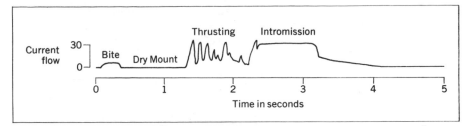

The mating behavior of rabbits can be recorded electrically, and the individual actions distinguished from one another on the basis of the amount and duration of current flow.

technique was that pelvic thrusting occurred at a constant rate, 14 thrusts per second. This was true no matter which animal did the thrusting, how long the thrusting lasted, or how many thrusting episodes preceded the measured one.

The automatic technique also revealed that rabbits mate in bursts, or runs. The first run of copulations almost always starts within ten minutes of the time that the animals are placed together, and there may be as many as 15 copulations during the first hour. As time goes on, the interval between matings becomes longer and longer. After five to ten hours, during which the animals may have mated 30 or more times, an hour may elapse between matings. Generally all mating stops by the time 18 hours have passed.

This gradual decrease in rate of mating reflects the sexual capabilities of the male. Almost all mammalian males have a period of time after an ejaculation during which they cannot ejaculate again, and the length of this refractory period increases after each successive ejaculation. Although a male rabbit may be able to ejaculate twice in a span of two or three minutes when he first is stimulated sexually, after he has ejaculated 30 times no amount of stimulation will result in another ejaculation, until at least half an hour has passed.

The fact that the female does not have a similar refractory period can be demonstrated by a simple experiment. If a male is allowed to mate freely with a female, they will copulate at a high rate during the first few hours; by the fifth hour, however, the rate will have slowed considerably. If we now replace the male with a fresh buck who has had no contact with a female for several days, the new male and female will immediately start to mate at the same high rate demonstrated by the original pair at the start of the session. If we again exchange the males, bringing back the first one, the rate will fall again. Thus it is the male that determines the frequency of matings within a run of copulations.

Although the male determines the frequency of copulations within a run, it is the female who determines when a run will occur. The female rabbit has periods of sexual receptivity during which, if a male is available, she will mate. The receptive periods are comparatively short, and they are separated by longer periods of sexual nonreceptivity during which the female actively avoids the sexual advances of males [see illustration, page 82, top]. No copulatory behavior occurs during the nonreceptive periods, the duration of which varies considerably even in the same female. For example, one female was housed in a small chamber with a male for two months. They copulated more than 200 times during that time, in nine distinct runs. At times only 12 hours, at other times as much as 20 days, separated two consecutive runs.

Sexual Receptivity

Why did the durations of the female's nonreceptive periods vary so widely? The variations cannot be ascribed to changes in the environment: the temperature was always 74°; the lights were always on; and, except for ten minutes each day when food and water supplies were replenished, the animals were never disturbed. Therefore the explanation must be physiological.

Sexual receptivity in the female rabbit is determined by the level of sexual hormones in the blood. This hormonal control of behavior is complex: several hormones act simultaneously, some to enhance receptivity and others to inhibit it, and receptivity is determined by the balance of these antagonistic hormones which prevails at the time in question. If the balance is artificially disturbed, as by the injection of a hormone, behavior will be affected accordingly. For example, in rabbits an injection of estrogen will enhance receptive behavior; on the other hand, an injection of progesterone will inhibit it.

Although we do not yet know what causes day-to-day variations in the receptivity of female rabbits, we do know

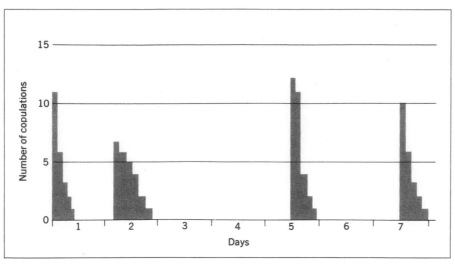

During the week charted here, this female rabbit had fairly regular periods of sexual receptivity. Sometimes, however, a female will be receptive twice in one day and then unreceptive for as long as twenty days.

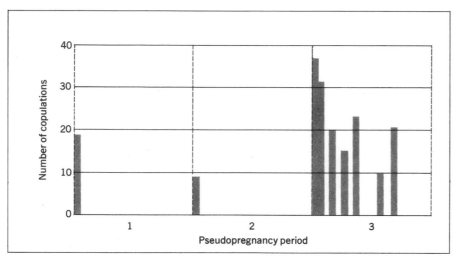

During a 16- to 20-day pseudopregnancy, a female rabbit will sometimes have one receptive period and sometimes many.

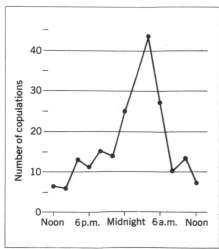

Rabbits prefer to mate in the middle of the night.

From *JEAB* (see bibliography), copyright 1967 by the Society for the Experimental Analysis of Behavior, Inc.

two occasions on which receptivity can be expected: immediately after a female gives birth to a litter and at the end of a pseudopregnancy. The receptive period following a litter, called postpartum estrus, apparently results from a decrease in the amount of progesterone in the blood. Progesterone is produced by the corpus lutem, a structure which develops in the ovary after ovulation and remains active until the end of pregnancy. Then it degenerates; as it degenerates, the production of progesterone decreases and the female becomes sexually receptive.

Pseudopregnancy

The second predictable receptive period occurs after pseudopregnancy, which is a physiological reaction to a sterile mating. Even if a mating is not fertile—if no sperm are present—the female will ovulate after copulation. Ovulation stimulated by sterile matings, like ovulation stimulated by fertile matings, results in the development of the corpus lutem, which produces progesterone. The female looks and acts pregnant. Her mammaries develop and she pulls hair from her body to build a nest. Except that fetuses are not developed, the physiological and behavioral changes in the rabbit exactly parallel those of true pregnancy. However, pseudopregnancy does not last as long as true pregnancy —16 to 20 days as opposed to 28 to 32. And, of course, there is no litter.

Although the corpus lutem produces progesterone throughout pregnancy and pseudopregnancy, female rabbits frequently become sexually receptive while in these conditions. It is not known what stimuli produce these receptive periods, which occur at irregular and unpredictable intervals [*see illustration at middle left*]. It is known, however, that they tend to occur late at night or early in the morning.

In fact, rabbit sexual behavior in general—even when the female is neither pregnant nor pseudopregnant—follows a nocturnal pattern. The pattern becomes evident only after the animals have been paired for about 24 hours and the initial burst of sexual activity has subsided. Subsequent mating tends to occur at night even when obvious clues to the time are absent. In a study of 13 different pairs of animals in an environment where neither lighting nor temperature varied with the time of day, about 75 per cent of the matings took place between dusk and dawn [*see illustration at bottom left*].

Our knowledge of rabbit sexual behavior has evolved from careful observation and experimentation. The knowledge is useful, and the methodology is useful as well. For example, a full understanding of human sexual behavior cannot be had without the kind of research which has given us an understanding of animal sexual behavior: direct observation, under experimental conditions, of the behavior as it occurs. William H. Masters and Virginia Johnson have made a start in this vital area of research. With more researchers of their ability and courage, perhaps eventually we can clear the mist which still shrouds the subject of sex in man.

... and grows. One rabbit family can produce 130,000
descendants in two years.

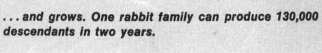

COPULATION IN RATS

By Gordon Bermant

The musings of poets aside, animals do not languish for lack of love and sexual union. If an animal fails to eat, he rapidly deteriorates and dies. If he fails to drink, he dies even sooner. But if an animal repeatedly fails to copulate, he neither gets sick nor dies. As far as life-sustaining functions are concerned, copulation fulfills no physiological need and is not necessary for the survival of the animal. Why, then, do animals copulate?

Whenever we ask *why* a behavior occurs, there are really two different questions we could have in mind: *What for?* or *How come?* To the question *What for?*, we expect an answer in terms of the function or purpose that the behavior serves; to *How come?*, we want a description of the events that cause the behavior.

The *What for?* of copulation is simple...

It serves the function of transmitting sperm cell to ovum, thereby playing a crucial role in the continuation of animal species. We might at first imagine that we could answer the question "Why do animals copulate?" by saying that they do it with the intention of reproducing. However, this explanation of copulation would certainly be incorrect if we applied it to subhuman species. Only man has developed the skills in thought and language that are required to comprehend and express the relation between copulation and reproduction. Whereas men and women may copulate with the intention of producing offspring, nonhuman animals do not. Therefore, when we ask why animals copulate, we are really searching for the *How come?*, for the *determinants* of the behavior: the physiological and environmental conditions that cause the complex postures and motions of copulation. For the past several years I have been

investigating some of these determinants of copulation in a number of animal species, primarily the laboratory rat.

Why Study Rats?

Rats have been the favorite experimental subjects of American animal psychologists for many years, and hence we know a great deal about their behavior. In addition, the study of rats has contributed much of what we know about the physiology of reproduction, particularly the roles played by the gonadal and pituitary hormones. And finally, certain rather unique features of the rat's copulatory pattern allow us to perform experiments that would be impossible with other species. These advantages make the small, inexpensively maintained rat an ideal subject for experimental investigation of copulatory behavior.

A word about definitions: I shall use the term *copulatory behavior*, not *sexual behavior*. Sexual behavior is best defined as any behavior that distinguishes males from females; copulatory behavior refers specifically to activities directly associated with the transfer of sperm.

Behavioral Description: The Male

The first stage in an investigation of this sort is a careful description of the behavior and its temporal organization. Social behaviors such as copulation are intricate nonverbal dialogues. There is a continuous interchange of action and reaction between the animals. In describing the behavior we must pay close attention to the reciprocating effects that the behavior of each animal has on the other.

In the copulatory behavior of the rat, the male usually appears to take the initiative. It is therefore convenient to organize the behavioral description around the responses of the male.

Suppose that a male rat, with previous copulatory experience, and a receptive female are placed together in a small enclosure. Within a minute or less, the male normally begins the preliminaries which lead to copulation. This often involves nothing more than a brief nuzzling of the female's flank or genital area. Such stimulation produces in the highly receptive female a short, jerky forward motion and a lordosis response (*see illustration, opposite*). The male may then move behind the female and mount her. He grasps her flanks with his forelegs

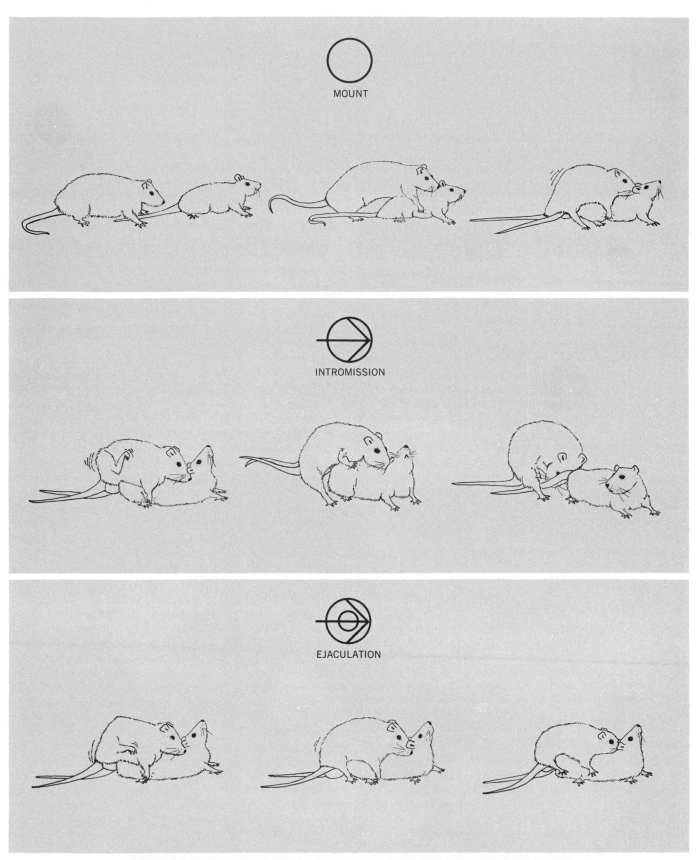

Three behavioral events involved in the copulatory sequence of the rat are shown here: mounting, intromission, and ejaculation. Each event is represented by a special symbol.

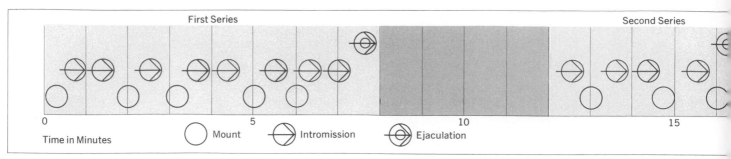

First Series   Second Series

0   5   10   15

Time in Minutes   ⊖ Mount   ⊕ Intromission   ⊕ Ejaculation

The time course of normal copulatory behavior in the rat involves about five ejaculatory series (three are shown here, light gray

and begins a series of rapid, shallow, pelvic thrusting movements. At this point two possibilities arise: either he will penetrate the female or he won't. If after several rapid thrusts he fails to penetrate, he dismounts by pushing away rather slowly and turning at a slight angle to the female. But if penetration occurs, the male makes a single deep thrust and immediately thereafter pushes vigorously up and away from the female. Under normal conditions the duration of penile insertion during the single deep thrust and withdrawal is between two- and three-tenths of a second (200-300 milliseconds). The energetic, almost acrobatic dismount following the single deep thrust is one of the most consistent features of the copulatory sequence. Unless special (electronic) methods of detection are used, the form of this dismount is the only reliable indication that the male has achieved penetration.

So far we have seen two of the male's responses: a mount without penetration, which is called simply a *mount;* and a brief penetration, which is called an *intromission.* The male does not emit semen during these brief intromissions. When, then, does the male ejaculate?

After his initial intromission the male withdraws from the female and engages in genital grooming and other noncopulatory behavior for 20 to 60 seconds. Then he reapproaches the female and either mounts or achieves another intromission. This pattern of brief copulatory responses separated by relatively long periods of inactivity usually continues until the male has achieved between eight to fifteen intromissions. Then his behavior shows a dramatic change.

Now, after mounting and penetrating, the male does not throw himself off, but thrusts deeply as many as five times. The last of these thrusts is accompanied by an orgasmic spasm of the male's

hindquarters at the moment of deepest penetration. Only now does he ejaculate. For a few seconds following the ejaculation, the male clutches his partner, often so tightly that they do not separate if the experimenter tries to lift them from the cage. This time the male dismounts very slowly, usually within five seconds after the ejaculation.

Following ejaculation, the male does not approach the female for about five minutes (five to ten times longer than after each of his previous brief penetrations). Then the male mounts again to achieve an intromission—and begins his second ejaculatory series. In this series the male makes fewer mounts and intromissions, and ejaculates sooner than in the first series.

If the male is allowed to remain with the original female for several hours, he may ejaculate five times or more. However, the period of time between an ejaculation and the next intromission (the *post-ejaculatory interval*) rapidly increases in length, suggesting that the male is becoming tired. *(See illustration above.)* Later we shall see that physical fatigue is only partially responsible for this waning of copulatory activity.

This description highlights four basic questions that need to be answered: 1) What prompts the male to approach and mount the female for the first time? 2) What determines whether a male will succeed in achieving penetration? 3) Why does the male require so many intromissions before ejaculating? 4) What causes the male to slow down and eventually stop his copulatory responding? Much of my research has centered around the last three of these questions.

Sensory Feedback: The Primary Determinant of Intromission

In order to determine what factors facilitate penetration by the male, we ana-

lyzed intromission further and then performed some experiments.

The intromission response itself is divided into two stages or components: 1) a series of rapid shallow thrusts followed by 2) a single vigorous deep thrust and withdrawal. The distinction between shallow and deep thrusting was first studied in detail in 1940 by Calvin Stone and Leonard Ferguson of Stanford University. On the basis of high-speed photography they made estimates of the duration of penetration. It seemed to them that penetration took place even during the early portions of the shallow thrusting stage. This is important because it determines the duration of penetration, and hence the amount of genital sensory feedback. To be sure of the answer, I refined Stone and Ferguson's experiment in 1963, in Frank Beach's laboratory. The refinement consisted of small electrodes attached to each animal so that direct genital contact, with the aid of an electronic circuit, illuminated a lamp that was photographed along with the animals.

My films generally confirmed Stone and Ferguson's findings, but with one crucial exception: The males made very little if any direct genital contact during their shallow thrusting. Whenever the lamp lighted to indicate successful penetration, the male ceased his shallow thrusting and executed the single deep thrust. This meant that shallow thrusting did not contribute substantially to the stimulation of the penis but served to orient the male properly for executing the deep thrust. It seems, therefore, that shallow thrusting is the detection component of the response, and deep thrusting the stimulation component.

I went on to test this conclusion by experiment. Norman Adler and I reasoned that if feedback from the penis is required for the release of the deep

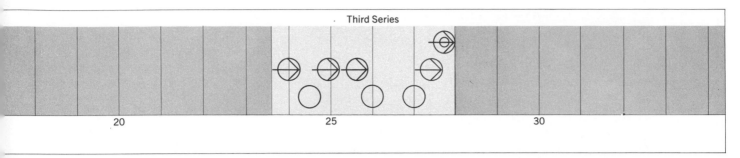

Third Series

20   25   30

ne pauses between an ejaculation and the beginning of the next ejaculatory series (darker gray) become progressively longer.

thrust response, then by preventing feedback by anesthetizing the penis we should be able to block the response. Sure enough, a topical anesthetic applied to the male abolished the deep thrust without interfering with mounting and shallow thrusting. Sven Carlsson and Knut Larsson of Goteborg University have obtained identical results using a liquid local anesthetic.

The necessity for feedback prior to full penetration is not restricted to the rat. Madeline Cooper and Lester Aronson of the American Museum of Natural History have shown that male cats surgically deprived of feedback from the penis are incapable of successfully penetrating a female. As with rats, these males continue to mount, but their orientations are inadequate for penetration. In these cases the motivation to perform remains unaffected but the capacity for successful performance is hampered.

The Ejaculatory Mechanism

What is the relation between intromissions and ejaculation? The most obvious suggestion is that one produces the other. The series of intromissions preceding each ejaculation somehow changes the internal state of the male so that the ejaculatory response becomes more and more likely. But how to discover the physiological mechanisms producing these changes?

In 1956 Frank Beach suggested a model for the underlying mechanism that was later further developed by the Swedish psychologist Knut Larsson. The basic idea is that the stimulating effects of each short intromission are not immediately forgotten but are stored somewhere in the nervous system. Because some of the excitation aroused by each intromission stays with the rat, the total level of excitation increases during the series of intromissions. When the amount

of accumulated excitation reaches a critical level, the next penetration results in enough additional excitation to produce ejaculation.

Larsson suggested that the level of stored excitation increases spontaneously for several minutes following a single intromission, even if the male does not achieve another intromission during that time. This spontaneous growth becomes progressively slower and eventually declines unless the male augments the process by achieving another intromission (*see illustration, page 90*).

Larsson arrived at his theory by observing the behavior of males who were experimentally separated from the female after each intromission. (Normally, when the animals were not separated by the experimenter, the males achieved an intromission every twenty to thirty seconds and ejaculated after ten to twelve intromissions.) When a separation of between two and three minutes was enforced, the males ejaculated after only four or five intromissions. When the separation was seven minutes or more, the number of intromissions needed to achieve ejaculation became very large. Indeed, some males failed to ejaculate even after several dozen intromissions. Larsson concluded that the short, enforced separations of three minutes had allowed the excitation from each intromission to grow spontaneously to its maximum. Therefore the total number of intromissions required to reach the ejaculatory level of excitation had been reduced to a minimum. Longer enforced separations allowed a decline in excitation. (*See illustration, page 91.*)

This "accumulating excitation" model has achieved partial support from the results of several experiments. For example, I showed in 1964 that if the male were separated from the female only once during an ejaculatory series, then

he ejaculated after fewer intromissions than when no interval was enforced. Yet the number of intromissions required was greater than when separation occurred after each intromission. This is the result predicted by the theory.

The basic assumption of this model of the ejaculatory mechanism is that the number of intromissions preceding ejaculation is determined only by the time interval between the intromissions (*see illustration, page 92 top left*). However, I believe this model is oversimplified. It would be surprising if nothing more were involved in the control of such a complex sequence of behavior, and in fact, the results of several experiments have shown that it does oversimplify the picture. We are forced to acknowledge that other factors must be involved in determining the number of intromissions required for ejaculation.

Our understanding of how these factors operate has been aided by physiological data collected by Benjamin Hart of the University of California, Davis. Hart has shown that male rats whose spinal cords have been separated from their brains are still capable of showing strong reactions similar to ejaculation. This means that the neural machinery associated with ejaculation is organized in the spinal cord. It may be, as Hart suggests, that these responses are normally checked or inhibited by higher brain centers, and the function of genital excitation is simply to release them.

This physiological information can be incorporated into the original excitation model in a straightforward way. Earlier we assumed that the critical level of excitation for ejaculation was always the same. Now we can see that this level may increase or decrease as more or less inhibition is impressed on the spinal ejaculation reflex by the brain. The amount of inhibitory influence at any time can be

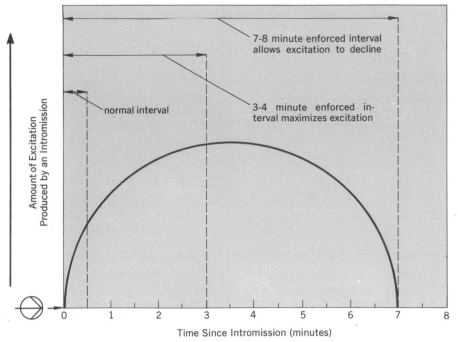

Every intromission produces a spontaneous build-up of excitation in the male rat. The excitation begins to decay after reaching a peak (unless another intromission occurs).

Graph labels:
Amount of Excitation Produced by an Intromission (vertical axis)
Time Since Intromission (minutes) (horizontal axis: 0 1 2 3 4 5 6 7 8)
normal interval
7-8 minute enforced interval allows excitation to decline
3-4 minute enforced interval maximizes excitation

expected to change with many changes in the environment; therefore, we need to do experiments that will tell us in detail how the environment controls inhibitory influence on ejaculation.

Cessation of Copulation: Exhaustion or Boredom?

In 1956 Frank Beach and Lisbeth Jordan allowed 12 male rats to copulate with single females until the males appeared exhausted (that is, until 30 minutes passed without the occurrence of a copulatory response). After each exhausted male was allowed from 24 hours to two weeks of rest, the males were placed with new receptive females and again allowed to copulate until exhausted. The experiment showed that a 24-hour rest period was not enough: only one of the 12 males ejaculated again, and only three achieved intromission. In fact, 10 to 15 days of rest seemed necessary for the males to regain original levels of copulatory performance.

Then, in 1958, Allen Fisher of the University of Pittsburgh reported a startling and paradoxical finding. Fisher found that if he replaced the original female with a new one immediately after the male reached exhaustion, the "exhausted" male began to copulate immediately and could achieve ejaculation with no difficulty; moreover, if the male were continually supplied with new females at regular intervals, he could double or triple his total number of ejaculations before exhaustion.

This dramatic restoration of copula-

tory behavior established beyond doubt that the gradual cessation of copulation with the first female is not produced simply by physical exhaustion or by the inability to copulate further. "Copulatory exhaustion" is now seen to be at best a relative term. The male simply does not exhaust himself with only one female. Instead he becomes progressively more disinterested in the stimuli she provides—until they no longer elicit his copulatory behavior. Another female provides a novel set of stimuli capable of rekindling the male's interest. And so does still another female after that.

Fisher's result is puzzling in the light of the findings of Beach and Jordan. It appears that male rats are potentially more active copulators immediately after prolonged copulation than after 24 hours of rest. How to resolve this paradox?

As a first step toward understanding this, Dale Lott, Linn Anderson and I did the following experiment. We first allowed males to "exhaust" themselves with single females. Then we introduced a second female immediately, or after periods of rest ranging up to 24 hours. The males were allowed to copulate with the second female for as long as they had with the first. The design of this experiment permitted us to trace the time course of changes in copulatory behavior. When the second female was introduced immediately after the removal of the first, the male would mount her virtually immediately. However, after a 24-hour delay, males took substantially longer to begin copulation. (*See illustra-*

tion, page 92, top right.) In fact, some of the males refused to mount at all. Although the males in this experiment were more likely to copulate after a 24-hour delay than the males in Beach and Jordan's experiment, they were certainly slower to begin copulation after this period of rest than when they had been given no rest at all.

We saw that a substantial number of rats copulated to ejaculation with the new female. We now look at the period of time that elapsed from this ejaculation to the next intromission. Do these post-ejaculatory intervals also show evidence of recovery? Does changing females affect the male's ability to recover from ejaculation? It turns out (*see illustration, page 92, center right*) that the intervals are always greater with the second female than with the first: Changing females did not improve the male's ability to recover from ejaculation. In fact, even following the 24-hour rest period the post-ejaculatory interval is only beginning to return to its original value.

Here, then, is a partial resolution of the paradox. We can see that the "novelty" produced by the introduction of the second female immediately after prolonged contact with the first causes the male to approach her promptly and commence copulation. But this novel stimulation does not re-establish the male's original ability to recover rapidly from ejaculation. This recovery comes only with time. It is not complete even after 24 hours. Also, it is clear that the ability of the second female to arouse the male to achieve intromission dwindles substantially within 24 hours; the immediacy of the change in females is a part of the novelty that induces the male to copulate. Males copulate with the second female not *in spite* of her immediate introduction but *because* of it.

The Female's Motivation

We have so far concerned ourselves exclusively with the male's behavior. But the success of the male in achieving intromission and ejaculation also depends on the response of the female to his attempts—the female must be properly receptive. What are the characteristics of the female's receptivity?

Female rats, like the females of many other mammalian species, are receptive to copulatory behavior only at the time they are capable of reproducing—that is, the time of ovulation. Under normal laboratory conditions, female rats ovulate once every four or five days. For ap-

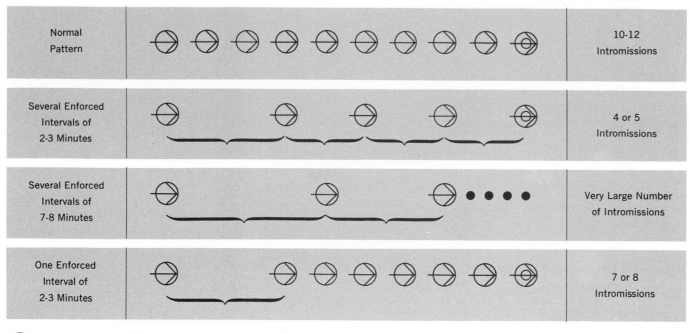

Normal Pattern		10-12 Intromissions
Several Enforced Intervals of 2-3 Minutes		4 or 5 Intromissions
Several Enforced Intervals of 7-8 Minutes		Very Large Number of Intromissions
One Enforced Interval of 2-3 Minutes		7 or 8 Intromissions

⊕ Intromission　⊕ Ejaculation

The number of intromissions required for ejaculation may be changed by separating the male and female for varying lengths of time during the copulatory sequence.

proximately 19 hours during this time, the female will allow the male to mount and achieve penetration.

The most characteristic response of the receptive female is *lordosis:* an arching of the back that produces a pronounced elevation of the hindquarters and genital area. Lordosis and a sideward deflection of the tail permit the male to achieve penetration.

The lordosis response is not under voluntary control in the female. It is a reflex response that usually occurs only when the male grasps the female's flanks. The female rat does not spontaneously present herself to the male in her copulatory posture, as for example female monkeys do. Instead she is dependent upon the male for the elicitation of this response. But it is only in this one sense that the female rat is the passive member of a copulating pair.

When a receptive female is placed with a vigorous male, she does not appear to have much to do with the selection of intercopulatory or post-ejaculatory intervals. The male seems to control the pace of copulation. Receptive females will occasionally approach sluggish males and circle them or perhaps nuzzle them a little. But this sort of approach is exceptional. It is, in itself, insufficient evidence that the female is positively motivated for copulation. In fact, considering both the reflexive nature of the lordosis response and the male's predominant role in determining when the events will occur, it is clearly possible that the female might not have

positive copulatory motivation at all. How could this problem be put to a direct experimental test?

One method is to attempt to train the female to perform some arbitrary response (for example, to press a lever) in order to be exposed to a vigorous male. If a female can be trained to seek copulation, then we can safely state that she has positive copulatory motivation. In 1960, at Harvard University, I discovered that female rats would press a lever in order to receive a single copulatory contact (mount, intromission, or ejaculation) from a male. The training procedure was essentially the same as that used to teach animals to press levers for food. Each time the female pressed the lever, I placed a male in the cage and allowed him to achieve one contact. I then removed him and waited to see if the female would press the lever again. Under these conditions females would usually maintain their lever-pressing behavior until they had received five ejaculations. Clearly the female is motivated.

Complications appeared immediately, though, for at this same time Trevor Pierce and Ronald Nuttall of the Social Relations Department at Harvard demonstrated that female rats would work, not only to achieve copulatory contact, but also to avoid it. They placed a receptive female in a small arena containing several vigorous males. At one end of the arena was an elevated platform. The female was allowed to jump onto this "balcony" at any time, but the males were forced to remain in the arena below. The

presence of several males in the arena ensured that the female would be under almost continuous invitation to copulate.

Under these conditions the female made regular trips to and from the balcony. Immediately upon jumping down she would be approached by a male who would mount, intromit, or ejaculate. The attempt of a second male would usually follow very shortly thereafter. The female rarely accepted the second male but instead dodged her way through the other animals to the balcony, where she remained for a period of time before jumping down again. The female was clearly motivated both to achieve copulation and to prevent repeated copulations from occurring within brief intervals. Each female established a set of "preferred intervals" for copulation.

A careful examination of the behavior in the lever-pressing and balcony situations reveals that the amount of time a female chooses to wait between copulatory episodes is consistently related to the kind of stimulation she has just received from the male (*see illustration, page 92 bottom right*). Whenever a female was mounted without penetration, she would press the lever again (or return to the arena) after a pause of 20 seconds or less. If she received an intromission, she was likely to wait about one minute before seeking the next contact. And if the male had ejaculated, the female would usually delay her next contact for between two and five minutes.

This close relation between the type of copulatory contact and the female's

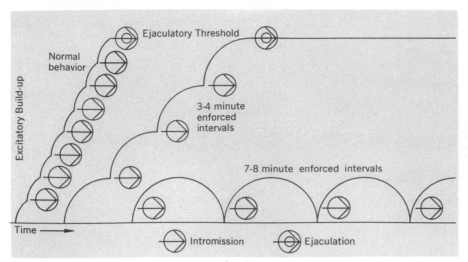

Larsson's theory of excitatory build-up accounts for the effects of enforced intercopulatory intervals. The number of intromissions needed to produce an ejaculatory excitation level depends upon the amount of excitatory build-up after each intromission.

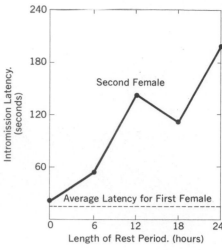

After copulating extensively with the first female, a male takes longer to begin copulating with a second female as the amount of rest between females is increased.

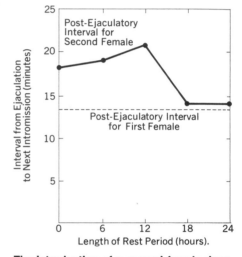

The introduction of a second female does not permit the male to recover from ejaculation more rapidly. The male shows recovery only after a rest of about 24 hours.

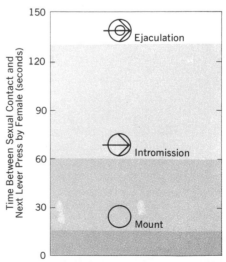

If a receptive female is allowed to control the time between sexual contacts by pressing a lever, she will press the lever again sooner after a mount than after an intromission, and sooner after an intromission than after an ejaculation.

subsequent pause allows us to conclude that females can detect the difference between mounts, intromissions, and ejaculations. More important, it suggests that the more genital stimulation a female receives from a single contact, the longer she will wait before responding again.

In 1963, William Westbrook and I began a series of three experiments to obtain more exact information on how changes in the quantity of copulatory stimulation affected the female's tendency to initiate further contact. Our hypothesis was that if we reduced the amount of stimulation afforded by copulatory contact, the females would seek subsequent contacts earlier. In all three experiments, we used the lever-pressing technique. In the first experiment we concentrated on the effect of ejaculation.

When the male rat ejaculates, his seminal fluid coagulates almost immediately to form a viscous plug in the female's vagina. Sometimes this "vaginal plug" falls out of the female within a few minutes. At other times it is pulled out during subsequent copulation. In any case, the presence of the plug in the vagina seems an obvious place to look for a substantial contribution to the prolongation of the female's post-ejaculatory intervals. Following up this reasoning with experimentation, we injected males with a drug that prevented the emission of seminal fluid at the time of the ejaculatory response. With this treatment, males showed all the behavioral signs of ejaculation. But no semen was emitted. When females received no vaginal plugs, they recovered from ejaculation sooner than they did when plugs were deposited. The plug plays a functional role in determining the female's post-ejaculatory interval. It appears to

contribute quite a bit to the amount of vaginal stimulation.

In our next experiments we attempted to reduce the amount of available stimulation one step further. First we partially anesthetized the female's vagina and external genital area, and noted that they then responded more rapidly after all three types of contact than they did while unanesthetized. Finally, we reduced copulatory stimulation to a bare minimum by placing the females with males whose penises had been anesthetized. This treatment, we said earlier, prevents full intromission as well as ejaculation. Under these conditions, receptive females actively sought copulatory stimulation at extremely short intervals throughout a full hour.

The basic determinant of copulatory receptivity in female rats is the hormonal state of the animal around the time of ovulation. Without this, she will not permit copulation. Our experiments indicate that superimposed on this basic receptivity are short-term changes in responsiveness caused by the amount of genital stimulation the female receives.

These experiments show that both male and female rats impose on copulatory activities their own sets of temporal limitations, each set largely determined by the amount of sensory feedback afforded by previous contact. The temporal requirements of each partner mesh neatly and naturally together so that effective copulation and reproduction proceed efficiently from generation to generation. This is yet another of nature's wise prearrangements of compatible connections between animals. The experimental psychologist seeks to explicate these relationships, and in so doing concludes by admiring them. ∩

THE
HUNGRY
FLY

By Vincent Dethier

HYPERPHAGIA, over-eating, is a comparative business. That which is over-eating in one animal is normal in another. Animals that feed infrequently may appear to over-indulge in the eyes of animals that feed frequently and regularly. The python that swallows the hog, the tick or leech that gorges itself on blood, human beings of certain tribes who eat themselves into a stupor when an elephant is killed and practically starve between slaughters—for all of these, "over-eating" is a normal adaptation to particular environmental circumstances. Occasionally, in the normal course of events, some animals that eat normal sized meals on a regular schedule become hyperphagic for limited periods. Certain migratory birds do precisely this prior to long flights with the result that considerable energy reserves are accumulated. Hibernating mammals over-indulge seasonally in preparation for a long lean winter. Some animals, notably people, not uncommonly become abnormally or pathologically hyperphagic.

These cases, normal and abnormal alike, dramatically illustrate what we often take for granted—the fact that the vast majority of animals regulate their feeding within remarkably precise limits. The nature of the regulatory mechanism is one of the most fascinating problems in physiology and physiological psychology today.

Although the most direct path toward understanding man is formed through the study of man, there is always hope that the study of a basic phenomenon in a so-called lower or simple organism will assist us in locating the more direct pathway. Buoyed by this hope we have spent many years studying the feeding behavior of the black blowfly, *Phormia regina* Meigen [*see illustration page 97*]. The black blowfly is an unusually fine experimental animal for the study of feeding mechanisms because it is essentially an energy machine with few requirements. To live out its maximal life span of 60 days it requires only oxygen, water, and carbohydrate. Since it does not grow, it has no other needs that are not already bequeathed to it by its larval stage. The blowfly is, however, quite small—only 8 mm long.

We started our investigation with the simple assumption that feeding is influenced by oral factors (taste) and post-ingestion factors. If the characteristics and interactions of these factors could be understood, we felt that we would be able to construct a reasonably complete picture of the operation of normal feeding behavior. We approached the problem using behavioral, electrophysiological, and surgical techniques (including the induction of experimental hyperphagia).

Tasting With Their Feet

We first needed information about the physiology of the sense of taste in the blowfly. Although it had been known since the eighteenth century that insects could taste and smell, no one, up to the time when our work began, had ever knowingly seen a taste or olfactory receptor. There were, of course, many surmises and inspired guesses, but no proof. The sequence of events that finally led to the discovery of taste receptors began about 45 years ago with the observation of Dwight Minnich of the University of Minnesota that butterflies and flies could discriminate sugar from water merely by stepping in the solutions. After a long series of exquisitely controlled experiments Minnich concluded that these insects bore organs of taste on their feet. Many biologists were reluctant to accept the conclusion, and little came of the work at that time.

Ten years later Eltringham in England and Tinbergen in the Netherlands, examining butterflies and flies respectively, inferred from microscopic structure that certain delicate, transparent hairs were the taste organs of the legs. About the same time, Minnich himself arrived at similar conclusions regarding the taste organs of the fly proboscis. However, another lapse, nearly 30 years, occurred before unequivocal proof was forthcoming. In 1953 Casmir Grabowski and I set out to settle the matter of identity once and for all. Examination of the legs of *Phormia* revealed that the only structures that could conceivably have a sensory function were the variously sized and shaped hollow hairs thickly clothing the legs. Remembering Minnich's observation that sugar applied to the whole leg elicited proboscis extension, we reasoned that stimulation of individual hairs might achieve the same result if indeed any of the hairs were gustatory organs. By the laborious method of counting all of the more than 100 hairs on each leg, placing minute drops of sugar on the tips of individual hairs, and observing whether or not the proboscis extended, we discovered that the hairs described by Tinbergen and Minnich were in fact the taste organs of the legs and mouth respectively.

Specific Receptors

By this time it was common knowledge that flies could distinguish among water, sugar, and salt. But did it follow that there were specific water, sugar, and salt hairs which were analogous to the different kinds of taste buds in the mammalian tongue? Again, by exploiting the behavioral criterion of proboscis extension, we were able to show that each chemosensory hair was sensitive to all stimuli, touch included. To demonstrate this, we treated a thirsty, hungry fly as follows. One hair on the proboscis was stroked gently with a dry needle; the fly responded by extending its proboscis. After stroking had been continued for several seconds, the response ceased. Waning of the response could have indicated sensory adaptation, central nervous system adaptation, or muscle fatigue. When a neighboring hair was stroked, however, the response resumed immediately, indicating that the earlier waning reflected sensory adaptation. Next, a hair adapted to touch was stimulated with a small drop of water rolled onto the tip. Proboscis extension occurred immediately, indicating that although the hair was adapted to touch it was not adapted to water. Repeated stimulation with water eventually resulted in adaptation, which was again shown to be sensory. The adapted hair was then stimulated with sugar. The response occurred.

These behavioral experiments indicated that each hair is a complex organ possessing multiple specific receptors. Under appropriate circumstances the touch, water, and sugar receptors trigger proboscis extension, the first act in feeding. Without this oral stimulation the fly does not attempt to feed regardless of how hungry it may be.

Flies will not ingest sugar or water that has been adulterated with compounds of the sort that we ourselves find distasteful. Salts, acids, and hundreds of other compounds have been shown to inhibit proboscis extension and to shut off feeding if proboscis extension has already taken place. It was conceiv-

Cutting the recurrent nerve produces overeating—hyperphagia—and a bloated, fat fly. Sometimes the fly will eat so much it actually bursts.

able that unacceptable compounds like salt acted by interfering with water and sugar receptors. Again, however, behavioral methods supplied evidence of the presence of a salt receptor in each hair. After proboscis extension was elicited by stimulating one hair with sugar, salt was applied to an adjacent hair. The result was proboscis retraction.

The experiments just described demanded that each hair possess a minimum of four receptor cells. Fortunately, microscopic examination revealed that each hair is in fact multiply innervated. There are five bipolar neurons. The dendrites of four extend to a pore in the tip of the hair; the fifth dendrite terminates in the hair socket. This last is the mechanoreceptor; the others are the water, salt, and sugar receptors, and a fourth chemoreceptor whose sensory characteristics are not yet known. [See illustration page 98.]

Electrophysiology of the Receptors

As is characteristic of all receptors these labellar receptors generate electrical changes that can be detected with appropriate instruments. When a chemical stimulus reaches the terminal pore in the hair, it initiates a change in the permeability of the membrane of the dendrite. Depolarization of the membrane occurs. This depolarization spreads as a slow wave down to the underlying cell body. Here, repetitive, abrupt, all-or-none changes in potential are generated. These electrical volleys, the action potentials, travel along the nerve in both directions—along the axon to the central nervous system and back up the dendrite where the initial depolarization occurred. As early as 1937 I had attempted to record electrophysiological events in insect chemoreceptors, but equipment available at the time was unequal to the task. In 1955 Edward Hodgson, Jerome Lettvin, and Kenneth Roeder, working at Tufts University, devised a unique technique that made detection of action potentials possible. Independently, Hiromichi Morita and his associates at Kyushu University in Japan, who had been conducting with the admiral butterfly *Vanessa indica* a long series of experiments paralleling the blowfly studies, invented the same technique. These workers had discovered that action potentials generated by the chemoreceptors could be recorded through the tip of the hair.

The technique is ingeniously simple. An isolated blowfly head or proboscis is impaled on a fine silver wire or a small, salt-filled glass pipette into which a sil-

ver wire is inserted. This pipette serves as an indifferent electrode. Another glass pipette with a tip diameter of 4-10 microns, also salt-filled and connected with a silver wire, is slipped over the tip of a hair. This pipette serves simultaneously as a recording electrode and as a carrier for the stimulus.

Hodgson and his associates found that when the recording pipette contained salt solution alone, only one of the five neurons fired action potentials. These were of uniform amplitude and frequency. As the concentration of salt in the pipette was increased, the frequency of firing increased. When the pipette contained sugar in addition to salt, a second spike appeared on the record. It had a smaller amplitude than the first. Its frequency of firing was not appreciably affected by changes in salt concentration but did increase in an orderly fashion as sugar concentration was increased. Clearly then, there was one neuron sensitive to salt and another one sensitive to sugar.

In time, electrophysiological studies confirmed all of the behavioral findings. Myron Wolbarsht, working in our laboratory, demonstrated activity from the mechanoreceptor, and David Evans and Deforest Mellon found the water receptor. Finally, Edward Hodgson and Richard Steinhardt at Columbia University and Frank Hanson in our laboratory showed that behavioral rejection of non-electrolytes (for example, alcohols) was not mediated by the salt receptor but occurred because the sugar and water receptors became temporarily inoperative. These discoveries were facilitated by Morita's development of a still more clever recording technique which consisted of inserting an electrode through a minute hole bored through the side wall of the hair. This invention freed experimenters from the restriction of mixing stimulus and electrolyte since pure stimulus solutions could now be applied to the tip of the hair while the recording electrode was in the side.

There remained only one major gap in our understanding of the chain of peripheral events triggering and driving feeding. Once the fly has extended its proboscis most of the chemoreceptive hairs of the labellum are no longer in contact with the solution because the oral lobes are spread. Inside on the oral surface there are minute papillae long suspected of being organs of taste. Because of their inaccessibility and extremely small size they had long defied experimental analysis. Electrophysiological recording was further complicated

because the papillae are *inside* and are moist. After many failures Hanson and I finally succeeded in proving that a papilla, like a hair, contains specific receptors for touch, sugars, and salts. By squeezing the body of the fly between thumb and forefinger we were able to force enough blood into the head to cause eversion of the proboscis. A ligature tied at the base of the everted proboscis then prevented redistribution of the blood when squeezing ceased. The problem of the moisture on the papillae was met by adding agar to the test solution and while the mixture was still boiling hot forcing it into the recording pipette where it rapidly jelled.

Finding and Feeding

The factors inducing and driving ingestion are now well understood. In nature the food of the fly consists of nectar from flowers, honey dew secreted on leaves by aphids, sap from the wounds of trees, fermenting fruit, and many kinds of decaying material. For egg laying and ingestion of protein flies assemble at carrion, offal, and feces. A fly locates its food by random searching or by orienting to odor. Flies are great explorers. They land on many surfaces and investigate. When food does possess an odor, as is the case with carrion and fermenting materials, the fly flies upwind to the source. Regardless of how the fly initially locates the food, it sooner or later steps in it thus stimulating the taste hairs of the feet. This stimulation triggers proboscis extension causing the taste hairs of the labellum to be stimulated in turn. This sensory input results in eversion of the oral lobes. Now the papillae are stimulated and sucking commences. The whole process up to this point is completely under peripheral sensory control. A unique feature of ingestive behavior is the fact that the whole complex process of proboscis extension, oral lobe spreading, sucking, and swallowing can be triggered and maintained by activity from a single neuron, the sugar cell of any hair.

Tests of the stimulating effectiveness of more than 80 carbohydrates, correlated with studies of the nutritional adequacy of these compounds, revealed that the effectiveness of sugars as taste stimuli bears no orderly relation to nutritional value. In fact, one of the more effective stimulating sugars is fucose, a methyl pentose, which is totally inadequate as a nutrient. In tests a fly will ingest non-nutritive, highly stimulating fucose in preference to poorly stimulating, highly nutritious mannose and starve to death.

What Stops It?

Ingestion obviously does not continue forever. What causes the blowfly to stop sucking? By analogy with human experience any number of factors might be involved in terminating feeding: a full gut, internal pressure against the body wall, rise in blood-sugar level, changes in hormonal levels. To understand how these might operate it is necessary to follow the course of food within the fly. This can be accomplished by slitting the fly from end to end to expose the alimentary canal because a fly in this condition will still feed. It is even possible to remove surgically the entire alimentary canal and observe its operation in a saline bath.

The force of sucking drives food into the oesophagus. Waves of peristalsis drive the food back to a point where the gut bifurcates [*see illustration page 98*]. One channel of the bifurcation is a thin duct leading into a dead-end, impermeable storage sac, the crop. The other channel is the main course of the alimentary canal, the mid- and hindguts. Almost all absorption takes place in the midgut. During feeding, the food arriving in the oesophagus is diverted into the crop by a synchronized system of valves. After ingestion has ceased, food is transferred from the crop to the midgut intermittently over a period of several hours. Churning and kneading motions in the crop cause food to be driven back into the oesophagus every time the crop valve opens. When the crop valve closes, the midgut valve opens and peristalsis in the oesophagus drives the slug of fluid into the midgut.

As time passes the crop becomes progressively more empty. Originally, rate of emptying was studied by feeding a large number of flies a known volume and concentration of sugar, sacrificing a few individuals periodically, removing the crop and weighing it. Because the crop is like a tough little impervious plastic bag, precise values convertible to volume were obtained. A more ingenious method permitting continuous measurements in a living fly was subsequently perfected by George Green in our laboratory. He simply mixed an opaque material with the food, periodically X-rayed the flies in two planes and calculated volume from area.

A close correlation was found to exist between the rate of crop emptying and the fly's acceptance threshold for food. For example, a newly fed fly may have an acceptance threshold for sucrose at concentrations in excess of 2 moles. De-

This blowfly is extending its proboscis (arrow) in response to chemical stimulation of a taste hair. The fly is attached to a wax block to prevent gross bodily movements during stimulation.

Photomicrograph of the blowfly labellum shows several taste hairs (dark protrusions), with bipolar neurons evident at the base of each hair.

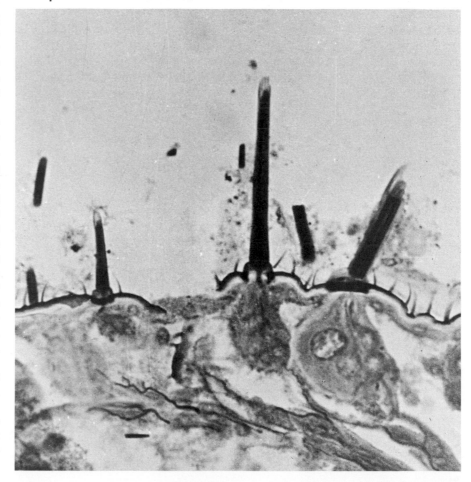

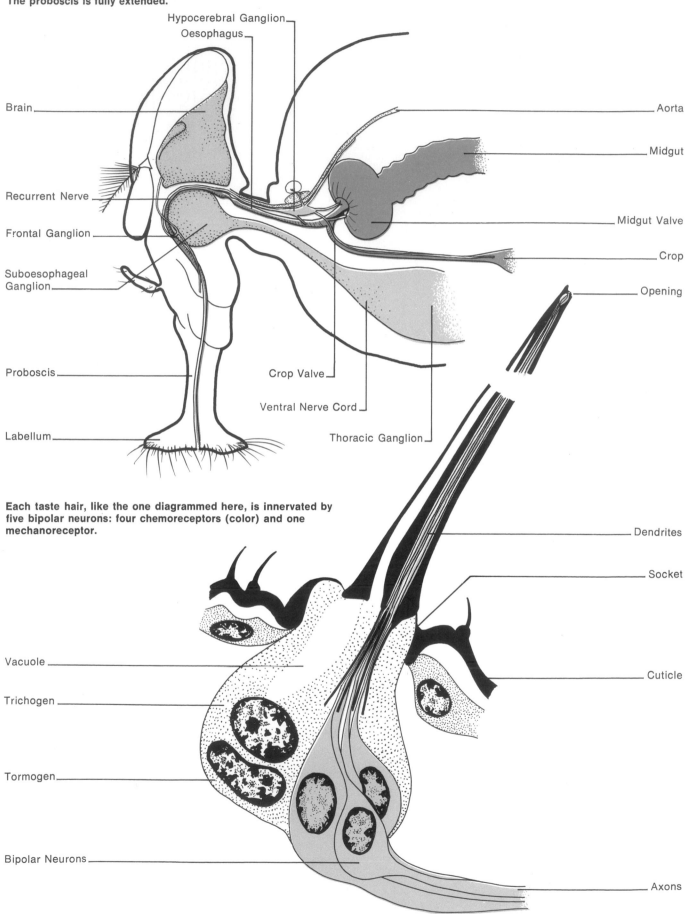

The alimentary canal (dark color) and the central and stomatogastric nervous systems (light color) are shown in this diagram of the blowfly's head, thorax, and anterior abdomen. The proboscis is fully extended.

Hypocerebral Ganglion

Oesophagus

Brain

Recurrent Nerve

Frontal Ganglion

Suboesophageal Ganglion

Proboscis

Labellum

Crop Valve

Ventral Nerve Cord

Thoracic Ganglion

Aorta

Midgut

Midgut Valve

Crop

Opening

Each taste hair, like the one diagrammed here, is innervated by five bipolar neurons: four chemoreceptors (color) and one mechanoreceptor.

Dendrites

Socket

Vacuole

Trichogen

Cuticle

Tormogen

Bipolar Neurons

Axons

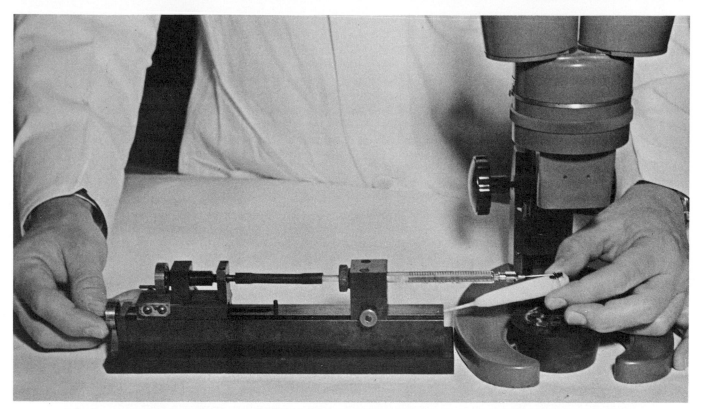

Injecting sugar solution directly into the blood cavity of the fly, using this apparatus, makes the fly metabolically satiated without having ingested any food. Despite resulting high blood-sugar level, the fly remains hungry.

prived for 90 hours the fly then has a threshold of 10^{-7} moles. Since electrophysiological studies have proved that there is no change in the threshold of the sense organs that drive feeding, we concluded that it is a central threshold that is changing. Some change associated with crop emptying results in central inhibition of chemosensory input.

We naturally suspected that fullness of the crop might provide the signal that results (in the central nervous system) in inhibition of sensory input. To test this idea we designed experiments in which the crop was either ligated, and thus functionally isolated, or removed entirely. A fly was placed on a wax block, ventral side up, held by two strips of plasticene, one across the thorax and one across the posterior abdomen. A small incision was made in the skin of the abdomen at the juncture of the thorax and abdomen, and the crop was carefully brought to the outside. A silk loop was slipped over the exposed crop and the duct tied. The crop was then pushed back through the wound. In some cases a second ligature was tied around the duct, a cut made between the two, and the crop removed.

When an empty crop was ligated or removed, sugar ingested by the fly filled the foregut and midgut. The acceptance threshold was elevated to the normal level. The crop need not contain sugar, therefore, to shut off feeding. Con-

versely, when full crops were removed, thresholds did not drop immediately as might have been expected if crop pressure were the inhibitory factor. The threshold did, however, drop after four to six hours. The same rapid decrease occurred if the full crop was ligatured. This acceleration in the drop in threshold was attributed to the fact that sugar in other regions of the gut could not be replenished after depletion. It was possible, therefore, that the presence or absence of sugar in the midgut was the critical factor shutting off ingestion.

Midgut Preparations

Surgery and manipulation of the midgut is extremely difficult; remember that the entire fly is only 8 mm long. However, Dietrich Bodenstein, now at the University of Virginia, had over the course of many years perfected exceptionally delicate surgical techniques applicable to insects. Together he and I conducted a series of experiments involving ligation, removal, and loading of the midgut. For ligation or removal a fly was placed dorsal side up in a depression in a wax plate. A small wedge of muscle tissue was removed from the prothorax. Removal of the wedge exposed the gut in the region of its bifurcation. A drop of physiological saline solution was placed in the wound. The cut-out wedge was also placed in solution. After the midgut was lifted into view, silk, roughly the

diameter of baby hair, was slipped under it, brought around, and tied tightly. If the gut was to be cut, a second ligature was applied and a transection made between the two. The cut-out wedge was then replaced and the incision closed. After a period of recovery flies were fed.

Following feeding, the thresholds remained high for four hours. Obviously the presence of food in the midgut was not necessary to maintain elevated thresholds. In another experiment the midgut was loaded with sugar by giving flies enemas. Deprived flies with guts loaded via this route still acted hungry, so food in the midgut does not terminate feeding.

Parabiotic Flies

David Evans and I had shown earlier that blood-sugar levels rose rapidly after feeding. Could this rise play a role in the termination of feeding? One way of testing this hypothesis was to alter blood-sugar levels independently of feeding. We therefore prepared parabiotic flies. A small drop of paraffin was placed on the dorsal surface of the thorax. Here it was puddled with a hot needle so as to form a wax crater. Next, the floor of the crater together with the underlying cuticle was excised exposing the hemocoele—the blood cavity. The crater was filled to the rim with saline. Another fly, similarly prepared, was placed against the first so that the rims of the two craters fit snugly together. The junction was sealed with a hot needle. The two flies now shared a common blood supply. After one was fed to repletion, the acceptance thresholds of both were tested. The fed fly refused food; its unfed partner sucked avidly. Not only did this experiment tend to rule out the direct influence of blood-sugar in terminating feeding, it also weakened any hypothesis suggesting a role for hunger or feeding hormones. As a final check, some hungry flies received large quantities of sugar injected directly into the blood cavity [see *illustration page* 99].Despite the fact that these flies were now metabolically satiated, they remained behaviorally hungry.

One small section of the alimentary canal had thus far escaped experimental scrutiny. This was the foregut, the region extending from the pharyngeal pump to the diverticulum. Does the presence or absence of food in this re-gion, or the passage of food through this region, play a role in the termination of feeding? We could investigate this possibility by loading the foregut with food that had by-passed the mouth or by eliminating the foregut entirely. The foregut, however, lies within the fly's neck, a narrow corridor only 0.5 mm wide crowded with many essential struc-tures. Moreover, the foregut has so small a diameter (0.05 mm) that successful loading with food was never accom-plished. The thought occurred to Boden-stein and myself that we could isolate the foregut physiologically by cutting its nerve supply.

The foregut, indeed the entire ali-mentary canal, is innervated by the stomatogastric nervous system, the ana-logue of the vertebrate autonomic sys-tem [see *illustration page* 98]. The stomatogastric system commences as a small ganglion, the frontal ganglion, situ-ated anterior to the brain. Bilateral con-nectives join it to the brain. From the frontal ganglion a large trunk extends anteriorly for a short distance then re-verses direction and passes posteriorly beneath the brain along the dorsal wall of the oesophagus. This trunk is the re-current nerve. Its diameter ranges from 5 to 10 microns. In the region of the bifurcation of the gut the recurrent nerve joins the hypocerebral ganglion. Here there are nerves serving the walls and valves of the alimentary canal, the aorta, the foregut itself, and the princi-pal endocrine complex, the corpus alla-tum and the corpora cardiaca. If we could transect the recurrent nerve in the anterior region of the foregut, we would essentially have deprived the brain of all information originating in the area of the foregut.

After a large number of practice trials we perfected the surgical procedure. What at first was a very tricky under-

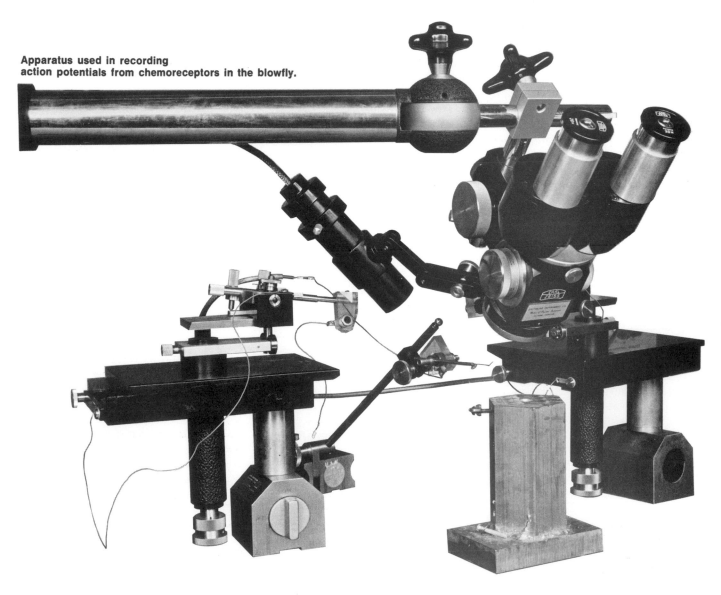

Apparatus used in recording action potentials from chemoreceptors in the blowfly.

taking has now become routine. Entrance is made through a dorsal slit in the neck. The exposed aorta is gently displaced to one side; adhesions supporting the two main tracheal trunks carrying the head's sole supply of oxygen are severed in order to free the oesophagus; the superficial neck muscles are stretched apart. These manipulations expose the recurrent nerve, which can now be cut.

As a consequence of cutting the recurrent nerve, the feeding behavior of the fly undergoes an extraordinary change—the fly is unable to control its ingestion. We had produced surgical hyperphagia.

Until It Bursts

A hyperphagic fly continues to eat until the crop expands into the entire body, until all other organs are squashed into a thin mass pressed against the hind end of the body cavity, until the fly becomes so bloated that the thin intersegmental folds of cuticle separating the plates of the external skeleton stretch to a point where the fly becomes a turgid, spherical, transparent ball [see illustration page 95]. At this point the pharyngeal pump can no longer work effectively against the hydrostatic and elastic back pressure. Attempts at ingestion persist, but no fluid actually accumulates. If, however, the pump is made to work harder by increasing input from the oral receptors that drive it, by stimulating with a higher concentration of sugar, the fly actually bursts.

It is clear that transecting the recurrent nerve interferes with a mechanism that normally shuts off ingestion. Bodenstein and I proposed that there are receptors in the foregut that monitor post-ingestive transfer of fluid from crop to midgut and that information from these receptors counteracts input from the oral taste receptors. When the fly is deprived of this inhibitory feedback, there is no way to shut off oral stimulation. It is shut off temporarily when the sense organs adapt but is reinstated as soon as disadaption occurs. Since feeding in the operated fly is driven by unrestricted sensory input, it races out of control.

It is interesting to compare surgical hyperphagia in the fly with that which can be produced in the rat. In the rat a lesion in the lateral hypothalamus causes the animal to starve to death while a lesion in the ventromedial hypothalamus results in tremendous overeating. These and other experiments suggest that there are excitatory and inhibitory areas in the central nervous system

of the rat that play an important role in the regulation of feeding. In the fly there is no evidence for the existence of central feeding centers. Instead, there is a balance between two sensory systems. The peripheral oral system initiates feeding; the internal foregut system inhibits feeding.

The Inhibitory Receptors

Our interpretation was favored by the fact, known from previous operations for excision of crop and midgut, that merely cutting those branches of the recurrent nerve that served other regions of the gut failed to interfere with the normal pattern of ingestion. It did, however, suffer from two weaknesses: first, the recurrent nerve at the site of transection carries fibers from the endocrine complex to neurosecretory cells in the brain, and, despite the earlier evidence from experiments with parabiotic flies, might conceivably transmit some indication of endocrine change associated with ingestion; second, no receptors had been found in the walls of the foregut.

It was not long before both of these weak points were shored up by experiment. It will be recalled that the recurrent nerve takes its origin from the frontal ganglion anterior to the brain. At this point it does not contain fibers from the endocrine glands because these enter the posterior part of the brain. If the recurrent nerve could be cut anteriorly, the point would be settled. After many false starts the operation was perfected. I lifted a skin flap between the eyes, went in through the fat body obscuring the frontal ganglion, and cut the recurrent nerve there. After the skin flap was returned to normal position, the fly was permitted to feed. The outcome was the same spectacular hyperphagia that had occurred after the posterior cut. The endocrine system is not involved.

An intensified search for receptors in the foregut finally turned up two likely candidates. In precisely the region indicated by hypothesis there is a pair of large multipolar neurons in the gut wall which resemble in appearance known stretch receptors found elsewhere in the body. In the meantime, Alan Gelperin demonstrated by an elaborate series of experiments that the postulated receptors must monitor stretch in the foregut as food is transferred through the region. It remains for us only to consolidate the conclusion electrophysiologically.

The Complete Picture

Our understanding of the regulation of feeding in the blowfly seemed to be in

tidy order until the recent appearance of a report by Nuñez demonstrating that hyperphagia can also be produced in flies by transecting the ventral nerve cord, the analogue of the vertebrate spinal cord, in the region of the neck. We were soon able to confirm this report. It occurred to Gelperin and myself that even though both recurrent nerve section and ventral cord section resulted in hyperphagia, the pattern of hyperphagia might be different. And indeed it is. A fly lacking information from the foregut takes a normal size initial meal, but, instead of gradually reducing further feeding to zero as the normal fly does, it continues to take many short meals over the next few hours. A fly with its ventral cord interrupted takes one interminable first meal. Thus, although sensory adaptation normally shuts off feeding when reinforced by central inhibitory feedback, it is unable to accomplish braking alone. Part of the contribution of the central nervous system is information regarding the extent of distension of the body wall because when nerves to the body wall are cut the fly overeats in much the same way as it does following ventral cord transection.

The picture that emerges, therefore, of feeding regulation in the blowfly is one of balance and imbalance between fluctuating chemosensory input and fluctuating inhibitory input from foregut and body wall stretch receptors. Chemosensory input varies as levels of adaptation and disadaptation in the taste receptors rise and fall. Inhibitory input varies as the rate of fluid transfer from crop to midgut decreases with deprivation and increases with feeding, and as distension of the body wall varies accordingly. When inhibitory feedback predominates, feeding ceases; when oral excitation predominates, feeding commences.

We see in the fly a relatively simple system operating by means of antagonistic sensory systems, one chemical and peripheral and the other, mechanical and internal. Somewhere in the central nervous system the incoming information is integrated. At the moment there is no need to postulate, nor is there any evidence for, feeding centers of the sort found in the hypothalamus of vertebrates. The fly system is primitive in the sense that it is not tied in directly with nutritive values and metabolic changes. Yet the fact that in the fly's world high sensory stimulating value and nutritive value are normally correlated and metabolic state and distension (gut and body wall) are normally correlated insures that energy needs are met efficiently.

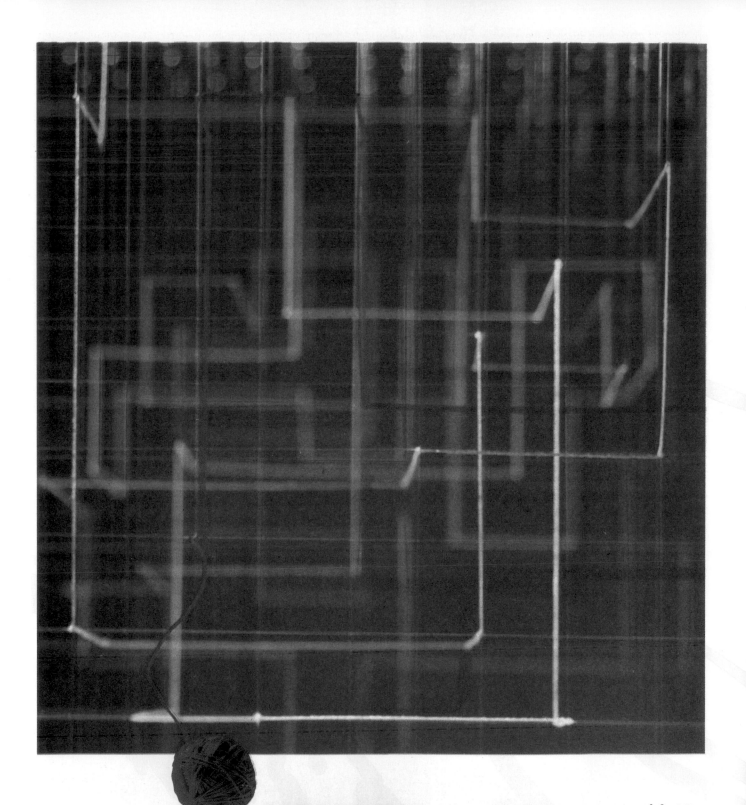

MEMORY: A MOLECULAR MAZE

By Ward C. Halstead
and William B. Rucker

REMEMBER THE LEGEND of the Minotaur—the half man, half bull monster of ancient Crete that lived at the heart of a vast labyrinth? Every year, seven youths and seven maidens were sent as sacrifice into the labyrinth, which was so full of twisting passages and blind alleys that none were able to find their way back out. But one year the hero Theseus fought and killed the beast. Having slain the Minotaur, Theseus was faced with the additional problem of extricating himself from the depths of the labyrinth. Fortunately his lover, Ariadne, had given him a ball of thread to unwind as he descended into the maze, thus providing him a way of retracing his steps.

Labyrinths, some of which existed in fact as well as in myth, were practical outgrowths of man's preoccupation with his sometimes mystifying ability to remember—and then to forget. The huge mazes they constructed can be considered as monuments to the formidable intricacy and unreliability of the memory process, whose physical complexities are only now being explored. Their builders —and their victims—might well have an empathetic smile for the researchers who are probing the chemistry of the brain for the secret of the memory process. These modern counterparts of Theseus have found themselves exploring a biochemical labyrinth as complex as the Minotaur's. The reader is here invited to follow part of the route, to view the progress, and to judge for himself whether it is the way of Ariadne's thread.

We assume that memory depends upon three functions; registration, retention, and retrieval. First, we select information from a continuous avalanche of sensory data and encode or register it in the nervous system. Secondly, the encoded information is filed and stored for later use. And lastly, when we have need of it, we can search the rather complex filing system and retrieve that specific information.

When we fail to remember an event, it is often difficult to determine which of the three functions is at fault. This difficulty applies not only to everyday cases of forgetfulness, but also to cases of amnesia, as described by George Talland (*see Section V*).

The human brain contains an estimated 10 billion nerve cells, or neurons. Each neuron communicates with about 400 other neurons, sending or receiving messages across junctions called synapses. Researchers working with lower animals have shown that as the embryonic brain grows, a large number of these synapses form according to an inherited or predetermined wiring pattern. A possible way for information to be encoded in the brain is to have the sensory input directed to particular neurons.

The making of a memory begins at the sensory organs, which receive and transform energy such as light, heat and sound into electrical nerve impulses. For example, light intensity in the eye is encoded in terms of the rate of nerve im-

pulses, and pattern perception results in part from the interaction of many nerve cells, each receiving information about different areas of the stimulus pattern. Our understanding of vision is the result of patient and brilliant investigations of many men, three of whom—Ragnar Granit of Stockholm, Haldan K. Hartline of Rockefeller University, and George Wald of Harvard—shared the 1967 Nobel prize for their work in this field.

We are able to follow the path of the coded nerve impulse as far as the sensory cortex of the brain. At this point, single neurons have been found that respond in distinct ways only to specific patterns of input. How the information is coded at higher levels of perception, thought and imagination is still largely unknown. It does seem, however, that registration of the information in the brain depends upon which neurons or synapses are activated, and how much activation takes place. Learning new information or new responses could involve a change in the sensitivity or ease of transmission in the synapses, as J. Anthony Deutsch proposed in the next article in this section.

Memory is generally described in terms of its age: short-term memory for recent events, and long-term memory for remote events. Early observers, including Freud, stressed the quantitative difference between the two, for example, that memories of recent events are more detailed than memories of remote events. However, the fact that memories are more fragile in their youth suggests that there may be a qualitative difference as well. A study of 1,000 patients treated for head injuries found that almost three-fourths of the patients had forgotten events that occurred just before their injuries, while only one-sixth had forgotten earlier events. Interestingly, patients were more likely to recall details of their accidents if they were questioned immediately after the accidents had occurred.

What sort of change within the nervous system might be responsible for the difference between short-term and long-term memory? One view, advanced by Donald O. Hebb of McGill University, is that the nervous system records a sensory input by means of a *pattern* of neural activity. He postulates that a reverberating circuit is established in randomly connected neurons, and that the nerve impulse must circulate many times in a closed, self-exciting circuit until some type of permanent anatomical change has occurred in the synaptic con-

nections between the neurons. At some later time the same group of cells will fire when stimulated again by the same type of sensory input. [*See illustration, page 107.*]

Hebb's model of the memory process is divided into two phases: a reverberating circuit for short-term memory, and some form of permanent change in the synaptic connections for long-term memory. This theory can be tested by disrupting the activity of the neurons shortly after their stimulation. If the theory is correct, the disruption should prevent consolidation of the long-term memory trace. For instance, an experimenter can teach an animal a task (preferably a task that can be learned in one trial, so the time of learning can be pinpointed), then disrupt neural activity by an electroconvulsive shock.

In a typical experiment, a mouse is placed on a small platform under a very bright light. To escape this intense light, the mouse steps into the hole, it completes an electric circuit and receives a foot shock. The next day when placed on the platform again the mouse will hesitate for some time before running into the escape hole. Once shocked—twice shy: and it is this hesitation that indicates that the mouse remembers the previous day's punishment. However, if the mouse is given an electroconvulsive shock immediately after the foot shock, the next day the mouse will *not* hesitate to run into the hole to escape the intense light. This indicates that the mouse has forgotten the punishing foot shock. Furthermore, if the electroconvulsive shock is given some later time after learning, the effect on the mouse's memory is much less. These findings support the idea that disrupting neural activity may interfere with the formation or consolidation of long-term memory.

The two-stage model of the retention process of memory is probably too simple. In the study of head-injured patients mentioned earlier, some patients were able to recall details of their accidents if they were questioned within a few minutes of the event—even though half an hour later they appeared to have forgotten completely what had occurred. Since the loss of long-term memory implies disruption of the short-term phase, or dynamic trace, it seems that their memory must have been stored in some other form just after the accident. In other words, there may be yet another phase of memory, an intermediate phase with an independent life of its own, which holds information during the period while the dynamic trace is dissipating and the permanent or consolidated trace is still being constructed.

The three-phase model of memory is supported by the research results of Leon J. Kamin of McMaster University. He trained both bright and dull rats to avoid punishment in a shuttle-box apparatus. The rats showed good retention of learning when tested one minute, 30 minutes, 24 hours and 20 days after learning. But all the rats showed a sharp drop in performance when tested one hour and six hours after learning. This dip in performance, sometimes called the Kamin effect, may be attributed to the unequal rates of decay and growth of the intermediate and long-term memory processes. Apparently the intermediate phase of memory (strong at 30 minutes) fades and if the consolidated phase of memory does not become established rapidly, there is a period (at 3 to 6 hours) when a memory gap occurs. Kamin's results also show that bright rats may have been able to consolidate their learning faster than dull rats [see illustration, page 107].

Retention of memory, then, appears to have three phases: the dynamic phase, the intermediate phase, and the permanent, or consolidated phase. According to our model these phases operate sequentially, and there is likely some overlap between succeeding phases as one fades and the next grows [see illustration, page 107]. Also, our model indicates that at least the intermediate and the consolidated phases may not depend upon each other for their existence. Total retention at any time is the sum of the retention in each phase. Whenever this total falls below the threshold for recall, such as during the Kamin effect, there is a temporary loss of memory. Only the consolidated phase of memory is capable of maintaining itself, and it is this phase about which we will be most concerned.

Much of the experimental logic supporting the three-phase model of retention comes from the work of D. J. Albert of British Columbia, who demonstrated the differences between the intermediate and consolidated phases of retention. Albert also has investigated the factors that control the rate of consolidation. By applying a positive electrode (anodal polarization) directly to an area of the cortex, he apparently has been able to accelerate the rate of consolidation. By applying a negative electrode (cathodal polarization), he could decelerate the rate. He found that the rats whose memory was being lost because of an overly

slow rate of consolidation would benefit immensely from anodal polarization therapy.

Another important contribution of Albert was his demonstration that disrupted memory could be restored under some conditions. He was able to conclude that although consolidation may be initiated by the activity *between* neurons, it must be carried to completion *within* individual neurons, independently of the other neurons in the circuit.

Do nerve cells behave as if they learn and retain memories? One possible indication that nerve cells do "learn" is the change in their rate of firing. For example, James and Marianne Olds of the University of Michigan have found that certain nerve cells in the rat's brain can be conditioned to increase their rate of firing by stimulating the reward center in the hypothalamus just after the nerve cells have fired spontaneously. That is, the cells behave as if they have learned to fire faster.

The electrical properties of the membranes of single-celled animals, such as paramecia, are very similar to those of nerve cells, and several investigators have reported evidence that single-celled animals can learn simple responses. For example, Beatrice T. Gelber of the National Institutes of Health has shown that paramecia can learn to cling to a platinum wire. If a clean wire is lowered into a paramecia culture, they generally will avoid it. However, if the wire is coated with bacteria on which the paramecia feed, they will begin to cling to it. After a coated wire has been used a number of times, when a clean wire is offered again, more paramecia will cling to it than before the training.

It is interesting to note that the memory retention of paramecia follows a pattern similar to the Kamin effect—that is, retention has two peaks. Two hours after training, a relatively large number of paramecia will cling to the wire, but four hours after training, the paramecia count drops significantly. The number of paramecia rises to a second peak at nine hours, then falls back to the pretraining levels at 19 hours. If the second peak is analogous to consolidated memory, this could mean that the paramecia have not evolved a way to maintain a memory permanently.

So far, we have presented two arguments that memory may be encoded in single cells: (1) that long-term memory does not appear to depend on the interaction between neurons; (2) and that

single cells behave as if they learn and retain. What, then, are the mechanisms that are available to the cell for carrying out these functions? The most promising possibility at this time seems to be the synthesis of new proteins within the cell.

Proteins are essential to all life as we know it. Certain proteins are essential to the structure that a particular cell assumes, while other proteins, called enzymes, control the rate of virtually every chemical reaction that relates a cell to its environment. The excitability and conductivity of nerve cells depends both on structural proteins and on enzymes. Thus, it is not surprising that biochemists have found an extraordinarily high rate of protein synthesis in nerve cells. Researchers have been able to manipulate the pattern of protein synthesis in the brain by varying the kind and amount of stimulation given to an animal.

We know that cells can learn from experience to produce a particular kind of protein. In the immune response, for example, some body cells learn to produce a specific new protein—an antibody—to combat some foreign material such as a transplanted organ. Also, embryonic cells arising from a single fertilized egg respond to the chemical stimuli in their environment and learn how to specialize as heart cells or liver cells or brain cells, each of which must produce specific types of proteins. This learned pattern of protein production becomes independent of the original stimuli and sometimes is retained for the lifetime of the cell.

So we can ask, is it possible that individual neurons produce new and specific proteins to record a memory trace? Is this, perhaps, what occurs in the consolidation of memory? Such a possibility was suggested by Ward Halstead and Joseph J. Katz in 1947 at the American Psychological Association's brain and behavior symposium in Detroit. They suggested that a neuron could only become a full partner in the permanent recording of an event by making a new protein. This protein would then substitute in part for the original stimulus, and the activity of the neuron would become independent of the original stimulus, as it did in the Olds experiment with the reward center. Since proteins normally are destroyed continuously in the cell, they also had to postulate some mechanism for the continued production of the new protein.

Molecular biology was in its infancy in 1947 and the Halstead-Katz model of memory had to await the further development of the knowledge of how cells control protein synthesis. And develop it did, as witnessed by the extraordinary number of Nobel prizes awarded in the last 20 years to scientists who found the answers to this fascinating puzzle. Today we know that the genetic message for making a particular protein is encoded in desoxyribonucleic acid molecules (commonly called DNA), which are found in the nucleus of the cell. The DNA molecule acts as a template, or mold, for the production of another similar molecule called ribonucleic acid or RNA, which carries the message to the protein factories in the cytoplasm of the cell. This messenger RNA, or mRNA for short, activates the factory to produce a specific kind of protein, thus completing the translation of the genetic message.

Using the new knowledge about protein synthesis, Josefa B. Flexner and Louis B. Flexner of the University of Pennsylvania have proposed a modification of the Halstead-Katz model of memory. They suggest that the electrical impulse code triggered by a sensory stimulus causes the neurons to produce a chemical agent. This chemical agent induces a previously inactive strand of DNA to begin producing a specific mRNA, which in turn causes the production of a specific protein. The protein plays a dual role: first it allows the original impulse code to be triggered when the memory must be recalled, and second, it keeps the DNA continually active so that more of the same protein can be made to replace that which is naturally destroyed in the cell. The consolidated memory, therefore, will be self-regenerating and permanent. [*See illustration, right*.]

If memory is retained in a cycle of macromolecular synthesis, then it should be possible to enhance or disrupt memory with drugs that aid or interfere with the production of mRNA or proteins.

Two drugs, 8-azaguanine and actinomycin-D, have been used by psychologists to interfere with the synthesis of mRNA in the brain. These and similar drugs have not reliably been found to affect either short-term or intermediate memory, and it appears that only the final, or consolidated, phase of memory may depend upon protein synthesis.

The Flexner-Halstead-Katz model predicts that memory should be permanently destroyed by drugs that affect mRNA production, since the mRNA is necessary for protein production, and the protein is necessary to activate the DNA and continue the cycle. Although

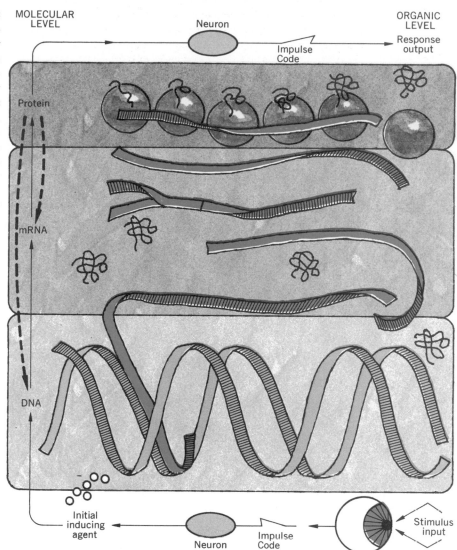

MOLECULAR MODEL OF MEMORY! Permanent memory may be stored in a feedback cycle involving protein synthesis. An incoming nerve impulse code triggers the release of an agent that causes DNA to make messenger RNA, which in turn makes protein. This protein can trigger the original impulse code when the memory must be recalled.

some researchers have reported this type of effect, others have reported the contrary effect.

In fact, the intercerebral injections of actinomycin-D actually improved the performance of carp in one memory test. Another drug, magnesium pemoline, the so-called "memory pill," was originally reported to facilitate the production of RNA and to enhance memory retention in rats and people. However, these findings have been challenged, and the conflict of views has yet to be resolved experimentally.

The research evidence indicates that long-term memory may be partially independent of DNA-produced RNA. This means that the Flexner-Halstead-Katz model of memory is probably incomplete. It seems necessary to postulate a special mechanism for the synthesis of RNA that does not entirely rely on the

DNA template. This mechanism might be similar, perhaps, to that used by RNA viruses, which can reproduce inside a host cell without needing a set of DNA instructions. We suggest the possibility, therefore, that long-term memory may be maintained by RNA synthesis under the direction of another RNA, as well as by RNA synthesis by DNA. Specifically, in this model the protein would have a third role to play [*see illustration, above*]. In addition to allowing the original impulse code to be triggered on demand and keeping the DNA actively producing mRNA, the protein would also activate mRNA to reproduce itself.

Some support for this special mechanism comes from research with tricyanoaminopropene, a drug that does *not* affect DNA synthesis of RNA. When injected into animals, this drug increases the RNA content of nerve cells as much as 25 per cent. It also has been shown that the drug increases the rate of consolidation of memory in rats under certain conditions. However, further research is still needed to determine the role played by RNA in memory consolidation.

The evidence that long-term memory depends on the synthesis of proteins is more convincing. Bernard W. Agranoff and his associates at the University of Michigan have used goldfish trained in a "shuttle-puddle" to study memory consolidation. The goldfish are trained to avoid a shock by swimming from one compartment to another. After learning this task, the goldfish are injected intracranially with a drug such as puromycin or acetoxycycloheximide (AXM), which interferes with the production of protein from mRNA. The researchers found that the drugs blocked both brain protein synthesis and the fixation of long-term memory in goldfish. Agranoff has suggested that the consolidation of memory will cease entirely if protein synthesis falls below a certain rate.

Although comparable results have been reported using mice as subjects, the Flexners recently have turned up some unexpected results. They have found that injection of large amounts of AXM either alone or together with puromycin into mouse brains will block protein production without permanently blocking memory recall. They also found that injection of a saline solution from two to 60 days after treatment with puromycin results in improvement of memory. The explanation of these results must await experimental clarification, and may lead to further refinement of the molecular model of memory.

If permanent memory is stored in a macromolecular cycle such as the one we have proposed, the proteins and mRNA extracted from the brains of trained animals should show some evidence of the memory trace. This hypothesis could best be tested by two critical experiments. First we would have to extract the coded molecules without damaging the cells they come from and show that, without them, the animal does not remember its training but is as capable of learning as it was before the extraction. Second we would have to return each molecule to the cell from which it came and show that the animal now remembers without retraining.

The drug experiments in which amnesia is induced by drugs such as puromycin and AXM fulfill some of the requirements of the first experiment: during the drug-induced amnesia the animals were still capable of learning. However, we are unable as yet to extract molecules from cells without damaging the surrounding tissue, and we do not know how to return molecules to their cells of origin. What we can do is extract chemicals from the brains of trained animals (donors) and administer them to untrained animals (recipients). If the behavior of the recipients can be related to the training of the donors, this will support the theory that the extracted molecules participate in memory retention. It may also help to answer a related question: is there a different protein produced to aid each synapse on each neuron in the memory circuit, or is the same protein produced by many neurons to serve entirely different synapses?

The first transfer-of-training studies were reported by James McConnell of the University of Michigan. He showed that when trained flatworms were fed to untrained flatworms, transfer of the learned task occurred. This was followed by other experiments in which RNA extracted from the brains of trained rodents was injected into untrained animals, and some of these experiments seemed to confirm the occurrence of transfer of learning. But some scientists were unable to replicate these results using the RNA extracts. This led to transfer of training experiments in which the entire brain of the donor animal was homogenized and a portion injected into recipient animals, and these experiments have had considerable success.

Frank Rosenblatt of Cornell University, working with rats, has demonstrated that a wide variety of trained tasks, including Pavlovian conditioning, operant conditioning, and discrimination, can be transferred to untrained rats by injecting them with a homogenate extract from the brains of trained rats. Georges Ungar of Baylor University has used homogenates to transfer habituation to a sudden sound or to an air blast, and training to enter either the right or the left alley of a T-maze. The behavior of the recipients in these experiments was directly related to the training of the donors.

Both Rosenblatt and Ungar have tried by treating the homogenate to chemically identify the specific biochemical agent that is responsible for the transfer of learning. Their evidence indicates that one ingredient involved in information coding must be a protein, possibly a polypeptide containing from 10 to 40 amino acids. If this is true, then there may be as many as 10^{15} different polypeptides that a nerve cell might use in preserving memory—a very large number, but not large enough so that every piece of information can be encoded with a different polypeptide. However, it may be that the same polypeptide is used in different ways by different neurons.

Some recent experiments have uncovered another phenomenon: negative transfer of training. Under certain conditions, injection of brain extracts will incline an animal to make responses *exactly opposite* to those the donor was trained to make. Working with rats whose natural preference was to turn left, Ungar trained these rats to turn right instead. Then he injected extracts from the brains of the trained rats into untrained rats. If the recipient rat also had a natural preference to turn left, transfer of training occurred and the recipient rat would turn right. But if the recipient rat's natural preference was to turn right, the injection had either no effect or actually caused him to turn in the direction opposite to donor training, that is to the left.

To explain this bizarre result, Ungar has hypothesized that the extract carries two conflicting instructions: anti-bias, and directional. The recipient rat with a natural preference the same as the donor's (to turn left) receives the instructions "Don't run left" (anti-bias) and "Run right" (directional). But the anti-bias instruction for the rat whose natural preference is to run right is "don't run right" and the directional instruction is "Run right," and either the two instructions cancel each other or the anti-bias instruction wins out.

Another set of experiments with injection of RNA brain extracts, conducted in Denmark by Einar Fjerdingstad, had similar strange results. The RNA extracts were taken from three groups of donor rats: untrained, trained to run into a lit alley in a maze, and trained to run into a darkened alley. As might be expected, rats that received an injection from trained donors learned more quickly than rats who received an injection from untrained donors. However, when the donor's training was the *opposite* that given to the recipient rat—that is, if the recipient was trained to run into a lit alley when the donor training had been to run into the darkened alley—then the recipient's learning was significantly faster than a recipient who was trained to make the same choice as the donor.

When we learned of the Danish experiments, we began to suspect that two antagonistic effects might be operating, and that these effects could be related both to the *kind* of training and to *how much* training the donors had received. To test this, we carried out an experiment in which donor rats were divided into four groups. All of the rats were trained to choose the lit door in a discrimination box, but the rats in each group received a different number of training trials (9, 54, 108, 162). A control group of rats received no rewarded training. We first tested the recipients' preference, without reward, for the lit or the unlit door. Then we rewarded the recipients for choosing the darkened door—the opposite of the training that the donors had received.

Preference testing *before* rewards showed that recipients of extracts from little-trained donors initially preferred the lit door (positive transfer of training), while rats injected with extract from overtrained rats initially preferred the darkened door (negative transfer of training). These findings suggest that two qualitatively different agents are involved in the transfer process. One comes from early learning, and the other from later learning. The fact that no transfer of training was observed in rats receiving extracts from donors trained to the intermediate level indicates that the two agents are antagonistic in their actions. In rewarded training recipients of extracts from little-trained donors (9 and 54 trials) and from over-trained donors (162 trials) learned more rapidly than recipients of extracts from the control donors (0 trials). But no transfer of training was observed with extracts from the donor groups with an intermediate (108) level of training. It appears that recipients of extracts from the little-trained donors used the transferred information in different ways during unrewarded preference testing and rewarded training.

Both negative transfer of training and the existence of antagonistic agents in early and late learning are difficult to explain in terms of the macromolecular model of memory. Preliminary experimental data indicate that it may be possible to separate the antagonistic agents by chemical procedures. It may be that we will discover that negative transfer and antagonistic agents are part of a unique biochemical process evolved to aid the brain to process information during learning and consolidation phases of memory.

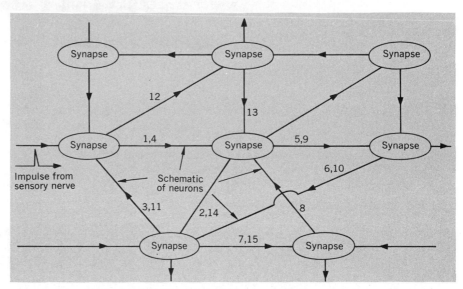

HEBB'S REVERBERATING CIRCUIT. Impulse from a stimulus may be relayed through many neural pathways (sequence indicated by numbers) until closed circuit is set up.

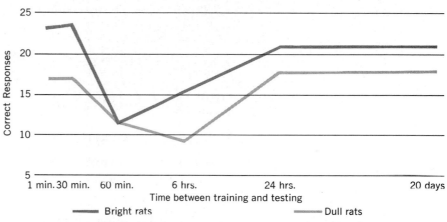

KAMIN EFFECT. The dip in performance by rats a short time after learning may be due to unequal rates of growth and decay of successive phases of memory retention.

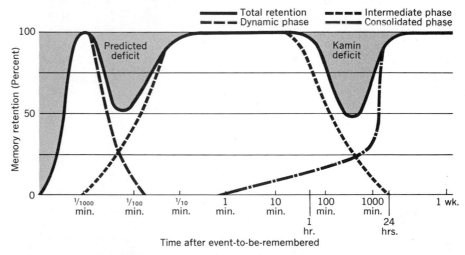

THREE-PHASE MODEL OF MEMORY. Theoretical model by Halstead-Rucker postulates three phase memory: dynamic, intermediate, and permanent. The model predicts deficits in memory (such as the Kamin Effect) in intervals between successive phases.

Research into the molecular basis of memory has recently taken an unexpected turn, and it is becoming apparent that new paths must be explored.

Perhaps one day soon, we may find the path that will lead us to the center of one of nature's most sophisticated labyrinths—the molecular maze of memory.

NEURAL
BASIS
OF

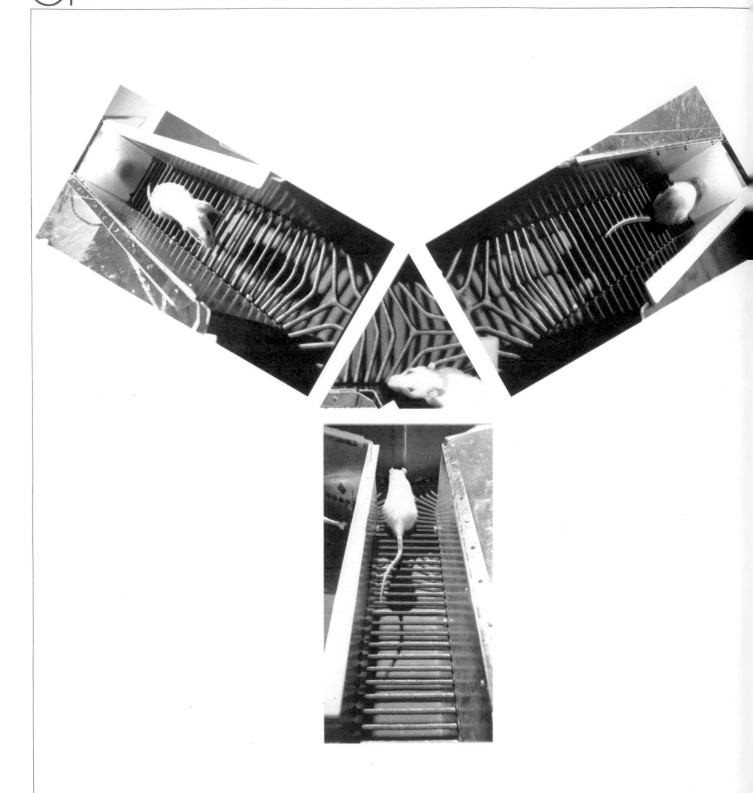

By J. Anthony Deutsch

At present the physiological basis of learning is unknown. We know that time alters the stability of memory, and this alteration presumably reflects in some way the underlying physical process. Many theories have been advanced to explain these changes, but only recently have discoveries been made that permit us to test the validity of the theories.

An old but still influential theory, put forward by an Italian physiologist, E. Tanzi, in 1893, postulates that the passage of nerve impulses causes some kind of physical change in the connections between nerve cells. The connections between the nerve cells, or neurons, are called synapses. While it is possible to show in the laboratory that the *functioning* of synapses can be affected by excessive use or disuse, these experiments do not show that changes occur in actual *learning*. A different kind of evidence is needed to show this, and I shall describe how such evidence has been obtained in some of my recent research.

We know that whatever changes produce the physical basis of memory, at least some of them must occur relatively slowly. Remarkable evidence for this comes from everyday accidents. For example, a person who has struck his head violently in an automobile accident may suffer from retrograde amnesia. He may be unable to remember what happened during the week before the accident, but he is able to remember what happened two weeks, two months or two years before. The gap in memory covers a continuous stretch of time, with one end anchored to the time of the accident. As memories return, those most distant in time always return first.

This indicates that as a memory gets older it becomes more difficult to dislodge. So the physical change that underlies memory must alter slowly with time. If this change is an alteration in the *sensitivity* of a synapse, then it should be possible to show this by the use of drugs.

To understand how this can be done,

we must briefly sketch what happens at a synapse when a message is transmitted from one nerve cell to another. The synapse is a microscopic gap (a few hundred angstroms, or less than a millionth of an inch) between adjacent neurons. Inside the neuron itself, a message is transmitted as an electrical impulse or disturbance. When this traveling electrical impulse reaches the synaptic region, it triggers the release of a chemical substance from vesicles at the end of the nerve cell. This chemical transmitter then travels across the narrow synaptic cleft to the receiving nerve cell. The chemical transmitter fits into certain sites on the second nerve cell as a key fits into a lock, mainly because the transmitter molecules have a specific size and shape.

The transmitter, it is believed, depolarizes the membrane of the receptor cell and initiates a new electrical impulse in the second neuron. The electrical impulse then travels along the neuron to the next synapse, triggering the release of a chemical transmitter, and so on [*see illustrations page 111*].

There are many different types of synapses in the brain, and they may use different kinds of transmitters, such as acetylcholine or norepinephrine (a chemical related to adrenalin). One of the best understood synapses uses acetylcholine (ACh) as the transmitter. ACh is present in relatively high concentration throughout the central nervous system. One of the strange things about this transmitter is that when too much of it accumulates on the synaptic part of the receptor cell, the transfer of messages across that synapse is blocked. To prevent a breakdown in transmission across the synapse, ACh must be inactivated as soon as it has performed its function. This is accomplished by an enzyme called acetylcholinesterase (AChE), which rapidly destroys ACh after it has been ejected.

There are two classes of drugs that interfere with synaptic activity, each in a distinctive way. One kind acts directly on the receptor nerve cells, while the other interferes with the destruction of the transmitter. The first kind is called

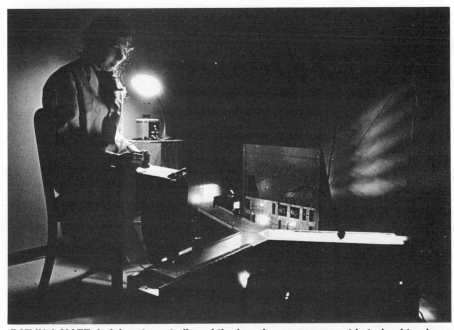

RAT IN A MAZE. In laboratory studies of the learning process, a rat is trained to choose the correct branch of a Y-maze either to escape an electrical shock or reach a reward of some kind. It takes about 30 trials for a rat to make 10 correct decisions in a row.

the anticholinergic drugs, or blocking agents. These drugs fit into the same sites on the receptor nerve cells as does ACh. However, although these blocking agents fit into the same sites, they do not initiate an electrical impulse in the second neuron. In addition, these blocking agents are not rapidly destroyed by the enzyme AChE. This means that the drugs can put parts of receptor cells out of action. The larger the dose of a blocking agent, the more sites are inactivated. The effect of the blocking agent, then, is to subtract from the effectiveness of the transmitter ACh.

A number of blocking agents are found in plants. Scopolamine is found in henbane, whose effects were known to the ancient Greeks. In high doses, scopolamine is a nerve poison: it completely stops transmission across synapses. In lower doses it simply reduces the amount of transmission and can be used medicinally to relieve such disorders as stomach cramps. Atropine, another blocking agent, is found in the deadly nightshade or belladona plant. In low doses, it is used to relieve muscular spasms and to dilate the pupil of the eye.

Drugs of the second kind that affect transmission across the synapse are the anticholinesterases, or inhibitors of the enzyme AChE. Since the function of AChE is to destroy the transmitter chemical ACh, inactivation of AChE will lead to an accumulation of ACh at the receiving sites of the synapse. As indicated previously, accumulation of too much transmitter at the receptor will block the synapse.

Another interesting effect of inhibitor drugs occurs when a neuron ejects too little transmitter to trigger an electrical impulse in the receptor cell. With the addition of the enzyme inhibitor, the transmitter is destroyed less rapidly and the amount of transmitter at the receptor cell builds up until it triggers an electrical impulse in that nerve cell.

This boosting effect is used in the medical treatment of myasthenia gravis, a disorder marked by progressive weakening of the muscles. A patient with this disorder may be unable to move, even though there is nothing physically wrong with his nerves or his muscles. The muscular weakness is caused by the release of too little ACh at the junction between nerve endings and muscles. By inactivating the enzyme that destroys the transmitter, enough of the transmitter can build up at the receptor sites to initiate muscle contraction, and paralysis disap-

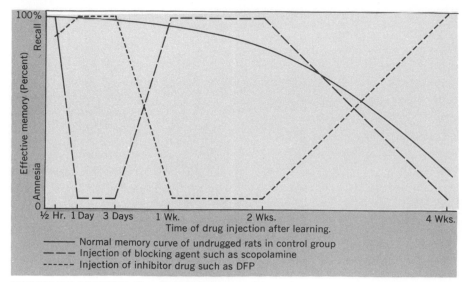

EFFECT ON MEMORY. Results from rat experiments in Y-mazes show how two types of drugs—blocking agents (anticholinergics) and inhibitors (anticholinesterases)—can each produce amnesia or recall, depending upon the time of injection after learning.

pears. However, the dose of the inhibitor drug is critical. If the dose is too large, too much of the transmitter will pile up at the receptor sites, causing a block, and paralysis will return.

We therefore have drugs that enable us to track changes in the efficiency of transmission across a synapse. Blocking agents, or anticholinergics, can completely stop transmission when relatively small amounts of transmitter are released. Yet this same dose of a blocking agent should not interfere with transmission when the amount of transmitter is high. On the other hand, addition of drugs that inhibit the action of the enzyme AChE, which destroys the transmitter, should not hinder transmission when levels of the transmitter are low. In fact, enzyme inhibitors may even improve transmission in this situation. But when the level of transmitter is high, the same dose of inhibitor should block transmission because of the excessive build-up of transmitter at the receptor sites.

Another way of looking at this is to suppose that learning causes changes in the *sensitivity* of the receptor cell rather than changes in the amount of transmitter released. In some respects, this is a more attractive explanation, but we will follow both interpretations in our guided tour of some of my laboratory experiments to discover the physical basis of learning.

In one set of experiments, I studied the effect of drugs on learning in rats: a rat is placed in a maze on a mildly electrified grid. To escape from the electrical shock, the rat must choose whether to run into a lit alley or into a dark alley.

If it runs into the lit alley it escapes the shock. If it runs into the dark alley, the shock continues. It takes about 30 trials for a rat to learn to choose the lit alley. In these studies, learning is defined as the ability to make 10 correct decisions in a row.

After a number of rats have passed the learning test, they are put back into their cages. The rats are divided into several groups. Some are injected with a drug half an hour after the learning trials, others after one day, three days, seven days, or 14 days. A control group does not receive any drugs. Although the rats receive their drug treatment at various times after learning, they all are tested at the same time interval after the drug injection.

It should be noted that the drug doses used in the experiments cause no apparent change in the rats' ability to learn. Groups of rats injected with the drug will later perform as well as untreated rats in learning tests.

When rats are injected with an inhibitor drug, such as diisopropyl fluorophosphate (DFP) or physostigmine, which inactivates the AChE enzyme that destroys the ACh transmitter in synapses, some interesting changes in memory occur.

Rats injected with the drug half an hour after the learning trials forget only a little. They take more trials to relearn the maze than rats from the control group, but require far fewer trials to learn than rats that have never been trained.

When rats are injected with the inhibitor drug one and three days after training, they show perfect retention of learning. But rats treated with the drug seven and 14 days after training lose their memory of the training almost completely. A control group of rats not drug injected, still remembers to choose the lit alley after seven or 14 days.

We might conclude that the inhibitor drug causes premature forgetting. However, this is too hasty a conclusion. If we retest undrugged rats four weeks after they have learned to run the maze, we find that they have forgotten which path to take. But if we then inject them with an inhibitor drug in the same dose as previously caused forgetting, the rats regain their memory almost perfectly. In this case, the injected drug could be called a "memory improver."

We know that the injected drug prevents the enzyme AChE in the synapse from destroying the chemical transmitter after it has been ejected. From these experiments, we can draw the following conclusions. After one day, the amount of transmitter released in the synapse is relatively small (or we could say that the sensitivity of the receptor cell is low). At three days, the amount is still low, since injection of an enzyme inhib-

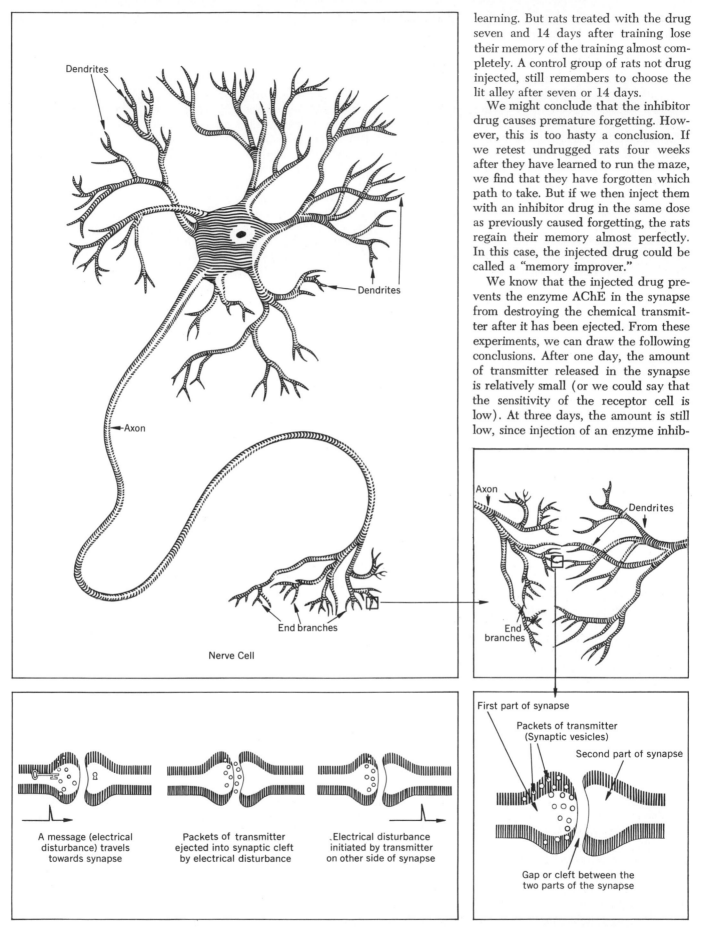

NEURAL PATHWAY. A message travels along a nerve cell (*top*) as an electrical impulse until it reaches the junction between the end branches of one neuron and dendrites of another. At the synapse, electrical impulse triggers release of a chemical transmitter.

itor does not cause a pile-up of enough transmitter at the receptor sites to block the synapse. But at seven days, the amount of transmitter (or sensitivity of the receptor) rises and remains high even at 14 days. Injection of the drug causes a pile-up of transmitter at the receptor and blocks the synapse. After four weeks, the level of transmitter (or sensitivity of the receptor) has dropped to such a low point that the rat has forgotten the learned task. Injection of the drug, however, enables the small amount of transmitter still present to become effective and the rat regains its memory.

These conclusions can be cross-checked by repeating the experiments, this time with blocking agents—drugs that fit into the same sites on the receptor cell as the ACh transmitter. A blocking agent such as scopolamine should abolish memory where we have concluded that synaptic transmission is weak, and leave recall unaffected in cases where we suppose that transmission is high.

In repeating the experiment with scopolamine, we found that memory is unaffected by a drug injection half an hour after learning. But a drug injection one or three days later completely knocks out memory of what was learned. This is what we would predict on the basis of our previous conclusion that the synaptic transmission level is low at one or three days after learning. At seven and 14 days, injection of scopolamine does not affect memory. This also confirms our interpretation that transmission is strong at seven and 14 days.

We can check our conclusion that synaptic transmission gradually improves during the week after learning without the use of drugs. Rats are given only a small number of learning trials in a maze so that correct choices are only partially learned. The rats are divided into several groups. Each group is given a different waiting period—one day, three days, five days, etc.—before it is brought back to the maze. In this session, the rats are allowed to learn the task completely, and we count the number of trials they need to do so. We find, interestingly enough, that the rats who wait seven days before the second session learn with a much smaller number of trials than rats who are tested after one day or three days. This suggests that there is spontaneous strengthening of memory in rats a week after learning.

If our theory is right, one of the things we can expect is that drug-induced disappearance of memory will be tempo-

rary. The action of the drug on the synapse should last only as long as the drug is present. And a number of experiments do show that memory returns when the effect of the drug wears off. There is also evidence that the inhibitor drugs, or anticholinesterases, do not completely inactivate the enzyme AChE in the dose strengths used in our experiments. It is likely that only a portion of the enzyme is inactivated and that the destruction of ACh transmitter is not halted but simply slowed down. If this is so, then the spacing of trials after the injection of the inhibitor should affect the degree of amnesia. If the trials are spaced farther apart, more transmitter should be destroyed between trials. Since too much transmitter at the receptor causes the block in the synapse, increased spacing of a well-learned task should improve recall. And, indeed, it

are millions of neurons in the nervous system and each neuron may have thousands of synapses on it. In the synaptic region, the neurons are intricately intertwined, much like a mass of spaghetti. Detecting changes made by a single learning task is almost impossible. A major difficulty is finding a way to observe the same set of synapses before and after learning—a task similar to finding a needle in a haystack, except that in this case we are trying to find a specific piece of hay.

Fortunately, we can again use drugs to determine whether learning affects the same set of synapses or a different set of synapses on each learning trial. If each trial increases the transmission across the same set of synapses, then the larger the number of learning trials (the more learned the habit), the greater the susceptibility of that learning to inhibitor

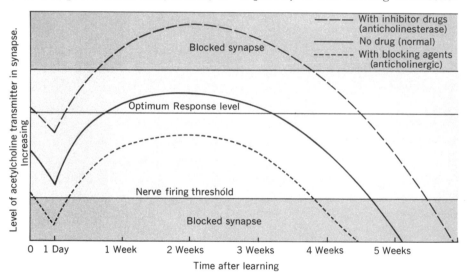

SYNAPTIC TRANSMISSION MODEL. Middle curve shows changes in synapse after learning. Inhibitor drug (*top curve*) or blocking agent (*bottom curve*) can block transmission at certain times. This model helps explain the drugs' paradoxical action.

turns out that this is what happens. In tests of drug-injected rats seven days after the learning session, when the trials are spaced 25 seconds apart, the rats exhibit almost total amnesia. When the trials are set 50 seconds apart, the rats remember their learned task.

From the results of our experiments, it looks as if learning changes a synapse's ability to transmit messages. Our experiments consisted of a large number of trials, and each learning trial could have affected a different set of synapses. On the other hand, each trial could have affected the same set of synapses over and over again. We cannot observe changes in the synapses directly, even with an electron microscope. A typical synapse may measure as little as one millionth of an inch in size. There

blocking. Also, if the same set of synapses is affected by learning, then a small number of learning trials should produce weak transmissions and therefore memory will improve with injection of the inhibitor drugs.

On the other hand, if each learning trial simply changes another set of synapses until enough synapses are altered to ensure correct performance, then the number of trials should not alter the susceptibility of the learned habit to blocking by an inhibitor drug. Each synapse will be altered in an all-or-nothing fashion, and each should be equally susceptible to the drug.

To test these two ideas, we trained three groups of rats. One group received 30 training trials, the second 70 trials, and the third 110 trials. The rats with only 30 trials could be considered undertrained. In their last 10 trials, they chose the correct path only two out of three times. Five days later, half of the rats in each group were given a dose of diisopropyl fluorophosphate, a drug that inhibits the AChE enzyme. The undertrained group injected with the drug performed very much better than their undertrained counterparts who were not given the drug. In their first 10 trials, the drug-treated rats performed almost perfectly. Drugged and undrugged rats from the group with 70 trials performed identically. Overtrained rats (110 trials) injected with the drug, however, performed much worse than their undrugged counterparts, and even worse than the undertrained rats that had been drugged.

In other words, a well-learned habit is blocked by injection of this drug, whereas recall of a poorly learned habit is improved. This indicates that the same set of synapses is stimulated more and more with each learning trial.

To show that the results had nothing to do with the *number* of trials but rather were concerned with the degree of learning, we performed another experiment in which the number of learning trials was the same for all rats. This was done by taking advantage of the rat's propensity to learn more quickly when the light in the safe alley of the maze is very bright. Groups of rats were given the same number of trials, but variations in the brightness of the light in the safe alley led to very different rates of learning. The group with a dim light had learned very little at the end of 30 trials, while a group with a very bright light had learned to make the right choice almost every time. Injection of the inhibitor drug produced the same results: the group with the well-learned habit forgot, the group with the poorly-learned habit performed better.

This seems to confirm that the same set of synapses is affected as learning of the same task progresses. The same synapses are stimulated more and more with each trial. As a result of this stimulation, the synapse becomes gradually more efficient at passing messages. This increase in efficiency occurs without any apparent need for practice or repetition of the learned responses.

Our evidence supports the theory that the physical change underlying learning is the increase of transmission efficiency in a synapse. But our experiments do not provide enough information to decide whether the increased efficiency is caused by increased sensitivity in the receptor or increased amounts of transmitter in the synapse.

We can, however, set up an experiment that will identify the correct explanation. There is a class of drugs that mimics the transmitter action of acetylcholine. One of these drugs is carbachol (carbaminoylcholine), a very close chemical relative of ACh. Carbachol is strongly resistant to destruction by the AChE enzyme. When injected in low doses, carbachol acts together with ACh to excite the receptor nerve. Higher doses of carbachol will block memory. Results of research to date indicate that injections of carbachol will improve new memories but block older ones. When the amount of transmitter is small, the injected carbachol teams up with it to improve memory. When the memory is one week old, if we assume that the amount of transmitter increases, then it is hard to explain why the same dose of carbachol results in a blocked synapse. It is unlikely that the increased amount of transmitter would cause the block, because the transmitter would be destroyed at the normal rate by the AChE enzyme. A more likely explanation is that the receptor becomes more sensitive (requires less transmitter to become activated) and that the carbachol blocks synaptic transmission because it alone can now keep the sensitized receptor nerve cell depolarized, which prevents initiation of new electrical impulses in that neuron.

So, although we have good evidence that learning improves transmission across synapses that use ACh as a transmitter, the evidence that this improvement is caused by an increase in the sensitivity of the receptor is much more tentative.

These findings suggest that some human memory disorders may be due to a lowered efficiency in transmission across synapses, particularly those using ACh as the transmitter. If this proves to be the case, some memory disorders may be improved with relatively simple drugs. But in spite of the effect of our drugs on the memory of rats, we have discovered no memory pill. While one day such a drug might be developed, it is not likely to be one of those used in our research. All these drugs are potent poisons; their effects are mixed—they improve some memories while blocking others—and their effects are transitory. Seekers for a pill to end practice and study forever will have to look elsewhere.

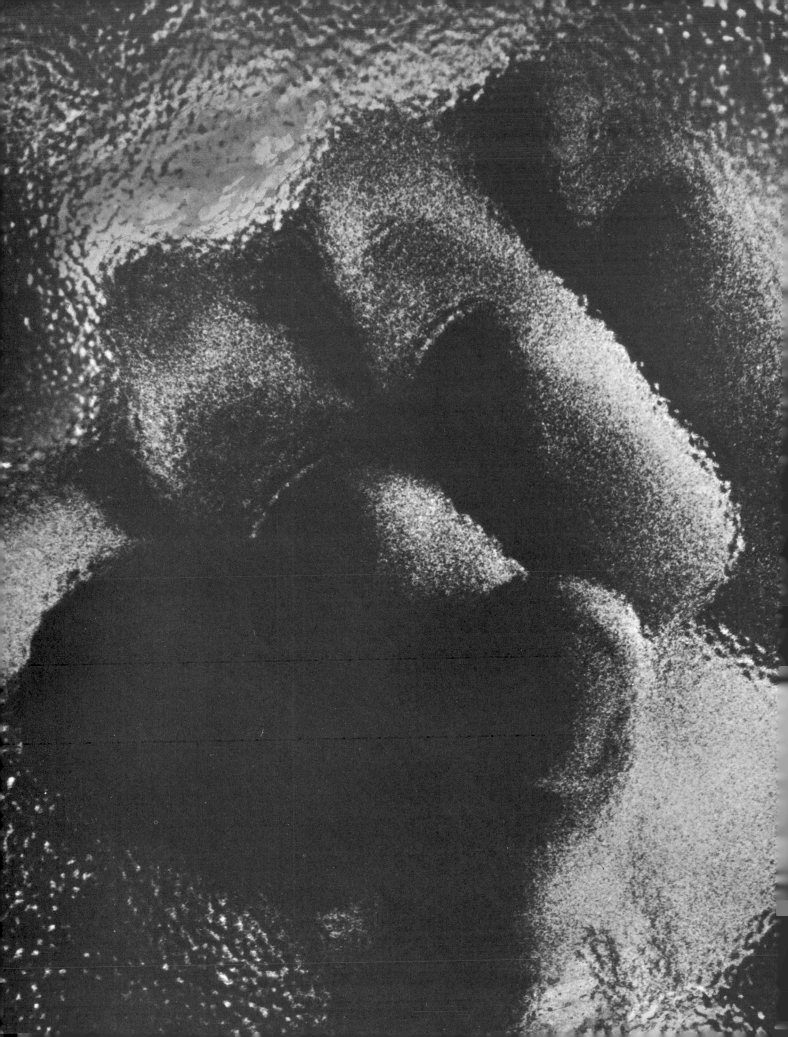

PAIN AND AGGRESSION

By NATHAN AZRIN

With the advent of nuclear weapons and man's power to annihilate himself along with much of the planet's "thin film of life," the behavior we call "aggression" is of more than academic interest. Sooner or later any debate on the possibility of a warless world turns into a debate on whether aggression in man is based on nature or nurture. Recent books such as *On Aggression* by Konrad Lorenz, which generalize animal behavior to man, arouse unusually heated controversy in which one may detect overtones of "Tain't so," or "I told you so," depending on whether the debater views man as but little lower than the angels, or but little higher than the apes.

In fact, however, we know very little about aggression. What do we mean when we speak of "aggressive behavior"? Warning? Threat? Attack? Predation? What kinds of stimuli produce an "aggressive" response? Can we scientifically measure the amount or intensity of aggression?

For many years experimental psychologists have used the operant conditioning procedures developed by Skinner, and extended by others, to study various animal behaviors—particularly learning—under carefully controlled laboratory conditions. These conditioning techniques are based on the principle that behavior can best be studied when it is analyzed in terms of the following question: Under what conditions will there be a change in the frequency of an observable, measurable bit of behavior? The "bit of behavior" is called a "response," the occurrence of which is largely controlled by *reinforcement*. In *positive reinforcement,* a given response increases in frequency if it is followed by a reward, such as food for a hungry animal. In *negative reinforcement,* a given response increases in frequency if it is followed by the termination of an aversive event, such as electric shock applied to an animal's feet. By using only measurable units of behavior, the occurrence of which can be controlled through various procedures and schedules of reinforcement, the experimentalist need not depend on intellectual constructs such as "instinct" or "intention" as explanations for behavioral processes.

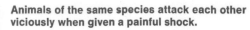

Animals of the same species attack each other viciously when given a painful shock.

Snapping Turtles   Ferrets

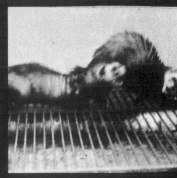

Snakes   Opossums

Serendipity

More than thirty years ago Lawrence O'Kelly and Lynde Steckle studied the "escape" behavior of rats by delivering an electric shock to their feet through an electrified floor-grid in the cage. They found that a single rat, alone in the cage, would attempt to escape or would "freeze" into immobility. But if a group of rats were shocked, they immediately began attacking one another, lunging, striking, and biting. However, since attempts by others to reproduce these results were only partly successful, there were no further tests of the puzzling report that foot-shock made rats "emotional."

About five years ago, at the Anna Behavior Research Laboratory, we were trying to see if negative reinforcement (escape from shock) could be used instead of positive reinforcement (food) in teaching two rats to interact with each other. Our plan was to slowly increase the intensity of shock to their feet until the rats happened to move toward each other, at which moment the shock would be abruptly stopped. By gradually changing the degree of proximity required to terminate the shock, we thought that the rats would learn to approach each other as a means of escaping the unpleasant shocks. Instead, much to our surprise, the rats violently attacked each other as soon as the shock became painful and before the experimenter had time to terminate it. This behavior did not occur all the time or with all rats, but so disruptive were these scrambling, attack-like episodes when they did occur, that we had to abandon our original objective.

Our interest was now aroused in this seeming relation between pain (foot-shock) and attack. Was the attack merely the result of random, agitated movements causing accidental collisions

between the rats, or could we produce this shock-attack behavior whenever we wished? Was it produced only by foot-shock, or would other types of shock or aversive events produce it also? Was it an all-or-none reaction? Was it learned or innate? How was it affected by hunger? Did it occur only with male rats? Would it have occurred if the rats had lived peaceably together since infancy? Would it eventually die out as the rats became accustomed to the shock? Was such shock-attack behavior peculiar to rats alone—was it "species-specific," as is their well-known tendency to crawl into a hole? My colleagues, Roger Ulrich, Don Hake, Ronald Hutchinson, and I embarked on a series of studies to explore this seeming relation between pain and aggression or, more precisely, between shock and attack.

Measuring the Attack

Our first task involved "identification" and "quantification" of what we wished to study, so that our investigation could be orderly and disciplined, and so that other researchers could test our results by repeating our experiments exactly. We had, therefore, to define what we meant by "pain" and "aggression," and find ways of measuring them. To define and measure pain was easy: we knew that it was produced by electric shock, and that we could measure its intensity by the intensity of the shock. Our major problem was that of defining "aggression" and measuring its intensity or amount. The phenomenon we had observed was that of attack—but to identify it seemed impossible in the beginning, as we observed the rapid and seemingly random actions of the rats. But closer observation and slow-motion pictures showed that there were elements of consistency. Immediately upon receiving the shock, a rat would stand erect on its hind legs, face another rat,

open its jaws so that the front teeth were clearly visible, and make physical contact with the other by striking with its forepaws.

This posture and these movements were observed only when another rat was present; otherwise a shocked rat held its jaws sufficiently closed so that

the teeth were not visible, and usually kept all four feet on the floor. The posture and movements of a shocked rat in the presence of another rat were distinctive enough so that observers could be reasonably definite in judging that a particular episode constituted an attack. Each of these attack episodes lasted for about one second; the best method for quantifying the attack seemed to be a simple counting of the number of attack episodes.

Getting Down to Cases

Our first objective was to see if there was a relation between the intensity of the shock (pain) and the degree of aggression (number of attacks). Was it, we wondered, an all-or-none reaction, occurring in full intensity whenever some pain-threshold was reached, and not at all below that threshold; or would

| Ferret and Rat | Opossum and Hamster | Snake and Monkey | Opossum and Rat |

They will also attack animals of a different species— even those normally feared and avoided.

the number of attacks increase as the shock-produced pain intensified? It turned out that there was a direct relation between the intensity, duration, and frequency of the shock and the amount of aggression—and this was limited only by the physical incapacity of the rat at high shock-intensities. As experimentalists, we were especially surprised and gratified to find that at optional shock-intensities, an attack accompanied almost every shock; having identified the appropriate stimulus conditions, we could produce this complex attack-response in almost "push-button" fashion.

We found, too, that the rats did not adapt to the shock; its effect did not wear off and the rats continued to attack—sometimes to the extent of several thousand a day—as long as we delivered the shocks. This demonstrated that the attack was not a startle-response to a novel stimulus, but was a strong and enduring reaction.

But was it "innate" or learned? That is, had our rats learned, through association with other rats, to respond with attack to painful events or threatening situations? If so, then rats that had been isolated from other animals from infancy on would not display the shock-attack response. Not so. Social isolation did reduce the number of attacks somewhat, but did not eliminate them. We found, too, that rats that lived together attacked one another just as often as rats that had been caged separately. Sexual competition or attraction was not involved in the reaction, either, for males and females attacked members of the opposite sex or members of the same sex. Nor was this a predatory reaction, for hunger did not appreciably affect the number of attacks. We concluded at this point, therefore, that the shock-attack response is a reflex-like reaction in which a specific stimulus (pain) produces a

fairly stereotyped response (aggression), which is relatively independent of normal learning experiences.

Rats Are Not the Only Ones

Now we wanted to find out if this shock-attack response is confined to rats or whether it is widespread in the animal kingdom. In other words, how far could we generalize our findings with regard to this particular psychological process?

First, we found that this response occurred in many different strains of rats. Then we found that shock produced attack when pairs of the following species were caged together: some kinds of mice, hamsters, opossums, raccoons, marmosets, foxes, nutria, cats, snapping turtles, squirrel monkeys, ferrets, red squirrels, bantam roosters, alligators, crayfish, amphiuma (an amphibian), and several species of snakes including the boa constrictor, rattlesnake, brown rat-snake, cottonmouth, copperhead, and black snake. The shock-attack reaction was clearly present in many very different kinds of creatures. In all the species in which shock produced attack it was fast and consistent, in the same "push-button" manner as with the rats. In testing other species, however, we found that the shock-attack reaction is not as easily generalizable as the above results might lead one to suppose. First, it does not reflect the general tendency to aggressiveness of a particular species; rather, it appears to be a special process. For example, many species that normally attack in their natural state frequently did not attack when shocked; fighting cocks and Siamese fighting fish are well known for their proclivity to attack members of the same species, yet shock not only failed to produce attack in either of these species, but tended to suppress it.

Nor did shock produce attack in many other species known to attack under nor-

mal conditions: iguanas, skunks, rhesus monkeys, tarantulas, chickens, hawks (and several other species of birds), and fish, including the flesh-eating piranha. Further study may show that these animals failed to attack only because the experimenter failed to discover the condition that produces pain in these animals—a difficult task at best because different species vary greatly in sensory endowment. All we can say at this time is that the shock-attack reaction is present in a great variety of species, but we cannot as yet say that it is synonymous with aggressiveness in general.

Where shock did produce attack, we found that the reaction was not a stereotyped reflex—that is, each species attacked in its own distinctive way. The monkeys used their hands; several species slashed with their forepaws; the opossums hissed; and the snakes often hissed and sometimes encircled the target of their attack. But biting was common to all the attacks, and it appears that the aim of the attack is not merely to ward off or defend, but to injure or destroy, by whatever means the animal possesses.

Shocked Animals Are Not Choosy

Ethological studies of animals in their natural environment have demonstrated that many innate behavior patterns are "triggered" by specific physical characteristics of another animal. For example, the red, swollen belly of the female stickleback triggers courting behavior in the male. We wanted to find out, therefore, whether the shock-attack reaction is similarly related to specific physical attributes of the "target," or whether it is the expression of a general tendency to destroy. If the attack-response to pain is triggered, then slight changes in the appearance of the target should change or eliminate the reaction. To test this, we conducted a long series of studies in

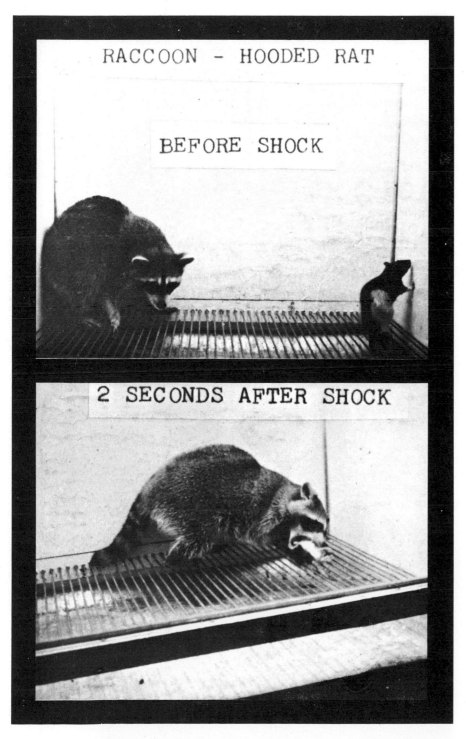

RACCOON - HOODED RAT

BEFORE SHOCK

2 SECONDS AFTER SHOCK

which various animals were paired with target-animals of a different species. For example, we shocked a rat caged with a target guinea pig, a racoon with a rat, a monkey with a mouse, a monkey with a rat, a rat with a rooster, and an opossum with a rat. In every instance, the shocked animal attacked the target, showing that the characteristics of the target animals are not relevant.

And this raised the question of whether, indeed, a live animal was needed; might not a model do as well? Stuffed dolls produced the same shock-attack reaction. Did the model have to be similar to an animal? We used the simplest geometric form, a sphere with no animal-like features—in actuality, a tennis ball. The animals attacked the tennis ball. It seems, therefore, that under the stimulus of pain, animals will attack and try to destroy almost any "attackable" object in the environment—animate or inanimate—regardless of its attributes.

Problems, Problems . . .

Though our studies had provided us with much information, they had also raised some serious methodological problems. First of all, the attack-episodes had been identified and counted by a human observer; thus our results depended entirely on gross observation and subjective interpretation. And in the second place, the behavior of the target animal influenced the attacks. Attacked, the target animal often fought back, and in some cases the results were even more disconcerting. For example, often at the very first shock, the rat attacked the snake with which it was paired. But there was no second try, for the snake would fatally injure the rat. The selection of rats as our initial subjects was fortunate, since they usually do not inflict serious injury, but if we were to study more destructive animals, we

would have to eliminate both counter-aggression and the likelihood that one animal would destroy another.

The "Bitometer"

The discovery that pain would produce aggression against an inanimate object enabled us to solve both of our problems, for it provided us with a means to record attack-behavior objectively, and it allowed us to test the attack-responses of very destructive animals. We suspended a tennis ball or other object from a cord that was attached to a switch. Whenever an animal struck or bit the ball, the switch closed and provided an output signal to a recording device. An even more direct and useful method of automatically recording attack was the "Bitometer"—a pneumatic tube that could be bitten by the shocked animal, giving us a direct measure of the number of bites as well as a measure of their duration and forcefulness. These and similar devices made it possible for us to study the shock-attack reaction of a single animal during many months, encompassing thousands of attack episodes, without injury to the subject or to the target, and eliminated the problems of counter-aggression and reliance on human observers.

We developed a specialized apparatus for monkeys, and modified it for several other species. Restrained in a chair, yet permitted considerable freedom of movement, the monkey is positioned so that it faces the target—the "Bitometer" —and is maintained at a fairly close but fixed distance from it. [*See illustration p. 120.*] The "Bitometer" yields an output signal only if the monkey bites it; pulling, striking, or pushing it displaces too little of the enclosed air to produce an output. Since we had found that there is a direct relation between the intensity of the shock and the amount of aggression, we precisely controlled the

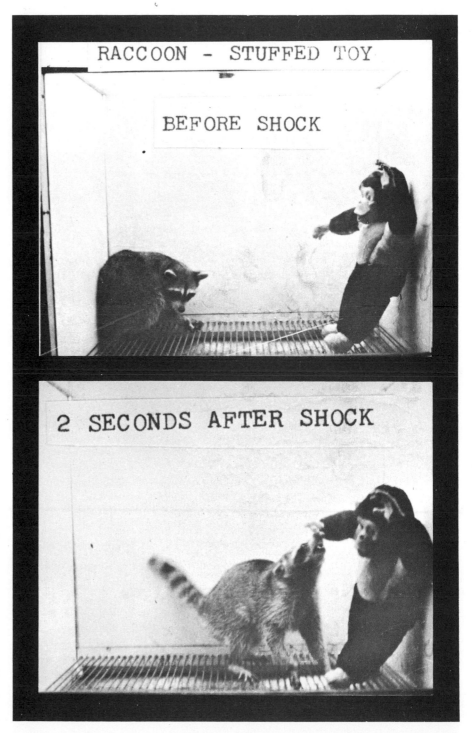

RACCOON - STUFFED TOY

BEFORE SHOCK

2 SECONDS AFTER SHOCK

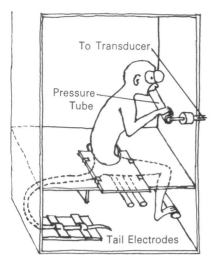

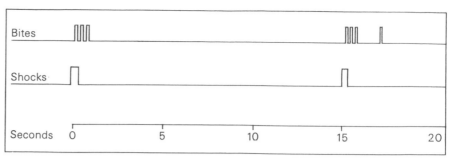

A Typical Bitometer Record

Laboratory equipment was designed to measure aggression automatically. The test box (left) is equipped with a restraining chair and a Bitometer, which, when bitten, activates a recorder. Electrodes attached to the monkey's tail deliver electric shocks.

intensity of the shock by fastening surface electrodes on the monkey's tail.

As Long As It Hurts . . .

Because electric shock is a novel experience for an animal, seldom if ever encountered in its natural state, we wondered whether the novelty of the stimulus, or perhaps the postural imbalance caused by foot-shock, might account for the attack-reaction. Would attack be provoked by other painful stimuli? Shock delivered to rats and monkeys by means of surface or subdermal electrodes produced attack as before, eliminating postural imbalance as a cause; intense heat produced attack in rats; and a physical blow provoked it in monkeys. Clearly, it seems, attack is a reaction to many types of painful experience, and is not distinctively related to electric shock.

But is attack provoked only by events which produce physical pain, or might "psychologically" painful experiences have the same effect? For example, hungry pigeons have been trained to peck at a disk by reinforcing them with a few pieces of grain. Several observers have noted that when the reward for this response is abruptly stopped, the pigeon appears to become agitated. Might this abrupt shift from expected reward to no reward be psychologically painful enough to produce attack? We tested this possibility by exposing a hungry pigeon to this "frustrating" situation—with a target pigeon in a restraining box close by. The box was pivoted on a switch in such a way that if the target were attacked, the impact closed the switch and provided an automatic measure of the attack. When the experimenters failed to reward the pigeon with the expected grain, the bird first made a flurry of vigorous attacks on the wall disk, and then turned around and with beak and wings attempted to attack the

target bird [*see illustration opposite page*]. The same thing happened when a stuffed pigeon served as target. Because the recording procedure was completely automatic, we could study how the degree of hunger and the number of preceding rewards affected the amount of aggression.

This discovery that abruptly terminating a rewarding situation produces aggression greatly modified our view of the pain-attack reaction, for it provided experimental evidence to suggest that withdrawing reward is equivalent to physical pain. Thus attack will be precipitated by the psychological pain resulting from simple changes in the frequency of reward, as well as by physically painful events.

Since this sort of psychological pain seems to be more common in human experiences than are extremes of physical pain, these findings may help us understand some of the mechanisms which produce aggression in man. Being scolded, being fired from a job or expelled from school, losing a sexual partner, running out of gas, having one's allowance cut down or stopped, losing money to a vending machine, being thwarted by a stuck door—who has not experienced these noxious events and felt like kicking the door, taking a hammer to the vending machine, or just smashing the nearest thing?

Fight vs Flight

"He who fights and runs away may turn and fight another day." How is the pain-attack reaction related to other effects of noxious stimuli such as escape or avoidance? More simply, when does pain produce fight and when flight? To answer this question, rats and monkeys were exposed to a variety of procedures which provided them with a target for attack, as before, but which also made available a response which would allow

them to escape or avoid the electric shock. The results all pointed in the same direction: the shocks produced attack only when the animals could not avoid them, because (1) no avoidance-response was possible, (2) it was possible but not yet learned, or (3) the avoidance-response was excessive. Once the rat or monkey learned that by pressing a lever he could avoid the shocks, the avoidance behavior (flight) was predominant, and the attacks (fight) took place only on those few occasions when a shock was delivered. Thus it appears that the attack reaction to pain can be eliminated by establishing effective avoidance behavior. Or, in everyday terms, it seems that pain-evoked aggression can be controlled or eliminated by establishing effective, peaceful means for avoiding the pain.

Aggression and Counter-aggression

Attack need not be opposed to escape, however, as a reaction to pain; this is illustrated by the situation in which the aggressor inflicts injury on the target. For the injury causes pain to its victim, and this should lead to counter-aggression—and the counter-aggression will be rewarded if it eliminates the source of the initial pain. Counter-aggression is thus analogous to pressing the lever that stops the shock. According to this analysis, then, counter-aggression should be a very strong and quickly acquired reaction to aggression. We investigated this possibility by using the "Bitometer" as the target for monkeys to whom we delivered an electric shock; however, in these studies, the biting attack postponed the next shock. These monkeys learned almost immediately that biting was a way of avoiding shock, and their biting attacks did not decrease even when the shocks could no longer be avoided that way. When the pain-attack reaction is rewarded by escape

"Psychologically" painful experiences can cause the attack response. A pigeon taught to peck a key for grain rewards becomes agitated if the rewards are discontinued, and will vigorously attack a nearby target pigeon. If no target is provided, the pigeon can be taught to peck a second key in order to obtain a "victim."

from pain or avoidance of further pain, the two together produce strong and lasting counter-aggression that continues even when the counter-aggression no longer serves its original purpose. A vicious circle is formed that can be broken only by interpolating a non-aggressive means of escaping or avoiding pain.

The Urge to Kill

How flexible is this pain-attack reaction? Can it provide a means for teaching new behaviors? If not, we would have to consider it to be stereotyped and reflex-like, but if it could serve as the basis for acquiring new behaviors, this might explain the variations in the mode of attack. We explored this possibility in monkeys by using the appearance of an attack target as a reward. We put each monkey in a compartment without any target, and then shocked him. Hanging nearby was a chain; if the monkey pulled the chain immediately after being shocked, a target appeared—the tennis ball. Did the monkey learn to pull the chain every time he was shocked, thus providing himself with a target for his aggression? Yes. This study confirmed our earlier findings that the pain-attack reaction is not stereotyped behavior. Rather, pain seems to create a changed state in the animal during which it is rewarding for him to injure or destroy.

What Does It All Mean?

What began as an accidental observation that some rats scrambled and attacked one another upon receiving a painful electric shock, has led to the discovery of a psychological relationship that has much greater generality than we could have anticipated. To sum up, these studies indicate that pain tends to provoke attack behavior (aggression) in many different species, and possibly in man as well. It is provoked both by physical and by psychological pain; it is

directed at animate and inanimate parts of the environment; it can serve as the basis for learning new behaviors; and it can be eliminated by providing the animal with a non-aggressive means of escaping or avoiding pain. From the standpoint of evolution, pain-provoked aggression seems to have survival value, since it causes the animal to react instantly and vigorously to noxious events —and in a way that is likely to terminate them.

Aggression, like much other social interaction, is difficult to study with any exactitude. Because many individuals are usually involved, because the attacks are usually violent, brief, and quickly delivered, and because they can be manifested in a variety of ways, it has been difficult for human observers to agree as to what constitutes an act of

aggression. Thus an important outcome of this study is the development of procedures for measuring and identifying aggression; valid automatic recording techniques can be used to quantify this important but complex social behavior, and to subject it to controlled laboratory analyses.

The discovery that pain provokes aggression and that the pain-attack reaction is not stereotyped or reflexive behavior, is of major importance. Though it is but one of the many factors to be considered in analyzing aggression, it appears to be among the most amenable to laboratory study. If we can understand the many causes of aggression we may hope, eventually, to learn how to use it constructively for the further advance of our own species, rather than for our destruction. ◖

III. psychological development

Without question the most now field of theoretical and experimental study in modern psychology is the area of human development. The contributions collected here focus on the primary interest of this area—the child. Bruner and Kagan, professors at Harvard, reflect their differing though complementary concerns in the papers "Up From Helplessness" and "The Many Faces of Response." Neither offers, nor pretends to offer, a complete account of the developmental process. The emphasis, as in most of modern psychology, is on the systematic exploration and exposition of small yet central topics within the developmental field.

Children are born, grow, and die in all cultures, in all parts of the world. It is not peculiar, therefore, to find that cross-cultural studies of ideas about development and education reveal more agreement than disagreement. The Coles' account of practices in Russian nursery schools strikingly reveals the chasm between American and Russian approaches to education. It is noteworthy, however, in showing how small the chasm really is: many bridges of similarity already appear across it.

Even in the area of development, the lower animal makes its contribution. The Harlows discuss several aspects of the intellectual and emotional development of monkeys.

The focus of developmental psychology continues, of course, to be the child. The mysteries of the child's intellectual development are explored by Wohlwill. Then Rhoda Kellogg, the internationally known collector of children's art, writes about understanding both the creativity and the formal content of a child's artistic production.

When it comes to interpretation, not all observers of the child psychological scene find themselves in agreement. In this collection, both Israel Goldiamond and Lawrence Kohlberg look at the moral stance of children. While finding essentially the same substantive content, they differ radically over its developmental interpretation. Kohlberg is the European traditionalist, drawing from the school of Jean Piaget and seeing development as a succession of organized stages. Goldiamond is the American behaviorist, drawing from the school of B. F. Skinner and seeing development as an outgrowth of the principles of learning and the conditions of reward and punishment to which the child has been subjected.

Few things are sadder than a sick child, and the saddest of all is a mentally sick child. The articles by Ferster and by Bijou discuss two kinds of children's mental disease. They hold out hope of bringing the autistic child toward normality and of improving the lot of the mentally retarded child.

Experimentation in natural educational settings is probably as old as schools themselves. More freedom, less freedom; more teachers, fewer teachers; longer hours, shorter hours—many combinations have been tried in an attempt to change the direction of education. One of the most successful attempts is described in A. S. Neill's account of England's unique Summerhill school.

Some have asked if children have political attitudes. Robert Hess of Stanford believes that they do, and he offers a discussion of them.

The infant
learns to control
his environment
on his way...

Up from Helplessness

by Jerome Bruner

I T IS A WORKING PREMISE of mine that infant development cannot be understood without considering what it proceeds from and what it moves toward. The human infant has behind him a long process of primate evolution, which has endowed him with certain biological capacities. In front of him, in adulthood, lie not only the behavior man shares with other primates but the use of a culture that is uniquely human. Human culture, as Claude Levi-Strauss pointed out, is based on three types of exchange, carried out through language, kinship arrangements and economies. They are used by all men and by men alone.

From his evolutionary inheritance, then, the newborn child develops the capacity to use a culture that is exclusively human. This is not to say that evolution or culture *causes* infants to develop as they do, but merely to point out the central position that the infant in fact occupies.

It may seem that this view of infant development places a large burden on a very small pair of shoulders. The equipment and the actions at a child's disposal when he begins his enormous task look, at first glance, rudimentary. To illustrate, the research I am about to describe focuses on sucking and looking, reaching and grasping, and prelinguistic communication—little acorns indeed.

Through these activities, however, the infant develops four abilities that are crucial to the use of human culture. He develops, first, voluntary control of his behavior, a highly complex matter that requires the anticipation of an outcome, the choice of a means to achieve it, and the ability to start and sustain a chosen series of acts. Second, he gains internal control of his attention,

so that he can direct it toward solutions to problems instead of following the dictates of external stimuli. Third, he learns to carry out several lines of action simultaneously. Fourth, he establishes reciprocal codes that pave the way for speech and other forms of human exchange.

Before I discuss how these abilities develop, I should point out that there are certain inequities in the young child's situation. For example, the infant's sensory equipment provides him with more information than his motor system can use: he can look at a toy well before he can reach out his hand to take it. Similarly, his motor system has more slack, more degrees of freedom for movement, than he can control. He begins to learn by cutting down drastically on his available neuromuscular freedom, developing that form of clumsiness so characteristic of human infancy. Initial learning, then, may be learning to reduce the complexity of response in order to gain control.

Sucking and Looking

The human infant is notorious for his helplessness, but one thing he can do from birth is suck. Sucking begins as a reflex action, and the infant uses it for several functions apparently preordained by evolution: nutrition, discomfort reduction and exploration. Even on the first day of life, however, the child has some control over his sucking and can adapt it to changes in the environment. If milk is delivered to a day-old child in response to

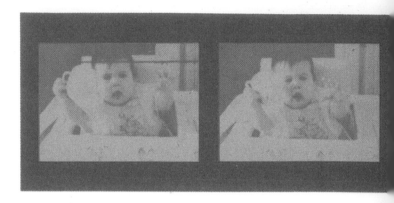

only a little pressure on the nipple, the baby will almost immediately reduce the amount of pressure he exerts.

Another thing the child can do almost as soon as he is born is look, but he cannot look and suck at the same time. The newborn infant sucks with his eyes tight shut. If he begins to look at something, he stops sucking. By two or three months of age, when a burst-and-pause sucking pattern has become established, the baby will suck in bursts and look during the pauses between. At four months, he seems able to suck and look simultaneously, but this turns out to be not quite true. Though suctioning stops when the baby looks, a mouthing of the nipple continues. This phenomenon is called place-holding. By maintaining one feature of an ongoing activity, the infant seems to remind himself to resume that activity after he has carried out a different one. His ability to suck-(look)-suck is probably part of a general decrease in the extent to which one activity pre-empts all others.

One way to test an infant's voluntary control is to see whether he will use an action as a means to some new end. Infants as young as one or two months old show considerable ability to use sucking for a novel purpose. They can learn to suck on pacifiers in order to bring about visual clarity—to increase the illumination of a picture in a darkened room (as in E. R. Siqueland's experiment at Brown University), or to bring the picture into focus (as in one by Kalnins in our laboratory at Harvard).

Watching infants do this has taught us something about how they learn to coordinate the two ordinarily independent activities, sucking and looking. A six-week-old baby will suck the picture into focus, but then he starts looking and stops sucking, so that the picture drifts back out of focus again. He may try to resolve this dilemma by sucking without looking until the picture is in focus and then looking and sucking together for a brief period. As soon as he stops sucking, and the picture starts to blur, he averts his gaze. Gradually, the amount of time he can spend both sucking and looking increases. What the child seems to be learning here is not so much a specific response as a sequentially organized, adaptive *strategy* of responses.

Grasping, like sucking, is one of the infant's very early reflexes. By the time he is four weeks old, he automatically catches and holds an object that touches his hand. What role this reflex plays in the development of *voluntary* grasping is a matter of considerable controversy. Some psychologists see a very close relation between the two: they say that voluntary grasping develops from reflexive grasping through a purely internal process of maturational unfolding. Others see little or no relation; they say that a voluntary grasp develops only through interaction with the environment.

In my opinion, both views are false. The existence of prepared reflex machinery clearly facilitates the acquisition of voluntary motor control. For one thing, as T. E. Twitchell of Tufts Medical School has observed, voluntary control often starts with the self-evocation of a reflex, much as in the recovery pattern of hemiplegics. But to leave the matter at that ignores one crucial aspect of

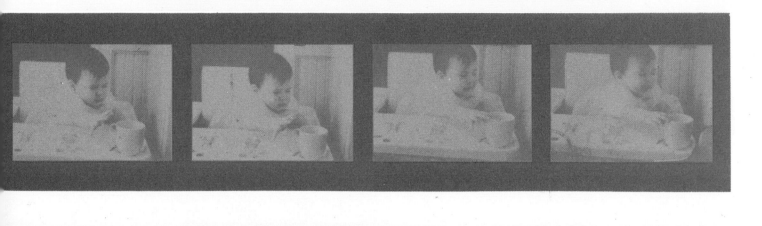

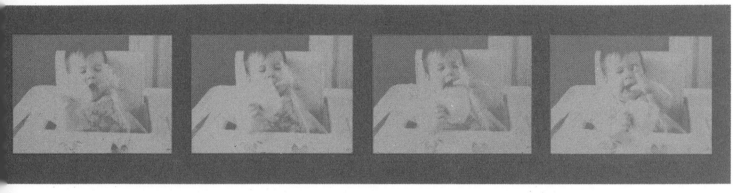

voluntary control: intention. Much of the infant's earliest voluntary activity is characterized by the *absence* of aid from prepared reflex mechanisms. Instead, it begins with diffuse activity that bears less resemblance to organized reflex responses than to athetoid behavior (the wormlike movements of fingers, toes, hands and feet seen in certain brain-damaged children). Even when a reflex pattern does precede voluntary control, there is a period of diffuse, athetoid activity before voluntary control begins.

Once it has begun, how does it proceed? As I mentioned earlier, the infant has much more freedom of movement than he can control. His strategy for increasing his control is to impose severe restrictions on his freedom—to keep his elbow locked as he reaches for something, for instance—and to reduce the restrictions as he consolidates his skill within them.

The child uses this strategy as he learns to reach. If an object crosses the visual field of a month-old child, he will move his head in pursuit. As the object approaches him, he changes his level of activity, becoming quieter if he was active or more active if quiet before. Tension in the child's trunk increases. In a six-week-old, this tension takes the form of an attempt to lift the shoulders and arms, even though the child has had no experience reaching for or retrieving objects. By 10 or 12 weeks, the approach of the object makes the infant pump his arms, shoulders and head, staring at the object and

working his mouth at the same time. From this position, he may launch swiping movements toward the object, keeping his hand clenched in a fist. I have seen babies blink in surprise as they execute the swipe, as if the "connection" between intention and act were unexpected, that is, as if a "reafference copy" of the act had not been widely distributed to supporting sensory and motor systems.

At about four months, the child has enough control to execute a less explosive, slow reach. He extends his arm toward the object, hand wide open now. His mouth and tongue are working, and his intention is clearly to put the object in his mouth. Indeed, a slow reach always follows the same sequence: activation, reach, capture, retrieval to the mouth and mouthing. If you insert a finger for him to close on, you will bring the action to a stop.

The open mouth and wide-open hand serve a placeholding function similar to that of the rhythmic mouthing of the nipple which reminded the younger infant to resume sucking when he had finished looking. The open mouth keeps the terminus of the act in evidence during the execution of its components; the rigidly opened hand, which is a step forward from the more primitive closed fist, maintains in exaggerated form an intention whose fulfillment has been delayed. As with so much early development, processes that later become internal, such as intention and attention, have external motor representations at first.

A word here about reaching and looking. A seven-month-old may begin a reach with visual guidance, but he is likely to execute the reach without it. When one of our seven-month-olds, Kathy, is in the midst of reaching for a cup, her eyes are closed. If a reach involves some conflict between the line of vision and the course the hand must follow (detour-reaching), the child is especially likely to look away or close his eyes as he reaches. Also, when Kathy tries to get both hands around a cup already held with one hand, she reduced degrees of freedom drastically by the simple expedient of shutting her eyes (*see the illustrations that precede on pages 128 and 129*).

The Use of Tools

Kathy and her cup can show us a little about how the infant begins to develop an ability to use tools. When a seven-month-old starts to use a cup, he has no appreciation of the problem of holding the cup level as he lifts it to his mouth. By 14 months, he solves this problem by making four to six jerky adjustments of his hands and arms as he raises the cup. By 27 months, the choppiness is gone, and the child keeps the rim of the cup horizontal in a smooth movement all the way up.

This is "tool-use" of a sort, but it is quite crude. Several preliminary skills are still missing. An experiment with two-year-olds, performed at Harvard by A. R. Jonckheere, suggests what they might be. We wanted to see whether two-year-olds would use strings as tools to get prizes, a task that required them to pull strings with prizes at the ends toward them in preference to other unbaited strings. They would not. They either pulled in all the strings, or they pulled just the one closest to them.

Three things seemed to make it difficult for the children to maintain problem-solving behavior long enough to retrieve their prizes. First, they tended to play with the strings, the edge of the playpen, and so forth: they altered their goals to suit the means at hand, instead of altering means to meet the requirements of a fixed goal as problem-solving requires. The situation reminded us of the lobotomized cook who could never get to the center of the city to shop because of all the tempting things she encountered en route. Second, the children preferred to use adults as "tools" instead of the strings. They would plead for help, stretching their arms toward the prizes and crying, rather than pull in the strings by themselves. Third, the problem seemed to include too many features for the children to handle. They would look at the prizes, the strings, the bars of the playpen, and seem to be overwhelmed.

Before a child can learn to use tools, then, he must be able to adapt means to ends instead of ends to means; he must do this in preference to asking for help; and he must have enough control of his attention to keep a goal in mind while he decides how to reach it and carries through his plan. We are now at work on several studies dealing with these capacities and will be ready to report on them soon.

Codes and Language

We come now to the acquisition of codes that precede the rules of syntax. There is a sharp distinction, in the first year or so of life, between "doing" behavior and "communicating" behavior—between behavior addressed to things and behavior addressed to persons. For instance, eye contact, which is a major link between parent and child, has no counterpart in "doing" behavior, and neither do smiling, crying and vocalization.

Either the infant has an innate predisposition to expect reciprocation of some kind to these gestures, or he acquires that expectation very quickly. When the expectation is fulfilled by an adult's response to the child's initiative, that seems to convert the child's behavior into a signal, and he proceeds to conventionalize it by stripping it down to its essential elements. For example, the quality of his crying changes, becoming less intense, once it has started to serve as an effective signal.

It is easy to fool oneself into seeing a connection between prelinguistic and linguistic behavior. What an infant does before he can speak may be quite different from what he does when he begins to speak, even within the category of verbalization itself. When a baby starts to babble, for example, he acquires front vowels and back consonants first, and back vowels and front consonants last. But when he learns to speak, the reverse is true. In speech, vowels come in from back to front, starting with /a/, and consonants from front to back, starting with /p/. As David McNeill has said, the baby completes his vocabulary of phonemes by filling in the space between the two.

It is almost surely true, however, that early interaction codes are the basis for some aspects of later communication and language. The channel for any kind of signal system, prelinguistic or linguistic, must derive from the enrichment of these interaction codes.

But the *form* the signal system takes must come from elsewhere. I believe that it constitutes a refinement of human sensorimotor skill. Indeed, the growth of phonology itself requires the refinement of a neuromuscular skill: the ability to delineate the sounds between those produced by the mouth as a funnel opened outward (the voiced /a/) and as a funnel opened inward (the unvoiced /p/).

I would even suggest that the modularization present in phonology, which can be described as the formation of binary oppositions, can be seen in cruder form in the development of other human skills. The way the infant moves his hands progresses from the "babble" of athetoid movement of the fingers to the sharply contrasting tight-fisted and then wide-open hand during reaching. Also, the infant's early attempts to combine syntactic structures are reminiscent of the choppy movements of his arm and hand as he first tries to keep his cup level. In both cases, there is a division of part acts into roughly equal time segments, and then the coordination of part acts into a smooth sequence.

It is even possible to conceive of a nonlinguistic origin for so essential a rule of language as predication. All languages, without exception, employ this principle, which involves dividing an event into a topic and a comment. For instance, in the statement "John is a boy," John is the topic and his boyhood is the comment on the topic.

There are two homologues in human nonlinguistic behavior that might predispose us toward language that uses predication. One of them concerns information processing; the other has to do with manipulative skill.

Many cognitive theorists distinguish between focal attention and a more diffuse sort of sensing. They postulate that we organize events by synthesizing successive focal attendings. Each instance of focal attention requires the extraction of one or a few features from a more general sensory input and is, therefore, a "comment" on a "topic." Other theorists say that, when we direct our attention toward something, we do so because we have noted a deviation from a "neural model" of some steady state. When deviation reaches some critical level, we attend or orient. The deviation, then, is a "comment" on the neurally represented steady state, or "topic."

The parallel between predication and the use of the hands is based on the distinction between a power or holding grip and a precision or operating grip. Many primates have no precision grip at all, though it is well developed in the great apes. But only man is predisposed to use one hand (usually the right) for the precision grip and the other for the power grip. Once specialization has begun, which is not until the infant is about a year old, the child works out many routines for holding an object with one hand and working on it with the other. This is a predicative procedure, and it probably has a profound effect on tool-use and tool-making.

Let me risk the speculation that the differentiation between holding and operating on what is held may follow the same rule as the differentiation between focal and diffuse attention, and that both may presage the use of topic and comment in language. The same rule may also undergird the other two systems of exchange that are unique with man, kinship and economy.

This examination of infant development has shown, I hope, that the infant's behavior is intelligent, adaptive and flexible from the outset. The degrees of freedom the child can control at first may be few, but the strategies he devises for working within his limitations are typical of a species that plainly is different from other primates. Infancy may be a limited enterprise, but it already has within it the pattern that makes possible man's growth as a user of culture.

Christopher

The Many Faces of Response

By Jerome Kagan

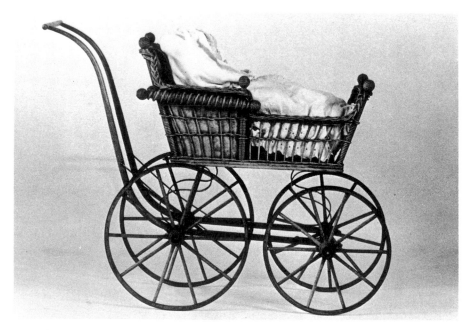

E ach generation of psychologists seems to discover a fresh set of phenomena and a sparkling new object to study. The favorite of the academic psychologist during the opening years of this century was the adult trained to report sensations of color, lightness, and weight. Then, as psychology decided that learned habits and biological drives were more critical than feelings and sensations —and easier to objectify—the white rat captured the stage. The current star is

the human infant, and the theme centers on his emerging mental life.

The human child has become a favorite subject for many reasons. Historical explanation always has been basic to American psychology. The belief that early learning governs later behavior stems in part from our recently strong commitment to behaviorism, and from our hope that bad habits which are learned early in life can be unlearned, or at least that good habits can be taught to the next generation.

The work of Harry Harlow and his colleagues with monkeys and terrycloth mothers has intensified psychologists' concern with the effects of early experience on later behavior, as has the heavy stress that psychoanalytic theory places on the first five years of life.

Interest in the young child clearly rests on more than one base. But a major catalyst for experimentation with the infant was the work of Robert Fantz of Western Reserve University, which showed that by remarkably simple methods one could determine what a baby was looking at. To everyone's surprise, the infant turned out not to be perceptually innocent. The hope that we might be able to determine what a baby perceives led us to believe that we might begin to probe his mind.

Moreover, some psychologists believe that the infant provides a simple prototype of adult processes. After all, important discoveries about heredity in man were made by biologists who studied generations of fruit flies. The maxim that the easiest way to discover basic principles is through the study of simple forms has become a part of scientific catechism. Thus many hope that the infant will yield some of nature's basic truths about psychological functioning.

Three primary questions currently motivate infant-watching. Observation of the baby may lead to a better under-

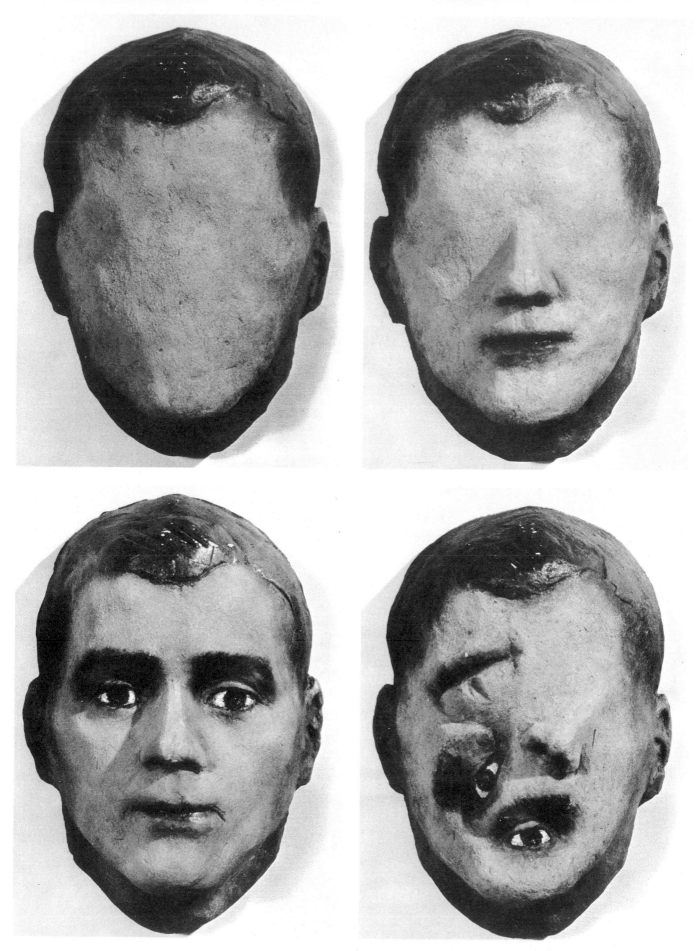

ATTENTION, PLEASE. These painted clay masks were shown to infants of varying ages and changes in reaction were recorded.

standing of the laws of perceptual processing and the principles of learning. In addition, the belief—which derives from the overwhelming differences among day-old babies — that variations among young infants preview the psychological structure and behavior in the older child requires validation.

Finally, there is the "early learning" hypothesis. How early during the first year of a child's life do different experiences begin to influence later behavior? This question was the main impetus for the research project that I shall describe.

There are many possible approaches to the problem. The one we chose was to study infants of divergent social classes in order to determine how early and in what form the lower-class child begins to behave differently from the middle-class child, and perhaps to detect the experiences that produced the differences. It already is known that by the time children are five years old differences from class to class are enormous.

Membership in a social class stands for a varied and complex set of experiences. One of its most predictable consequences is differences in the quality of mental performance. The lower-class child is likely to differ from the middle-class child in many aspects of intellectual functioning. If the specific areas of retardation could be diagnosed, remedial procedures could be suggested.

Our research group at Harvard has been attacking this problem through a longitudinal study of infants from lower-middle-, middle-, and upper-middle-class families. The major focus of the study was mental development. Specifically, the study was directed at differences in the rate and quality of the development of schema. (A schema can be defined as a kind of mental image or memory of an event. It is not a photographic copy, but a caricature of an event—a partial representation. It is somewhat like a diagram that represents only the essential aspects of an object.)

We presented the infants in our study with facsimiles of human faces and human forms. Then we recorded how long they looked, how much they babbled, how frequently they smiled, and how their hearts reacted to these stimuli. In essence, the focus of inquiry was the attentional behavior of the infant.

Several forces control the duration of an infant's attention to a visual event, and the relative importance of each force changes during the first two years of life. For the first six to nine weeks, the infant maintains long spans of attention to stimuli that move and to stimuli that contain

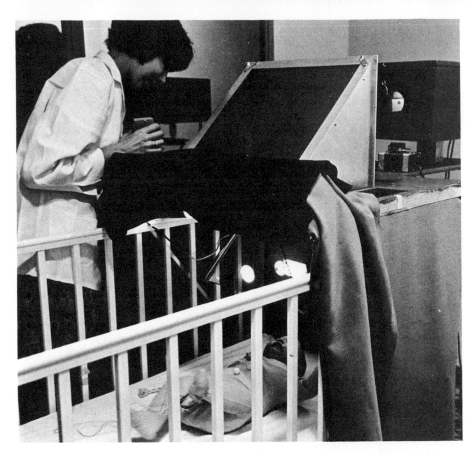

MASKS ABOVE THE CRIB. Four-month-old infants lay on their backs while at intervals Harvard researchers projected the painted clay masks above their heads.

a high degree of physical or black-and-white contrast. New-born infants tend to focus their eyes on the apex of a black triangle against a white background rather than on the center; that is, they focus on the border between the black triangle and the white background, which is where the physical contrast between light and dark is greatest.

The infant's initial study of the environment is directed by an unlearned preference, but this force soon gives way to a second that is dependent upon learning. Before the infant is four months old, the length of time he watches an object is governed by the degree to which what he is watching differs from an internal schema that he has now acquired.

Stimuli that resemble or are not very different from the infant's schema will attract and maintain his attention with the greatest intensity. Stimuli that closely match or have no relation to his schema will hold his attention for a much shorter time. It is not clear why this is true, but it may be that the sustained attention reflects the infant's attempt to match the somewhat novel event to his schema—an effort to assimilate or to understand it.

A third principle that governs early attention involves the nests of associa-

tions to particular objects and events built up during the child's first two years. During this period, he learns collections of reactions to objects. A two-year-old often labels and describes familiar objects in his environment. "Look at the cat," he says. "Look at the doggie eating," or "Baby is crawling out the door."

The child's attention often remains riveted on an event while a chain of associations is expressed. Since the child does not learn complex nests of symbolic associations until the second year, this factor would not be expected to exert a strong influence on attention until that time.

Each of these three processes—physical contrast, discrepancy between event and schema, and rehearsal of acquired associations—emerges at different times in the child's development, but each is always operative at least to some extent. It is reasonable to assume that these factors join together to affect attention. An event that presents high physical contrast, that differs from the infant's schema, and that elicits long nests of associations will hold his attention longest. Perhaps this is why the television commercial can capture the child's attention so effectively.

The data from our study lends support to this assumption. We studied 160 firstborn Caucasian infants, from families with different social-class backgrounds. In the lower-middle-class group, one or both parents had failed to finish high school, and the fathers were employed as unskilled laborers. In the middle-class families both parents had finished high school and some had attended college, and the fathers were either white-collar workers or skilled laborers. In the upper-middle-class group, both parents were college graduates and some had graduate training, and the fathers were employed in professional or executive jobs.

We observed the infants in the laboratory at 4, 8, 13, and 27 months of age. To date, all of them have been studied at 4, 8, and 13 months. Half have been assessed at 27 months. Mothers and children also were observed at home when the children were 4 and 27 months old.

Each time the infants came to the laboratory, we showed them a set of three-dimensional, flesh-colored clay faces [see illustration, p. 134]. The four-month-old infants were placed on their backs in cribs, and the masks were presented above them [see illustration, p. 135]. The older babies sat in highchairs that faced a screen, while their mothers sat beside them. Each face was displayed on the screen for 30 seconds at a time; then the field was blank for 15 seconds before the next face appeared. The child saw each mask on four separate occasions, and the four masks were presented in random order. During each episode we recorded the length of the child's fixation on the face, his vocalizations, smiling, fretting or crying, and changes in his heart rate.

One index of attention is the duration of an infant's fixation on the mask. The fixation times were highest at 4 months, dropped dramatically at 8 and 13 months, and then began to rise again at 27 months, a pattern consistent with the varying influences on early attention already discussed. Contrast and discrepancy are the two major factors governing attention at 4 and 8 months. At 4 months, the masks are very different from the child's schema of a human face, while at 8 months and 13 months his schema of a face is so well formed that discrepancy is not so great.

Two of the masks had eyes. Since the eyes provided physical contrast, four-month-old infants watched these masks longer than they did the two masks without eyes. But contrast is subordinate to discrepancy at 8 and 13 months of age. Thus the presence of eyes becomes less important at the older ages; by the time the child is 13 months old, the presence of eyes has no effect at all.

The richness of associations affects the length of time a child will study objects when he is 27 months old, but its effect is weaker at the younger ages. At 27 months, fixations were longest to the disarranged face; the richness of associations acted together with schema discrepancy to lengthen the attentional span.

Support for this conclusion comes from a related investigation. Gordon Finley, now at the University of British Columbia, has shown chromatic paintings of facial stimuli to one-, two-, and three-year-old middle-class children in Cambridge and to peasant Mayan Indian children living in the Yucatan Peninsula of southeastern Mexico [see illustration, top of page 137]. At all three ages, the American children showed longer fixation times than the Mayan children, and at two and three years of age the disarranged face elicited longer fixation times for both groups of children than did the regular faces [see illustration, bottom of page 137].

At both two and three years of age the American children vocalized much more to the masks than the Mayan children did. The American three-year-olds talked to the faces for an average of ten seconds; the Mayan children talked for only three seconds. This suggests that the longer fixation times of the American children were accompanied by rehearsal of associations to the faces.

Social-class differences in attentiveness emerge clearly during the first year of life, but the time at which they appear depends on the particular response studied. With infants of 4, 8, and 13 months, the association between social class and fixation times became stronger with age, and it was always higher for girls than for boys. One group of infants was tested at 4, 8, and 13 months. The stimuli seen first at 4 and 8 months were four human faces. At 13 months, the first stimuli seen were four human forms. [See illustrations, below.] The relation to social class was low at 4 months, moderate at 8 months for girls but low for boys, and high for both sexes at 13 months but higher for girls than boys.

The stronger association between social class and duration of fixation for girls has two possible interpretations. Perhaps girls are biologically more homogeneous at birth than boys are, and perhaps this means that differential experience in the world is more faithfully reflected in the behavior of girls. That is, if girls differ less than boys at birth, we might expect a more consistent relation in girls be-

SOCIAL CLASS DIFFERENCE. Attentiveness to visual stimuli is affected by social class. When infants of four and eight months were shown these faces and 13-month-old infants were shown these human forms, the association was clearly stronger for girls.

tween specific experiences that are presumed to promote attention and subsequent attentive behavior.

Consider the following analogy: Two hands are placed separately on two pieces of clay, each piece of clay representing an infant. One piece of clay is of uniform softness and pliability; the other is lumpy, and varies in pliability. If the two hands come down on the two pieces of clay with the same force, each makes a different impression. The homogeneous clay reflects more faithfully the force that was imposed on it than does the clay with variable pliability.

An alternative interpretation is not inconsistent with the first, but it requires no biological assumptions. It assumes instead that social class has a stronger influence on the way mothers treat their daughters than on the way they treat their sons. Observation of some of our four-month-old children in their homes supports this idea. Middle-class mothers talked substantially more to their daughters than lower-class mothers did; this difference was not present in lower- and middle-class mothers of sons. The longer fixation times at 8 and 13 months by the daughters of well-educated mothers may be a function, in part, of the greater face-to-face stimulation that the child may receive. Longer face-to-face contact may cause the child to show longer fixation times not only to interesting facial stimuli, but perhaps to all classes of interesting events.

A study by Judith Rubenstein, of the National Institute of Mental Health, supports this argument. On two occasions she visited the homes of 44 Caucasian babies five months old and observed the behavior of their mothers. The mothers were classified as high-attentive, medium-attentive, or low-attentive, depending upon the number of times they looked at, touched, held, or talked to their babies.

The babies with highly attentive mothers spent longer times studying and manipulating a novel stimulus than did babies of low-attentive mothers. It was as if the close reciprocal play experienced by the babies with highly attentive mothers established their interest in long explorations of interesting events.

The use of a decrease in heart rate to assess processes related to attention has a short but interesting history. One reason cardiac deceleration was not used earlier to measure attentional reactions can be traced to general arousal theory. This theory implies that when an organism is "tense" about anything—fear, sexual pas-

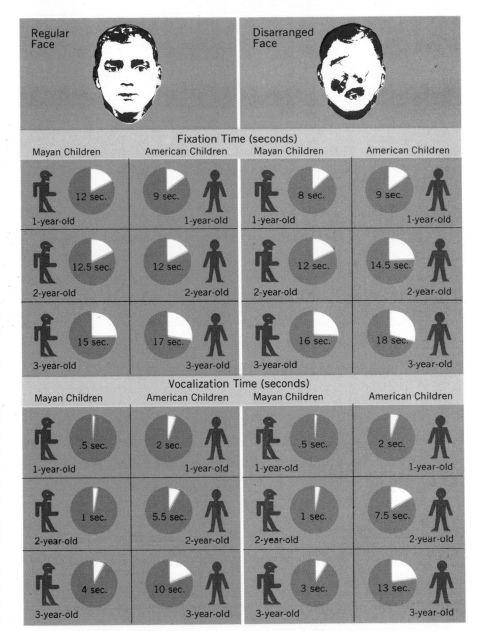

CULTURAL DIFFERENCES. American and Mayan children of the same ages, when shown paintings of human faces, showed consistent variations in reaction times.

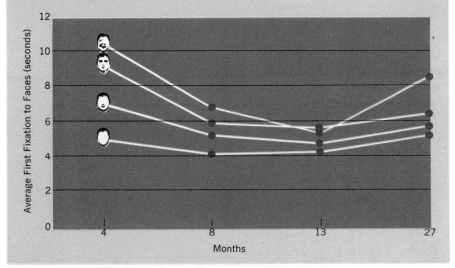

FIXATION TO FACES. The pattern of fixation times to the four masks shown by infants of varying ages corresponded to the known influences on early attention.

137

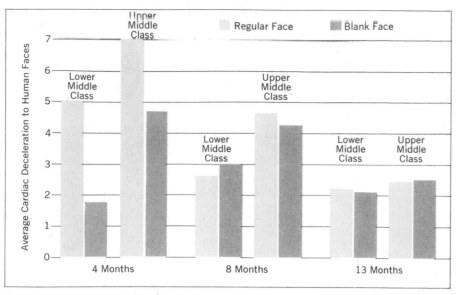

CARDIAC DECELERATION. Heart rate corresponded to social class at four months.

sion, or intense attention—it will show autonomic reaction patterns which reflect internal arousal. That is, among other things, it should show an increase in heart rate. Thus investigators did not search for *decreases* in heart rate in response to episodes that involved attention, and they often did not know how to interpret them when such did appear.

Then John and Beatrice Lacey of the Fels Research Institute demonstrated clearly that cardiac deceleration was a dominant reaction when an organism attended to external events. Once a relation between cardiac deceleration and attention to external events had been established in adults, it became useful with young children, who cannot tell you what they perceive.

In a recent study, Robert McCall of the University of North Carolina and I showed that an infant was likely to show a cardiac deceleration when the stimulus was moderately discrepant from an existing schema—when the event surprised the child, but not too much.

Bearing this hypothesis in mind, let us turn to the social-class differences noted in our study. The differences in cardiac deceleration between the lower- and upper-middle-class children in response to the clay faces were largest at 4 months, and statistically significant. The differences were smaller at 8 months and minimal at 13 months [see illustration above]. Thus the relation between social class and an attentive reaction to the faces increased with age for fixation time, but it diminished with age for cardiac deceleration.

The relatively large difference between classes on cardiac deceleration at 4 months is to be expected if we view

cardiac deceleration as most likely to occur when the infant is surprised by a stimulus that is a bit discrepant from his schema. If the lower-class child had a poorer schema for a human face, then these three-dimensional clay faces, particularly the blank faces, would bear minimal resemblance to his schema. A related point here is that, at 4 months of age, not one lower-class boy smiled at the blank face, whereas 22 per cent of the middle-class boys did. The smiles can be interpreted as signs of recognition, indicating some perception of similarity between the blank face and the child's schema for a face.

The absence of large cardiac decelerations at 13 months suggests that the faces were not surprising to these infants. However, neither large decelerations nor class differences in deceleration should be expected at that age. The long fixation times shown by upper-middle-class

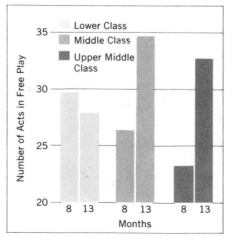

FREE PLAY. Social class affects activity in free play, so that the lower-class infants' responses decrease at a time of increased responses among higher social classes.

children at 13 months are a result of rich nests of associations. The less rich associations of the lower-class child lead to shorter fixation times.

Class differences in infant behavior show up not only in the laboratory, but in the playroom as well. At 8 and 13 months, the children were brought with mothers into a small room containing a variety of toys—a brightly colored wooden bug, a red plastic dog, a pail, a set of wooden blocks, a wooden mallet, a pegboard, a shaft of plastic quoits, a toy lawn mower, and a furry dog.

We recorded the number of changes of activities that each child made within the free-play period—that is, the number of times the child changed his active attention from one toy to another. The number of changes decreased in lower-class children between 8 and 13 months, but it increased in middle- and upper-middle-class infants [see illustration, bottom of this page].

These differences are interpreted to mean that the upper-middle-class children had a richer response repertoire at 13 months and thus did not tire of the toys as quickly as the lower-middle-class children did. This interpretation is congruent with the longer fixation times displayed in the laboratory by upper-middle-class children at 13 months. As with fixation time, the increase in the number of activity changes during play between 8 and 13 months was more striking for girls than for boys, paralleling the greater effect of social class on fixation time for girls.

Differences in the behavior of infants from divergent classes appear to emerge as early as the first year of life and in an expected direction. By the time the child is three years old, the differences are even more obvious. Lower-class children have a limited vocabulary, they speak less intelligibly, and they seem to be less involved in problem solving.

Our data suggest that these later differences may have their roots in the first-year period. It seems reasonable to begin educational procedures with lower-class mothers at this time in order to persuade them that the child learns schema for his environment from the first weeks on. The effect of educating mothers at a time when their children are experiencing rapid mental growth might help the infant, and it also might increase the emotional involvement of the mother with her child. Ultimately, it might facilitate the child's formation of those motives and standards during the preschool years that have such an important bearing on later development. ∩

Russian Nursery Schools

By Michael and Sheila Cole

In the Russian nursery school, a child is taught not only that red is different from blue but that red is the color of apples— and that red apples are ripe apples and ripe apples are edible apples.

IT WAS FREE-PLAY PERIOD at Preschool 67 in the northwest suburbs of Moscow, and it was early summer. Two three-year-old boys were building a castle in the sandbox, occasionally getting in the way of a little girl who was tunneling. A red-faced youngster was hard at work hauling pails of water for the boys from a nearby pond. In a far corner of the yard, two little girls were playing with dolls. Sitting under an arbor in another corner, alone, was a three-year-old girl with short, dark hair, singing softly to herself.

We had seen the girl spend the play period that way for several days, and we mentioned her to the teacher, a young woman who had been trained at one of the Soviet Union's pedagogical institutes. "Oh, that's Irichka," she replied. "Irichka is happy to be alone. She's that kind of child— quiet and able to amuse herself."

To us, it seemed odd that a woman who was supposed to be raising children in a collective should show such an easy acceptance of individualism. But the more we learned about Soviet nursery schools, the more apparent it became that we had brought with us from the United States a full bag of misconceptions.

We spent the summer of 1966 in the Soviet Union, chiefly to help with preparations for the 18th International Congress of Psychologists. In the United States at the time, Head Start programs were springing up all over, and the newspapers were full of heartwarming accounts of children listening to stories and receiving medical check-ups for the first time in their lives. A heated debate was also underway among teachers and psychologists about what kinds of program would best prepare these children for the public schools, whose task in turn would be to make them productive and socially useful members of our society.

Especially because of this situation at home, we were eager to find out all we could about Soviet nursery schools. We spent almost a week at Preschool 67, talking to the children, teachers and principal. Later, we visited the Institute of Preschool Education in Moscow and interviewed its director, A. V. Zaporozhets. The Institute is responsible for recommending a nursery-school program to the Soviet Union's Ministry of Education, and its psychologists perform the research on which the recommendations are based. Once the program has been adopted by the Ministry, it is used throughout the country.

Nursery schools have been part of the system of universal education in the Soviet Union since the time of the Bolshevik Revolution. Although they are not compulsory, preschools are the first link in the Soviet educational system. The Communist Party assigns to nursery schools the task of insuring the normal development of all children— preparing them for school and teaching them proper work habits, so that they, like their American counterparts, will grow into productive and socially useful members of their society.

Preschool 67 is just like thousands of nursery schools in the Soviet Union. Its drab, two-story building comes from a blueprint in use throughout the country for almost 10 years, and its educational program and goals are also identical to those in effect elsewhere.

The pupils range in age from two to seven; there are 150 of them, all from homes in the neighborhood of the school. One group of 25 lives in the school's small dormitory, going home only on weekends and holidays. The others arrive between eight and nine in the morning and leave between four and six in the afternoon.

There is a long waiting list at Preschool 67, as there is at most nursery schools, and admission is based on need. Priority is given to children who have two working parents and no grandmother or other baby-sitter, to orphans, and to children from very large families or from homes where there is sickness or some other problem. Payment, which is determined by the parents' income, ranges from $2.20 to $13.00 a month.

When we arrived at Preschool 67, the children were eating breakfast on one side of a large, airy, toy-cluttered room. The older children used cloth napkins and sat at tables covered with white cloths. These amenities, we were told by Sofia Shvedova, the warm, grandmotherly director of the preschool, were both a reward for good table manners and an incentive to improve. "We ask the children to see how clean they can keep the tablecloth," she said. "But we never shame them when they have an accident."

"We know that some children eat less than others, but we give them all the same amount anyway," Mrs. Shvedova went on. "We let them eat as much as they can. We occasionally feed the little ones. But we don't force a child to love all food. We try to teach him little by little."

"In nursery school, children should grow to be healthy, alert, life-loving, playful, agile individuals with good bearing."

FROM *PROGRAM OF EDUCATION IN THE NURSERY SCHOOL* (Ministry of Education, 1962)

At nursery school, the children receive three substantial meals a day—they are not supposed to eat at home on school days except for an occasional snack—and they take their naps there as well.

In other words, the nursery school is responsible for the health and physical development of the child. This lessens the burden on the working mother, and it also reflects the Soviets' very different view from ours of the relation between children and society. The Soviets believe that children are a natural resource, perhaps the most valuable resource a society has. Although the raising of the child is entrusted to the family, the ultimate responsibility for the child's development belongs to the State itself.

As the children finished their breakfast, they wiped their mouths on their napkins, asked the nanny if they could be excused, thanked her, and went to the other side of the room to play. A few children stayed behind; it was their turn to help clear the table.

Teaching the children to take care of their own needs, and to help with the chores and with the younger children, is an important part of the "work training" portion of the nursery-school program. The children do not receive concrete rewards for their "work," but they are profusely praised when they do a good job.

"They should all work well," Mrs. Shvedova said. "But we know that there are individual differences and that one child is not as capable as another. We try to measure them all against their own achievement. We can't give a

child a gold star when he breaks a plate, but we can say, 'Tolia did a very good job today. He tried very hard. He broke a dish, but he did it because he was trying so hard.'"

Surprising as it might seem to many Americans, Mrs. Shvedova's insistence on acknowledging individual differences and on judging the child against his own abilities is based on official ideology. The government-distributed manual for preschool teachers says that nursery schools should teach friendship and cooperation and also form individuality: the school's program of physical, intellectual, moral, work and esthetic training should take into account the age and individual characteristics of each child.

Later in the morning, a teacher took Preschool 67's three- and four-year-olds aside to read them a story. The

children listened intently. When the teacher had finished, she asked them to retell parts of the story and to answer questions about it, gently correcting their mistakes and insisting on answers that were complete, grammatical sentences. One little girl was over-eager: she shouted the right answer before a slower and shyer child could finish. The teacher restrained her gently and then encouraged the other child to answer by himself.

Teaching the children to speak Russian correctly and to express themselves fully is one of the major aims of the preschool program. Language training is a continuous process, carried on throughout the day by means of books, stories and direct contact with adults.

In another room, the older children followed their teacher's story in books of their own. Before the teacher began to read, she asked the children several questions about books and how they are used. During the story, she stopped often to ask what letter or sound a word began or ended with. Later, she requested summaries of the plot and descriptions of the characters.

For five- and six-year-olds, who will soon start school, there is great emphasis on skills like these. The preschool is in close touch with the grade-schools that the children will attend, and it teaches them the work habits and procedures that are used there. Reading and writing as such are not formally taught in nursery school, but reading and writing readiness are. The children learn to analyze the sounds they hear in the spoken language and to write the elements used in the letters of the Russian alphabet.

Elementary mathematical concepts are introduced gradually, through the use of concrete materials. The children learn to count to 10 by eye, ear, touch and movement; to answer questions of number, size and position in space; and to subtract or add one or two to any number up to 10. It is only in the last year of nursery school, when the children are six years old, that they begin to work with written numbers and with the symbols $+$, $-$ and $=$.

After lunch, we stood at the door of a dormitory crowded with high, white iron bedsteads and watched the children take their usual two-hour rest. They were supposed to be asleep, but they seemed determined not to succumb. Stripped to their underwear and covered with sheets, they tossed, turned, whispered, sucked their thumbs, asked the nanny for glasses of water, and requested permission to go to the potty—or reported that it was too late.

The nanny treated the bed-wetters and thumb-suckers matter-of-factly. If a child wet his bed, she changed his sheets and underwear with little fuss and no reprimands. She privately asked a few older children to take their thumbs out of their mouths, but when the thumbs were put back in a few moments she seemed not to notice.

After their naps, the children went outside to play. The yard was provided with swings, sandboxes and little pools of water; there were also gazebos and arbors, tables and chairs, and bookcases full of games, toys, books and arts-and-crafts materials.

One two-year-old boy, ignoring these enticements, began to wander off the nursery-school grounds. The nanny in charge, a motherly middle-aged woman, ran after him and brought him back. She scolded him affectionately, threatening to punish him by making him sit still.

"He's such a little one," she said. "He really doesn't understand. It's impossible to really punish him."

Mrs. Shvedova told us later that punishment is meted out only if the children hurt someone or are very disobedient. "The first time a child is bad, we don't do anything. We try to understand. But after a while we must punish, because of the other children. We try to suit the punishment to the child and the situation. We know the children well, and we know what each one will consider a punishment." Corporal punishment is frowned on in the Soviet Union, and the usual method of discipline is the temporary withdrawal of affection and praise.

During the play period, one group of girls five or six years old went to an arts-and-crafts area to color. They

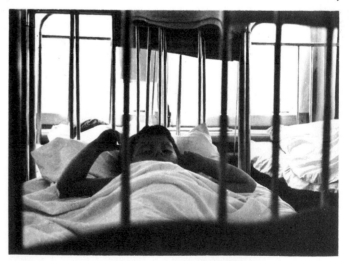

were eager to please and to show us their work, which was very neat. When one girl offered to draw us a picture to take home to our daughter, we requested a dog. "I can't," she said. "No one has taught me how."

In Soviet nursery schools, drawing is a lesson—something to be learned. There are exercises on how to draw straight lines, circles and other forms, and simple figures. These exercises are not considered play, and the teacher

"Teachers should teach the children to respect people and work, and to be interested in work, community life and nature." FROM *PROGRAM OF EDUCATION IN THE NURSERY SCHOOL*

keeps a little folder of each child's work to encourage a serious attitude toward it.

Looking through these folders, we found that the children's drawings were all the same. The teacher had shown them how to draw a house, a person, or whatever, and they had done it. Unlike most Americans, who believe that a child will be creative "naturally" if he is given the chance, the Soviets believe creativity is more than a matter of opportunity. It requires training. But they are quick to point out that the object of training is not stilted, narrow drawings like those in the folders at Preschool 67. How to teach creativity properly is a problem now being studied at the laboratory of esthetic education of the Institute of Preschool Education.

However, the development of creativity does not seem to be very high on Soviet preschools' list of priorities. When we asked Mrs. Shvedova what goals Preschool 67 had for its children, she replied, "We want them to be

smart and honest. If they are honest, they will be fair. We want them to love beauty, to be real people. We don't want them to be all alike, but originality and creativity are not that important."

One thing that *is* important is sensory training, which the Soviets define rather more broadly than we would. At the preschool one morning we watched a row of three-year-olds, seated on small benches under an arbor, receive a lesson in sensory training that was also a lesson in language. The teacher showed the children five vegetables and named them: an onion, a beet, a carrot, a cabbage and a potato. Then she put the vegetables in a cloth sack and asked a child to draw one out and name it.

When each child and the teacher had named the vegetables several times and repeated the names in unison, the teacher told the children that the five objects together were called vegetables. The class said the word "vegetable" several times and was dismissed.

The four- and five-year-olds had a harder task. After they chose a vegetable from the sack they were asked, without looking at it, to name it and tell everything they knew about it—its color, its shape, how it grows and how it is eaten. The rest of the children in the group corrected and helped them.

According to the Russians, perception is more than the physical reception of energy by the sense organs. It also involves the organization of perceptual signals—the way a person selects and systematizes certain characteristics of perceptible reality so that he can use them in such activities as speech, music, art and work. For the Soviets, then, perception means not only "perception" as we usually think of it; it includes a number of cognitive functions as well. When a child learns to perceive, he learns to orient himself in the world of the senses.

The Russians will allow that this can occur spontaneously, as a by-product of normal activity. But they do not believe that spontaneous development is very efficient or very effective. As A. V. Zaporozhets, director of the Institute of Preschool Education, explained when we talked with him, "Our nursery schools differ from most of those in the West, where there is no special program of education and it is believed that, given the chance, a child will ask questions and learn through his own initiative."

Soviet psychologists, Zaporozhets continued, disagree with both Jean Piaget and Maria Montessori. According to Piaget, the kind of thinking a child is capable of depends on his age. If beans are poured from a short, fat jar into a tall, thin one, a child of four is likely to think the tall jar contains more beans, while a child of six or seven will not be fooled. Piaget attributes this to the fact that the older child understands the principle of conservation.

The Russians, Zaporozhets said, do not agree "that a child cannot do such and such until a certain age. We think that teaching plays a decisive role in learning, and that a child can do quite a bit more than we previously imagined he was capable of."

They do think it is *easier* to develop certain abilities at certain ages, although they are not sure which abilities are easiest to develop at which age. As a working policy, they try to develop intuition and sensory abilities in early childhood, leaving abstract thought for later on. "We believe that thought is a hierarchical structure. For a complete intellect, the entire system, from the most concrete

143

to the most abstract, must exist. You don't have to rush to the third stage when you haven't gotten through the first."

Like Montessori, Zaporozhets said, the Soviets think sensory abilities should be developed during early childhood. But "Montessori believed that the child is born with all his sensory abilities and that training will simply strengthen them. We think this is incorrect."

As the handbook for nursery-school teachers written by Institute psychologists, *Sensory Training*, explains, the Russians find the Montessorian system of training too formal, too "pure," too far removed from the everyday world in which the child must use his senses. They believe it is not enough to acquaint the child with an endless variety of sensory data. He must be taught a generalized method of orientation and investigation—an approach to the world of the senses—which will efficiently give him the information he needs. This is best done informally, within the context of regular nursery-school activities such as making models, drawing, constructing things with sand or blocks, singing, dancing and storytelling.

Abstract exercises in which the child discriminates triangles from circles in an unanalyzed way are thought to teach him very little. In the Russian nursery school, a child is taught not only that red is different from blue but that red is the color of apples and, indeed, that red apples are ripe apples and ripe apples are edible apples.

The child is taught to use his senses, and he is also taught what the things he perceives mean and what words he can use to describe his sensory experiences precisely. At the same time, he is encouraged to generalize and categorize on the basis of his immediate sensory experience—he is taught, for instance, that onion-beet-carrot-cabbage-potato equals vegetable.

Here is a typical elementary exercise in sensory training, used with two- and three-year-olds. The object of the exercise, which is preliminary to developing the kind of perception the Soviets are talking about, is to teach the child to use his sensory apparatus to the fullest.

The teacher gives the child two cardboard circles (or triangles, or squares) that are the same size but different colors. She asks the child to put one circle on top of the other so that the edges are even, and to run his finger along the edges of the figures so that he can tell whether he has aligned them correctly or not. Then she gives the child a circle and a square of the same color—say, blue—and shows him a *red* square. His task is find which of his figures has the same *shape* as hers. The child makes his choice and verifies it by placing it on the teacher's model. If it fits, the child is praised; if not, the teacher suggests he try the other figure.

As *Sensory Training* points out, the object of perceptual training is to prepare the child for future activity. In short, the Russian approach is highly pragmatic and task-oriented. Perhaps for this reason, the schools make considerable use of construction exercises. Like drawing, building requires the child to perform a detailed visual examination of the form, size, and spatial arrangement of an object, but *Sensory Training* warns that there is an important distinction between construction and pictorial tasks. A picture always reflects the exterior characteristics of an object as it is visually perceived; construction serves a practical purpose. "Garages are built for cars, barns for animals, houses for dolls. Constructions are made by children to be used—acted with."

"Children's moral traits and the character of their personality should be formed while they are in nursery school." FROM *PROGRAM OF EDUCATION IN THE NURSERY SCHOOL*

Thus a teacher might provide the children with bricks, have the children pile them up in different ways and test the stability of the piles, and then suggest the construction of a road. Or she might give the children beams of different lengths and ask them to build a corral. She would point out the various factors the children should consider if the corral is to serve its purpose—that it must be high enough to prevent the animals from jumping out, that the beams must be close enough together to keep the animals from squeezing through, and so forth.

Although the stress in exercises like these is on purpose and practicality, note that it is also on *activity,* and particularly on physical activity as an important way to develop perceptual skills. The child is an active agent in his own development. *He* places the geometric figures together and runs his fingers around the edges; *he* piles the bricks and builds the corral.

This emphasis on the role of active experience in the child's development has its counterpart in contemporary American developmental theory. Richard Held of M.I.T., for example, has shown that there is a close relation between motor experience and visual perception, especially when one must coordinate what one sees with what one does. In one well-known experiment, Held provided a man and a woman with special glasses that shifted their visual fields to the right. Then he had the woman sit in a wheelchair while the man pushed the chair around the

campus. When the two were tested later, the man—who had had motor experience with the visual shift—was much better than the woman at correcting for the distortion that the glasses created.

In a similar experiment, Held placed two kittens in a circular box whose walls were painted with vertical stripes. One kitten sat in a cart; the other wore a yoke and walked around the box rather in the manner of a water buffalo, moving the cart around as he did so. Although the kitten who got the free ride saw the same things as the walking kitten, the walking kitten seemed to learn more. When the two were tested later, the kitten that had the motor experience showed superior ability to perform a number of tasks that required visual-motor coordination.

The notion of the child as an active agent in his own development also occurs in the work of Jerome Bruner of Harvard. Just telling the child a set of facts, Bruner says, does not produce real learning. The child must operate on his environment in such a way that he discovers solutions to the problems it poses. As the child searches for solutions, his approach becomes more sophisticated and also more effective. For example, young children who have not learned how to gather information efficiently play 20 Questions by asking about specific items: "Is it the dog?" "Is it Mommy?" Older children try to structure their questions so that each yields a maximum amount of information: "Is it a living American man?" Through a process of active searching, the older children have learned generalized techniques for gathering information.

Much of the research now being done by Zaporozhets and his colleagues at the Institute is based on this general premise that activity leads to learning. There are experiments, for example, on teaching cooperation and consideration of others through role-playing. Several children who are not friendly with each other are asked to perform a joint task—to tell a story together, or to put on a puppet show—in the hope that they will be friendlier after than they were before.

We arrived in the Soviet Union with a mental image of a monolithic preschool system, chiefly Pavlovian in theory and rigid, regimented and stifling in practice. Soviet psychology does include some Pavlovian concepts, and Soviet preschool programs do follow a common outline, but these are a much smaller part of the whole picture than we had supposed. In fact, the theoretical and empirical research conducted at the Institute would command the respect of developmental psychologists in Geneva or New York, and the care given the children of Preschool 67 could serve as a model anywhere—anywhere, that is, where children are treated as one of society's most valuable resources. ∩

The Young Monkeys

Harry &
Margaret
Harlow

When we watch a newborn rhesus monkey with its mother, the infant seems to display signs of affection almost at once, clinging to the mother's body and climbing into her arms. The slightly older infant cries pitcously when separated from its mother. Still later, as the maternal bond weakens, the young monkey reaches out to others its own age for companionship and, finally, for sexual satisfaction.

These examples illustrate the three basic social responses of primates — affection, fear, and social aggression. In fact, the responses usually emerge in that order as the infant monkey matures.

Affection, the reaction to cuddling, warmth, and food, comes first in these broadly based and sometimes even overlapping categories. Then comes fear, as the infant begins to explore a sometimes dangerous world. And finally, there is social aggression when the monkey is older, more exploratory, and better able to handle itself.

These responses obviously are not the simple component behavior patterns which B. F. Skinner has described, nor are they like Pavlovian reflex reactions. Rather, they are highly complicated and built-in patterns of behavior which can be modified by learning. Under certain circumstances, normal development can be blocked, and the patterns disrupted. When this is done under experimental conditions, we can learn more about the sensitive, vital process of socialization.

Certainly monkeys are not people, but they are the highest form of animal life except for humans, and we can perform complex experiments with them in which we manipulate their environment with more freedom than we can when using people as subjects. For example, we can put monkeys into isolation as they develop, we can add to or take away from their basic emotional needs. And as we learn more about the basic emotions of monkeys we can profit from this knowledge, in our ever-active search to find out more about ourselves and the world of life we live in.

The Beginnings of Affection

The first sign of affection by the newborn rhesus monkey is a reflex action which facilitates nursing. The infant grasps its mother's fur and moves upward on her body until restrained by her arms. This brings the baby monkey's face close to the mother's breast, and the infant begins to nurse. Throughout the first two or three weeks of life, the response of infant to mother continues to be based on reflexes, although the baby gradually gains voluntary control of its motor behavior. But even after the young monkey is skilled enough to walk, run, and climb by itself, it continues to cling to its mother. The bond of affection between infant and mother continues to grow stronger instead of weaker during the next few months.

The mother monkey warmly returns her infant's affection, and this reciprocal affection operates in a way that helps prepare the young monkey for participation in a more complex social environment. The mother shows her fondness by cradling, grooming, caressing, and protecting her baby. At first, this affection is primarily reflex behavior and is stimulated by the touch, sound, and sight of the baby. Interestingly, the baby need not be the female monkey's own, for pre-adolescent, adolescent, and adult females are attracted to all the infants in their group. Given the opportunity, even females who have not recently borne young will adopt infants, and this indicates that hormonal changes associated with parturition are not essential to the establishment of maternal affection.

Fear

Fear responses show themselves after the young rhesus has matured intellectually and has had enough experience to recognize objects which are strange and dangerous. In its first two months a young rhesus shows little or no fear. But by the third or fourth month of life, unfamiliar places, persons, and objects as well as loud or unusual noises make the infant screech and cling to its mother. Young monkeys separated from their mothers will cry frequently and clasp themselves. An infant that has previously known only its mother can be frightened by other monkeys, but if the young rhesus has previously been part of a group, it will be afraid of other monkeys only when threatened by them, or actually hurt.

Making Friends

By the time they are two months old, young monkeys that have been allowed to live in groups show an interest in other monkeys, especially infants. First contacts are usually brief, beginning with physical exploration which can be one-sided or mutual. From these early experiences come more complex play behavior and the development of affection for other young monkeys. Emotional attachment to monkeys of the same age usually appears before the emergence of fear. However, if such attachments are not permitted to develop — if, for instance, the young monkey is kept apart from his peers—there is some possibility that this friendly emotion will not emerge at all. Nevertheless, the infant that has received a good deal of maternal affection can sometimes make friends even when the normal age for doing so has passed.

Emotional bonds among those of the same age usually grow stronger as the maternal relationship begins to ebb. The infant's first emotional experience, the attachment to its mother, is quite distinct from later emotional ties. For example, the peer relationship originates in and develops through play. Young monkeys that have not been permitted to establish relationships with other infants are wary of their playmates when finally allowed to be with them, and these deprived monkeys often fail to develop strong bonds of affection. Yet monkeys that have been deprived of mother love but provided with early contacts *can* develop ties with their peers which seem comparable to the bonds formed by mother-reared infants.

Affection of age mates for one another is universal within the entire primate kingdom. It starts early in all species of monkeys and apes, and it is evident throughout the life span. The beginnings of human sociability, however, are more variable because children's opportunities to contact their age mates differ from family to family and from culture to culture. Four decades ago, research by Charlotte Buhler and her associates in Vienna showed that human infants in their first year of life generally are responsive to one another. This can be confirmed informally by anyone who looks in on a pediatrician's waiting room where healthy young children contact one another quickly. If held, they strain toward one another, and if close together, they reach out to one another. They smile at each other, and they laugh together.

Sex Roles

In early infancy, the child's sex is relatively unimportant in social interactions: Human boys and girls, like male and female monkeys, play together indiscriminately at first. But though this continues for several years in humans, behavioral differences begin to appear in monkeys by the third or fourth month and increase steadily until the animal is mature.

Male monkeys become increasingly forceful, while the females become progressively more passive. A male will threaten other males and females alike, whereas females rarely are aggressive toward males. During periods of play males are the pursuers, and the females retreat. As they grow older, increasing separation of the sexes becomes evident in friendship and in play.

During their juvenile period, one to two years of age, and even after, rhesus monkeys as a rule form pairs and clusters of friends of the same sex. Only in maturity when the female is in heat does the pattern change, and then only temporarily. Male-female pairs dominate until the mating period ends. And then the partners return to their own sex groups. With humans, too, friendships with those of the same sex predominate in childhood, adolescence, and maturity. Even when men and women attend the same social event, men often cluster together with other men, while women form groups by themselves. Clubs for men only, or for women only, further demonstrate this sexual split.

At both the human and subhuman levels, this separation is undoubtedly based on common interests which in turn are based on anatomical and physical differences between the sexes. For example, male primates of most species are larger and stronger than the females and better-equipped physiologically for feats of strength and physical endurance. This probably leads the male to more large-muscle activities. Culture influences do not create differences in behavior between the sexes, but they do mold, maintain, and exaggerate the natural differences. Thus boys, not girls, are encouraged to become athletes, and women boxers and shot-putters are generally regarded as oddities.

The importance of peer relationships in monkeys cannot be overemphasized. All primates that live in groups achieve much of their communal cohesiveness and adult sexual social behavior through affectionate relationships with others of the same age. Monkeys learn their sex roles through play. By the third or fourth month of life, male and female sexual behavior is beginning to be different. By the time they are a year old, most monkeys who have been reared in groups display mature and specialized sexual behavior, except that male intromission and ejaculation do not occur until puberty, at about four years of age.

Social Aggression

Sexual differentiation usually is learned by monkeys before social aggression appears. After numerous and varied studies at the University of Wisconsin, we have concluded that unless peer affection pre-

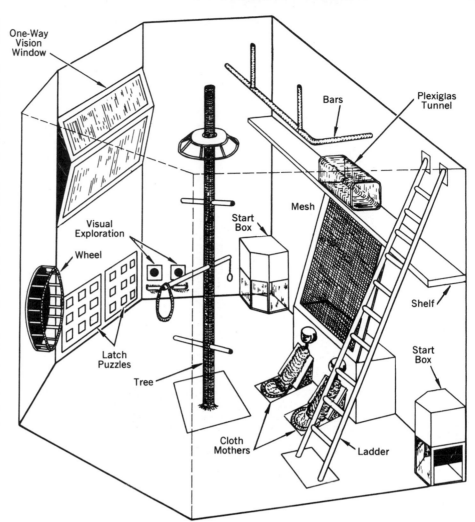

Social playroom for the young monkeys.

cedes social aggression, monkeys do not adjust; either they become unreasonably aggressive or they develop into passive scapegoats for their group.

Rhesus monkeys begin to make playful attacks on one another almost as soon as they are old enough for actual contact, and their aggression increases steadily throughout the first year of life. The young monkeys wrestle and roll, pretend to bite one another, and make threatening gestures. But they do not hurt each other, even though their teeth are sharp enough to pierce a playmate's skin.

If the young rhesus has had normal group contact during infancy, it will show restraint toward both friends and strangers. Only if threatened or to protect weaker members of its group will it fight.

While in the group the young try to find a place in the hierarchy, and as dominance is established a relative peace ensues. In contrast, monkeys who have been socially deprived may seriously injure one another when placed together at this stage.

Isolation Breeds Fear

One experimental rearing condition which throws much light on the problems of aggression and peer affection is total social isolation. At birth, the monkey is enclosed in a stainless steel chamber where light is diffused, temperature controlled, air flow regulated, and environmental sounds filtered. Food and water are provided and the cage is cleaned by remote control. During its isolation, the animal sees no living creature, not even a human hand. After three, six, or twelve months, the monkey is removed from the chamber and placed in an individual cage in the laboratory. Several days later it is exposed for the first time to peers—another monkey who has been reared in isolation and two who have been raised in an open cage with others. The four are put in a playroom equipped with toys and other apparatus designed to stimulate activity and play; they spend usually half an hour a day in the room five days a week and these sessions go on for six months.

Fear is the overwhelming response in all monkeys raised in isolation. Although the animals are physically healthy, they crouch and appear terror-stricken by their new environment. Young that have been isolated for only three months soon recover and become active in playroom life; by the end of a month they are al-

Cuddling and caressing help create the maternal bond between mother monkey and baby. The affection is quite mutual.

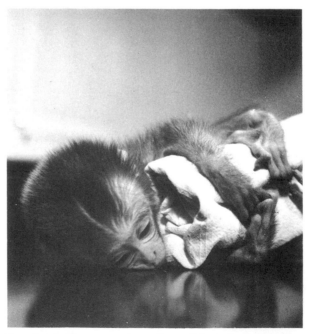

Deprived of a normal mother, this infant monkey forms a strong emotional attachment to an artifical, cloth mother.

When a six-month-old monkey, raised in total isolation from birth, is finally put together with other normal monkeys his own age, the infant cowers in fear and never learns to play.

By the time they are two months old, young monkeys begin to explore the world—and each other. They make friends and play. The maternal bond weakens.

Two baby monkeys, raised from birth together, become like Siamese twins; they cling together chest to chest. If artificially separated from each other, they clamor to resume clinging.

When several baby monkeys are raised together from birth, they often cling together in a choo-choo line. They tend to play together a great deal and to develop sexually at an early age.

most indistinguishable from their control age mates. But the young monkeys that had been isolated for six months adapt poorly to each other and to the control animals. They cringe when approached and fail at first to join in any of the play. During six months of play sessions, they never progress beyond minimal play behavior, such as playing by themselves with toys. What little social activity they do have is exclusively with the other *isolate* in the group. When the other animals become aggressive, the isolates accept their abuse without making any effort to defend themselves. For these animals, social opportunities have come too late. Fear prevents them from engaging in social interaction and consequently from developing ties of affection.

Monkeys that have been isolated for twelve months are very seriously affected. Although they have reached the age at which true aggression is normally present, and they can observe it in their playmates, they show no signs of aggression themselves. Even primitive and simple play activity is almost nonexistent. With these isolated animals, no social play is observed and aggressive behavior is never demonstrated. Their behavior is a pitiful combination of apathy and terror as they crouch at the sides of the room, meekly accepting the attacks of the more healthy control monkeys. We have been unable to test them in the playroom beyond a ten-week period because they are in danger of being seriously injured or even killed by the others.

Our tests have indicated that this social failure is not a consequence of intellectual arrest. In the course of thirty-five years of experimentation with and observation of monkeys, we have developed tests of learning which successfully discriminate between species, between ages within species, and between monkeys with surgically-produced brain damage and their normal peers. The tests have demonstrated that the isolated animals are as intellectually able as are monkeys of the same age raised in open cages. The only difference is that the isolates require more time to adjust to the learning apparatus. All monkeys must be adapted to testing, but those coming from total isolation are more fearful and so it takes longer for them to adjust to the situation.

And Aggression

We continued the testing of the same six-

and twelve-month isolates for a period of several years. The results were startling. The monkeys raised in isolation now began to attack the other monkeys viciously, whereas before they had cowered in fright. We tested the isolates with three types of strangers: large and powerful adults, normal monkeys of their age, and normal-one-year olds. The monkeys which had been raised in the steel isolation cages for their first six months now were three years old. They were still terrified by all strangers, even the physically helpless juveniles. But in spite of their terror, they engaged in uncontrolled aggression, often launching suicidal attacks upon the large adult males and even attacking the juveniles —an act almost never seen in normal monkeys of their age. The passage of time had only exaggerated their asocial and antisocial behavior.

In those monkeys, positive social action was not initiated, play was nonexistent, grooming did not occur, and sexual behavior either was not present at all or was totally inadequate. In human terms, these monkeys which had lived unloved and in isolation were totally unloving, distressed, disturbed, and delinquent.

And Sexual Inadequacy

We have found that social deprivation has another long-term effect which is particularly destructive—inadequate sexual behavior. This is found in all males and most females reared in total or semi-isolation. Whereas some of the females that have been in semi-isolation still show a certain amount of sexual responsiveness, this is probably due to their easier role in copulation. The separate actions required for copulation begin to appear in young infants, but these actions are not organized into effective patterns unless early social play—particularly of a heterosexual nature—is allowed. Monkeys that fail to develop adult sexual patterns by the time they are 12 to 18 months old are poor risks for breeding when they are mature.

For example, we found in one study that semi-isolated females that are placed with breeding males avoid social proximity and do not groom themselves. They often engage in threats, aggression, and autistic behavior such as clutching and biting themselves, and they frequently fail to support the male when mounting occurs. In contrast, normal females seldom threaten males, are

not aggressive, and do not engage in autistic behavior; they maintain social proximity, groom themselves, and provide adequate support for the mounting male.

Parallel tests with males show that socially deprived males are even more inadequate than their female counterparts. Compared to the normal males, they groomed less, threatened more, were more aggressive, rarely initiated any sexual contact, engaged in unusual and abnormal sexual responses, and—with one exception—never achieved intromission.

The sexual inadequacies of the socially deprived monkeys did not come from a loss of biological sex drive. High arousal was often seen, but it led to inappropriate responses—autistic behavior, masturbation, and violent aggression—all in a frenetic sequence lasting only a few seconds.

Monkeys Without Mothers

In another series of experiments on the emotional bases of social development in monkeys, we raised some infants with continuous peer experience and no mothers. Two, four, and six monkeys were reared together in groups. The groups of two tended to cling together in the first few weeks, chest to chest, and this behavior persisted long after normally raised infants would have stopped clinging to their mothers. The two young monkeys moved about like Siamese twins joined at the chest. When some external force turned up to break the two apart or one rhesus attempted to explore an object, the other quickly tried to resume the clinging posture. This immature behavior continued until the animals were put in separate cages, although we found that it could be drastically reduced if the pairs were reared together for a fixed period of time, separated for another specified time, and then subjected to alternate togetherness and separation.

We also found that four or six infant monkeys living together in one cage tend very soon to form a line in which one rhesus leans forward and the others get behind him in a single file, each clinging to the back of the animal in front of him. If the first monkey moves without breaking loose, the whole group usually moves in unison with it, but if the lead rhesus frees itself, the pattern breaks up, to be re-formed shortly.

While monkeys reared in pairs play very infrequently—the tight clasp they have on one another restricts movement —the infants raised in larger groups play extensively. In one respect, the monkeys which have been raised in the larger groups are quite precocious: Their sexual behavior is perfected at an early age and as adults they breed readily. This is in sharp contrast with the absence or insufficiency of sexual activity in male and female isolates.

Throughout our studies, we have been increasingly impressed by the alternative routes monkeys may take to reach adequate social behavior, which by our criteria includes affection toward peers, controlled fear and aggression, and normal sexual behavior. In protected laboratory conditions, social interaction between peers and between mother and child appears to be in large part interchangeable in their effect on the infant's development. A rhesus can surmount the absence of its mother if it can associate with its peers, and it can surmount a lack of socialization with peers if its mother provides affection. Being raised with several age mates appears to com-

pensate adequately for a lack of mothering, although it is likely that animals reared in this way would be at a disadvantage if confronted by monkeys that had had a mother and early experience with others their age as well.

From an evolutionary point of view, there is an advantage to the animal in having two independent sources of affection—mother and peers. Each in part compensates for the deficiencies of the other. Mothers vary considerably in the depth and type of their attachment to their children. A rhesus mother denied normal affection in her early life may be so detached from her infant and, in many cases, may be so brutal that the effects could be devastating for her infant unless there were companions available for play. Human mothers may also exhibit detachment and physical abuse, which pediatricians refer to as the "battered baby" syndrome—a much more prevalent phenomenon than police and court records indicate.

Isolation studies which begin at birth and continue until some specified age

provide a powerful technique for the analysis of maturational processes without interference from an overlay of learning. Indeed, the isolation experiment is one of the few methods by which it is possible to measure the development of complex behavior patterns in any pure or relatively pure form. While it is commonly thought that learning shapes preestablished, unlearned response patterns, this is barely half of the picture, at least as far as social learning is concerned.

One of the most important functions of social learning in primates—and perhaps in all mammals and many other classes of animals as well—is the development of social patterns that will restrain and check potentially asocial behavior. These positive, learned social patterns must be established before negative, unlearned patterns emerge. In this sense, social learning is an anticipation of later learning: The inappropriate exercise of negative behavior can be checked within the social group while the same behavior is permitted toward intruders threatening from without. ◖

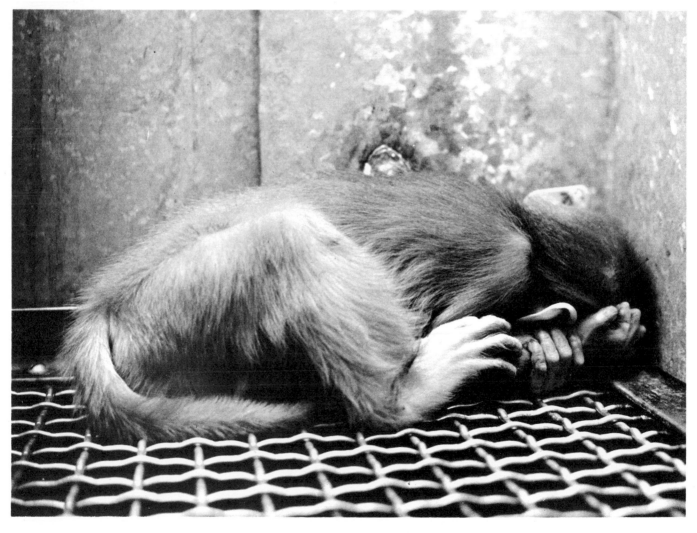

THE MYSTERY OF THE PRE LOGICAL CHILD

A five-year-old girl, Mary, has been taken out of her kindergarten class to participate in a psychological experiment. She is seated in front of a table on which two brightly colored necklaces lie side by side; they are of equal length, and their ends are neatly aligned. "Let's pretend that the blue one is yours," the psychologist tells her, "and the red one is mine. Who do you think has the longer necklace, you or me?" Mary slightly puzzled, replies with conviction, "We both do!"—her way of asserting that the two lengths are equal. "That's right, but watch carefully," says the experimenter as she picks up her own necklace and forms a circle out of it. "Now tell me, Mary, whose necklace is longer, or is mine still just as long as yours?" Mary stretches out her arms to illustrate length, and beams: "Mine is longest! You made yours into a ring, and mine is all *this* long."

By Joachim F. Wohlwill

In an experiment which Jean Piaget (below) made famous, children of different ages are shown two identical glasses, each containing an equal amount of lemonade or orange soda. When the lemonade is poured into a tall thin container, the average five-year-old insists there is more lemonade than orange soda; the six-year-old becomes confused; and the seven-year-old knows the meaning of conservation of liquid.

In schools, psychological laboratories, and child-study centers across the country and throughout the world, children are participating in such experiments in our attempts to answer one of the most difficult and puzzling questions about child development: How does the uniquely human capacity for logical thought develop? How does the child's thinking evolve from a pre-logical stage to one defined by the rules of adult logic? Children are being asked questions about lengths, weights, amounts, and numbers, and about space, time, and probability to see if they use a qualitatively different type of reasoning from that used by adults, or if children—naive realists that they are—place undue trust in appearances.

By the time she is six or seven, Mary will know that the length of a string of beads is conserved—that is, its length will not change even if its longness disappears when both ends are joined in a circle. How does she gain the concept of length as a dimension so that she ignores the perceptual cues presented by changes in shape? Does understanding of dimension, class, probability, and the like come from a natural process of maturation or from extensive teaching and experience? A generation ago the child-mind was pictured either as an empty shell that gradually fills with knowledge picked up piece by piece from the environment, or as an adult-mind-in-miniature which grows to its full size as the child develops. Today, many psychologists believe that neither view is correct. Instead, they see a structured mind, internally consistent yet externally illogical—a kind of Alice-in-Wonderland world where lengths, weights, and distances have as much constancy as the shape of "silly putty."

This new picture has aroused widespread and vigorous debate, not only among child psychologists, but also among educators because it raises a host of questions about our understanding of mental processes in general and about child development in particular. Do we develop in specific stages on our way to adult reasoning? Is this development

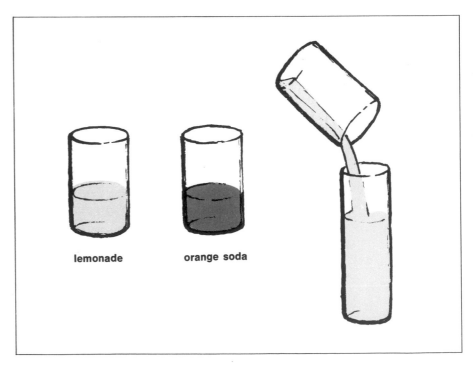

lemonade   orange soda

"pre-set" as is a child's physical growth, or can it be speeded up by teaching and experience? If so, by what methods of teaching and by what kinds of experiences? Since what we call intelligence involves to a large extent conceptual thinking, our inquiry holds important implications for our understanding of this much-debated subject.

Jean Piaget— Explorer of a New World

The current concern with the conceptual world of childhood and with the child's mode of reasoning has been inspired very largely by the work of Jean Piaget at the Institute Jean-Jacques Rousseau in Geneva, Switzerland. During the past 30 years, Piaget and his collaborators have mapped out, step by step and book by book, the dimensions of the curious and fascinating world which exists in the child's mind.

Let us sit in on one of Piaget's experiments. On the table in front of Johnny, a typical five-year-old, are two glasses identical in size and shape. Piaget's glass is half full of orange soda and Johnny's glass is half full of lemonade. Piaget puts a tall, thin glass on the table and pours Johnny's lemonade into it [see illustration, p. 156]. "Now who has more to drink, you or me?" the famous experimenter asks the five-year-old. "I have," Johnny says. "There's more lemonade in mine because it's higher in the glass." The five-year-old is convinced that he has more lemonade in his new glass even when he is asked: "Are you sure it just doesn't look as though there is more?" Piaget points out that his own glass is wider than Johnny's new glass, but the child replies, "Yes, but this one goes way up to here, so there's more." Pointing to the original lemonade container, the experimenter then asks: "Suppose we pour your lemonade back into the glass it came from—then what?" Johnny remains firm: "There would still be more lemonade."

The responses of Lonny, a typical six-year-old, are interestingly different. When the lemonade is poured into the taller, narrower glass and Piaget asks, "Do we both have the same amount to drink?" Lonny, on thinking it over, says, "Well, no." Asked to explain why, he says, "Your glass is bigger." But he becomes confused when the experimenter points out that the new glass is taller: "I guess there's more lemonade in the tall glass." Piaget asks, "Suppose we poured your lemonade back into the glass it came from?" Shades of Alice-in-Wonderland, the answer is, "Then we'd have the same amount to drink."

But now here is Ronny, a year older than Lonny. When the lemonade is poured into the narrow glass, Ronny is sure that there is still the same amount of lemonade as there was before. The conversation goes this way:

"How do you know it is still the same?"

"Well, it was the same before."

"But isn't this new glass higher?"

"Yes, but the old glass is wider."

What do these three tests tell us? Five-year-old Johnny's insistence that there is more to drink in the tall, narrow glass comes from his preoccupation with the most salient fact about the liquids—the difference in their heights. He blithely ignores the difference in the widths of the two glasses. Six-year-old Lonny shows some confusion. He seems to recognize that both the height of the liquid and the width of the glasses must be taken into account, but he can focus only on one aspect of the situation at a time. He recognizes, however, that if the lemonade is poured back into its original container, equality will be restored. But seven-year-old Ronny has no doubts. He *knows* the amount of liquid remains the same because he understands the compensatory relationship between height and width; he understands the concept of conservation of amount.

The Idea of Logical Necessity

Ronny's *understanding* is the critical point for Piaget. It is not merely that Ronny, at seven, can simultaneously perceive both the height and the width of the containers, but also that he can understand the inverse relationship between the two dimensions and can thus recognize that conservation of amount is a logical necessity. Some children may express this recognition without referring to dimensions at all: "You only poured my lemonade into that glass; it's still just as much." Or, "Well, it's the same as it was before; you haven't given me any more lemonade."

The conservation of amount—which Ronny understands at seven—is but one of a set of dimensions for which children acquire the concept of conservation at different ages. The more important of the "conservations" and the ages at which children, on the average, first show understanding of them, are the following:

Conservation of number (6-7 years): The number of elements in a collection remains unchanged, regardless of how the elements are displaced or spatially rearranged.

Conservation of substance (7-8 years): The amount of a deformable substance such as dough, soft clay, or liquid remains unchanged, regardless of how its shape is altered (as in transforming a ball of clay into a long, narrow snake).

Conservation of length (7-8 years): The length of a line or an object remains unchanged, regardless of how it is displaced in space or its shape altered.

Conservation of area (8-9 years): The total amount of surface covered by a set of plane figures (such as small squares) remains unchanged, in spite of rearranging positions of the figures.

Conservation of weight (9-10 years): The weight of an object remains unchanged, regardless of how its shape is altered.

Conservation of volume (14-15 years): The volume of an object (in terms of the water it displaces) remains unchanged, regardless of changes in its shape.

It must be emphasized that the ages given above are only gross averages; first, because children vary considerably in the rate at which their thinking develops, and second, because their recognition of the concept depends to a certain extent on the way the problem is presented. For example, children may recognize that the number of checkers in a row remains unchanged when the length of the row is expanded, but fail to recognize it when the checkers are stacked in a pile.

The Stage of Concrete Operations

The responses of young children to tests such as those I have described give us a fascinating glimpse into processes which we, as adults, take so much for granted that they scarcely seem to involve thinking at all. But what is the significance of the conservation problem for an understanding of mental development? Piaget holds that the attainment of conservation points to the formation of a new stage in the child's mental development, the stage of concrete operations. This stage is manifested by conservation, and in a variety of other ways which attest to a new mode of reasoning.

For example, if children who have not yet reached the stage of concrete operations are presented with a set of pictures [see illustration, right] comprised of seven dogs and three horses, and are asked, "How many animals are there?" they will readily answer, "Ten." They are quite able to recognize that both the subsets—dogs and horses—are part of a total set—animals. But if asked, "Are there more dogs or more animals?" these "pre-operational" children will maintain there are more dogs. They translate the question into one involving a comparison of majority to minority subsets and have difficulty in comparing the elements of a single subset with those of the total set.

For Piaget this indicates that these children as yet lack mental structure corresponding to the logical operation of adding classes—or to use modern jargon, they are not "programmed" to carry out this operation.

The various manifestations of the stage of concrete operations do not necessarily appear at the same time. As we saw, concepts of conservation are attained for various dimensions at different age levels, and one concept may consistently lag behind another closely related concept. Suppose we present a child with two balls of modeling clay, identical in appearance and weight. Let us flatten one of the balls and roll it out into the form of a sausage. Now we will ask the conservation question for two different dimensions, substance—"Is there still as much clay in the ball as in the sausage?"—and weight—"Does the ball still weigh as much as the sausage?" The same child often will give opposite answers to these questions, and in such cases the child almost invariably asserts conservation for substance while denying it for weight. Thus it appears that the mode of reasoning involved in recognizing conservation of substance precedes that for weight.

The Young Child: Pre-Logical or Merely Naive?

Piaget holds, first, that these phenomena represent qualitative developmental changes in the child's mode of thinking; and second, that they are largely spontaneous and occur independently of teaching or of specific experiences. His views have aroused controversy as vigorous and at times as heated as did the views of Freud. Piaget's descriptions of the phenomena themselves—the diverse ways in which children respond to conceptual tasks—have been on the whole verified and accepted as essentially correct. The controversy rages over the explanation for them. Can the young child's lack of conservation be explained as resulting from a qualitatively different mode of reasoning, characteristic of the pre-operational stage? Or is it merely the result of a naive trust in perceptual cues, combined with a strong tendency to respond to the most obvious, or perceptually salient, aspect of a situation?

For example, the sight of liquid rising in a narrow glass to a height well above that of the shorter, wider glass from which it came conveys a compelling impression of difference in quantity. It is easy to lose sight of the compensating difference in the width of the two glasses. Moreover, in the child's every-day life, glasses tend to be fairly similar in size; thus the height of liquid in a glass is a reasonably reliable index to its amount. There is indeed some evidence to support "naiveté" as an explanation. Studies carried out at Harvard suggest that children who initially lack the notion of conservation can recognize it if the misleading perceptual cues are screened out—that is, if the child cannot see the level of liquid as it is poured into the new container. It must be said, however, that other investigators who replicated this experiment did not obtain similar results.

Martin Braine of Walter Reed Medical Center conducted experiments using the ring-segmented illusion [see illustration, right] which showed that children can learn to resist perceptual cues when they are induced to differentiate between appearance and fact. Two shapes, A and B, are first superimposed so that the child can see that B is bigger. A is then placed above B; the child now will assert that A both looks bigger and really is bigger. As a result of a series of such problems in which the experimenter corrects all erroneous responses, the child will learn to pick B as really bigger than A, in the face of the contrary evidence of the senses.

These experiments suggest that the child is inclined to respond naively to perceptual clues, but is this really the whole truth? In collaboration with a student, Michael Katz, I recently carried out the following experiment on the class-inclusion (set-subset) problem described earlier. Instead of presenting pictures of animals, we asked five- and six-year-old children, "Suppose that on a farm there are seven dogs and three horses. Are there more dogs or more animals?" Lo and behold, when the problem was presented in purely verbal form, avoiding perceptual cues, many of the children did consistently better than they did when asked to solve the problem on the basis of pictures [see illustration, right].

On the face of it, this finding is the reverse of what might be expected. It is generally considered that at this age

Top illustration: When children are shown a picture containing seven dogs and three horses, and then asked whether there are more dogs or animals, "pre-operational" children maintain there are more dogs. However, when asked the same question in purely verbal form—without visual "aids"—many of these same children do considerably better.

Bottom illustration: In the ring-segmented illusion—in which segment B is really larger than segment A—children gradually learn to resist perceptual cues when they are induced to differentiate between appearance and fact.

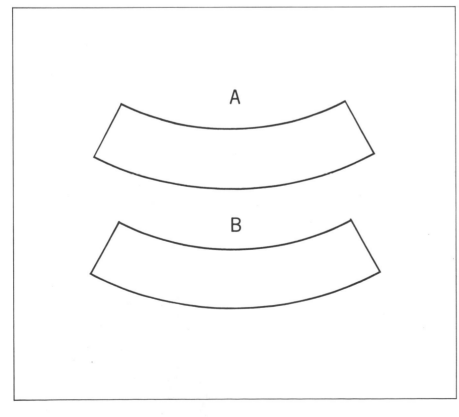

children's thinking is highly concrete, making it difficult for them to deal with purely hypothetical situations. However, it may be that the children did better when the problem was presented verbally because the pictures offered perceptual cues which strongly impelled the children to compare the two subsets. This explanation is in line with the view that children have difficulty with such tasks not because their reasoning is faulty but simply because they focus on the compelling aspects of appearance.

Nevertheless, further data uncovered in our studies seem to show that the interpretation is at best a gross oversimplification of the situation. When we tabulated the results for each child and compared scores on the verbal and the picture tests, we found the following: Among the large number of children who did not give any correct answers at all on the picture test, almost half also failed to give any correct answers in the verbal test. But of those who did give at least one correct answer to the picture test, 90 percent scored higher on the verbal test.

Eliminating the perceptual factor did *not* guarantee that a child could relate the subsets to the total set. These children seemed quite incapable of recognizing that an object can belong to two classes at once. Improved performance on the verbal test seems to indicate that there is an intermediary phase in the establishment of the class-inclusion concept. During this phase the perceptual cues are still dominant enough to bias the child's recognition of the concept.

Moreover, it is difficult to interpret the results of Piaget's experiment with the two balls of clay on the basis of perceptual cues alone. Why should the change in shape from sphere to sausage, with length becoming salient, bias the child toward thinking that the *weight* has changed and yet not bias the same child with respect to the *amount of substance?* The question becomes even more significant when we ask ourselves why one concept precedes another.

If we assume that conservation concepts are acquired primarily through

experience, we would be led to the conclusion that weight-conservation should be acquired first. The weight of an object, or more particularly the difference in weight between two objects, can be verified directly by weighing an object in one's hand; experiencing differences in the weight of objects begins in infancy. On the other hand, how does one *know* that amount-of-substance is conserved with change in shape? Yet the child recognizes that this "unexperienced" abstraction, "amount of clay," is conserved and does so well before he agrees that the readily-defined, often-experienced entity, *weight*, is conserved.

Conceptual Development— Taught or Spontaneous?

The problems just discussed raise a more general question. Let us return to the types of reasoning displayed by Johnny, Lonny, and Ronny. I did not choose these names just to create a nursery-rhyme effect; I intended to suggest that the three boys could very well have been the same child at five, six, and seven years old. For, in the normal course of events, we expect Johnny to come to think as Lonny did, and Lonny, as he matures, to reason as Ronny did. Yet these changes usually occur spontaneously. In the course of play activities and everyday experience, children pour liquid from one container to another, roll balls of modeling clay into snakes, form rings with strings of beads. But five- and six-year-olds rarely ask themselves questions—or are asked questions by others—which lead them to ponder about things like the conservation of length. They are even less likely to be given direct information about such questions involving conservation.

Somehow, therefore, these logical notions must be acquired indirectly, by the back door, as it were. The question is, where *is* the back door? If we assume that these seemingly spontaneous changes in mode of thinking do not occur in a vacuum, what sorts of experiences or activities can we postulate that may mediate them? What facets of his experience play a role in the child's ac-

quisition of logical principles? It is this question which has been the subject of a great deal of concentrated discussion and research the world over.

Can such rules be taught before the child has discovered them for himself? A great deal of ingenuity has been expended to devise approaches aimed at teaching children "the logical facts of life," especially the conservations. Many such attempts have met with indifferent success, although recent studies have been more encouraging. Nevertheless, even where the zealous psychologist has succeeded in demonstrating the beneficial effect of this or that type of training, the results have been quite limited. That is, the learning has rarely been shown to have much transfer, even to similar concepts or tasks.

There is a real question, then, whether such restricted, short-term training offers sufficient conditions for establishing the basic rules of thought which, according to Piaget, are "of the essence" in the child's mental development. At least equally important, however, is the question—do such experiences represent *necessary* conditions for the development of logical thought?

If we look at what children actually do during the years in which changes in their mode of thinking take place, the answers to our questions may not be quite so difficult to find. For example, children do gain considerable experience in counting objects and so it does not seem unreasonable to suggest that the child comes to realize—quite implicitly—that *number* is a dimension, totally independent of the perceptual aspects of a situation. But doesn't this directly contradict the suggestion that such concepts are not established through knowledge gained from experience? What I am suggesting is this: Through his experience in measuring, counting, and the like, the child may develop a *conceptual attitude* toward dimension in general. Then, confronted with a conservation-type question, he is able to ignore the perceptual cues which had previously been predominant, and can respond only to those aspects which, as a result of

his experience, have now become dominant. Thus for Johnny, at five, the situation was dominated by a single perceptual cue—height of liquid in the glass. By the time he is seven, Ronny has, one might say, become an operationist; his concept of quantity is determined by the criteria he utilizes in measuring—for instance, as with the number of glasses of equal size that could be filled with the contents of a jar.

Ronny has developed a concept of quantity, furthermore, which may be of sufficient generality to encompass related dimensions that cannot be directly measured. This is particularly true if the dimension that is difficult to measure—for example, amount-of-substance—is assimilated to one that is easily measured —for example, quantity-of-liquid. Indeed, conservation for substance and liquid do appear at about the same time! It is interesting to note that the conservation-promoting attitude can go astray by dint of overgeneralization—a square and a circle made from the same piece of string do not have the same areas, counter to what even many adults assume.

Counting, Measuring, Ordering, Classifying

This interpretation of the way young children form logical concepts suggests that we may better understand their development by looking at activities such as counting and measuring and ordering or seriating, for these are clearly relevant to concepts of quantitative attributes like weight, length, area, and the like. In a similar vein, classifying or sorting are relevant to understanding class and subclass relationships.

Counting, measuring, sorting, and the like are usually part of children's spontaneous, unprogrammed, everyday experience along with the more formal instruction they may receive in school. In research currently under way at Clark University, we are focusing on an intensive study of these activities and on their possible relationships to concepts like conservation and class-inclusion.

For instance, we want to see the extent to which children will arrange spontaneously a set of stimuli according to some plan or order. Children are offered a set of nine blocks with different pictures on each face representing six classes of pictured objects—houses, birds, flowers, vehicles, stars, and dolls. Each class is subdivided according to size, color, and type; for example, there are three kinds of flowers, each pictured in one of three colors. The child is given a board divided into nine compartments, in a 3 × 3 layout, into which he can place the blocks in whatever way he thinks they should go, though he is asked to do so in successively different ways. [*See illustration, page 163.*]

We are interested in seeing how many categories the child constructs and how much internal order is displayed in each arrangement. In addition, we want to see how actively and systematically he handles the blocks (for example, in searching for a particular face). Not surprisingly, there is a close relationship between the two aspects of a child's performance: Children who receive high scores for recognition of categories and internal order generally go about their task in a much more systematic manner and manipulate the blocks more actively than the low scorers.

A perfectly consistent arrangement, showing three rows and three columns filled with pictures belonging to the same category, would earn a score of six. The five- to seven-year-olds we have studied thus far tend to be relatively unsystematic in their handling of the blocks, and lacking in consistency and order. On any one trial the median number of rows or columns filled with pictures in the same category is only 0.6. In one study carried out with a group of lower-class children from a day-care center, we found, however, that their scores could be substantially raised by intensive experience in responding to dimensions of order and to relationships of identity and difference in a set of stimuli.

Thus far, we have not found an unequivocal correlation between these measures of block-sorting behavior and conservation. However, we did find that

of those children who were very poor in ordering the blocks, only 25 percent showed number conservation. Whereas among the children who did somewhat better at ordering the blocks, 64 percent did show number conservation. The relation between block-sorting scores and performance on the class-inclusion task is much closer, as would be expected, since the two tasks are similar.

In other experiments we looked at children's approach to comparing and

measuring lengths, heights, and distances. In general, almost no kindergartners and few first-graders showed awareness of the function of a unit of distance or a reference object. They failed to make use of a plastic ruler to measure distance. In many instances they did not even think of placing two objects side by side to see which was longer. In other words, since they had as yet no real understanding of length as a dimension, it is not surprising that many lacked conservation.

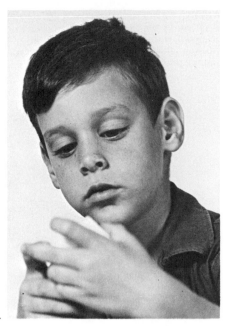
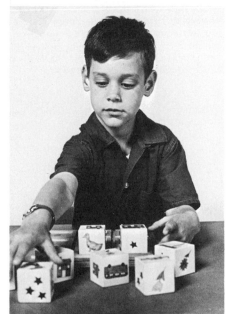

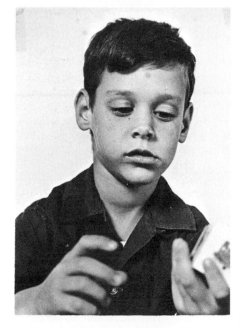

When faced with the set of dowels at the left, most children place the dowels of varying lengths into the constant-size holes in the base—and form an ordered pattern of decreasing heights. However, when faced with the set of dowels on the right in which both the lengths of the dowels and the depths of the holes vary, most children become confused—and cannot produce either of the two ordered arrangements shown.

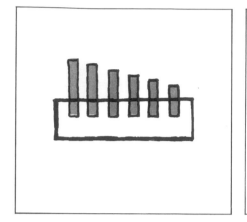

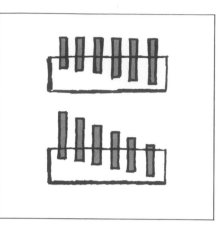

Other interesting insights were provided by experiments with the dowel-board [*see illustration, at left*]. When children are given a set of red dowels of different lengths and asked to put them any way they like into the holes of the accompanying wooden base, a majority come up with an ordered series. They are then given an identical set of blue dowels, but the holes in the accompanying base vary in depth, matching the variations in the lengths of the dowels. Thus, if they like, the children can arrange the blue dowels in a series identical to that of the red dowels or, by matching the lengths of the dowels with the depth of the holes, they can produce a series of equal height. Many children find this "problem" highly puzzling. Their behavior often becomes so disorganized and erratic that they produce no sort of order whatsoever. Of the 35 children we tested, 25 were unsuccessful. Again, comparing this kind of ordering ability with conservation-of-number ability, we found that, of the 25 unsuccessful children, 16 lacked number conservation, whereas among the 10 successful children, only 2 lacked conservation of number.

Though our research is still in its early stages, the results thus far obtained encourage us to believe that our approach may help solve the mystery of the prelogical child, and tell us something about how the conservations and other concepts manifested in the stage of concrete operations come into existence.

Our finding that children's scores could be raised by intensive experience suggests a profitable focus for instruction in the primary grades, where little attention is generally given to cultivating the child's measuring and classifying skills. Our guess is that concerted efforts to encourage and guide children's activities in this area might well pay handsome dividends. Beyond merely speeding the development of the skills themselves, an imaginative approach should provide children with a sounder, more broadly based foundation on which subsequent learning of mathematical and scientific concepts can be built.

Can We Teach Personal Morality?
Can We Train the Human Conscience?

And Can We Free the Human Spirit?

Moral Behavior: A Functional Analysis

By Israel Goldiamond

WHEN WE SPEAK OF SOMEONE as following the dictates of his conscience, making a moral decision, we are usually speaking of a puzzling relation between behavior and its consequences. For example, a young man is captured by the enemy, who demand that he betray his fellows. If he gives in, he will be rewarded handsomely. If he does not, he may be tortured or killed. Yet he does not inform. Because he chooses torture over reward, we consider his behavior moral, and we respect him. Even if he is a criminal shielding his accomplices, we may respect him, grudgingly.

In milder form, this kind of nonordinary correspondence between behavior and its consequences is frequent enough to be designated by specific names, such as moral decisions, conscience, altruism, loyalty. We often admire such action, possibly because the cohesiveness of society to a large extent rests upon its occurrence, and possibly because there is something special about it, namely, it violates the customary relation between behavior and its overt consequence.

Violation of this relation is not confined to choice of punishment over reward. The scientist who persists dog-

165

gedly at his task despite failure after failure exemplifies what would be called, in laboratory terms, the persistence of nonreinforced behavior, or the persistence of behavior in the face of extinction. In common-sense terms, we speak of this relation as indicating determination, will power or strength of character—traits which are not, of course, limited to scientists. There are yet other cases where it is so difficult to specify the overt consequences that we talk of self-satisfaction and inner-direction, as when we solve a puzzle for the sake of solving it.

At times such behavior is called irrational. We can imagine a soldier's captors urging the prisoner to behave sensibly, or reasonably, by revealing what he knows. The captors are not being strictly opportunistic when they use such terms to gain compliance, since a common definition of rational behavior involves weighing the consequences according to some decision rule.

When we talk of conscience, or morality, we usually are speaking of behavior in anomalous relation to its overt consequences. The anomaly is posed by our expectations which are based on common sense and on such systematized relations of consequences to behavior as classical economics and behaviorist learning theories.

It is becoming increasingly possible to develop operant programs for behaviors which are relevant to human social problems. Since these procedures require systematic use of consequences, to what extent are they relevant to moral outcomes which are related to consequences in an anomalous way?

Laboratory Expectations

Operant behavior may be loosely defined as behavior whose rate or form is governed by its (overt) consequences. The behaviors which concern decision theory are, accordingly, operants. In operant laboratories, one or more behaviors are chosen for measurement, and events which are of consequence to the organism are made *contingent* on these behaviors. With these methods, it has been possible to maintain selected behavior for extended periods of time.

At first glance, it is difficult to conceive of such anomalous goals in the experimental animal laboratory. If a rat has a choice between two levers, and pressing the one will bring him food, while pressing the other will bring a brief, intense electric shock, we would regard it as unusual if the rat chose shock and spurned the food.

If humans sometimes act otherwise, it may be argued that laboratory procedures are irrelevant to human behavior described as dictated by conscience. It might be stated that, yes, we may be able to utilize operant technology to program arithmetic and reading, and possibly even to eliminate problems such as stuttering. But when it comes to conscience, morality, altruism and regard for others, behaviorism falls short. These behaviors—which make us human—cannot be related to a system of overt and manipulatable consequences.

Rather than adopting this sweeping negation, we might state that consequences *do* enter into the outcomes discussed, but that they are *internalized.* On an intuitive level, we avoid guilt-feelings and remorse by behaving appropriately, and, indeed, conscience makes cowards of us all by suppressing those behaviors that would lead to internal punishment. The captive who would not betray his colleagues has set up an internal psychological economy in which the loss of his life is outweighed by the lives of his colleagues.

Psychoanalytic theory separates the internal psychological economy governed by the avoidance of anxiety or attainment of gratification from the consequences described as *secondary gain,* which may be external. A neurotic symptom (behavior) may be maintained by the secondary gain (explicit reinforcement) of social control it produces. The symptom may, however, be a defense against certain disastrous internalized consequences. The development of the superego may be partly considered as internalization of external relations.

Such internalized concepts have been extended to explain nonordinary behavior in laboratory animals. The pigeon who pecks continually under extinction, after working on an intermittent schedule, is considered by some theorists to be maintained by hope. Eventually, the reality principle takes over and the hope is replaced by despair. He extinguishes.

Observable conditions that are explained by internalization seem, like human conscience, to be marked by nonordinary relations between behavior and its consequences. However, it is becoming increasingly possible to state the conditions under which they occur and can be programmed. They can be categorized under three major headings: alternate contingencies and consequences; behavioral consequences; and programming variables.

Decision theory has been used to ration-

alize many of the problems of classical psychophysics through signal detection. In research involving decision theory, the organism makes either of two responses. A person may, for example, buy a stock or a bond. Either purchase may result in gain or loss. For given market conditions a pattern of purchases may be stipulated which optimizes net income or follows some other decision rule.

In our laboratory we have flashed on a screen rectangles analogous to market conditions of ambiguous sizes to observers. The rectangles we call Small (stocks) vary in size around a small mean size, and the rectangles we call Large (bonds) vary in size around a larger one.

In the training program, a single rectangle is presented each time. The observer is taught to press a button or lever on the left when a small rectangle appears and a button or lever on the right when a large rectangle appears. The distributions then overlap: a rectangle from the large end of the small series will be larger than one from the small end of the large series, but we will treat it as Small, regardless of its objective size. The situation is similar to that created by a single radar blip which cannot be distinguished as either a Russian or an American plane. A discriminative response, a decision, must be made and the decision will have consequences. If the observer calls it Large (by responding in the right) the response is considered a False Alarm and is penalized. Different consequences are attached to all four possible combinations of responses Large and Small to the rectangles so classified.

Decision theory specifies a criterion (a pattern of behavior whereby the organism tends to respond Large to any rectangle over a given size). A variety of boundaries or criteria between Small and Large is possible, and in each the net from profits and losses will differ. As we shift the overlap between small and large distributions and change the payoffs, our observers shift their criteria, continuing to optimize net gain.

The subjects in our experiments were humans working for money — and baboons and patis monkeys who worked for food pellets obtained only during Hits responding right to Large. A False Alarm made the apparatus inoperative (time out) for as long as 120 seconds, resulting in varying delays of the opportunity to earn further reinforcement.

Any criteria set when distributions overlap will produce Hits, but also errors. Our observers suffered long runs of such losses, *produced by their own behavior,* but these were more than counterbalanced by the long-term gains. Indeed, this same argument of long-term gains often is raised in support of moral behavior. The point is that we were able to program such behavior for laboratory monkeys by manipulating the program of reinforcement.

Avoidance Behavior

Another relevant behavioral pattern is called Sidman Avoidance. A timer may deliver a shock every five seconds. Pressing the bar postpones the shock 15 seconds. By responding at least once every 14 seconds, shock is completely avoided. Perfect avoidance is maintained over extended periods.

Complex internalized explanations have been proposed to explain such behavior when there is no environmental change. One explanation is that anxiety builds up as the time for shock approaches. A response at that time, since no shock follows, terminates the inner anxiety and reinforces the behavior, exactly as when a response ends a shock.

A very simple explanation emerges when we examine possible alternatives. If the person or animal in the experiment does not respond, he will get shocked. If he responds, there is no shock. Hence, he responds.

To assess the extent to which alternatives rather than anxiety control behavior, we might substitute consequences not related to anxiety, such as presentation of positive reinforcement, for the electric shock. In our laboratory, Donald M. Thompson is doing precisely this. Food is automatically presented every 15 seconds to a pigeon. When he pecks a disc, he postpones its delivery for five seconds, that is, obtains food five seconds later. If he waits 14 seconds and then responds, the food will have been delivered 19 seconds after the last delivery. Accordingly, he waits for delivery, then responds, gets food five seconds later, responds again, and so on. The animal learns in accord with this schedule, exactly as does the shocked animal. In this case, the pigeon maximizes reinforcement frequency, and in the avoidance case, he minimizes shock frequency. No special explanation is required to the effect that internalized escape from anxiety is being built up. Alternatives may also explain some choice of punishment, as Nathan H. Azrin and his colleagues at Ama State Hospital have demonstrated. When they shocked a pigeon every time it pecked, pecking increased. But when punishment was absent, pecking stopped. Such behavior appears masochistic. The explanation is that when shock followed each response, food was also sometimes delivered. When shock was absent, there was no food.

A second key was then made available which provided food without shock. The pigeon switched pecking to this key. If undergoing punishment is the only way to obtain reinforcement, then the animal or a human being may set up the conditions for punishment. If there is an alternative of reinforcement, a better way, without punishment, he will choose that instead.

It has been argued, in the human case, that the patient in therapy desires to maintain the disturbing behavior, but wants to shed the punishing consequences attached. Our observations suggest that reformulation is required. The disturbing behavior is punished, hence the request for treatment. The suggestion for treatment is to identify, from the disturbing behavior, the maintaining consequence, and make the consequence depend on desirable behavior.

In other words, disturbing or "emotional" behavior may not be irrational. One four-year-old, who could complete a fluent sentence in five seconds, took as long as 20 seconds when he stuttered. His parents, by scrupulously behaving in exactly the same attentive manner whether he stuttered or not, actually reinforced his stuttering. Operant analysis suggested that the stuttering was a means for getting attention. If his parents attempted to extinguish the response by not reinforcing it, another symptom might be substituted. Instead, the parents were urged to continue reinforcing stuttering with attention, but to supply massive reinforcement whenever the child spoke fluently. Within three weeks he was totally fluent.

Results from research on alternate contingencies and consequences pose problems for an analysis in terms of overt consequences if one defines reinforcement only in terms of presentations (or withdrawals) immediately following the response. Implicit acceptance of this narrow equation may have driven reinforcement underground, or, rather, underskin. A broader definition of consequences accounts for the data, and preserves their observable, and therefore, manipulatable, nature. As we shall see, yet another restriction supports internalization.

When a rat runs an exercise wheel, where is the reinforcing stimulus? When the child works on a puzzle for the fun of it, the same question may be raised. And being virtuous for its own sake, rather than for external blandishments, is a test of moral upbringing, as is resistance to temptation. In such cases, there has been discussion of *intrinsic* reinforcement, or *autonomous* behavior or *autotelic* behavior. There have been numerous attempts to reformulate these terms into stimulus-response links and chains. These attempted reformulations, as well as frankly internalized terms, may rest upon the equation of consequential events with consequential stimuli.

Behavior as a Consequence

Research by David Premack of the University of California, Santa Barbara, has led to formulation of the principle bearing his name. One form of the principle states that given two *behaviors* with differing probabilities of occurrence, the high probability behavior may be used to reinforce the low probability behavior if it is made contingent upon it. In one experiment, for example, a rat only occasionally pressed a lever (no food was attached) but he often operated a running wheel. The running wheel was now made operative for only a short period of time; pressing the lever released the brake. Lever pressing increased, exactly as it does when it is rewarded with food.

The Premack principle is not a trivial restatement. It rests on a procedural and functional definition of scientific terms. If identical behavior results when we (a) manipulate the presentation of a stimulus (which defines it as a reinforcing event), and when we (b) similarly manipulate the opportunity to behave, then the opportunity may also be defined as a reinforcing event. If I withdraw the opportunity to work on a puzzle from a child, and require specified behaviors to produce this opportunity, and the behaviors then increase as they do with similar manipulations of food for pigeons, then the scientific status of the two consequential procedures is identical, and both are reinforcers.

The Premack principle has tremendous practical implications. It suggests that by observing anyone's behavior carefully we may discover what his reinforcers are. These may be the behaviors which he often persistently engages in, and are to be distinguished from high frequency behavior which produces punishment as well as reinforcement, such as stuttering and other disturbing behaviors. The engineering problem is to make the behavioral reinforcers depend upon the behaviors we want the organism to emit.

There is a further implication. All the procedures developed in the laboratory to transfer reinforcing properties from one stimulus to another, to maintain their effects over extended periods of time, and to schedule them, may now be used for behavioral reinforcers. Behaviors which seem to be goals in and of themselves can be used as reinforcers to increase and maintain other behaviors.

The Program as a Variable

If we establish a behavioral pattern by reinforcing each occurrence, as we typically do, and then arrange it so that long periods of behavior are not reinforced, the behavior may extinguish. If, however, we gradually program toward this goal, we can maintain control; Jack Findley of the Institute for Behavioral Research was able to maintain behavior when 20,000 responses were required for reinforcement. When the periods between presentations of reinforcement vary, and we decide to extinguish, behavior will persist for extraordinary periods of time. This persistence creates a theoretical puzzle by the narrow definition of reinforcement as a separate event attached to behavior (where is the reinforcement?), and solves the puzzle by internalizing the reinforcement. We would say the pigeon is hopeful or expects reinforcement. When he finally extinguishes, despair has overcome him.

We can, however, explain the behavior on the basis of the schedule and the program used to control it. This explanation is not limited to the hopeful pigeons. On the contrary, it is a statement of tremendous generality. It holds for a variety of species, for a variety of behaviors, and for a variety of different reinforcers. Such resistance to extinction will characterize the behavior of almost any organism programmed toward such an intermittent schedule. Since a scientific explanation describes a functional relation and the conditions under which it holds, we have provided a very explicit explanation which encompasses a variety of findings by stating that the behavior is a function of the program used.

We might state that the pigeon who persists in a task despite the absence of payoff is stubborn or stupid (the snarl words) or has character (the purr word for the same data). Indeed when a person persists despite frustration (which is one of the nontechnical terms for extinction) and despite defeats, we state that he doesn't know when he's been licked, or that he has character, depending on our relation to him. The programming of intermittent reinforcement suggests to us how we can establish character.

Practically every behavior of the Cub Scout is reinforced. Requirements for merit badges are gradually increased, to the prodigious feats required of Eagle Scouts. The scouting movement builds character.

From the learner's viewpoint, we are speaking of his past history. From the investigator's viewpoint, we are speaking of a *program* used to alter the learner's repertoire, and the program itself is a critical variable.

A dimension along which we may consider the programming variable is the probability of built-in error. This may range all the way from a high probability to almost zero.

Typically, in the laboratory, we establish a new behavior or a new discrimination by reinforcing the correct response and by not reinforcing the incorrect response. Errors are so characteristic of this trial-and-error procedure that the number of errors or number of trials needed to establish the response (which often is saying the same) is used as a measure of learning.

It has been argued that error is indispensable for learning, for it supplies the necessary information and knowledge of results. However, errorless programming procedures systematically investigated by Herbert S. Terrace of Columbia University have questioned this statement. It is possible to train in complex discriminations in such a manner that the trainee never makes a mistake. The program capitalizes upon current strengths by requiring behavior under very similar conditions. The requirements are changed gradually so that we finally wind up with a totally different repertoire, produced in small steps, each within the organism's grasp.

While it is possible to establish identical end-discriminations by either trial-and-error or errorless programming, other factors may indicate the superiority of one method of programming over another in some instances.

A child who has been trained to swim by throwing him into a deep lake, pulling him out as he goes under and dunking him again, may learn to swim as well as a child gradually introduced to water

in current swimming instruction programs. But children taught by the two methods are likely to have very different responses and other behaviors associated with swimming.

Errorless procedures have been used to program a variety of behaviors with humans in both individual and social settings. The learning in these situations occurs without the frustrations and emotional concomitants of extinction.

In the laboratory, given an identical discrimination, say choosing yellow instead of green, which is produced by trial-and-error learning or by errorless programming, there will be differences in the generalization gradients when other colors are presented, as well as other differences. Ensuing behavior, as well as the possibility of learning in some cases, become functions not only of the task, but of the program, that is, how the task was taught. Theoretically, the question that errorless programming raises is the generality of learning formulations derived from investigations characterized by error during acquisition. The formulations may be quite valid for the value of the programming dimension represented by error. The extent to which the formulations extend to the value represented by errorless programming, remains to be seen.

A Better Way to Morality

The substitution of errorless programming for trial-and-error learning may be considered part of a social trend which has gradually seen the substitution of reinforcement procedures for aversive control. It is only recently that slavery has been abolished. As Harvard's B. F. Skinner has pointed out, a wage society has substituted the maintenance of work through positive reinforcement for the slave society's maintenance of work through the negative reinforcement of avoiding the lash, and there is no question as to which is the more productive. It requires far more ingenuity to maintain and alter behavior through continual reinforcement than through extinction and aversive control.

Our discussion has centered around procedures which can be used to establish and maintain the behavioral relations with subtle consequences which define our use of terms such as conscience, morality, altruism and character. If we can explicitly define these relations, we may be able to start developing programs in which such behavioral relations are our objectives. We would start with the current repertoire of the organism, and step by step reinforce approximations, explicitly specified, in the desired direction. By changing the program where it does not work, we might learn what is involved in the establishment of conscience, and how to develop programs toward this end, like other programmed courses now available. Training takes place at present, of course, but the programs may be implicit, may contain irrelevant and unsuccessful items, and often employ aversive control. Rather than exhort or punish, we might try to train effectively.

The possibility of errorless programming of such terminal repertoires, and the probability that much of our programming to date, whether explicit or haphazard (called development of morality), has involved errors, extinction and aversive control, raise some interesting questions.

Certainly, much of the training involved in teaching a child to respond to the dictates of conscience and teaching him to internalize outer effects, known as the development of the superego, rests to a large extent upon the use of punishment or its threat, and it is this that may have been picked up by psychoanalysts and systematized around castration anxieties. A task that therapists often face in the case of a person unable to live existentially (that is, respond to immediately available as well as to postponed consequences) and to respond fully to his environment is to release him from such crippling bonds of the superego. The crippling bonds have been regarded as a necessary accompaniment of training processes. It may very well be that these bonds are connected, not with the training process itself, but with the use of extinction and aversive control in the establishment of the behavior-consequence relations we call conscience.

Laboratory research in behavior analysis suggests that we might turn our attention to the possibility of establishing moral and other discriminations without extinction and aversive control, by using errorless procedures that provide continual reinforcement. It may thereby be possible to program behavioral relations with the environment which are dictated by conscience, which are moral, and which are altruistic, but at the same time are spontaneous, existential and free, since they have been programmed without fear or threat. ∩

Understanding Children's Art

By Rhoda Kellogg

DURING the last hundred years, there has been increasing interest in children's drawings and paintings. Adults flock to gallery or museum shows of children's art, delighting in its freshness and originality and in the glimpse it offers of the child's world. Moreover, ever since Freud drew attention to the ways by which repressed psychological material is overtly expressed, psychologists have used children's drawings as a means of understanding child development in general, and the problems of individual disturbed children. And for many years

the ability of the child to copy simple forms or to "draw a man" has been widely used as a test of intelligence for preschool children.

My study of children's art began more than 20 years ago, primarily out of a desire to understand very young children, my favorite people. I had already read many books on psychoanalysis, among them the works of Carl Jung who believed that mandalas, or designs based on a crossed circle, were of great human and psychological significance. When I first noticed that three-year-olds were drawing crossed circles, my interest in child art was intensified and I wanted to know what kinds of drawings preceded the crossed circle, and what kinds followed it. Thereafter, no scribblings made in the Golden Gate Nursery Schools, which I direct, landed in the wastebasket; each child's dated drawings were filed, and I began to sort a few hundred scribblings into look-alike groups.

Since then, I have seen more than a million pieces of children's art, half

produced by children below the age of six and the rest by grade-school children. About a third of these works are now housed as the Rhoda Kellogg Child Art Collection at the Phoebe A. Hearst Pre-School Learning Center in San Francisco, and the rest are still in storage elsewhere. More works by some 300 children between the ages of two and 12 who attend the nursery school, or the child art classes at the Center, are being collected.

To most people, "child art" calls to mind the stick figures which children draw as representations of people. Contrary to popular belief, however, the stick man is not a spontaneous product of child art. It is a figure children learn after the age of five from adults or from other children. Because there are such important differences between the work done by pre-schoolers and that done later, I call the former *self-taught child art*. This article will emphasize the early art which children under six teach themselves before adults start showing them "how to draw."

For generations, adults have viewed children's scribblings as no more than the natural products of random motor activity. Most adults rate a child's

drawing according to how well it represents a person or a familiar object. This representational approach has prevented adults from appreciating the wealth of structured, non-pictorial work which children teach themselves to produce before they begin to pictorialize.

Because most adults consider the ability to draw representationally to be an exceptional talent possessed by only a few individuals, and because almost every child possesses the capacity for scribbling, it is very difficult for us as adults to see that early scribblings can be valuable documents for understanding the origins of art. Some parents may save their children's pictorial drawings, but few save their children's scribblings. From my recent analysis of these non-pictorial, early works produced before age three, I have concluded that early scribblings are essential to understanding all forms of graphic art as well as child art.

As I studied the self-taught art work of children from all over the world, the main sequential stages of child development in art became evident. In 1955 I reported my findings for the work of three- and four-year-olds in a book, *What Children Scribble and Why*. Not until 1965, however, did I understand

the work of two-year-olds; therefore the *why* of scribbling is much better explained in my new book, *Analyzing Children's Art*, which will be published this year.

At this point you may ask: By what criteria can the term "art" be applied to the scribblings of two-year-olds? I answer that graphic art of whatever kind is produced by the human hand moving over a surface with a marking instrument. Any number of descriptive labels can be applied to these markings—scribblings, designs, gestalts, motifs, charts, symbols, signs, compositions, abstractions, representations, or pictures. The label depends upon who does the labeling and in what context the work is viewed.

Basic Scribbles

Every form of graphic art, no matter how complex, contains all the lines found in children's work, which I call the 20 *Basic Scribbles*: vertical, horizontal, diagonal, circular, curving, waving or zig-zag lines, and dots. Basic Scribbles can be made whether or not the eye controls the movement of the hand, for

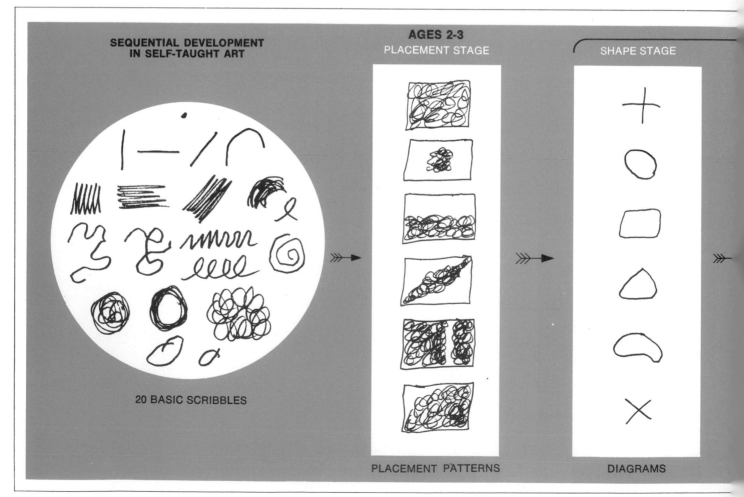

SEQUENTIAL DEVELOPMENT IN SELF-TAUGHT ART

20 BASIC SCRIBBLES

AGES 2-3

PLACEMENT STAGE

PLACEMENT PATTERNS

SHAPE STAGE

DIAGRAMS

scribbles are the product of a variety of directional muscular movements which human beings make even before the age of two. Basic Scribbles are not learned from adults—they are spontaneous human "events" which take place when a finger or marking instrument moves over a surface and leaves a record of the movement. Not until I had studied child art for many years did I realize that though these early scribblings are visually meaningless to adults, they are visually significant to the child who makes them.

The Basic Scribbles are the building blocks out of which all graphic art, pictorial and non-pictorial, is constructed. And when the child looks at his scribblings, he sees them as visual wholes or entities.

Before young children can draw the figures called a "man," a "horse," "a dog," and so forth, they will not only have scribbled, but will have constructed many abstract components and designs. I now know that children's first pictorial drawings are not early attempts to draw specific objects as the sight of those objects registers in the mind. Instead, children gradually realize that certain objects resemble their own designs,

and observe that adults call some of these designs "houses," "boats," "people," "flowers." Thus children learn which drawings are pictorial and which are not. Drawing "from life" comes at a much later time. All children spontaneously scribble and make designs, but adults must teach them how to "copy nature."

It is difficult for adults to appreciate and understand self-taught art because the minds of children and of adults are so different. Through years of living, adults have accumulated a store of rich associations which children have yet to acquire. For example, when a child looks at an ⬡ he has drawn, he sees only ◯ a round form, or gestalt, but the adult may see this as a scribble, a letter, a circle, an ornament, a symbol, a sign, a wheel, a ring. . . . The famous psychologist, Arnold Gesell, once said that our knowledge of the child is about as reliable as a 15th century map of the world. The scribblings of children can help adults gain a more reliable map.

Sequential Development in Self-Taught Art

As children progress from scribbling to picture-making, they go through four

distinguishable stages: the Placement Stage, the Shape Stage, the Design Stage, and the Pictorial Stage.

Placement Stage. Even the very earliest scribblings are not placed on the paper by happenstance. Instead, most of them are spontaneously drawn on the paper in *placement patterns,* that is, with an awareness of figure and ground relationships. I have detected 17 different placement patterns. The Spaced Border Pattern is shown below, and six

others are shown in the illustration at the bottom of the page. The 17 patterns appear by the age of two, and once developed are never lost.

Shape Stage. Placement patterns produce overall gestalts, or forms, which result from the location of the scribblings on the page. These gestalts contain implicit shapes. For example, the Spaced Border Pattern usually implies a rectangular shape:

By age three, most children can draw these implied shapes as single-line outline forms, called *diagrams,* and have reached the Shape Stage. There are six

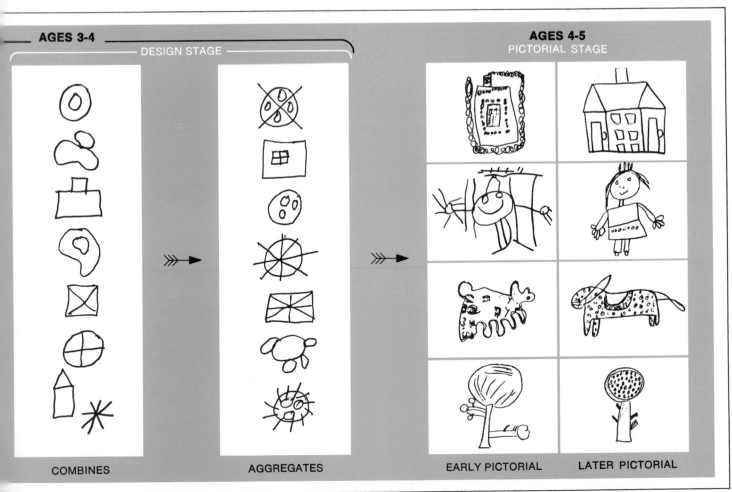

AGES 3-4
DESIGN STAGE

COMBINES

AGGREGATES

AGES 4-5
PICTORIAL STAGE

EARLY PICTORIAL   LATER PICTORIAL

diagrams: circles (and ovals), squares (and rectangles), triangles, crosses, X's, and odd forms.

Design Stage. As soon as children can draw diagrams, they almost immediately proceed to the Design Stage in which they put these simple forms together to make structured designs. When two diagrams are united, the resulting design is called a *combine*:

and when three or more are united, the design is called an *aggregate*:

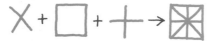

Pictorial Stage. Between the ages of four and five, most children arrive at the Pictorial Stage, in which their structured designs begin to look like objects which adults can recognize. The Pictorial Stage can be divided into two phases: the first contains *early pictorial* drawings, and the second contains *later pictorial* drawings.

The early pictorial drawings differ from the gestalts of the Design Stage in that they are suggestive of "human figures," "houses," "animals," "trees," and the like. The later pictorial drawings are more clearly defined and are easily recognized as familiar objects by adults. The later pictorial drawings do not necessarily represent a more advanced stage of artistic development; they are merely those pictorial drawings which adults recognize and approve of.

In his pictorial drawings, the child is not necessarily trying to draw representationally, but is more concerned with creating esthetically satisfying structures. For example, a Multiple-loop Scribble (smoke) might appear more pleasing to him if it circles around a square aggregate (a house). Logical consistency does not become his concern until adults restrict his expression along lines considered to be "proper."

From Humans to Rockets

The child's first drawings of the human figure look very odd to adults; the figure is round like a ball and the arms come out of the head. The reason for this lack of likeness is that the child is not drawing persons as seen, but is modifying the mandalas and suns of the late Design Stage in order to give his familiar gestalts a new look.

Mandala is a Sanskrit word denoting a "magic circle," though crossed squares and concentric circles or squares are also

174

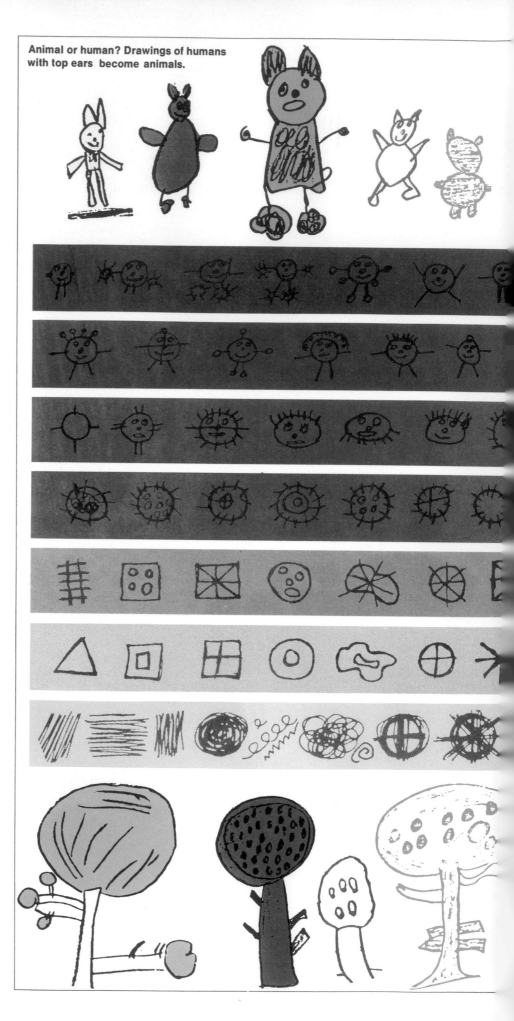

Animal or human? Drawings of humans with top ears become animals.

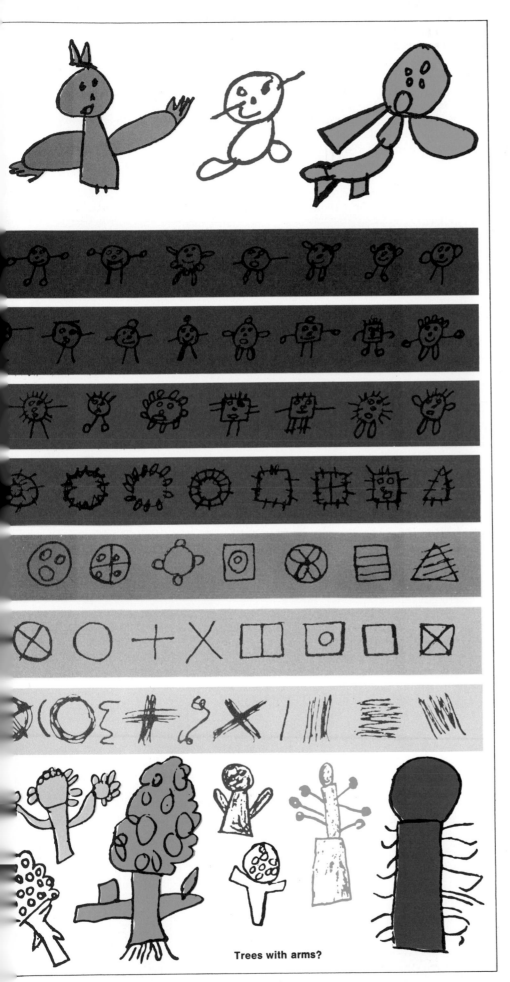

Trees with arms?

mandalas. The distinguishing characteristic of a mandala is its perfect balance, and mandala balance is dominant in self-taught art. The child's mandalas are prominent in the combines and aggregates, and are a departure point for proceeding to draw suns, radials, and human figures. The mandala gestalt (1) suggests the sun gestalt (2) and the two of them evolve into the first human figure (3). In the first drawings of humans, the arms are attached to the head and there are markings on top to balance the legs. Later the child omits arms from his drawings, perhaps in the effort to relieve the monotony of mandala balance. But actually almost all drawings of humans that children create before age six do fit nicely into an implied circular or oval shape, no matter what distortions of anatomy are required. This leads me to conclude that the child is not at all concerned with trying to draw his "humans" so that they look like people; he is striving for variety within a set of esthetic formulas. [*See illustration this page.*]

Drawings of human figures are followed by drawings of animals which are only modified gestalts of humans. For example, when the ears are on top of the head the human becomes what adults call an animal. [*See illustration this page.*]

In the same way, the "buildings" which children spontaneously draw are not attempts to depict real houses. Instead, these gestalts are interesting variations on designs made up of squares and rectangles. This applies to drawings of boats, cars, trees, airplanes, and rockets.

Before age five there are no differences between art gestalts produced by boys and girls. From then on, however, cultural influences lead them to draw different subject matter.

Is Picasso Right About Child Art?

The child's production of art gestalts collides head-on with the conception of art which adults have learned after age six and have passed on from one generation to another, according to the approved formulas of the local culture. Adults who coach children to draw real-life objects are not really being helpful; they may even be causing harm. The child's purpose is not that of drawing what he sees around him; rather, he is probably a very experienced master of self-taught art, concerned primarily with the production of esthetic combinations which are often the envy of adult artists. In fact, Picasso says that adults should not teach children to draw, but should learn from them.

It is very difficult to convince adults that art is not essentially a matter of portraying reality. A deep appreciation of art derives from an appreciation of both the explicit and the hidden esthetic gestalts present in all art; the pictorial aspect of art is important, but it is not the ingredient which separates mundane art from great art.

Children left alone to draw what they like, without the interference of adult "guidance," usually develop a store of gestalts which enable them to reach the culminating stage of self-taught art. From there, if they are especially gifted, they may develop into great artists, unspoiled by the stenciled minds of well-meaning adults. Few children, however, are given this opportunity, and most relinquish art after the first few years in school.

Child Art and Learning to Read

Failure to allow self-taught art to take its natural course of development after age six causes confusion in the child mind and misunderstandings between children and adults, both of which interfere with learning and discipline in school. The child whose ability to create art gestalts has been developed usually learns to read quickly and well. Since neither parents nor educators know the value of scribbling, they fail to provide a place, under proper supervision, for the very young to scribble. This is unfortunate, because scribbling and drawing develop the child's ability to perceive abstract gestalts, an ability so necessary for learning to read. The teaching of reading and writing has never been based on any awareness of the child's interest in abstract expression. Children who have been free to experiment with and produce abstract esthetic forms have already developed the mental set required for learning symbolic language.

As the child learns to read, he is expected to comprehend difficult systems of gestalt-making, each with its own order and rules: (1) the written and printed language system of the culture; (2) the simple art gestalts that teachers and parents make and which the child is supposed to copy; (3) adult art used as illustrations in books; (4) gestalts as they appear in photographs, movies, and television; and (5) gestalts as they appear in charts, graphs, diagrams, and maps.

Reading and writing primarily involve visual skills, yet prevalent teaching methods emphasize association of the spoken word with the graphic symbols for those words. I believe that teaching the alphabet and stressing phonetics may be the wrong approach. Reading can better be taught by recognizing the importance of the child's inherent gestalt-making system as it is developed in self-taught art, and then by building upon it. Allowing a child to draw what he likes for at least 30 minutes every day in school might very well free him to continue developing his capacity to perceive abstract gestalts. This would lay the groundwork for improving his reading, and would improve his writing ability also, because scribbling and drawing develop the fine muscle skills required for making precise markings on paper.

Using Child Art to Test Intelligence

In our country today, drawing is widely used as the basis for measuring general intelligence in young children.

These "intelligence" tests can be categorized according to the kinds of drawing abilities which they emphasize. In the Goodenough test, the child is rated by his ability to draw a man; in the Bender test, he is rated by his proficiency in copying visual gestalts; and in the Lantz test, his spontaneous art is subjectively judged by an "expert." Because we fail to understand the nature of child art, these tests are imperfect instruments of measurement.

For example, the Goodenough Draw-a-Man test, devised in 1926 and recently revised by Dale Harris, is based on such erroneous conceptions of the child mind and of child art that its use today is pure psychological ritual with no scientific validity. Scientific statistical treatment has been given to data so meager and so highly selected as to be absurd, but the human mind finds ritual comforting where knowledge is lacking. [See "Water Witching," by Ray Hyman and Evon Z. Vogt, *Psychology Today*, May 1967.] For the last 40 years the intelligence of many American four-year-olds

has been measured by the Goodenough test which is "standardized" on only 119 drawings of children of that age. The test itself was devised on the basis of but 2306 drawings, made for the most part by children of various ages who lived on the wrong side of the tracks in Perth Amboy, New Jersey. In revising the test, Harris standardized 3000 more drawings, but his conceptions of how children should draw the parts of the body—that is, the 71 features to be scored—resemble neither anatomy nor natural child art. The use Goodenough and Harris made of child art cannot be justified on rational grounds because both of them refused to consider the esthetic components of children's drawings as being relevant.

Before a child can learn to draw from the stimulus of an adult's drawing—that is, learn to copy—he must have developed certain skills of hand-eye-brain coordination. Gesell found that few three-year-olds could copy perfect circles and squares, and he claimed that children could not draw: ⊠ until the age of seven. (Yet five-year-olds will commonly draw this mandala in non-test situations.) The Bender Motor Gestalt test consists of a set of tricky gestalts which the child is asked to copy, but which no one would ever draw outside of a test situation. Few children or adults can complete the test perfectly. The Bender test is not a good test because it fails to take into consideration the natural development of child art. The gestalt: would look wrong to any child, for: ◯◇ is the natural ◯ way to combine a square and ☐ a circle. Another gestalt might ☐ look to a child somewhat like an awkward diagonal cross, for which a substituted graceful cross is a "failure."

Still another test based on art is the Lantz Easel Age Scale which is standardized on 3000 paintings of such subject matter as houses and boats—because drawings of the human figure are too complicated to rate. The test is "satisfactorily correlated" with the Goodenough test and has been given the usual statistical treatment so that it looks scientific. The ratings on the test are based on an Easel Age Score, which is said not only to measure intelligence, but to measure it quantitatively. I do not see how this is possible when even adults, whose intelligence has been proved by their functioning, are not able to "draw a man," make paintings of houses, or copy designs perfectly in the

Bender test. Another flaw in the test arises from the fact that children who persist in painting abstract works called "Q" paintings, are said to be in need of help of a special psychological or medical nature. This discourages the natural development of artistic expression and may send perfectly healthy children into unnecessary clinical treatment.

A Proposed Child Art Test

I am not sure that we need more tests for children, but if we must have them they should be as accurate and as harmless as possible. A child's artistic creations could be used as the basis for assessing more general mental functioning if the usual drawbacks associated with the testing situation were eliminated. Since any child's file of drawings shows that he can waver between scribbles and suns from one day to the next, it is unreasonable to suppose that the child's "intelligence" can be assessed on the basis of his performance during a short test period [see illustration below].

Spontaneous drawings done over a period of several weeks should be examined for the presence or absence of certain gestalts considered to be "normal" at certain age levels.

In order to set up the standard against which the child's performance would be evaluated, a large number of children's works would have to be studied to determine the age range for the first appearance of particular gestalts. A frequency distribution of selected aggregates, mandalas, suns, and human figures could then be plotted as a function of age level. Any child's stage of artistic development could then be compared with the norm to determine his relative performance.

This test would be particularly useful for diagnosing mental retardation—and pseudo-retardation. Often I have been able to convince the parents of a supposedly retarded child that their child was perfectly normal in his art development and hence probably perfectly normal in intelligence.

Universals and Universities

Parents, educators, and psychologists are not the only adults who fail to understand the significance of the origins of art in childhood. Art historians, anthropologists, and archeologists, who encounter the motifs of self-taught art in their studies of primitive and past cultures, usually view these gestalts as products of the adult mind, rich in symbolic meaning, and characteristic of local cultures. For example, Giedion, the noted art historian, interprets triangular diagrams as vulvas and fertility symbols; and Margaret Mead believes that "art comes from art,"—that each generation teaches its favorite gestalts to the next generation. A better understanding of these ancient gestalts could be achieved through a greater knowledge of the universal nature of self-taught child art.

Human beings throughout the world, from Paleolithic times to the present, have used some of these basic motifs of child art. Pictorial drawings made by children in many lands are remarkably similar because they are the outgrowths

Each pair of drawings compares one child's "best" and "poorest" drawing of a human done within one week's time.

178

of earlier scribblings and designs [*see illustration below*]. Since this early art is so uniform in expression, from country to country, culture to culture, past to present, I conclude that the child's early abstractions (as well as later, derivative, pictorial drawings) are the products of innate patterns of neurological growth and human development.

Indeed, Max Knoll has discovered that the phosphenes, or light patterns which adults experience when the cortex is electrically stimulated, are similar to children's scribblings. This suggests that there are some inherent neurological mechanisms that enable us to produce and to perceive the basic line-gestalts out of which art forms are produced. Several studies, have shown that infants only a few weeks old can respond with movements of their eye muscles to the stimulus of abstract patterns, and it is now generally agreed that the mind at birth is not a blank, nor is it a "blooming buzzing confusion," as William James suggested.

Live Art Scribbles

Children's scribblings and drawings contain a voluminous written message, a message which has not yet been completely deciphered. It may turn out that "live art scribbles" are as important as The Dead Sea Scrolls.

I believe that the hidden message in child art, when properly understood, will free us to recapture the un-*adult*-erated esthetic vision of the child. Perhaps the day will come when adult and child can enjoy self-taught art together, not as "cute" or "remarkable" products of the childish mind but as the ground-work of all art. Then adults will not make stencils for children to fill in, nor will they patronizingly laugh at what they do not understand.

Children are happy when they can draw objects to fit into implied esthetic shapes. What the great artist struggles to achieve, the child creates naturally. ∩

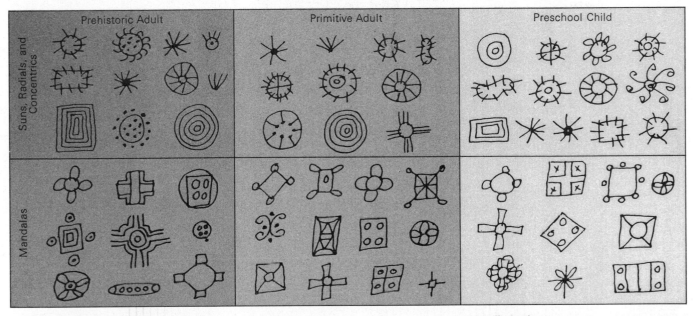

The universality of basic art motifs from past to present (above) and from country to country (below).

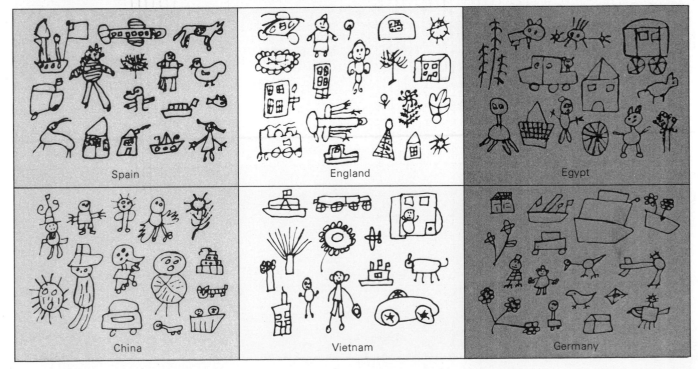

You're a good man, Charlie Brown!
You have humility, nobility and a
sense of honor that is very rare indeed.
You are kind to all the
animals and every little bird.
With a heart of gold, you believe
what you're told, every single
solitary word. You bravely face
adversity; you're cheerful through
the day; you're thoughtful, brave
and courteous. You're a good man
Charlie Brown! You're a prince, and
a prince could be a king.
With a heart such as yours
you could open any door —
if only you weren't so wishy-washy.

The Child as a Moral Philosopher

By Lawrence Kohlberg

How can one study morality? Current trends in the fields of ethics, linguistics, anthropology and cognitive psychology have suggested a new approach which seems to avoid the morass of semantical confusions, value-bias and cultural relativity in which the psychoanalytic and semantic approaches to morality have foundered. New scholarship in all these fields is now focusing upon structures, forms and relationships that seem to be common to all societies and all languages rather than upon the features that make particular languages or cultures different.

For 12 years, my colleagues and I studied the same group of 75 boys, following their development at three-year intervals from early adolescence through young manhood. At the start of the study, the boys were aged 10 to 16. We have now followed them through to ages 22 to 28. In addition, I have explored moral development in other cultures — Great Britain, Canada, Taiwan, Mexico and Turkey.

Inspired by Jean Piaget's pioneering effort to apply a structural approach to moral development, I have gradually elaborated over the years of my study a typological scheme describing general structures and forms of moral thought which can be defined independently of the specific content of particular moral decisions or actions.

The typology contains three distinct levels of moral thinking, and within each of these levels distinguishes two related stages. These levels and stages may be considered separate moral philosophies, distinct views of the socio-moral world.

We can speak of the child as having his own morality or series of moralities.

181

Adults seldom listen to children's moralizing. If a child throws back a few adult cliches and behaves himself, most parents—and many anthropologists and psychologists as well—think that the child has adopted or internalized the appropriate parental standards.

Actually, as soon as we talk with children about morality, we find that they have many ways of making judgments which are not "internalized" from the outside, and which do not come in any direct and obvious way from parents, teachers or even peers.

Moral Levels

The *preconventional* level is the first of three levels of moral thinking; the second level is *conventional*, and the third *postconventional* or autonomous. While the preconventional child is often "well-behaved" and is responsive to cultural labels of good and bad, he interprets these labels in terms of their physical consequences (punishment, reward, exchange of favors) or in terms of the physical power of those who enunciate the rules and labels of good and bad.

This level is usually occupied by children aged four to 10, a fact long known to sensitive observers of children. The capacity of "properly behaved" children of this age to engage in cruel behavior when there are holes in the power structure is sometimes noted as tragic (*Lord of the Flies, High Wind in Jamaica*), sometimes as comic (Lucy in *Peanuts*).

The second or *conventional* level also can be described as conformist, but that is perhaps too smug a term. Maintaining the expectations and rules of the individual's family, group or nation is perceived as valuable in its own right. There is a concern not only with *conforming* to the individual's social order but in *maintaining*, supporting and justifying this order.

The *postconventional* level is characterized by a major thrust toward autonomous moral principles which have validity and application apart from authority of the groups or persons who hold them and apart from the individual's identification with those persons or groups.

Moral Stages

Within each of these three levels there are two discernable stages. At the preconventional level we have:

Stage 1: Orientation toward punishment and unquestioning deference to superior power. The physical consequences of action regardless of their human meaning or value determine its goodness or badness.

Stage 2: Right action consists of that which instrumentally satisfies one's own needs and occasionally the needs of others. Human relations are viewed in terms like those of the marketplace. Elements of fairness, of reciprocity and equal sharing are present, but they are always interpreted in a physical, pragmatic way. Reciprocity is a matter of "you scratch my back and I'll scratch yours" not of loyalty, gratitude or justice.

And at the conventional level we have:

Stage 3: Good-boy—good-girl orientation. Good behavior is that which pleases or helps others and is approved by them. There is much conformity to stereotypical images of what is majority or "natural" behavior. Behavior is often judged by intention —"he means well" becomes important for the first time, and is overused, as by Charlie Brown in *Peanuts*. One seeks approval by being "nice."

Stage 4: Orientation toward authority, fixed rules and the maintenance of the social order. Right behavior consists of doing one's duty, showing respect for authority and maintaining the given social order for its own sake. One earns respect by performing dutifully.

At the postconventional level, we have:

Stage 5: A social-contract orientation, generally with legalistic and utilitarian overtones. Right action tends to be defined in terms of general rights and in terms of standards which have been critically examined and agreed upon by the whole society. There is a clear awareness of the relativism of personal values and opinions and a corresponding emphasis upon procedural rules for reaching consensus. Aside from what is constitutionally and democratically agreed upon, right or wrong is a matter of personal "values" and "opinion." The result is an emphasis upon the "legal point of view," but with an emphasis upon the possi-

bility of *changing* law in terms of rational considerations of social utility, rather than freezing it in the terms of Stage 4 "law and order." Outside the legal realm, free agreement and contract are the binding elements of obligation. This is the "official" morality of American government, and finds its ground in the thought of the writers of the Constitution.

Stage 6: Orientation toward the decisions of conscience and toward self-chosen *ethical principles* appealing to logical comprehensiveness, universality and consistency. These principles are abstract and ethical (the Golden Rule, the categorical imperative); they are not concrete moral rules like the Ten Commandments. Instead, they are universal principles of *justice*, of the *reciprocity* and *equality* of human rights, and of respect for the dignity of human beings as *individual persons*.

Up to Now

In the past, when psychologists tried to answer the question asked of Socrates by Meno "Is virtue something that can be taught (by rational discussion), or does it come by practice, or is it a natural inborn attitude?" their answers usually have been dictated, not by research findings on children's moral character, but by their general theoretical convictions.

Behavior theorists have said that virtue is behavior acquired according to their favorite general principles of learning. Freudians have claimed that virtue is superego-identification with parents generated by a proper balance of love and authority in family relations.

The American psychologists who have actually studied children's morality have tried to start with a set of labels—the "virtues" and "vices," the "traits" of good and bad character found in ordinary language. The earliest major psychological study of moral character, that of Hugh Hartshorne and Mark May in 1928-1930, focused on a bag of virtues including honesty, service (altruism or generosity), and self-control. To their dismay, they found that there were *no* character traits, psychological dispositions or entities which corresponded to words like honesty, service or self-control.

Regarding honesty, for instance, they found that almost everyone cheats some of the time, and that if a person cheats in one situation, it doesn't mean that he *will* or *won't* in another. In other words, it is not an identifiable character trait, *dis*honesty, that makes a child cheat in

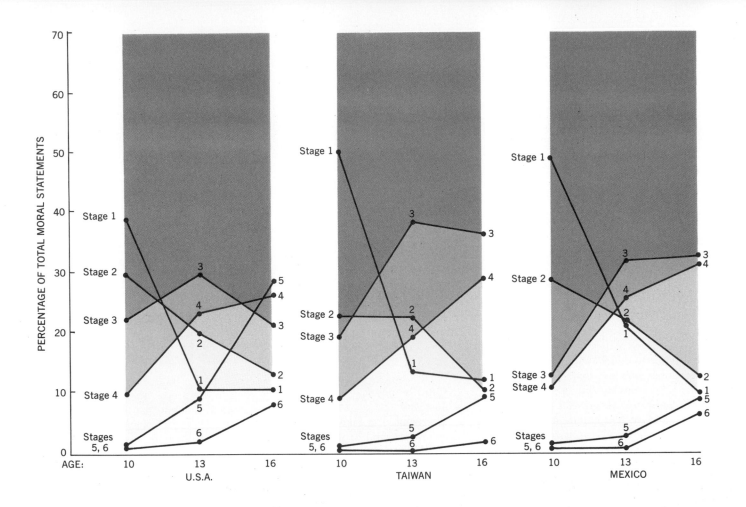

1. Middle-class urban boys in the U.S., Taiwan and Mexico (*above*). At age 10 the stages are used according to difficulty. At age 13, Stage 3 is most used by all three groups. At age 16 U.S. boys have reversed the order of age 10 stages (with the exception of 6). In Taiwan and Mexico, conventional (3-4) stages prevail at age 16, with Stage 5 also little used.

2. Two isolated villages, one in Turkey, the other in Yucatan, show similar patterns in moral thinking. There is no reversal of order, and preconventional (1-2) thought does does not gain a clear ascendancy over conventional stages at age 16.

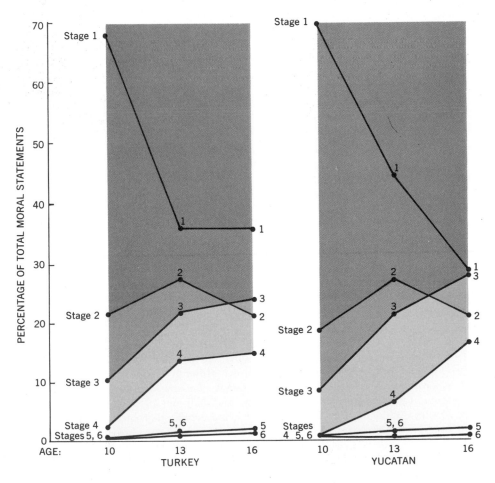

a given situation. These early researchers also found that people who cheat express as much or even more moral disapproval of cheating as those who do not cheat.

What Hartshorne and May found out about their bag of virtues is equally upsetting to the somewhat more psychological-sounding names introduced by psychoanalytic psychology: "superego-strength," "resistance to temptation," "strength of conscience," and the like. When recent researchers attempt to measure such traits in individuals, they have been forced to use Hartshorne and May's old tests of honesty and self-control and they get exactly the same results —"superego strength" in one situation predicts little to "superego strength" in another. That is, virtue-words like honesty (or superego-strength) point to certain behaviors with approval, but give us no guide to understanding them.

So far as one can extract some generalized personality factor from children's performance on tests of honesty or resistance to temptation, it is a factor of ego-strength or ego-control, which always involves non-moral capacities like the capacity to maintain attention, intelligent-task performance, and the ability to delay response. "Ego-strength" (called "will" in earlier days) has something to do with moral action, but it does not take us to the core of morality or to the definition of virtue. Obviously enough, many of the greatest evil-doers in history have been men of strong wills, men strongly pursuing immoral goals.

Moral Reasons

In our research, we have found definite and universal levels of development in moral thought. In our study of 75 American boys from early adolescence on, these youths were presented with hypothetical moral dilemmas, all deliberately philosophical, some of them found in medieval works of casuistry.

On the basis of their reasoning about these dilemmas at a given age, each boy's stage of thought could be determined for each of 25 basic moral concepts or aspects. One such aspect, for instance, is "Motive Given for Rule Obedience or Moral Action." In this instance, the six stages look like this:

1. Obey rules to avoid punishment.
2. Conform to obtain rewards, have favors returned, and so on.
3. Conform to avoid disapproval, dislike by others.
4. Conform to avoid censure by legitimate authorities and resultant guilt.

5. Conform to maintain the respect of the impartial spectator judging in terms of community welfare.
6. Conform to avoid self-condemnation.

In another of these 25 moral aspects, the value of human life, the six stages can be defined thus:

1. The value of a human life is confused with the value of physical objects and is based on the social status or physical attributes of its possessor.
2. The value of a human life is seen as instrumental to the satisfaction of the needs of its possessor or of other persons.
3. The value of a human life is based on the empathy and affection of family members and others toward its possessor.
4. Life is conceived as sacred in terms of its place in a categorical moral or religious order of rights and duties.
5. Life is valued both in terms of its relation to community welfare and in terms of life being a universal human right.
6. Belief in the sacredness of human life as representing a universal human value of respect for the individual.

I have called this scheme a typology. This is because about 50 per cent of most people's thinking will be at a single stage, regardless of the moral dilemma involved. We call our types *stages* because they seem to represent an *invariant developmental sequence.* "True" stages come one at a time and always in the same order.

All movement is forward in sequence, and does not skip steps. Children may move through these stages at varying speeds, of course, and may be found half in and half out of a particular stage. An individual may stop at any given stage and at any age, but if he continues to move, he must move in accord with these steps. Moral reasoning of the con-

ventional or Stage 3-4 kind never occurs before the preconventional Stage-1 and Stage-2 thought has taken place. No adult in Stage 4 has gone through Stage 6, but all Stage-6 adults have gone at least through 4.

While the evidence is not complete, my study strongly suggests that moral change fits the stage pattern just described. (The major uncertainty is whether all Stage 6s go through Stage 5 or whether these are two alternate mature orientations.)

How Values Change

As a single example of our findings of stage-sequence, take the progress of two boys on the aspect "The Value of Human Life." The first boy Tommy, is asked "Is it better to save the life of one important person or a lot of unimportant people?". At age 10, he answers "all the people that aren't important because one man just has one house, maybe a lot of furniture, but a whole bunch of people have an awful lot of furniture and some of these poor people might have a lot of money and it doesn't look it."

Clearly Tommy is Stage 1: he confuses the value of a human being with the value of the property he possesses. Three years later (age 13) Tommy's conceptions of life's value are most clearly elicited by the question, "Should the doctor 'mercy kill' a fatally ill woman requesting death because of her pain?". He answers, "Maybe it would be good to put her out of her pain, she'd be better off that way. But the husband wouldn't want it, it's not like an animal. If a pet dies you can get along without it—it isn't something you really need. Well, you can get a new wife, but it's not really the same."

Here his answer is Stage 2: the value of the woman's life is partly contingent on its hedonistic value to the wife herself but even more contingent on its instrumental value to her husband, who can't replace her as easily as he can a pet.

Three years later still (age 16) Tommy's conception of life's value is elicited by the same question, to which he replies: "It might be best for her, but her husband—it's a human life—not like an animal; it just doesn't have the same relationship that a human being does to a family. You can become attached to a dog, but nothing like a human you know."

Now Tommy has moved from a Stage 2 instrumental view of the woman's value to a Stage-3 view based on the husband's distinctively human empathy and love for someone in his family. Equally clearly, it lacks any basis for a universal human value of the woman's life, which would hold if she had no husband or if her husband didn't love her. Tommy, then, has moved step by step through three stages during the age 10-16. Tommy, though bright (I.Q. 120), is a slow developer in moral judgment. Let us take another boy, Richard, to show us sequential movement through the remaining three steps.

At age 13, Richard said about the mercy-killing, "If she requests it, it's really up to her. She is in such terrible pain, just the same as people are always putting animals out of their pain," and in general showed a mixture of Stage-2 and Stage-3 responses concerning the value of life. At 16, he said, "I don't know. In one way, it's murder, it's not a right or privilege of man to decide who shall live and who should die. God put life into everybody on earth and you're taking away something from that person that came directly from God, and you're destroying something that is very sacred, it's in a way part of God and it's almost destroying a part of God when you kill a person. There's something of God in everyone."

Here Richard clearly displays a Stage-4 concept of life as sacred in terms of its place in a categorical moral or religious order. The value of human life is univer-

sal, it is true for all humans. It is still, however, dependent on something else, upon respect for God and God's authority; it is not an autonomous human value. Presumably if God told Richard to murder, as God commanded Abraham to murder Isaac, he would do so.

At age 20, Richard said to the same question: "There are more and more people in the medical profession who think it is a hardship on everyone, the person, the family, when you know they are going to die. When a person is kept alive by an artificial lung or kidney it's more like being a vegetable than being a human. If it's her own choice, I think there are certain rights and privileges that go along with being a human being. I am a human being and have certain desires for life and I think everybody else does too. You have a world of which you are the center, and everybody else does too and in that sense we're all equal."

Richard's response is clearly Stage 5, in that the value of life is defined in terms of equal and universal human rights in a context of relativity ("You have a world of which you are the center and in that sense we're all equal"), and of concern for utility or welfare consequences.

The Final Step

At 24, Richard says: "A human life takes precedence over any other moral or legal value, whoever it is. A human life has inherent value whether or not it is valued by a particular individual. The worth of the individual human being is central where the principles of justice and love are normative for all human relationships."

This young man is at Stage 6 in seeing the value of human life as absolute in representing a universal and equal respect for the human as an individual. He has moved step by step through a sequence culminating in a definition of human life as centrally valuable rather than derived from or dependent on social or divine authority.

In a genuine and culturally universal sense, these steps lead toward an increased *morality* of value judgment, where morality is considered as a form of judging, as it has been in a philosophic tradition running from the analyses of Kant to those of the modern analytic or

"ordinary language" philosophers. The person at Stage 6 has disentangled his judgments of—or language about—human life from status and property values (Stage 1), from its uses to others (Stage 2), from interpersonal affection (Stage 3), and so on; he has a means of moral judgment that is universal and impersonal. The Stage-6 person's answers use moral words like "duty" or "morally right," and he uses them in a way implying universality, ideals, impersonality: He thinks and speaks in phrases like "regardless of who it was," or ". . . I would do it in spite of punishment."

Across Cultures

When I first decided to explore moral development in other cultures, I was told by anthropologist friends that I would have to throw away my culture-bound moral concepts and stories and start from scratch learning a whole new set of values for each new culture. My first try consisted of a brace of villages, one Atayal (Malaysian aboriginal) and the other Taiwanese.

My guide was a young Chinese ethnographer who had written an account of the moral and religious patterns of the Atayal and Taiwanese villages. Taiwanese boys in the 10-13 age group were asked about a story involving theft of food. A man's wife is starving to death but the store owner won't give the man any food unless he can pay, which he can't. Should he break in and steal some food? Why? Many of the boys said, "He should steal the food for his wife because if she dies he'll have to pay for her funeral and that costs a lot."

My guide was amused by these responses, but I was relieved: they were of course "classic" Stage-2 responses. In the Atayal village, funerals weren't such a big thing, so the Stage 2-boys would say, "He should steal the food because he needs his wife to cook for him."

This means that we need to consult our anthropologists to know what content a Stage-2 child will include in his instrumental exchange calculations, or what a Stage-4 adult will identify as the proper social order. But one certainly doesn't have to start from scratch. What made my guide laugh was the difference in form between the children's Stage-2 thought and his own, a difference definable independently of particular cultures.

Illustrations number 1 and number 2 indicate the cultural universality of the sequence of stages which we have found. Illustration number 1 presents the age trends for middle-class urban boys in the

**"Socrates, Lincoln, Thoreau
and Martin Luther King tend to speak
without confusion of tongues."**

U.S., Taiwan and Mexico. At age 10 in each country, the order of use of each stage is the same as the order of its difficulty or maturity.

In the United States, by age 16 the order is the reverse, from the highest to the lowest, except that Stage 6 is still little-used. At age 13, the good-boy, middle stage (Stage 3), is not used.

The results in Mexico and Taiwan are the same, except that development is a little slower. The most conspicuous feature is that at the age of 16, Stage-5 thinking is much more salient in the United States than in Mexico or Taiwan. Nevertheless, it *is* present in the other countries, so we know that this is not purely an American democratic construct.

Illustration 2 shows strikingly similar results from two isolated villages, one in Yucatan, one in Turkey. While conventional moral thought increases steadily from ages 10 to 16 it still has not achieved a clear ascendency over preconventional thought.

Trends for lower-class urban groups are intermediate in the rate of development between those for the middle-class and for the village boys. In the three divergent cultures that I studied, middle-class children were found to be more advanced in moral judgment than matched lower-class children. This was not due to the fact that the middle-class children heavily favored some one type of thought which could be seen as corresponding to the prevailing middle-class pattern. Instead, middle-class and working-class children move through the same sequences, but the middle-class children move faster and farther.

This sequence is not dependent upon a particular religion, or any religion at all in the usual sense. I found no important differences in the development of moral thinking among Catholics, Protestants, Jews, Buddhists, Moslems and atheists. Religious values seem to go through the same stages as all other values.

Trading Up

In summary, the nature of our sequence is not significantly affected by widely varying social, cultural or religious conditions. The only thing that is affected is the *rate* at which individuals progress through this sequence.

Why should there be such a universal invariant sequence of development? In answering this question, we need first to analyze these developing social concepts in terms of their internal logical structure. At each stage, the same basic moral concept or aspect is defined, but at each higher stage this definition is more differentiated, more integrated and more general or universal. When one's concept of human life moves from Stage 1 to Stage 2 the value of life becomes more differentiated from the value of property, more integrated (the value of life enters an organizational hierarchy where it is "higher" than property so that one steals property in order to save life) and more universalized (the life of any sentient being is valuable regardless of status or property). The same advance is true at each stage in the hierarchy. Each step of development then is a better cognitive organization than the one before it, one which takes account of everything present in the previous stage, but making new distinctions and organizing them into a more comprehensive or more equilibrated structure. The fact that this is the case has been demonstrated by a series of studies indicating that children and adolescents comprehend all stages up to their own, but not more than one stage beyond their own. And importantly, *they prefer this next stage.*

We have conducted experimental moral discussion classes which show that the child at an earlier stage of development tends to move forward when confronted by the views of a child one stage further along. In an argument between a Stage-3 and Stage-4 child, the child in the third stage tends to move toward or into Stage 4, while the Stage-4 child understands but does not accept the arguments of the Stage-3 child.

Moral thought, then, seems to behave like all other kinds of thought. Progress through the moral levels and stages is characterized by increasing differentiation and increasing integration, and hence is the same kind of progress that scientific theory represents. Like acceptable scientific theory—or like *any* theory or structure of knowledge—moral thought may be considered partially to generate its own data as it goes along, or at least to expand so as to contain in a balanced, self-consistent way a wider and wider experiential field. The raw data in the case of our ethical philosophies may be considered as conflicts between roles, or values, or as the social order in which men live.

The Role of Society

The social worlds of all men seem to contain the same basic structures. All the societies we have studied have the same basic institutions—family, economy, law, government. In addition, however, all societies are alike because they *are* societies—systems of defined complementary roles. In order to *play* a social role in the family, school or society, the child must implicitly take the role of others toward himself and toward others in the group. These role-taking tendencies form the basis of all social institutions. They represent various patternings of shared or complementary expectations.

In the preconventional and conventional levels (Stages 1-4), moral content or value is largely accidental or culture-bound. Anything from "honesty" to "courage in battle" can be the central value. But in the higher postconventional levels, Socrates, Lincoln, Thoreau and Martin Luther King tend to speak without confusion of tongues, as it were. This is because the ideal principles of any social structure are basically alike, if only because there simply aren't that many principles which are articulate, comprehensive and integrated enough to be satisfying to the human intellect. And most of these principles have gone by the name of justice.

Behavioristic psychology and psychoanalysis have always upheld the Philistine view that fine moral words are one thing and moral deeds another. Morally mature reasoning is quite a different matter, and does not really depend on "fine words." The man who understands justice is more likely to practice it.

In our studies, we have found that youths who understand justice act more justly, and the man who understands justice helps create a moral climate which goes far beyond his immediate and personal acts. The universal society is the beneficiary. 𝄞

By C. B. Ferster

the autistic child

There are children who live in a world no one can enter. Is there any way to reach them?

THE AUTISTIC CHILD lives in a cage of unbreakable glass. He cannot reach out, and no one can reach in. A good part of the time the child does nothing but sit quietly in a chair, or sleep, or lie huddled in a corner. At other times he is active, sometimes violently so, but his activity affects only, himself. He may spend hours compulsively rubbing a rough spot on the floor, moving his fingers in front of his face, babbling to himself, licking his body like a cat, or flipping sand to produce a visual pattern. He may beat his head against the wall, hit himself until he is covered with bruises, or use his fingernails and teeth to tear his own flesh.

Some autistic children are mute. Others make inarticulate sounds or echo bits of the speech they hear around them. But they do not talk to or with other people. When an autistic child does try to communicate, it is by biting, kicking, screaming, having tantrums—primitive forms of behavior, called *atavisms*, which create a situation others will go to almost any lengths to eliminate.

If one were to watch an autistic child for a day and then watch a normal child for a month, one would see much of the autistic child's behavior reproduced by the normal child. Almost any child, on occasion, will gaze out the window for an hour or more, make bizarre faces or have severe tantrums. Any child may run sticks over picket fences, step on (or over) all the cracks in the sidewalk, or chew a piece of rubber balloon to shreds.

But normal children are only out of touch with their surroundings once in a while, and primitivisms are not their only form of behavior. They interact with their physical and social environment in many different ways. The autistic child's behavior is far more restricted. He has very few ways of changing and being changed by the world around him.

Since his behavioral repertoire is so small, what there is of it is used over and over again. It is the *frequency* of withdrawn, self-stimulatory or atavistic behavior, not simply the fact that it occurs, which distinguishes the autistic child from the normal one.

Autism is a very rare disorder, affecting only one child out of 50,000 or 100,-000. We need to know how autism comes about and how it may be treated not only because these few children desperately need help but because the study of autism contributes to our understanding of other forms of behavior. There are parallels, for example, between the development of autism in young children and the development of schizophrenia in adolescents. In addition, the past experiences of the autistic child, like his present behavior, differ from those of the normal child not so much in *kind* as in *intensity* and *frequency*.

We do not know yet whether the causes of autism are biological or environmental, or both. Parents of autistic children sometimes report that the child seemed "different" from birth, that he stiffened each time he was picked up. Some autistic children have shown neurological anomalies such as abnormal EEG patterns. So far, however, the evidence for an inborn biological deficiency is meager.

A child's environment can have very dramatic effects on his behavioral development. This has been shown repeatedly. There have been infants who spent most of their early lives locked in closets and became primitive, animal-like children. There also have been primitive, animal-like children who have learned new forms of behavior when a new environment was arranged for them. Thus it makes sense to examine the surroundings of the autistic child for circumstances that might explain the gross deficiencies in his behavior.

The major processes by which behavior is acquired and lost are *reinforcement* and *extinction*. If a rat receives a pellet of food when it presses a bar, the rat will press the bar more and more often. When the pellets are no longer delivered, bar-pressing decreases in frequency and finally stops. Similarly, a person's ordinary speech usually is reinforced by the reply it gets, and a speaker who gets no reply soon stops talking. Behavioral processes are harder to observe in a natural social environment than in an experimental laboratory, but they operate similarly.

The very limited repertoire of the autistic child may come about because his behavior is not successful. Ted is an example of an autistic child whose behavioral development was thwarted because little of his behavior was reinforced. At first this was hard to see, because Ted's mother did not seem unresponsive. She was a very active woman who moved busily around the house, accomplishing many tasks and talking a great deal.

The child, however, was prevented from completing any action he happened to begin. When he reached for a lamp, his mother appeared as if by magic to seize his hand and hold it back. When

he reached for the doorknob, again she intercepted him. When he approached his brothers and sisters, his mother separated them. When he held out a receipt he had gotten from the newsboy, she walked past and left him standing with the slip of paper in his hand.

Even the mother's speech did not make contact with the boy. While the boy was in the living room, his mother called him from the kitchen. "Ted, come over here," she said. "I want to read you a story. Ted, Ted, don't you want to read a story? Ted, come over here and read a story. TED, where are you?"

Ted paid no attention. After five minutes of calling, the mother came into the living room and picked up the book. She continued to call, "TED, TED, TED. . . . Come on and read your book." When he happened to wander near enough, she took hold of him, sat him down next to her, and began to read.

The boy did not object and seemed happy to sit with his head against his mother's shoulder. But it was obvious that the physical contact was what kept him there. The reading was irrelevant, as was most of the mother's speech.

In short, only a tiny part of the mother's behavior had a reinforcing effect on the child. Furthermore, by interrupting or ignoring his attempts to do things for himself she was preventing him from successfully completing an action—any action—of his own.

Sometimes a child's behavior succeeds only under very specific conditions—with one particular person, for example. If the circumstances suddenly change, a great deal of behavior can be lost. This happened to a little girl of four, who spent a year in the care of a teen-age baby-sitter.

The girl's mother was a very disturbed, nearly psychotic, woman. She remained in the home while the baby-sitter was there, but she had nothing whatever to do with the child. If the child said "Mom, can I have a cookie?" there was no answer. If she said "Janet, can I have a cookie?" Janet said yes and gave her a cookie. If the girl said "Let's go out," the mother did not answer. Janet might reply and take the child outside.

This situation might be compared to that of a laboratory pigeon being trained to peck a green key instead of a red key. If the pigeon pecks the green key, a piece of grain appears, but if it pecks the red key, nothing happens. After a while the pigeon doesn't bother pecking the red key at all.

When the baby-sitter left at the end of the year, this child lost almost her whole behavioral repertoire. She became incontinent, she talked less and less, she could not be kept in nursery school. Eventually she needed chronic care at a state home for the retarded. The reason for this massive loss of behavior was not just the sudden switch in caretakers but the fact that the mother had been present the *same time* as the baby-sitter. If the mother had been away for the year and had been able to respond normally to the child when she returned, there probably would have been only a slight, temporary break in behavior. If the mother had been away but had *not* been able to treat the child normally when she came back, the same severe loss probably would have occurred, much more slowly.

Parents and children constantly influence each other's behavior. Even punishment is usually more productive than no reaction to the child at all.

This is not to say that punishment is a desirable form of behavioral control. Although its main effect is to *strengthen* behavior that avoids or ends the punishment, punishment can weaken behavior if all positive reinforcement is withdrawn. If a parent not only spanks a child but refuses to speak to him for the rest of the day, he may reduce the frequency of parts of the child's repertoire that he did not intend to affect.

In addition, punishment can promote less advanced forms of behavior. Punishment is most likely to be dispensed when a child is doing something fairly active, such as finger painting on the wall or trying to drive his parents' car. A child who sits on the kitchen floor studying his fingers will probably be left alone. If a child is consistently punished when he tries to have a strong effect on the environment, such attempts will begin to produce considerable anxiety. So the child may substitute simpler activities, such as rubbing a spot on the floor.

He may also resort to primitive controlling behavior, like screaming and tantrums. If he finds that he *can* affect his environment in this way, he is likely to keep on using atavisms in preference to other behavior.

When one sees the amount of control some autistic children exert over their parents by means of tantrums and other atavisms, it is hardly surprising that the behavior is so durable. One child's parents told us that they took turns standing guard all night at the door of his room because a tantrum started if

they left and ceased only when they moved back. Another mother slept with her arm over her child every night for five months, so that she could stop him when he woke and clawed at his face.

Everything described so far—lack of reinforcement, sudden changes in its source, the withdrawal of approval, and practices that encourage primitive behavior—also occurs in the lives of children who do not become autistic. Accounting for the autistic child's massive failure of development therefore presents a problem. The explanation seems to be that the autistic child has faced more severely damaging situations more often than the normal or nearly normal child. Most of the evidence that this is true is anecdotal, but compelling.

One often finds, for instance, that autistic children have parents who are completely unable to respond to the child's behavior. A parent who is a drug addict, an alcoholic, chronically ill or severely depressed may not even acknowledge the child's existence for days on end. One also finds parents who have beaten, tortured, starved or incarcerated their children for long periods of time. One woman kept her child in a dog run.

When we look at the child rather than the parents, we often discover a history of serious or chronic illness during infancy. In such cases, the child's standard way of communicating with the parents usually has been to cry and fret. After the child recovers, the crying may persist, and the parents may very well keep on reacting. So the child deals with the parents through primitive behavior, and the parent responds in order to end the behavior. The child's development, already retarded by his illness, may progress no farther.

A child is not usually identified as autistic until some complex form of behavior (such as speech) fails to develop—that is, until the child is two, three or even four years old. Although this does not prove that autism was not present earlier (indeed, parents occasionally report deviant behavior in very young infants), it does suggest a careful examination of that period in the child's life when the disorder may express itself.

A two-year-old is at a stage of development when his behavior is especially vulnerable to disruption. For one thing, he is more likely than a younger child to provoke a negative reaction from his parents. The activities of a baby are simple and relatively unobtrusive. But when a child begins to crawl, walk, reach for ashtrays and lamps, and cry loudly when crossed, he may also begin to frighten and upset his parents and thus to invite the kind of treatment that weakens behavior.

Furthermore, the child's new behavior is not at all firmly established. New behavior develops fastest when it has a consistent, reliable effect on the environment. Since the child can only approximate what he is trying to do at first, his

efforts succeed only part of the time. If an enthusiastic parental response is lacking too, the child may very well abandon the behavior.

Sometimes a parent will praise the child's first nonsense syllables but become angry a month later when the child still cannot speak in complete, intelligible sentences. This sudden shift in the performance required for reinforcement can have the same effect on the child as suddenly requiring a laboratory pigeon to peck 300 times instead of 25

for a piece of grain: the behavior stops.

However, sudden changes in the kind and amount of behavior required for reinforcement are more likely to occur in adolescence than in early childhood. A 10-year-old may need do no more than hold out his hand for his allowance or run next door to find a playmate. A 16-year-old is expected to work for his money and to master an elaborate courtship ritual. At school, where assignments used to be frequent and short, the teenage student may have to work for weeks or months before he finds out from the teacher how he is doing. In general, the adolescent must perform a substantial number of specific acts before his behavior is reinforced, often without benefit of a complete series of intermediate, transitional experiences.

If the change in kind or amount of behavior an adolescent must deliver is too sudden or too large, the effect on his development can be disastrous. One can-

not build the Empire State Building if there is only a toothpick holding up the 20th floor. One schizophrenic boy had a job as a truck driver before he was hospitalized; he would not stop at the restaurant where the other drivers ate because he did not know how to order food from the waitress. Another young man in the ward had frequent and violent temper tantrums; their source turned out to be his inability to tie his shoelaces.

Autistic children are very difficult to treat. Until recently, they were considered virtually hopeless. So much of the normal repertoire is missing; a long history of experiences must be recreated; dealing with a six-year-old child as if he were one or two years old presents innumerable problems. Some therapists have succeeded with prolonged residential treatment. In addition, recent experimental attempts have sometimes produced dramatic changes in the children's behavior. Even when these experiments are not entirely successful from a therapeutic point of view—when, for example, the changes do not last—they represent progress, because they show the child's potential for development.

One promising approach to rehabilitation is illustrated by a project that I am participating in at the Linwood Children's Center for autistic children, located between Washington, D.C. and Baltimore. The Director of the Center, Jeanne Simons, is chiefly a clinician, and I am chiefly an experimentalist. What we are trying to do is produce a kind of model for cooperative work between the two fields.

During our collaboration we found that our methods are a great deal alike. I tend to approach an experiment, even in the animal laboratory, from a clinical point of view; Miss Simons manipulates the environment in her clinic much as I do in the laboratory. I might be called a sheep in wolf's clothing, and she a wolf in sheep's clothing.

Miss Simons is an unusually gifted therapist. Like many gifted therapists, she has trouble explaining to other workers how she gets her results. Her metaphors—"Walk behind the child so that you can see where he is going"—describe the principles of operant reinforcement very well, but they helped the staff little in everyday dealings with the children.

Here was an area where an experimentalist could help. A functional analysis of Miss Simons' methods, in objective language, would make it easier for the staff to understand and evaluate them. It would also give Miss Simons a new perspective on her own work.

As I watched Miss Simons deal with the children, I saw the application of every principle of behavior that I know. But I did not always recognize them at first. There was one boy who teased Miss Simons by pulling her hair. When she continued to give him her full attention, I wondered why. It seemed clear that her attention was reinforcing the annoying behavior. But when I looked more closely, I saw that Miss Simons was holding the boy's wrist close to her hair so that he couldn't pull it. She released her grip only when he made a move toward some more desirable kind of behavior.

To illustrate the kind of thing Miss Simons does (and the way behavioral language can clarify it), I will describe an encounter she had with an autistic girl named Karen.

Karen was mute and she had very little contact with her environment. She would cry continuously and softly, and she had a doll that she always carried with her.

The encounter took place only a short time after Karen arrived at Linwood, and it was the child's first sustained interaction with another person. It lasted for about half an hour. During that time, there were perhaps 200 instances in which Miss Simons' behavior was clearly contingent on that of the child. The general therapeutic goals were to diminish Karen's crying, weaken the compulsive control of the doll, and begin developing more constructive forms of behavior that Karen could use to manipulate the environment herself. The third goal was the most important, and during the encounter it became clear that the extinction of the crying and the weakened control of the doll were by-products of the reinforcement of other behavior.

Miss Simons placed Karen on a rocking horse in the playroom and began to rock her and sing to her. The rocking and singing stopped the child's crying. Then, for brief periods, Miss Simons kept on singing but stopped rocking. She sensed very accurately how long the pause could be without the child's beginning to cry again.

After a few minutes of this, the therapist took the doll from the child and placed it on a table. But she moved the table very close to Karen so that the child could easily take the doll back again. When she leaned over to do so,

Karen rocked *herself* slightly. From then on, Miss Simons sang only when Karen rocked herself, which Karen did more and more frequently.

Miss Simons placed the doll on the table several times and the child calmly took it back. Then Karen *herself* put the doll on the table. Miss Simons began to rock the horse vigorously. The intensity of her voice as she sang kept pace with the rocking.

Up to this time, Miss Simons sang whenever the child rocked herself, but now she occasionally did not sing even though the child rocked. As this new situation began, Karen took the doll back off the table—having been without it for more than a full minute for the first time since her arrival at Linwood.

As she picked up the doll, it accidentally dropped to the floor. Karen began

to cry. "Do you want to pick it up?" Miss Simons asked. "I'll help you." She lifted Karen off the horse and the *child* picked up the doll. When Miss Simons asked if she wanted to get up again, Karen raised her hands and Miss Simons helped her climb back into the saddle.

Karen dropped the doll again, and again Miss Simons helped her pick it up and get back on the horse. This time Karen came closer to mounting by herself, though Miss Simons still provided some support. The therapist rocked the horse vigorously and moved the doll to a couch, not far away but out of reach, and she stopped the rocking for a moment. Karen glanced at the doll and then withdrew her attention. Miss Simons picked up the doll and tapped it rhythmically; Karen looked at her, made a sound, and began to rock in time with the tapping. Miss Simons gave her the doll.

The next time the therapist took the doll away, Karen cried but kept on rock-

ing. Miss Simons began to sing, which stopped the crying. Then she took the child off the horse so that Karen could get the doll from the couch. They sat together on the couch for a few moments, the child on the therapist's lap. When Karen tried to persuade Miss Simons to go back to the horse by pulling her arm in that direction, Miss Simons smiled and picked the child up but carried her in another direction.

Here there seemed to be a deliberate switch in contingencies. Miss Simons had developed a repertoire of performances in Karen that involved the rocking horse. Now she had shifted to a new set of reinforcers, picking Karen up and interacting with her through body contact and singing. She did not reinforce any attempts to go back to the horse. I don't know what Miss Simons would have done if Karen had struggled in her arms and continued gesturing toward the horse, but I suspect she knew this was improbable before she made the shift.

Even though the behavioral processes that operated here were the same ones I knew from laboratory experience, I would not have been able to put them into practice as Miss Simons did. For example, I might have kept Karen on the horse, without the doll, until her crying stopped. What Miss Simons did instead was wait until Karen's behavior was strongly controlled by rocking and singing before she took the doll away. Later, when Karen dropped the doll and began to cry, Miss Simons reacted at once and used the doll itself to reward the girl for picking it up.

Observation of Jeanne Simons' therapy has taught me many new ways in which the behavior of autistic children can be developed. As for her, she says she is more aware of her own actions. She sees more clearly the individual elements in her complex interchange with a child and has a better understanding of the specific effect of each small act. This helps her refine and modify her procedures and also allows her to describe them more clearly for the staff.

"I think I can explain little step-by-step procedures now so that people don't just look blindly at me with awe," she says. "I'm not even sure intuition is so mysterious. I think it's having eyes all over the place and seeing the tiny little things that children are doing. . . . And I am able to see the tiny little steps and explain much better what I am doing with the children. So the magic is out of Linwood—which I think is wonderful!"

By Sidney W. Bijou

The Mentally Retarded Child

TRADITION HAS IT that mental retardation is a symptom of something deeper—of something called "defective intelligence," "clinically inferred brain damage" or "familial factors." This view has lost ground in recent years. The more modern one that is replacing it regards retardation not as a symptom but as a form of behavior: limited behavior that has been shaped by past events in a person's life. The new method does not assume that we can know what goes on inside a person. Instead, it concentrates on what can be scientifically observed.

No special theory is necessary to analyze the behavior of a mentally retarded person. The same principles apply to the development of all people—retarded, normal and accelerated. Psychological development, according to behavior theory, consists of interactions between the behavior of the individual as a total functioning biological system and environmental events. It follows then that retardation is the result of conditions that prevent, reduce or delay the development of effective ways of interacting with the environment.

In addition to being a total functioning biological system, an individual is a complex behaving system that changes his environment, and also a source of stimuli that affect his own behavior and the behavior of others toward him. The second characteristic suggests that a person carries around with him part of his environment. This is indeed the case, as we shall see.

When I refer to environmental events, I mean the specific events that are actually related to a person's behavior. This is not the usual definition of environment. The dictionary defines environment as "an aggregate of surrounding things and influences," or as "external conditions." In this analysis, the environment, and synonymously, environmental events, refer only to those stimuli *that can be linked with the behavior of an individual.*

There is one other critical difference in the way behavior theory uses the term. Environment usually refers to the social, cultural and physical conditions that influence a person's life. These conditions are part of the word *environment* as it is used in behavior theory, but so is another category—the biological. This biological environment, the one that a person carries with him all the time, is made up of stimuli that emanate from one's own anatomical structure and physiological functioning.

As the so-called normal individual develops, opportunities become available to him for contact with a succession of environmental events. The rate at which the normal person takes advantage of these opportunities, and to what extent, is more or less typical of his culture. In addition, the normal person's biological structure and physiological functioning are adequate, and they mature at the usual rates. For the retarded person, on the other hand, the pace of successive social, physical and biological conditions is slowed down, and the effectiveness of many contacts is almost nil.

It is the quantity and quality of opportunities for contacts that determine a person's rate of development. The more extreme the restrictions on opportunities, the more extreme the retardation. The factors that contribute to delays and failures in development are therefore a major concern of scientists who hold the behavioral theory of retardation. I shall discuss these factors here in terms of (1) abnormal anatomical structure and physiological functioning, (2) insufficient reinforcement and discrimination histories, (3) the disadvantageous reinforcement of "undesirable" behavior, and (4) severe aversive stimulation.

The four categories will be presented separately for the sake of clarity; in reality, they interact with each other constantly, and in many complicated ways.

Anatomy and Physiology

A person who is biologically abnormal may well have altered response capabilities that affect the nature and progression of stimulating conditions. Since biological anomalies range from mild to severe, their effect on psychological development extends in turn from inconsequential to devastating.

Obviously, responses to stimuli are likely to be affected by impairments of the responding parts of the body and of internal coordinating systems such as the central nervous system. A child cannot possibly learn a response if it requires an anatomical part that the child does not possess or a physiological function of which he is incapable. A child with impaired vocal cords cannot be trained to make all the sounds necessary for normal speech. (He may, of course, be able to learn different responses that will serve the same purpose in the sense that they will affect the environment in the same way.)

Not so obviously, the stimulus that precedes a response may also be affected adversely by biological impairment. When skills in body management and locomotion are inadequately developed, the number and type of physical and social stimuli available for contacts are limited. Restricted mobility generates fixed behavioral repertoires. A child limited to lying on his back can only experience stimuli that are above his body or brought into his line of vision, while a child who can roll from side to side and sit up can interact with stimuli over a greatly extended range. Similarly, a child who can reach, grasp and retrieve an object can have infinitely more experiences than a child who has yet to develop manual coordination and skill. The child who can move about can become involved in a great many novel situations compared to a physically handicapped child who must depend upon the good will of others for his locomotion. The biological impairment of some children makes certain stimuli forever inaccessible to them; for others, the stimuli will become available on a delayed time-schedule.

The stimulation of the physically impaired child may also be restricted because of the way the child *looks* to others —because of his social stimulational characteristics. If the child's physical appearance is repugnant or unappealing, people may avoid him, leave him as quickly as possible, or ignore him. As Donald Zimmerman has commented, "These results superimpose social deprivation upon physical defect."

Because our society likes to think it demonstrates concern for the physically impaired, aloof behavior is often made to appear unavoidable. For example, a physically disabled youngster · can be without positive social interactions for long periods because his parents are too "busy" looking after the other children and his siblings are too "bogged down" with homework to engage in extended play with him. The children in the neighborhood exclude him from their games because he cannot "keep up with them." And the school principal bars him from school because he is not "ready."

Avoidant, abbreviated and dutiful social relationships deprive any child, physically impaired or not, of the basic intellectual and social interactions that only people can provide. For example, complex behavior, such as thinking in abstract terms or solving problems, develops in later childhood and beyond only if people are available to arrange and rearrange stimuli (set up problems, bring dissimilar things together and point out similarities and differences), to stimulate responses (ask questions, offer hints and prompts), and to react appropriately to the responses given (confirm correct responses, assist in changing incorrect responses). Innumerable interactions of this sort, some very subtle, occur every day in the life of a normal child in the home, neighborhood and preschool. For example, a mother on her way to the store may see a cow grazing in the pasture and say to her preschooler, "What is that over there?" To the response, "Doggie," she may say, "No, that's a cow," and describe the differences between the two animals. Similarly, the development of appropriate emotional behavior patterns seems to require, among other things, repeated experience with social contingencies such as attention, praise, approval and affection for desirable behavior; with social support following adverse events, such as consolation after injury or frustration; and with corrective procedures that do not generate new emotional problems.

Structural and functional biological impairment is a fact of life, and many of the children it affects will always have limited behavioral repertoires: They will always be developmentally retarded.

The important thing is that their development should progress as far as possible, and behavioral scientists will always be interested in ways of helping them accomplish this objective.

Reinforcement and Discrimination

Reinforcement is a difficult word to define to everyone's satisfaction. It is roughly synonymous with "reward," but only very roughly. As used here, reinforcement refers to a stimulus environmental event following a response that increases the probability of a similar response in a similar situation in the future. Behavior that is sensitive to such consequent stimulus events is called *operant behavior*. It includes verbal, motor, social and intellectual responses as well as much emotional behavior.

The stimulus following operant behavior is called a *stimulus event*, to emphasize that some identifiable change has occurred. The change may add something to the situation (giving a glass of orange juice to a child following his request, "Mother, may I have a glass of juice?") or removing something from it (taking off a child's sweater in response to, "My sweater itches"). Stimulus events that strengthen operant behavior are called *reinforcing stimuli*, and they are said to have a reinforcing function.

Reinforcement does not take place in isolation. Other events occur at the same time, creating conditions that increase or decrease the probability that operant behavior will occur. Of particular interest here are stimulus events that occur immediately before the response that is likely to be reinforced. They are called *discriminative stimuli* (or cues) and are said to have a discriminative function, because they provide the signal for behaving in a way that will probably produce reinforcement. Reinforcing stimuli and discriminative stimuli are therefore interdependent.

One stimulus can serve *both* functions: it can be both a discriminative and a reinforcing stimulus. A smile from a parent in response to a child's good table manners may increase the probability of good table manners in the future (a reinforcing stimulus). A smile from the same parent in the living room may serve as a cue for the same child to climb onto the parent's lap (a discriminative stimulus). In the same way, receiving a sweet may be a reinforcing stimulus that strengthens the preceding behavior, which was the statement, "I want a cookie." The same cookie on a plate may be a discriminative stimulus

for reaching, grasping and bringing to the mouth. Because of the interlocking relationship between discriminating and reinforcing stimulus functions, we consider them together as conditions that retard or promote development.

In general, a child's progress in building a repertory of discriminations (as well as one of motor skills) depends on four things: the number and kind of opportunities made available to the child by the action of people (particularly parents); the properties of available physical objects; the characteristics of the child's structure and physiological functioning; and his maturational and health condition. On the one hand, interactions that reinforce, discriminate and interrelate culturally serviceable behavior are expected to produce people with large repertories of socially, intellectually and vocationally valuable (highly reinforceable) behavior. Reports by Lewis Terman and his co-workers on the background and achievements of high I.Q. children and their offspring support this contention. On the other hand, environments with meager opportunities for reinforcement, discrimination, and the development of complex motor and verbal behavior are expected to produce children with limited repertories of socially serviceable behavior. With respect to the role of meager opportunities, Charles Ferster says:

"Under this category belong individuals who are not making contact with important parts of their environment simply because their history did not include a set of experiences (educational) which could develop these performances during the normal maturation of the individual. Especially in the area of everyday social contacts, considerable skill is necessary for producing social reinforcements, and the absence of this skill either results in an individual without a social repertoire or one who achieves effects on his social environment by indirect means, as, for example, using aversive stimulation to gain attention."

On the basis of inferences from behavioral principles, there are at least three sets of circumstances under which inadequate behavior of this type may evolve: when reinforcements, particularly social reinforcements, are infrequent and weak; when reinforcements are lacking (extinction) or given indiscriminately; and when programs for the development of essential discrimination and skills are lacking or ineptly arranged.

Infrequent and Weak Reinforcements.
Under-staffed child-care institutions may be responsible for one set of circumstances in which reinforcements are infrequent and given in small amounts. For example, Wayne Dennis and Pergouchi Najarian observed children one to four years old in three Iranian institutions, each of which used different child-rearing practices. In two of the institutions, the children were markedly retarded in motor skills; in the other there was little evidence of such retardation. The investigators summarized their findings as follows:

"The extreme retardation in Institutions I and II was probably due to the paucity of handling, including the failure of attendants to place the children in the sitting position and the prone position. The absence of experience in these positions is believed to have retarded the children in regard to sitting alone and also in regard to the onset of locomotion. The lack of experience in the prone position seems in most cases to have prevented children from learning to creep; instead of creeping, the majority of the children in Institutions I and II, prior to walking, locomoted by scooting. In Institution III, in which children were frequently handled, propped in the sitting position and placed prone, motor development resembled that of most home-reared children. The retardation of subjects in Institutions I and II is believed to be due to the restriction of specific kinds of learning opportunities."

In a later study of a similar institution in Beirut, Lebanon, Yvonne Sayegh and Wayne Dennis reported that additional stimulation given to infants could accelerate development. In their words, "appropriate supplementary experience can result in rapid increases in behavioral development on the part of environmentally retarded infants."

Inadequate reinforcement—and the retardation that it leads to—may also occur in a home where, except for basic biological care, the child is left to his own resources because his parents are preoccupied with outside activities or with serious physical or mental health problems. Ferster has discussed how such child-rearing practices contribute to behavioral deficits in the early development of a severely disturbed child:

"The most fundamental way to eliminate a kind of behavior from

an organism's repertoire is to discontinue the effect the behavior has on the environment (extinction). A performance may also be weakened if its maintaining effect on the environment occurs intermittently (intermittent reinforcement). Behaviors occurring because of their effects on the parent are especially likely to be weakened by intermittent reinforcement and extinction, because the parental reinforcements are a function of other variables and behavioral processes usually not directly under the control of the child."

He went on to point out that speech and social behaviors are those most likely to be adversely affected by extinction (non-reinforcement) and intermittent reinforcement, because at this early stage of a child's life the parents are the most important source of reinforcers for the development of those behaviors.

Note that I referred to parent-child interactions that create behavior deficits in severely *disturbed* young children. How does this relate to the task of analyzing retarded development? Simply this: there is good evidence that the conditions and processes contributing to severe behavioral disturbances in children also slow down development. Failure to perpetuate a behavior eliminates that particular behavior—one that the child has already established for dealing with current situations—from the child's repertory. It also puts him at a disadvantage in learning new behavior that requires a foundation of responses of the sort lost. Verbal development is a case in point. Because it is basic to so much other behavior, inadequate reinforcement of early verbal behavior can result in deficits in intellectual, social, emotional and even motor development.

Many retarded children are also behaviorally disturbed, and practically all severely maladjusted children are also developmentally retarded. We distinguish between the behaviorally disturbed and the developmentally retarded only for practical purposes in grouping children for residential care and for educational and training programs.

There is another condition that may produce weak social reinforcement on a sparse schedule: the physical appearance of a child considered repulsive by the social community. As I mentioned earlier, an atypical biological makeup can result in a shortage of adequate social contacts and experiences with physical objects. As a result, the markedly

unattractive child does not have adequate opportunities to develop relationships with new reinforcing and discriminative stimuli.

Indiscriminate Reinforcement, or None.
One of the ways behavior (particularly that supported by weak social and sensory stimulation) is eliminated is by withholding reinforcement. This process is called *extinction*. One might say that the extreme case of intermittent reinforcement is extinction.

There is a wide variety of behavior supported by scattered social interactions (a nod, a smile, a pat for showing commendable perseverance) and by the stimulation of physical things made available in interesting ways. When a family must struggle with poor health, adjustment difficulties, drug addiction, alcoholism and the like, it may not provide the social interactions or physical objects necessary to reinforce behavior.

Behaviors may also be weakened or remain undeveloped if reinforcements are delivered indiscriminately, with no relevance to the response the parent wishes the child to learn. An example with which we are all familiar is the child who is chronically sick, disabled or incapacitated. The parents, understandably concerned, react by maintaining close supervision and responding almost continuously, and without question, to each and every one of the child's needs or demands, reasonable or unreasonable. If the child screams for no obvious reason, the parent comes running, thus reinforcing the screaming; if the child spews out his food, the parent coaxes him to eat another mouthful; if the child demands constant companion-

ship, someone is stationed nearby. This situation also tends to reduce the child's exploratory behavior, with consequences that will be discussed below.

Poor Development of Skills.

If there are few or no occasions for the child to interact with responsive people and interesting things, then there are few opportunities for him to acquire and retain serviceable behavior supported by reinforcement processes. Serviceable behavior includes skills in body management, manual dexterity, crawling, walking, running, jumping, skipping, climbing and skating; the transformation of sounds into words, phrases and sentences; and the relating of words, spoken or written, to things, symbols and other words.

In a number of situations, severe restrictions on a child may retard his development. Here are a few.

(1) *When a child is treated as though he were abnormal or chronically ill.* A study of a four-year-old girl in a laboratory nursery school showed that the infantilization practices of the parents resulted in the complete absence of speech, and in gross motor incoordination to the point where she was unable to move about without stumbling and falling.

(2) *When the parent engages in abnormal or idiosyncratic practices.* In a classic case, Kingsley Davis described an example of a deaf-mute mother who kept her illegitimate child in isolation. Mother and child spent most of the time together in a dark room, shut off from the rest of the family. The situation was discovered when the child was six and a half years old. She communicated with her mother by gestures and made only "strange croaking sounds." Efforts to determine whether the child could hear were at first inconclusive; later it was established that her hearing was normal. She displayed fear and hostility toward others, particularly men. As one might expect, reactions to objects were unusual: when presented with a ball, she used it to stroke the interviewer's face. Psychological testing yielded a mental age on the Stanford-Binet of one year and seven months, and a social age on the Vineland Social Maturity Scale of two and a half years.

(3) *When the environment is thinly populated with stimulating people and intriguing things.* A sparse social environment not only reduces the frequency of social reinforcing stimuli, it limits the opportunities for a child to engage in programmed activities that result in discriminations normally expected in his

particular culture. People are necessary to arrange the environment so that the child can learn intellectual skills and develop a store of knowledge. People are necessary to create opportunities for the development of manners and morals. People are necessary to provide circumstances that establish values, interests and attitudes appropriate for community life.

(4) *When the necessary physical and cultural components of the environment are absent because of economic and social circumstances.* The detrimental effects on development of economic and cultural deprivation have now been recognized and are being stressed in programs designed to help children from underdeveloped areas and disadvantaged surroundings.

Reinforcement of 'Undesirable' Behavior

In some situations, retardation may develop because "undesirable" behavior has been reinforced. Presumably no parent would *want* to develop "bad" behavior in a child, but it may evolve precisely because the parent dislikes it and finds that attending to it reduces or eliminates it. In the long run, though, this type of interaction strengthens both the "bad" behavior of the child and the attending behavior of the parent. The child is positively reinforced by the parent's action, and the parent is negatively reinforced by the action that has terminated the child's "bad" behavior. A familiar example is the child who gets what he wants by having a temper tantrum. Chances are that tantrum behavior was strengthened by the parents' compliance with the condition that instigated the tantrum. Chances are, also, that the parent "gave in" to terminate the distasteful or even alarming behavior displayed by the child. So the parent's response to the tantrum strengthened tantruming on the part of the child, and the child's termination of the current tantrum strengthened "giving in" on the part of the parent.

This may be a plausible technical account of how a parent can strengthen undesirable behavior, but how does it relate to retarding development? First, undesirable behavior may become the child's main way of responding. If a child is constantly screaming or having tantrums, his learning of new socially and educationally desirable behavior will be slow or even static. Furthermore, the results of formal and informal tutorial interactions will be reduced; effective

attention and work spans will be relatively short, and even minor nonreinforcement episodes such as correcting a color-naming error may set off strong and prolonged aversive behavior. A report by Montrose Wolf and his colleagues on the behavioral treatment and rehabilitation of a preschool boy diagnosed as autistic, retarded and brain-injured described many instances in which strong aversive behavior had to be weakened considerably, or even totally eliminated, before the boy could be retrained. Second, unpleasant behavior may well make the child socially repugnant and so discourage people from approaching and participating in prolonged educational and social interactions with him. This, in turn, will limit his repertory of behavior. Children who display obnoxious behavior are often considered unteachable, or nearly so. They find themselves in a situation similar to that of a child who is avoided because he is physically repellent.

Severe Aversive Stimulation

Another kind of interaction that may retard development is called *contingent aversive stimulation*. This refers both to the practice of administering strong punishment to stop a particular behavior and to hurts and injuries that may occur, for example, during medical treatment or in a serious accident.

Aversive stimulation can have several consequences. First, aversive stimulation can stop ongoing behavior—it may suppress the behavior that preceded it. If the stimulation is moderate, the suppressed behavior is likely to reappear. A skinned knee slows down an active youngster only for minutes. If the stimulation is severe, however, suppressive effects may remain for some time. More than one clinical account has been given of a young child who stopped talking for weeks, months or years following severe punishment by an intoxicated or disturbed parent.

Second, the setting in which aversive stimulation occurs may become aversive in itself: formerly neutral or positive situations can become distasteful or frightening. (After being thrown from his favorite horse, the youngster now reacts to the animal with fear.) The removal of such stimuli is negatively reinforcing. It strengthens the tendency to get away from the aversive situation or thing, to avoid it, or to become immobile when it arises. (If attempts to put the child back on the horse are discontinued because the youngster cries and hollers, then crying and hollering behavior is strengthened and fear of the horse and of things associated with it remain.)

One cannot predict which classes of behavior will be strengthened by negative reinforcement, but it is certainly clear that excessive avoidant behavior can restrict the range of interactions available to a child. In many instances the interactions that are terminated may be needed for further development (speaking, for example), and the situations that are avoided may be critical to a normal child-rearing environment (such as those involving the father) and may affect other similar aspects of the environment (all male adults). Thus, stimuli and responses that were not directly involved in the aversive interaction may come to have aversive properties in themselves.

Third, aversive stimuli may evoke physiological responses (such as gastric reactions to a fear-producing event) that affect biological functioning of the child and thereby reduce his potential for serviceable interactions.

While the consequences of strong aversive stimulation are most frequently discussed in the literature of child psychopathology under the heading of severe emotional disturbances (referred to as psychoneurotic, psychotic and autistic), they are discussed here because aversive stimulation also retards development. Just as biological anomalies and social insufficiencies limit opportunities for development, so do strong avoidant reactions. All three foreclose many occasions for a child to make new adjustments.

I have singled out for discussion here the retarding effects of abnormal ana-

tomical structure and functioning, inadequate reinforcement and discrimination histories, reinforcement of undesirable behavior, and severe aversive stimulation. There are, however, other processes. For example, there is the possibility that the termination (say, through death) of interactions with a mother-figure after a strong affection bond has been established can have strong retarding effects. It can weaken or even eliminate well-established behavior by removing the cues on which the behavior depended. It should be emphasized, however, that these other processes do *not* include assumed conditions such as "defective intelligence," "clinically inferred brain damage" and "familial factors."

By A. S. Neill

Can I come to Summerhill?

I hate my school.

JUST OVER 20 YEARS AGO I had two books published in New York, *The Problem Teacher* and *The Problem Family*. So far as I could make out each issue sold a few hundred copies and the rest were sold as remainders at a few dimes each. The press notices I got were either lukewarm or hostile. One called the books old hat. "We have lived through this in the States and there is nothing new for us." Twenty years later the book *Summerhill* became a best seller in the States. Why? I have no idea. I like to think that the U.S.A. has come up to date rather than that I have gone out of date. I do not know why I get so large a mail from the U.S.A. It is mostly from young people and in the seven years since the book was published I can recall only two hostile letters. Many are from school children. "Can I come to Summerhill? I hate my school. It is all pressurization. The teachers make every lesson dull and dead and originality is frowned upon." Oddly enough, although our British education is all wrong, I never get letters from home children.

The mystery to me is this: Why has America become conscious that its education is not good enough? Why now and not 20 years ago? Surely the schools have not changed all that much. But is it a case of a change of society? Is society sicker than it was a couple of decades ago? I fancy that that is the deep reason. In all countries youth is rebelling. Alas, too often rebelling against all that does not matter. The hippies, the flower merchants show their protests, not against war, not against race discrimination, not against the stupid learning we call education; no, all the challenge is the right to wear long hair and leather jackets and blue jeans. That is the impression I get in this country, but from what I hear and read about America the young, especially in the universities, are challenging real evils—the insane dollar values, the dead uniformity of the people who have been molded and indoctrinated so much that they are automatic slaves to any ideas thrown out by the press and the TV screens. In Britain I think that the average TV program is geared to a nation of 10-year-olds. Our B.B.C. refused to put on *The War Game* because it told of the horrors of an atomic war and it might upset the nice folks who want to think that God is in his Heaven and all is right with the world. The young feel that they have been cheated by the old, lied to, castrated by their parents and teachers. They no longer accept glib answers—

in Vietnam we are saving the world from Communism; in South Africa we are preserving the God-given rights of the superior whites; in the U.S.A. we are battling to preserve the white civilization. It is significant that all these reasons involve hate and war and possibly ultimate death to humanity. Youth sees a world full of savagery. Hitler's six million Jews paved the way for a world that accepted torture and death as almost commonplace factors in our modern life. In short, the world is very very sick, and youth feels it but, alas, cannot do much about it. Summerhill's good friend Joan Baez, recently in prison, has no power over the hate merchants; all she can do is to march in protest and then be carted to prison. It is the helplessness of youth that so often brings despair.

In this American *Stimmung* the book *Summerhill* was launched in 1960. It caught on because it was voicing what so many of the young had felt but had not intellectualized, had not made conscious. For its theme was freedom—real freedom, not the sham thing so often called democracy. Freedom for all to grow at their own pace; freedom from all indoctrination, religious, political, moral; freedom for children to live in their own community, making their own social laws. To many a youth Summerhill became synonymous with Paradise. I hasten to say that it isn't—*Gott sei dank!* Most of the rebellion stems from home, from what Wilhelm Reich called the compulsive family, the family that strangles youth, fears youth, often hates youth. From my mail I am led to believe that the American family is more dangerous than the British one. I never get the sort of letter I had two days ago from New York. "I am 17 and I am allowed no freedom at all. I have to be in at certain hours and if I am late my father hits me. I hate my parents." A girl of a middle-class family. I have had scores of similar letters. A boy of 15 writes, "I hate school and cannot concentrate on my work and my parents bully me all the time because they say that I must go to college and get a good job." I have no idea how much truth is in Vance Packard's *The Status Seekers* but even if a 10th is true it gives a terrible picture of American civilization. A Cadillac-civilization with its sequel, dope and drugs and misery for those who cannot accept the god of cars and furs and wealth.

This looks like an attack on a country by an outsider and it may well be

I do not know the answer; all I know is that when children are free they do not kill life.

resented by some readers, but I do not mean it as an attack; it is a case of trying to think aloud the answer to the question: Why did the Summerhill book catch on in the U.S.A.? At home we have our own miseries and troubles. The growing race hate due to the immigration from Jamaica. The futility of a culture that dwells on bingo and football crowds, on infantile TV programs; a culture that gives the cheap sensational press millions of readers while the more cultured papers—*The New Statesman,* the *Observer,* the *Sunday Times*—too often struggle to keep themselves alive. World sickness is not confined to North America. Russia has its teen-age gangsters also.

One reason why Summerhill appealed to the U.S.A. may be that it is, so to say, anti-education. The great American educationists, Dewey, Kilpatrick and their kind, were mostly pre-Freudian in their outlook. They kept linking education to learning, and today in all countries educational journals concentrate on the learning process. I escaped that trap. I was and I am ill-versed on what the educationists did. I never read Rousseau or Pestalozzi or Froebel; what I read in Montessori I did not like, partly because it made play the mate of learning. Learn-

We are all in the trap and only the more aware of us try to find a way out.

ing what? Summerhill is not a seat of learning; it is a seat of living. We are not so proud of David who became a professor of mathematics as we are of Jimmy who was hateful and antisocial and is now a warm-hearted engineer with much charity and love to give out. Summerhill puts learning in its own place. I have more than once written that if the emotions are free the intellect will look after itself. What a waste it all is! Sixty years ago I could read some Latin and Greek. Today I can't decipher the Latin words on a tombstone. Our schools teach children to read Shakespeare and Hardy and Tennyson and when they leave school the vast majority never read anything better than a crime story. For my part I'd abolish nearly every school subject, making geography and history matters for the school library, and quadratic equations a luxury for the few boys and girls who loved maths. Abolish exams and my school will have only creative teachers—art, music, drama, handwork, etc.

Every man has a bee in his bonnet. It was comforting to read in Erich Fromm that Freud had to be in the station an hour before his train was due. My original bee was psychology. In the 1920s my home was Vienna and my associates the psychoanalysts. Like all young fools I thought that Utopia was just 'round the corner. Make the unconscious conscious and you have a world full of love and fellowship with no hate. I grew out of that phase but did retain the belief that education must primarily deal with the emotions. Working for many years with problem children made my belief stronger. I saw that the aim of all education must be to produce happy, balanced, pro-life children, and I knew that all the exams and books in a million classrooms could not do a thing to make children balanced. A B.A. could be a hopeless neurotic—I am an M.A. myself. A professor could remain at the age of 10 emotionally. What the emotional level of the British Cabinet or the American Pentagon is is anyone's guess; my own guess is a low one. Today in any school anywhere it is the head that is educated; every exam paper proves the point.

Now one cannot flee from reality. I could not say to prospective parents, "Exams and school subjects are not education and I refuse to teach the ordinary school subjects." That is what the Americans would call flunking out, and, by the way, I get too many letters from students in the U.S.A. saying, "I can't go on with my college career. The teaching is too dull; I am flunking out. I want to be a child psychologist." I answer that they won't let one be a child psychologist unless one accepts their qualification demands. I wrote to the last man who had flunked out, "If you haven't the guts to walk through the muck heaps, how can you ever expect to smell the roses you value so much?"

I do not find this flunking-out element in old Summerhill pupils. One of my first pupils spent two years standing at a mechanical belt in a car factory. He is now a successful engineer with his own business. His brother who wanted to be a doctor had to pass an exam in Latin. In just over a year he passed the matriculation exam in Latin. "I hated the stuff but it was in my way and I had to master it." That was over 40 years ago when students did not as a rule flunk out. I do not think that youth has become defeatist; rather it is that society has reached a point of futility and cheapness and danger where youth, frustrated by the mundane standard of success, simply gives up in despair. "Make Love not War" is a most appropriate motto for youth even if youth feels it is a hopeless cry, and it is a hopeless cry; the hate men who make wars force youth to die for country but when the young demand freedom to have a sex life, holy hypocritical hands are held up in horror. Youth is free to die but not to live and love.

I fear I am rambling, not sticking to the point. My consolation—too many who stick to the point make it a blunt one. I ramble because I am trying to evaluate Summerhill as a factor in the sick world, really asking what value freedom has for youth. One is naturally apt to think that one's geese are swans; one tends to forget or ignore the outside world, so that when a lecturer in education in an American college wrote and told me that over 70 per cent of his students thought that Summerhill was all wrong it came as a shock. I had repressed the idea that when the young are conditioned and indoctrinated from cradle days, it is almost impossible for them to break away, to challenge. Few can stand alone without a supporting crowd behind them. "The strongest man is he who stands most alone." Ibsen.

I like to think that freedom helps one to stand outside the maddening crowd. Symbolically one sees differences. The conventional suburban office-goer with his striped trousers and his neat tie and his neater mind on one side. On the other, the creator, the artist to whom exterior things mean but little. Compare the tailoring of L. B. J. with that of a film director or a Picasso. Symbols, but characteristic. Put it this way: Summerhill gets hundreds of visitors but I do not think that any visitor ever notices that my staff never wear ties. Summerhill hasn't got to the Old-School-Tie stage. But one cannot carry such phantasying too far; my old friend Bertrand Russell wears a tie, and no one would claim that he is a crowd man.

I think that one aspect of Summerhill is that it, rightly or wrongly, gives pupils an anti-crowd psychology. I could not imagine any old pupil following a Hitler or for that matter a Kennedy or a Reagan. This sounds incongruous because the chief feature of Summerhill is the self-government, the making of laws by one and all from the age of five to 84. Pupils become ego-conscious and at the same time community-conscious. Bill can

do what he likes all day long as long as he does not interfere with the freedom of anyone else; he can sleep all day if he wants to but he is not allowed to play a trumpet when others want to talk or sleep. It is as near democracy as one can get; every child is a member of parliament able to speak "in the house." No doubt because this democracy is real and honest our old pupils cannot tolerate the sham we name politics. Because politicians have to rely on votes nearly every urgent reform is delayed for two generations. In England an M.P. has—say—a predominantly Catholic constituency or a Baptist one. How can he act honestly when faced with some reform—a bill to abolish punishment for homosexuality, a much-needed reform of the divorce and abortion laws? Was any great man a politician? Any Darwin, any Freud, any Einstein, any Beethoven? Was any big man ever a crowd-compeller, a demagogue?

When children are free they become wonderfully sincere. They cannot act a part; they cannot stand up in the presence of a school inspector because they will not countenance insincerity and make-believe. Tact forces them to make minor adaptations as it does with you and me. I dutifully doff my hat to a lady although I realize that it is a meaningless, even dishonest, gesture, hiding the fact that in a patriarchal society a woman is inferior in status, in pay, in power. To tell a social white lie is often a necessity but to live a lie is something that free people cannot do. And my pupils feel that to be a member of a crowd must involve living a lie.

This crowd psychology angle is important. It is at the root of the sickness of the world. A neighboring country insults your flag and many thousands of young men die for the honor and glory of their fatherland. National hatreds everywhere, Greek v. Turkey; Israel v. Arabs; Rhodesian white v. Black. And it is not only the nationalism crowd. Our football grounds are full of irrational, partisan hate and violence. Gang warfare is not confined to Chicago. Yet in a way violence is minor. It is the violence that a crowd inflicts on its members that frightens, the violence of intimidating, of molding. A school uniform means: We are members of a crowd, a crowd that will not tolerate opposition. We must all dress alike, think alike, act alike. For the great law of any crowd is: Thou shalt conform. The world is sick because its crowds are sick.

Education therefore should aim at

abolishing crowd psychology. It can do this only by allowing the individual to face life and its choices freely. Such an education cannot lead to egocentricity and utter selfishness, not if the individual is free within the confines of the social order, an order made by himself. The slogan "All the way with L. B. J." shows the iniquity of the crowd, a system that makes crowd members sheep who can feel the most elementary emotions without having the intellectual capacity to connect such emotions with reason. Today our schools educate the head and leave the emotions to the crowd-compellers—the press, the radio, the TV, the churches, the commercial exploiters with their lying advertisements. Our pop heroes and film stars have become our leading schoolmasters, dealing with real emotions. What teacher in what school could have a few hundred hysterical females screaming their heads off when he appeared?

The danger today is undeveloped emotion, perverted emotion, infantile emotion. Millions scream in Britain every Saturday afternoon when their favorite football teams take the field. If the evening paper had a front page in big lettering "Atom War Very Near," most of the spectators would turn to the back page to see the latest scores. Crowd emotions are not touched by news of starvation in India or China. It is this same unattached unrealized emotion that makes the crowd numb to any realization of a likely atomic war. Crowd emotion is not shocked by our inhuman and un-Christlike treatment of criminals in prison; it does not even realize that the inhumanity is there. And none of us is guiltless. I do not cut down my tobacco and give the savings to the starving nations. We are all in the trap and only the more aware of us try to find a way out. My own way is Summerhill or rather the idea behind Summerhill, the belief that man is originally good, that, for reasons no one so far knows, man kills his own life and the lives of his children by harsh and anti-life laws and morals and taboos. It is so easy to cry, "Man is a sinner and he must be redeemed by religion" or what not. God and the Devil were comfortable explanations of good and evil. One thing I think Summerhill has proved is that man does not need to become a "sinner," that man does not naturally hate and kill. The crowd in Summerhill is a humane one. In 47 years I have never seen a jury punish a child for stealing; all it demanded was that the value of the theft be paid back.

**Youth sees
a world full
of savagery.**

When children are free they are not cruel. Freedom and aggression do not go together. I have known a few children who were reared with self-regulation, that is, without fear and outside discipline and imposed morality. They seem to have much less aggression than most children have, suggesting to me that the Freudians with their emphasis on aggression must have studied the wrong children.

Even in Summerhill, where very few pupils were self-regulated, there is a peacefulness, a minimum of criticism, a tolerance that is quite uncommon. When a Negress pupil came from the States not even the youngest child seemed to notice her color. Our TV showed white

faces full of hatred when black pupils were being stoned in the Deep South. This is alarming. We can condition children to hate and kill by giving them a hate environment. But we can also give them another sort of environment —were I a Christian I'd call it a love-your-neighbor environment. But then, what is a Christian? Catholics and Protestants beat children in home and school —didn't Jesus say suffer the little children? The Christians see that they suffer, all right. But to narrow the life negation to religion is wrong. A humanist can hate life and children; he can be as anti-sex as any Calvinist.

Summerhill has not answered many questions, the biggest one being: Why does humanity kill the life of children, why does it take more easily to hate than to love? Why did jackboot Fascism conquer a nation of 60 million?

One answer to the question of world sickness is sex repression. Make sex a sin and you get perversions, crime, hates, wars. Approve of children's sex as the Trobriand Islanders did under a matriarchal system and a Malinowski will fail to find any trace of sex crime or homosexuality before the missionaries came and segregated the sexes. Wilhelm Reich, to me the greatest psychologist since Freud, dwelt on the necessity for a full natural orgastic life as a cure for the sickness of an anti-life society. Then came the new American Interpersonal Relationship school of Sullivan and Horney, with long case histories of patients who seemed to have no sex at all. I have a book on problem children written by an Adlerian; I failed to find the word sex in it. And in all this divergence of views on sex, what can one believe? One can make the guess that the torturers of German Jews were sex perverts, but can one safely conclude that the men in the Pentagon are Hawks because of their sex repressions?

I have gone through many phases in the last 50 years, the most exciting my long friendship with Homer Lane and then with Reich. Now, at 84, I simply do not know the truth about sex. Is a teacher who canes a boy's bottom a repressed homosexual or a sadist or simply a man who has never been conscious of what he is doing? I ask because my father in his village school tawsed children with a leather strap and when I became a teacher I automatically did likewise without ever once wondering if it were good or bad. Looking back now I see that one motive was fear, fear of losing one's dignity, one's power;

fear that any slackness would lead to anarchy. I cannot see anything sexual in my tawsing.

Summerhill society is a sex-approving society. Every child soon learns that there is no moral feeling about masturbation or nudism or sex-play. But every adolescent is conscious of the fact that if approval meant the sharing of bedrooms by adolescents the school would be closed by the Establishment. One old boy once said to me: "The fear of closing the school if pregnancies occurred gave us a new form of sex repression." The difficulty was and is this: How far can a school go in being pro-sex in an anti-sex society? Not very far, I fear. Yet one factor is of moment; the pupils are conscious of our attitude of approval. They have had no indoctrination about sin or shame, no moralizing from Mrs. Grundy. Their free attitude shows itself in minor ways. In our local cinema a film showed a chamber pot. The audience went into fits of obscene laughter but our pupils did not even smile; one or two asked me later why the people laughed. Free children cannot be shocked—by cruelty, yes, but by sex, never.

Summerhill products are often said to be quiet, unaggressive, tolerant citizens, and I wonder how much their rational attitude on sex has to do with their calmness of life. They prove that censorship is the product of a life-hating civilization. I never see our adolescents taking from the school library *Lady Chatterley* or *Fanny Hill*. A girl of 16 said they were boring.

Most of our old pupils are pacific. They do not march with banners against the H-bomb or against racial discrimination. I cannot imagine any of them ever supporting warmongers or religious revivalists or play censors. But how much this has to do with a free attitude to sex I cannot know. Certainly sex is the most repressed of all emotions. Most of us were made anti-sex when in our cradles our hands were taken from our genitals, and it is an arresting thought that the men who have the power to begin a nuclear war are men who were made sex-negative long ago. Anglo-Saxon four-letter words are still taboo in most circles, maybe partly for class reasons; a navvy says fuck while a gentleman says sexual intercourse.

I confess to being muddled about the whole affair of sex. I do not know if we all experienced Reich's perfect orgasm there would be an end to war and crime and hate. *I hae ma doots.* Yet it is true that people who have a pro-sex attitude to life are the ones most likely to be charitable, to be tolerant, to be creative. Those who do not consider themselves sinners do not cast the first stone. For charity I would go to Bertrand Russell rather than to Billy Graham.

Billy naturally leads to religion. Summerhill has no religion. I fancy that very few religionists approve of it. A leading Church of England priest once called it the most religious school in the world, but few parsons would agree with him. It is interesting to note that I have had many letters of approval from Unitarians in the U.S.A. I asked one Unitarian minister what his religion was. Did he believe in God? No, he said. In eternal life? "Good heavens, no. Our religion is giving out love in this life," and I guess that is exactly what the Church of England priest meant. It is our being on the side of the child (Homer Lane's phrase) that has aroused so much antagonism among religionists. The other day a Catholic school inspector told a meeting of Catholics that corporal punishment was practiced much more in their schools than in Protestant ones. "We beat the body to save the soul." In the days of that life-hater John Knox I would have been burned at the stake. The widening interest in the freedom that Summerhill stands for fits in with the lessening belief in religion. Most young people, outside the R.C. faith, have no interest in religion. To them God is dead. God to them was father, molder, punisher, a fearful figure. The gods and fathers were always on the side of the suppressors. In Britain the enemies of youth, those who call for the return of beating with the cat, those who want to censor plays and films and language, those who demand strict punishment for the teen-age delinquents, they are not the young; they are the old, the old who have forgotten their teen-age period.

I am sure that the growing interest in freedom for children coincides with modern youth's rejection of a joyless, repressive religion. A religion that has become perverted. Christ's "love your neighbor as yourself" has become: Okay, so long as he isn't a Jew or a Black. "Let him who is without sin among you cast the first stone" has become: Censor plays and novels and measure bathing costumes. Owing to the threat of universal incineration youth today is possibly more pro-life than it has ever been. Juvenile crime is really at bottom an attempt to find the joy of life killed by morals and discipline and punishment. In the days when Summerhill had many delinquents they went out cured simply because they were free from adult standards of behavior. Religion must be rejected because it tells the young how to live, but it does not need to be religion; I have known humanists who gave their children sex repression; I know agnostics who believe in beating children. Really what one believes does not matter; it is what one is that matters. After all religion is geographical; had I been born in Arabia I'd have had three wives and, alas, no whisky.

There is a comic element in religion even if there isn't a joke in the Bible or the Prayer Book. The true believer must know that Bertrand Russell will roast in hell for eternity while Billy Graham sits at the right hand of God. With Russell to look after, the familiar words "poor Devil" will have a real significance.

What is the outlook for freedom? Will the minority ever take over from the majority? And if it does, will it retain its belief in freedom? Doesn't Ibsen say somewhere that a truth remains a truth for 20 years, then the majority takes it up and it becomes a lie? Summerhill has 64 children who are free from molding: the world has millions of children who have little or no freedom, millions of adults who frankly are sheep. One tragedy of life is that men have followers. Men who remain disciples are always inferiors. The Pharisee who thanked God that he was not as other men may have been a conceited ass but on the other hand he may have got hold of something. There is something wrong when millions who praise the Beatles never heard of Milton or Freud or Cézanne, when millions kill the life of their babies, when thousands of young men die in a battle for they know not what. Anti-life is all around us, and I wish I knew why. I wish I knew why mankind kills what it loves. I do not know the answer; all I know is that when children are free they do not kill life; they do not condemn their fellow men. They do not want to tell others how to live. It is significant that old pupils do not seek jobs where they will boss others; few have gone into business. I used to daydream of one's becoming a tycoon and endowing the school, knowing all the time that he would be so hard-boiled that he would not endow anything.

I am not trying to sell Summerhill. I am trying to say that the cure for the sickness of man does not lie in politics or religion or humanism; nay, the cure is freedom for children to be themselves. Like many others I once thought that the Russian Revolution would bring Utopia to youth, for it began with freedom for children, self-government in the schools. Then, according to Reich, the psychologists took charge and youth became sacrificed to political anti-life, so that today communism has no connection with individual freedom to grow naturally. Indeed I often wonder why the Americans are so scared of communism. Both systems believe in the terror of the bomb; both discipline and castrate children; both believe that education means subjects and exams and acquired knowledge. The only difference I can see is who takes the profit? The Russian Revolution proved that the sickness of the world cannot be cured by politics.

The only answer that I can think of is freedom for children, individual freedom, social freedom, sexual freedom as

I saw that the aim of all education must be to produce happy, balanced pro-life children.

in a small way practiced in Summerhill.

I said that I thought Wilhelm Reich the greatest psychologist since Freud. His diagnosis of man's sickness is deep and wise. Man flees from natural sex by armoring himself against joy in life, stiffening his body, fearing any signs of genitality, changing good emotions into "emotional plague," in short, becoming anti-life, hence wars and many diseases and child-beating. Even if one accepts Reich's diagnosis the question arises: What can be done about it? How can we prevent folks from becoming anti-sex and anti-life? Analysis of any school is not the answer. What effect on humanity have all the case histories ever published? Do all the things Melanie Klein found in babies have any bearing on the education of children? So far psychology has been a matter of diagnosing without any salient suggestions for a cure. Ah, yes, some cases of cures of individual neurotics, but the cure for a sick world, none. A Scientologist has just told me that he could cure any problem child in my school in 10 days.

Are we all fakers? Self-deluders? Do the hundreds of books on psychology published every year have any effect at all? I am inclined to say none, but I am biased, for I cannot read a book on psychology now.

The psychologists have narrowed the science—or is it an art? The doctors have limited psychology to the consulting room and the rich and those with time to spare. How many psychoanalysts have opened schools? A few—Anna Freud, Susan Isaacs, e.g., but the main body of Freudians has done nothing in the way of prophylaxis. The Summerhill Society of New York issues a list of schools claiming to have self-regulation and self-government. Some may be excellent but, as I have not seen any of them, I cannot give an opinion pro or anti. I do not think that they belong to any special schools of psychology and I sincerely hope that they don't. I am sure that the list does not contain the name of the school that claimed to be Summerhillian and washed out a boy's mouth with soap and water when he swore.

The future of psychology should lie not in the consulting room or the hospital for neurosis but in the infant bedroom and the infant school. Mr. Brown's phobia of spiders may fascinate his analyst but his phobia is as nothing in a world of millions of half-alive children.

To return to Summerhill, it went through the stages of the Century—the faith in analysis, the futile attempt to find the original trauma in a young thief. I read them all—Freud, Jung, Adler, Rank, Stekel, Reich—and got more and more confused by their psychological jargon. I never learned the meaning of words like manic-depression, compulsive neurosis, hysteria, etc. Never knew how specialists could draw the line between one and another. Oh, so many were brilliant in their diagnosis and treatment, but in the end what did one learn? And today I feel as confused about the Interpersonal Relationship folks, for, if men like Stekel seemed to overemphasize sex, they seem to denigrate it altogether. So I left schools of thought and concentrated on Summerhill, forgetting theory and avoiding words like complex. "Everyone is right in some way," Reich used to say, the corollary being that everyone is wrong in some way.

Let us face the truth, that we are all little men, even the greatest among us. We do not know how and why the super Rolls Royce, the human body, ticks. We know nothing about life and how it began, nor can we account for the universe. We do not know why Brown dies of cancer and his brother of diabetes. In the psychological realm we cannot account for a Bach or a Milton or a Hitler. We know little about heredity or the origins of love and hate. A doctor does not know what causes a headache. So that we should be wary of panaceas of all kinds—Zen Buddhism, Scientology, Theosophy, psychoanalysis, Moral Rearmament, and a few score of other isms and ologies. We must go on enquiring, searching for the truth, but if we follow a creed, if we become disciples, if we label ourselves Freudian or Reichian or Hubbardian or any other ian we have stopped growing, stopped enquiring; we become "yes" men. It worries me to hear of schools in the U.S.A. that call themselves Summerhills. One should take from others what one feels is good. No one should accept any creed, religious or political or psychological. I got much from Homer Lane; later I got much from Reich. But in both men were views that I could not accept, and thus I escaped discipleship. If a teacher claims that Summerhill inspired him, good, I wish him luck, but if a school claims to be a new Summerhill I fear it will fail. There is a pioneer in each of us, an explorer, a visionary. As in sport we pay others to play the game for us, so in pioneering; we find it easy to look for a leader and be content to be a humble follower of Billy Graham, Sigmund Freud, Barry Goldwater, Karl Marx.

Fans are arrested creators, arrested pioneers. And the big question is: in a world in which the vast majority are fans, how can a few independent people set about "curing" the Establishment?

We must remember that the Establishment has the ultimate power. A bureaucratic Ministry of Education could close my school on material grounds alone: not enough lavatories, not enough cubic feet per child in a bedroom. But, to be fair, the Ministry has not interfered with me in the 44 years Summerhill has been in England. But now that the National Union of Teachers and many Labor M.P.s demand the closing of all private schools, pioneering in education is going to have a bad time. Had there been no private schools there could not have been a Summerhill; the State, the Establishment will allow new methods of teaching history or maths but it is unlikely to tolerate new methods of living in a school. Really I should vote Tory, for the Tories will not lightly give up their Etons and Harrows, and as long as we have the public schools like Rugby the smaller private schools will be protected. Alas, the private school is I fear doomed by lack of finance alone. Summerhill would have died seven years ago had not the publication of *Summerhill* in the U.S.A. brought a flood of American pupils. Today people in England do not have the money to support private schools. Those who do, select the established schools, the public schools and the big co-ed schools with their well-equipped libraries, labs, etc. Parents, like teachers, still look on education as learning in all countries East and West. Educational journals seldom mention the child or freedom or creation. When I write a letter about the teaching of English I get quite a few replies, but when I write an article on the psychology of the child no teacher answers.

I want to claim that Summerhill has for 47 years demanded that character is of more moment than the ability to learn subjects. I have never denigrated learning; all I have done is to put it in its second or 10th place. But what effect the school has had on education I cannot judge. Some say that the permissiveness of some schools stems from Summerhill. Who can know? I like to think that it isn't Summerhill, that it is the *Zeitgeist*, the longing of youth for freedom. Maybe some *History of Education* in the year 2000 will have a footnote about a school called Summerfield run by a mad Scot called S. A. Neale. Sorry I won't be there to laugh at the footnote. 𝄞

Political Attitudes in Children

Do our schoolteachers subvert solid social growth?

by Robert D. Hess

"Sandra, in what way could our country be harmed?"

"By war, we can be harmed, and if the President of the United States don't do the right job that he should be doing he can lead us into trouble too."

"Which is worse?"

"I think war is worse. No, wait—I don't think war is worse. I think the other one is worse, because in war you can fight back but when the President doesn't do his job right, there can be nothing done about it. You just can't get a new President—you just have to wait."

Sandra is a sixth-grade girl from the working class, the daughter of a police detective in a large Midwestern city. She is somewhat more sophisticated about political matters than many children her age. It is unusual for an elementary school child to suggest the possibility that the President might not "do his job right." More typical is Sandra's implicit assumption that the United States would be on the defensive side in the event of war. Most young children believe that the Government and its representatives are wise, benevolent and infallible, that whatever the Government does is for the best, and that the United States is a highly effective force for peace in the world.

The average child would agree with Sandra that, if something *is* wrong, "you just have to wait." They know that a citizen can write letters to the President and to Congress, but they see virtually no other way to influence political affairs in the period between elections. They know almost nothing about pressure groups, for instance. In fact, group political activity of any sort, including that of political parties, seems unimportant to them. They believe that the way the citizen affects the Government is through the vote, the individual vote; that is almost the only thing that counts, and it counts very heavily indeed.

Political socialization, the process by which attitudes like these are learned, is a special, socially oriented form of political learning. It is accomplished *by*

the society and *for* the society, mostly through the institution of the schools. Its purpose is to transmit to each new generation the political attitudes and behavior patterns that the society deems useful in its adult citizens. That is, political socialization is based on and is intended to preserve stability and consensus in the adult population.

In the United States today, stability and consensus are conspicuously lacking. There is strong, open conflict between ethnic groups and the dominant society, between the affluent and the poor, and between generations. The conflict concerns wealth and other material resources, but the basic issue is the division of political power.

In my opinion, children in this country are being socialized in ways that contribute to the very fragmentation which political socialization is meant to prevent.

In 1961 and 1962, David Easton and I, together with Judith Torney and Jack Dennis, collected data on the political knowledge, attitudes and behavior of

12,000 children in grades two to eight. The children were from eight cities, two in each major region of the United States. In each region we used a large city and a small one; and in each city, two schools from working-class areas and two from middle-class areas.

We found, among other things, that elementary-school children have a highly idealized view of the Government and a very high estimate of the power of the individual vote, combined with an ignorance of other legitimate channels of influence. These views are unrealistic (a fact that is becoming increasingly obvious today to children themselves) and they do not offer a good foundation for active, effective participation in a democratic process. They seem to point more toward compliance and complacency on one hand, and toward disillusionment, helplessness, anger and perhaps even rejection of the system on the other.

The child's early conception of the nation and its Government is vague but very favorable. In the early grades, al-

WHO DECIDES WHAT LAWS ARE MADE? Children have a low opinion of the power of most groups to influence law-making, but a high opinion of the power of the individual. Eighth-graders rate the average citizen's influence as greater than that of big companies, rich people, newspapers and churches; only the President and unions have more.

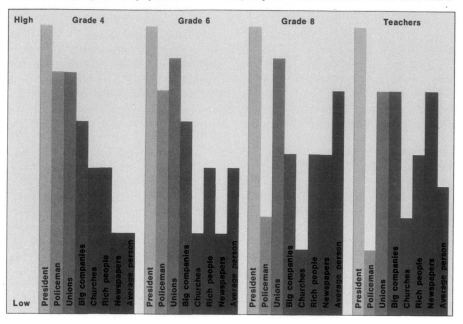

most all children agree that "the American flag is the best flag in the world," and that "America is the best country in the world." As one girl put it, "if it wasn't for the United States, there probably would be a lot of wars and regular Dark Ages."

"President" and "Government" are almost synonymous for the young child. Both are regarded as powerful and benevolent, though there is some confusion about the functions they perform:

"Judy, do you know of anyone in the United States Government?"

"Well, the President."

"What do you know about the President?"

"Well, that a . . . oh, dear . . . he . . . ah, makes laws and a . . . and . . . ah . . . well, he tries to do good."

"Tommy, what is the Government?"

"The Government is like the President, but he isn't actually a President. . . . Maybe he makes the laws of the country. Maybe he tells the numbers on the license plates. . . . I heard on the radio that he's in charge of the income tax. He can higher it or lower it."

"What does he spend the money on?"

"How should I know? Like the Government doesn't know what we spend our money on. He spends it for food,

clothing, things for his wife, and that sort of thing."

In the second grade, the average child believes that the President would be nearly as helpful to him as a policeman or his father if he were in trouble. Children express strong emotional attachment to the President and expect him to protect them. They think he is personally responsive to children's wishes; if necessary they could even go to the White House and talk to him.

Responses to one question show especially clearly how concerned children think the President is about them. The question was "If you write to the President, does he care what you think?"; the possible answers were that he cares "a lot," "some" or "a little." Three-fourths of the children in second grade and 43 per cent of those in eighth answered "a lot." (Interestingly this answer was also chosen by 47 per cent of the teachers.)

Laws, like Government, are viewed as powerful and benevolent. They are helpful and protective, just and unchanging. Most young children think laws were made a long time ago, probably by the President, and his stamp of approval carries weight: "The President okays them before they're obeyed, so

I guess if it is good enough for him, it is good enough for anybody."

The young child's idealization of the figures and institutions of Government is supported by what he learns in school, but it does not seem to originate there. Its source is probably the child's psychological need to compensate for his own inferior and vulnerable place in the system. Attachment to the President, for example, begins with an awareness that there is a very powerful "boss" of the United States. If he is benevolent and concerned with the child's welfare, the child need not be afraid of him. The child apparently sees his position in the nation as similar to his position in the family, a conclusion borne out by what we learned from children with working-class backgrounds. Working-class children tended to have less positive attitudes toward their fathers than children from the middle and upper classes, and to invest the President with correspondingly more paternalistic qualities. They expressed very strong emotional ties to him.

In the later grades, children begin to transfer their allegiance from officials to offices and institutions. The average seventh-grader thinks that the Supreme Court and the Government know more and are less likely to make mistakes than the President. Since support for offices rather than for particular officials is an important ingredient in peaceful political change, the transfer of allegiance from personal figures to roles and institutions is a step toward political stability.

However, older children have not abandoned their belief in the benign qualities of governmental authority so much as redirected their expectations of protection toward institutions. In all grades, 80 to 90 per cent of the students agreed that "the United States Government knows what is best for the people." Agreement on a related item, "What goes on in Government is all for the best," declined with age, from 90 per cent in grade three to 76 per cent in grade eight, but this is still a very high percentage. (Among teachers, agreement had dropped to 46 per cent).

An idealized acceptance of the authority, omniscience and benevolence of

"The Government is like the President, but he isn't actually a President. Maybe he makes the laws of the country. Maybe he tells the numbers on the license plates."

the political system does not fit well with the need, in a democratic society, for a critical examination of public policy. Without abandoning his positive attachment to Government, law and structures designed to regulate dissent, the citizen must see a need to watch—and to influence—the Government's actions.

Older children do show more awareness that all is not necessarily perfect than younger ones. Though agreement with positive statements about how the system *should* be stays high in all grades, perceptions of how things actually are become more realistic with age. Most children in all grades agree that the policeman's job is to make people obey laws, but the belief that punishment inevitably follows crime declines from 57 per cent in second grade to 16 per cent in eighth (and to two per cent in teachers). Similarly, children of all ages agree that "laws are to keep us safe," but there is more and more reluctance to agree that "all laws are fair." In general, responses to idealized statements of how things ought to be were more stable than perceptions of the way the system really functions.

How Does the System Work?

This discrepancy between the ideal and the actual could be the basis for disillusionment and cynicism, but it might also be an incentive to act. Let us assume the latter—that at least some older children are motivated to do more than admire the status quo and comply with the law. Let us also assume (for the moment) that these children have two other prerequisites to political action, a view of themselves as effective and a view of the system as responsive. What then?

Children believe that democracy is "rule by the people," but they have a limited understanding of how this rule operates. As one sixth-grade boy tried to explain it, "Oh, in the United States the people are supposed to rule the Government . . . but that is kind of complicated because the Government rules over the people. . . . It is kind of mixed-up, but it's a good set-up, but yet there's no real rule. Everybody has power; that is, everybody's power is limited."

The idea of a reciprocal relationship between an individual citizen and the Government is difficult to grasp, even for adults. Young children do not try: they see Government at the top and themselves at the bottom, with influence moving down but not up. In general, children in the early grades say that the duties of the citizen are compliance and "good" behavior. Asked what a citizen can do to help the country, one fourth-grader replied, "Well, follow the laws, don't get in accidents, and do practically everything as hard as he can." Children this age, presented with a list of seven characteristics of the good citizen and asked to choose two, opted for "helps others" (48 per cent) and "always obeys laws" (44 per cent).

Older children said that the good citizen "is interested in the way the country is run" (65 per cent) and "votes and gets others to vote" (45 per cent). Almost all eighth-graders think it is important to vote, and most of them are convinced that the ideal citizen "makes up his own mind" about a candidate, rather than turning to parents, teachers, television, newspapers and so forth. Just where the ideal citizen *does* turn for political information is unclear, though estimates of usefulness of the mass media began to rise in the later grades.

A similar spirit of independence shows itself when eighth-graders are asked what they think of voting along party lines. The ideal citizen, they say, votes for "the man, not the party," and he splits his ticket.

Parties and Pressure Groups

Attitudes toward political parties are fairly late in developing. Most children first learn the words "Democrat" and "Republican" when they label a Presidential candidate as one thing or the other. Young children identify the party with the candidate rather than vice versa; since they see the candidates as different, they also believe the parties are different.

To older children, the Democratic and Republican parties look almost identical. "Well, basically they both want the same things," said an eighth-grade girl. "Just peace and happiness and want our country to be free."

Children are eager to minimize political conflict of all sorts. They usually take sides in a campaign and hope their man wins, but this does not mean they condone strong disagreement between the candidates. Unity and cohesion should surely reign *after* an election, and perhaps before as well. Here, for instance, is what one seventh-grader remembered about the 1960 election: "[I remember] the morning of the election when Kennedy was elected, and Nixon said that Kennedy would be a nice President. Kennedy said how sorry he was that Mr. Nixon wasn't elected. He would have been just as good a President as he was himself, and that he wished they could both be President together. I would have liked them to go together instead of going through this big thing that they go out in the streets and talk to all the people and giving the impression that they got a better impression than the other one. It would have been easy if they both went together. Then there wouldn't have been much quarreling and fighting."

Conflict between parties is just as undesirable as conflict between candidates. One question we asked the children was, "If the Democrats and Republicans disagreed on important things, would it be good or bad for the country?" On a scale from 1 (very bad) to 5 (very good), the responses ranged from a little under 2 in the fifth grade to a little over 2 in eighth. Teachers were better able to tolerate disagreement, and the difference between them and eighth-graders on this item was one of the largest in our data.

Although most older children believe that adults should belong to parties, they think a decision between the two should be deferred until after high-school graduation. Asked to specify the party they would join if they were adults, 32 per cent specified "sometimes Democrat, sometimes Republican." This percentage is somewhat higher than estimates of the number of independent voters in the adult population, though much lower than the 55 per cent of teachers who reported themselves "sometimes Democrat, sometimes Republican."

Very little material on partisanship and political conflict finds its way into the

" Oh, in the United States the people are supposed to rule the Government, but that is kind of complicated because the Government rules over the people . . . "

AFFECTING THE GOVERNMENT. As a child grows, his confidence in his ability to affect the Government increases steadily. But a child with low social status and low I.Q. feels much less effective than others.

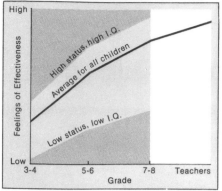

elementary-school curriculum. Teachers apparently stress the virtue of independent political action oriented toward an assessment of candidates' worth rather than an alignment with a party. They may do this from a desire to avoid controversial issues or to present political material without bias. But the result for the students is an awareness of the need for consensus and majority rule without a complementary appreciation of the role of debate, disagreement and conflict.

As for pressure groups, children's understanding of the role they play in government is shown in the illustration on page 26. Until the seventh grade, children rated the policeman's influence in law-making as higher than that of any other individual or group except the President and labor unions. In a clear demonstration of faith in the importance of the individual, older children saw the average citizen's influence on law-making as equal or superior to the influence of big companies, rich people, newspapers and churches. Teachers differed greatly from eighth-graders on this matter, rating the influence of unions, big companies, rich people and newspapers nearly equal, and much greater than that of the average citizen.

The sharp divergence between students and teachers suggests that this topic, like partisanship, is not discussed at school. Schools concentrate on the formal aspects of Government, teaching that Congress makes the laws but not recognizing the influence of interest groups. It is not easy to teach children

that groups which promote their own (as opposed to the public) interest can be influential, even decisive, in legislative matters, but it would make for a more realistic view of how a complex democracy operates.

Effectiveness

Exerting an effect on the course of Government requires more than an awareness of the need to do so and a knowledge of how to go about it. As I mentioned earlier, it also requires a belief in one's own effectiveness and in the Government's responsiveness. A child who thinks the Government is benevolent and protective may fail to see why he *should* interfere, but he also believes that if he *does* speak, the Government will listen. And a child who thinks the Government pays more attention to the average person than to, say, U.S. Steel or *The New York Times* may confine his political activities to the voting booth, but he unquestionably has a high opinion of his own effectiveness.

There is a house-of-cards air to this structure of beliefs; misguidedly or not, however, most children do believe that the Government is responsive and that they, as individuals, can be effective in the political arena. Most, but not all. For example: *"Richard, if the President did something that people didn't like, what could they do?" "The people can't do anything. They can't go to the White House and tell him what to do because he makes all the decisions. If the people don't like it, too bad for them."*

Richard is from a working-class home. A difference in feelings of effectiveness was one of the most striking social-class discrepancies in our data, one of the few variables on which there was considerable difference between the middle- and the low-status groups. Even in third and fourth grade, low-status children see themselves and their families as having substantially less ability to influence Government than high-status children award themselves, and the difference increases with age.

Differences between I.Q. groups on effectiveness were even more marked than those between social classes, and they also increase with age. Children of

low intelligence were three or four years behind children of high intelligence in developing a sense of effectiveness, and the eighth-grade child of low intelligence was scarcely above the highly intelligent third- or fourth-grader.

On effectiveness, as on most matters where there were variations by both social class and level of intelligence, the difference between low- and high-status children was less than, but in the same direction as, the difference between children of low and high intelligence (*see illustration, left*). In addition to feeling less effective, children from the lower class and children with low I.Q.s tend to be more loyal, accepting and compliant and less interested and involved in politics than children from the middle and upper classes and children with high I.Q.s—in short, to be more trusting and apathetic.

Another way of putting it is to say that children from low-status homes and children of low intelligence are retarded in their socialization to effective participation in the political system. But perhaps they are only a little more retarded than children from other groups.

Children of all classes and all levels of intelligence seem to be learning an incomplete, simplistic and cognitively fragmented view of the political process, and the situation is likely to persist as long as the schools stress values and ideals, the individual and his vote and the need for compliance and consensus at the expense of social realities, the role of groups, and the uses of controversy and argument.

The strength of current protests against social and political conditions, and the fact that they are focused on institutions, is a sign of vigor: it indicates at least a hope that remedies can be found short of full revolution. However, under the circumstances it makes very little sense to instill in children a superficial faith in the institutions under attack, to gloss over social realities, and to obscure many of the routes effective action can take. More useful would be a candid acknowledgment of political and social facts and, especially, a clear explanation of the ways that institutions can be influenced and changed. ∩

"If it wasn't for the United States, there probably would be a lot of wars and regular Dark Ages."

iv. the sensory world

When you turn the page, you will participate in an experiment in perception. Bela Julesz of the Bell Telephone Laboratories has studied the physical conditions of three-dimensional perception for years and has moved beyond laboratory studies to the fashioning of a striking demonstration. His article makes you, the reader, one of his subjects. Moreover, he explains why his demonstration has made you see what you saw.

One method of studying human perception is to distort it. Perception, after all, is almost always an instantaneous event, and it has proved difficult to perform instantaneous experiments. But when perception is intentionally distorted, as in Irvin Rock's experiments, the individual slowly adapts to the distortion. The manner in which the adaptation takes place often indicates the nature of fundamental principles of undistorted perception.

The sensory psychologist usually sits in his small, well-controlled laboratory and studies the reactions of people to very carefully controlled physical stimulation of a single sensory modality such as hearing, vision, smell, or touch. On occasion, however, events in the world outside of the laboratory become either so interesting or so nationally important that the scientist is drawn out to apply his observational and experimental methods to them. The sonic booms produced by high-speed aircraft are such a problem. In his article, Green describes both the physical basis of sonic booms and the psychological basis of our reactions to such loud, unexpected, and perhaps even damaging sounds. He also begins to explore the sociological implications of noise pollution and the hopes we have for controlling it.

In "Body English" Frank Geldard of Princeton University summarizes studies of sensory communication through the skin. Instead of presenting lights and sounds to the eye and ear, Geldard studies how information can be transferred from the outside to the inside of an individual by presenting stimuli to the individual's skin. Work that began in the 1940s as an attempt to invent methods of communicating with fighter pilots who could not hear radioed instructions over the noise of their aircraft's engines has contributed significantly to the pure science of the skin.

It is of both practical importance and scientific interest to investigate the sensory world of lower animals. Included here are two fascinating examples. Burghardt's work on the chemical perception of snakes not only advances sensory psychology but also hints strongly at a new basis for zoological classification. James Simmons explores the sensory world of night-flying bats, who perceive objects by means of an intricate self-generating system of acoustical radar.

All in all, the world of sensory psychology is the straightest of marriages of physics, psychology, and the simplest reactions of a human or animal observer. Occasionally, though, laughter can be heard from the laboratory, as when Paul Herman encountered "the terrible tenrec."

Experiment in

MOST OF US TAKE it for granted that objects will look much the same whether we view them with one eye or with both eyes. Except for a certain loss of depth perception, the world we see when we shut one eye is almost identical to that we see with our normal two-eye, or binocular, vision. Shapes, textures and contours of the objects about us don't change much when we view them with one eye shut.

But what would our perceptual experience be like if somehow we could create an environment that looked entirely different, depending on whether we looked at it with one eye or with both eyes? If we could separate monocular and binocular cues, what could we learn about the laws of perception?

And would the results differ from the established findings of classical psychology, with its centuries of studying images in which the monocular and binocular perceptual cues are not separated?

Intrigued by these ideas, I have been working since 1959 to devise techniques that would permit creation of images in which the monocular and binocular information are independent of each other. I have been able to "eclipse" the powerful monocular visual cues and thus reveal a previously hidden psychology of binocular vision.

It was particularly challenging to find a way to create complex stereographs with no apparent shapes or contours when viewed with one eye but which would yield predetermined shapes when seen with both eyes.

For more than a century we have known that binocular parallax—the relative difference in the horizontal location of corresponding points in the left eye and the right eye—is the principal binocular depth cue. Because the distance between the two eyes and the focal length of the eyes at a given fixation are constant for any individual, there is a simple trigonometric relationship between the parallax shift and the actual distance of the object. In traditional investigations, the aim has been to relate the amount of parallax shift to the amount of depth perceived.

It is commonly thought that the problem of depth perception is relatively simple because of the analogy between the eyes and a range finder. The most intriguing part of this problem is not the relationship between binocular parallax and depth, but rather how the brain *matches* corresponding points in the two monocular fields so that the disparity can be perceived.

In traditional investigations of stereoscopic vision, images with only a few dots or lines ordinarily are used. These present only a few visual targets, and so the question of which dot in the left eye's view belongs to which dot in the right eye's view does not arise. My previous interest in stereo radar systems (that use two or more search beams) taught me that the "false target probability" increases as the number of targets increases. When there is one "blip" on the stereo radar screen, there is no problem in matching the blip to the target. But if many blips appear, the chances of assigning a blip to the wrong target increase tremendously.

This false target probability problem also occurs in perception. For example, when four targets cast their projections on the retinae, there are 16 possible ways the brain can combine the information it receives. In this case, only four of the target localizations are correct, and 12 are false, yielding a false target probability of 0.75. The probability of making a false target localization approaches 100 per cent as the number of targets

**EXPERIMENT 1
THE FLOATING SQUARE**

**OBJECT: To demonstrate that depth perception can occur even when no contours or shapes are visible to either eye alone.
METHOD: Take out the anaglyphoscope. View anaglyph, opposite page, through red *or* green filter, with one eye shut. You will see no shapes in this 20,000-dot figure. With both eyes (red filter/left; green/right eye) view from arm's length or more. Within minutes, you will see a center shimmering square. Try to bring center square dots into sharp focus; concentrate on dots that seem higher than surrounding square. Gradually, the center square will float toward you. Take your time. The depth effect does not occur quickly. Please be sure there is no glare on the page. Next, reverse filters (green/left; red/right). The square will appear as beneath a glass surface. Focus through the "glass" onto dots that seem lower than others. The square will move back.
RESULTS: The usual monocular contour or depth cues are unnecessary to perceive shape or depth. Implication: Visual fields from each eye are first combined in the cortex, and binocular processing occurs on the combined field.**

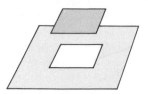

By Bela Julesz

Perception

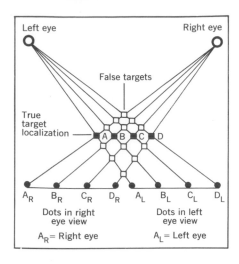

domly selected black and white dots. The dot patterns in the left and right images are identical, except for a center square in one image that has been shifted a few units to one side, as if it were a solid sheet. Because of this shift, an area is uncovered, and this area is filled with randomly selected dots. [*See illustration left.*] The horizontal shift of the center square corresponds to binocular parallax.

The task of producing these stereographs is an ideal job for the computer —which can print out and manipulate patterns containing thousands or even millions of dots. Without the computer, these studies would have been extremely difficult, and probably impossible. With enough patience, of course, one could turn out a random-dot stereograph by hand. The pointillist painter Georges Seurat painstakingly placed tiny dot after tiny dot of color on a canvas until he created the overall effect he sought. The sheer magnitude of creating a single finished painting by this method explains why there are so few Seurats.

Our computer-generated dot patterns can be made to appear completely random when viewed with one eye. But if viewed binocularly, certain correlated areas are seen in depth. I have created a number of such stereographs, and my research with them at Bell Telephone Laboratories over the past nine years has borne out my earlier expectations that when monocular cues are *eclipsed* a new aspect of the visual system emerges, which in some ways is richer than any known before.

We are now ready to begin our experiments with binocular fusion and depth perception.

First Computerized Anaglyphs

Examine the left and right images of the *stereo image pair*. When viewed with one eye, the dot distribution in each of the two images appears to be uniform. However, when these images are fused binocularly (a feat that some of the readers will be able to do without a stereoscope), the hidden center square emerges in vivid depth above the larger surrounding square.

To facilitate binocular fusion, a similar stereograph is reprinted as a red-and-green anaglyph in EXPERIMENT 1.

Anaglyphs are composite pictures printed in two colors, usually red and green; they produce a three-dimensional effect when viewed through red-and-green spectacles. Anaglyphs are well-known in the printing industry, but are difficult to produce because any areas

increases. [*See first illustration above.*]

How does our perceptual process eliminate these ambiguities? In determining binocular parallax, do we first scan the monocular patterns in the right and left eyes individually, and then fuse them? Or are the two visual fields first combined in some manner, and all further processing conducted on the fused field? Or do we use a combination of both processes? [*See illustration, opposite.*]

One possible way we process visual information is by *form recognition*. It has been tacitly assumed that in the act of recognizing form, we combine thou-

sands of dots in each eye's view into gestalts—or unified patterns. These gestalts then are identified in each eye's view as corresponding to each other.

For example, a person looking at a football crowd obtains a binocular picture presumably by matching corresponding faces that he recognizes and identifies separately in his left eye and right eye images.

To test this theory, I developed stereographs that contain no recognizable forms or shapes when viewed with one eye. A computer was programmed to print a square containing 10,000 ran-in which the red and green overlap must be printed in yellow. With the aid of computer-controlled printouts, we are presenting here for the first time anaglyphs in which no red and green dots overlap.

The anaglyph illustrations in this article have been set up as experiments, which you, the reader, can perform. Each experiment is self-contained, with a full description of the procedure and explanation of the results.

Pause for a moment now and carry out EXPERIMENTS 1 and 2.

Since the stereographs in EXPERIMENT 1 and EXPERIMENT 2 appeared completely patternless when viewed with one eye, it appears that monocular gestalt organization is not necessary for binocular fusion. These experiments also demonstrate that complex surfaces as well as simple depth planes can be binocularly portrayed by this technique. However, one still might argue that something simpler than gestalts, such as line segments and small clusters of dots, could be extracted from each monocular field and then compared during binocular fusion. Some sort of preprocessing of the images in each eye could occur before binocular fusion. This hypothesis is tested in EXPERIMENT 3 [*found on page 217*].

The results show that even in the total absence of small clusters of dots, binocular fusion still can occur. Thus, for these examples at least, there is no preprocessing of the separate monocular images, either at the macro or micro levels before binocular fusion takes place. This shows that binocular depth perception results from the brain's processing of the combined images.

How, then, do we relate the dots in the left eye's view with the dots in the right eye's view when all the usual monocular cues have been removed? With two squares, each with 10,000 dots, there are theoretically billions of ways that binocular fusion could take place. One plausible hypothesis is that binocular fusion occurs where the black and the white dots in the two images happen to be in identical positions. In a random-dot stereograph, such as the *stereo image pair*, by chance 50 per cent of the dots are in identical positions in the left and right images. These dots are said to have "zero disparity." The majority of the remaining dots can be matched at either +1 or −1 unit disparities, since nearly all of these remaining dots are located either one unit to the right or one unit to the left of a "zero disparity" dot.

Therefore, in the fused binocular percept we might expect to see three planes staggered next to each other in depth: the zero disparity plane, the +1 disparity plane, and the −1 disparity plane. Also, because only 50 per cent of the dots in any of the three depth planes have the same disparity, the planes should appear semitransparent, or lace-like.

However, this is not what we actually perceive in this stereograph. What we do see is not three planes, but two—the plane of the center square and the plane of the surrounding square—at considerable depth. And these two planes are solid, not transparent.

This indicates that when visual images are fused binocularly, the fusion mechanism prefers to look for dense surfaces. Thus, the binocular process consists, in part at least, of matching clusters of adjacent dots in each eye's view. In other words, the fusion process consists of locating as many dots as possible with the same disparities. For example, in EXPERIMENT 1, while there are probably many tiny clusters of dots with the same disparity values, only two large areas have dots with the same disparities—the center square and the surrounding square.

Depth Fields

One simple model of binocular depth perception [*see illustration, p. 220*] to explain these findings is: In the brain (cortex), the left and the right retinal images are *subtracted* point-by-point from each other. The "difference" is scanned for dot clusters of similar horizontal disparities. The cortex creates several difference fields by horizontally "shifting" the images prior to each subtraction. These difference fields are stacked in depth above each other. For example, take the stereograph with a displaced center square (EXPERIMENT 1). Of the several difference fields created, only two contain dense clusters of dots. The zero disparity field is perceived as the surrounding square, and the field displaced one unit is seen as the center square. There are no dense clusters of dots with similar disparities in the other difference fields. And so these fields play no part in forming the stereoscopic image. What we see, then, is the center square in depth either above or below the surrounding square.

This simple model based on difference fields has been tested in a practical application. A computer program based on this model, called AUTOMAP-1, has been developed for automatically com-

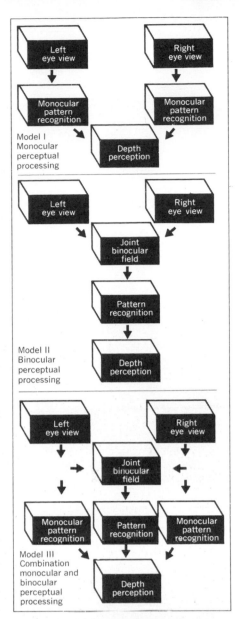

MODELS OF PERCEPTION. Random-dot stereograph experiments show depth perception and pattern recognition can occur according to second hypothetical model.

piling three-dimensional maps from two-dimensional aerial photographs. Each exposure is taken from a different aircraft position to produce the proper amount of parallax shift in the images. Previously, contour maps had to be made by clerks who plotted the contours point-by-point. The clerks fused two aerial photographs of the terrain with the aid of a stereoscope and then subjectively tried to align a floating point of light with the three-dimensional percept of a mountain top or valley bottom. The successful automation of this task frees people of a tedious and time-consuming chore. The fact that an object does not

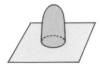

EXPERIMENT 2—THE EXPANDING DOME

OBJECT: To demonstrate the dramatic sensation of perceiving a paraboloid dome in great depth by viewing an array of one million random dots.

METHOD: View anaglyph, below, at arm's length or more. When seen through red filter only, the dots appear speckled and randomly distributed. Seen through filters with both eyes (green/right; red/left) the center circle takes on a translucent quality of indeterminant depth. Locate the higher dots in the circle and bring them into sharp focus. The surface of the dome will take shape slowly. Initially, it looks like a transparent bubble with dots scattered on the surface. As you watch, the bubble will elongate until it has grown about six inches from the page. Move your head from side to side and watch the dome move with you. Keeping the dome in focus, move back slowly. The dome will follow you. If you have difficulty in raising the dome, hold a pencil tip a half inch off the page and over the circle. Focus on the pencil tip and watch for dots that seem to rise to the pencil. As the dots rise, slowly lift the pencil as though pulling up the dots. Watch patiently, the dome will emerge. Next, reverse filters (red/right; green/left). The circle will seem to be covered by a glass. Look through the glass and try to find dots below the surface. The dome will expand back into the page in great depth.

RESULTS: Continuous complex surfaces, as well as single planes, can be portrayed in depth with random-dot, computer-generated stereographs.

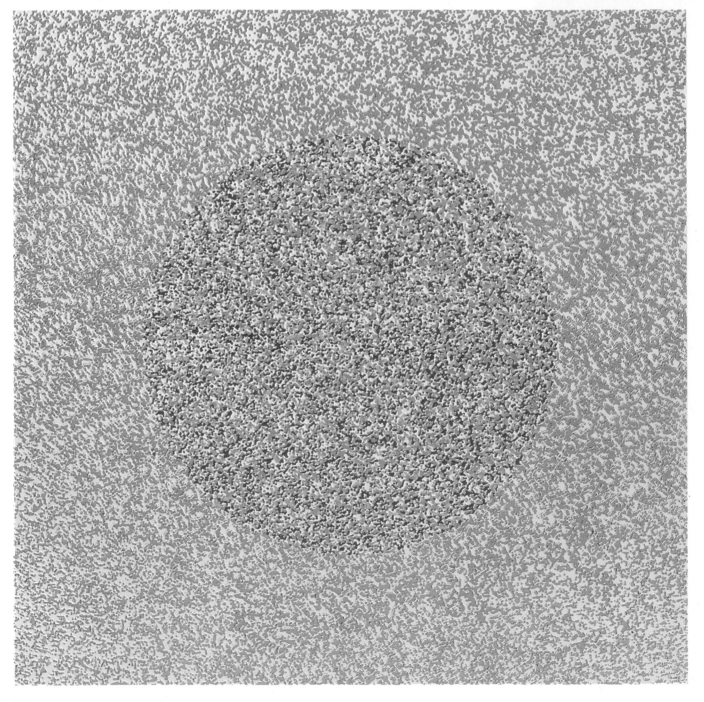

216

EXPERIMENT 3—GHOST SQUARES

OBJECT: To determine if binocular depth perception occurs when the left and right eye images have no clusters of dots that are similar.

METHOD: View anaglyph, below, through the anaglyphoscope. Notice every small cluster of dots is different in each eye's view. Next, view anaglyph through filters with both eyes (red/right; green/left). Look for dots that seem higher than others. Gradually, a full plane of dots will rise above page. Higher yet, look for faint dots. As you focus on them, a third "ghost" plane will appear. You now should see three transparent planes stacked in depth. Reverse filters (green/right; red/left). The three planes descend into page.

RESULTS: Since the images seen by each eye are totally different, there are no monocular cues that can be recognized before binocular fusion. Thus monocular preprocessing is not required for depth perception.

EXPERIMENT 4—LOST SYMMETRY
OBJECT: To demonstrate the effect of monocularly visible patterns on binocular fusion.
METHOD: View anaglyph, below left, through red filter only. The top half is a mirror image of the bottom half. View through filters with both eyes (red/left; green/right). Gradually, horizontal stripes will emerge in depth and scramble the symmetry. Next, view the anaglyph, below right, through red filter only. A four-fold symmetry becomes visible. View through filters with both eyes (green/right; red/left). Gradually, a transparent plane floats up and obscures the symmetry.
RESULTS: The suppression of the monocular pattern by the binocular percept indicates that binocular fusion dominates monocular pattern recognition.

EXPERIMENT 5
BROKEN CONNECTIVITIES
OBJECT: To demonstrate that binocular fusion can occur on a point-by-point basis without extracting features such as lines.
METHOD: Anaglyph, right, is derived from stereo image pair (p. 214) and a portion is reprinted below, top left. Bottom left image is derived from the image above it by breaking the diagonal connectivity of the dots. Now, view anaglyph through red filter only, then green filter only. The images are strikingly different even though only 16 per cent of the dots are different. Viewed through filters with both eyes, a center square is seen in depth.
RESULTS: Binocular fusion can occur on a point-by-point basis.

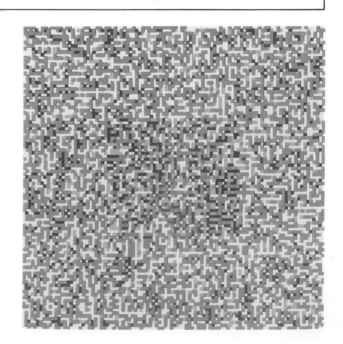

218

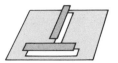

EXPERIMENT 6—BINOCULAR ILLUSION

OBJECT: To study the origin of an optical illusion.

METHOD: View anaglyph through red or green filter with one eye shut. No shapes are visible. Next, view with both eyes through filter (red/right; green/left). Gradually, a horizontal bar near the bottom will emerge above the paper. A vertical bar in the center takes longer to emerge. (Vertical shapes are more difficult to fuse.) After bars have risen above the page, compare their lengths. Although both are exactly the same length, the vertical bar appears much longer. Reverse the filters (green/right; red/left) and the bars will descend into the page.

RESULTS: The origin of this illusion (and most "optical" illusions) is not in the eye but in the cortex, and occurs after binocular fusion.

219

have to be recognized in order to locate it in space makes conceivable the automation of many tasks that now require humans as operators or observers.

Competing Cues

In the first three experiments, we have learned that binocular fusion and depth perception are possible even when all monocular pattern cues are eliminated. But what happens when monocular cues, such as shapes or symmetry, are present in one or both of the stereograph images? Do monocular cues affect binocular fusion? In the next experiment, we will explore a new class of computer-generated images in which symmetrical patterns are visible when viewed with one eye.

EXPERIMENT 4 demonstrates what happens when images of this type are fused binocularly. When viewed with one eye as instructed in the directions, the top half of the first stereograph appears to be a mirror image of the bottom half. In the other stereograph, a fourfold symmetry is visible when it is viewed with one eye. When these stereographs are viewed binocularly, the symmetry is scrambled in the fused binocular image. In a similar experiment which I conducted in my laboratory, a word or text is clearly visible when the stereograph is viewed with one eye, but fragments into random dots and disappears when the stereograph is viewed binocularly.

This phenomenon should not be confused with binocular rivalry, which oc-

curs when two dissimilar images, say a page of print and a picture, are presented simultaneously, one to each eye. The two images can be fused in a stereoscope, or the two objects can be placed side by side on a table, separated by a vertical sheet of paper and viewed so that the left eye sees only the left object and the right eye sees only the right object. We do not see the two images at the same time but rather we alternately see one object and then the other. This rivalry, or alternation, does not occur during the binocular suppression of monocular images. Once binocular fusion takes place, it remains stable. This indicates that if binocular fusion occurs, it precedes or dominates recognition of monocular patterns or gestalts.

These findings do not exclude the possibility of certain simple preprocessing of monocular cues prior to binocular combination. For example, research by physiologists David H. Hubel and Torsten N. Wiesel of Harvard has shown that receptor cells in the retina carry out considerable preprocessing of stimuli. They have discovered "line detectors" in the retina that are directly connected to certain cells in the cortex of the brain. These line detectors respond primarily to lines of light with specific orientations.

To find out if simple monocular preprocessing interferes with binocular fusion, we made a stereograph using short diagonal line segments. [*See illustration opposite.*] Fusion can be easily obtained —the process can operate by extracting features such as lines or edges. Never-

theless, we must emphasize that binocular fusion can operate on a point-by-point basis without extracting monocular features. We have demonstrated this in the laboratory, with stereographs in which the diagonal connectivity is one of the images that is deliberately destroyed. That is, wherever three diagonal dots in the left and right images were identical, the middle one was changed to its complement: black to white, or white to black. Only 16 per cent of the dots in the two images are different, when viewed monocularly, but the two images look strikingly different. [*See* EXPERIMENT 5.] Binocular fusion is easily obtained, demonstrating that fusion can occur on a point-by-point basis.

Random Dot Movies

Experiments with random dot stereographs can be extended to motion pictures. For example, a film can be made of a stereograph with the raised center square. When viewed with one eye, the motion picture appears to be no more than the "snow" often seen on empty television channels. But when viewed binocularly, not one but two "snowstorms" appear. The center square appears in depth above the larger surrounding square.

By employing the proper sequence of random dot images, a binocular illusion of movement can be created. The center square can be made to move up and down through the surrounding square. Watching the center square, a viewer experiences a unique sensation of movement, in which an object appears to move independently of its texture.

New perceptual phenomena different from those obtained with classical stimuli can be produced with this film technique. For instance, a classical stroboscopic experiment alternately presents pictures of two lines in different positions. If the rate of presentation is slow enough, each line is seen successively in its proper position. If the rate of presentation is increased, the viewer thinks he sees a single line jumping back and forth. At a still faster speed, the viewer sees the two lines simultaneously. This experiment performed with a random-dot stereograph containing two bars produces almost identical results—with a very interesting exception.

At the point where the viewer sees a single bar jumping back and forth above the background, as the speed of presentation is increased the movement of the bar appears to slow down. Eventually it

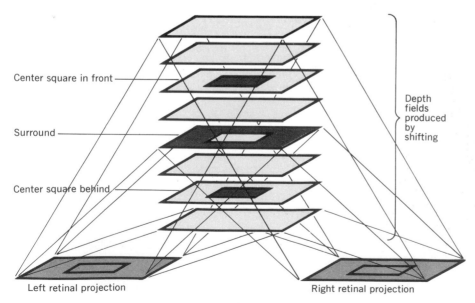

Center square in front

Surround

Center square behind

Left retinal projection

Right retinal projection

Depth fields produced by shifting

DEPTH FIELDS. A possible explanation of depth perception is that the right and the left retinal images are compared and then "subtracted" on a point-by-point basis. The resulting "difference field" is scanned for dot clusters of similar disparities. A stack of difference fields is created by mentally "shifting" the images prior to the subtraction.

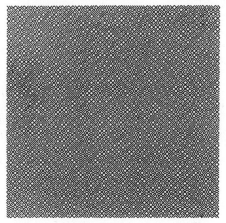

DIAGONAL-LINE STEREOGRAPH. Stereo images are created by having the computer randomly select diagonal line segments instead of dots. When seen through a stereoscope, a center square emerges above background square, as shown in Experiment 1.

appears to stand still while the surrounding margin jumps back and forth.

Seymour Papert of M.I.T., using the random-dot motion picture technique, has determined the perceptual level at which the "waterfall illusion" occurs. If you stare long enough at a waterfall and then close your eyes, you will appear to see movement in the opposite direction to the waterfall. This effect is commonly explained as the result of fatiguing of the motion detectors in the retina or just beyond. The waterfall illusion can be created using movies of the random-dot stereographs. Since there are no moving patterns perceivable at the retinal level in these films, this strongly suggests that the illusion is caused by some process in the cortex that occurs after binocular fusion.

Panum's Fusional Area

Do these results with random-dot stereographs mean that the findings of classical depth perception studies are wrong? The answer is no. In the classical investigations, the images used had only a few dots or lines, while the experiments described in this article use complex images containing thousands of dots. The relationship between classical research and the present studies can be likened to the relationship between atoms and molecules. And just as experimental findings about molecules do not disprove the findings on a single atom, neither do the findings with complex random-dot stereographs disprove those obtained with simpler images. The questions raised in studies using random-dot stereographs are at a different hierarchical level than the questions posed in classical studies.

In another experiment, Derek Fender, of the California Institute of Technology,

and I have shown how much a perceptual phenomenon depends on the particular stimuli used. This experiment alters one of the basic physical findings of stereoscopic perception—Panum's fusional area, named after the 19th Century Austrian physiologist, P. L. Panum. He found that two images on the left and right retinae could be distinguished as separate images only if they were farther apart than six minutes of arc (1/10th of a degree). If the two images were registered within six minutes of arc —Panum's fusional area—then the two images seemed as one.

In our experiment, four graduate students submitted to the discomfort of contact lenses fitted tightly to their eyeballs. With mirrors attached to the contact lenses and with optical projectors, we stabilized the location of images on the students' retinae, despite ever-present eye motion. We began by projecting left and right stereograph images onto the left and right retinae. The students had no control over what they saw. When the images were brought within Panum's fusional area, the student experienced binocular fusion. Then we pulled the images apart slowly.

We found that the images remained fused binocularly until they were separated horizontally by 120 minutes of arc (2 degrees, or 20 times Panum's fusional limit). At this point they break apart suddenly. The images had to be brought back to within six minutes of arc alignment before they fused again.

Thus, the area of maintaining fusion for random-dot stereographs is much larger than Panum's fusional area. Because of this experiment, the notion of the limits for corresponding points must be changed. Two dots that are 120 minutes of arc apart can be considered cor-

responding points if they are part of a dense structure that has been previously fused binocularly (but not if they are part of a simple structure). The binocular fusion mechanism has a sort of memory—once fusion has been obtained, it tends to be maintained.

In retrospect, it is not surprising that when we use thousands or millions of dots or lines, we can study a deeper structure of the visual system than we could by using only a few lines or dots.

Depth Blindness

This article serves merely as an introduction to the growing field of complex stereographs.

In random-dot stereographs, all of the monocular depth cues can be eliminated. These are so powerful that the illusion of depth persists even when we use only one eye. Monocular cues include: interposition (near objects blocking part of the background); motion parallax (near objects appear to move more rapidly than objects far away); perspective (parallel lines seem to meet in the distance); texture; and shadowing.

With the random-dot stereographs, for the first time it is possible to make an objective, quantitative test of stereoscopic vision based only on binocular disparity. Our tests of several thousand people indicate that there may be as many people who are "depth blind" as are color blind. Clinical tests for "depth blindness" in applicants might be useful for certain jobs—jet pilots, for instance, or heart surgeons. The random-dot stereograph also can be used to learn more about color perception, optical illusions, perceptual learning, and eye movements.

Our last experiment for the reader illustrates how this technique can be used to study the origin of optical illusions. In EXPERIMENT 6, a well-known vertical-horizontal optical illusion is portrayed without any monocular cues. From the results, we can conclude that the origin of this illusion is not retinal but probably in the brain [*see p. 219*].

In my investigations, I have developed techniques to "paint" binocular shapes in which the monocular shape cues are eclipsed. Although I started out to explore the problem of binocular depth perception, these techniques now can be used by psychologists to explore any visual phenomena involving our perception of shape. Out of these investigations, using stimuli with a richer structure than can be obtained with simple line targets, we may hope to get a deeper understanding of our visual system. ⌻

When the World is Tilt
Distortion—How We Adapt

By Irvin Rock

SUPPOSE YOU WERE FORCED to wear goggles with prisms inserted. Everything would be fringed with color; straight lines would seem curved, and all objects would appear to the side of their actual location. Would objects around you forever appear distorted or would you, in time, begin to see the world as it normally looks? Would you ever adapt to such a world?

To answer this question, let us consider first how we see the world without prisms. We all learned in school that the eye functions like a camera, with an image formed by the lens at the back of the eye and transmitted to the brain. There is much truth in this common explanation. And yet the camera theory cannot fully explain the way we see the world. Think about the problem of the perception of size. It is true that if we look at one cube that is twice as large as a cube beside it, the image of the larger cube on the retina will be twice as big as the image of the smaller, and we will perceive the large cube as twice as big.

But suppose the large cube is farther away? We know that the more distant an object is, the smaller its image is in the eye. But even if the larger cube is moved so far away that its image on the retina is the smaller, it still will seem larger. Psychologists call this size constancy.

The size of the image cast on the retina does vary with distance, but the perceived size does not change appreciably. And so the size of a retinal image is not the only basis for our perception of size. It would seem that the brain also takes into account the distance of an object before "deciding" on the size to perceive.

Constancy of size is not an exception, but rather a typical example of the way we see the world. When the sun goes behind a cloud, the light reaching our eyes from everything around us diminishes, but white objects continue to look white, gray continues to look gray (achromatic color constancy).

When we see a circle at a slant, the shape of its image becomes elliptical, but the perceived shape changes only slightly, if at all (shape constancy).

When we move, the image of everything in our field of vision shifts across the retina, but the objects do not seem to move (position constancy). Therefore, an explanation based purely on the photographic image cast on the retina does not explain adequately how we see.

You may argue that I have described not the act of seeing, but of knowing. You might well say that we do see the distant object as smaller, but judge it to be larger because we have learned about perspective and the effect of changing distance, or that we do see the world moving when we move, but know that we are moving, not the world.

But your argument is wrong. We do tend to see in terms of these constancies.

This point is illustrated by a photograph originally devised by Edwin G. Boring of Harvard University. In our illustration, the girl seated down the corridor looks much larger than we would predict from the small image she casts. This is borne out when the picture of the girl in the distance is cut out and placed alongside the other, at the same distance from the observer [see illustration, page 225]. In the first picture, you take distance into account in reaching an impression of the girl's size.

Is the fact that the distant girl in the first picture looks larger than the same girl in the second merely a matter of knowing? Such a claim constitutes a forced and false description derived from what we think we ought to see based on our implicit acceptance of the camera model of vision. This model maintains that vision is directly determined by the retinal image and must be constant when the image is the same and change whenever the image changes. Years ago, psychologists such as Edward Titchener were caught up in precisely this tendency of altering the facts to fit their theories of perception.

Recently, T. G. R. Bower of Harvard has shown that two-month-old infants perceive on the basis of constancy, namely that they take distance and slant into account in perceiving size and shape. The behavior of chickens, fish and many other species suggests that they also see in terms of constancies rather than in terms of the physical properties of their retinal images. It is difficult to believe that lower organisms and infants see in terms of the changing image, but behave otherwise because they know better.

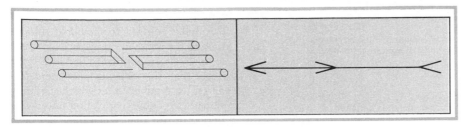

Research like this has led psychologists to claim that there is a separate discipline of perception. They believe that there are laws of perception that must be discovered and that these laws cannot come from the elementary facts of vision, or be understood as factual knowledge gained about the world.

One further argument may be mentioned. Optical illusions cannot be explained on the basis of the retinal image, since the image accurately mirrors the objective state of affairs. Nor can the illusions be based on knowledge; they defy knowledge. For example, we *know* the two line segments in the familiar Müller-Lyer illusion are of equal length, but even after we have confirmed our knowledge with a ruler, one segment still looks longer than the other [*see illustration, above*]. Therefore, all optical illusions attest to the impotence of knowledge about a situation to affect its appearance.

Does this mean that perception is not based on past experience? Not necessarily. I have argued that we cannot reduce perception to *knowing*; we *see* the world on the basis of certain complex central processes that take into account information about things like distance, slant, illumination, or our own movement. We cannot rule out the brain's use of past experience in achieving these perceptual experiences.

The two tablets shown suggest that past experience plays a role in what we see [*see illustrations, below*]. One tablet contains cuneiform writing in *bas-relief*; the other contains the same writing in *intaglio*. Yet the figure on the right is the one on the left turned upside down. The point I wish to emphasize is that we *see* the writing in this way: it looks as if it protrudes in one case and is indented in the other. The knowledge I have just given you—that these are pictures of the same object—has essentially no effect on the way they look. This illusion is based on the position of the shadows (shadow underneath—object protrudes; shadow above—object is indented).

There is reason for believing that this perceptual effect *is* based on past experience. Both sunlight and indoor artificial light typically come from above. Logically, then, a bump on a flat surface usually will be shadowed on the bottom and highlighted on the top. So we could learn—though quite unconsciously—that shadows are associated with protrusion and indentation.

One rather bold experiment supports this theory. E. H. Hess of the University of Chicago reared chickens from the time of hatching in cages where the only light came from below. These chickens, unlike normally reared chickens, pecked more at photographs of grain with the shadow at the top, suggesting that these photographs looked to them like protruding objects—and, therefore, like grain.

But this experiment is the exception. Even after a century of work dominated by psychologists—and before them, philosophers—who believed we *learn* to see the world the way we do, there is little solid evidence to support this belief.

In fact, there now is rather good evidence that form and depth perception are innate, that form and depth are perceptible at birth or soon thereafter. Bower's work shows that even perception in terms of constancy of size and shape is either not learned in humans or learned quickly—soon after birth—in some completely unknown way.

But what about the prismatic spectacles and the like that distort the world by refracting light? It has been known since the days of Herman von Helmholtz and Wilhelm Wundt in the last century that, if you continue to look through the prism, you will adapt to the distortions. Soon things no longer appear either as displaced or as curved as when you first looked through the prism.

This would appear to be a clear case of *learning* to perceive. If so, if we can demonstrate the effects of such experience on seeing in the adult, then perhaps we can conclude that perception in the young infant develops similarly. Study of adaptation to prismatic distortion now takes on real importance. In the laboratory we can produce, in a relatively short time, the effect of experience on perception. The next step would be to investigate the conditions necessary to induce these effects.

Many laboratory attempts have been made to study adaptation to visual distortion. As early as 1896, George Stratton at Berkeley undertook to view the world through an inverting lens system. His retinal image was reinverted—since the normal retinal image is an inverted one—and the world appeared upside

down. He hoped to discover whether, in time, the world would appear normal —or right side up—again. Stratton wore the device continuously for eight days, never permitting himself to see the world except through the lenses. To judge from his day-to-day description of his experiences, the outcome was not altogether clear.

This difficult and trying experiment has been repeated about once every decade since and—in my opinion—the results still are not clear. Stratton claimed he adapted or was well on the way to a complete righting of the scene. Others after him seemed to get no such effect, though T. Erismann and Ivo Kohler of Innsbruck recently claimed their observers did adapt.

There are several difficulties with Stratton's experiment. No objective methods were used to supplement and to clarify the observer's often unclear introspections. The choice of optical distortion—*complete* re-inversion of the retinal image—compounds the difficulty. A less drastic change would have been advisable, because it is difficult to imagine partial adaptation with complete re-inversion. The world will look upside down or right side up, but not tilted by some lesser magnitude. A further difficulty is the confusion between changes in behavior and changes in perception.

In addition to the altered appearance of things, lenses or prisms also lead to incorrect movements at the outset. Stratton reached upward for things that were

actually below the head, and vice-versa. Or he reached leftward for things that were actually to the right, and vice-versa. One may learn to correct these errors and nevertheless continue to *see* the world upside down.

Indeed, everyone who has undertaken this experiment has adapted behaviorally. Incorrect movement tendencies have disappeared and some observers have learned to bicycle and to ski while wearing the inverting lenses. Whether they adapted to the distorted appearance of things is another matter. This is not to deny that these two aspects of adaptation are related.

Except for these sporadic experiments on re-inversion, no systematic work on adaptation to distortion was done until recently. This delay in systematic investigation probably can be traced to the work of J. J. Gibson of Cornell University, who set out in 1933 to study the ability of observers to reestablish sensory-motor coordination when they viewed the world through prisms. However, his observers reported that straight lines that were curved by the prisms later tended to appear less curved. Gibson therefore shifted his focus of interest to this problem. Reasoning that a prism creates a curved retinal image and that this curved image later appears to straighten, he felt that the crucial thing was the curved image. His next—and plausible—move, one that I believe had an important historical impact, was to abandon the prism technique in favor of looking at a truly curved line. Surprisingly enough, he found that if you stare at a curved line for a few minutes, it will look less curved. If a straight line is then introduced, it will look curved in the opposite direction. This is the now well-known Gibson normalization effect. (He made a similar discovery about a tilted line.)

Gibson reasoned that objects tended to approach the norm from which they are departures. Since lines can curve symmetrically in either direction, a straight line is the norm or neutral point. If a curved image tends to lead eventually to an impression of straightness, then we may suppose that the entire coordinate system has shifted to a new neutral point. If this shift occurs, a straight image will no longer appear straight.

Prismatic distortion was no longer the focus of study. The prism seemed irrelevant to Gibson's work; it was only one method of creating a curved image. The normalization effect could not be

adaptation to a distorted world based on learning to see the world more accurately. In this effect the observer came to see *less* accurately, for after a while the truly curved line looked less curved. Therefore, it was not learning in the usual meaning. Interest shifted from prism adaptation to adaptation effects based on fixating curved and tilted lines.

The field of prism adaptation had to be rediscovered. Investigators had to realize that there *is* a class of effects such as Stratton first studied: Perceptual change based on learning to see a distorted world more correctly. The work of Erismann and Kohler played a major role, for when their observers wore the distorting devices over weeks or even months, they encountered dramatic changes and equally impressive after-effects when at last the prisms were removed. Richard Held of M.I.T. gave this work impetus by developing objective techniques for studying change and by showing experimentally that normalization effects of the kind Gibson discovered could not account for the changes that take place in wearing prisms.

A typical modern adaptation study is divided into three parts: pre-test, exposure period, and post-test. In the pre-test, the experimenter establishes just how each observer judges the perceptual property under investigation.

For example, the observer is asked to indicate when a flexible, luminous rod appears straight. Because he is shown the rod in a darkened room, he must respond in terms of the absolute appearance of the rod. He cannot compare it with other contours in his field of vision. Several measures are taken and the average computed. Then the observer puts on the prisms, set in goggles, and his exposure period begins. He performs relevant activities, more often than not merely walking through the laboratory corridors. For the post-test, he is brought back to the darkened room, his goggles are removed, and once more he views the flexible rod. The difference between pre-test and post-test is the measure of adaptation. Any adaptation will be revealed by an after-effect. In this experiment, a curved rod will appear straight, since a curved image has—during exposure to the prisms—come to yield an impression of straightness.

It is also possible to conduct all three stages with the observer wearing prisms. Adaptation in this procedure is revealed by the selection of a curved rod in the pre-test and a straight rod in the post-test. It can be argued that, if the ob-

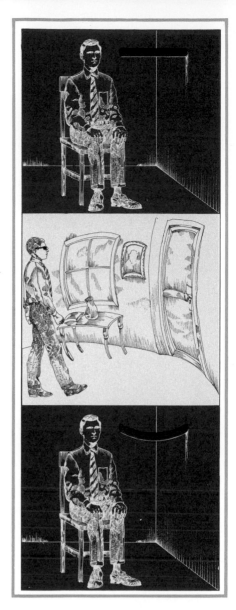

observers will adapt to a *tilted image,* a superior procedure to Stratton's 180-degree transformation. In the pre- and post-test, the observer sets a luminous line until it appears vertical. Exposures of a half-hour to an hour induce changes of from three to 10 degrees, providing objective data that an image need not be in its usual position for the observer to see it as upright. Stratton's belief thus appears to be confirmed.

Adaptation to altered curvature exists, but is relatively small. In one study, adaptation was only 30 per cent of the total distortion after observers wore prisms for 42 days. Nevertheless, the adaptation—and this is also true for tilt —is greater than the Gibson normalization effect can explain. Within a very short time, there is also appreciable adaptation to distortions of *size.*

The curve of adaptation levels off after the first day or two of exposure. After that adaptation increases very little. The reason for this is unknown, nor do we know whether adaptation other than that to displacement will be complete if the exposure is continued indefinitely.

Erismann and Kohler reported certain dramatic effects such as simultaneous adaptation to blue filters on the left side of both goggles and to yellow filters on the right; simultaneous adaptation to compression of images on one side and expansion on the other. However, it has not been possible to reproduce the color effect and we still lack adequate confirming evidence about the compression-expansion effect and other effects of this kind.

We must now consider the theoretical problem of adaptation to distortion. Are we to suppose that perception is so malleable that no matter how we distort the retinal image, the observer ultimately will adapt and see the world as we do? If this is true, how can we reconcile it with the findings that many perceptual attributes are present at birth and do not depend on learning? What mechanism underlies such changes in appearance?

I believe the answer is that perception is not completely malleable. We can adapt only to certain kinds of distortion. The information within the retinal image *does* supply us with the necessary core of what we see.

Suppose we hypothesize that the retinal image provides crucial information about *relationships* between objects. Consider the following example. Imagine you are looking at two straight lines, A and B, with line A being vertical and line B tilted, and A being longer than B

[*see illustration below*]. Assume that line A is straight ahead of you. In terms of the *relationship* of the image of A to that of B, we can say that A is longer than B and that A and B diverge, being closer at one end than the other. That is all.

Now if you look at this same configuration through a wedge prism, holding the position of your eyes still, the image will be distorted [*see illustration below*]. The entire pattern will be displaced sideways on the retina, and A and B will be curved. But the basic relationships are preserved: A remains longer than B, and A and B diverge from one another. If you look at the pattern through a lens that magnifies or minifies the lines, then, while the absolute size of the two images will be altered, the relationship of their sizes to one another will not be affected. If you look at the same pattern through an optical device that tilts the entire retinal image, the relationship of tilt of the lines *with respect to one another* will not be altered [*see illustration below*].

Therefore, if the crucial information given by the image is relational, the kinds of distortions that are being studied are not distortions at all! On the other hand, if a more drastic kind of distortion were introduced, such as a random scattering of points on the image [*see illustration below*], I think you will agree it is unlikely that an observer will ever adapt. He would never come to see A and B as we do.

But, if perception depends only on the relationships within the image, why does the world look distorted when *first* we look through prisms? This point has been completely overlooked by investi-

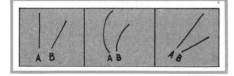

gators, who have assumed that it is intuitively self-evident that the world looks distorted because the image is distorted.

Let us consider this previously ignored problem of the initial distortion. Perhaps the absolute aspects—not the relationships of the two lines—will explain the distortion. Lines A and B produce images of specific size at any specific distance; A's image on the retina is vertical,

server wears prisms during the testing, he will try to discount the known distortion in order to give the "right" answer. Without prisms, he has no reason to compensate and adaptation will be revealed by an "error." Thus, the aftereffect obtained without prisms gives impressive evidence that a change in the nervous system does take place.

The findings of various adaptation studies indicate that adaptation to *displacement* occurs readily. If the observer is given enough exposure, this adaptation will be more or less complete. When an object straight ahead is prismatically displaced, the observer must turn his eyes to look at it. Many investigators agree that this kind of adaptation is based on the observer's interpretation of the turned position of his eyes as *not* turned. Hence, after exposure, an object fixated with eyes turned appears straight ahead.

There is now fairly good evidence that

B's is tilted; the images of both A and B are straight. Perhaps the visual experience of a lifetime associates these absolute aspects with their corresponding perceptual properties: the size of the image with the perceived size; the orientation of the image with the perceived orientation; the curvature of the image with the perceived degree of curvature. Such associations are preserved in the form of enduring memory traces, and these traces are faithful representations of the absolute features of the retinal image and the associated perceptual properties.

If this is true, A appears tilted when first viewed through a tilting prism, not for any innate reason, but because a

formation of a new association while wearing prisms becomes plausible. Through learning, a curved image is associated with a straight line.

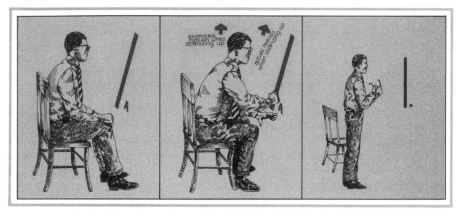

vertical orientation of the retina has become a sign of the perceptual vertical in the neural organization underlying perception. (Orientation here is with respect to the observer. The prism does not change the orientation of A with respect to B.) A appears smaller when viewed through a reducing lens, not because a smaller image innately demands a smaller percept, but because the specific size of the image has become a sign of a specific perceptual size. A and B appear curved when first viewed through a wedge prism, not because a curved image innately suggests a curved line, but because only a straight image has become a sign of a perceptually straight line.

Given this explanation, it is obvious how we adapt to prisms. It is only when the perceptual properties of absolute tilt, size, curvature and the like are *not* linked innately to absolute features of the retinal image that a theory of adaptation makes sense. For it would be hard to understand why, if image curvature innately determines perceived curvature, the perception of curvature is subject to change. But if the relationship of image curvature to perceived curvature is a *learned* one in the first place, then the

We have not yet explained how the observer forms these new associations. It is not enough to say he does so by looking through prisms. To illustrate this point, imagine a stationary observer who looks at A and B through a tilting prism. Suppose that he can see only this pattern; everything else being invisible. A will look tilted and B almost horizontal, and they will continue to do so. Unless information is provided that tilted A is vertical and horizontal B is tilted, no new associations can be formed. The observer would not adapt.

Suppose, however, the observer now can see his own body. The image of his body, seen through the prisms, will un-

dergo the same tilting transformation. It, too, will appear tilted [see *illustration above*]. Consequently, he now can learn that the tilted image of A is actually "vertical," for it is parallel to his body.

Other information than direct sight of the body can lead to adaptation. Movement by the observer could be an important clue. The seated observer who can see only A and B through the prisms has no reason to see the lines as they really are. But suppose he stands up [see *illustration left*]. Since A appears tilted with respect to himself, he would expect to move obliquely away from A. Instead, he finds that he remains directly in front of A; the direction of his movement is clearly in alignment with A. (A is in fact vertical and the observer is in fact moving directly upward.) From his movement, he learns that A is indeed vertical with respect to himself.

The same informative value of movement applies to curvature distortions. Imagine an observer who looks through curving prisms at a horizontal straight line on a wall. If he sits or stands still and sees only the line, there is no reason for its curved appearance to change. But if he walks parallel to the wall, peculiar changes of the line's image will occur [see *illustration below*]. That part of the line that had been in front of him will appear to move upward, and the part he is approaching will move downward. In other words, the lower-

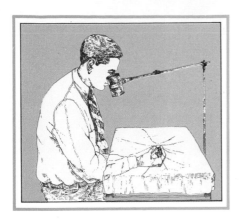

most bulge of the line will always remain directly in front of him. This is because the line *is* straight. Wherever he is, the tendency of the prism will be to displace that part of the line to his side upward to a greater degree than the part straight ahead. These changes in the image of the line inform him that its curvature is parallel to the direction in which he is moving. Because he moves in a straight path, the line must be straight.

We have not yet considered an obvious source of information—what we can find out from our other senses, particularly from touch. Suppose the observer who looks at A through tilting prisms then runs his hand along the line. You would expect that it would be easy for him to tell that the line is actually vertical.

In fact, in both philosophy and psychology there is a long tradition that can be traced to Bishop Berkeley of belief in the educating role of touch in the development of adequate visual perception. We see correctly in spite of the logical limitations of the retinal image as a source of information—for example, the image is two-dimensional, but vision is three-dimensional—so that it has seemed plausible to believe we learn to see by touching things and moving around in the environment.

But running the hand along the tilted line does not lead to visual change. Quite the contrary. The line will *feel* tilted. So dominant is vision that the impression yielded by our sense of touch is distorted to conform with our visual impression, even when it is wrong.

In our laboratory we have presented an observer with a conflict between vision and touch. In a simple experiment, the observer views a square through a lens that reduces the image to half its actual size. A one-inch square appears as a half-inch square. The observer is allowed to grasp the square, but a cloth below the square prevents him from seeing his hand. And he is not told that

he is looking through a reducing lens [*See illustration left.*]

In this conflict between two senses, the observer experiences only what he sees, and the *feel* of the square conforms to the *look* of it. The "feel" is captured by vision. As for adaptation, if the observer is given a prolonged exposure to this contradictory experience, vision does not change at all. Touch changes! The impression of size by touch alone—with the eyes closed—has changed following exposure to the conflict. The one-inch square now feels smaller than it did before the experiment began. It is therefore hard to believe that adaptation to prismatic distortion can be based on touch.

Contrast this failure to adapt visually to a reduced image with a different experiment. The observer is exposed to a reduced image, but he is given visual information. He does not have to rely on his sense of touch. In this experiment, the observer looks through a convex mirror that makes everything appear diminutive. Through this, he sees a good portion of his own body and an array of familiar objects, such as playing cards or checkers and checkerboard [*see illustration below*]. Tests of size perception are conducted before and after exposure to this optically reduced scene.

During the exposure period, which can be as brief as 10 minutes, the observer either remains stationary or plays solitaire or checkers. The reduced images of objects lead increasingly to an impression of normal size. In the test following exposure, the observer judges a luminous line of about 10 inches in length seen in the dark to be about 12 inches long, suggesting that considerable adaptation to the reduced image has taken place.

I believe that the crucial information here consists of sight of the body and the array of familiar objects. If the observer saw only a rectangle through the convex

mirror, it no doubt would continue to look about half its actual size. But when he sees a playing card maintain its normal size in relation to other objects, particularly to his own minified hand, he receives information that the reduced image is of a much larger object than first it seemed to be.

If perceptual adaptation is a fact, and if my suggested hypothesis concerning memory traces is plausible, a difficult question remains. How can memories affect the way things look? I cannot answer this question, but it is interesting to consider other cases where memories probably have such effects.

Consider the familiarity and meaningfulness of objects. Logically, it must be the case that a figure "4" *looks* familiar and meaningful because of memories associated with it. If so, these memories

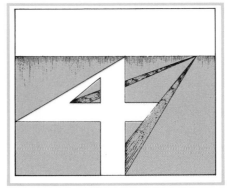

must enter into the neural organization underlying such perceptual experience. Even more to the point, because it involves space perception, is the drawn figure of a cube. The memories of three-dimensional cubes apparently are aroused by the sight of the drawn figure, and these memories then must enter the neural organization that leads to the visual impression that a two-dimensional drawing is three-dimensional. Recall the photographs of the cuneiform carvings. The memories of how shadows fall on three-dimensional objects must play a determining role in the way these photographs appear to us.

These are examples of past experience contributing to present perceptual experience. It is in this way, I would speculate, that adaptation effects can be understood. In our laboratory experiments, memories of how a tilted or curved line "behaves" somehow affect the way these lines look to our observers after prolonged exposure. On the other hand, our perception of the *relationships* between objects in the environment is in all probability innately determined. Not learned, but there all the time. ◪

Sonic Booms

Jangled Jet Nerves and the Thundering Future   By David M. Green

For most of us, the menacing bang and vibrations that we call sonic booms are only an irritation and a nuisance. But in the future these booms certainly may become destructive to property, far more frequent, and far more jangling to anyone sensitive to noise.

About a dozen persons were injured not too long ago by flying glass when a sonic boom caused by a low-flying airplane shattered more than 200 windows at the Air Force Academy, in Colorado. And in France, three people were killed when *le bang* from a supersonic jet caused the collapse of the roof of an old farmhouse.

We can all think of other sonic-boom disasters, and the future brings the possibility of a vast increase in sonic booms. There may be larger, faster fighters and bombers, and more frequent military air traffic over the United States. But by far the most serious increase in the jet thunder is likely to come from the next generation of commercial aircraft. Already the French and British have unveiled a large four-engine jet aircraft, the Concorde, which will have a maximum cruising speed of 1,450 miles per hour. In our own country the Federal Government is heavily subsidizing development of a supersonic transport—the SST—which will be even bigger and fly even faster (1,780 miles per hour) than the Concorde. If airlines are permitted to schedule overland flights of these planes most of the nation will be exposed to as many as 20 sonic booms a day or nearly one boom every half-hour.

And, barring an effective technological advance in aircraft design, the sonic booms will probably become several times as intense as they are now. With the new speed transports, the sonic boom will be equivalent to the noise from a large commercial jet flying at about 800 feet over a listener's head! The prospect of such noises for even a moment, when the moment is repeated again and again during the day, is likely to be of more than passing interest to the reader.

It is time we knew what the sonic boom is all about.

How a Sonic Boom is Generated

The physical principles responsible for a sonic boom are quite simple. Any projectile, like a bullet or an airplane, moving through the air faster than the speed of sound will create a sonic boom. As the projectile moves, it displaces air molecules and hence a normal sound wave is generated. This sound wave travels in all directions like an expanding balloon. When the velocity of the projectile is less than the speed of sound (about 720 miles per hour), then the sound wave will outrace the projectile and a listener would hear a continuous noise. When the velocity of the projectile is faster than the speed of sound, it races ahead of its own sound waves. The sound waves in the wake of the projectile join together to generate a single wavefront called a bow wave. It is exactly analogous to the surface wave generated by a speedboat as it knifes through the water. When the sonic bow wave passes by a listener, the listener hears a sharp crack—which we call a sonic boom.

The Boom on the Ground

Just as the wave of a speedboat spreads until it reaches the shore of the lake, so the cone of the bow wave generated by the airplane grows in size until it reaches the ground. Thus a very wide path along the ground can be affected by the sonic boom produced by a single aircraft. It is estimated that the SST will cut a 50-mile-wide swath—quite a continental boom corridor. The height of the aircraft, of course, influences the width of the corridor. The weather, the wind and the conditions of the atmosphere also influence sonic-boom

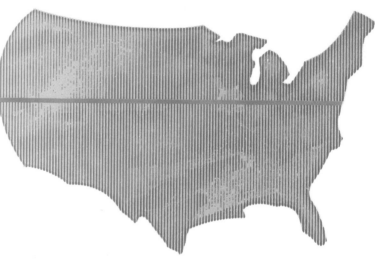

CONTINENTAL SONIC BOOMS. Each flight of the new supersonic transports will generate a boom path 50 miles wide across the country. Below is only the San Francisco-Washington corridor.

SONIC BOOM BIRTH. When a plane travels faster than its sound, normal sound waves join to form a wavefront like a motorboat. As wave washes over us, we hear a sharp crack—the sonic boom.

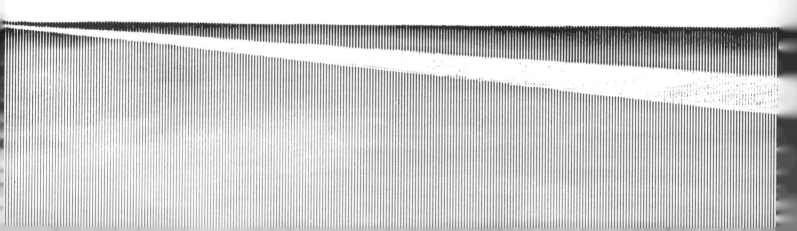

intensity, at times focusing the wave and leading to abnormally large, even super, booms.

Suppose we stand on the ground with a microphone and record a sonic boom. The recording would be analogous to the record we would get if we stood on the shores of a quiet lake and measured the height of waves from the wake of a distant speedboat. In both cases the recorded form of the wave generated by the bow resembles an N, and so we call it an N wave. With a sonic boom, there is first a rapid increase of pressure, then a slow decrease to below normal pressure, and finally a quick return to normal. It is the rapid rise above and the return to normal pressure that probably are the most significant parts of the N wave when we hear the boom outdoors. The usual measure of the boom's intensity is the peak overpressure, how much the air pressure generated by the sonic boom rises above the normal atmospheric pressure.

Peak overpressure of the boom is measured in pounds per square foot (psf). A boom produced by a small fighter plane (F-104) at a few thousand feet altitude may measure only 1 psf. Flying the plane at lower altitudes would make the intensity of the boom much greater. In general, a sonic boom is louder when the aircraft is larger, when the plane flies closer to the ground, and when it passes directly overhead.

A boom intensity of one pound per square foot is fairly small as booms go, but it is enormous when compared to the sound intensities for normal hearing. The relative loudness of a sound heard by the ear is measured in decibels, a unit named after Alexander Graham Bell.

Ordinary conversation in a room generates a noise level of about 60 to 70 decibels. On this scale, the peak overpressure in a one pound per square foot sonic boom is equal to 128 decibels—just about as intense as a pneumatic riveter at close range (*see chart, page* 235).

A sound level higher than 120 decibels is considered to be highly discomforting, if not downright painful. But before we jump to any conclusions we must take into account the fact that the sonic boom is not continuous; it is an impulsive sound of short duration.

Impulse and Steady-State Sounds

From scales based on physical measurements, we have developed reasonably good techniques for assessing the noisiness of fairly steady sounds. The effects of short sound impulses depend on the *energy* of the sound wave,

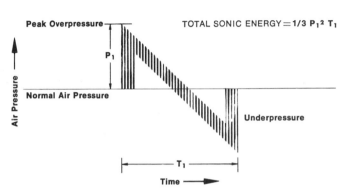

THE SONIC BOOM. Idealized boom recordings resemble an N and show the rise and fall in atmospheric pressure. The energy of a boom depends on both peak pressure and duration.

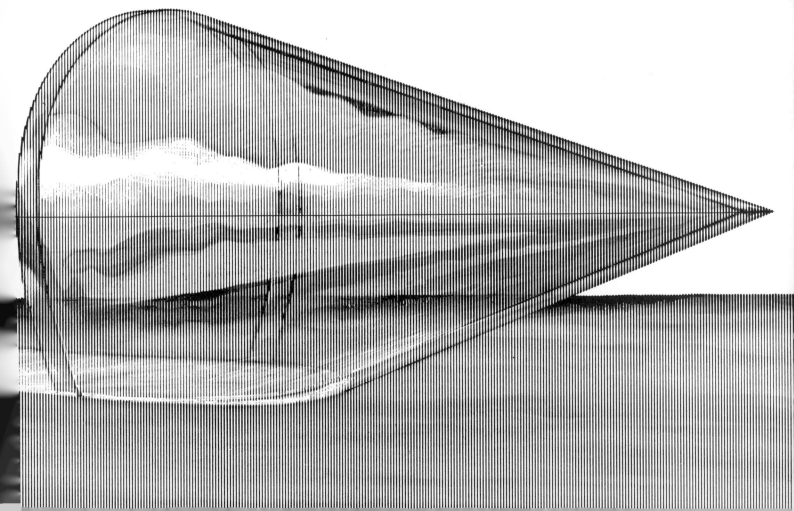

that is, both its duration and peak pressure—its power. Also important is how the energy is distributed over sound frequencies, because the ear is not equally sensitive to all frequencies. Few people hear sounds above 20,000 cycles per second and enormous intensities are needed to make sound audible below 10 cycles per second. We are most sensitive to sounds in the region of 1,000 to 3,000 cycles per second. The energy needed to just hear a brief sound at 100 cycles per second is roughly a million times more than the energy needed to hear the same brief sound at 2,000 cycles per second.

Recordings were made of sonic booms from three types of planes—a small fighter (F-104), a light bomber (B-58), and a large experimental bomber (B-70).

Each plane generated the same peak overpressure of about two pounds per square foot. But the duration of the boom varied according to plane size—0.1, 0.2, and 0.3 of a second, respectively. When the peak overpressure is the same, the total energy of a sonic boom is

area. Even airport noise from landings and take-offs is localized and minor by comparison.

Noise pollution is similar to water or air pollution. A single industry can change—drastically—the environment of large segments of the population. Lakes and rivers are spoiled. And we have formulated no clear policies to control such massive effects on our natural resources. Even with our tardy recognition of smog-generated health hazards, our control over the pollution of the air we breathe is weak and ineffectual.

The boom is bad enough, but the rumors about it are worse. Let us lay to rest the new wives' tale. Sonic booms are very unlikely to damage our hearing. The peak pressures are high, but the total energy is many times smaller than the energy from a pistol shot, and only a very small fraction of target shooters suffer any noticeable damage to their hearing.

Many people believe that the shock response to sonic booms may cause, indirectly, both physical and psycho-

proportional to its duration. This means that a boom lasting 0.3 second has about three times as much energy as a boom lasting 0.1 second.

However, the higher energy of the longer sonic boom is not distributed equally across all frequencies, and the amount of energy generated in the audible frequency range was roughly the same for all three planes. The recording showed that, as the duration of the boom increases, more energy appears in the lower sound frequencies to which the human ear is relatively insensitive.

This means that if the peak overpressure is the same, the noisiness of the boom heard outdoors will be approximately the same whether it is generated by a small fighter plane, such as the F-104, or by a larger aircraft, such as the B-58. But consider the boom heard inside a house. Although our ears are insensitive to the very low frequency energy, the windows, walls and roofs of our homes are not. They absorb this energy. Our walls move. Our windows and doors rattle. Thus, the magnitude of the boom as heard inside the house depends both on the peak overpressure and on the duration of the sonic boom, because both parameters affect the total effective energy delivered to the house. Two sonic booms that seem equally loud outdoors can have greatly different apparent intensities when heard inside a building.

In fact, a sonic boom that is hardly noticeable outdoors may seem like a momentary earthquake indoors.

Noise Pollution

How will people respond to the frequent, intense booms of the future? Will we become a nation of jangled jet nerves? In principle, the sonic boom is no different from any other noisy nuisance. Local legislation can limit the noise of trucks and construction machinery. But the sonic boom creates a disturbance over a much wider

logical damage. And this aspect of the problem is less clear. There is little information concerning startle reactions to sonic booms, although there has been a great deal of research on the startle reflex to acoustic stimuli like pistol shots. People can become used to sudden sounds and stop reacting—at least overtly. And we simply do not know yet whether adaptation or increased sensitivity would occur with frequent exposure to booms.

Surveys conducted in metropolitan areas where booms are heard frequently provide a better direct source of information concerning the acceptability of booms. One of the earliest such studies was in St. Louis, Missouri, under the sponsorship of the Air Force, the National Aeronautics and Space Administration, and the Federal Aviation Agency. Over a 10-month period residents of that city were exposed to approximately 150 sonic booms. A definite flight plan was adopted and measurement of the N wave was made at a variety of ground locations within the boom corridor. Most were from a B-58 bomber, with peak overpressures of 0.4 to 3 pounds per square foot.

The National Opinion Research Center conducted thorough interviews with some 1,000 families in various parts of the city. The interviews were described as part of a general community survey, not as sonic boom research. Interviewers classed unfavorable responses to the booms as either interfering or annoying, depending upon the intensity of the resident's response. In families where the booms were considered interfering, 93 per cent reported the house shook, 74 per cent were startled, 42 per cent were wakened abruptly, and about 20 per cent had their rest and relaxation, conversation, or radio and television reception interrupted. In about 40 per cent of the interviews, residents reported annoyance at the booms.

SOUND INTENSITIES. Sounds are measured in decibels (db); over 120 db are painful. Common sonic boom—peak overpressure, one pound per sq. foot—creates unpleasant 128-db boom.

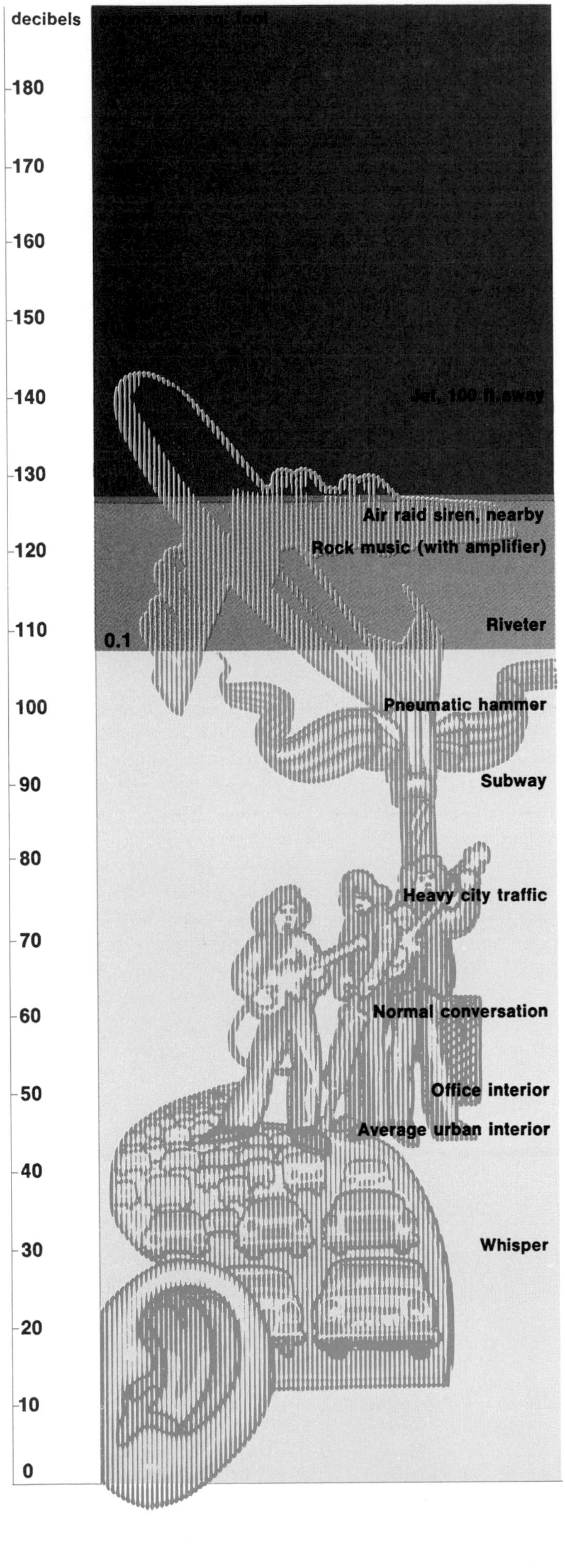

decibels

- 180
- 170
- 160
- 150
- 140 Jet, 100 ft. away
- 130
- 120 Air raid siren, nearby
         Rock music (with amplifier)
- 110 Riveter
   0.1
- 100 Pneumatic hammer
- 90   Subway
- 80
- 70   Heavy city traffic
- 60   Normal conversation
- 50   Office interior
- 40   Average urban interior
- 30   Whisper
- 20
- 10
- 0

It is difficult to apply the results of this survey to regular commercial flights by SSTs. Because a public information program was held before the tests, the public believed the booms were caused by a military exercise. And even though there were booms as intense as SST booms, they were infrequent and irregular, unlike projected SST flights.

Another interesting survey was conducted during a program of overflights in Oklahoma. With eight flights per day at fixed times, the intensity of the boom was gradually increased from about one pound per square foot during the first few weeks of test to about 1.5 pounds per square foot for the middle 15 weeks of tests, and finally to about two pounds per square foot the last six weeks. Local residents were asked on three separate occasions to report on whether they thought they could learn to live with eight booms a day from a *civilian* supersonic airplane. The percentage of people who felt that they "very likely" would learn to accept the boom declined from about 80 to 60 per cent during the course of the tests. The percentage who replied that they couldn't learn to accept the boom increased from about five to nearly 20 per cent. It is not clear, though, whether this change in attitude represents a sensitization to the boom because of repeated exposure or simply reflects the increase in intensity of the boom over the several weeks of the test.

Psychoacoustic Tests

The final source of information concerning man's reaction to the sonic boom makes use of psychophysical tests and employs the same methods that were used to construct the current scales of loudness or noisiness. Dr. Karl Kryter of the Stanford Research Institute applied these methods to sonic booms in tests at Edwards Air Force Base in the summer of 1966.

A large group of people were asked to compare the annoyance difference between a sonic boom and the noise of a low-flying plane. Some people were inside their homes during the tests. Others were outdoors. Some worked at the Air Force base; others lived in towns 70 miles away.

There is frequent criticism of the comparison of dissimilar sounds. Certainly, the task of comparison is more difficult if the sounds are qualitatively different, but Kryter's data show that it can be done. If the intensity of a boom drops by 10 decibels, the number of people judging that the boom is more acceptable than a conventional low-flying plane will rise from 20 to 80 per cent. Kryter's data indicates that a change of one decibel in noise level will change five per cent of the judgments and, further, that measured differences greater than five decibels are probably very reliable. Kryter's results also showed that we are more irritated by sonic booms we hear when we are in our homes than by the same intense boom heard when we are outdoors. This is because of the way our homes "react" to the sound. Houses keep out a good deal of conventional flyover sound. But they absorb sonic-boom energy, converting some of the inaudible sound energy to audible sounds. And what a shaking thing that is!

The Edwards Air Base tests seem to show that we may build up a tolerance for sonic booms. People living at the base had been exposed every day for two years to regular sonic booms—sometimes eight in a day. They were consistently more tolerant of aircraft noises than were the people who lived 70 miles away. Of course the sample may be skewed: the base residents earned their livings from the noisy aircraft, and had they been unable to tolerate such noise, they would have left for quieter work.

Will the SST Fly Overland?

The new SSTs seem ideal for transocean flights. The plane can decelerate and approach land at subsonic speeds, and thus no boom need be generated over populated areas. Any attempt to restrict the SST to only overseas travel, however, will be subject to strong pressure.

The greatest pressure for overland use of the SST will be economic. By 1977, about $4.5 billion will have been spent on developing the SST. The estimated price to build one plane is about $40 million—five times the cost of any current commercial aircraft. Some 300 planes must be sold before the manufacturer and the government can recoup their enormous development costs. A natural way to increase sales is to broaden the market—not to declare domestic flights off-limits.

William A. Shurcliff, a Harvard physics researcher who has organized a "Citizens League Against the Sonic Boom," stresses the sad but sound fact that a single overland SST flight from Los Angeles to New York would cut a sonic boom swath that would shock up to 20 million people with its thunder.

In 1967, the Air Force paid out $440,000 to settle over 3,300 claims for damages from sonic booms. The Citizens League estimates that a daily schedule of 150 SST flights over the U.S. would cause $1 million damage per day. (Frankly, I am somewhat skeptical about this estimate which probably is considerably inflated.)

To those who are by nature sanguine, the most hopeful avenue is to attempt somehow to decrease the level of the SST boom, and research is presently underway to streamline the plane and minimize the bow wave it creates. Unfortunately some of the best designs to minimize the size of the bow wave also decrease the lift of the airplane.

The Future

In the near future, barring technological breakthroughs, we can expect to hear 20 booms per day, each as loud as a flyover of a conventional jet at 800 feet altitude.

The projected level of exposure is so extreme that it may be tempting to conclude that it will never be permitted. Such a view, in my opinion, is wrong. Certainly there is nothing in the history of noise control in this country to inspire such confidence. Nor would a similar review of the history of air and water pollution support such optimism.

The increase in noise exposure will be gradual, not abrupt, and will parallel the increase in air pollution over the last 30 years. I am certain that had anyone asked a resident of New York or Los Angeles if he would endure the levels of air pollution now present in those cities he would have answered with an emphatic no. Yet today, the residents do endure these conditions and it is only in extreme cases that they are moved to positive action.

The basic problem is that any prior recognition of the danger is based on projections, and projections are simply guesses about the future. Certainly the preceding projection of sonic-boom exposure has many uncertainties and may generate disagreements just as any other 10-year look into the future. Each factor in the preceding projection might be challenged and if new estimates were substituted, the entire outlook could change.

Further research is particularly needed on the psychological responses of people to prolonged exposure to sonic booms. The need for this kind of research has been emphasized in a recent report by the National Academy of Science, authored by Professor Raymond Bauer of Harvard. But unless some major breakthrough in technology occurs, we are in for a noisy future. Ω

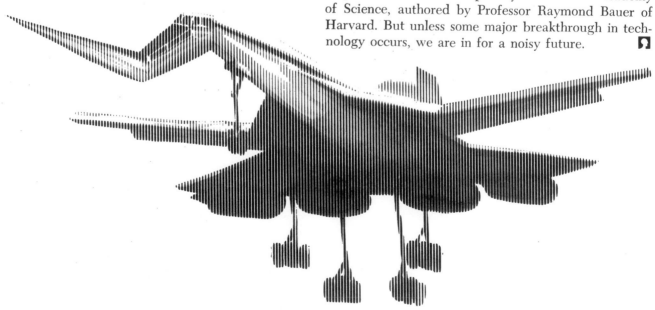

Can the skin learn a language?
Why not?
Then touch will tell.

bod′y Eng′lish

by Frank A. Geldard

WHAT KIND OF LANGUAGE can the skin understand? Well, most people would say, the skin can understand the "language" of texture—the rich, complex, unmistakable feels of silk, velvet or tweed. Or the "language" of hot and cold, the "message" of the insect's sting, the language of warning, the affectionate touch on the shoulder, or the small number of pokes and jabs which can mean anything from, "Shhh—the boss is coming" to "Isn't that the most ridiculous thing you've ever heard?"

But what about language in a narrower sense—can skin receive and understand a complex impersonal system of symbols like Morse, semaphore or even English?

And even if the skin can handle language in the communications sense, aren't the eyes and ears enough?

Eyes and ears were not enough during the early years of World War II, when fighter pilots were shot down too often because they could not hear their wing commanders, and they did not peel away fast enough when enemy planes closed in. Thus research was begun to find out if warning signals could be built into cushions so that pilots could "hear" by the seat of their pants.

Certainly it is painfully obvious that the eyes and ears are not enough if you are blind or deaf or both. Braille, for instance, is an arbitrary, very difficult language to learn, and most blind people do not read well in it. It is also obvious that there are a myriad of conditions in which even the nondefective eye or ear may be absorbed, or baffled, or in some way at a grave disadvantage—you can't hear when the water's running or bombs are falling or crowds are screaming. You can't see in the dark or in the fog. The human voice is wildly distorted by helium under deep-sea pressure, and so on.

Assuming then the practical need to explore all possible channels of communication, we can and should ask: What can the skin do? What kinds of signals can it handle? What kinds of discriminations can it make? How can these discriminations be used as the building blocks of a sophisticated, easily intelligible vehicle for hard information?

The Compromising Skin

As a receiving instrument, the skin combines the best abilities of the eye and ear; it doesn't perform quite as well as the eye and ear do in their specialized fields, but it is the body's only receptor that can handle both fields fairly well.

By the ear's field, I don't mean sound—the blessed human voice, for instance, or the divine noise of the Prelude to Parsifal—I mean time. Within a continuous sound, the ear can detect a break or silence only two to four thousandths of a second long. The ear has a rather poor space-sensing ability, however; more often than not

237

We can begin to talk about a skin language that uses discrimination in time and space as vocabulary items.

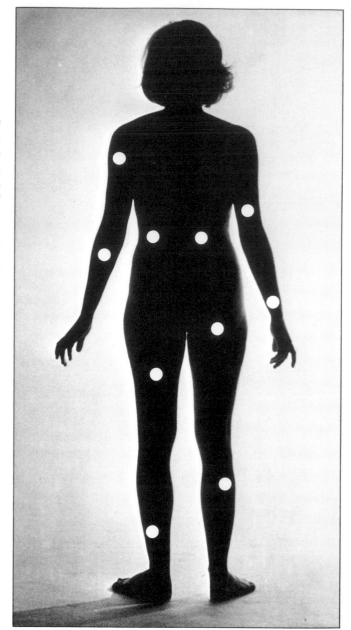

VIBRATOR SITES. These sites, far enough apart and devoid of bone, form recognizable elements of language in spatial terms.

we speak of a sound coming from "somewhere." Space is the eye's province: the eye can be fooled, of course, but it can make extraordinarily fine discriminations—indeed the finest the human organism is capable of. On the other hand, the eye is a sluggish time organ; home movie screens which reflect only 24 discrete flashes of light per second are seen as a continuous picture or blaze of light.

The skin handles time almost as well as the ear. Under proper conditions, the skin can detect a break of about 10 thousandths of a second in a steady mechanical pressure or tactile buzz. For the eye, comparable time discriminations are much slower; eye discriminations are about 25-35 thousandths of a second. (Ball-park figures for the ear, for the eye, and for the skin are thus .003, .030, and .010 seconds, respectively.)

In terms of space, the skin can identify and distinguish between coded signals delivered from five to seven different locations within the chest area. The ear cannot identify the source of a sound (provided this sound is produced at some distance from the hearer) with anything like the same fineness, as anyone who has ever tried to "spot" a buzzing insect by ear can testify.

The Skin's Vocabulary

Given the skin's fairly accurate spatio-temporal perception, we can begin to talk about a language that uses discriminations in time and space as vocabulary items. The skin's time sense provides us with two vocabulary elements—duration and frequency.

When using duration in a system of signals, it is not worth considering vibratory pulses or buzzes shorter than 0.10 second (they are not felt as buzzes, and could easily be mistaken for an accidental poke or jab); at the other end, buzzes lasting more than two full seconds would slow any signaling system to a crawl. Between these limits, the skin can distinguish some 25 discrete, just-noticeable differences in length, at least four or five of which can be judged with absolute correctness. When presented in isolation, these four or five signals are felt to have a distinctive length—short, medium-short, medium, and long, for instance. These distinctive lengths can be coded and hence become meaningful elements in a language.

Frequency is a somewhat finer aspect of temporal discrimination, analogous to heard pitch. Such felt frequency depends primarily on the rate at which successive impacts are delivered to the skin. Usable or "hearable" frequency ranges for the skin are rates below 150 impacts per second, which is of course below the frequencies present in speech or the mid-musical range. But within this limited range, the skin does almost as well as the

ear; for example, a frequency or pitch of 40 impacts per second can be distinguished from one of 39.5 or 40.5 impacts per second! Sixty impacts per second provides a good general carrier frequency or note upon which pitch variations can be played conveniently.

Another valuable vocabulary item or codable discrimination is that of intensity or "loudness." Sensitivity to loudness or softness varies from one location to another on the skin, so that figures have to be specified for particular body sites. But, in general, from the threshold below which nothing is felt, to a safe distance under the discomfort level, the average subject can detect some 15 just-noticeable differences in intensity. As with duration, some of these intensities can be recognized as having a unique value, like soft, medium and loud, for instance, even when there is nothing to compare them with, and hence can be suitably coded to mean something.

The fourth useful dimension in cutaneous talk is loca-

The vibratese code proved quite efficient... it could be handled about twice as fast as Morse Code.

tion or space. There are a number of problems connected with the skin's space sense that are only now being investigated. (For example, when two chest vibrators are activated simultaneously, they are felt as one, but more about this later.) But so long as they are buzzed in sequence, with just a tiny time differential separating the signals, as many as seven vibrators may be placed on the chest and used as codable signal elements.

Vibratese—A Workable System

Vibratese was a language having 45 separate signals; three intensities (weak, medium, strong), and three durations (short, medium, long), were delivered to five different spots on the chest. (All steps could be combined with all others, $3 \times 3 \times 5$, giving 45 steps or signals.) Letters of the alphabet were each assigned a signal representing a unique combination of duration, intensity and location. The times were kept short—0.1, 0.3, 0.5 seconds for short, medium and long, respectively. The most frequently occurring language elements were assigned shorter durations, enabling the system to "fly" at a rapid pace. The code proved quite efficient, since the all-important vowels were assigned each to its own vibrator, and since letters followed each other promptly, with none of the wasteful silences that are built into International Morse.

The vibratese alphabet could be mastered in only a few hours, and it was not long before two- and three-letter words could be introduced, and then short sentences. Trainees found that, as with radio or telegraphic codes, they could "follow behind" and combine letters and words into larger patterns. When the training sessions were finally discontinued—not because the learning limit had been reached, but because the sending equipment could go no faster—one subject was receiving at a rate about twice that of proficient Morse reception.

The vibratese experiment taught some valuable lessons but, more importantly, it raised questions about the possibility of making far better use of the space dimension. Could vibrators be scattered all over the body? Could they be activated simultaneously? These questions had to remain open, given the purely technological limitations imposed by the equipment then available—the vibrators were extremely cumbersome, and the chest area was the only place to put them.

By the time the Cutaneous Communication Laboratory at Princeton University was established in 1962 (hitherto most work in this field was done at the University of Virginia), a major technological breakthrough had taken place. A small, compact, yet powerful vibrator somewhat like a hearing aid was developed in 1959 by R. C. Bice at the University of Virginia. Later, a more

rugged and reliable vibrator of the same general type was developed at Princeton by Carl Sherrick. Both these instruments can be attached quite simply and firmly at any desired body site, and can be counted on to perform accurately over long periods.

It is possible that systems using only coded variations in spatial location can provide languages thoroughly adequate for many purposes—simple warning or tracking systems, for example.

In one experiment at Princeton we placed the vibrators on 10 different body sites (*see illustration, opposite page*). These sites weren't arbitrarily selected, and many others were tried. It was surprising how far from each other vibrators had to be in order to act in relative independence of one another. It was also surprising how many potential sites had to be abandoned because they provided ready paths to the ear; subjects complained of hearing, rather than feeling, the vibratory bursts. Though we really don't know as yet whether exactly corresponding points on the two sides of the body need to be avoided—as they are, intentionally, in the illustration—general neurological principles seem to suggest this.

Subjects were exposed to patterns consisting of two vibratory bursts one fifth of a second long, and separated by a half-second silence. Each of these two bursts activated from one to nine sites at the same time. In some of these patterns, both bursts were identical: exactly the same sites were involved, as in:

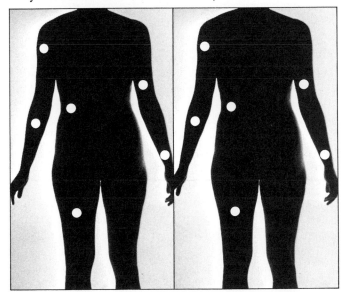

In other patterns, the two bursts were different in varying degree. The same number of sites were involved, but they weren't the same ones. Altogether, 1,000 patterns were presented (more than half a million are possible); 500 were "sames" pairs and 500 were "differents." The subject's task was merely to report which were which.

"The letter W...sweeps vividly across the body, shoulder to ankle, shoulder to ankle, like a sort of tactile neon sign."

The really important error-causing factor turned out to be not the sheer number of sites involved, but rather the extent to which successive bursts had elements in common. That the number of sites alone was not primarily the culprit became evident when patterns utilizing no more than four vibrators were consistently misjudged to be the "same" because they had three sites in common:

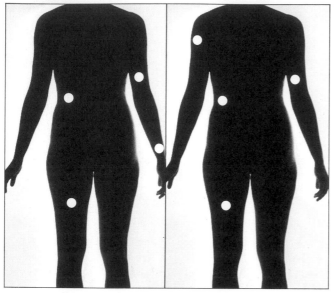

More elaborate patterns were discriminated perfectly, so long as they were different enough.

Space-Time Cooperation

It is clear now that tactile communication not only permits, but fairly demands, the coordination of both spatial and temporal variations. A peek into the future reveals at least one of the many possibilities to be explored.

At Princeton, we developed an instrument called the optohapt. The symbols supplied by a typewriter are transmuted into sequences and combinations of vibratory bursts distributed over the body surface. Nine of the locations (*see illustration, page 238*) are used.

A glance at the circular inset (*see illustration, opposite page*) will reveal the essential mode of operation. In the case of an E passing steadily from right to left, the vertical backbone of the letter first activates in a single burst the entire array of nine vibrators, then continues on with #1 (*top*), #5, and #9 (*bottom*). The middle one quits a little sooner than the top and bottom vibrators because of the shorter middle branch of the E. A distinctive spatio-temporal pattern is thus created, one which belongs exclusively to the E, though differing from an F only by the inclusion of a long burst on one vibrator (#9). Some of these time-space patterns are extremely attention-getting, to say the least; the letter

W, for instance, sweeps vividly across the body, shoulder to ankle, shoulder to ankle, like a sort of tactile neon sign.

Actually, letters do not provide the best material. Punctuation signs and a variety of literary and business symbols are more distinctive and more readily learned.

In the exploratory stage, we examined a group of 180 symbols, searching for the most easily understandable signals. The final survivors for alphabetic coding are shown in the illustration below. These, if presented at the optimal speed—optimal means having suitable "zip" and vivid movement—are easy to learn and retain. They are also easy to combine into word-forming sequences.

The optohapt represents only one limited set of possibilities for presenting spatio-temporal patterns; typefaces arbitrarily dictate the patterns flashed to the skin, and the typewriter carriage moves only one way, of course. The Cutaneous Communication Laboratory is just now putting into operation a tape system which tells a different story. The new device—speedy, accurate, and reliable—will provide what appears to be the ultimate

E	.	D	‖	P	..
T	⌣	U	ı	B	→
A	‖	C	/	V	V
O	■	M	Ш	K	..
I	ı	F	–	X	Γ
N	▬	G	🏛	J	J
S	◇	W	\	Z	⌐
R	∏	Y	:	Q	⸲
H	÷				
L	—				

→■ᵢᵢ: . ▬🏛–I◇÷

BODY ENGLISH

THE OPTOHAPT ALPHABET. These symbols can be flashed to the skin rapidly and vividly; they are easy to learn and "read."

challenge to the skin, a set of patterns containing far more elements than even the most rabid dermophile would ever claim to be within the skin's ability to conquer. Experiment will shortly decide if we shall ultimately arrive at a completely satisfactory "Body English."

A Friendly Look Backwards

In terms of research history, we have made a good deal of progress since 1762, when Jean-Jacques Rousseau proposed that the skin might serve as a channel of communication. In his revolutionary educational treatise, *Emile*, Rousseau drew attention to the common observa-

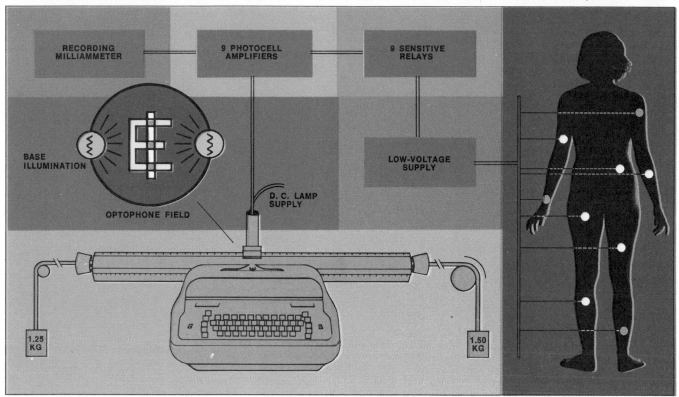

THE OPTOHAPT. It transforms photoelectric impulses from typewriter symbols into sequences and combinations of vibratory bursts which are played upon the skin as though upon a piano keyboard. The skin reads the bursts as a spacetime "tune."

tion that the vibrations of the cello can be felt by the hand and fingers and that "one can distinguish without the use of eye or ear, merely by the way in which the wood vibrates and trembles, whether the sound given out is sharp or flat, whether it is drawn from the treble string or the bass." He asked whether "we might in time become so sensitive as to hear a whole tune by means of our fingers." Beyond that, he estimated that "tone and measure" might ultimately become "the elements of speech" for communication with the deaf.

The idea that the skin ought to be trainable to receive complex vibratory patterns never really was lost sight of in the more than two centuries since *Emile*. People continued to suggest that speech and music might be impressed on the skin much as it is delivered to the eardrums. Indeed the argument was an evolutionary one: the eardrum is basically a derivative from skin, and the tactile sense should therefore be able to learn to do, at least crudely, what the tympanic membrane does so superbly.

During the first third of this century there were elaborate and painstaking experiments, both in America and in Germany, aimed at teaching the skin to recognize complex chains of vibrations delivered to the fingertips. In the most extensive of these, words and sentences were spoken into a microphone which activated a small crystal speaker, an instrument known as the teletactor, which imparted its vibrations to the fingers. But the results were disappointing: only a series of poorly discriminated rhythmic accents could be learned, and not too effectively. In the mid-'30s the whole effort was abandoned, and it was many years before it was learned why these experiments had failed. Now we know that the frequencies important in speech are all but impossible for the skin to discriminate. The skin was being asked to do something at which it is quite inept.

The long course of research and speculation has led us to the knowledge that the skin can handle time and space discriminations fairly well. We have put this knowledge to the test, and have shown that the skin can receive rapid and sophisticated messages. There is every likelihood that skin languages of great subtlety and speed can be devised and used.

But the point is that we have much more in the way of basic fact than anyone has yet put to work. This fairly solid ground floor of data is available for a host of applications, and I have touched obliquely on a few of them—warning signal systems, supplementary directional systems, a sophisticated language for the blind or deaf, and, of course, all sorts of secret military or commercial uses. But I confess to a certain sympathy with the classic remark attributed to Michael Faraday on the occasion of his being asked what good his induction motor was: "Maybe you can tax it some day." ♎

Chemical Perception in Newborn Snakes

By Gordon M. Burghardt

A FACE IN A CROWD, a familiar voice in a busy conversation, a delicate perfume in a summer evening's breeze, a hint of spice in a culinary masterpiece—each of these sensations leaps forward forcefully into our consciousness. We see the face, not the crowd; we hear that special voice, not any of the others; we smell the perfume, to the momentary exclusion of Summer's other scents; we taste the spice, for a moment forgetting the impression of the dish as a whole. Out of what William James called the blooming, buzzing confusion of our raw sensory experience, we selectively admit into our consciousness only some of these myriad perceptions.

It is not simply a matter of our being especially sensitive to these salient perceptual events. Each face in the crowd, for example, is equally large and equally bright—perhaps even equally interesting on close examination. Rather, some events excite our interest and attention because they have particular meaning to us as individuals.

One source of this meaning is, of course, our past experience. The mother has come to recognize and respond to her baby's cry among all those in the nursery; the chef comes to detect the missing spice in the complex aroma rising from the stew; the wine taster comes to sense the particular essence that identifies the truly great vintage. All of us, highly trained or not, constantly select perceptual events from all the hundreds of stimuli imposed on us—and in so doing we project a perceptual structure onto the entire outside world.

The perceptual world of the normal human adult seems at first glance to be largely a matter of experience. Each of us finds a different face in the crowd to be particularly exciting and interesting. But perception also is tempered by natural, inherited limitations and sal-iences. It is true that a musician learns by experience to appreciate a great composition, but the range of tones which he can hear and the discriminations between tones which he can make are determined largely by the inherited structure of his ear. It also is true that each individual develops his own personal set of appreciated forms and colors. But commonly shared illusions and hallucinations suggest commonly inherited characteristics within both our visual and nervous systems.

In fact, perhaps the most amazing and instructive cases of imposed perceptual structure are those which are not learned by a lifetime of experience but rather are dictated by nature through generations of evolutionary experience. The young child, for example, without any specific training or experience, will select a balanced diet from a multitude of offered foods, even if left solely to his own devices. My research with snakes has shown that the infant snake is peculiarly fitted out by its inheritance to snap at and eat specific nutritious objects from among the countless hundreds of objects which it will encounter in its first few days of life. More important yet is the finding that the snake seems prepared by nature to eat only those objects which it normally will encounter in its natural habitat. The wisdom of generations of evolutionary development has imposed on these small animals a perceptual structure which facilitates their survival from the moment of birth.

Releasers and Perception

We owe most of our knowledge of this form of natural perceptual selectivity to the ethologists who have elaborated the concept of the "releaser." Basically, they have discovered that a given behavior often is critically dependent on just one aspect of the stimulus situation, while other equally perceivable qualities are without effect. For example, the red belly feathers of the male British robin trigger an attack by another male robin. A dummy, accurate in all respects except that the belly is not red, elicits no attack, but a bundle of red feathers alone is sufficient to release the behavior.

There are many other examples of these critical relations. From them, pioneers of ethology such as Jacob von Uexküll and Konrad Lorenz arrived at a seminal concept known as the releasing mechanism. This mechanism is "keyed" to respond to perceptual cues from the relevant stimulus object, and these cues are known as releasers or sign stimuli. Another aspect of interest was that in many cases these releaser-response relations did not have to be learned in any normal sense during the individual organism's life. Eckhard Hess, at the University of Chicago, has shown that newborn inexperienced chicks prefer to peck at some colors rather than at others. Why this should be is not known yet, but the point is that previous pecking experience was not necessary; releasing mechanisms are innate. It is almost as if there is an Innate Perceptual Schema somewhere inside the organism, to which the environment must correlate in order for a response to occur. Thus nature imposes structure on the organism's perceptual world.

Whereas most work on releasers is and was concerned with vision, my research has been with chemical releasers, odors, which elicit behavior patterns.

The Sense of Smell

The chemical sense of smell is perhaps the most interesting and intriguing sense that we possess. We are certainly selective in our response to odors, many of which elicit profound emotional experiences. Why is there such a mystery surrounding perfumes, and why do only a small proportion of those developed win lasting favor? Why do some smells repel us, while others brighten our outlook throughout the entire day? Yet the mechanisms of smell, even the stimuli themselves, are little understood. There are even authorities who believe that, through generations of disuse and societal taboos, Western man has become insensitive to his sense of smell.

When we try to study smell in man, methodological problems appear immediately. These include the inaccessibility of the sensory receptor itself, the difficulty of presenting an odor in a standardized manner, problems of adaptation and conditioning, and our inability to specify what in the physical stimulus correlates with the subjective impression. There have been some ingenious attempts to overcome these problems. For instance, John Amoore, with the U.S. Department of Agriculture, has had considerable success in correlating the smell of a substance with its molecular shape. But the fact remains that at present man is not a very good organism to use in the study of the chemical senses. Man's reliance on other sensory modalities confounds the precise assessment of the role and mechanism of smell.

Enter the Serpent

What would be a good experimental animal other than man? Many mammals below the primates rely on the chemical senses, but with them a behavior is rarely completely dependent upon olfaction. Most closely related to the mammals are the reptiles, the behavior of which is without question the least studied of all the vertebrate classes. Nevertheless, no one questions the great importance of the chemical senses to snakes. Snakes evolved from lizards and have reached a degree of specialization of the chem-

ical sense unrivaled by any other group of terrestrial vertebrates.

Snakes possess numerous advantages as experimental animals and many species do very well in captivity. Since some species such as garter snakes are viviparous and often give live birth to 60 or more babies at a time, they are especially useful in the study of early development. Nevertheless, snakes have been neglected as experimental subjects, probably because of society's antipathy toward them. The Biblical story of the Garden of Eden probably didn't help. But perhaps a different attitude is needed. As Robert G. Ingersoll put it back in the year 1872:

> If the account given in *Genesis* is really true, ought we not, after all, to thank this serpent? He was the first schoolmaster, the first advocate of learning, the first enemy of ignorance, the first to whisper in human ears the sacred word "Liberty," the creator of ambition, the author of modesty . . of inquiry . . of doubt . . of investigation . . of progress . . and of civilization.

Snakes, besides having a well developed sense of smell, have another modality derived from their olfactory nervous apparatus. The receptor for this modality is known as Jacobson's organ or the vomeronasal organ. It is present in some amphibians, reptiles, and mammals, but it reaches its highest degree of specialization in snakes. The organ consists of a pair of sacs which open into the anterior roof of the mouth. The epithelial lining of the sacs contains typical olfactory cells and their cytoplasmic extensions form a branch of the olfactory cells which terminates on a specialized portion of the olfactory bulb.

The chemical senses in snakes and their behavioral importance were studied by a number of workers 25-45 years ago. While the discussion of the indi-

vidual contributions of such scientists as Baumann, Kahmann, Noble, Weidemann, Wilde, and Bogert is not possible here, we can list what seem to be the major results of often conflicting research. First, taste seems to be of rather minor importance and plays a role only when food objects are actually in the animal's mouth. Secondly, Jacobson's organ functions in conjunction with the tongue. The snake's frequent tongue-flicking is a mechanical means of picking up and transferring chemical substances to the vicinity of Jacobson's organ within the mouth. (Of interest is the fact that snakes have an indentation in the upper lip which allows them to flick the tongue without opening the mouth at all.) The third point is that many behaviors in snakes—including prey trailing and courtship—seem to involve both Jacobson's organ and normal olfaction. However, Wilde in 1938 demonstrated that the attack on prey by the adult common garter snake is dependent almost totally upon Jacobson's organ. By severing various nerves, Wilde was able to show that only when Jacobson's organ was functioning did an attack take place. Olfaction alone was neither necessary nor sufficient. To prove that only a chemical stimulus was involved, he used a clear and colorless solution of earthworm mucus, which was presented to the snakes on cotton attached to glass rods. The snakes, which normally ate earthworms, attacked this cotton as they would a normal prey object. Wilde's research inspired ours. The behavior pattern and its elicitation were clearly commensurate with the ethological concept of the releasing mechanism. Perhaps feeding behavior in newborn snakes could tell us a great deal, not only about serpent behavior but also about the potentialities and functioning of chemical sensory mechanisms in general.

Analysis of Prey Attack Behavior in Newborn Snakes

We started by asking questions: Would newborn garter snakes respond to chemical stimuli from worms with prey-attack behavior before they ever had experience with any type of food object or its odor? Would they respond to extracts from other normally-eaten classes of prey? And if the above answers were affirmative, was this stimulus-response connection reasonably permanent? If the answer to these three questions were yes, then we would be dealing with a highly precise biological relationship which would offer limitless opportunities for studying, among other things, learned versus unlearned factors in chemical perception, the relations of selective chemical releasers to evolution and ecology, and the development of a behavioral bioassay technique for chemical stimuli.

Using a litter of three-day-old previously unfed garter snakes (*Thamnophis s. sirtalis*), we found that the answer to all three questions was yes. The chemical stimuli were prepared by placing a standard weight of either redworms, minnows, mealworms (larvae of a beetle), or horsemeat into warm distilled water for one minute. The prey then were removed, and the resulting water solution filtered and refrigerated until use. Of the four items, the first two (redworms and minnows) readily are eaten in nature by this species of snake; the other two are rarely, if ever, eaten.

Naive newborn snakes dramatically attacked a cotton swab that had been dipped in either worm or fish extract. They did not attack swabs dipped in the insect extract, meat extract, or pure water. The attack response, given an effective stimulus, comprised the following: The snake increased its rate of tongue flicking and then lunged forward at the swab with its jaws wide open at about a 45° angle. [*See illustration, p. 247.*] This response was identical with that seen toward live redworms and small fish. Moreover, although these young snakes normally refused to eat pieces of horsemeat, they readily attacked and ate horsemeat dipped in the worm extract. The inexperienced snake somehow can recognize, on the basis of chemical stimuli alone, what it "should" attack as a potential prey object.

The stability of the response to chemical stimuli first was tested in completely naive snakes from the same litter by presenting the worm extract at five-minute intervals for 20 trials. An attack was given every time and no progressive weakening of the response was apparent. In a later test for stability, 40 trials were given to a snake with still no weakening of the response. [*See illlustration, p. 246.*] Naturally, the response cannot be elicited indefinitely at such short intervals. However, the stability shown is more than sufficient for the testing of the same individual repeatedly with the same or with a different extract.

After we obtained the above results, we were convinced that this phenomenon was worthy of intensive study. A series of experiments was designed to investigate various aspects of chemically released attacks by newborn snakes.

One of the first experiments concerned the role of vision in eliciting this behavior. With the same litter, we investigated the responses to visual aspects of prey animals from which the snakes could obtain no chemical information. A variety of small sealed glass vials was introduced into the home cage of each individual snake. Vials were either empty or contained a type of small organism, which was either dead or alive. The results were as follows: If there were moving organisms in the vials, the snakes would orient themselves, flick their tongues, and explore; however, they never opened their mouths or tried to attack the animals through the glass. Further, the amount of interest in the vial shown by the snakes was clearly proportional to the amount of movement going on in the vial at the time. For instance, quickly-swimming guppies elicited the greatest response, while dead guppies of exactly the same size and coloration elicited no response. This response to movement in the vials disappeared rapidly when the vials were reintroduced a short while later, indicating that the novelty of the moving animals was involved. Indeed, at this point we can conclude that the role of vision is limited to the orientation toward and exploration of a potential food object, particularly if moving, but that the attack of prey can be elicited in naive subjects only by chemical stimuli.

Further experiments with inexperienced garter snakes whose eyes or nostrils (or both) had been artificially closed showed that neither olfaction nor vision is at all necessary for the prey-attack response to occur. Jacobson's organ is apparently responsible. Naturally, the attacks of blind snakes were not well-directed, but attacks they were.

Comparative Studies

One of our main interests has involved the study of species of snakes which have feeding habits in nature and captivity that are quite different from those of the garter snakes with which our work began. Would newborn young of these species respond to chemical stimuli from animals which the species normally ate? We began by looking at other species of snakes in the garter snake group, the genus *Thamnophis*. In this large and widespread group of snakes are found forms with very different food habits. We tested seven species and subspecies

on a series of extracts from prey representing most classes of animals known to be eaten by at least some species in the genus. The congruence between the responses of the inexperienced newborn young and the known feeding habits of the species was very close. For instance, the Chicagoland garter snake (*Thamnophis sirtalis semifasciatus*) will eat fish, worms, amphibians, and leeches very readily and we obtained highly significant responses to those extracts, but not to extracts of slugs, mice, insects, and

crayfish, which in fact this species rarely, if ever, eats. [*See illustration, p. 248.*] As in many snakes tested, there was a big difference in the relative effectiveness of larval and adult salamanders. It appears that during metamorphosis changes occur in the chemicals from the skin which elicit prey-attack behavior.

Consider another species, the eastern plains garter snake, *Thamnophis r. radix*, which has similar habitat and feeding preferences. We tested a litter of 22 newborn young and obtained the profile

of responses to various extracts. [*See illustration, p. 249, top.*] Again, all extracts were significantly higher than the water control but for those of the baby mouse, slug, cricket, and metamorphosed salamander. Although no extensive ecological studies have been done on this species, it appears that earthworms, amphibians, fish, and leeches are eaten readily, with worms being probably most common in the natural diet. Extracts from three kinds of earthworms and three kinds of fish were tested.

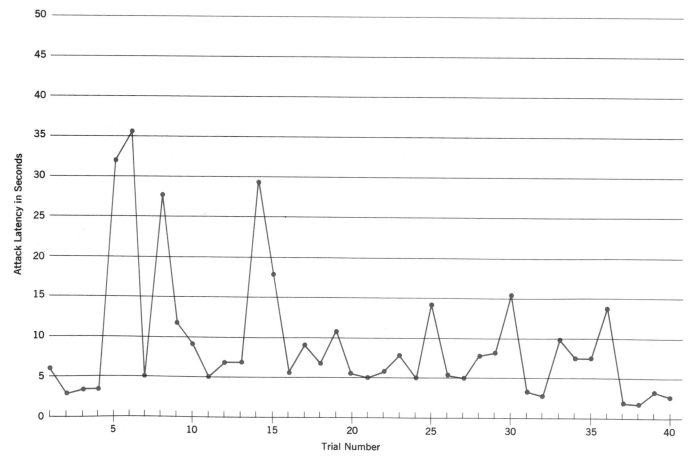

Newborn garter snakes reliably and repeatedly attack a swab dipped in an extract made from worms normally eaten by adult garter snakes. Inexperienced snakes attacked on 40 successive trials at five-minute intervals. No habituation took place.

In a characteristic attack on a swab dipped in extract from a prey, the garter snake orients toward swab and increases its rate of tongue-flicking (upper photographs), lunges toward swab (middle photographs), and bites swab (bottom photographs).

Again, it was found that the larval salamander had a higher releasing value than the adult form. This is a relationship which frequently has been found in species of newborn snakes that include amphibians in their normal diet. It may represent evolution's discovery that larva are tasty, while adults are tough—and perhaps dangerous.

In sharp contrast to the above were results obtained from the western smooth green snake (*Opheodrys vernalis blanchardi*). This species, unlike others we studied, is oviparous instead of bringing forth young alive. In one experiment, eggs were laid and hatched in captivity. The young were tested at the same ages as were the plains garter snakes, and with the same extracts. The same extracts were presented to the green snake as to the plains garter snake. [*See illustration, opposite, bottom.*] The cricket extract was the most potent; indeed, it was the only extract to which actual attacks were made and the only one significantly higher than the water control on the basis of the tongue flick-attack score. The result becomes more meaningful when it is realized that, out of all the extracts presented, the cricket extract is the only one which represents an organism eaten by the green snake. In fact, it appears that this species will eat nothing but insects, spiders, and soft-bodied arthropods.

The differences between the smooth green snake and the plains garter snake are striking. In contrast to green snakes, plains garter snakes never eat insects, and the cricket extract received the lowest score of all the extracts. It is obvious, therefore, that clear and biologically useful differences exist between the chemical perceptions of food objects by these two species of snakes.

The green snake and the plains garter snakes are rather widely removed from each other both taxonomically and ecologically. The common garter snake, discussed first, and the plains garter snake are much more closely related, live in similar habitats, and appear to eat the same food. With these two species, the extract-response profiles show no clear differences. Is it possible to find differences between closely related forms? Just how precise is the technique? A final answer to the last question cannot be given yet, but it is possible to generate some dramatic differences between species of the same or related genera. Let us look at a couple of examples:

Two species of garter snakes and one of the brown snakes (*Storeria*) were ex-posed to extracts from three earthworms, three fish, and one slug. We tested eight inexperienced newborn midland brown snakes (*Storeria dekayi wrightorum*), known to eat only worms and slugs. The second species of naive young tested was Butler's garter snake (*Thamnophis butleri*). We tested a litter of 15 from a female caught in southern Michigan. In captivity, Butler's garter snake readily eats worms and fish but not slugs. The third species to be compared on these three classes of extracts was the western aquatic garter snake (*Thamnophis elegans aquaticus*), known to eat only fish. We tested a litter of nine from a female found in southern California.

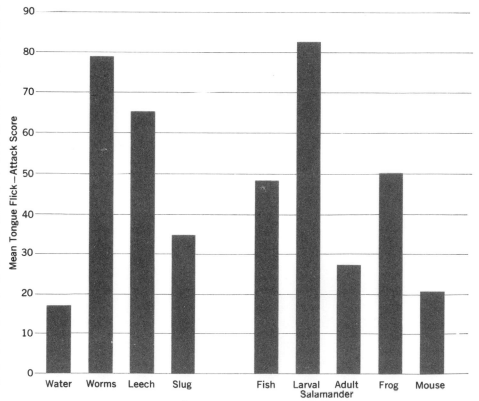

Newborn Chicagoland garter snakes were tested on extracts from common prey, scored high for prey normally eaten by adults (color), low for prey rarely eaten (grey).

The results were clear. The responses of the different species of inexperienced snakes to skin extracts parallels the feeding habits manifested by specimens freshly caught in the field. [See illustration, page 250.] Scores for the brown snake were on a different scale from the garter snakes—about half as high, due to a lower frequency of tongue flicking. This reduction also was found in another species from the same genus.

Turning to the water snakes (Natrix), we found some more remarkable differences. Most water snakes (such as Natrix s. sipedon, the common banded water snake) eat fish and amphibians, but Graham's water snake (Natrix grahami) and the queen snake (Natrix septemvitatta) eat practically nothing but crayfish, and newly molted ones at that. Here the newborn young attacked only crayfish extracts and even gave a greater response to extracts from newly molted crayfish. [See illustration, page 251.]

Taken together, these results dramatically indicate the species-specific nature of chemical perception in newborn snakes. That these are related to the natural feeding ecology of the different animals is equally clear. But what do these comparative results mean? First of all, they can best be understood in terms of evolutionary principles. By natural selection each kind of newborn snake comes to recognize, by chemical cues, the type of prey that it is best adapted to eat. Our present interpretation is that there is an Innate Perceptual Schema, or releasing mechanism, based upon genetic information which enables the newborn snake to recognize, by chemical cues, the type of prey that it should eat. Differences between species then easily can be seen as ecological adaptations that have evolved through natural selection. As such, they can be as useful in the study of the relationships and differences among species, such as skeletal structure, scale patterning, or other morphological characteristics. For instance, the two species of water snakes responding to crayfish extract are closely related by the usual taxonomic criteria. But too facile an evolutionary interpretation does not do justice to the data. This technique shows that a naive snake will respond to chem-

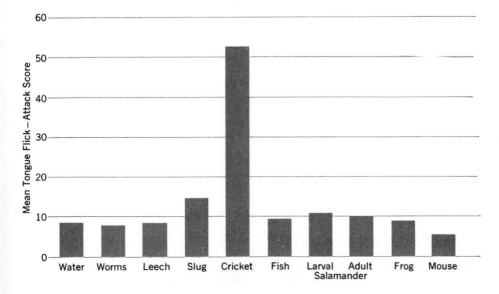

Strikingly different attack profiles were obtained with babies from two different species of snakes, the eastern plains garter snake (above), and the western smooth green snake (below). Nevertheless, the babies attacked extracts of prey normally eaten by the adult of the species (color) but did not attack the other extracts (grey).

ical cues that cannot or do not figure in the normal feeding behavior of the species. For instance, where it is found, the aquatic garter snake would rarely, if ever, encounter the guppy, yet the newborn young responded to the guppy extract readily. However, since the aquatic garter snake normally eats fish, it is probable that the guppy possesses chemical cues similar or identical to those found in fish which the snake normally eats.

In Butler's garter snake the situation is quite different. An extensive field study by C. C. Carpenter, now at the University of Oklahoma, showed that in nature the diet of this species comprises only worms and leeches. Yet captive specimens readily eat fish and amphibians, and newborn young respond to extracts from all four groups. Indeed, the complete profile of responses to extracts by Butler's garter snake is very similar to those of the plains garter snake or the common garter snake, which does eat all four types of prey in nature. It is apparent, therefore, that the normal feeding habits and ecology of a species are not sufficient to "explain" the response to chemical cues in newborn young. But we should remember that evolution is a process of time and that the past may exist in the present. A feasible hypothesis in this instance is that Butler's garter snake has retained the perceptual side of a releasing mechanism which appears to be of no selective advantage in its present mode of life. Of course, retention of the potential of naive snakes to respond to chemical cues from fish would be advantageous if a change in the environment occurred so that fish became a necessary or more easily obtainable food source. The same could be true for amphibians in this species. It is interesting to note, in this connection, that on the usual taxonomic

criteria several authorities feel that Butler's garter snake has evolved from the plains garter snake.

We are beginning the construction of species profiles based upon the responses of newborn young to a series of extracts. So far we have investigated over 15 forms from seven genera. It is by looking at very closely related forms, however, that the most valuable comparative conclusions may be gleaned, since here the traditional taxonomic canons of anatomical distinctions among species may be only of limited value.

Other Considerations

The problem of how these responses by naive snakes can be modified through subsequent experience is interesting, and work is underway in this area. However, the strength of these innate releaser-response ties is often more striking than

is their lability. For instance, a large litter of garter snakes was divided into two groups. One group was tested on the standard series of extracts during the first week of life and then released. As with all our testing, it was possible to rank the stimuli in order of effectiveness. The rest of the litter was raised for either 64 or 191 days on an artificial, unnatural diet (strained liver). Since they would not eat this food, we periodically forced it down their throats. At the end of the predetermined number of days on the artificial food, the snakes were tested in an identical fashion on the same series of extracts as were the snakes in the litter tested at birth. Remember that for this period of time these snakes had never had the opportunity either to receive a chemical stimulus normally eliciting an attack response nor to perform the attack response itself. In

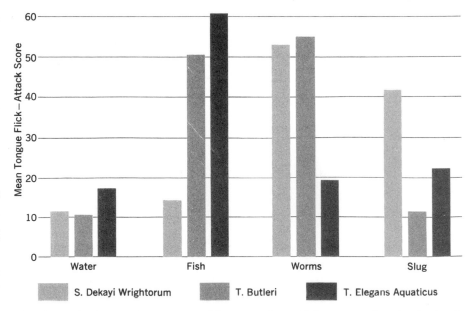

Attack profiles for newborn snakes of three species tested on three classes of extracts reflect diets of adult snakes. (Scores for S. Dekayi Wrightorum are doubled.)

nature a similar amount of deprivation would have resulted in the early death of the snakes. Yet the snakes in both deprived groups attacked the same extracts in the same way as did their littermates tested earlier. No degeneration of the releaser-response system had taken place during the long periods of inaction. The artificial diet, by the way, was refused at the end of the experiment as it had been at the beginning.

There is some evidence, however, that early feeding experience can influence subsequent behavior if the snake actually attacks and eats the prey object. Further experiments are in progress on this aspect of the problem.

Currently, studies also are being carried out, in collaboration with John Law of the biochemistry department at the University of Chicago, on the chemistry of the effective extracts. Once we know the nature of the chemical stimuli involved in this behavior, it should be possible to study stimulus structure and releasing value on a molecular level.

If the chemical perception of the newborn snake is so well adapted to the ecological and evolutionary aspects of its existence, it is reasonable to inquire into the possibility of similar situations elsewhere in the animal kingdom, including man. But many psychologists, while admitting the existence of complex inherited sources of stimulus information in birds, fish, and insects, feel that mammals, especially humans, are so perceptually and behaviorally plastic that evolutionary considerations of the type discussed here are unimportant or irrelevant, or perhaps even dangerous. Possibly a new approach is needed. Gene Sackett, at the University of Wisconsin, recently has shown that rhesus monkeys raised in visually restricted environments respond in species-specific fashion when confronted with pictures of monkeys having certain expressions such as threat. Robert Fantz has shown that the newborn infant brings into the world more complex visual abilities than previously thought and, on the physiological level, David Hubel and Torsten Wiesel have demonstrated the extensive visual abilities built into the newborn kitten. Daniel Freedman and Eibl-Ebesfeldt are directing our attention to the implications of evolutionary, ethological thought for our understanding of human behavior.

But as concerns the chemical senses we only can speculate. Probably no odor would elicit as specific an overt response in man as in the snake. But many of the responses of men to situations and stimuli are internalized. Feelings and affective states replace the motoric responses necessarily measured with animals. Perhaps many of the feelings aroused daily in the odoriferous world of man are influenced in part, at least, by evolutionary memories recorded in the genes many ages ago, fleeting emotional bonds with our ancestors. And this memory might be a little bit different for each of us, for we all have had a unique voyage from the past.

The highly precocial nature of young snakes and their dependence upon the chemical senses allow the phenomenon to be elucidated clearly. But the point is that we should not be concerned just with whether the newborn organism has or has not certain perceptual abilities of vision, olfaction, etc. We would like to know if he can use these abilities innately to recognize stimuli having biological and evolutionary significance. In many cases we may never find out. Nevertheless, the search is both exciting and meaningful. ♫

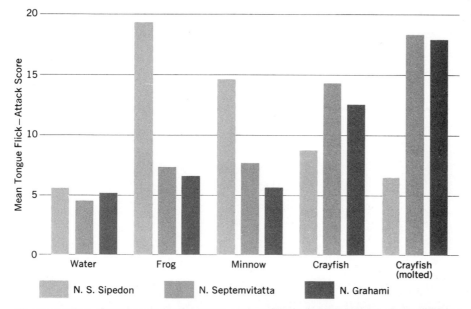

Three species of snakes from the same genus, *Natrix* (water snakes), have different natural diets. The attack profiles of the newborn young show the same differences.

By James A. Simmons

The Sonar Sight of Bats

LIVING CREATURES have developed a remarkable variety of ways to obtain information about their environments. An animal's surroundings contain many different forms of energy and a variety of substances. As different animals go about their daily or nightly activities, they sense an impressive number of these energies and substances. Every aspect of behavior in any animal is under direct, immediate control by the information abstracted from the light, the heat, the vibrations, the chemical concentrations, the physical environment.

Nature has been particularly ingenious in providing ways for animals to detect objects without having to move up to them and bump them. Vision serves a wide range of different animals, from the invertebrates to the most elaborate mammal. Airborne and waterborne sound provides many organisms with information about things somewhere in their vicinity. Vibrations of the ground also act as stimuli for terrestrial animals. The sense of smell tells many animals that something is near, and the rattlesnake can even detect heat radiated from a source warmer than the rest of his surroundings.

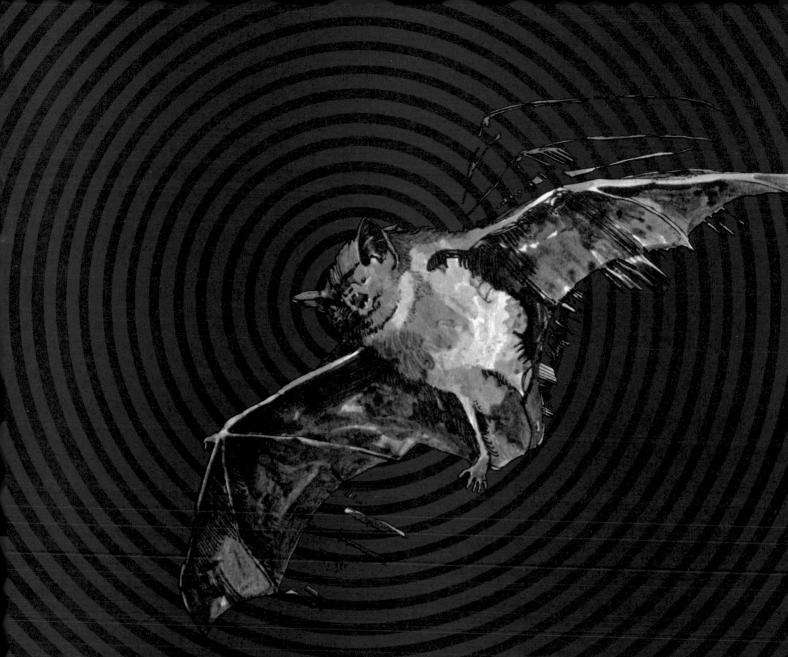

In a few instances, nature gives animals portable sources of energy with which to explore the environment. Orientation by self-emitted energy is analogous to a man exploring a dark room with a flashlight. Whirligig beetles, insects that live on the surface of water, detect objects by rippling the water and picking up reflections of these ripples. Some species of fish generate electrical fields in the water around their bodies and detect objects by means of the disturbances the objects cause.

The most famous and best-studied type of emitted-energy orientation is found in bats. These little animals, already interesting to zoologists in their means of locomotion, reproductive processes, and choice of living quarters, find their way around with a full-fledged sonar system. For a number of years research on the hearing and perceptual capabilities of bats has been under way at the Auditory Research Laboratories of Princeton University.

Bats are creatures of the night. They sleep by day in caves, abandoned mines, culverts, attics, old barns, trees and any of a hundred other quiet, sheltered places in which they can hang. In the evening they emerge to seek food and water. Their nocturnal habits have resulted in their inclusion with other beings of darkness and the supernatural in most of our folklore.

The bats owe their enormous biological success to the night and to their peculiar adaptations to life in darkness. With hardly any light with which to see, they fly at daredevil speeds through trees, bushes and jungle thickets, dart about in the air catching small flies and mosquitoes, and fly in and out of deep caves, often through winding passages and in the company of hundreds and hundreds of other bats. Yet a bat rarely bumps a branch or misses a meal.

In geographic range, in numbers of individuals, and in the number and variety of different species bats are indeed flourishing. They have existed in basically the same form for over 50 or 60 million years. Although often regarded as rodents, "mouse-angels," bats are in fact a separate group of mammals, distinct from rats, mice and squirrels. Zoologists classify bats in the order Chiroptera (wing-handed). The order is divided into two groups.

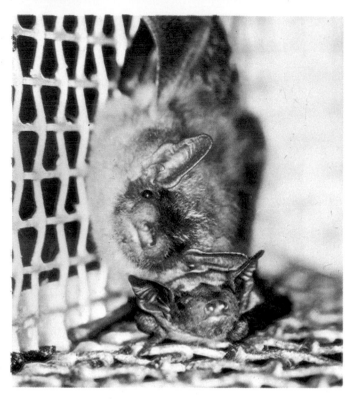

One of the suborders, Megachiroptera, is composed of bats less specialized for flight than the other. Megachiropterans have excellent vision and live on a diet of fruits. Perhaps the best-known of these is the "flying-fox," a large fruit-bat with a wingspread of five feet.

The other suborder, Microchiroptera, consists of bats that are well equipped for life in the air. They have powerful wings, and they also seem to have relatively poor vision and habits that usually keep them well away from light. Microchiropterans differ considerably in their diets. Some eat insects captured in the air or on the ground, some eat fruit or the nectar of flowers, and some capture and eat small birds and mammals, including other bats. The vampire bats are so specialized they eat only the blood of mammals or birds. To get by without being able to see, the various bats of the suborder Microchiroptera have evolved a remarkable way of getting information about objects in the environment.

The Bat Problem

The little, insectivorous bats of North America and Europe have long been zoological curiosities. Their proficiency in moving around at night attracted some attention. In the 18th Century an Italian monk, Spallanzani, and several of his collaborators discovered that blinded bats could live and fly around without any apparent trouble. They found that impairment of hearing was the only way to disorient a bat. The science of the day reacted against the unconventional implication that bats "saw" with their ears, and most of Spallanzani's contemporaries assumed that the bat's skill in flying arose from touch sensitivity to near-by objects.

Little more became of the question of how bats found their way about until the 20th Century, when knowledge in acoustics provided a basis for renewed speculation.

In 1912 the British inventor Hiram Maxim suggested that the bat detects obstacles by feeling echoes of the sounds of its wing beats as they reflect back from objects. Several years later, H. Hartridge, an English physiologist, proposed that bats navigate with a kind of sonar, emitting high-frequency sounds and detecting echoes of these sounds.

In 1938, Donald R. Griffin, a zoologist then working at Harvard University, found that bats do indeed emit extremely high-frequency cries, often much higher in frequency than the upper limit of human hearing (or 20,000 cycles per second). Griffin and Robert Galambos worked together for several years on the discovery and established that the bat's ears can respond to such high-frequency sounds, and that the basis for obstacle avoidance in bats is the detection of echoes of its cries.

Bats navigate with a sophisticated biological sonar, called *echolocation*. They emit a series of short, sharp cries that contain frequencies from 25,000 cycles per second to well over 100,000 cycles per second. Some kinds of bats emit loud sounds, some emit soft sounds, some emit sounds of almost constant frequency, some emit frequency-modulated sounds, and some emit sounds rich in harmonic frequencies. All of the Microchiropteran bats use echoes of their own characteristic cries for sensing objects in the environment (*see illustration, p. 255*).

Echolocation is an active process in which the bat generates a sound and identifies objects and obstacles with the reflected echoes. Although many animals can detect and locate near-by objects by picking up sounds that the objects themselves may emit or by sensing changes in the environmental noise level near the objects, relatively few animals use active sonar. The excitement stirred up by the discovery of the bat's echolocation led to the discovery of the use of sonar by porpoises and to the possibility that other animals, including some birds and terrestrial mammals, might also echolocate. Man himself can echolocate, as has been shown by several experiments on blind persons and on blindfolded subjects. To be sure, man can also echolocate with apparatus built for that purpose, as in the cases of ultrasonic scanning devices in medicine and underwater sonar systems.

We are accustomed to *seeing* objects in our surroundings. It is ordinarily with vision that we locate and iden-

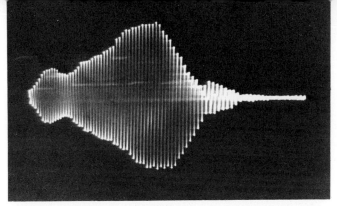

ECHOLOCATION CRY. Photograph of oscilloscope trace of a bat cry, which lasts about 2 milliseconds; is frequency-modulated.

tify objects, navigate from place to place and find our way around obstacles. Qualities such as size, shape, distance and texture have underlying visual cues like relative size, visual angle, perspective, parallax and stereoscopic vision. These visual cues are in turn based on the physical properties of the light that stimulates our eyes.

Hearing is another important human sense, but not entirely the same way as vision. We use hearing for communication, for detecting, locating and identifying sound sources, and for music.

But bats use hearing in place of vision to gather information about distant objects. Banished for its own good to a life away from light, the bat perceives the important qualities of objects not with the intensity, wave length and distribution of light striking the retina, but rather with the intensity, frequency and time of arrival of sounds at the ears. The bat "sees" near-by objects, in terms of the physical parameters of the echoes of its own cries as they return from the objects. The ears and brain of the bat have become highly specialized for rapidly processing the auditory cues in the echoes so that the essential details about obstacles or targets are detected in time to catch a moth or avoid a branch.

The bat's behavior is exquisitely controlled by the perceptions of the environment it derives from echolocation. We can inquire about the bat's mode of perception in much the same way as we traditionally have investigated vision. What kinds of judgements can a bat make about objects that it perceives with sonar? Animals that use vision easily can perceive object size, shape, location and distance. Can the bat also detect such things? The bat's performance in flight and skill in hunting of course suggest immediately that it readily can perceive size, shape, movement, etc., but can we demonstrate some of these perceptions experimentally?

In an attempt to learn more about the extent to which echolocation can substitute for vision, I have been working on the ability of several species of bats to make judgements of the size of objects, the shape of objects, and the distance to objects. I have found that when examined by the methods normally reserved for visual perception, the bat's sonar is very versatile, every bit as flexible as would be expected from the performance of bats in nature.

The species that I have used for the study of distance, size and shape discrimination is the big brown bat, *Ep-*

tesicus fuscus. This hardy insectivorous bat thrives in captivity, easily adapts to discrimination training, and can echolocate with great skill. It emits sounds that sweep in frequency from just under 50,000 cycles per second down to about 25,000 cycles per second, and its cries easily can be detected, even with crude, homemade condenser microphones (*see illustration, left*).

Since bats are among those mammals that occasionally carry rabies, all our staff members are vaccinated against the disease, and no one handles any bat without protective gloves.

When beginning discrimination studies with bats, there is one important experimental precaution to consider. The visual capabilities of echolocating bats are not well known. Available evidence suggests that bats are probably not very good at visual pattern perception, but no one is certain. To eliminate the possibility that vision may be used in discrimination learning experiments, at least some of the bats must be deprived of sight. For most species, the best way to do this is actually to remove their eyes while they are anesthetized. The operation is safe, and the animals appear to recover completely. In discrimination experiments with dozens of bats of several species, no instance of the use of vision has come up. That is, blinded bats and normal bats do *not* perform differently on discrimination experiments.

Sonar Perception of Object Size

To find out whether an animal's vision is sufficiently acute to perceive the size of a stimulus, you can try to train the animal to distinguish between a large stimulus and a small stimulus. If it can learn to respond to one of the two stimuli, say the larger, but not to the other, then you have demonstrated that in some way the animal is able to perceive the relative size of each stimulus and to identify correctly the larger one. This technique is called *simultaneous discrimination learning,* and it is a basic tool for the study of sensory and perceptual capabilities in animals.

Although size discrimination is a problem usually encountered in connection with visual perception, there is no reason why we cannot try to train echolocating bats to discriminate between objects differing in size. A sim-

BAT RESPONDING TO STIMULI. The mouth is open for emission of sonar cries in experiment for distance-discrimination.

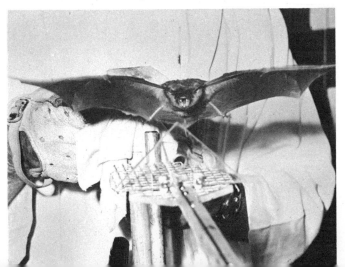

SIZE DISCRIMINATION EXPERIMENTAL SET-UP. Bat sits on the single platform at left and examines the two landing platforms and targets with its sonar. It responds by flying correctly to whichever platform carries larger triangle more than 90 per cent of the time.

ple experimental set-up can be used for training bats to distinguish between a large stimulus and a small one (*see illustration, above*). The bat is taught to sit on the platform at the left and to examine the other two platforms and the triangular shapes mounted on them. The targets are 30 centimeters away from the bat. Notice that one of the triangles is larger than the other.

Each time the bat flies from the starting platform to the landing platform that has the large triangle, he is rewarded with a choice bit of food—a piece of an insect. The positions of the triangles are "randomly" interchanged from right to left and back again to ensure that the bat is responding to the size of each stimulus and not to its position. After a week or two of training the bat can choose the platform with the larger stimulus more than 90 per cent of the time.

Acuity of Size Perception

We used a series of triangles to demonstrate that the big brown bat can distinguish between objects of different sizes with surprising accuracy (*see illustration top left, p. 257*). We first showed the bat a pair of triangles that differed greatly in size. Each bat was trained to fly to the large triangle in this pair until it could do so with a minimum of errors for 75 trials. As expected, the bats learned to discriminate between the triangles easily.

Then we transferred the bat to a pair slightly closer in size. We carried out 50 trials on this second pair, rewarding the bat with food for every correct response. Pair by pair, with 50 trials on each pair, the bat moved through a series of six additional pairs of triangles.

As each new pair was shown to the bat, the size difference between the larger and the smaller triangle became a little bit smaller. Finally, the bat came to the seventh pair, in which the size difference was reduced to zero; the triangles were equal in size. As the size difference got progressively smaller, it became harder and harder for the bat to pick correctly the larger of the two triangles. Eventually, the size difference became too small for the bat to choose the larger triangle. The bat responded half of the time to one triangle, and half of the time to the other.

We charted the performance of three bats trained on the entire series of triangles (*see illustration, top right page 257*). Using an *arbitrary* level of 75 per cent correct responses, we established the threshold of size discrimination for the bats. This threshold is an approximation of the smallest size difference that the bat can detect with any kind of consistency. The light level in the lab was very low for the sessions with sighted bats.

One of the three bats that had been trained was blinded and run on the series of triangles again. The

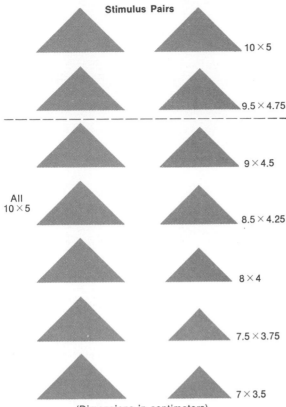

Stimulus Pairs

10 × 5

9.5 × 4.75

9 × 4.5

All
10 × 5

8.5 × 4.25

8 × 4

7.5 × 3.75

7 × 3.5

(Dimensions in centimeters)

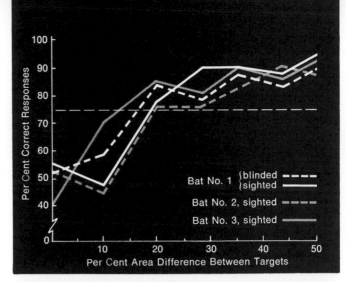

TARGET SELECTION. Bat is trained to respond to the large triangle in the bottom pair (*see chart at left*) and its ability to correctly pick the larger triangle in each of the other pairs is measured. Chart above clearly shows that the bat does not need to use its vision for these consistent-size discriminations.

blinded bat had a threshold of about 16 per cent difference in stimulus surface area, which was almost the same as the average threshold for the three normal runs.

It is clear that visual cues did not play a decisive part in the discrimination performance of the bats. (Bats that were blinded from the start of training perform the same as these three bats, so it appears that *Eptesicus* simply does not need to use vision at all for these size discriminations.)

The threshold difference for the blinded bat lies between the fifth and sixth pair of triangles shown to the bat (*see illustration top left, above*). By looking at the outlines and dimensions of the stimuli, you can see that the bat's sonar appears to be an adequate substitute for vision as far as size is concerned.

By bouncing artificial sounds off the triangular targets used in the experiment, you can learn something about the auditory cues the bats used to discriminate the triangles. The targets in the pairs turn out to differ in the intensity of the echoes they reflect. The triangles in the most easily discriminated pair differ by about eight decibels in the intensity of their echoes. As the size difference gets smaller, pair by pair, the echo intensity difference gets smaller, too.

Sonar Perception of Shape

As we have seen, an echolocating bat can determine the relative size of one of two stimuli with a good deal of acuity. If the stimuli were the same in size but different in shape, could the bat still learn to choose between them? To see if echolocation can be used to tell something about the shape of an object, I have used triangular stimuli of the same kind used in the size experiments.

One stimulus was an isosceles triangle 10 centimeters wide and five centimeters high, the same size as the largest triangle in the first experiment. The other triangle was five centimeters wide and 10 centimeters high. Both targets had the same surface area, but one was short and wide and the other was tall and thin. These triangles were mounted on landing platforms and used in the same way as before.

Both sighted and blinded bats learned to discriminate between the two different shapes. When the training was carried out exactly as in the size discrimination experiment, the level of performance reached by the bats corresponded to an intermediately difficult size discrimination, something like the fourth pair of triangles in the size experiments.

What about the echoes that the bats use to distinguish the shapes? Over the frequency range used by the big brown bat, the echoes differ somewhat in intensity. The difference is from one to three decibels, depending on the frequency. These intensity differences are about the same as the difference between the members of the fourth pair of triangles in the first experiment. It seems quite possible that the shape difference was detected by means of the echo intensity differences.

Depth Perception by Sonar

Humans find it rather easy to judge the distance to an object with vision, and there exists a large variety of visual depth cues. Can bats use their echolocation to determine how far away an object is? Considering the exceptional ability of many species of bats accurately to track flying insects, one expects them to be able to judge the range of a target. The discrimination procedure used for size and shape perception was adapted to the study of range determination by bats.

Just as before, the bat was placed on a starting plat-

257

form and confronted with two landing platforms and targets. The triangles on the platforms were identical in size and shape, both were 10 centimeters wide and five centimeters high. The distance to the targets previously was fixed at 30 centimeters. Now it was the distance to the targets that the bat had to discriminate.

The bat was trained to fly to whichever platform was closer. At first, the near target was 20 centimeters away, and the far target was 30 centimeters away. The distances were alternated left and right in the same "random" fashion as were the sizes and the shapes. After the bat learned to discriminate between targets that differed in distance by 10 centimeters, the difference was reduced by moving the nearer target back to 21 centimeters. A number of trials were completed, and then the distance difference was reduced by another centimeter, moving the nearer target to 22 centimeters. In steps of about a centimeter, the difference in distance between the targets was further reduced to seven centimeters, then six centimeters, and so forth until the two

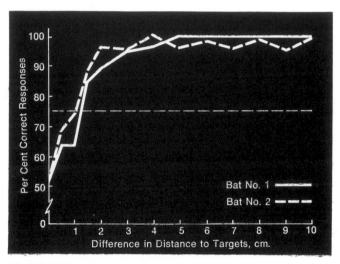

DISTANCE ACCURACY. Two blinded bats were trained on a series of special distance discrimination tests beginning with a difference of 10 cm. and gradually proceeding down to zero.

targets were finally presented to the bat at equal distances. This procedure allowed us to estimate the range difference threshold for two stimuli presented at the same time.

We trained two blinded specimens of the big brown bat on a series of distances beginning with a difference of 10 centimeters and proceeding down to zero (*see illustration, above*). Large differences, between 10 centimeters and three centimeters, were easily discriminated; the bat flew to the closer platform on nearly every trial. When the range difference fell below three centimeters, however, the bat's discrimination performance declined. The average threshold for a large number of specimens of *Eptesicus* is 1.2 centimeters. This threshold, a measure of the accuracy of the bat's determination of distance, is only four per cent of the total distance of 30 centimeters.

The extreme accuracy of the bat's determination of the range of a target is not restricted to *Eptesicus*. In addition to the insect-eating *Eptesicus*, a European insectiv-

orous bat, *Rhinolophus*, and a carnivorous, tropical bat, *Phyllostomus*, have also been studied. These other bats are about as accurate as *Eptesicus* in judging distance.

Besides the great accuracy of the bats' discriminations, there were several other surprises in the range experiment. Suffice it to say that the results of this experiment, together with more recent ones, show that the bat determines which target is closer by the difference in arrival time between echoes from the nearer and farther targets. The signal processing done by the bat on echoes from targets separated by a few centimeters is a complicated matter, and current experiments on sonar ranging by bats are only just beginning to clarify what happens.

Echolocation: A Biological System

As we have seen, echolocation does a creditable job of providing a way for bats to appreciate objects in the environment without vision. Their sonar allows bats to do a lot more than merely to detect the presence or absence of objects "out there." They can make rather fine distinctions between objects both as to the nature of the object and also its location. There are other questions that arise. Can a bat localize an object horizontally and vertically as well as it can in distance? Does a bat get information about the texture of objects? Experiments now in progress are hopefully going to answer such questions.

In addition to the straightforward study of stimulus perception by sonar, there is the problem of the basis for echolocation in the bat's hearing. New techniques for electronically simulating targets by presenting faked echoes to the bat are proving very useful in analyzing the auditory cues used in the exploration of targets. These techniques are designed to study the mechanisms of echolocation, and perhaps they will even tell something of the brain processes of the bat's sonar.

The 20th Century has been a century of surprises for scientists. This is no less true for the student of animal behavior than for the particle physicist, molecular biologist, or neurophysiologist. The unearthing of the means of orientation in bats has been one of the more unexpected events for zoologists and comparative psychologists.

Interest in bat sonar is but an example of a general trend. Scientists have rediscovered biology in a very big way in recent years. The ingenuity in design and function of biological systems has attracted many people to research on living systems. Discoveries in sensory physiology and psychology, in the molecular basis of genetics, and in many other areas of biological activity have highlighted the impression that really challenging problems are to be found in the study of organisms and their workings. The more that we find in the processes of living creatures, the more humble we may feel as fabricators of mechanism and machinery. What man can yet compress a multi-purpose sonar system into the form of a lump of jelly about as big as your thumb, make that system seek out its own operating power, and even more, use such a system to produce others like it as a by-product of its own operation? 𝛀

Science is a glamour career and psychology is golden, but be warned by

THE TERRIBLE TENREC

A shaggy insectivory story   *By Paul N. Herman*

As PART OF A LONG-RANGE comparative investigation of sensory physiology, we frequently have reason to look at the acoustic talents of various animals. Some are quite conventional, others fall into the realm of the near exotic. Over the past few years we have looked at bats, rats, kangaroo rats, chinchillas, lizards of all sizes, monkeys, dolphins, raccoons, agoutis, and a host of others. This is a story about the tenrec. Experimentally speaking, it is a sad story.

In the spring of 1966, Edwin Gould, a Johns Hopkins University biologist, went to Malagasy—the island of Madagascar—on an expedition. There he gathered and sent to our Auditory Research Labs at Princeton 15 specimens of the Tenrec, a strange and rare insectivore slightly smaller than a rat. The tenrec is special because it can produce sounds by rubbing together sharp spines clustered along its lower back.

Gould earlier had investigated the possibility that the tenrec used this technique to bounce sounds off objects and thus determine their location. He observed spine sounds in the tenrec with microphone and oscilloscope and reported frequencies from ten to 70 kilocycles. He also suggested that the spine sounds might be the way tenrecs communicate while gathering food or for social activity. To test this theory, we proposed to investigate the streaked tenrec's auditory apparatus and sensitivity.

The streaked tenrec, *Hemicentetes semispinosus*, gets his common name from the markings on his back—seven lengthwise bands, alternating black and light yellow. His head and back are protected by sharp spines distributed among hairs of about the same length. The tenrec's coat is about a half inch long, except for a ruff over the neck and shoulders, which is about two to three times as long. When the animal is disturbed, the spines are erected, especially those on the ruff; the forepart of the body is thrust upwards in a quick, jerky fashion. This "humping" has the effect of thrusting the ruff spines into the skin of an enemy that approaches from above. Even with a thick leather glove, the handler often finds himself impaled on a spine or two that has been forced through the leather.

The sound-making organ consists of a group of about 14 spines in three rows along the lower middle back. These spines are heavier than the others, about 0.3 millimeter in diameter at their thickest region as compared to about 0.1 millimeter for the others. Moved vigorously by underlying muscles, their tips rub together too rapidly for the eye to follow, and high-frequency sounds are produced. Any disturbance or sudden stimulus, a quick movement or an attempt to pick up the tenrec, immediately provokes this stridulation.

We planned our investigation of the tenrec's hearing and stridulation in the conventional manner. We would concern ourselves with both the gross anatomy of the external, middle, and inner ears, and microscopic analyses of finer cochlear structures, that part of the inner ear which is the seat of hearing. We planned also to measure the tenrec's sound emissions, both from tongue and lip movements and from the stridulatory organ, and to see if he could detect sounds within that range.

His sensitivity would be indicated by recordings of the cochlear potential, based on a technique developed nearly 40 years ago by E. G. Wever, Director of the Auditory Research Laboratory. In this relatively simple procedure, one electrode is placed on the round window membrane of the cochlea and another anywhere on the tissues of the animal, usually in the head or neck area. The inner ear's electrical responses to sounds of differing frequencies are then amplified and viewed on an oscilloscope in order to evaluate the relative sensitivity of the animal. We hoped to compare these electrophysiological responses with behavioral responses from a conditioning task. It was a perfectly straightforward problem with the procedures and techniques reasonably well worked out.

But we didn't know the tenrec! The first indication of something gone wrong appeared when we arrived at the airport to pick up our prickly project. Gould had sent 15 specimens from Malagasy, but 19 arrived. Four live births had occurred while enroute by Air France, and there was a discrepancy in the bill of lading. Despite the difficulties involved in straightening this out, we viewed the population increase as a favorable omen.

Then we had to convince the Public Health Department's representative that despite his dictionary's description of the tenrec as a sort of hedgehog—which was on the proscribed list — it *really* wasn't a hedgehog and so it could enter the country legally.

The tenrec's Princeton quarters had to be maintained at normal Madagascar temperatures of 80-85 degrees. The fact that tenrecs naturally are odoriferous beasts, and the aroma of decaying food remnants, made working in their room somewhat traumatic. Our animal caretaker was slightly anosmic and so he was unruffled.

We soon discovered that our tenrecs would eat worms. Only worms. Nothing else. Morsels of hamburger, mealworms, flies, lettuce leaves, and other laboratory hors d'oeuvres were rejected summarily. They would eat nothing but live, juicy nightcrawlers. It soon became obvious that the tenrecs' prodigious appetites— 40 to 50 worms per day per adult animal —would exhaust the local worm supply quite quickly. I contacted a worm farm in Georgia and was assured that adequate supplies of earthworms could be shipped to New Jersey. Our storage facilities for worms were limited, and the worms had to be reasonably fresh. We even contemplated an earthworm airlift, but a sudden drop in the tenrec population grounded our plans.

Shortly after their arrival, all four of the baby tenrecs died, as did one of the adults. Our population was reduced to 14. Then a power failure in the building cut off all heat and took the lives of three of our remaining tenrecs. We suspected that one of these three must have been the leader of the pack, for fighting soon broke out among the survivors to establish a new pecking order. By the time peace was reestablished, all but five of the tenrecs were dead.

Placing an electrode on the round window of the cochlea generally is far from complex, but there often are considerable differences among species, and it is helpful to have as much advance information as possible concerning the best surgical approach. When we dissected the three tenrec power failure casualties and the adult that died during the first week, we discovered that the implant approach for the tenrec was most difficult. The round window was in a region far back on the skull and was overhung with a bony shelf which would make electrode placement precarious.

By this time we had lost 14 of the 19 animals without making any headway and so we decided to start immediately. We began by observing the stridulatory output and found that, although the range varied somewhat, it extended from about 15 to 60 kilocycles, with the principal energy output being between 25 and 45 kilocycles.

In view of anticipated difficulties in reaching and maintaining an electrode on the round window, we decided to use the remaining animals only for cochlear potential data and not to attempt any serious behavioral work. We did, however, make some preliminary observations to discover what responses and rewards to reinforce desired behavior might be appropriate for possible future work with other tenrecs. We found that, although the tenrec puts away a prodigious number of worms each day, he satiates quickly and prefers numerous small snacks to regular meals. This makes it inconvenient for the researcher who wishes to use food reward. The tenrec also can survive well for protracted periods without water, and further, his tough paw pads, adapted for scratching and digging, render him untouched at customary animal shock levels. The tenrec, it seems, is not only virtually untouchable, but it is also unteachable.

There appeared to be no regular response in his repertoire that was appropriate for behavioral training work, with the possible exception of his head and neck thrust. Pairing of tone with finger approach to his head, however, resulted only in the placing of several spines in the experimenter's finger and showed no indication on the part of the tenrec that he could be conditioned. He thus may be consigned to the same category as the guinea pig, who is untrainable but at least has no spines.

The next experimental difficulty was with anesthesia. On the first tenrec we tried ethyl carbamate, on the second sodium pentathol, two anesthetics used customarily with small animals. The dosage levels were small for body weight, but both tenrecs died. Ethyl carbamate did work as an anesthesia for the remaining three animals, but two of these died from other causes before we could obtain any scientific data. We successfully obtained a proper anesthesia level and placed an electrode on the round window in only one of our original 19 animals.

At last we were able to record the cochlear potential measurements. We found that the tenrec's sensitivity to sound increased until frequency reached 10 to 15 kilocycles. Then the sensitivity declines. The tenrec, it seemed, was not most sensitive to the sounds produced by stridulation, but he apparently *could* hear sounds in this range at short dis-

tances. His area of greatest sensitivity corresponded to the frequency of the tongue clicks he made during searching activity, a range that already had been established by Gould at from 11 to 16 kilocycles.

Sometimes all goes well. But with new and untried animals, you expect setbacks and accept them. This is the everyday work of science. Nevertheless, we breathed a sigh of relief at having been able to extract *any* data from this unfortunate combination of bad luck and chance. We chalked the experiment up to experience and were pleased at the thought of no longer working with the smelly, unlovable tenrec.

But one day, a fellow from Princeton's Public Relations Department said: "It's a great human interest story. Let me write it up."

I saw his story as a description of the ups and downs of everyday scientific activity. As such, it was a situation in science that might well be shared with the public. After submitting the story for approval, he released it to the wire services late in June 1967.

Repercussions were immediate and astounding. On July fifth, a Newark paper headlined: "Miserable Little Beasts Bring Misery To Science." On July sixth, the New York *Daily News,* on page two, inquired, "Anyone for Tenrec? Scientists find critter net loss," again not the sort of attitude we expected. "Tenrecs foil science," crowed a local paper, emphasizing a different aspect. No one yet had picked up our intended emphasis that things can and do go wrong in the laboratory. The following day a *New York Post* editorial declared firmly ". . . the little beast's staunch defense of its right to privacy has triumphed. Tenrec, we salute your spirit . . ."

Now, it is one thing to be misinterpreted, but behavioral scientists don't think of themselves as villains. I was surprised and distressed. After all, what was there in a relatively innocuous news release to provoke this much response and response of this kind? Local coverage perhaps is expected, but an editorial in a New York City daily?

Response continued to mount. In August, a note arrived from a colleague in Jerusalem to say how sorry he had been to read about our difficulties in the overseas edition of the *New York Times.* And in that same month, I received a letter from an old friend in Oklahoma who had read our story in the local paper. At the same time the saga was reported in another New Jersey newspaper and in the pages of *Popular Science.* Toward the end of the month, Gene Sheppard of radio station WOR, New York, applauded the tenrec for holding out information. He also suggested that investigators might spend more time on human, practical problems and less in pursuit of the elusive tenrec. Gradually, press comments became more biting, implying violation of privacy. Fortunately, no one formally called the use of electrodes a case of wiretapping.

Up to this point, the comments were directed exclusively at the investigators. But in September Russell Baker devoted his "Observer" column in the *New York Times* to the story, calling it: "The Beasts Who Outwitted Princeton." "Here are these beasts too dumb to even talk," he wrote, "yet they instinctively sense the dangers of cooperating with science. 'Come across with the information about those quill noises,' science commanded them. And their mute answer was, 'Not on your life.'"

What was there in the news release to trigger this scathing response? Perhaps the tenrec has, after all, done a greater service. Perhaps he has made clear a need for a social scientist's study of why the public reacts so strongly to the stimulus of beast defeating behaviorist. Several possibilities come to mind. The popular image of the scientist is that of a modern magician, valued for his contributions to comfort and convenience, yet distrusted. He stands for the different (he doesn't even work regular hours), the unknown (if God had intended . . .), and the bizarre (he might create a Frankenstein monster). The public is ambivalent about this orderly, intellectual, precise, studious, but not exactly charming, friendly, or humorous fellow.

People are reluctant and even fearful to accept the idea that Science may falter occasionally, but chortle when the tenrec or any other subject slips a banana peel under the foot of the investigator. Is this David defeating Goliath, the lowly humbling the exalted, or the vast electronic might of science frustrated by the pure at heart?

Lest it be thought that the tenrec has plunged me into paranoia, let me interject one last paragraph from Russell Baker. "The example of their [the tenrecs'] refusal to talk is a mockery of every man who has never been able to resist the electrode, the laboratory camera, the deprivation experiment. . . . Worst of all, their example forces us to

"I think there's something he's not telling us."

ponder our habit of pursuing the trivial by skirting the monumental."

Tenrecs aside, consider the matter of values in science. Who is wise enough to judge what is trivial and what is not, or what is a valid area for research and what is not? This is not to deny that there may be poorly designed studies or even failure. But we must acknowledge that much of what we do is done not to shake the world, but for the same reason that Sir Edmund Hillary climbed Mt. Everest: simply because it is there.

This bristly beastie has made me ponder: If the public sees the behavioral scientist as a cold, precise sort of fellow, then we may need Madison Avenue to come up with a lovable image for us. We need a Smokey the Bear or a Tony the Tiger—something that is wise but also cuddly, cute, warm, and even playful. Arthur the Otter? Flipper? Puffy the Pigeon? But it definitely should not be Tommy the Tenrec.

v. human function

the psychology of human functioning is central both to psychology and to each of us as individuals. By no means do psychologists working with animals, with physiological variables, or with developmental studies of children expect their work to contribute necessarily to the psychology of adult human functioning. Rather, every psychologist shares with the layman an intrinsic interest in his own and others' existence as human beings. Of overriding importance to the human existence is the psychology of language. A man is unique, if at all, as the beast who speaks. Several of our selections illustrate the variety of modern approaches to man the talker.

The late George Talland put his years of study of amnesia—the terrifying and isolating inability to remember—to the task of imagining a world without continuity. For most readers, the unsettling prospects of amnesia will be only imperfectly compensated for by Mehrabian's discussion, "Communication Without Words." An individual's inability to communicate with words robs him of much of his essence as a person. It is therefore comforting to find psychologists working on remedies.

In "Language and the Mind," Noam Chomsky investigates what the scientific study of the structure of language can expose as principles of mental functioning. Language is so highly ordered and grammar is so highly regular that there must be at the basis of linguistic functioning something that all human minds share in common. What this something is, how it came to be, and how it works make up the field of study of modern psycholinguistics.

Even the apparently most unimportant of human experiences may turn out, under study, to play its own role in the totality of experience. Singer suggests that daydreaming, enjoyed by all and generally regretted by most, has a unique importance of its own.

The prospect of the mind's triumph over matter has excited the curiosity of the parapsychologist (see Part I), the religious thinker, and recently the physiological psychologist. Kamiya discusses and analyzes an individual's conscious control over the electrical activity of his own brain. Whereas parapsychology has been concerned with the influence of one mind on another or on material structures outside of the individual, Kamiya's work concerns the influence of one mind on its own intrinsic electrical activity. Man may yet discover that he can control himself.

Fear fascinates psychologists not only because it is a common point of individual experience but also because its effects are never either benign or simple. Fear is an emotion that can at once be induced or reduced by a variety of circumstances. "The Psychopharmacological Revolution" by Jarvik shows man's dawning ability to control such emotions as fear with drugs. The scientific study of drug-induced states bears the same helpful relationship to the study of emotion and motivation as the distortion of perception (see Part IV) bears to the study of normal perceptual experience.

But the undisciplined use of drugs for purposes of emotional and motivational manipulation of oneself or of others raises ethical, moral, and evolutionary questions both for the present and for the future of man. As Irving Janis points out, a modern contradiction is the fact that fear may be healthy in some circumstances. Tinkering with the natural order of emotional things must eventually result in great knowledge and benefit, but it may also unleash horrors of destruction—or horrors of apathy—never before seen.

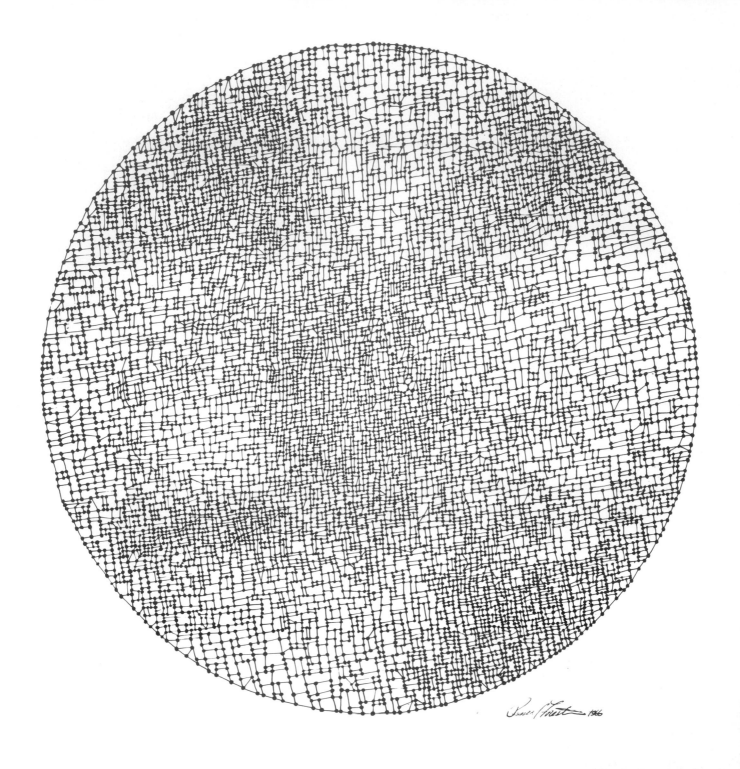

By GEORGE TALLAND

AMNESIA: a world without continuity

EVERYONE, AT SOME TIME or other, experiences a puzzling lapse of memory. A name or a date, or the details of an experience, unaccountably vanish from our mind. "It's right on the tip of my tongue," we say, or "I know it as well as I know my own name," and we rummage around in our minds for clues, but to no avail. "Don't try to remember it," someone may say comfortingly, "it'll come back if you stop trying so hard." And sure enough, mo-

ments or hours or even days later, the forgotten information may pop back as unexpectedly as it had vanished.

If we were never conscious of having forgotten something, we might never be curious about how we remember things—about the nature of memory, its mechanisms and laws. And by the same token, studies of amnesia—a prolonged or permanent loss of memory for previous experiences—have provided us with fascinating

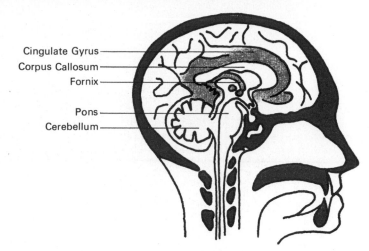

Diagrams of the brain show the functionally continuous circuit (color) implicated in memory. Removal of the pons and cerebellum in the enlargement at the far right exposes the complete circuit: cingulate cortex, hippocampus, fornix, mammillary body, mammillothalamic tract, and thalamus.

Cingulate Gyrus
Corpus Callosum
Fornix

Pons
Cerebellum

and unique information about how memory functions.

Models of Memory

In attempts to conceptualize so mysterious a function as memory, people have turned to a variety of models. Perhaps the oldest is that of grooves incised in a wax tablet. In the same way that wax tablets are liable to decay, it was thought that the substance in which memories were engraved would deteriorate, causing memories to blur and fade.

Another simple model is that of a container in which an infinite collection of items — memories — are stored. Containers can leak, and if they are filled too full the contents spill out over the brim. Thus forgetting holds no mystery for those who believe that our capacity to accumulate memories is limited. It is a reasonable belief, and appears to be supported by ample evidence from observation, but it is of little value unless we can define the limits of storage capacity, and discover in what way memories are stored.

The way these memories are related to each other, how one leads to another, has for some centuries been accounted for by the laws of association; and ever since the early 1880's, when Ebbinghaus systematically investigated his own performance in tests of memorization, a steadily expanding body of experimental studies has increased our knowledge of these laws. While we can speculate only in the most tentative fashion about how information is recorded in and extracted from memory, we do know a good deal about the effects of one kind of learning on another. We know that some kinds of learning can hinder as well as help another sort, and this is important because it offers an alternative to earlier notions that forgetting is a spontaneous process.

Recently, the computer has provided us with a new and useful model for thinking about the twin processes of remembering and forgetting. In computers, memories do not fade, but they can become inaccessible through some fault in the circuitry or some error in the program. Then either no information at all is forthcoming, or the wrong kind of information is printed out in place of that which is sought. While the computer model does have some features in common with human remembering, it certainly does not parallel memory processes in all important respects. The great virtue of this model is that it shifts the emphasis from the storage of memory to the processes of input and retrieval. It reminds us that unless information is properly programmed for access it will not be available on demand, and that a reliable system for storing memories is of little use if the program for reactivating them is defective. The study of various type of amnesias has shown that this is true of human memory—that is, that forgetting does not result so much from the "loss" of static memories as from the disruption of a complex on-going process.

Amnesia

The term "amnesia" usually evokes the image of a shell-shocked soldier or, more recently, the victim of an auto accident, who has no memory of the circumstances in which he sustained his injury, and often of anything that happened over some time preceding it. *Traumatic amnesia*, as this type of memory loss is called, involves loss of memory of the accident itself and is usualy accompanied by some degree of *retrograde amnesia* — the inability to recall events that occurred prior to the onset of the trauma. In such cases, the memory loss is limited and the recovery tends to be quite orderly. Step by step, more of the lost information returns, beginning with the events most remote in time, and closing in on the events that immediately preceded or involved the accident.

The memory loss in such instances is puzzling, because it usually extends to information that, quite clearly, the victim had registered up to the very moment of the accident—things he had said or done, questions he had answered. This type of amnesia suggests that information and experiences are not immediately placed on permanent record, but that the processes by which they enter into enduring memory take some time to be completed. Evidently there is a labile phase of information-intake, during which a powerful interference such as a concussion can prevent the experience from being permanently filed or consolidated in the memory system.

It is still a matter of debate how long information remains in this labile state. Very likely it varies with the individual, with the circumstance, and with the subject matter to be recorded, but its duration is on the order of seconds or minutes, and at the most, a few hours. This is also the range of the retrograde amnesia that typically follows a shock, but it does not represent the full extent of all retrograde amnesias, nor are the recovery patterns the same.

Amnesic Syndrome

In the retrograde amnesias following other types of brain insult — an operation, a vascular accident, or disease — the memory loss is apt to be extensive. An amnesic patient may have no recollection of having been married, although he had shared a home with his wife for several decades; he may have no memory of ever having had children, though he reared several. There is no ground for believing, as has been suggested, that this type of forgetting is motivated, that is, that such patients fail to remember because for some reason they do not want to remember; nor can

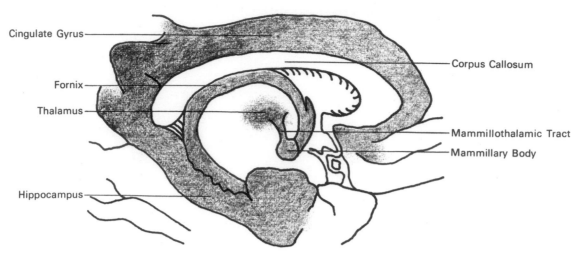

Cingulate Gyrus

Fornix

Thalamus

Hippocampus

Corpus Callosum

Mammillothalamic Tract

Mammillary Body

their forgotten life experiences be restored to memory with hypnosis or other aids. And memories of this type, though obstinately missing for a considerable length of time, may suddenly re-emerge for no discernible reason.

The amnesic syndrome is also known as *Korsakoff's disease*, named for the Russian psychiatrist who first identified this disorder as a specific mental illness and published a detailed description of it. This is a chronic disorder; its manifestations and prognosis differ from those of the amnesias following shock. Several of Korsakoff's patients who displayed this disorder, and most of those observed by other investigators, happened to be alcohol addicts whose disease was a direct outcome of this addiction and the associated nutritional deficiencies. Other cases have been reported to result from tumors and vascular accidents, or from degenerative or inflammatory disease, all of which affect one or another site in the brain along a *functionally continuous circuit*.

The relation between this circuit and the memory-process is only beginning to be understood; here, we will only point out that it comprises the cingulate cortex, the hippocampus, fornix, hypothalamus, mammillothalamic tract, and thalamus [*see illustration above*]. Although the analogy is quite loose, it is apparent that in the brain, as in the computer, a fault in the circuitry can disrupt the orderly retrieval of stored information.

One of the characteristic manifestations of the amnesic syndrome is "fast forgetting"— the inability to recall new information after a very short lapse of time. This has suggested that the amnesic syndrome results from a permanent impairment of the mechanisms by which information enters the memory-storage system. Other theories stress the damage in the processes of information retrieval, but neither explanation can account for

all the characteristic manifestations of this disease: an inability to acquire new information; loss of temporal and situational context; lack of initiative; neglect to test for contradictions; susceptibility to interruptions; and the failure to retrieve information in an orderly manner from the memory bank.

The explanation I prefer regards the amnesic syndrome as an expression of the patient's inability to set up and carry through an action plan, either for retrieving a memory, or for acquiring new ones.

Recovery of a Mental Map

As an example of the amnesic syndrome and recovery from it which may occur after severe but reversible brain damage, let us take the case of a patient whom I studied through the course of his disorder and partial recovery. This young man had suffered a vascular accident in the brain. Shortly after a successful operation he displayed a number of the signs characteristic of the initial phase of the amnesic syndrome. He was entirely disoriented about the place in which he found himself, about his age, the date and year, about the persons in his surrounding. He confabulated freely, that is, he answered questions and carried on conversations without the least regard to factual truth, producing irrational and partly fictitious autobiographical material. Most of what he said was palpably impossible or improbable, contradictory and confused. Gradually these anomalies cleared up, but the memory disorder improved much more slowly. The patient remembered virtually nothing of his daily experiences, could not learn more than the odd name, and that not very reliably, and had forgotten much of what he had experienced and known before his illness.

After some months in the hospital, his very severe disturbance in memory and

general orientation lessened sufficiently so that he could be discharged from the hospital and, in due course, return to work. During his spare hours, this young man used to drive a taxi in the suburb where he had lived for some four years prior to his illness. He had therefore possessed an excellent mental map of the area. When he was released from the hospital, though the skills he needed to drive a car were immediately available to him, he could not drive by himself because he was quite unable to find his way around. He had grown up in the neighboring city, however, and once he crossed the boundary into the city, he knew exactly how to get about. It was at least a year before he could dispense with someone to pilot him in the suburb where he lived, but eventually he regained his mental map of his home town.

The complex operations by which memories are rendered accessible may be permanently lost owing to irreversible brain damage, as with Korsakoff's disease. In these cases the processes governing both the acquisition of new information (learning) and the search-and-find operations of retrieving previously-stored material, remain seriously disrupted.

Alcohol addicts who develop Korsakoff's disease are typically delirious during the initial phase, grossly disoriented, and either completely apathetic or quite agitated. They are so far out of touch with their environment, so difficult to engage in an interview, that their memory disorder is scarcely apparent. Undoubtedly the memory disturbance is present and is as grave as it will be in the later, chronic stage of the disease, but it is overshadowed by the patient's total incomprehension of the situation in which he finds himself, his inability to keep his attention on any topic, and his tendency to confabulate — to jumble fragments of factual information derived

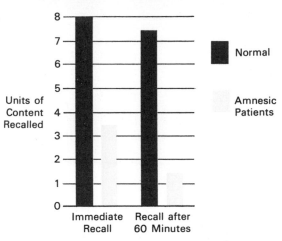

After being read a short story (see text), amnesic patients remember far fewer of 16 units of content than do normal people.

from the most diverse settings and to mix them with purely imaginary matter.

While with most patients, communication is usually restricted to a fleeting moment during the first stage of the disease, the attention of some can be held for a short while. One woman, who was able to carry on a reasonably coherent interview the first day after admission, gave me her married name correctly and answered several other questions with fair accuracy. However she stated that she was unmarried and lived in her mother's house. Since her medical chart indicated that she had been married for ten years, and that her mother had been dead for quite some time, I pointed to her wedding ring, asking why she was wearing it. After a moment's bewilderment, the patient listed the names of three men in rapid succession, presenting each as her husband, and relating some plausible enough circumstances surrounding each "marriage," such as parental opposition to the man in question. Remarkably enough, the list did not include the name of her actual husband whom, however, she remembered perfectly well the next day.

A World Without Continuity

One could speculate about the emotional significance to the patient of the three imaginary husbands and try to discover what roles these men had played in her life. The point of immediate interest, however, is the manifold contradiction to which the patient was quite indifferent. In the later phase of the disease, as the gross disorientation subsides, examples of such utterly irrational discourse are rare. Nevertheless, one of the most salient characteristics of the amnesic patient is his propensity to make contradictory statements and to leave them unresolved. Not uncommonly a patient may talk about his grownup children and grandchildren and in the next sentence refer to himself as a 25-year-old. One man, in his sixties, widowed for many years, would always tell me that his wife had been buried only a few days before, and would describe his children as if they were in their teens until I reminded him of his real age. This he remembered accurately enough, and his logic was sufficiently sound so that he realized that his children must be adults by now.

Since many of these patients retain their capacity for reasoning and judgment, such irrational statements must be attributed to false premises they hold about the current moment in their life history. Theirs is a world without continuity. With no memories of the recent past, amnesic patients lose their anchorage in time, and in their waking hours are as apt, as we are in our dreams, to mistake the present for the past, or confuse two periods of the past with each other. This is illustrated by the wizened old woman who looked forward to going out to dances on Saturday nights once she was released from the hospital. She thought of herself as the young girl who had been helping her father run his shop, and had completely forgotten the years of her married life.

The memories of the amnesic patient are fragmented; they seem to float free of any contextual constraints. This allows them to be recombined into patterns that have little relation to actual events in the patient's life. Indeed, the manner in which these new patterns are produced may resemble the processes of artistic creation, but their content is strikingly unoriginal, and the process itself does not seem to be experienced as a creative act; there is no conscious attempt at rearrangement, no search for meaning or order. The patient who confabulates, who errs in the temporal placement of an event, is unaware of his error and makes no attempt to correct it. He does not test a specific memory for accuracy of fit as we do when we are in doubt —"It was just before the war started; no, it must have been a week or so afterwards, because I remember . . ." He does not test or check alternate solutions to a problem of reconstructing a memory sequence. The amnesic patient does not seem to experience the sense of doubt, the sense of imperfect closure, the need for resolution that often precedes correct recall and recognition in normal people. The amnesic patient may fail to test for "fit" because he is not aware of the contradiction, but neither does he apply the test when the contradiction is pointed out to him.

Reconstruction from Fragmentary Memories

These examples of confabulation and of errors in temporal placement not only represent an anomaly characteristic of amnesic patients, but they also point to a fundamental attribute of all remembering—its creative or constructive nature. This quality illustrates Sir Frederic Bartlett's thesis that "all remembering is a reconstructive effort after meaning." The crude and often grotesque errors in recall, characteristic of the amnesic patient, differ only in degree but not in kind from those made by normal people.

This is demonstrated by one of the studies I carried out in the course of an extensive research on amnesia. This study involved a group of some 20 patients in the chronic phase of Korsakoff's disease. Although their memory function was impaired, they had all recovered from the disorientation and other grave symptoms that are so prominent in the early stages of this illness. They were quite able to engage in an interview and follow instructions. To probe their learning and retention, I used several short narrative texts, one of which was the following news report:

Twelve cards with different (but similar) designs are used to test the ability of amnesic patients and control subjects to remember and recognize one design (g) previously memorized.

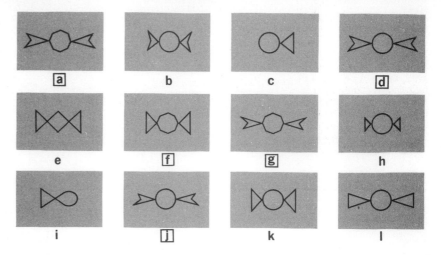

In a city in India, several thousand school children paraded in the main square to celebrate the sixty-eighth birthday of the prime minister. While reviewing the parade the prime minister released a number of doves, the symbols of peace, from the cages in which they had been kept. The white doves flew over the heads of the young marchers. One of them, however, perched atop the prime minister's head while he took the salute.

This text was read aloud to each of the patients at a measured pace, with the instruction to memorize it for reproduction; their ability to do so was compared to that of a control group of healthy people who had no memory disorder.

Even when their recall was tested immediately after the text had been read to them, few of the amnesic patients remembered more than four of the 16 units of content; they had forgotten almost all of them at the end of an hour; and many completely missed the gist of the story. The control group recalled twice as many items, and retained most of that information over the following hour [see illustration, page 271].

Quantitative measures, however, furnish only part of the evidence. When they are supplemented by an analysis of the kinds of errors in recall, we find many examples of simplification, such as the following account of the elaborately staged peace ceremony: "A group went to India to see the prime minister. They kept birds there." One patient started his report with "a man and wife celebrating his sixty-eighth birthday"; another made the principal actor a "maharajah," and a third gave the exact number of children as 5000. In the descriptions of the ceremony, there were several examples of elaboration with some gratuitous fabrication of details. These ranged from

speculations about the symbolic significance of the final incident, or comments about its amusing feature, to one observation about the children watching the dove until it flew away, and another about the cheering, followed by the remark, "The prime minister thought they were cheering him; they were actually cheering the dove." An example of immediate reproduction, notable alike for its brevity and for the variety of distortions within its narrow compass was this: "Prime minister had 68 doves to celebrate his birthday. When he went to count the doves, one was missing, as it was perched on his head."

Those in the control group were quite likely to omit some of the content, but they always retained enough of it to reconstruct a coherent account, and produced nothing comparable to the distortions of the amnesic patients.

The Telephone Game

It is possible, however, as the following study shows, to create in normal people something very much like the ambiguity and loss of direction that follow from the rapid and extensive forgetting in amnesic patients. One way to produce this effect is the method of "serial reproduction," known outside psychological laboratories as the "telephone game."

Thanks to the cooperation of my colleagues, I was able to set up seven chains composed of healthy men and women, rather above the average in intelligence. Each chain consisted of three persons; the first member of every chain was presented with the report about the Indian peace ceremony and asked to wait for a day, then pass on to the next member of the chain all that he remembered of it. The second passed on his version, after another 24 hours, to the third, who again waited for a day and then wrote down what he remembered of the story.

Under these conditions our superior normal subjects produced distortions that were remarkably similar to the immediate recall of the amnesic patients. References to the peace ceremony ranged all the way from a "large party for children" to "a party celebrated with fireworks"; references to the central figure included his designation as a maharajah. There were gratuitously exact estimates — 64 white doves; 2000 pigeons; 30,000 school children who were excused from classes to attend; there were elaborations, such as various interpretations of the significance of the episode, or comments on how amusing it must have looked. One subject produced a story that closely paralleled the fabrication of one of the amnesic patients: "In honor of this occasion he released a flock of doves, 44 in number; 43 turned up, the 44th he couldn't find, for it was perched on his head." The following gem of fabrication, however, had no match among the patients: "During the course of the celebration many more doves were released, and one of them laid an egg which hit Nehru on the head."

Experiments in Recognition and Recall

Since amnesic patients retain their vocabulary unimpaired, verbal tests of their learning and memory show their deficit in the kindest light. But if they are asked to reproduce figure drawings from memory, as a test of recognition and recall, the distortions of their drawings often compound the effects of forgetting with those of faulty execution. The amnesic patient's poor observation and retention are more evident from the following experiment in recognition that demanded no skillful performance. A set of 12 cards, each bearing a different design [see illustration above] was used with 16 patients in the chronic condition of Korsakoff's disease and with 16 con-

Recall is tested by having subjects pick out the correct design from a set of 12 designs. Amnesic patients show poor recall, particularly as the time between learning and testing is increased. These patients made errors by choosing four simplified versions (a, d, f, j) of the correct design (g).

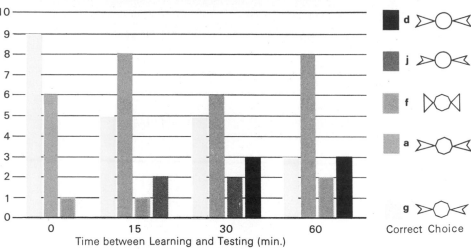

trol subjects matched in age; the latter were patients in psychiatric treatment for their problems of alcohol addiction, but none had any impairment of their memory function.

Each subject was shown the card bearing the design marked "g," and was allowed to study it until he felt certain that he could remember it. Then the entire set of 12 cards was placed in front of him in the order shown and he was asked to point to the design he had seen before. The same test was repeated after 15, 30, and 60 minutes; each time the order of the cards was changed, and at no time was the subject told whether he was wrong or right. One member of the control group always chose design "a," but none of the others made a mistake in any of the four trials. On the other hand, the responses of the amnesic patients were much less consistent, and they made far fewer correct choices [see illustration above].

Their mistakes were by no means random; all arose from the choice of designs that were similar, in principal outlines, to that of the model but were simpler and more symmetrical.

The amnesic patient's characteristic inability to learn new material, as well as his rapid rate of forgetting, is demonstrated by tests of memorizing lists of meaningful and nonsense syllables. Sixteen Korsakoff patients and 16 control subjects were given lists of 10 meaningful monosyllabic words (for example, hat, sun) or of 10 nonsense syllables (cuz, meb) to be learned for periods of three minutes. The subject was then instructed to recite as many of the words or syllables as he remembered, in any order he chose. Repeated tests of recall were given after different time intervals during which the subject was unoccupied. The results show the wide differences between the amnesic and control groups in initial acquisition, and a steep

rate of forgetting in the amnesic patients during the first few minutes [see illustration, page 274].

Susceptibility to Interruption

In another experiment both groups were asked to memorize a 10-word sentence; in this case, however, the subjects were occupied with a variety of tasks during the five-minute interval between the initial and the delayed test of recall.

In this experiment the immediate recall of the amnesic patient equalled or surpassed that of the control group. On the delayed tests, however, their recall never matched that of the control subjects, and the amount of material they had forgotten depended on the character of the intervening activity [see illustration p. 275]. The amount forgotten was least when they were not given any task, somewhat greater when they were engaged on a manual task (working a tally counter), still greater when a learning task was interpolated, and greatest of all after a brief interview in which they were asked a few questions such as where they had gone to school as children, who their teachers were, or the address of their childhood home.

The reason why the amnesic patients remembered the test sentence least well after the interview is that the questions took their minds off the experimental task. Whereas normal people have no difficulty in reverting to an interrupted activity, amnesic patients rarely manage to pick up the thread once it is dropped. This was quite apparent from a simple experiment which required that they count slowly from one to 22, stop for three minutes, and then continue counting up to 37.

This experiment was run under two conditions; in one, the break was occupied by rest, in the other by drawing a picture. In both conditions all the instructions were given in advance, that is,

at the end of the break the subject was told only, "now go on counting." One or two of the amnesic patients failed to stop when they reached 22; of the remainder, 10 completed their assignment without error after a rest, and two made errors of one or two places only. After three minutes of drawing, however, only four of the 16 remembered where to resume counting and where to stop.

Several other experiments demonstrated the difficulties these patients have in switching from one task to another and back again, and their disinclination to resume a task after interruption—although while engaged in an activity they persist with it, no matter how demanding it may be. This inability to depart from the track they are following is probably at the root of their failures to correct errors in the temporal placement of memories. It prevents them from exploring the contextual setting which invests each memory with its unique character.

When, on their twelfth to fifteenth visit to my laboratory, I asked the amnesic patients I was studying how many times they had been there, none of them came even close to the correct answer. Eight thought they had been there once before, and another 10 believed it was two or three times. Devoid of its contextual or associational cues, each visit is, of course, like any other, and blends with the rest into a composite memory. Experiences so incompletely registered cannot be reconstructed in retrospect, or will be reconstructed with low fidelity to the original event. The dearth of original learning and the rapid dissipation of the little that has been learned are characteristic features of the amnesic syndrome; even more characteristic than forgetting the content of an experience is forgetting its setting. This anomaly can be observed much better in clinical rather than in laboratory situations.

273

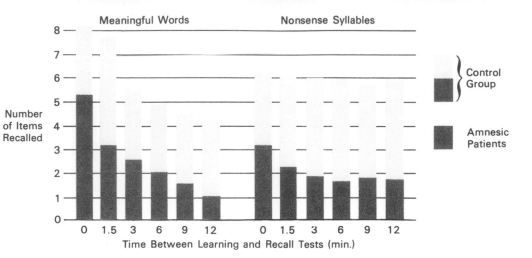

Amnesic patients and normal subjects spent three minutes memorizing each of several lists of 10 words (or 10 nonsense syllables). Repeated tests of recall after different intervals of time reveal marked differences: amnesic patients learned fewer items initially and forgot much more rapidly.

Meaningful Words   Nonsense Syllables

Number of Items Recalled

{ Control Group

Amnesic Patients

0 1.5 3 6 9 12   0 1.5 3 6 9 12
Time Between Learning and Recall Tests (min.)

Forgetting the Context

Some amnesic patients never learn the name of their doctor, and a few may not even recognize him after innumerable encounters. More typical still are those instances in which the patient is uncertain whether he knows his doctor, or recognizes him confidently, and correctly names him, but believes that they had met in some social setting other than the hospital. Errors of this kind can persist for years, and are resistant alike to correction and to chance fluctuations in content. One woman, whom I have studied for more than 10 years, always gives my name correctly and always insists mistakenly that we had first met at her neighbor's home. Another patient, when asked how long she has been in the hospital, invariably answers that she came in yesterday for examinations and expects to be sent home later in the day. When I first confronted her with the fact that she had been in the hospital for four years, she accepted the correction but remarked that she felt as if it had been yesterday. The incident made no lasting impression on her, for each time I repeated my question during the following seven years, she has answered that she "came in yesterday."

In another example Moyra Williams and Honor Smith reported on a patient who had been through a training program prior to developing the amnesic syndrome as a result of tuberculous meningitis. Some time after his discharge from the hospital, he received a group photograph of his fellow trainees, and though he could name each of them correctly, he had no idea of where he had met them. Williams and Smith also describe another patient who always obediently rolled over on his side when the trolley with the instruments for a lumbar puncture was brought into the room; but as soon as the needle was withdrawn he would deny that he ever had anything done to his back. Jacques Barbizet reported a similar case, that of a Korsakoff patient who had been receiving shock treatments; he always seemed angry and upset at the sight of the electric shock apparatus, insisting each time that he had never seen it before.

There are several reports in the literature about amnesic patients who could play an expert game of chess or could solve quite difficult mathematical problems. Once such patients have begun a task, they can apply their well established skills to complete it. Few observations illustrate this residual capacity more impressively than Oscar Kohnstamm's report of a patient who had been buried in a shell crater during World War I and had developed an amnesic syndrome, probably as a result of carbon monoxide poisoning. Although he was a trained teacher, this man could not answer the simplest questions about geography or recent history. He was able, though, to solve problems in arithmetic, to play cards, to read music, and learn new pieces on the piano. One evening he participated in a hospital concert, accompanying one of the singers on the piano, but the next morning he had no recollection of the concert itself or his part in it.

Loss of Self-Reference

It is clear that the memory defect manifested in the amnesic syndrome is not the same as the everyday forgetting of normal people. It does include the unavailability of the correct response, yet quite often the patient gives the overt response required, but is unaware of having done so, or cannot remember an earlier experience that prompted his correct response.

An experiment conducted by Edouard Claparede furnishes one more example that illustrates this characteristic disturbance. Claparede thought that the puzzling behavior of amnesic patients might be due to a loss of a sense of familiarity. To test this hypothesis, he once hid a pin between his fingers so that when he shook hands with one of his patients her hand was jabbed by the pin. A few minutes later, when he again extended his hand to her, she refused to take it. Pressed for an explanation, the woman said she was afraid she might be jabbed with a pin. She seemed entirely unaware of the fact that this was precisely what had happened to her. All she would say, to justify her apparently irrational suspicion, was that it had occurred to her that such a thing might happen, for people sometimes do hide pins between their fingers.

Perhaps the ultimate in amnesia is reached when a person correctly performs a required task, instantly forgets that he did so, and believes that the task was actually performed by the person who asked him to undertake it. This happened during the course of an interview in which I probed a patient's memory, both for some events that had taken place a few months prior to his illness, and for others that were quite recent. The first set of questions concerned an accident in which his brother had been killed; the second set concerned the forthcoming marriage of another brother. In reply to my uninformative questions —"Where?" "When?" "What is her name?" and the like—the patient gave me detailed and accurate answers relating to both events. I remarked, "You see, your memory is not so bad after all; you could remember pretty well these events in your family." The patient just stared at me with a puzzled expression, and then said, "But it was you who just told me about them." When I assured him that it was indeed he who had provided the information, he remained visibly unconvinced. Half an hour later I

274

The types of tasks that amnesic patients were required to perform during the five minutes between the learning of a list of 10 words and a subsequent test of recall produced various degrees of forgetting. Interviews proved to be the most disruptive activity.

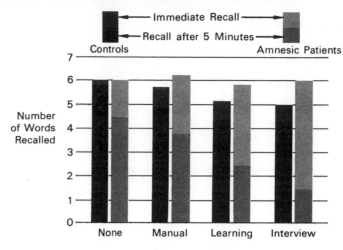

Remembering: An Action Program

Not only was this patient able to produce the information required, but afterwards he also remembered the topic of discussion. Nevertheless, he had no recollection of his own active part in the interview. His recall was factually accurate, and it was in the proper context, but he did not register it as a performance in remembering. How can we account for the absence of the experiential quality, for his mistaking the active for the passive role—and this after almost no delay, and in regard to a subject matter of profound personal significance? It seems likely that he did not experience his performance as an active one, but perhaps more like the automatic exercise of a habitual skill. Although he produced all the information, it was I who *programmed his behavior* with my questions. His recall depended on external activation. He exemplified in that interview the behavior so typical of amnesic patients, that of a completely respondent organism.

For over and above their manifold and unusual memory disorders, these patients are also notable for showing little emotion and no spontaneity whatsoever. Although on rare occasions they become visibly upset or angry, they almost immediately regain their placidity and indifference. They seldom initiate an action and seem quite happy sitting about, even when surrounded by others, saying nothing, doing nothing for hours on end.

When, instead of addressing specific questions to the patient mentioned above, I asked him to talk about his brothers, leaving my questions open, he could not tell me nearly so much about them. Whereas a normal person, in at-

repeated my questions; he again answered them correctly; and again he was convinced that it was I who had just told him about those events.

tempting to retrieve a memory, sets up an action program and executes it as well as he can, checking and testing alternatives, the amnesic patient at best carries out plans imposed on him by someone else—and then only as long as the plans demand no modification or choice along the way. An interruption, a momentary distraction, is likely to loosen the amnesic patient's grasp of the action plan, and if his hold is lost, there is no prospect of its recovery. We saw examples of this in the studies described above where the action required was that of remembering a 10-word sentence.

The retrieval of a specific memory involves setting up and executing a plan. Much-practiced skills, such as those employed in dressing, eating meals, speaking or writing, and overlearned information, such as certain salient public or private events of the years past, are all as readily available to amnesic patients as they are to normal people. But information that cannot be retrieved without a plan of action is beyond the reach of amnesic patients. They may hit on it immediately, but if they do not, further efforts to find it will prove useless. Indeed, there is little evidence that they even make such efforts.

Registration of Memories

Just as an action plan is required to recover information, it is also required for registering new information so that it can be available for future reference, that is, remembered. Judging from the evidence provided by studies of amnesic patients, it is not enough to perceive a message correctly, or even to respond to it overtly in the correct manner, in order to remember it at some later time. The acquisition of memories demands some further operations which can be interrupted by a violent blow, or can be permanently lost as a result of certain irreversible brain lesions. We may only

speculate about these operations, but it seems reasonable to view them as some process of cross filing which defines the multiple association—that is, the context of any one event—and thus establishes its uniqueness. Multiple filing also increases the accessibility of a memory which can thus be reached from many directions, along several routes.

A systematic investigation of the amnesic syndrome leads to the discovery of a number of unexpected facts. But in this instance, fuller knowledge of a mental disease does not offer remedies. The principal value of such studies is that they increase our understanding of normal memory function. The information we can gain about human memory from animal experiments or laboratory studies with human subjects is necessarily limited. Research in abnormal memory function offers new leads, some of which can be followed up in the laboratory. For example, the finding that a faultless overt response is not sufficient proof of intact memory is one that students of normal human subjects are unlikely to discover; experimenters using animal subjects cannot even formulate the problem.

The close association between lack of spontaneity and memory defects also becomes apparent only in studies of abnormal function. Yet it is an important observation, for it stresses the crucial part played by the execution of an action program, both in the registration and in the retrieval of memories. It reminds us that, quite apart from the associational factors involved, remembering is often primarily an operation of search, requiring flexibility, persistence, the capacity to check information for its accuracy, as well as access to its storage. The student of amnesic disorders recognizes the truth in the White Queen's comment to Alice: "It is a poor sort of memory which only works backwards."

COMMUNICATION WITHOUT WORDS

By Albert Mehrabian

SUPPOSE YOU ARE SITTING in my office listening to me describe some research I have done on communication. I tell you that feelings are communicated less by the words a person uses than by certain nonverbal means—that, for example, the verbal part of a spoken message has considerably less effect on whether a listener feels liked or disliked than a speaker's facial expression or tone of voice.

So far so good. But suppose I add, "In fact, we've worked out a formula that shows exactly how much each of these components contributes to the effect of the message as a whole. It goes like this: Total Impact = .07 verbal + .38 vocal + .55 facial."

What would you say to *that?* Perhaps you would smile good-naturedly and say, with some feeling, "Baloney!" Or perhaps you would frown and remark acidly, "Isn't science grand." My own response to the first answer would probably be to smile back: the facial part of your message, at least, was positive (55 per cent of the total). The second answer might make me uncomfortable: only the verbal part was positive (seven per cent).

The point here is not only that my reactions would lend credence to the formula but that most listeners would have mixed feelings about my statement. People like to see science march on, but they tend to resent its intrusion into an "art" like the communication of feelings, just as they find analytical and quantitative approaches to the study of personality cold, mechanistic and unacceptable.

The psychologist himself is sometimes plagued by the feeling that he is trying to put a rainbow into a bottle. Fascinated by a complicated and emotionally rich human situation, he begins to study it, only to find in the course of his research that he has destroyed part of the mystique that originally intrigued and involved him. But despite a certain nostalgia for earlier, more intuitive approaches, one must acknowledge that concrete experimental data have added a great deal to our understanding of how feelings are communicated. In fact, as I hope to show, analytical and intuitive findings do not so much conflict as complement each other.

It is indeed difficult to know what another person really feels. He says one thing and does another; he seems to mean something but we have an uneasy feeling it isn't true. The early psychoanalysts, facing this problem of inconsistencies and ambiguities in a person's communications, attempted to resolve it through the concepts of the conscious and the unconscious. They assumed that contradictory messages meant a conflict between superficial, deceitful, or erroneous feelings on the one hand and true attitudes and feelings on the other. Their role, then, was to help the client separate the wheat from the chaff.

The question was, how could this be done? Some analysts insisted that inferring the client's unconscious wishes was a completely intuitive process. Others thought that some nonverbal behavior, such as posture, position and movement, could be used in a more objective way to discover the client's feelings. A favorite technique of Frieda Fromm-Reichmann, for example, was to imitate a client's posture herself in order to obtain some feeling for what he was experiencing.

Thus began the gradual shift away from the idea that communication is primarily verbal, and that the verbal message includes distortions or ambiguities due to unobservable motives that only experts can discover.

Language, though, can be used to communicate almost anything. By comparison, nonverbal behavior is very limited in range. Usually, it is used to communicate feelings, likings and preferences, and it customarily reinforces or contradicts the feelings that are communicated verbally. Less often, it adds a new dimension of sorts to a verbal message, as when a salesman describes his product to a client and simultaneously conveys, nonverbally, the impression that he likes the client.

A great many forms of nonverbal behavior can communicate feelings: touching, facial expression, tone of voice, spatial distance from the addressee, relaxation of posture, rate of speech, number of errors in speech. Some of these are generally recognized as informative. Untrained adults and children easily infer that they are liked or disliked from certain facial expressions, from whether (and how) someone touches them, and from a speaker's tone of voice. Other behavior, such as posture, has a more subtle effect. A listener may sense how someone feels about him from the way the person sits while talking to him, but he may have trouble identifying precisely what his impression comes from.

Correct intuitive judgments of the feelings or attitudes of others are especially difficult when different degrees of feeling, or contradictory kinds of feeling, are expressed simultaneously through different forms of behavior. As I have pointed out, there is a distinction between verbal and vocal information (vocal information being what is lost when speech is written down—intonation, tone, stress, length and frequency of pauses, and so on), and the two kinds of information do not always communicate the same feeling. This distinction, which has been recognized for some time, has shed new light on certain types of communication. Sarcasm, for example, can be defined as a message in which the information transmitted vocally contradicts the information transmitted verbally. Usually the verbal information is positive and the vocal is negative, as in "Isn't science grand."

Through the use of an electronic filter, it is possible to measure the degree of liking communicated vocally. What the filter does is eliminate the higher frequencies of recorded speech, so that words are unintelligible but most vocal qualities remain. (For women's speech, we eliminate frequencies higher than about 200 cycles per second; for men, frequencies over about 100 cycles per second.) When people are asked to judge the degree of liking conveyed by the filtered speech, they perform the task rather easily and with a significant amount of agreement.

This method allows us to find out, in a given message, just how inconsistent the information communicated in words and the information communicated vocally really are. We ask one group to judge the amount of liking conveyed by a transcription of what was said, the verbal part of the message. A second group judges the vocal component, and a third group judges the impact of the complete recorded message. In one study of this sort we found that, when the verbal and vocal components of a message agree (both positive or both negative), the message as a whole is judged a little more positive or a little more negative than either component by itself. But when vocal information contradicts verbal, vocal wins out. If someone calls you "honey" in a nasty tone of voice, you are likely to feel disliked; it is also possible to say "I hate you" in a way that conveys exactly the opposite feeling.

Besides the verbal and vocal characteristics of speech, there are other, more subtle, signals of meaning in a spoken message. For example, everyone makes mistakes when he talks—unnecessary repetitions, stutterings, the omission of parts of words, incomplete sentences, "ums" and "ahs." In a number of studies of speech errors, George Mahl of Yale University has found that errors become more frequent as the speaker's discomfort or anxiety increases. It might be interesting to apply this index in an attempt to detect deceit (though on some occasions it might be risky: confidence men are notoriously smooth talkers).

Timing is also highly informative. How long does a speaker allow silent periods to last, and how long does he wait before he answers his partner? How long do his utterances tend to be? How often does he interrupt his partner, or wait an inappropriately long time before speaking? Joseph Matarazzo and his colleagues at the University of Oregon have found that each of these speech habits is stable from person to person, and each tells something about the speaker's per-

sonality and about his feelings toward and status in relation to his partner.

Utterance duration, for example, is a very stable quality in a person's speech; about 30 seconds long on the average. But when someone talks to a partner whose status is higher than his own, the more the high-status person nods his head the longer the speaker's utterances become. If the high-status person changes his own customary speech pattern toward longer or shorter utterances, the lower-status person will change his own speech in the same direction. If the high-status person often interrupts the speaker, or creates long silences, the speaker is likely to become quite uncomfortable. These are things that can be observed outside the laboratory as well as under experimental conditions. If you have an employee who makes you uneasy and seems not to respect you, watch him the next time you talk to him—perhaps he is failing to follow the customary low-status pattern.

Immediacy or directness is another good source of information about feelings. We use more distant forms of communication when the act of communicating is undesirable or uncomfortable. For example, some people would rather transmit discontent with an employee's work through a third party than do it themselves, and some find it easier to communicate negative feelings in writing than by telephone or face to face.

Distance can show a negative attitude toward the message itself, as well as toward the act of delivering it. Certain forms of speech are more distant than others, and they show fewer positive feelings for the subject referred to. A speaker might say "Those people need help," which is more distant than "These people need help," which is in turn even more distant than "These people need our help." Or he might say "Sam and I have been having dinner," which has less immediacy than "Sam and I are having dinner."

Facial expression, touching, gestures, self-manipulation (such as scratching), changes in body position, and head movements—all these express a person's positive and negative attitudes, both at the moment and in general, and many reflect status relationships as well. Movements of the limbs and head, for example, not only indicate one's attitude toward a specific set of circumstances but relate to how dominant, and how anxious, one generally tends to be in social situations. Gross changes in body position, such as shifting in the chair,

may show negative feelings toward the person one is talking to. They may also be cues: "It's your turn to talk," or "I'm about to get out of here, so finish what you're saying."

Posture is used to indicate both liking and status. The more a person leans toward his addressee, the more positively he feels about him. Relaxation of posture is a good indicator of both attitude and status, and one that we have been able to measure quite precisely. Three categories have been established for relaxation in a seated position: least relaxation is indicated by muscular tension in the hands and rigidity of posture; moderate relaxation is indicated by a forward lean of about 20 degrees and a sideways lean of less than 10 degrees, a curved back, and, for women, an open arm position; and extreme relaxation is indicated by a reclining angle greater than 20 degrees and a sideways lean greater than 10 degrees.

Our findings suggest that a speaker relaxes either very little or a great deal when he dislikes the person he is talking to, and to a moderate degree when he likes his companion. It seems that extreme tension occurs with threatening addressees, and extreme relaxation with nonthreatening, disliked addressees. In particular, men tend to become tense when talking to other men whom they dislike; on the other hand, women talking to men *or* women and men talking to women show dislike through extreme relaxation. As for status, people relax most with a low-status addressee, second-most with a peer, and least with someone of higher status than their own. Body orientation also shows status: in both sexes, it is least direct toward women with low status and most direct toward disliked men of high status. In part, body orientation seems to be determined by whether one regards one's partner as threatening.

The more you like a person, the more time you are likely to spend looking into his eyes as you talk to him. Standing close to your partner and facing him directly (which makes eye contact easier) also indicate positive feelings. And you are likely to stand or sit closer to your peers than you do to addressees whose status is either lower or higher than yours.

What I have said so far has been based on research studies performed, for the most part, with college students from the middle and upper-middle classes. One interesting question about communication, however, concerns young children from lower socioeconomic levels. Are these children, as some have suggested, more responsive to implicit channels of communication than middle- and upper-class children are?

Morton Wiener and his colleagues at Clark University had a group of middle- and lower-class children play learning games in which the reward for learning was praise. The child's responsiveness to the verbal and vocal parts of the praise-reward was measured by how much he learned. Praise came in two forms: the objective words "right" and "correct," and the more affective or evaluative words, "good" and "fine." All four words were spoken sometimes in a positive tone of voice and sometimes neutrally.

Positive intonation proved to have a dramatic effect on the learning rate of the lower-class group. They learned much faster when the vocal part of the message was positive than when it was neutral. Positive intonation affected the middle-class group as well, but not nearly as much.

If children of lower socioeconomic groups are more responsive to facial expression, posture and touch as well as to vocal communication, that fact could have interesting applications to elementary education. For example, teachers could be explicitly trained to be aware of, and to use, the forms of praise (nonverbal or verbal) that would be likely to have the greatest effect on their particular students.

Another application of experimental data on communication is to the interpretation and treatment of schizophrenia. The literature on schizophrenia has for some time emphasized that parents of schizophrenic children give off contradictory signals simultaneously. Perhaps the parent tells the child in words that he loves him, but his posture conveys a negative attitude. According to the "double-bind" theory of schizophrenia, the child who perceives simultaneous contradictory feelings in his parent does not know how to react: should he respond to the positive part of the message, or to the negative? If he is frequently placed in this paralyzing situation, he may learn to respond with contradictory communications of his own. The boy who sends a birthday card to his mother and signs it "Napoleon" says that he likes his mother and yet denies that he is the one who likes her.

In an attempt to determine whether parents of disturbed children really do emit more inconsistent messages about their feelings than other parents do, my colleagues and I have compared what these parents communicate verbally and vocally with what they show through posture. We interviewed parents of moderately and quite severely disturbed children, in the presence of the child, about the child's problem. The interview was video-recorded without the parents' knowledge, so that we could analyze their behavior later on. Our measurements supplied both the amount of inconsistency between the parents' verbal-vocal and postural communications, and the total amount of liking that the parents communicated.

According to the double-bind theory, the parents of the more disturbed children should have behaved more inconsistently than the parents of the less disturbed children. This was not confirmed: there was no significant difference between the two groups. However, the *total amount* of positive feeling communicated by parents of the more disturbed children was less than that communicated by the other group.

This suggests that (1) negative communications toward disturbed children occur because the child is a problem and therefore elicits them, or (2) the negative attitude precedes the child's disturbance. It may also be that both factors operate together, in a vicious circle.

If so, one way to break the cycle is for the therapist to create situations in which the parent can have better feelings toward the child. A more positive attitude from the parent may make the child more responsive to his directives, and the spiral may begin to move up instead of down. In our own work with disturbed children, this kind of procedure has been used to good effect.

If one puts one's mind to it, one can think of a great many other applications for the findings I have described, though not all of them concern serious problems. Politicians, for example, are careful to maintain eye contact with the television camera when they speak, but they are not always careful about how they sit when they debate another candidate of, presumably, equal status.

Public relations men might find a use for some of the subtler signals of feeling. So might Don Juans. And so might ordinary people, who could try watching other people's signals and changing their own, for fun at a party or in a spirit of experimentation at home. I trust that does not strike you as a cold, manipulative suggestion, indicating dislike for the human race. I assure you that, if you had more than a transcription of words to judge from (seven per cent of total message), it would not.

Language

And The Mind

By Noam Chomsky

ow does the mind work? To answer this question we must look at some of the work performed by the mind. One of its main functions is the acquisition of knowledge. The two major factors in acquisition of knowledge, perception and learning, have been the subject of study and speculation for centuries. It would not, I think, be misleading to characterize the major positions that have developed as outgrowths of classical rationalism and empiricism. The rationalist theories are marked by the importance they assign to *intrinsic* structures in mental operations—to central processes and organizing principles in perception, and to innate ideas and principles in learning. The empiricist approach, in contrast, has stressed the role of experience and control by environmental factors.

The classical empiricist view is that sensory images are transmitted to the brain as impressions. They remain as ideas that will be associated in various ways, depending on the fortuitous character of experience. In this view a language is merely a collection of words, phrases, and sentences, a habit system, acquired accidentally and extrinsically. In the formulation of Williard Quine, knowledge of a language (and, in fact, knowledge in general) can be represented as "a fabric of sentences variously associated to one another and to non-verbal stimuli by the mechanism of conditioned response." Acquisition of knowledge is only a matter of the gradual construction of this fabric. When sensory experience is interpreted, the already established network may be activated in some fashion. In its essentials, this view has been predominant in modern behavioral science, and it has been accepted with little question by many philosophers as well.

The classical rationalist view is quite different. In this view the mind contains a system of "common notions" that enable it to interpret the scattered and incoherent data of sense in terms of objects and their relations, cause and effect, whole and part, symmetry, gestalt properties, functions, and so on. Sensation, providing only fleeting and meaningless

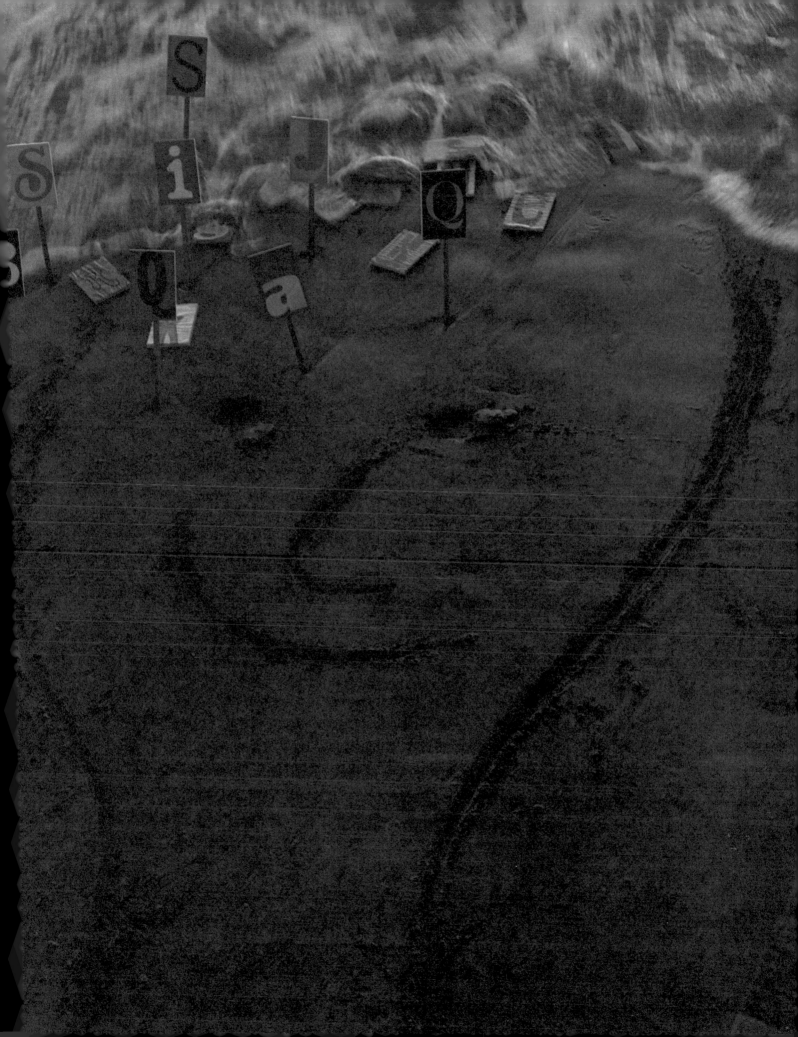

images, is degenerate and particular. Knowledge, much of it beyond immediate awareness, is rich in structure, involves universals, and is highly organized. The innate general principles that underlie and organize this knowledge, according to Leibniz, "enter into our thoughts, of which they form the soul and the connection . . . although we do not at all think of them."

This "active" rationalist view of the acquisition of knowledge persisted through the romantic period in its essentials. With respect to language, it achieves its most illuminating expression in the profound investigations of Wilhelm von Humboldt. His theory of speech perception supposes a generative system of rules that underlies speech production as well as its interpretation. The system is generative in that it makes infinite use of finite means. He regards a language as a structure of forms and concepts based on a system of rules that determine their interrelations, arrangement, and organization. But these finite materials can be combined to make a never-ending product.

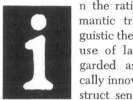n the rationalist and romantic tradition of linguistic theory, the normal use of language is regarded as characteristically innovative. We construct sentences that are entirely new to us. There is no substantive notion of "analogy" or "generalization" that accounts for this creative aspect of language use. It is equally erroneous to describe language as a "habit structure" or as a network of associated responses. The innovative element in normal use of language quickly exceeds the bounds of such marginal principles as analogy or generalization (under any substantive interpretation of these notions). It is important to emphasize this fact because the insight has been lost under the impact of the behaviorist assumptions that have dominated speculation and research in the twentieth century.

In Humboldt's view, acquisition of language is largely a matter of maturation of an innate language capacity. The maturation is guided by internal factors, by an innate "form of language" that is sharpened, differentiated, and given its specific realization through experience. Language is thus a kind of latent structure in the human mind, developed and fixed by exposure to specific linguistic experience. Humboldt believes that all languages will be found to be very simi-

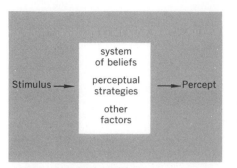

MODEL FOR PERCEPTION. Each physical stimulus, after interpretation by the mental processes, will result in a percept.

lar in their grammatical form, similar not on the surface but in their deeper inner structures. The innate organizing principles severely limit the class of possible languages, and these principles determine the properties of the language that is learned in the normal way.

The active and passive views of perception and learning have elaborated with varying degrees of clarity since the seventeenth century. These views can be confronted with empirical evidence in a variety of ways. Some recent work in psychology and neurophysiology is highly suggestive in this regard. There is evidence for the existence of central processes in perception, specifically for control over the functioning of sensory neurons by the brain-stem reticular system. Behavioral counterparts of this central control have been under investigation for several years. Furthermore, there is evidence for innate organization of the perceptual system of a highly specific sort at every level of biological organization. Studies of the visual system of the frog, the discovery of specialized cells responding to angle and motion in the lower cortical centers of cats and rabbits, and the somewhat comparable investigations of the auditory system of frogs—all are relevant to the classical questions of intrinsic structure mentioned earlier. These studies suggest that there are highly organized, innately determined perceptual systems that are adapted closely to the animal's "life space" and that provide the basis for what we might call "acquisition of knowledge." Also relevant are certain behavioral studies of human infants, for example those showing the preference for faces over other complex stimuli.

These and other studies make it reasonable to inquire into the possibility that complex intellectual structures are determined narrowly by innate mental organization. What is perceived may be determined by mental processes of considerable depth. As far as language

learning is concerned, it seems to me that a rather convincing argument can be made for the view that certain principles intrinsic to the mind provide invariant structures that are a precondition for linguistic experience. In the course of this article I would like to sketch some of the ways such conclusions might be clarified and firmly established.

here are several ways linguistic evidence can be used to reveal properties of human perception and learning. In this section we consider one research strategy that might take us nearer to this goal.

Let us say that in interpreting a certain physical stimulus a person constructs a "percept." This percept represents some of his conclusions (in general, unconscious) about the stimulus. To the extent that we can characterize such percepts, we can go on to investigate the mechanisms that relate stimulus and percept. Imagine a model of perception that takes stimuli as inputs and arrives at percepts as "outputs." The model might contain a system of beliefs, strategies for interpreting stimuli, and other factors, such as the organization of memory. We would then have a perceptual model that might be represented graphically [*see illustration at left, above*].

Consider next the system of beliefs that is a component of the perceptual model. How was this acquired? To study this problem, we must investigate a second model, which takes certain data as input and gives as "output" (again, internally represented) the system of be-

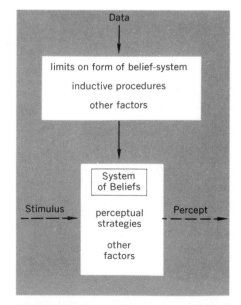

MODEL FOR LEARNING. One's system of beliefs, a part of the perception model, is acquired from data as shown above.

liefs operating in the perceptual model. This second model, a model of learning, would have its own intrinsic structure, as did the first. This structure might consist of conditions on the nature of the system of beliefs that can be acquired, of innate inductive strategies, and again, of other factors such as the organization of memory [*see illustration at left, below*].

Under further conditions, which are interesting but not relevant here, we can take these perceptual and learning models as theories of the acquisition of knowledge, rather than of belief. How then would the models apply to language? The input stimulus to the perceptual model is a speech signal, and the percept is a representation of the utterance that the hearer takes the signal to be and of the interpretation he assigns to it. We can think of the percept as the structural description of a linguistic expression which contains certain phonetic, semantic, and syntactic information. Most interesting is the syntactic information, which best can be discussed by examining a few typical cases.

he three sentences in the example seem to be the same syntactic structure [*see illustration at right*]. Each contains the subject *I*, and the predicate of each consists of a verb (*told, expected, persuaded*), a noun phrase (*John*), and an embedded predicate phrase (*to leave*). This similarity is only superficial, however—a similarity in what we may call the "surface structure" of these sentences, which differ in important ways when we consider them with somewhat greater care.

The differences can be seen when the sentences are paraphrased or subjected to certain grammatical operations, such as the conversion from active to passive forms. For example, in normal conversation the sentence "I told John to leave" can be roughly paraphrased as "What I told John was to leave." But the other two sentences cannot be paraphrased as "What I persuaded John was to leave" or "What I expected John was to leave." Sentence 2 can be paraphrased as: "It was expected by me that John would leave." But the other two sentences cannot undergo a corresponding formal operation, yielding: "It was persuaded by me that John would leave" or "It was told by me that John should leave."

Sentences 2 and 3 differ more subtly. In Sentence 3 *John* is the direct object of *persuade*, but in Sentence 2 *John* is not the direct object of *expect*. We can show this by using these verbs in slightly more complex sentences: "I persuaded the doctor to examine John" and "I expected the doctor to examine John." If we replace the embedded proposition *the doctor to examine John* with its passive form *John to be examined by the doctor,* the change to the passive does not, in itself, change the meaning. We can accept as paraphrases "I expected the doctor to examine John" and "I expected John to be examined by the doctor." But we cannot accept as paraphrases "I persuaded the doctor to examine John" and "I persuaded John to be examined by the doctor."

The parts of these sentences differ in their grammatical functions. In "I persuaded John to leave" *John* is both the object of *persuade* and the subject of *leave*. These facts must be represented

 study of such examples, examples characteristic of all human languages that have been carefully studied, constitutes the first stage of the linguistic investigation outlined above, namely the study of the percept. The percept contains phonetic and semantic information related through the medium of syntactic structure. There are two aspects to this syntactic structure. It consists of a surface directly related to the phonetic form, and a deep structure that underlies the semantic interpretation. The deep structure is represented

---

(1)	I told John to leave
(2)	I expected John to leave
(3)	I persuaded John to leave

First Paraphrase:

(1a)	What I told John was to leave (ACCEPTABLE)
(2a)	What I expected John was to leave (UNACCEPTABLE)
(3a)	What I persuaded John was to leave (UNACCEPTABLE)

Second Paraphrase:

(1b)	It was told by me that John would leave (UNACCEPTABLE)
(2b)	It was expected by me that John would leave (ACCEPTABLE)
(3b)	It was persuaded by me that John would leave (UNACCEPTABLE)

(4)	I expected the doctor to examine John
(5)	I persuaded the doctor to examine John

Passive replacement as paraphrase:

(4a)	I expected John to be examined by the doctor (MEANING RETAINED)
(5a)	I persuaded John to be examined by the doctor (MEANING CHANGED)

SUPERFICIAL SIMILARITY. When the sentences above are paraphrased or are converted from active to passive forms, differences in their deep structure appear.

---

in the percept since they are known, intuitively, to the hearer of the speech signal. No special training or instruction is necessary to enable the native speaker to understand these examples, to know which are "wrong" and which "right," although they may all be quite new to him. They are interpreted by the native speaker instantaneously and uniformly, in accordance with structural principles that are known tacitly, intuitively, and unconsciously.

These examples illustrate two significant points. First, the surface structure of a sentence, its organization into various phrases, may not reveal or immediately reflect its deep syntactic structure. The deep structure is not represented directly in the form of the speech signal; it is abstract. Second, the rules that determine deep and surface structure and

their interrelation in particular cases must themselves be highly abstract. They are surely remote from consciousness, and in all likelihood they cannot be brought to consciousness.

in the mind and rarely is there a direct indication of it in the physical signal.

A language, then, involves a set of semantic-phonetic percepts, of sound-meaning correlations, the correlations being determined by the kind of intervening syntactic structure just illustrated. The English language correlates sound and meaning in one way, Japanese in another, and so on. But the general properties of percepts, their forms and mechanisms, are remarkably similar for all languages that have been carefully studied.

Returning to our models of perception and learning, we can now take up the problem of formulating the system of beliefs that is a central component in perceptual processes. In the case of language, the "system of beliefs" would now be called the "generative grammar," the system of rules that specifies the sound-meaning correlation and generates the class of structural descriptions (percepts) that constitute the language in question. The generative grammar, then, represents the speaker-hearer's knowledge of his language. We can use the term *grammar of a language* ambiguously, as referring not only to the speaker's internalized, subconscious knowledge but to the professional linguist's representation of this internalized and intuitive system of rules as well.

ow is this generative grammar acquired? Or, using our learning model, what is the internal structure of the device that could develop a generative grammar?

We can think of every normal human's internalized grammar as, in effect, a theory of his language. This theory provides a sound-meaning correlation for an infinite number of sentences. It provides an infinite set of structural descriptions; each contains a surface structure that determines phonetic form and a deep structure that determines semantic content.

In formal terms, then, we can describe the child's acquisition of language as a kind of theory construction. The child discovers the theory of his language with only small amounts of data from that language. Not only does his "theory of the language" have an enormous predictive scope, but it also enables the child to reject a great deal of the very data on which the theory has been constructed. Normal speech consists, in large part, of fragments, false starts, blends, and other distortions of the underlying idealized forms. Nevertheless, as is evident from a study of the mature use of language, what the child learns is the underlying ideal theory. This is a remarkable fact. We must also bear in mind that the child constructs this ideal theory without explicit instruction, that he acquires this knowledge at a time when he is not capable of complex intellectual achievements in many other domains, and that this achievement is relatively independent of intelligence or the particular course of experience. These are facts that a theory of learning must face.

A scientist who approaches phenomena of this sort without prejudice or dogma would conclude that the acquired knowledge must be determined in a rather specific way by intrinsic properties of mental organization. He would then set himself the task of discovering the innate ideas and principles that make such acquisition of knowledge possible.

It is unimaginable that a highly specific, abstract, and tightly organized language comes by accident into the mind of every four-year-old child. If there were not an innate restriction on the form of grammar, then the child could employ innumerable theories to account for his linguistic experience, and no one system, or even small class of systems, would be found exclusively acceptable or even preferable. The child could not possibly acquire knowledge of a language. This restriction on the form of grammar is a precondition for linguistic experience, and it is surely the critical factor in determining the course and result of language learning. The child cannot know at birth which language he is going to learn. But he must "know" that its grammar must be of a predetermined form that excludes many imaginable languages.

The child's task is to select the appropriate hypothesis from this restricted class. Having selected it, he can confirm his choice with the evidence further available to him. But neither the evidence nor any process of induction (in any well-defined sense) could in themselves have led to this choice. Once the hypothesis is sufficiently well confirmed, the child knows the language defined by this hypothesis; consequently, his knowledge extends vastly beyond his linguistic experience, and he can reject much of this experience as imperfect, as resulting from the interaction of many factors, only one of which is the ideal grammar that determines a sound-meaning connection for an infinite class of linguistic expressions. Along such lines as these one might outline a theory to explain the acquisition of language.

s has been pointed out, both the form and meaning of a sentence are determined by syntactic structures that are not represented directly in the signal and that are related to the signal only at a distance, through a long sequence of interpretive rules. This property of abstractness in grammatical structure is of primary importance, and it is on this property that our inferences about mental processes are based. Let us examine this abstractness a little more closely.

Not many years ago, the process of sentence interpretation might have been described approximately along the following lines. A speech signal is received and segmented into successive units (overlapping at the borders). These units are analyzed in terms of their invariant phonetic properties and assigned to "phonemes." The sequence of phonemes, so constructed, is then segmented into minimal grammatically functioning units (morphemes and words). These are again categorized. Successive operations of segmentation and classification will lead to what I have called "surface structure"—an analysis of a sentence into phrases, which can be represented as a proper bracketing of the sentence, with the bracketed units assigned to various categories [*see illustration, page 283*]. Each segment—phonetic, syntactic or semantic—would be identified in terms of certain invariant properties. This would be an exhaustive analysis of the structure of the sentence.

With such a conception of language structure, it made good sense to look forward hopefully to certain engineering applications of linguistics—for example, to voice-operated typewriters capable of segmenting an expression into its successive phonetic units and identifying these, so that speech could be converted to some form of phonetic writing in a mechanical way; to mechanical analysis of sentence structure by fairly straightforward and well-understood computational techniques; and perhaps even beyond to such projects as machine translation. But these hopes have by now been largely abandoned with the realization that this conception of grammatical structure is inadequate at every level, semantic, phonetic, and syntactic. Most important, at the level of syntactic organization, the surface structure indicates semantically significant relations only in extremely simple cases. In general, the deeper aspects of syntactic organization are representable by labeled bracketing, but of a very different sort from that seen in surface structure.

There is evidence of various sorts, both from phonetics and from experimental psychology, that labeled bracketing is an adequate representation of surface structure. It would go beyond the bounds of this paper to survey the phonetic evidence. A good deal of it is presented in a forthcoming book, *Sound Pattern of English*, by myself and Morris Halle. Similarly, very interesting experimental work by Jerry Fodor and his colleagues, based on earlier observations by D. E. Broadbent and Peter Ladefoged, has shown that the disruption of a speech signal (for example, by a superimposed click) tends to be perceived at the

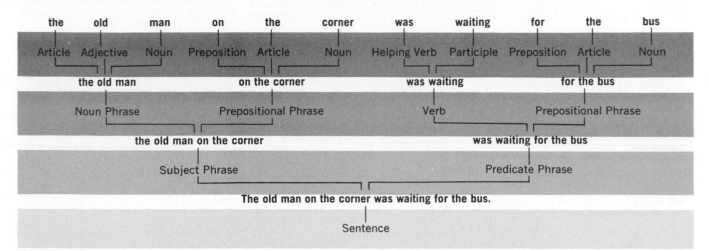

SURFACE STRUCTURE ANALYSIS. A type of sentence analysis now abandoned as inadequate at every level is this labeled bracketing which analyzes the sentence by successive division into larger units with each unit assigned to its own category.

boundaries of phrases rather than at the point where the disruption actually occurred, and that in many cases the bracketing of surface structure can be read directly from the data on perceptual displacement. I think the evidence is rather good that labeled bracketing serves to represent the surface structure that is related to the perceived form of physical signals.

Deep structures are related to surface structures by a sequence of certain formal operations, operations now generally called "grammatical transformations." At the levels of sound, meaning, and syntax, the significant structural features of sentences are highly abstract. For this reason they cannot be recovered by elementary data-processing techniques. This fact lies behind the search for central processes in speech perception and the search for intrinsic, innate structure as the basis for language learning.

ow can we represent deep structure? To answer this question we must consider the grammatical transformations that link surface structure to the underlying deep structure that is not always apparent.

Consider, for example, the operations of passivization and interrogation. In the sentences (1) John was examined by the doctor, and (2) did the doctor examine John, both have a deep structure similar to the paraphrase of Sentence 1, (3) the doctor examined John. The same network of grammatical relations determines the semantic interpretation in each case. Thus two of the grammatical transformations of English must be the operations of passivization and interrogation that form such surface structures as Sentences 1 and 2 from a deeper structure which in its essentials also un-

derlies Sentence 3. Since the transformations ultimately produce surface structures, they must produce labeled bracketings [see illustration above]. But notice that these operations can apply in sequence: we can form the passive question "was John examined by the doctor" by passivization followed by interrogation. Since the result of passivization is a labeled bracketing, it follows that the interrogative transformation operates on a labeled bracketing and forms a new labeled bracketing. Thus a transformation such as interrogation maps a labeled bracketing into a labeled bracketing.

By similar argument, we can show that all grammatical transformations are structure-dependent mappings of this sort and that the deep structures which underlie all sentences must themselves be labeled bracketings. Of course, the labeled bracketing that constitutes deep structure will in general be quite different from that representing the surface structure of a sentence. Our argument is somewhat oversimplified, but it is roughly correct. When made precise and fully accurate it strongly supports the view that deep structures, like surface structures, are formally to be taken as labeled bracketings, and that grammatical transformations are mappings of such structures onto other similar structures.

ecent studies have sought to explore the ways in which grammatical structure of the sort just described enters into mental operations. Much of this work has been based on a proposal formulated by George Miller as a first approximation, namely, that the amount of memory used to store a sentence should reflect the number of transformations used in deriving it. For example, H. B. Savin and E. Perchonock

investigated this assumption in the following way: they presented to subjects a sentence followed by a sequence of unrelated words. They then determined the number of these unrelated words recalled when the subject attempted to repeat the sentence and the sequence of words. The more words recalled, the less memory used to store the sentence. The fewer words recalled, the more memory used to store the sentence. The results showed a remarkable correlation of amount of memory and number of transformations in certain simple cases. In fact, in their experimental material, shorter sentences with more transformations took up more "space in memory" than longer sentences that involved fewer transformations.

Savin has extended this work and has shown that the effects of deep structure and surface structure can be differentiated by a similar technique. He considered paired sentences with approximately the same deep structure but with one of the pair being more complex in surface structure. He showed that, under the experimental conditions just described, the paired sentences were indistinguishable. But if the sequence of unrelated words precedes, rather than follows, the sentence being tested, then the more complex (in surface structure) of the pair is more difficult to repeat correctly than the simpler member. Savin's very plausible inference is that sentences are coded in memory in terms of deep structure. When the unrelated words precede the test sentence, these words use up a certain amount of short-term memory, and the sentence that is more complex in surface structure cannot be analyzed with the amount of memory remaining. But if the test sentence precedes the unrelated words, it is, once understood, stored in terms of deep structure, which is about the same in both cases. Therefore the same amount of memory remains, in the paired cases, for recall of the following words. This is a beautiful example of the way creative experimental studies can interweave with theoretical work in the study of language and of mental processes.

n speaking of mental processes we have returned to our original problem. We can now see why it is reasonable to maintain that the linguistic evidence supports an "active" theory of acquisition of knowledge. The study of sentences and of speech perception, it seems to me, leads to a perceptual theory of a classical rationalist sort. Representative of this school, among others, were the seventeenth-century Cambridge Platonists, who developed the idea that our perception is guided by notions that originate from the mind and that provide the framework for the interpretation of sensory stimuli. It is not sufficient to suggest that this framework is a store of "neural models" or "schemata" which are in some manner applied to perception (as is postulated in some current theories of perception). We must go well beyond this assumption and return to the view of Wilhelm von Humboldt, who attributed to the mind a system of rules that generates such models and schemata under the stimulation of the senses. The system of rules itself determines the content of the percept that is formed.

We can offer more than this vague and metaphoric account. A generative grammar and an associated theory of speech perception provide a concrete example of the rules that operate and of the mental objects that they construct and manipulate. Physiology cannot yet explain the physical mechanisms that affect these abstract functions. But neither physiology nor psychology provides evidence that calls this account into question or that suggests an alternative. As mentioned earlier, the most exciting current work in the physiology of perception shows that even the peripheral systems analyze stimuli into the complex properties of objects, and that central processes may significantly affect the information transmitted by the receptor organs.

The study of language, it seems to me, offers strong empirical evidence that empiricist theories of learning are quite inadequate. Serious efforts have been made in recent years to develop principles of induction, generalization, and data analysis that would account for knowledge of a language. These efforts have been a total failure. The methods and principles fail not for any superficial reason such as lack of time or data. They fail because they are intrinsically incapable of giving rise to the system of rules that underlies the normal use of language. What evidence is now available supports the view that all human languages share deep-seated properties of organization and structure. These properties—these linguistic universals—can be plausibly assumed to be an innate mental endowment rather than the result of learning. If this is true, then the study of language sheds light on certain long-standing issues in the theory of knowledge. Once again, I see little reason to doubt that what is true of language is true of other forms of human knowledge as well.

There is one further question that might be raised at this point. How does the human mind come to have the innate properties that underlie acquisition of knowledge? Here linguistic evidence obviously provides no information at all. The process by which the human mind has achieved its present state of complexity and its particular form of innate organization are a complete mystery, as much of a mystery as the analogous questions that can be asked about the processes leading to the physical and mental organization of any other complex organism. It is perfectly safe to attribute this to evolution, so long as we bear in mind that there is no substance to this assertion—it amounts to nothing more than the belief that there is surely some naturalistic explanation for these phenomena.

There are, however, important aspects of the problem of language and mind that can be studied sensibly within the limitations of present understanding and technique. I think that, for the moment, the most productive investigations are those dealing with the nature of particular grammars and with the universal conditions met by all human languages. I have tried to suggest how one can move, in successive steps of increasing abstractness, from the study of percepts to the study of grammar and perceptual mechanisms, and from the study of grammar to the study of universal grammar and the mechanisms of learning.

In this area of convergence of linguistics, psychology, and philosophy, we can look forward to much exciting work in coming years.

FOCUS ON FANTASY

May we now explore the world of wonder, of daydreams and night-mares, and the miracle of words that conjure up images to last as long as the mind of man? What, then, is fantasy? It is where you live.

"I have my own yacht
and plan a cruise
of the Eastern seaboard."

THE IMPORTANCE OF DAYDREAMING

BY JEROME L. SINGER

"George, I've asked you three times to empty the garbage and you haven't moved."

"Sorry, Darling, I guess I didn't hear you. I must have been daydreaming."

"But you were looking straight at me!" Mrs. Brown hears voices coming from five-year-old Timmy's bedroom. Momentarily startled, she soon realizes that Timmy merely is playing a game by himself, acting out the roles of the good guys and the bad guys.

The mother smiles proudly at Timmy's cleverness in shifting voices. Then she feels a pang of anxiety. Is something wrong with her son? Should he be talking to himself at his age? Isn't this a symptom of some emotional conflict?

These two cases illustrate a phenomenon most common to human experience. Daydreams intrude suddenly into the waking thoughts of almost everyone during a normal day and certainly surge into prominence in those quiet or solitary moments when we ride on trains, sit in waiting rooms, or prepare for bed.

The nocturnal dream, more vivid and dramatic, has been the focus of much attention in folklore, literature and science from the days of Joseph in Pharaoh's court to the recent flurry of neurophysiological experimentation on sleep. Its paler cousin, the fleeting fantasy or distracting image we call the daydream, has always been of interest to creative artists but has been virtually ignored by scientific researchers.

These two hypothetical but typical cases point up some of the unknowns about daydreaming. Is George's reverie simply an escape from the unpleasant reality of taking out the garbage? Is his failure to hear his wife the sign of worthwhile, creative thinking, or is it a psychological defense against the humdrum character of his life?

And what is the nature of the fantasy play activity in which young Timmy is indulging? Is he abnormal? Is his taking of several roles the creation in effect of a world around Timmy which is not really there; is it something that prepares him for skills in later life, or is it a passing characteristic of childhood. What kinds of cultural patterns foster such imaginative play or prevent its continuation?

Clearly, some systematic scientific understanding of the scope and function of daydreaming in children and in adults is called for. But how does one catch hold of so insubstantial a bit of fluff as a daydream for any kind of scientific study? Science usually requires objectivity, repeatability of the phenomenon, measurement and experimental control. How to squeeze a daydream into that mold has so baffled psychologists that very little formal research on daydreaming has been done.

Well before the turn of the Century, Sir Francis Galton proposed to study the range of human imagery and William James called attention to the stream of thought as a significant human phenomenon. Psychoanalysts have of course made frequent use of their patients' daydreams in diagnosis and therapy. But behavioral scientists have devoted surprisingly little effort to examining daydreams or related types of self-generated internal stimulation experienced by the average person.

Indeed, in our action-oriented nation, the term "daydreaming" has assumed a negative connotation. But it does not seem likely that fantasizing is inherently pathological or even defensive. It seems more reasonable that daydreaming is a fundamental human characteristic, an autonomous ego function. Daydreaming is more than a readily available defense or escape; it is a valuable method we all use to explore a variety of perspectives.

My own interest in daydreaming evolved out of an earlier interest in the nature of imaginative behavior as shown clinically in such "projective techniques" as the Rorschach inkblots and the Thematic Apperception Test. Both of these techniques require a person to project his own feelings and ideas into an interpretation of ambiguous images—inkblots in the first case and nondescript drawings in the second. Presumably in doing so he reveals his general behavioral style and his dominant motivational pattern.

Especially interesting to me was Herman Rorschach's observation that people who look at inkblots and report seeing human beings in action—the so-called M determinant—are imaginative people, inclined to an original, rich inner life. The Rorschach M response has interesting implications for an understanding of imagination. Nevertheless, with the Rorschach data we still are dealing with an inferred measure of imagination based on reactions to inkblots—several steps removed from the underlying process which is of primary interest: the daydream itself.

Rather than attempting to explore daydreaming simply by making inferences from the Rorschach data, we decided to begin again and examine the phenomenon more directly. For some time now a program of research has been carried on under my direction at the City College of the City University of New York, with the close collaboration of various colleagues, in particular Professor John Antrobus.

My first step was to devise a questionnaire, based on what I could learn from clinical literature and from the experiences of friends, relatives and patients, as well as from my own introspections. This questionnaire consisted of a large number of actual daydreams; the person answered it by indicating how frequently he indulged in the various kinds of daydreams described. Over a period of time the questionnaire was improved and polished, and administered to almost 500 men and women, most of them college-educated. No data on persons of other socioeconomic levels are available at this time.

The questionnaire included such sample daydreams as these:

"I have my own yacht and plan a cruise of the Eastern seaboard."

"I suddenly find I can fly, to the amazement of passersby."

"I see myself in the arms of a warm and loving person who satisfies all my needs."

"I picture an atomic bombing of the town I live in."

"I see myself participating with wild abandon in a Roman orgy."

In analyzing the responses to the questionnaire, we saw at once that almost all adults engage in some form of daydreaming every day. Most of these daydreams take the form of fairly clear visual images. They occur chiefly during private moments, just before bedtime or during rides on buses or trains.

Most people report that they enjoy their daydreams. In content their fantasies stick fairly close to simple possibilities, although a very high proportion admit wildly improbable dreams such as inheriting a million dollars. A sizable minority report such fantasies as "being the Messiah," obtaining homosexual satisfactions, and murdering family members. Those individuals with a pronounced tendency to daydream seem to run the gamut of both realistic and bizarre fantasies. Apparently nothing human is alien to the imaginative realm of the accomplished daydreamer.

Men and women vary little in the frequency of their daydreams, but there is an understandable difference in the content of their fantasies. Women's daydreams clearly show their interest in fashions, while those of men display their enthusiasm for heroics and athletics. A recent independent study by Morton Wagman of the University of Illinois,

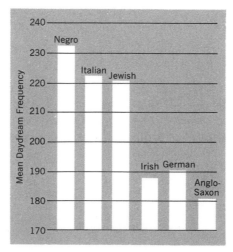

DAYDREAMING FREQUENCY: Order strikingly reflects the relative insecurity.

using the same questionnaire, indicates that men report more explicitly sexual daydreams than women, while women have daydreams involving passivity, narcissism, affiliation (need for personal contact) and physical attractiveness.

Marriage precipitates no special pattern of daydreaming, but there are changes in the frequency of fantasy as people grow older. The peak of daydreaming seems to be in mid-adolescence, and then it falls off gradually, although fantasy persists well into old age. In later years daydreaming takes on a retrospective quality, for future possibilities are not only limited but rather frightening to the aged.

We compared the daydream responses of adults from several socio-cultural groups—people from Italian, Irish, Jewish, Negro, Anglo-Saxon and German subcultures. All of them were well-educated, middle-class Americans born of at least the second generation, but with both parents from the same national-origin background.

The order of daydreaming frequency reported was, from high to low, Negro, Italian, Jewish, Irish, German and Anglo-Saxon. This order strikingly reflects the relative upward mobility, insecurity and even the pattern of immigration of the various groups to the United States. The latter three groups represent subcultures which have pretty well "made it," socially and economically, in America [see illustration below].

Interesting differences in the content of the fantasies also emerged. The Irish showed a tendency toward religious, extremely fantastic or heroic daydreams. The Negroes fantasized about sensual satisfactions, eating well, comfort, fine clothes and cars.

What other personality characteristics, we asked, might be associated with the tendency toward frequent daydreaming? Psychoanalytic theory suggested one hypothesis: that relative closeness to one's mother might lead to greater inhibition and fantasy.

In order to examine this theory and to evaluate relevant personality factors, we gave the subjects a series of additional tests. All subjects answered a questionnaire designed to explore their attitudes about self, mother, father and ideal self. They also filled out Cattell and Minnesota Multaphasic questionnaires which provided information on anxiety, repressive defenses and self-awareness. They kept logs of their night dreams for a month, a technique developed by Rosalea Schonbar of Columbia University. In

"I suddenly
find I can fly,
to the
amazement
of passersby."

addition they wrote Thematic Apperception Test stories or gave accounts of fantasies which were scored by judges for imaginativeness and creativity.

In general, findings with the questionnaire and with projective measures support psychoanalytic theory. Men and women who report closeness to or identification with their mothers, or a rejection of their fathers' values, tend to daydream more frequently. They also remember more of their night dreams. On the projective tests, such individuals rate as more creative storytellers, are generally more self-aware and anxiously sensitive, and are less inclined to employ defense mechanisms such as repression.

When we analyzed the results of some 40 personality tests taken by college freshmen and matched them with the subjects' daydreaming patterns, we discovered that there were seven categories of daydreaming.

General daydreaming reflected a predisposition to fantasy with great variety in content and often showed curiosity about other people rather than about the natural world.

Self-recriminating daydreaming was characterized by a high frequency of somewhat obsessional, verbally expressive but negatively-toned emotional reactions such as guilt and depression.

Objective, controlled, thoughtful daydreaming displayed a reflective, rather scientific and philosophically inclined content, and was associated with masculinity, emotional stability and curiosity about nature rather than about the human aspects of environment.

Poorly controlled, kaleidoscopic daydreaming reflected scattered thought and lack of systematic "story lines" in fantasy, as well as distractibility, boredom and self-abasement.

Autistic daydreaming represented the breakthrough into consciousness of material associated with nocturnal dreaming. It reflected the kind of dreamy, poorly controlled quality of inner experience often reported clinically by schizoid individuals.

Neurotic, self-conscious daydreaming revealed one of the clearest patterns— the one most closely associated with measures of neuroticism and emotional instability. It involved repetitive, egocentric and body-centered fantasies.

Enjoyment of daydreaming was characterized by a generally positive and healthy acceptance of daydreaming, an enjoyment of fantasy and the active use of it for both pleasure and problem solving.

People who scored high on introversion showed a strong inclination to respond to internally generated material. Their daydreams were either fantastic and fanciful or controlled, orderly and objective. This vividly calls to mind C. P. Snow's much discussed contrast of the literary-humanist scholar with the scientist-engineer. Both are given to inner activity, but they are very likely at opposite poles of the daydreaming dimension.

Daydreaming is not confined to adults; it also enters into the games of children. If we observe young children in a nursery or at a playground, those whose play is directly involved with physical reality can be separated from those who introduce make-believe characters, scenes or times into their play.

In one of our investigations, children between six and nine years of age were interviewed and observed in a series of situations. From their responses to questions about play habits, imaginary companions, and "pictures in your head," we classified them into high- and low-fantasy groups. We then told the children that we were looking for "astronauts of the future." We pointed out that astronauts have to sit quietly in a confined space for long periods of time and asked the children to remain seated in a simulated space capsule as long as possible.

The high-fantasy group were far better at sticking it out, presumably because they could create internal games to pass the time. These children also showed more creativity in storytelling and more achievement motivation. They were more likely to be firstborn or only children; they reported greater closeness to one parent, and they indicated that their parents played fantasy games with them and told them bedtime stories.

Clinically, the high-fantasy children were evaluated as more obsessional in character structure, with greater likelihood of Oedipal conflicts. The low-fantasy children more often were rated as hysterical personalities with pre-Oedipal conflicts—that is, problems with need satisfaction or aggression control, rather than problems relating specifically to parental figures.

Another study in this series, carried out by Bella Streiner and me, compared the dreams and fantasies of congenitally blind children with a matched group of sighted children. As could be anticipated, the variety and complexity of the dreams, daydreams and imaginative play of the blind children was greatly limited. Their dreams, cast of course in verbal and kinesthetic imagery, stayed close to

"I see myself participating with wild abandon in a Roman orgy."

their own immediate life situations. The sighted children were off on rocket ships or flying carpets, but for the blind children a trip to the supermarket became a source of adventure in fantasy.

The contrast emerged when two children, one blind and one sighted, imagined an airplane flight. The blind child spoke of the fact that the boy in his fantasy did not know what an airplane was but that he had a pleasant trip and enjoyed traveling with his mother. The sighted child told of the plane hitting an air-pocket, the pilot's unconsciousness, and the parents taking over controls of the ship.

Blind children, we discovered, were more likely to have imaginary companions, and to keep them to a later age than the sighted children. This is understandable when one remembers how dependent these children are on their parents or siblings for even simple maneuvers outside the home. Clearly, they develop make-believe companions, invariably sighted, as a comfort for the times when they are left alone.

Still another study, carried out under my direction by Sybil Gottlieb of the City University of New York, sought to determine whether children imitate adults in producing fantasy material. Several hundred children, who differed initially in fantasy predisposition, were divided into three groups. They were shown an experimental color movie in-

volving a lot of activity by abstract figures. After they had seen the movie, an adult discussed the film with each group. One group was given a very *imaginative* interpretation of the film; the second group was provided with a *realistic* type of story, and the third was given merely a literal description of the "events" of the movie with a *neutral* content.

Then a second abstract film was shown and the children were instructed to write something about it. We were looking for answers to these questions: (1) In describing the second film, to what extent would the children imitate the adult interpretations of the first film? (2) What effect would their initial imaginative predisposition have on their response? and, (3), Would the age level of the children make a significant difference?

Results were rather clearcut. The elementary-school-age children showed a strong imitative effect. Direct mimicry was rare, but the story content which emerged showed that the adults' versions of the first film had a decided impact on the way the children responded to the second. Their fantasy predisposition was less influential than the content of the adults' stories.

The older children were less influenced by the adult models. Rather, their imaginative predisposition was the deciding factor in how they described the second movie. Regardless of which adult version they had heard, those junior-high-school children who were rated high in fantasy showed far more imagination in their stories.

These and other experiments lead us to believe that fantasy play is indeed a kind of cognitive skill, a fundamental potentiality of all children. Normal development seems to require some aspects of imaginative play. The child combines novel associations with scraps of adult behavior and weaves them into his limited repertory of concepts. Fantasy play is one way in which a child carries out his explorations, not only through interaction with his environment but also through playful combinations and reexaminations of new ideas.

As a child develops a game such as "house" or "knights attacking a castle," he acquires mastery over the elements of the game and thinks of better ways to play it. Whether alone and talking to himself or with a companion, he gains verbal feedback from the game and he may develop a more differentiated vocabulary and a wider repertory of images.

As he grows older and the pressure increases for socializing his play, the child gradually "internalizes" his fantasy. When parents accept his imaginative play, or when the child is not shamed away from such activity, he may continue his fantasy play into late puberty, becoming quite skillful at this form of self-entertainment.

Predictably, children in the middle of large families are less inclined toward fantasy play. They are caught up in direct imitation of other children. It takes time and solitude to develop a rich imaginative life. Indeed, the indications that slum children show less complex fantasy play than other children may be attributed to the facts that their lives are spent in crowded conditions and that they lack consistent adult models for imaginative activity.

Freud theorized that fantasy processes grew out of early hallucinatory experiences of children during periods of drive arousal when gratification was delayed. The child gradually would experience the fantasy of gratification, partially reducing the drive and enabling him to "hold out" until sustenance arrived.

Seymour Feshbach made some ingenious attempts to test Freud's theory that fantasy partially reduces an aroused aggressive drive. His subjects, having been angered by insults from the experimenters, showed less residual resentment after being given an opportunity to write aggressive Thematic Apperception Test stories or to view an aggressive prize-fight film.

Richard Rowe and I applied this approach specifically to daydreaming rather than to projective fantasy. In our study we aroused anxiety instead of aggression. Our subjects were students who had to take surprise midterm examinations. Immediately after their test papers were collected, some of the students were allowed to engage in daydreaming. Others were assigned a distracting task. Results suggested that daydreaming did not reduce anxiety. If

"I picture an atomic bombing of the town I live in."

anything, daydreaming increased anxiety because the subjects could not avoid thinking about the situation in fantasy form.

But in other situations, daydreaming can reduce anxiety. In another study, Rowe placed subjects in a medical laboratory, taped electrical wires to them, and told them they shortly would receive an electric shock. Those subjects who daydreamed to divert themselves showed a reduction of the aroused heart rate caused by the threat of shock. But subjects who had no chance to daydream continued to show an accelerated heart rate. The subjects who were strongly predisposed to daydreaming, as measured by the daydream questionnaire, showed significantly less arousal in response to the experimental situation than those with little inclination to fantasy.

An elaborate study by Ann Pytkowicz, Nathaniel Wagner and Irwin Sarason of the University of Washington used sub-

jects rated high and low in daydreaming. They were subjected to insults, then given a chance to daydream or to tell Thematic Apperception Test stories. The experimenters found that both TAT fantasy and daydreaming worked equally well in reducing anger, but they worked best for those persons already inclined toward daydreaming. Contrary to a simple drive-reduction hypothesis, the investigators noted that the amount of aggression was not reduced. As the subjects engaged in fantasy activities, they shifted their aggression from the experimenter to themselves.

It may be that practiced daydreamers can engage in distracting imagery in the fantasy realm, or work out resolutions of their fear or anger. Thus, fantasy changes their mood, rather than reducing the amount of drive energy. Those not skilled in the use of fantasy, who are left to their own devices during a period of stress or while angered, actually may become more uncomfortable.

The issue of the functional role of daydreaming in relation to motivational or emotional processes is far from resolved. Moreover, the problem has broader implications, such as the effects of violence or sex in literature, art or movies. There is a general belief that sexual fantasy material is arousing and therefore ought to be limited to "mature audiences." But no restrictions are imposed on aggressive material presented to children. In effect, our folklore seems to argue that fantasy is drive-arousing in the sexual area, and drive-reducing in the area of aggression.

This latter notion has been seriously questioned by the work of several researchers. But it is still not known whether predisposition to fantasy might be a critical factor. Perhaps the daydreaming child is less likely to be aroused to direct action after witnessing violence in life or in a movie than the child who has little experience in fantasy play.

Another series of studies in this program dealt with daydreams in relation to information processing. Let us assume that daydreaming represents a special case of "noise" produced by the unceasing activities of our active brains. Ordinarily we are forced to ignore these "signals" in order to steer our way through our physical and social environments.

But when the flow of external information to be processed is markedly reduced, as when we prepare for sleep, there is a dramatic upsurge in awareness of one's interior monologues, self-generated imagery, or elaborate fantasy. Memories of the day's events flood into consciousness, touching off associations to earlier events or important unfinished business, leading to fantasies about what tomorrow will bring.

The results of a series of experiments, designed to examine fantasy processes, suggested distinct values in daydreaming and unearthed a wealth of materials about the process of fantasizing and free-association. In one experiment subjects seated in a small, dark, sensory-restriction chamber reported their thought content every 15 seconds. These signal detection and vigilance studies gave us a sample of thought that was independent of any stimulus and unrelated to any task. Reports were filled with fantasy like content, following the predictions of information theory. In another experiment, the electroencephalograph was used to record the eye-movement of subjects. Each person was left to think naturally, but whenever the polygraph showed periods of little or of considerable eye-movement, he was interrupted and asked to report his thought content. Tests were also made during periods of instructed fantasy, when the subject was asked to imagine that his deepest secret wish was coming true, and during conscious suppression, when he was asked to suppress his secret wish as if he wanted no one to read his mind. The Rapid-Eye-movement studies made under the opposed conditions were compared. As a result of the study of these comparisons, we now can make a number of generalizations.

Daydreaming can keep us entertained or reasonably alert under dull, monotonous conditions, but at the cost of missing some of what is going on "outside." When extreme alertness is demanded in a complex environment, daydreaming is less useful and may even become dangerous. It is as if the individual makes rapid estimates of the degree to which he will have to pay attention to his environment, and then allows himself some appropriate margin of time or "channel space" to indulge in fantasies, interpretative glosses on the scenery or his situation, or some other form of self-stimulation.

The situation is analogous to that of a driver. On a road he knows well, with little traffic, he feels free to drift off into an extensive daydream. On an unfamiliar city street where external information is irregular and not readily anticipated, too much attention to his thought-stream could be fatal.

To engage in a daydream, a person must withdraw part of his attention from his environment. When he is awake and in a normal environment, he somehow must screen out the material surrounding him. Perhaps he does this by fixing his gaze steadily at a spot in front of him, so that the image fades. With less external material to process, he can deal more effectively with internal material. This may account for the blank stare which tells us that someone with whom we're conversing really isn't listening but is lost in thought.

One of the important conclusions drawn from our program of research is that the ephemeral fantasy need not be so elusive a phenomenon. The properties of man's inner experience can be systematically studied by formal methods as well as by clinical observation. While the scientist may never see the actual inner imagery any more than he can see an electron, it should be possible to employ certain physiological or reporting measures in a sufficiently systematic fashion to ensure that we are indeed zeroing in on private experience.

The early psychoanalytic view that daydreaming is compensatory, defensive or drive-reducing does not seem either general enough or precise enough to become the basis of a model. Today it seems more reasonable to regard daydreaming as a consequence of the ongoing activity of the brain, and to apply models that relate to man's cognitive and affective environmental adaptation and his requirements for varied stimulation.

Very likely man's capacity to daydream is a fundamental characteristic of his constitution. Like other abilities—perceptual, motor or cognitive — it is there to be developed depending on circumstances.

The practiced daydreamer has learned the art of pacing so that he can shift rapidly between inner and outer channels without bumping into too many obstacles. He has developed a resource that gives him some control over his future through elaborate planning, some ability to amuse himself during dull train-rides or routine work, and some sources of stimulation to change his mood through fanciful inner play.

This heightened self-awareness also may bring to consciousness many things that less internally sensitive persons can avoid: awareness of faults, failures or the omnipresent threat of global destruction. The daydreamer thus pays a price for his highly-developed inner capacity. But perhaps it is well worth it.

"I see myself in the arms of a warm and loving person who satisfies all my needs."

Conscious Control of Brain Waves

By Joseph Kamiya

A YOUNG GIRL SITS ALONE. Her eyes are closed and electrodes are pasted to her skull. By consciously producing a particular brain wave, she turns on a steady tone that fills the darkened room. When she ceases to produce the brain wave, the room falls silent.

This is not a scene from a science-fiction drama, but an experiment in operant conditioning. Just as rats can be taught to press a bar, so people can be taught conscious control of their brain activity in a relatively short time. My studies indicate that by combining methods adapted from experimental psychology, computer technology and electrophysiology, we can increase our knowledge of the brain's function and of the elusive dimensions of consciousness, and can teach man to perceive and to control some of his brain functions.

The brain produces electrical activity from the moment of birth, and this activity can be recorded easily by means of the electroencephalograph. An electroencephalogram, or "EEG," shows a continuously changing series of wave patterns, waxing and waning in both size and rapidity of fluctuations and produced in seemingly random sequence. A number of these wave patterns—the alpha, beta, theta and delta rhythms—have been identified and named according to the number of cycles per second and the amplitude of the wave.

My experiments have been concerned with the alpha wave, a rhythm between eight and 12 cycles per second, with an amplitude up to about 50 microvolts. The alpha wave is the most prominent rhythm in the whole realm of brain activity and tends to come in bursts of a few waves to many hundreds. When one opens his eyes and reads or stares at something, the alpha rhythm disappears and is replaced by a random, low-voltage, mixed-frequency rhythm. Alpha rhythm is recorded most prominently from silver disk electrodes pasted to the scalp at the back of the head. These

MONITORING EEGS. Author Kamiya traces subject's control of alpha rhythms.

electrodes are connected to equipment in another room by means of wires.

While conducting experiments in sleep in 1958 at the University of Chicago, I compared EEGs made during the sleeping and waking states. I became fascinated by the alpha rhythms that came and went in the waking EEGs and wondered if, through laboratory experiments with this easily traced rhythm, a subject could be taught awareness of an internal state.

We began with a single subject. He was placed in a darkened room, told to keep his eyes closed, and his EEGs were monitored continually with equipment in an adjacent room. He was told that a bell would ring from time to time, sometimes when he was in state A (alpha) and at other times when he was in state B (non-alpha). Whenever he heard the bell, he was to guess which of the two states he was in. He was then told whether he was right or wrong.

The first day, he was right only about 50 per cent of the time, no better than chance. The second day, he was right 65 per cent of the time; the third day, 85 per cent. By the fourth day, he guessed right on every trial—400 times in a row. But the discrimination between the two states is subtle, so subtle that on the 401st trial, the subject deliberately guessed wrong to see if we had been tricking him. In order to be sure that he was differentiating between the two states from internal clues, we tried the experiments again without the bell. Perhaps, we speculated, since alpha and non-alpha are physiological states, they are connected with the threshold of hearing. But again he discriminated between the two states, saying A or B as he changed from one to the other.

We investigated the possibility that eye position might be related to alpha activity. We found that whenever our subject raised his eyes, there was a burst of alpha. Another test was run. This time he was required to look straight ahead, and his performance dropped from 100 per cent accuracy to 80 per cent. Yet within 40 trials he was back up to 100 per cent. Whatever relationship had existed between his eye position and his discernment of the alpha state was now destroyed.

These tests were repeated with 11 other subjects, and eight reached a significant proportion of correct guesses within seven sessions of about an hour each, although none reached the level of performance of our first subjects. These results suggested that a conditioned, introspective response had been established. When asked to describe the difference between the two states, all those who had taken part in the experiment described various kinds of visual imagery or "seeing with the mind's eye" as occurring in the non-alpha state. The alpha state commonly was reported as "not thinking," "letting the mind wander," or "feeling the heart beat." The task demanded focused attention, for when trained subjects were asked to repeat the alphabet backward during the trials, their discrimination of alpha dropped dramatically.

Interestingly we found that when subjects had successfully learned to discern the two states, they were able to control their minds to the extent of entering and sustaining *either* state upon our command.

Our studies here at Langley Porter Neuropsychiatric Institute in San Francisco have been on a somewhat different basis. The goal of these experiments has been to see if subjects can learn to control their alpha waves without first going through discrimination training. With the aid of digital logic components, we devised a circuit to respond to the occurrence of alpha waves by sounding a tone. As long as the alpha waves per-

sisted, the tone sounded. When the alpha waves stopped, so did the feedback.

The volunteer was seated in a darkened, sound-deadened room and challenged to find a way to keep the tone sounding. It was explained only that certain mental states produced the tone. Overt muscular movements were not allowed. At the end of each minute-long trial, he was told the per cent of time that he had been able to sustain the tone. After five such trials, his task was reversed. He was to suppress the tone for five additional one-minute trials. After 40 such tests, eight of the 10 subjects were able to control the tone, emitting

tranquil, calm and alert when they are in the alpha state, and about half of our subjects report the alpha state as very pleasant. Some of them asked us to repeat the tests so that they could experience once again the high alpha condition.

The reports, so closely resembling descriptions of Zen and Yoga meditation, were so provocative that we invited seven practiced Zen meditators to participate in our experiments. These men, who were experienced in Zen meditation, learned control of their alpha waves far more rapidly than did the average person. Meditation means long periods

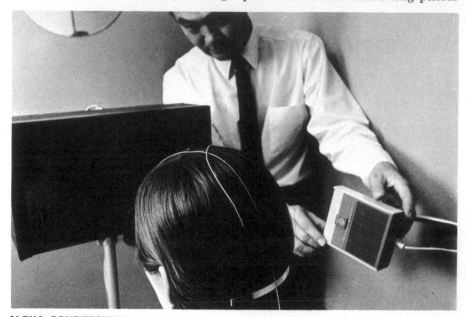

ALPHA CONDITIONING, CONTROL. Electrodes record when subject consciously produces particular brain wave. Graph, right, shows result of five one-minute trials in conditioning, graph, on far right, mean performance of 10 subjects in frequency control.

or suppressing alpha waves in accordance with our instructions. [*See illustration, center right*.] Again, visual imagery was reported as effective in decreasing the tone—and the alpha—while an alert calmness, a singleness of attention, and a passive "following" of the tone sustained it—and the bursts of alpha activity. Alpha waves apparently result from an alert, non-drowsy state, devoid of concrete, visual imagery.

This experiment on trained self-control of alpha waves has been confirmed at several other laboratories. Dr. Barbara Brown of the Sepulveda Veterans' Administration Hospital has successfully used a light instead of a tone to help people turn on their alpha waves with their eyes *open*. Each time the alpha train was interrupted, the light dimmed and went out. Even though visual imagery has an initial suppressive effect on alpha activity, her subjects also learned to control their alpha waves.

People describe themselves as being

of sitting still, of turning the attention inward, and of learning to control the mind and body, and so the conditions required for the experiment were perhaps not strange to this special group.

The work of Tomio Hirai and of Akira Kasmatsu of Tokyo University is especially interesting in this context. They found a high correlation between EEG patterns and the number of years of Zen practice and the proficiency rating of Zen masters. These two researchers described progressive changes in the EEG of Zen masters during meditation: prominent alpha activity (with eyes open); increased alpha amplitude, particularly in the central as opposed to the posterior cortical regions; the slowing of alpha frequency; and—in mystics with 20 years or more of Zen practice—the appearance of trains of theta activity. (The theta wave is even slower than the alpha wave and has a rhythm of five to seven cycles per second.) In another study, B. K. Anand, G. S. Chhina and Balden Singh of the All-India Institute of Medical Sciences in New Delhi, found that beginning Yoga students with pronounced alpha activity in their EEG patterns while they were at rest had an unusual aptitude for the practice of Yoga.

The great interest at present in comparing various subjective states with that state produced by psychedelic drugs—and the deliberate use of these drugs to alter states of consciousness—indicates a possible value in studies of alpha wave control during the LSD experience. A study by Barbara Brown indicates that, by listening to the subject's report of his drug experience, one can predict the

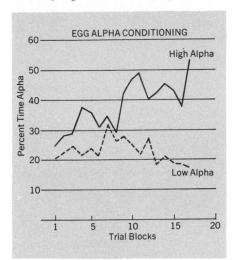

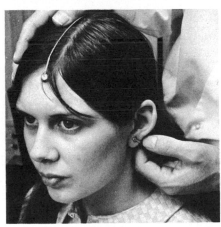

drug's effect on his alpha activity. If he reports only diffused states of feeling, his EEG will reveal little or no change; if he reports visual hallucinations, his EEG will show low alpha activity.

It must be stressed that there is no connection between alpha waves and extrasensory perception. People tend to associate the two because radio waves are involved in communication, but radio waves are generated at several thousand cycles per second, while brain waves range between a fraction of a cycle and about 100 cycles per second, with most of the energy limited to about 15 cycles per second. Also, the amount

of energy involved is so infinitesimal that a powerful receiver placed half an inch from the skull could never detect it. There is thus no evidence of electromagnetic radiation to the outside world by brain activity.

While the alpha rhythm covers the range from eight to 12 cycles per second, the dominant alpha frequency for each person is different and probably varies no more than half a cycle at any time. With this in mind, we tested the ability of 10 volunteers to increase or decrease consciously the frequency of their alpha rhythm. [*See illustration, below.*] Each volunteer heard a series of clicks instead of a steady tone. With digital logic devices we compared single alpha cycle durations with a standard duration preselected for the subject, so that about half of his cycle would be shorter than this standard. If the alpha rhythm took longer to complete its cycle than the individual's standard (fewer cycles per second), he heard a high-pitched click; when the rhythm was completed before his standard (more cycles per second), he heard a low-pitched click. The subject was told only that the clicks were generated by his brain waves and that his job was to increase the number of high clicks. Most people managed to control their average alpha frequency by this method, although they found it difficult to describe precisely what they did to gain control.

Since we first began experimenting at the University of Chicago, we have tested over 100 people. A few produced no alpha waves at all. Of those who did produce alpha waves, 80 to 90 per cent learned to control them to at least some degree. We found that people who were relaxed, comfortable and cooperative tended to produce more alpha waves than those who felt tense, suspicious and fearful, or who actively thought of what

was going to happen next. We found that people peak and then level off in the extent to which they can control the emission of alpha waves. Most of the people with whom we worked have been young, college-educated adults, from 18 to 45 years old. The youngest person we tested was 15, the oldest, 60.

More work needs to be done with other groups to determine what results can be obtained with uneducated people, people with low I.Q.s, and with professional groups such as bankers or insurance salesmen. It would be revealing to do a study with young children, who do not have a differentiated, sophisticated vocabulary and who lack abstract concepts for these internal states. They might give us a fresh look at what goes on inside our bodies, and they might prove even more skilled at controlling their own brain waves than adults.

We have only scratched the surface of a challenging new field. These studies need to be expanded even further into what might be called a "psychophysiology of consciousness." Each of the different brain rhythms could be investigated as we have studied the alpha wave. The activity of the autonomic nervous system is now being explored in my laboratories. The heart rate, visceral contractions, palm sweating, and muscle tension can be brought under control by this method. Our preliminary studies already indicate that the systolic blood pressure of some hypertensive patients may be subject to learned control.

Dimensional analysis of the specific psychological states associated with the control of physiological processes seems to be a worthy goal. This would require a computer that can store information, compare the relation among several measures in a single subject, and produce an instantaneous feedback. The fact that for many centuries mystics have been doing something measurably real suggests that the meditative tradition is worth examination. Learning the essence of this obscure, dimly comprehended tradition might strip it of much of its mystical quality.

We have expended very little systematic effort in our culture on teaching people to discern and control the inner workings of their bodies. Once we are able to control these body functions, immense possibilities suddenly lie before us. We then will have the tools for an intensive exploration of the consciousness of man. Different subjective states —anxiety, misery, euphoria or tranquility—might be mapped with the aid of trained subjects. Their reports of these various internal states could be related to their EEGs and to the various reactions of their autonomic nervous systems. Perhaps, through methods like factor analysis, we can discover that anxiety consists of a particular proportion of beta and a wave not yet identified, together with specific degrees of certain measurable autonomic responses. We suspect that tranquility and alpha activity somehow are connected.

Psychiatrists and psychologists, today's specialists on matters of the mind, disagree on most of the fundamental issues concerning consciousness. Through an intensive investigation such as we have proposed, the discontinuity between the subjective and the objective aspects of psychology and psychiatry might dissolve, and we would have a unified science. Someday it might be possible to examine a patient's physiological states and diagnose his neurosis just as the physician now detects tuberculosis by examining an X-ray. And if certain mental states can be defined, people can be trained to reproduce them. Instead of gulping a tranquilizer, one might merely reproduce the state of tranquility that he learned by the kind of training used in our studies. Perhaps our increasing concern over control of the individual by psychological persuasion could be diminished. People with full control of their internal states might be better prepared to resist external control. Studies of learning as a physiological process might disclose ways to increase the efficiency of learning in our schools and colleges. Trained control of bodily states might well be added to the curriculum, perhaps beginning as early as elementary school.

Suppose that we can measure the effect of a Beethoven concerto or a Shakespearean sonnet or a painting by Van Gogh. Would critics of the future be replaced by psychologists? They might at least be compelled to use a precise language. For the first time we might have a precise language for them to use because, to the extent that brain waves and other physiological states represent various states of mind, man would at last have an exact vocabulary for interpersonal communication.

Today we are little better informed about human consciousness than were Plato and Aristotle. By combining the methods of modern psychology and the advances in electronics and data-processing, perhaps one day we will make the same kind of stride physics has taken since the days of Democritus.

By MURRAY E. JARVIK

THE PSYCHOPHARMACOLOGICAL REVOLUTION

ONE HOT August evening in 1955, Helen Burney sat listlessly on her bed in the violent ward of the large Texas hospital where she had been confined for the past four months. During most of that unhappy time, Helen had been highly vocal, abusive, and overactive. Only the day before she had tried to strike a ward aide, but immediately several burly attendants had grabbed her, roughly tying her into a straitjacket and pinioning her arms against her chest. But today Helen's behavior was very different. Her incessant talking and shouting had stopped; all day long she spoke only when spoken to; most of the time she lay on her bed with her eyes half closed, moving little, and looking rather pale. However, she was unusually cooperative with the nursing personnel, got out of bed when told to, and went to the dining room without resisting. What had happened to bring about this remarkable change?

That morning she had received an injection of a new synthetic drug, chlorpromazine, which had been discovered a few years earlier in France. On the same day thousands of mental patients throughout the world were receiving the same drug, many of them for the first time. News of the drug's usefulness had spread rapidly in the preceding months, and it was being tried in mental hospitals throughout the world. Few of those taking or administering the drug realized that they were participating in a revolution in psychiatric treatment. In fact, many psychiatrists felt that this drug would be no more effective in treating schizophrenia than the other drugs which had previously been tried with little success. But they were wrong—and luckily, too—for there was little else they could offer the masses of impoverished patients who clogged the mental institutions all over the world. Soon it would be difficult to find a psychotic patient who was not receiving a drug of some kind for the treatment of his illness. The era of clinical psychopharmacology had begun, and the new drugs were hailed as the first real breakthrough in the treatment of one of man's most serious and mysterious afflictions—psychosis.

Until it was discovered that drugs could help the severely disturbed, almost the only recourse in the management of such patients was physical restraint. Philippe Pinel, the famous French psychiatrist, campaigning for humane treatment of the insane at the end of the 18th century, freed the inmates of the grim Bicetre mental hospital from their iron chains. Unfortunately, other physical restraints had to be substituted when patients became assaultive or destructive, and though the padded cell and the camisole, or straitjacket, may have been softer than chains, they allowed no greater freedom. Not until the mid-1950's did drugs finally promise total emancipation from physical restraint for

most patients. Despite the fears of some psychiatrists, psychologists, and social workers that the social and psychological factors contributing to mental illness would be ignored, the use of psychopharmaceuticals radically improved the treatment of the mentally ill within and without the hospital. Indeed, only with their use has it been possible for some families to be held together, for some individuals to be gainfully employed, and for some patients to be reached by psychotherapy.

Since 1955, psychopharmacology has burgeoned as an important scientific discipline in its own right. In the past 15 years, many new chemical agents have been developed for the treatment of each major category of mental illness. These drugs include phenothiazines, rauwolfia alkaloids, butyrophenones, propanediol and benzodiazepine compounds, monoamine oxidase (MAO) inhibitors, dibenzazepine derivatives, and many more. They have been found useful in the treatment of psychoses, neuroses, and depressions. Even autistic behavior, psychopathy, sexual deviation, and mental retardation have been attacked with drugs, but clinical psychopharmacologists feel that the surface has only been scratched in these areas. The search continues, though presently on a smaller scale than in the past, for more effective agents.

Folk-Psychopharmacology

Although as a full-fledged scientific discipline psychopharmacology is less than 15 years old, the psychological effects of drugs have piqued the curiosity of occasional researchers for almost a hundred years. Indeed, it is surprising that interest was so slow in developing, for man's empirical knowledge of the effects of drugs on behavior is both ancient and widespread.

The records of mankind, going back thousands of years, are filled with anecdotal and clinical reports of the psychological action of drugs obtained from plants. Though we can be sure that most of these folk remedies were merely placebos, a few have demonstrable me-

dicinal properties and are still in use today. The cuneiform tablets of ancient Assyria contain numerous references to medicinal preparations with psychological effects. For more than 5000 years, the Chinese have used the herb Ma Huang (yellow astringent), which contains the potent stimulant, ephedrine, and in the earliest writings of China, Egypt, and the Middle East there are references to the influence of various drugs on behavior.

In the first century before Christ, the Roman poet Horace wrote lyrically of the psychological effects of **alcohol:** "What wonders does not wine! It discloses secrets; ratifies and confirms our hopes; thrusts the coward forth to battle; eases the anxious mind of its burthen; instructs in arts. Whom has not a cheerful glass made eloquent! Whom not quite free and easy from pinching poverty!" And "In vino veritas" was already a familiar Roman adage when it was cited by Pliny.

Opium, an effective folk remedy, is mentioned in the Ebers papyrus, and Homer tells us that Helen of Troy took a "sorrow-easing drug" obtained from Egypt—probably opium. Although the

analgesic and sedative properties of opium were extensively described in classical literature, little was said about its addictive properties until Thomas de Quincy hinted at them, early in the 19th century, in his *Confessions of an English Opium Eater.* And while the chemical isolation of morphine and the invention of the hypodermic needle, in the middle of the 19th century, made profound addiction truly feasible, morphine is still considered by many physicians the most

essential drug they use — "God's own remedy."

Morphine and its derivatives and analogs (for example, heroin) are self-administered by countless thousands of people throughout the world, although in many countries, especially in the West, such use is illegal. The practice persists, nevertheless, perhaps for the reasons given by the French poet, Jean Cocteau, who was himself an addict: "Everything that we do in life, including love, is done in an express train traveling towards death. To smoke opium is to leave the train while in motion; it is to be interested in something other than life and death."

Like morphine, **cocaine** is another vegetable product discovered by primitive man. It is clearly not a placebo, and its use is illegal. The Indians of Peru have chewed coca leaves for centuries, and still do, to relieve hunger, fatigue, and the general burdens of a miserable life. The alkaloid cocaine was isolated in 1859, and its systematic use was not only practiced but advocated by such respected figures as Sigmund Freud and William Halsted, as well as by the legendary Sherlock Holmes. It is highly doubtful that the continued use of cocaine produces a physiological dependence. Today, cocaine-taking is relatively uncommon in the northern hemisphere.

On the other hand, an ancient drug which remains exceedingly popular, though its medical uses today are nil, is **marijuana,** the dried leaves of the hemp plant *Cannabis sativa.* Cannabis is so ubiquitous, and grows so easily, that its widespread use is not  surprising. Marco Polo is credited with bringing the "Green Goddess" to the Occident, although Herodotus tells us that the Scythians inhaled the vapor, obtained by heating hemp seeds on red-hot stones, and then "shouted for joy." To this day, cannabis is almost always smoked; this allows its active ingredients to be absorbed into the pulmonary blood circulation and, avoiding the liver, to be promptly carried to the brain. Similarly, the active ingredients of opium and tobacco are usually self-administered by inhalation of the vapors from heated plant products.

Hashish, derived from cannabis, and

smoked, chewed, or drunk, has been widely used for centuries throughout the Middle East. The Arabic term for a devotee of hashish is "hashshash;" from the plural, "hashshashin," comes the English word "assassin," for at the time of the Crusades, the Hashshashin were a fanatical secret Moslem sect who terrorized the Christians by swift and secret murder, after having taken hashish to give themselves courage. Richard Burton, the famous traveler, adventurer, and writer, described his experiences with hashish during a pilgrimage to Mecca at the end of the 19th century. About 50 years earlier, Moreau de Tours suggested that physicians should take hashish in order to experience mental illness and thereby understand it better. Claude Bernard, the great French physiologist, is said to have declared that "hashish is the curare of the mind." Today we know a great deal about the mode of action of curare and almost nothing about that of hashish, but Bernard suggested a working hypothesis. Perhaps cannabis, like curare, blocks some vital neurohumor in the brain.

Quantitative, objective studies of cannabis are rare, even today. However, a recent report by Carlini indicates that cannabis facilitates maze-learning in rats. In the absence of comparative studies, it is difficult to say how cannabis resembles or differs from other drugs; anecdotal reports suggest that it resembles lysergic acid diethylamide (LSD).

Another drug with a long history of use is **mescaline** or **peyote,** which the Aztecs are credited with having used five centuries ago, and which has been and still is used by certain Indians of Central America and the Southwest United States. Its effects resemble those of marijuana and LSD; they have also been compared with those of **psilocybin,** a drug which the Aztecs derived from a psychotogenic mushroom they called "teonanacatl," or "God's flesh."

The Chemical Era

Until the 19th century, the only drugs known to affect behavior were those de-

rived from plants and long familiar to mankind. With advances in chemistry during the first half of the 19th century, however, the general anesthetics, including nitrous oxide, diethyl ether, and chloroform were discovered and brought into widespread use; and by the time Emil Kraepelin began his psychopharmacological investigations in the 1880's, a few new sedatives, including the bromides and chloral hydrate, were available.

Nitrous oxide, an artificially prepared inhalation anesthetic, was investigated by Sir Humphrey Davy, who described its effects thus in 1799: "I lost all connections with external things; trains of vivid images rapidly passed through my mind and even connected with words in such a manner as to produce perceptions perfectly novel. I existed in a world of newly connected and newly modified ideas."

Inhaling nitrous oxide soon became a favorite student diversion, and enterprising showmen charged admission for public demonstrations of its effects; the popular interest in this gas reminds one very much of the current preoccupation with LSD. But though nitrous oxide was beguiling to thrill seekers, it never became as popular as LSD, perhaps because the gas is difficult to transport. Although **diethyl ether** was originally prepared in 1543 by Valerius Cordus when he distilled alcohol with sulfuric acid, its potential as an anesthetic remained unknown for 300 years until Crawford Long and William Morton first used it clinically in the 1840's. Ether parties subsequently became popular among students, although the drug's extreme flammability probably discouraged more widespread and persisting popular use. **Chloroform** was introduced about the same time as ether, but its toxic effects upon the heart, recognized almost immediately, discouraged its nonmedical use. It was not known for many years that the liver, also, is severely damaged by this drug.

Chloral hydrate, a powerful sleep-producing drug, was introduced into medicine in 1869 but has been generally ignored by experimental psychologists—though not by the underworld where, in the form of "knockout drops" mixed with alcohol, it has been the active in-

gredient of the "Mickey Finn." **Paraldehyde,** first used in 1882, has similarly been eschewed by psychological investigators, perhaps because of its extremely unpleasant odor; nevertheless, it has been used extensively for many years in mental institutions for producing temporary narcosis in dangerously violent patients, especially those with delirium tremens from alcohol withdrawal.

Bromides, particularly potassium bromide, slowly gained popularity during the 19th century to the point where millions of people were taking them as sedatives. Unlike the barbiturates, however, the bromides produce psychoses involving delirium, delusions, hallucinations, as well as a variety of neurological and dermatological disturbances. For a time, chronic toxicity resulting from continued use of these compounds became a leading cause of admission to mental hospitals. Bromide is still a common ingredient in headache remedies, "nerve tonics," and over-the-counter sleeping medications.

The Antipsychotic Drugs

With the antipsychotic drugs, as happens more often than is supposed, use preceded research. The ancient preparation, Indian snakeroot powder, mentioned more than 2500 years ago in the Hindu Ayurvedic writings, deserves at least as much credit for ushering in the era of clinical psychopharmacology as does the modern synthetic drug, chlorpromazine. According to the ancient doctrine of signs, since the roots of the plant *Rauwolfia serpentina* were snake-like, they were administered for snakebite. Snakeroot was also used for insomnia and insanity—quite rational uses,

in view of modern findings—as well as for epilepsy and dysentery which it actually aggravates, and for a host of other conditions for which its value is questionable.

The first scientific intimation that Indian snakeroot might be useful in mental illness came in 1931 when Sen and Bose published an article in the *Indian Medical World* entitled "*Rauwolfia serpentina,* a new Indian drug for insanity and high blood pressure." But this suggestion was not confirmed for almost a quarter of a century. Rauwolfia began to attract the attention of the Western world only in 1949, when Rustom Valkil advocated it for hypertension, and the Swiss pharmaceutical firm, Ciba, subsequently isolated the active ingredient which they named **reserpine.** In 1953 a Boston physician, Robert Wilkins, confirmed that reserpine was effective in the treatment of hypertension, and a year later a New York psychiatrist, Nathan Kline, announced that he had found reserpine useful in the treatment of psychotic disorders. Soon numerous psychiatrists in other parts of the world corroborated Kline's results, and the use of reserpine spread with amazing speed. When Frederick Yonkman at Ciba used the term "tranquilizing" to describe the calming effect of reserpine, the word "tranquilizer" entered all modern languages to designate a drug which quiets hyperactive or anxious patients.

The subsequent clinical history of reserpine is a strange one. Reserpine and chlorpromazine were twin heralds of the dawn of psychopharmacological treatment, but the popularity of reserpine in the treatment of mental disease has dwindled until today, a decade and a half later, its use has been practically abandoned for such therapy while chlorpromazine is still the leading antipsychotic drug. Yet there are many studies which attest to the efficacy of rauwolfia and its derivatives in the treatment of psychiatric disorders; probably its tendency to produce depression was one of

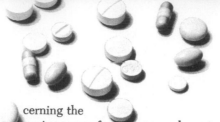

the chief reasons for its near demise. Furthermore, chlorpromazine has spawned scores of offspring-phenothiazines, widely used for the mentally ill.

Like reserpine, **chlorpromazine's** usefulness as an antipsychotic drug was discovered more or less by accident. In the early 1950's the French surgeon, Henri Laborit, introduced chlorpromazine into clinical anesthesia as a successor to promethazine, known to be a sedative antihistamine capable of heightening the effect of other drugs. It was noticed that chlorpromazine reduced anxiety in surgical patients and enabled them to face their ordeal with indifference. This led to its trial with agitated psychotics, whom it calmed with dramatic effectiveness. In 1954 the drug was released commercially in North America by Smith, Kline and French as an antiemetic, but shortly thereafter it was tried with psychiatric patients. Large-scale controlled studies by the United States Veterans Administration and by the Psychopharmacology Service Center of the National Institute of Mental Health showed chlorpromazine and the related phenothiazines to be useful in the treatment of acute schizophrenia. Other studies show that phenothiazines help discharged mental patients to stay out of the hospital. A drug with ubiquitous actions on all body systems, chlorpromazine has been used in the treatment of anxiety and tension, depression, mental retardation, senility, drug addiction, pain, nausea and vomiting, and spasticity. Since its mechanisms of action are still not known, it is difficult to delimit the validity of these applications.

Anti-Anxiety Drugs

Anxiety is such a common experience that everyone reading this article has a subjective understanding of the term. It may be defined as an unpleasant state associated with a threatening situation, and is closely allied to fear. Sedative hypnotic drugs including alcohol, barbiturates, bromides, and chloral hydrate, have frequently been employed for the treatment of anxiety. In 1955 a number of new drugs with properties common to the sedative hypnotics were introduced for the treatment of anxiety, but the most successful of these, by far, was **meprobamate,** popularly known as Miltown or Equanil. Many of the arguments con-

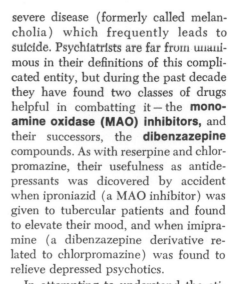

cerning the uniqueness of meprobamate revolve around its similarity or dissimilarity to the barbiturates. But since the properties of the various barbiturates differ from one another, it is not easy to compare the whole class to meprobamate. All, however, tend to produce sleep when used in large doses, to produce effects reported as pleasant, and to produce convulsive seizures as a consequence of sudden withdrawal after the prolonged administration of large doses. Giving meprobamate to a patient suffering from neurotic anxiety is not quite the same as inserting a nail into a broken bone to hold it together, or giving insulin to a diabetic. In giving meprobamate, we are employing a drug with a poorly defined action to treat a poorly defined condition. But the condition is widespread, important, and demands action, and the drug seems to help.

In any case, meprobamate's standing as the most popular tranquilizer was soon usurped by **chlordiazepoxide** (Librium). This compound strongly resembles meprobamate and the barbiturates, but there do appear to be differences which the experimentalist can measure. For example, Leonard Cook and Roger Kelleher recently reported an experiment in which rats could postpone a punishing shock by pressing a lever. Cook and Kelleher found that at some doses chlordiazepoxide will produce an increase in the rate of lever pressing whereas meprobamate does not. Also it has been shown with a Lashley jumping stand that rats will sometimes become "fixated" if the discrimination problem is made insoluble. Chlordiazepoxide seems to eliminate this fixated behavior whereas meprobamate does not. The possible differences in the behavioral effects of sedative hypnotic drugs have not yet been fully explored, and the study of these differences should tell us a great deal about the drugs themselves.

Anti-Depression Drugs

While depression, at least in a mild form, is an experience perhaps as common as anxiety, it can also constitute a severe disease (formerly called melancholia) which frequently leads to suicide. Psychiatrists are far from unanimous in their definitions of this complicated entity, but during the past decade they have found two classes of drugs helpful in combatting it—the **monoamine oxidase (MAO) inhibitors,** and their successors, the **dibenzazepine** compounds. As with reserpine and chlorpromazine, their usefulness as antidepressants was dicovered by accident when iproniazid (a MAO inhibitor) was given to tubercular patients and found to elevate their mood, and when imipramine (a dibenzazepine derivative related to chlorpromazine) was found to relieve depressed psychotics.

In attempting to understand the etiology of depression, it is ironic that biochemists have not hesitated to rush in where experimental psychologists fear to tread. What has emerged, based on a combination of clinical observations and animal studies, is the *catecholamine theory* of depression. Broadly interpreted, the theory says that a state of well-being is maintained by continuous adrenergic stimulation of certain receptors in the brain by catecholamines like norepinephrine and dopamine (hormones produced in the brain). For example, reserpine's so-called tranquilizing effect—indifference to surroundings, lack of appetite, and apparent lassitude—is attributed to depletion of catecholamines. Another compound, alphamethyltyrosine, which decreases the synthesis of catecholamines, has been found to produce "depression" in animals. On the other hand, some compounds have been found which produce an increase in the level of brain catecholamines. Administration of MAO inhibitors, which inactivate MAO and thus prevent catecholamine from being destroyed, produce increased levels of catecholamines and greater alertness, activity, and degree of electrical self-stimulation (in animals implanted with electrodes in "reward" areas of the brain). Administering the precursors of catecholamines—for example, dihydroxyphenylalanine (DOPA)—or MAO inhibitors, will prevent or reverse the depression caused by reserpine [*see illustration opposite page*].

The dibenzazepine compounds, typified by **imipramine** (Tofranil), do not change the level of brain catecholamines in animals, yet they are effective antidepressants. However, the mode of action of these compounds may be compatible with the theory. Studies show that the catecholamine level in the brain is reduced, not only by enzymatic de-

struction, (for example, by MAO), but also by reabsorption of the catecholamines into the neurons. It has been hypothesized that the dibenzazepine compounds potentiate the action of normally present catecholamines by preventing this reabsorption.

LSD

LSD shares the responsibility with reserpine and chlorpromazine for ushering in the psychopharmacology era. Albert Hofmann's accidental discovery of this substance at Sandoz Pharmaceuticals in Basel, Switzerland in 1943 is now well known. LSD is a semi-synthetic compound of plant origin, a derivative of ergot (a fungus which infects rye). Although its effects are similar to those of marijuana and mescaline, its outstanding characteristic is its extreme potency, and its ability to produce bizarre mental states picturesquely described by Humphrey Osmond as psychedelic or "mind-expanding." The ability of LSD to block 5-hydroxytryptamine (another amine resembling the catecholamines in some respects, abbreviated 5HT) and thus to change brain levels of 5HT, has excited interest. More recently Maimon Cohen has reported the frightening finding that LSD can damage chromosomes. The role of LSD in producing a psychotic state has not been established. Despite thousands of papers dealing with this substance, we have very little idea of what LSD does, and we don't know how it does it. It is unfortunate that legal restrictions and the manufacturers' understandable diffidence make this fascinating chemical inaccessible for research.

There is something in the use or action of psychotogenic or "hallucinogenic"

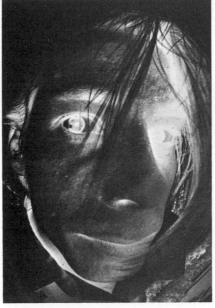

drugs which appeals to certain towering if unconventional figures in literature and the arts. From the time of Toulouse-Lautrec through the era of the expatriates (Gertrude Stein, James Joyce, Ernest Hemingway), bohemian Paris was not exactly abstemious nor did it restrict itself to alcohol for thrills or new sensations. Though the virtues of illicit drugs do not appear in paid advertisements in the public press, nevertheless very talented "copywriters" have turned out glowing testimonials to promote the use of these drugs. Thomas de Quincey and Samuel Coleridge, at the beginning of the 19th century, recommended opium, and Paolo Mantegazza in 1859 gave highly colored accounts of the beatific effects of coca. Freud also approved of cocaine and advised his fiancée to take it. Charles Baudelaire, called the "De Quincey of hashish," was supported

by Arthur Rimbaud and Paul Verlaine in acclaiming the beneficence of this drug; more recently Aldous Huxley declared that the "doors of perception" could be opened by mescaline and LSD. Many jazz, swing, bop, and other musicians claim that marijuana and other stimulant drugs enhance their playing or composing.

Whether drugs truly enhance creativity is a moot point. Artists, poets, scientists, and inventors will testify that LSD or marijuana or amphetamine inspired them to produce works of value, but controlled experiments to test these claims are lacking. Who would not like to find a magic drug that would turn an ugly frog into a handsome prince, or a Cinderella into a princess? Drugs can sometimes seem to have magic powers, but they do not ordinarily instill beauty, wisdom, and virtue into the taker. Yet estrogens can change a skinny adolescent girl into a beauty queen and, if one can extrapolate from cases of precocious puberty (or infant Hercules), super-androgens must be responsible for Clark Kent's transformation into Superman.

Drugs do change our perception of the world, and when this perception becomes unbearable, as in terminal cancer, drug use is clearly justified. The question is whether it is justified for the relief of unhappiness, dissatisfaction, or boredom. The religious uses of wine and peyote for sacramental purposes have, in part, inspired Timothy Leary to found a new religion, the League for Spiritual Discovery (LSD), which advocates the use of LSD and other so-called psychedelic drugs. The legal difficulties of this organization have spurred city, state, and federal legislative and enforcement bodies to enter the field of psychopharmacology in order to control the distribution and use of behavior-affecting drugs. But the government is trying to make rules about substances which are still poorly understood, and it rests with psychopharmacologists to clarify the action of psychotogenic drugs so that such rules can be made on a more rational basis.

The Birth of Scientific Psychopharmacology

Without the spur of clinical success, it is doubtful that basic research in the effects of drugs on behavior could have advanced very rapidly. During the first half of the 20th century, drugs were seldom used in the treatment of mental illness, since morphine, cocaine, barbiturates, and other sedative hypnotics had already been tried and proven generally ineffective. Other more physical

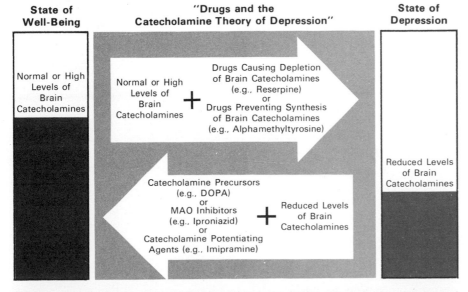

State of Well-Being	"Drugs and the Catecholamine Theory of Depression"	State of Depression
Normal or High Levels of Brain Catecholamines	Normal or High Levels of Brain Catecholamines + Drugs Causing Depletion of Brain Catecholamines (e.g., Reserpine) or Drugs Preventing Synthesis of Brain Catecholamines (e.g., Alphamethyltyrosine) →	Reduced Levels of Brain Catecholamines
	← Catecholamine Precursors (e.g., DOPA) or MAO Inhibitors (e.g., Iproniazid) or Catecholamine Potentiating Agents (e.g., Imipramine) + Reduced Levels of Brain Catecholamines	

Relationships between drug-produced changes in brain catecholamine levels and changes in mental states provide evidence for the "catecholamine theory of depression."

The classification of some major drugs and their properties are outlined in this table. Complex psychological and pharmacological effects require some multiple listings. Only one trade name is listed for each drug. The question mark (?) indicates unknown information.

approaches to therapy, including hydrotherapy, occupational therapy, and psychosurgery had been employed with varying results. Only electroconvulsive shock (ECS) seemed to be very successful, but its administration required considerable skill. Psychiatrists depended chiefly, therefore, on psychological methods (primarily communicative interactions) which, unfortunately, were usually inefficient and ineffective for the majority of severely psychotic individuals.

Experimental psychologists showed only an intermittent and desultory interest in the effects of drugs on behavior. A handful of drugs had already been investigated, but the results were of very little interest to the most influential psychologists who were busy, in the 1930's and 1940's, building their own psychological systems or attacking rival systems.

In fact, however, psychopharmacology had already been born more than half a century earlier. In 1879 the first laboratory of experimental psychology had been established at Leipzig by Wilhelm Wundt. One of Wundt's most famous students was Emil Kraepelin, sometimes called the father of modern psychiatry because he invented a widely used system for classifying mental disorders. Kraepelin might also be called the father of scientific psychopharmacology, for he applied Wundt's new experimental methods to investigate the influence of drugs on psychological functions. Kraepelin studied pharmacology at Tartu in Estonia, then a center of research in this field. During his stay there he demonstrated that alcohol, morphine, and other drugs impair reaction time and the mental processes involved in associational learning. It is an ironic coincidence that Kraepelin was interested in the two areas which finally coalesced 75 years later—basic, quantitative, experimental psychopharmacology, and the treatment of mental disease.

Though psychopharmacology had little scientific status at the beginning of the 20th century, Kraepelin's early work was continued by a few psychologists who studied the effects of alcohol, caffeine, cocaine, strychnine, and nicotine. In 1908 the Englishman, W. H. R. Rivers, reported on the influence of drugs

308

Drug Class	Group
PSYCHOTHERAPEUTICS These drugs are typical of many used in the treatment of psychological and psychiatric disorders.	
Anti-psychotic drugs are used primarily to treat major psychoses, such as schizophrenia, manic depressive psychoses, and senile psychoses.	**ANTI-PSYCHOTIC:** Rauwolfia alkaloids Phenothiazines
Anti-anxiety drugs are used to combat insomnia, induce muscle relaxation, treat neurotic conditions, and reduce psychological stress.	**ANTI-ANXIETY:** Propanediols Benzodiazepines Barbiturates
Anti-depressant drugs are effective in the treatment of psychiatric depression and phobic-anxiety states.	**ANTI-DEPRESSANT:** MAO Inhibitors Dibenzazepines
Stimulants (see **STIMULANTS,** below)	**STIMULANT:**
PSYCHOTOGENICS These drugs produce changes in mood, thinking, and behavior. The resultant drug state may resemble a psychotic state, with delusions, hallucinations, and distorted perceptions. These drugs have little therapeutic value.	Ergot derivative Cannabis sativa Lophophora williamsii Psilocybe mexicana
STIMULANTS These drugs elevate mood, increase confidence and alertness, and prevent fatigue. Analeptics stimulate the central nervous system and can reverse the depressant effects of an anesthetic drug. Caffeine and nicotine, found in beverages and tobacco, are mild stimulants.	Sympathomimetics Analeptics Psychotogenics Nicotinics Xanthines
SEDATIVES AND HYPNOTICS Most of these drugs produce general depression (sedation) in low doses and sleep (hypnosis) in larger doses. They are used to treat mental stress, insomnia, and anxiety.	Bromides Barbiturates Chloral derivatives General
ANESTHETICS, ANALGESICS, AND PARALYTICS These drugs are widely used in the field of medicine.	
General anesthetics act centrally to cause a loss of consciousness.	General anesthetics
Local anesthetics act only at or near the site of application.	Local anesthetics
Analgesic drugs, many of them addicting, typically produce euphoria and stupor, and are effective pain-relievers.	Analgesics
Paralytic drugs act primarily at the neuro-muscular junction to produce motor (muscular) paralysis, and are commonly used by anesthesiologists.	Paralytics
NEUROHUMORS (NEUROTRANSMITTERS) Adrenergic and cholinergic compounds are known to be synaptic transmitters in the nervous system. Other natural compounds (e.g., 5-HT, γ-aminobutyric acid, Substance P) may also be neurotransmitters.	Cholinergic Adrenergic Others (?)

308

Example	Trade or Common Name	Natural or Synthetic	Usage	How Taken	First Used	Evidence of Addiction?
reserpine	(Serpasil)	nat	greatly diminished	injected ingested	1949	no
chlorpromazine	(Thorazine)	syn	widespread	injected ingested	1950	no
meprobamate	(Miltown)	syn	widespread	ingested	1954	yes
chlordiazepoxide	(Librium)	syn	widespread	ingested	1933	yes
phenobarbital	(see SEDATIVES, below)					
tranylcypromine	(Parnate)	syn	diminished	ingested	1958	no
imipramine	(Tofranil)	syn	widespread	ingested injected	1948	no
amphetamine	(see STIMULANTS, below)					
lysergic acid diethylamide	(LSD, Lysergide)	syn	widespread?	ingested	1943	no
marijuana	(hemp, hashish)	nat	widespread	smoked	?	no
mescaline	(peyote button)	nat	localized	ingested	?	no
psilocybin		nat	rare	ingested	?	no
amphetamine	(Benzedrine)	syn	widespread	ingested injected	1935	yes
pentylenetetrazol	(Metrazol)	syn	rare	ingested injected	1935	no
lysergic acid diethylamide	(see PSYCHOTOGENICS, above)					
nicotine		nat	widespread	smoked ingested	?	yes
caffeine		nat	widespread	ingested	?	yes
potassium bromide		syn	widespread	ingested	1857	no
phenobarbital	(Luminal)	syn	widespread	ingested injected	1912	yes
chloral hydrate		syn	rare	ingested	1875	yes
alcohol		nat	widespread	ingested	?	yes
nitrous oxide	("laughing gas")	syn	rare	inhaled	1799	no
diethyl ether		syn	greatly diminished	inhaled	1846	no
chloroform		syn	rare	inhaled	1831	no
cocaine	(coca)	nat	widespread	applied ingested	?	yes
procaine	(Novocaine)	syn	widespread	injected	1905	no
Opium derivatives	(morphine, heroin)	nat	widespread	injected smoked	?	yes
d-tubocurarine	(curare)	nat	widespread	injected	?	no
acetylcholine		nat syn	laboratory	injected	1926	no
norepinephrine		nat syn	laboratory	injected	1946	no
5-hydroxytryptamine	(5-HT, Serotonin)	nat syn	laboratory	injected	1948	no

on fatigue; in 1915 the Americans, Raymond Dodge and Francis Benedict, and Harry Hollingsworth (1912, 1924) examined the effects of drugs on motor and mental efficiency. In 1924 even Clark Hull, one of the most influential psychologists of the mid-20th century, studied the effect of pipe smoking and coffee drinking on mental efficiency, before he turned his attention to building theoretical systems.

Psychopharmacological research was spurred in the 1930's and 1940's by the imminence and advent of World War II, which aroused military interest in the applications of drugs, particularly the amphetamines, and concern about the psychological consequences of anoxia, i.e., severe oxygen deficiency. Both allied

and German soldiers were given amphetamines to combat sleeplessness and fatigue; these drugs were found to diminish fatigue, but whether they could raise performance above normal levels was an open question which is still not fully answered. Insufficient supply of oxygen to the brain was shown to adversely affect reasoning, memory, and sensory functioning; for example, it renders the subject less sensitive to visual stimuli, and prolongs the time needed for the eyes to adapt to the dark. Such

impairment was particularly serious in military pilots for whom the loss of judgment and sensory function resulting from lack of oxygen at high altitudes could be disastrous.

More recently a number of factors have converged to make psychopharmacology a popular field for research. During the mid-1950's, Europe and the United States were prospering, and governmental support for health services and medical research began to expand at an unprecedented rate. Spurred by therapeutic success and the possibilities of large profits, and as yet unencumbered by severe governmental restrictions concerning drug safety and efficacy, pharmaceutical companies were eager to discover new drugs prescribable to millions of waiting patients. Support for research on new psychotherapeutic drugs became big business. In addition, the Psychopharmacology Service Center, established within the National Institute of Mental Health, contributed millions of dollars for research on the psychological effects of drugs.

With the rise of psychopharmacology, clinical psychologists immediately began to devise methods, such as rating scales and questionnaires, to evaluate the effects of the new drug therapies. However, some of the psychotherapeutic achievements credited to the action of drugs may also be attributed to reforms in mental hospitals and better programs of community mental hygiene.

Psychological Methods in Psychopharmacological Research

To screen out potentially useful drugs and characterize their action, psychopharmacologists have used a variety of procedures in studies carried out with rats and mice. Measures of spontaneous motor activity are widely employed, as are other observational and rating techniques. Among the most favored procedures are those based on operant conditioning, because they are objective, automatic, generally quite reliable, and permit extended investigation of a single animal. The chief apparatus is the Skinner box, a cage containing a lever-pressing mechanism. Depending on the experimental conditions, depression of this lever can produce either a positive reinforcement (food) or a negative reinforcement (electrical shock). Some investigators feel that the schedule, and not the kind or amount of reinforcement, determines a particular drug susceptibility. Some schedules require that the animal respond quickly, or slowly, or in certain patterns, in order to obtain food

or avoid shock. On the other hand, even before the phenothiazines and reserpine appeared on the market, it was shown that these drugs seemed to selectively impair conditioned responses controlled by aversive consequences (that is, punishing shock) but had less effect upon

unconditioned responses. It appears that the strength of the stimulus and the nature of the motor response required are vital factors determining the relative susceptibility to different drugs.

Many psychopharmacologists not trained in the Skinnerian approach use discrimination boxes and mazes to study the effects of drugs, and a number also use classical conditioning procedures; maze-learning was used in a recent study which demonstrated that analeptics (such as strychnine) facilitate learning. Similarly, work on the amnesia produced by intracerebral antibiotics was based on results obtained with mazes and shuttle-boxes. Even single-trial learning procedures are being increasingly used to study the effects of drugs. Psychological research has not yet reached a point at which any one method of measuring behavior can be considered superior to any other.

Chemistry and the Brain

Psychologists have subdivided behavior in different ways, but they are in general agreement about certain broad categories of functions. If different psychological functions depend upon discrete chemical substances, then we

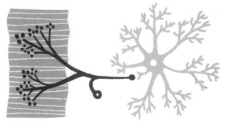

might expect to find specificity of drug action—that is, that certain drugs selectively affect certain functions. If the localization of psychological functions involves a grosser type of organization—if it depends, say, on complex neural connections—then we would not necessarily expect to find such specific relations between drug action and psychological function.

Certain sensory structures are clearly chemically coded. Taste and smell receptors obviously are and respond to specific drugs. Sodium dehydrochlorate and saccharin, even when injected into an antecubital vein, respectively produce a characteristic bitter or sweet taste on reaching the tongue and are used for measuring blood circulation time. Streptomycin and dihydrostreptomycin selectively, though not exclusively, attack the eighth nerve; visual effects are produced by santonin, digitalis, and LSD. Haptic sensations are said to be produced by cocaine ("cocaine bug"), but there is no good evidence that somesthetic sensory pathways are selectively affected by any chemical substance. Histamine and polypeptides, such as substance P or bradykinin, will at times produce itch or pain, and hint that sensory chemical specificity is a possibility.

Motor structures are also chemically coded and enable curariform drugs to have a selective paralyzing action. Similarly, autonomic ganglia can be affected selectively by different drugs and the vast field of peripheral neuropharmacology rests on such specificity.

We are beginning to learn how the central nervous system is organized neuropharmacologically. Histochemical, radioautographic, and fluorescent techniques are making such mapping possible. For example, it is known that the central nervous system pathways which control motivational mechanisms such as hunger, thirst, and sex, are susceptible to cholinergic, adrenergic, and hormonal substances. Further mapping of this kind is bound to result in better understanding of the relationship between drug action and functional localization in the central nervous system.

One can inhibit activity with a wide variety of depressant drugs or activate animals with stimulant drugs. No simple role can be ascribed to acetylcholine, norepinephrine, or 5-hydroxytryptamine (serotonin) in the control of behavior. What part, if any, these substances play in learning is even more mysterious. Some theorists have proposed an inhibitory cholinergic system balanced by an excitatory adrenergic system, and the facts seem to fit thus far. Of course, the brain is full of all species of chemicals which are waiting to be investigated by psychologists. Nucleic acids and particu-

larly ribonucleic acid (RNA) have been assigned a special role in learning by some, but evidence is conflicting. Proteins seem a more likely candidate, and such inhibitors of protein synthesis as puromycin and cyclohexamide do interfere with both memory and learning. The production of retrograde amnesia

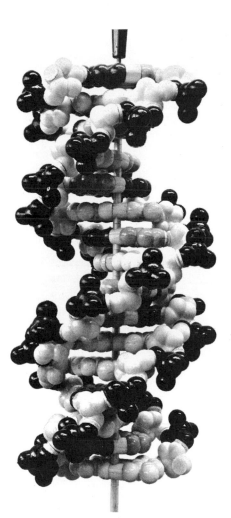

deoxyribonucleic acid (DNA)

and the post-trial facilitation of learning by drugs provide evidence for a consolidation process. [*See "Amnesia: A World Without Continuity," this section*]. But the experiments are difficult to perform, and many unspecified sources of variability will have to be identified before general mechanisms can be revealed.

The Future of Psychopharmacology

Ever since Loewenhoek's invention of the microscope, scientists have tended to believe that in the "ultra-fine structure" of an organism lie the explanations for its functioning. Hence it is not surprising that attempts to explain drug action are couched in terms of chemical binding to specific molecular receptors. However, behavior can no more be seen in a test tube full of brain homogenate, than can the theme of a mosaic be determined from an analysis of its stones. The Gestalt principle that the whole is something more than the sum of its parts is not always recognized by physical scientists who tend to be very analytical, to look at "parts" in their approach to explanation. The psychologist has an increasingly important role to play in psychopharmacology, for he must determine whether the particular sedative, antidepressant, psychotogenic, or facilitating drug which the biochemists and neurophysiologists want to study, really has the behavioral properties they think it does.

In the future it should be possible to say in what ways each important psychopharmaceutical influences behavior, and thus to characterize it by a behavioral profile, just as we can now describe a chemical in terms of its chromatographic pattern. Ultimately, it ought to be possible to look at the chemical structure of any new drug and predict whether it will be useful as an antipsychotic, an antifatigue agent, an appetite stimulant, and so forth. By the same token, the physiological determinants of behavior will be so well worked out that we will understand why a drug which causes alertness also depresses hunger, or why one that causes difficulty in doing arithmetic also causes peculiar sensations in the skin. One can envisage the day when drugs may be employed not only to treat pathological conditions (reduce pain, suffering, agitation, and anxiety), but also to enhance the normal state of man — increase pleasure, facilitate learning and memory, reduce jealousy and aggressiveness. Hopefully such pharmacological developments will come about as an accompaniment of, and not as a substitute for, a more ideal society. ◘

WHEN FEAR IS HEALTHY

THE DOCTOR WHO TELLS his patient that surgery "won't hurt a bit...and it'll give you a chance for a good rest" is likely soon to have an upset and angry convalescent on his hands. Instead of helping a threatened person to be brave, this sort of unrealistic promise may lull him into a false sense of security that ill prepares him for the distressing experience that lies ahead.

It is a widely held notion that the more fearful a person is about a stress situation, the less able he is to cope with it. But while it is true that too much fear puts one in a poor position to handle stress, research has begun to make us realize that too little fear also can have bad effects. It is the man, woman or child who faces impending stress with a moderate degree of fear who seems best equipped to handle it well.

My own interest in the importance of fear in preparing people for stressful events dates back to 20 years ago, when I began making some observations in the surgical wards of a general hospital. I noticed that patients who were completely unworried about an impending operation seemed less able to withstand the stress of their postoperative convalescence than were those who had been somewhat apprehensive prior to surgery.

To see if my observation was valid, I conducted a study in the surgical ward of a large community hospital. Twenty-three patients were interviewed intensively before and after they had major surgery. These interviews were supplemented with hospital records, including the physicians' and nurses' daily notes on each patient's behavior.

Three general patterns of emotional response emerged. The first was a relatively familiar pattern, found in those who were very apprehensive. Both before and after surgery these patients felt highly vulnerable to bodily damage. They seemed unable to develop inner defenses to help them cope with the threats of surgery. They could not sleep without sedation and, when the time came for routine postoperative treatments, they shrank back in fear or displayed stormy emotional outbursts. Most of these patients were found to have a history of neurotic disorder, including anxiety attacks. Therefore their emotional reactions following surgery appeared to be a continuation of their long-standing neuroses and not just a response to the dangers of surgery.

A second group of patients displayed very little fear before their operations. They were calm and felt invulnerable, apparently because they denied or minimized the possibility of danger and suffering. When the inescapable pain and harassment of normal recovery from major surgery began, they no longer could maintain their calm. They became upset—apprehensive, angry and resentful—and tended to blame the hospital staff for their suffering. Most of these patients seemed to be clinically normal. They had been told very little about the suffering that inevitably lay in store for them and they simply had avoided facing the implications of their situation. It seemed likely that these patients, if they had been given adequate warnings before surgery, would have been better able to cope with pain and stress.

The third group consisted of people who were moderately fearful before their operations. They asked for and received realistic information about what was going to happen to them so that the aftereffects of surgery were no surprise. After surgery they felt fairly secure, cooperated with the hospital staff, and were able to reassure themselves when their fears were momentarily aroused. As one patient reported, "I knew there might be some bad pains so when my side started to ache I told myself it didn't mean that anything had gone wrong."

The main hypotheses suggested by this series of intensive case studies were supported by a second study—a questionnaire survey conducted with more than 150 male college students who had recently undergone a surgical operation. Several measures were used to rate each patient's postsurgical stress reactions, including anger and resentment against the hospital staff, anxious preoccupation

with unpleasant operation experiences, and emotional disturbances when recalling the operation. Each of these reactions was examined in relation to what the patient had reported about his fear level before surgery.

When the indicators of postoperative stress are plotted against the anticipatory fear level, we see that the relationship is not monotonic—that is, greater anticipatory fear is not consistently related to greater tolerance of postoperative stress. Instead, both high fear and low fear are associated with low tolerance for stress, and the peak of the curve —high tolerance for stress—is located somewhere in the middle of the fear continuum, not at one end or the other. This shows that high stress tolerance is associated with moderate anticipatory fear. [*See illustration, page 315, upper left.*]

This type of relationship, which forms an inverted U-shaped curve, is familiar to experimental psychologists. They often have found a similar relationship between strength of motivation and efficiency of performance or learning. Moderately strong motivation seems to facilitate efficient performance, while very high motivation hinders it. Fear, like other motivational states, has been found to improve performance as long as it remains moderate. But it interferes when it reaches too high a level.

The outcome of the surgery research is in line with these findings. The findings clearly contradict the popular assumption that placid people—those who are least fearful about an impending ordeal—will prove to be less disturbed than others by stress. Those patients who were calmest and most confident about their invulnerability before the surgery tended to become much more upset than those who had been part-time worriers.

The patients who were moderately fearful were motivated to seek and take account of realistic information and assurances; this made convalescence a less difficult time for them. Were they such different patients from those who did not cope so well with the stresses of surgery? A careful check showed no significant

differences as to type of operation, the amount of pain, degree of incapacitation, type of anesthesia, or even the prognosis; nor were there differences between the groups as to age, education, sex, ethnic origin, or the number of prior hospitalizations.

But when I looked into the amount of advance information each patient had obtained, I found an important difference: patients in the low-fear group had little idea of what to expect, whereas those in the moderate-fear group had been far better informed.

To investigate this apparent relation between prior information and stress tolerance from another standpoint, I looked at the answers obtained from the questionnaire survey of young men who had recently undergone surgery. The questionnaire asked them how they had reacted after their operations.

Comparing "informed" and "uninformed," I found two important differences. First, more of the informed men reported that they had felt worried or fearful before surgery; second, fewer of the informed men said that they had become angry, resentful or emotionally upset after the operation. [*See illustration, page 315, upper right.*]

Since these are correlational data and are based on after-the-fact reports, they cannot be accepted as conclusive evidence. Nevertheless, they point in the same direction as the observations made in the intensive case studies, suggesting the following hypothesis: If no authoritative warnings are given and if other circumstances are such that fear is not aroused beforehand, the normal person will lack the motivation to prepare himself psychologically for danger and he will thus have a low tolerance for stress when the crisis is at hand.

The 'Work of Worrying'

In *Psychological Stress*, the book in which I published the findings of this research among surgical patients, I have suggested a theoretical concept—the "work of worrying"—to emphasize the potentially positive value of anticipatory fear. The work of worrying involves psychological processes similar to the "work of mourning," the term Freud used to describe the typical changes in normal persons as they come to accept the death of loved ones.

We can see more easily what the work of worrying accomplishes if we look at what is likely to happen if a person fails to undertake it.

Little or no anticipatory fear

↓

no mental rehearsal of impending danger

↓

feelings of helplessness when the danger materializes

↓

disappointment in protective authorities and increased expectations of vulnerability

↓

intense fear and anger.

Failure to carry out the work of worrying can be expected if a stressful event occurs under any of the following conditions: (1) if the person is accustomed to suppressing anticipatory fear by means of denial defenses, by overoptimism, and by avoiding warnings that would stimulate the work of worrying; (2) if the stressful event is so sudden that it cannot be prepared for; and (3) if an adequate prior warning is not given, or if strong but false reassurances encourage the person to believe that he is invulnerable.

Other studies on the psychological effects of severe illness, of community disasters, and of combat dangers provide many bits of evidence consistent with the findings of the surgery research described above. Like the surgery research, they suggest that if a normal person is given accurate prior warning of impending pain and discomfort, together with sufficient reassurances so that fear does not mount to a very high level, he will be less likely to develop acute emotional disturbances than a person who is not warned.

We know that there are exceptions, of course, such as neurotic personalities who are hypersensitive to any threat cues. But this does not preclude the possibility that moderately fear-arousing information about impending dangers and deprivations will function as a kind of emotional inoculation, enabling normal persons to increase their tolerance for stress by developing coping mechanisms and effective defenses. I call this process emotional inoculation because it may be analogous to what happens when anti-

bodies are induced by injections of mildly virulent viruses.

If these inferences are correct, we should find that a group of surgical patients given appropriate preparatory communications before their operations will show better adjustment to the stresses of the postoperative period than an equivalent group of patients given no special preparatory communications other than the information ordinarily available to any hospitalized patient. This prediction has been confirmed in two carefully controlled studies done in 1964, one conducted by Patricia Moran in the pediatric wards of the Yale-New Haven Hospital, and the other by Lawrence Egbert and his colleagues with adult surgical patients at the Massachusetts General Hospital.

In the latter study, 97 patients were divided randomly into two groups. The anesthetist who conducted the study gave the control group only a routine medical interview but provided the experimental group with an additional preparatory communication intended to facilitate their work of worrying. To insure that neither group would receive favored treatment, neither the surgeons nor the hospital staff was told about the experiment.

The differences between the two groups were remarkable. During the five days just after surgery, patients in the experimental group required only half as much sedation as did patients in the control group. [*See illustration, p. 315, lower left.*] They also complained less. They were judged to be in better physical and emotional condition, and their surgeons decided that they were well enough to be sent home an average of two and seven-tenths days earlier than the patients without the extra preoperative communication.

Similar results were found in another experiment recently completed by James C. Miller, one of my co-workers at Yale, who worked with dental patients before and after they had oral surgery. All these experiments on the effectiveness of preparatory communications support the conclusion that preparatory information is valuable for surgical patients. However, we must wait for additional field experiments to be certain that the relationship between fear-arousing information and stress-tolerance also holds in other stress situations.

The 'Proper Dose' of Fear

We turn now to another type of research that helps round out our under-

standing of the positive and negative effects of anticipatory fear. One important problem that experimental social psychologists have begun to investigate is the proper dosage of fear. Research on this problem is highly relevant to the issues I have just been discussing concerning psychological preparation for subsequent stress. To produce successful emotional inoculation it is necessary to interfere with the person's spontaneous efforts to ward off his awareness of the signs of impending danger. Unwelcome information has to be given in order to convey a realistic picture of the disturbing events the person is likely to experience. How can this be done without running the risk of provoking either panic or adverse avoidance reactions, such as defensive indifference and denial? The answer is most likely to come from systematic communication studies that assess the effects of different dosages of fear-producing material—for example, in warning messages about lung cancer that urge people to cut down on smoking.

Although a large number of relevant experiments have been reported, we cannot yet formulate any definitive rule about the intensity of fear arousal that is most likely to be effective. On the one hand, some attitude-change experiments show more psychological resistance and less acceptance of precautionary recommendations when strong fear appeals are used in warning messages than when milder ones are used. In our initial experiment on this problem, Seymour Feshbach and I gave equivalent groups of high school students three different versions of a dental hygiene communication, all of them containing the same set of recommendations about when and how to brush the teeth. The results showed that there were diminishing returns as the level of fear increased. A number of subsequent studies have supported our conclusion that when fear is strongly aroused by a persuasive communication, but is not fully relieved by reassurances, the audience will be motivated to ignore, minimize or even deny the importance of the threat.

On the other hand, there are similar experiments that show a gain in effectiveness when strong threat appeals are used, and these experiments point to the facilitating effects of fear arousal. Evidently, changes in attitude and the decision to adopt a recommended course of preventive action depend upon the relative weight of facilitating and interfering responses, both of which are likely

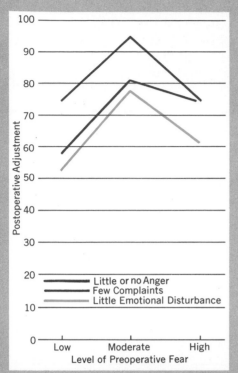

POSTOPERATIVE REACTION. Patients who were moderately fearful before surgery tolerated its aftereffects best.

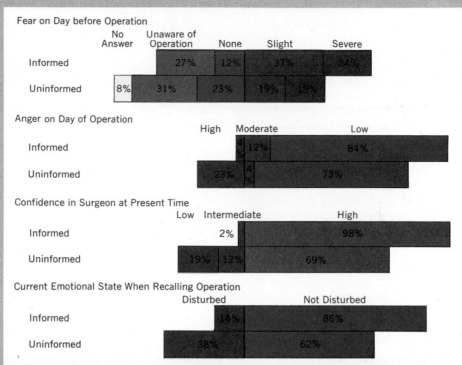

Fear on Day before Operation

	No Answer	Unaware of Operation	None	Slight	Severe
Informed		27%	12%	37%	24%
Uninformed	8%	31%	23%	19%	19%

Anger on Day of Operation

	High	Moderate	Low
Informed	4%	12%	84%
Uninformed	23%	4%	73%

Confidence in Surgeon at Present Time

	Low	Intermediate	High
Informed		2%	98%
Uninformed	19%	12%	69%

Current Emotional State When Recalling Operation

	Disturbed	Not Disturbed
Informed	14%	86%
Uninformed	38%	62%

FOREWARNED PATIENTS. Young men who were aware of what to expect after their surgery reported *more* prior fear, *less* later anger, resentfulness or emotional upset.

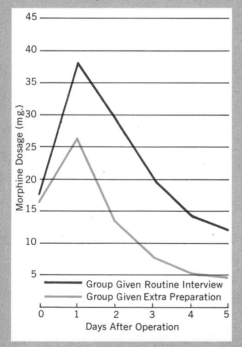

POSTSURGICAL SEDATION. Patients who had done the "work of worrying" required only half the sedation of those who hadn't.

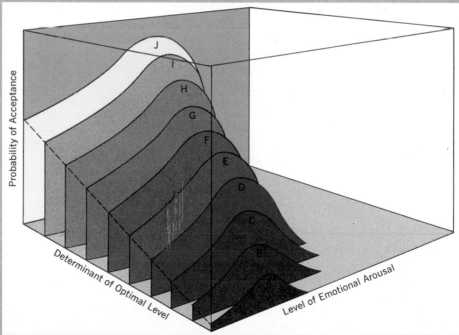

THREE-DIMENSIONAL MODEL. Acceptance of a message depends not only on how much fear is aroused *(left to right)*, but on how much can be tolerated *(front to back)*.

to be evoked whenever a communication arouses fear.

Consequently, we cannot expect to find any broad generalization that will tell us whether a high-threat or low-threat version will be more effective. Rather, we must expect the optimal level of fear arousal to vary for different types of warning communications and for different types of personalities.

By the optimal level of fear, I mean the point at which the facilitating effects of fear arousal are most powerful and outweigh the interfering effects. Once the level of fear arousal exceeds that optimal level, interference gets the upper hand and acceptance of the communicator's recommendations will be seen to decrease.

A Theoretical Model

On the basis of various theoretical considerations suggested by many research findings on the effects of fear-arousing communications, I have recently proposed a three-dimensional model made up of a family of inverted U-shaped curves, each of which is similar to the curve shown earlier from the surgical studies. [See illustration, page 315, lower right.] In the diagram of the three-dimensional model, each curve has a different peak (A, B, C, D, etc.). These peaks are assumed to vary as a function of any factor that influences the relative strength of facilitating and interfering responses. The third dimension in the diagram, labeled "determinant of optimal level," is intended to represent any factor that overcomes resistances and thus shifts the optimal level toward the maximum level of stress tolerance. A central task of research on the effects of emotional appeals is to discover these interacting determinants and to describe the way they affect acceptance.

Threat evokes vigilance and information-seeking. The more threatening the warning, the more likely it is that the recipient will scrutinize the message carefully and will look for a loophole so he can ignore the distressing warning. This type of reaction makes for a low optimal level of arousal. But by introducing impressive new arguments that eliminate obvious loopholes and that break down the usual efforts to evade distressing ideas, the communicator may be able to prevent the recipient from denying the personal relevance of what is being said and thereby raise the optimal level. Thus, elements of the message itself may determine whether a low or high degree of fear will lead to more acceptance.

The trustworthiness of the communicator also affects the amount of resistance evoked by a fear-arousing communication. The optimal level of arousal for a television commercial that urges smokers to avoid lung cancer by using a new type of filter might be near point A in the diagram, while that of the same message from a medical scientist might be at point D. Similarly, the optimal level would tend to be higher when the recommendation is known to be a workable, well-tested solution rather than one apparently based on guesswork. Other factors that determine whether the optimal level will be high or low also can be conceptualized as falling on the third dimension on the model.

The model enables us to reconcile some of the findings of past experiments that seemed to contradict each other. It also allows us to state more precisely the expected outcomes when we are dealing with interacting determinants of the optimal arousal-level. Such predictions pertain to any communication device that helps people tolerate a high level of fear without becoming so defensive and resistant that they reject the message.

Emotional Role-Playing

This model has influenced our recent research on fear arousal by inclining us to search for psychological techniques that will raise the optimal level by preventing resistances from being mobilized when the person thinks about future dangers that might require preventive action. One such newly discovered technique is called emotional role-playing. This procedure seems to stimulate empathy in a way that breaks down a person's usual defenses, making him more willing to take precautions recommended by health authorities.

In the first in a series of experiments, Leon Mann, now of Harvard, and I used 26 young women as subjects. All of them were cigarette smokers who had not expressed any intention of cutting down on their tobacco consumption. Half were assigned at random to the experimental group, half to the control group. None was aware of the purpose of the study.

We set up a psychodrama situation for the experimental group, in which each subject was asked to play the part of a patient suffering from the consequences of smoking. The investigator played the role of physician. To make the situation as realistic as possible, he wore a white coat and used impressive props such as an X-ray photograph of the lungs.

Five scenes were acted out. In one, the "physician" pointed out the X-ray indications of a malignant mass in the patient's lung as he gave her the bad news that diagnostic tests indicated the presence of lung cancer. [See illustration, page 312.]

In the last scene, the "cancer victim" was asked to think over the news while waiting for the physician to arrange for her hospitalization to undergo lung surgery. She was asked to express her spontaneous personal responses just as if the situation actually confronted her.

The women in the control group were exposed to the same information but they did not participate in the role-playing. Instead, they listened to a tape recording of a session with one of the experimental subjects.

Role-playing proved to be an extraordinarily disquieting experience but the subjects apparently were able to tolerate a high level of fear without mobilizing resistances. It reminded me of a passage in William Faulkner's novel The Town, where the character Ratcliff says: "This here is the kind of thing a man has got to know hisself. He has got to learn it out of his own hard dread and skeer . . . So I got to wait. I got to wait for him to learn it hisself, the hard way, the sure way. Then he will believe it, enough anyhow to be afraid."

The role-playing generated plenty of "dread and skeer," and it had a markedly greater effect in changing smoking habits than did the tape recording. In a follow-up study conducted 18 months after the role-playing episode, the experimental subjects continued to report a significantly greater decrease in the number of cigarettes smoked than did the young women in the control group. [See illustration, at right.] This long-term outcome indicates that a single one-hour session of emotional role-playing can have a profound long-term effect upon smokers who initially have no intention of cutting down on cigarette consumption. And the results suggest that significant changes in smoking habits may persist for years.

A recent study by Leon Mann indicates that this type of emotional role-playing is more effective with both male and female smokers than cognitive role-playing (enacting the role of a debater arguing against smoking). Mann also found that the amount of attitude change produced by this fear-arousing procedure increases when subjects are given the opportunity to verbalize their own ideas while acting.

All our studies support the general conclusion that emotional role-playing induces the person to "repackage" already available information in a way that changes his feelings of personal vulnerability to health hazards. For average people, enacting the role of victim in a realistic way probably reduces or bypasses psychological resistance, and thus they are able to tolerate a higher level of fear without becoming predominantly defensive. Here we have an example of one important implication of our theoretical analysis: If a warning communication is given in a way that prevents resistances from becoming dominant, the gain in motivation from strong fear

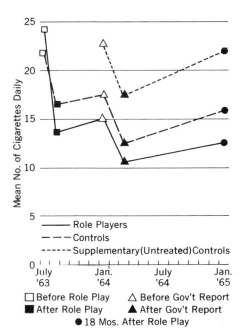

PSYCHODRAMA. After 18 months, girls who took roles of cancer patients continued to smoke less than girls who did not.

arousal will no longer be outweighed by interfering motivational effects. The results from the experiments on emotional role-playing make this implication plausible.

Perhaps the psycho-logic of the process when you take part in an emotional role-playing session is something like this: You already know that there is impressive evidence of a relation between lung cancer and smoking. But you get a great deal of pleasure out of smoking and have not felt willing to give it up. Playing the role of a lung cancer patient enables you to find out how you would feel if you discovered that you had cancer. It brings home to you the fact that you could develop lung cancer. Now you feel that it actually could happen to you, that you are vulnerable to the harmful effects of smoking. But you also know the danger is not inevitable, for there is reassurance in the message as well as threat. You want the reassurance of knowing that you have a good chance of avoiding lung cancer and so you decide to give up smoking.

A similar process is suggested by some of the experiments by Howard Leventhal of the University of Wisconsin and his co-workers ["Fear—For Your Health," reproduced in Section VIII], which indicate the effectiveness of a strong fear-arousing movie sequence depicting a young victim of lung cancer undergoing chest surgery. Their findings suggest that certain types of empathy-eliciting devices might augment the effectiveness of movies and other mass-media communications.

Insofar as the assumptions of the theoretical model appear to be plausible, we

are encouraged to continue the search for psychological devices that can break through a person's defensive facade. Research on emotional role-playing, as well as on emotional inoculation, points to the conclusion that when a warning is presented in a way that evokes a high optimal level of fear, it will have the effect of increasing the average person's tolerance for subsequent stress. Under appropriate conditions, a person's initial attitude of denial or unwarranted complacency can be transformed by strong fear arousal into a more adaptive attitude—an attitude that combines vigilance with high receptivity to precautionary recommendations.

It seems to me that the most important value of the new theoretical model is that it poses new types of questions for systematic research on the way emotional arousal influences attitudes and decisions. In earlier research we asked: "In what way is acceptance of a recommendation affected by changes in fear-level?" The theoretical model enables us to ask different questions:

"What are the various determinants of the optimal arousal-level for inducing acceptance?"

"What factors increase the optimal fear-level and facilitate coping with stress by enabling precautionary recommendations to function as effective forms of reassurance?"

Thus, the problem becomes that of investigating the interacting determinants for different kinds of threat, and of discovering psychological devices that can prevent resistance from interfering with the positive motivation that comes from realistic fear. 🎭

VI. personality

reud's ideas survive in the thinking of almost every branch of psychology, but the age of the global theory of personality seems finished. No longer do psychologists generate elaborate, closed, baroque systems to describe and explain why men appear and behave as they do. Great systems of the past still flourish, but their power to generate hot argument and their attraction for the new generation of psychologists have waned. Instead, psychologists of personality concentrate on methods for assessing personality characteristics of individuals, on studying such generally occurring but specific problems as aggression, on attempting to characterize the general personality tendencies of a whole generation of human beings in an almost sociological fashion.

At the start of this section, Frank McMahon considers some pitfalls in the construction and use of psychological tests, not to mention their interpretation. Cattell offers a sober evaluation of the measurement of I.Q., that single most dictatorial and controlling number stamped on all our records throughout our schooling. Intelligently measured or not, I.Q. and personality characteristics determine and control the placement of nearly every individual not only in school but also in the hierarchy of his daily work. These readings provide perspective on the measurements that others have used to place us where we are.

From time to time in the history of psychology, various diagnostic systems have purported to delineate individual personalities by means of relatively simple measurements of other individual characteristics. One such was phrenology, the child of Gall and Spurzheim. Phrenology made it possible to identify the personality of an individual by feeling, measuring, and interpreting the bumps on his skull. David Bakan ponders if this was (is) foolishness.

Try the following exercise, and you will be convinced that the way in which you write is so intrinsically yours that it may reveal something about your personality. On lined paper sign your name as you normally do on each of the first three lines. On the next line do not sign normally but attempt to copy your own signature, paying particular attention to its idiosyncrasies. Now notice that the first three signatures bear much more in common among themselves than does any one of them to the fourth, copied signature. This example, courtesy of the late Gordon W. Allport, illustrates clearly that unified expressive behaviors such as writing truly belong to the person who engages in them. No wonder that Anthony examines the validity of writing as an expressive behavior indicative of a writer's personality characteristics.

The tendency to concentrate theoretically and experimentally on specific problems in personality is admirably illustrated here by Leonard Berkowitz's essay on aggression. These experiments and reflections on man's aggressiveness join a long and distinguished line of works that have attempted not only to understand but also to control the unhealthy and destructive aspects of aggression.

Can an entire generation be grim? Can a revolution of the magnitude engulfing Americans of this generation be quiet? These questions are examples of attempts to characterize the personality of a generation. All of us have somewhat stereotyped notions—fostered by tall tales, TV, and movies—of the character of the American generation of the 1920s, of the German generation of the 1930s, of the Japanese warlords before the opening to the West. Robert Kavanaugh and the Uhrs suggest how the current generation of Americans is (or should be) viewed by its contemporaries and how it perhaps will be viewed by its progeny.

Psychological Testing— A Smoke Screen Against Logic

MANY YEARS AGO—but not long enough—I took Psychological Testing I and II, Projective Testing I and II and a couple of Advanced Testings I and II. I shall never forget the day the class was analyzing the results of a Rorschach ink-blot test and the professor became extremely excited over a response to one of the cards: ". . . and here," the patient had said, "I see a church steeple, over here a church, and down here is the grass."

"You see," the professor explained, "the church steeple represents a phallus; the grass, pubic hair; and we are dealing with a conflict between religious restriction and sexual desire."

And in another class, we discussed a sentence-completion item from another personality test: *"One night I . . . awakened and went to the refrigerator to get something to eat, a hot dog, I think."* Well, this was written by a young woman, and its interpretation I shall leave to the reader, whose wildest fantasies could not outdo those of the psychologists.

Or the objective test item: "I'm not as healthy as I used to be." (Checked true.) That one sent us scurrying through the other tests for indications of abnormal anxieties or mental disorders, never once giving even passing thought to the possibility that on that day the test taker may have needed an Alka-Seltzer.

One of the great geniuses of the psychological movement was Sigmund Freud. Freud helped everyone but the psychologist. To the psychologist Freud gave the psychoanalytic method, in which the analyst is free to roam the patient's subconscious without fear of successful contradiction. The Freudian method was a handle that the psychologist could grasp in all emergencies, a method that allows contradictory diagnoses and deceives the psychologist and alienates the patient. In interpreting a patient's subconscious, it is axiomatic that what is sought is unknown both to the patient *and to the psychologist*.

Granted, remarkable strides have been made as a result of Freud's work. We have, for example, pretty clear evidence that people are not always what they seem to be on the surface. The possi-

by Frank B. McMahon Jr.

322

"We obscure understanding and diagnosis by double talk and even triple talk."

bility that sexuality is a childhood trait as well as an adult preoccupation seems clearly established. But one of the leaders in current dream research, Calvin Hall of the University of California, Santa Cruz, made a list of sexual symbolism found in various psychology books and articles. There were 102 such objects, including anything resembling a gun or stick, and actions such as ploughing and flogging. Like cars, sexual symbols have suddenly become too numerous. What started as a good idea has suddenly swamped us in an asphyxiating smog. Sexual symbols and their interpretation have almost supplanted the patient himself.

On the other hand, the late Gordon Allport, Harvard professor and former president of the American Psychological Association, suggested that if we wanted to know about a person, the first step was to ask him directly. Unfortunately, his suggestion has gone by the wayside. We psychologists are afraid to re-

linquish our position of omnipotence in relation to the patient and to elicit his aid in understanding man.

Today, a mixture of fear and desire for power grips clinical psychology. The desire for power indirectly manifests itself in the American Psychological Association's valid attempts to have clinicians as expert witnesses at trials. A recent court victory has validated these attempts, solidifying clinical psychology's growing power base. On the other hand, fear indirectly manifests itself, making it seem clinicians have something to hide, in the restrictions against undergraduates purchasing Rorschach cards and in the incomprehensible jargon that has been set up to explain and understand psychological disturbances.

Psychologists have had a long and difficult struggle in gaining recognition. Unfortunately, the price of this recognition has been to obscure understanding and diagnosis by double talk or even triple talk. If this results in the patient being kept in the dark, it is immaterial because few psychologists feel the patient should have any say. Witness the common phenomenon at a hospital "staff" conference: heads nodding, slight smiles, everything short of cheering at a say-nothing statement such as, "He's fixated at this level because during these early years his father was stern, lenient, hos-

tile, neutral, castrating, overprotective." Choose any of the above. They all work!

With psychology now strong enough as a science, the sad part is that we do not go back and pick up the pieces. Are we really testing what we think we are testing?

Psychology has had a strange developmental pattern. In order to get rid of the idea that man is a completely rational animal, we stressed his inability to understand himself. We stressed that the fountain pen represented something other than itself—it represented a penis. Now that we have proved our point (that man is not always rational), psychologists are caught in an equally extreme myth that man is a spidery maze of disguised sickness.

We must go back and talk with the patient—if need be, about something as insignificant as the pen. "Tell me, Mr. Patient, what does this pen mean in your dream (or your Rorschach card)?" The patient may say it means that he wants to be a writer, that he feels his imagination and its expression are constricted.

Rather than loosen the hold on the past, however, we interpret elaborate psychological tests in the same way, over and over, searching most of all for hidden symbols, deep meanings. The patient knows this. That there is trickery involved is most obvious to him. The patient is on guard and legitimately so. The psychologist is on guard, and legitimately so. We have, then, a contest of who can outfox whom. The psychologist has the upper hand, of course, because he can interpret anything he finds in the tests any way he wants.

Another problem, repeatedly pointed out by men like Lee Cronbach, Hans Eysenck, Gordon Allport and Carl Rog-

"We interpret elaborate psychological tests in the same [old] way...searching most of all for hidden symbols..."

ers, is that we are playing roulette odds when we predict anything of substance via psychological tests as they now stand. For example, roughly half of the studies on the validity of Rorschach tests are positive, half are negative. Take your pick.

In any case, validity studies (which tell whether a test measures what it is supposed to measure) show personality tests to be of such low validity that the issue is often sidestepped. A validity of 1.00 is perfect and in the personality testing field a validity of .25 is often considered pretty good. Lee Cronbach, however, in *Essentials of Psychological Testing,* says a validity of .25 is poor. Depending on how a validity study is performed, who the test takers are, what their backgrounds and intelligence are, a validity of .25 can mean a personality test has little better than fifty-fifty accuracy. Reliability, which is closely related to validity, tells how *consistent* a test is in measuring what it is supposed to measure. The Minnesota Multiphasic Personality Inventory, which is considered the king of self-report tests, has reliability coefficients that begin as low as .50. [Self-report tests are ones where the patient reports on himself, by himself, via written answers to true-false questions like: I am contented with my sex life.]

Dr. Anne Anastasi, a prominent psychologist in the testing field, reports one reliability study (to note the extreme) on the MMPI Paranoia scale that was a minus quantity, −.05. She then explains that the scales don't mean what they say, anyway.

"For example, we cannot assume a high score on the Schizophrenia scale indicates the presence of schizophrenia ... moreover, such a score may appear in a normal person."

In the face of such evidence, I think there are two major reasons for the continued ingrowth of the psychological testing movement. First, in order to maintain a mythical sense of professionalism, we are overinterpreting, being overerudite and succumbing to a fear of *not* seeing something in a test. Second, and running counter to the first reason, to understand the infinitely complex hu-

man mind we would have to ask the patient for assistance and take some of what he says at face value, integrating his material with our testing. Unfortunately, some psychologists think this is like the surgeon asking the patient where to cut.

Basically, there are three types of psychological tests: objective, semi-projective and projective (true-false, sentence completion and ink-blot).

Examining these three types in 1959, K. B. Little of the University of Denver and Edwin Schneidman of the National Institute of Mental Health had 48 clinical psychologists assess the tests of persons already interviewed and tested by other clinicians who had diagnosed these persons as ranging from psychotic to normal. These 48 investigators found that the clinicians tended to "overinterpret" the tests of the normal group. The clinicians assigned to normal persons the diagnostic label of "neurotic."

Subsequently, I decided to do an experiment of my own to test further the hypothesis that clinicians "overinterpret." I ran a study comparing psychology graduate students as raters of test results with raters from outside psychology. Objective, semi-projective and projective material was abstracted from the tests of 36 individuals receiving psychotherapy and 27 who said they had never received psychological treatment. The 27 responded to a questionnaire, on which they did not have to put their name, to the effect that they had never felt the need of, or sought, treatment. Of course, statistically, there would be more "disturbed" persons among those who were receiving treatment. I selected replies of the 63 persons to each type of test, avoiding replies that appear infrequently in response to a given test stimulus. I gave the replies to 16 clinical psychology graduate students, all of whom had completed their course work

in psychological testing and were within a semester of receiving their Ph.D.s. I selected 16 business-administration majors at a comparable level of graduate study as the second group of raters.

The two sets of graduate students evaluated the replies of the "neurotic" and the "normal" groups according to whether they thought the test takers were "normal" or "neurotic."

Our finding was that in an overall evaluation of the replies to the Minnesota Multiphasic Personality Inventory and the sentence-completion test the business-administration students were able to differentiate "normal" from "neurotic" replies with approximately as much accuracy as were the students in psychology. What is possibly more interesting is that in differentiating between "normal" and "neurotic" on the Rorschach tests the business students outdid their counterparts in psychology.

Detailed examination showed that the psychology students interpreted the Rorschach replies of more intelligent

" '...the church steeple represents a phallus; the grass, pubic hair; and we are dealing with a conflict between religious restriction and sexual desire.' "

test takers as being more disturbed; they overinterpreted the symbolic content given by the brighter persons.

Considerable evidence from other studies shows that more intelligent people produce more symbols. If symbolic interpretation is indeed the primary factor in overinterpreting, then normal persons of higher intelligence are likely to receive abnormal ratings.

This is not meant to suggest that laymen are necessarily better at test interpretation than psychologists, but that psychologists are evolving ever more elaborate test interpretations that remove the clinician further and further from the reality of the patient.

One could go to the extreme of saying that in the case just cited clinical training was of no benefit to diagnosis. My contention, however, is that training has been aimed in the wrong direction. It encourages a preoccupation with digging out what may not even be in a person's psyche: elaborate and secret unconscious meanings. Instead, clinical training should be used in conjunction with both common sense and what the patient says of himself. In place of the tricky diagnosis, we should focus on what the patient is saying, in most cases taking his word for it (statistically better than roulette) and trying to integrate both sources into a comprehensible whole.

Oddly enough, although both groups of raters were able to distinguish "normal" from "neurotic" replies on the MMPI and the sentence-completion tests, the content of the test items themselves did not seem to be critical in the rating procedure. That is, if certain test

items consistently meant disturbance, these items should have been consistently rated as such. This was not the case. There were only 22 out of 376 test items that 75 per cent of the raters rated the same way.

This suggests that the content of the test items themselves is not being accurately interpreted. The traditional psychological test may not be pinpointing the content that is most meaningful to the patient and most enlightening to the psychologist.

In 1963, I published a new personality test designed to be administered on a "man-to-man" basis. Each and every question was completely transparent, or face-valid. The test taker could easily tell that a certain response would count "against" him. A face-valid item looks to the test taker to be what it is. An example of an item that is *not* face-valid is, "I used to like to play drop the handkerchief."

For this "man-to-man" technique to work, I had to avoid the ambiguity of the typical test. Therefore, after each traditional psychological test item I inserted a qualifier that the test taker could use to keep from feeling (and being) shoved behind the eight ball. For example, "Some people have it in for me," True or False, followed by: If true, "I can't seem to get them off my mind," True or False.

This couplet type of questioning means that if the individual checks both parts "true," he is acknowledging a problem in his life that is important enough to admit to twice. Obviously, the couplet does not make clear the deeper meaning of the item, nor can the meaning really be made clear by any self-report test. The couplet does signal areas in which the patient desires further discussion. More important, the couplet relies heavily on the patient himself.

The test is then scored, but instead of writing a report that is known only to the psychologist, as is customary, we return the test to the test taker for discus-

"The patient is on guard...
The psychologist is on guard...
We have a contest of
who can outfox whom."

6. a. I do not think there is a God.   T F
   b. IF TRUE: My life seems empty because there seems to be no purpose to i

7. a. I am not an important person— at least to those around me.   T F
   b. IF TRUE: I feel I am just about worthless.

8. a. I sometimes work so long at something until others lose their patience with me.
   b. IF TRUE: I often lose patience with myself over my persistence.   T F

9. a. I have made a satisfactory adjustment in my sex life.   T F
   b. IF FALSE: I feel capable of making such an adjustment in the near future.   T

10. a. I have periods of such great restlessness that I can't sit still.   T F
    b. IF TRUE: Most of the time I feel like a rubber-band stretched tight.   T F

11. a. I often worry about religious problems.   T
    b. IF TRUE: I feel depressed and confused about religion.   T F

12. a. In my family there is not much love and companionship.   T F
    b. IF TRUE: I get enough love and companionship from others (friends, other relatives, etc.).   T F

13. a. When I go to a party, I generally find myself either alone or with just one other person.   T F
    b. IF TRUE: Because of this, I feel "ill-at-ease" at most parties.   T F

14. a. The world seems more like a jungle than "civilization."   T F
    b. IF TRUE: I don't feel very safe or secure in my everyday life.   T F

COUPLET QUESTIONS. Above are samples of author McMahon's bold innovation, which was designed to combat trickiness and inaccuracy in psychological tests.

sion. To discuss each item on a standard objective psychological test would be a big job considering the large (more than 500 on the MMPI) number of items. But by using the couplet method, we can construct an effective test with just under 50 items. The psychologist may point out that certain of the test taker's replies to the test suggest problem areas. The discussion should further clarify the meaning and purpose of any test item and the extent to which an item, in the opinion of the psychologist or the test taker, should be further explored. I consider this discussion an essential ingredient of the testing process.

Psychologists using the test quickly found that it helped place the patient-doctor relationship on an above-board basis. The meaning behind the items and the methods of coping with the problems the items suggested could be explored with mutual confidence.

We further analyzed the test structure to determine what meaning was inherent in the single test item versus the couplet. For example, the traditional test item, "Some people have it in for me," was rated by a group of psychologists. Interpretations of its meaning ranged from "indicates an aggressive individual" to "he's got paranoid traits."

A second group of psychologists rated the same item, except that we added the couplet or qualifier, "I can't seem to get them off my mind," and marked it *false*. Interpretations changed considerably. Many fewer psychologists now thought

that the statement, "Some people have it in for me," indicated severe disturbance. Their interpretations, however, still varied widely.

At this point, I performed an informal validity study of my test. Patients who had discussed the test items with the therapists were asked, after three ses-

"In place of the tricky diagnosis, we should focus on what the patient is saying."

sions, to list important problems not covered so far in the therapeutic relationship. Only one of 32 persons indicated he had failed to touch on his major problems.

In numerous other validity studies, the couplet test has been compared with the longer and less face-valid type of objective tests. The results of these other tests were the same as those obtained with the couplet test in enough cases to yield correlations of between .80 and .95 (and none below .80), which are high. Other studies of the couplet test yielded validities in the .70 and .80 range. In these studies, therapists who were unaware of the results obtained with couplet tests rated patients with other diagnostic tools. Comparison of their results with the couplet test results showed the high validities.

Therapy with regressed patients has been most effective when the therapist takes the time to learn the specific language of the patient himself. [See "The Shattered Language of Schizophrenia," in Section XII.] He might have to learn, for instance, that the patient conceives of God as a Chinese four feet tall, with a mustache. This can take a great deal of time and effort and only a few therapists have been heroic enough to bother.

Similarly, most of us are not now allowing for the meaning that patients attach to their symbols when they take tests. I do not intend to imply that symbolism or hidden meaning is not of the utmost value. It seems only logical, however, that the patient should help us to understand the symbols. I think the reason for the high validities of the couplet test is that the test is neither clever nor tricky. It says to the patient, "You help me to understand you." Why not try him out?

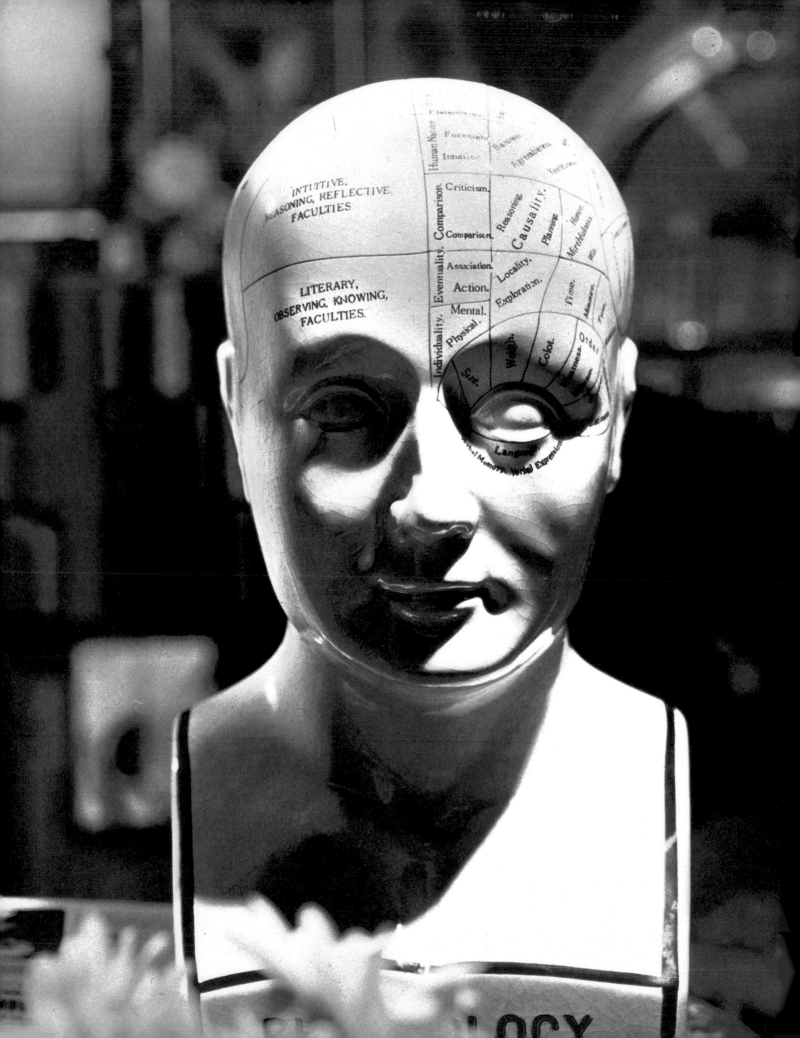

GEORGE COMBE

shrank from the slightest contact with it, to the extent of "repressing" its connection with the scientific research that continued to be done in both Europe and America.

Phrenology As Hooplah

Johann Spurzheim arrived in Boston on August 24, 1832. He gave many lectures and demonstrations, including a series of lectures at Harvard, with a special series for the medical faculty. As one contemporary observer put it, "the professors were in love with him." Some six frenzied weeks after his arrival Spurzheim died, mostly it would seem of exhaustion, his brains having been thoroughly picked by the Brahminical professors. There was a widely attended funeral, with most of intellectual Boston in attendance. A specially formed committee, headed by Josiah Quincy, the president of Harvard, expressed "a sense of the public loss sustained by the death of this distinguished man," and the Boston Phrenological Society was formed as a memorial to him.

In September of 1832, George Combe, a Scottish lawyer, came to America. Combe, though not a physician, had thoroughly studied the work of Gall and Spurzheim, and he could demonstrate Spurzheim's new dissecting techniques as well as all the extremely minute craniological measuring procedures. (Combe made important technical contributions to the methodology of Dr. Samuel G. Morton, whose works in physical anthropology are considered seminal.) This polished and witty man very favorably impressed Daniel Webster, William Emery Channing, Horace Mann, Dr. Samuel Gridley Howe, and many other leading New Englanders. He became the darling of that lecture-loving age, and spoke to large enthusi-

astic audiences in Boston, New York, Albany, Philadelphia, Baltimore, Washington and other eastern cities.

The initial enthusiasm for phrenological lectures was the property of that same fairly large, relatively homogeneous class of cultivated persons who were responsible for the burst of intellectual activity often referred to as the New England Renaissance, and having Boston-Cambridge-Concord as its hub. As this first vociferous enthusiasm on the part of the lyceum crowd began to wane —partly because phrenology ceased to be as novel as, say, mesmerism—the popularists saw a good thing and moved in.

The belief that science was a particularly direct and efficacious instrument for improving human life had been expressed and put into practice by Franklin and Jefferson; this belief had spread rapidly and taken deep roots, nurtured by the ripples of material prosperity resulting from the nation's first major industrial expansion. The ordinary citizen became increasingly receptive to anything that was "scientific." Phrenology was touted as scientific, promising to analyze a person thoroughly, quickly and sympathetically (that is, "democratically"). It guaranteed to show him, scientifically, the way to personal improvement and personal happiness.

The energetic tutelage to the nation of the firm of Fowler and Wells spread phrenology and enriched them. The huckstering mind is essentially the same in all times and climates, whether speak-

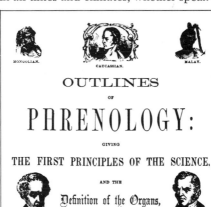

MONGOLIAN.   CAUCASSIAN.   MALAY.

OUTLINES

OF

PHRENOLOGY:

GIVING

THE FIRST PRINCIPLES OF THE SCIENCE,

AND THE

Definition of the Organs,

INCLUDING THEIR

USE, EXCESS, AND DEFICIENCY.

COMBE.   SPURZHEIM.

Know   Thyself.

DR. GALL.

BY FOWLER AND WELLS.

Phrenologists and Publishers,

308 BROADWAY,

NEW YORK.

RICAN.   AM. INDIAN.

ing from the back of a painted wagon or in front of a TV camera. And the vast majority of men have always wondered with varying degrees of intensity who they are and who their neighbors are, and how they can "perfect" themselves; just as surely they have welcomed anyone or anything that promises unambiguously to tell them. Thus phrenology came to enjoy an extraordinary popularity in mid-19th Century America. Fowler and Wells turned it into a national industry. They had "parlors" in New York, Boston and Philadelphia. They booked lecture tours for traveling phrenologists in every corner of the nation. The list of their publications on phrenology was virtually endless. They published all the classical literature, and they themselves were tremendously prolific; their *Phrenological Self-Instructor* was a best-seller. They sold all sorts of paraphernalia to be used in connection with examinations and demonstration:

SHOULD WE MARRY?

Are We

Well

Mated?

The most important question in connection with marriage should be in regard to mutual adaptation, physically, mentally and morally. Phrenology explains this, and therefore should be consulted. There are many works on the subject that can be read profitably by all, but the best work relating to this specially is

WEDLOCK; OR, THE RIGHT RELATION OF THE SEXES.

A Scientific Treatise Disclosing the Laws of Conjugal Selection and Prenatal Influences, also Showing Who Ought and Who Ought Not to Marry. By Samuel R. Wells, author of "New Physiognomy," "How to Read Character," etc. Price, $1.50; in fancy gilt, $2.

The Work being a Practical Guide to all the Relations of a Happy Wedlock, and it should be read by all, and especially those contemplating Marriage. Is handsomely printed and beautifully bound. Copies will be sent, postpaid on receipt of price, $1.50; full Gilt edges, $2.00.

Address, FOWLER & WELLS CO., Publishers,
775 Broadway, New York.

busts, pointers, charts, skulls, casts of famous heads. As the vogue spread from the salons of the East, popular phrenology became increasingly cluttered with these paraphernalia, each itinerant phrenologist adding, according to his genius, some additional gimmick. In the space of a few decades, popular phrenology became a rural entertainment whose quack-ridden charlatanry was a source of embarrassment to any thoughtful man.

But before popular phrenology got quite out of hand, it put into wide circulation one of the major devices associated with all psychometric movements, the printed rating-scale specifying clear alternatives. On each of these rating-scales or "test forms" the phrenologist would indicate the magnitude of each of the 37-odd functions or organs. The ratings varied from "small-medium-large" to nine-point values, sometimes further qualified by pluses and minuses. The scales were accompanied by complete explanations, so that the person phrenologized could read about himself in detail and gain a clear "mental daguerreotype," as a Fowler and Wells advertisement put it, of himself. It was a fundamental assumption of popular phrenology that one could infer the nature of mental functioning on the basis of information collected in an hour or so. This assumption met almost no resistance and is still retained in most modern psychometric methods.

The Cultural Interweave

The science of any period is a rich source of what are essentially images or metaphors that illustrate, if not shape, that period's view of itself. After a certain time-lag, these images or metaphors become the skeleton on which the articulate members of a culture unwittingly drape their various arguments and propositions. The influence of evolution and natural selection as Victorian metaphors has been widely discussed; "relativity," however vaguely understood, has impressed itself deeply on 20th Century culture as a metaphorical equivalent of "discontinuity," "isolation," or "loneliness." (It is only a short symbolic step from trains passing each other in the daylight to ships passing in the night.) As the most widely discussed science of its period, phrenology also provided a set of images or metaphors or formulaic ideas that could be applied to widely varying problems and situations.

The wide acceptance of phrenology as a valid science and as an exciting entertainment meant that its assumptions were assimilated on a large scale. You simply couldn't talk about phrenology intelligently and sympathetically unless you first accepted its fundamental premise that man himself could be studied scientifically and that the phenomena of mind could be studied objectively and explained in terms of natural causes. On a less articulate level, millions of people absorbed such a premise as they lined up to have the bumps on their skulls read.

From its beginnings in Gall and Spurzheim to its brassiest moments in the sideshow, phrenology expressed the notion that the different parts of the brain could be altered, trained or flexed

as the different parts of the body or musculature could be. Perceived as a sort of mental flash or headline — THE MIND IS A SET OF MUSCLES — this notion became a metaphor that was of immense practical use to all sorts of people.

Humane men and women were, for instance, desperately concerned with the plight of the insane. So long as the mind or brain was conceived of as a unitary, non-material entity—a disembodied bit of the Godhead—treatment of the insane could only take the form of horrified neglect or active punishment. The mind of the lunatic had been "taken back," divinely withdrawn in retribution for some secret sin or crime, and the devil(s) had moved into the vacuum. It was very difficult to square this idea with alternations of lunacy and lucidity without raising theological questions about a divine Indian-giving; treatment sometimes consisted in quite literally beating the devil out of the temporarily afflicted. Phre-

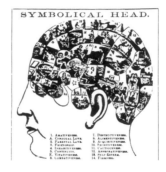

SYMBOLICAL HEAD.

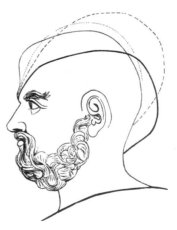

nology's simple assertion that only part of the brain was afflicted was accepted *because it worked;* it enabled people to argue quite sensibly for conditions in which a particular weakened faculty could in some way be modified by "exercise." You could no longer exile or punish people for insanity any more than you could punish them for more physical forms of weakness.

This image or metaphor of brain exercise applied equally well to criminals. Reformers armed with phrenological arguments objected to capital punishment or physical punishment of any sort, and advocated instead proper conditions for exercise and thus, interestingly enough, for the indeterminate sentence. In all cases they urged the modification of treatment with respect to the phrenological or mental characteristics of the individual criminal.

A more specific though less significant event might be chosen to illustrate the genuine *practicality* of phrenology in its time. Blind deaf-mutes were considered utterly beyond the reach of human aid. Dr. Samuel Gridley Howe, who became the head of the Perkins School for the Blind in Boston, had Laura Bridgman examined phrenologically. The analysis of her skull "proved" that she had an active, intelligent brain. Work was then begun that enabled Laura Bridgman to become the first systematically educated blind deaf-mute, work that continued long after the doctrine of the skull had dropped into the scientific limbo.

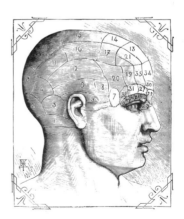

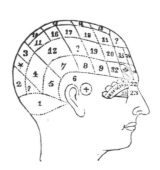

EDGAR ALLEN POE

WALT WHITMAN

Phrenologists took a deep interest in the psychology of learning and were well represented in the avant-garde of educational reformers. Horace Mann, who as the first secretary of the Massachusetts Board of Education revolutionized public instruction, was steeped in phrenological thought. (He had been so impressed by George Combe that he named a son after him.) Phrenologists urged a short school day, together with physical training and a good deal of free play; they were opposed to drill and the use of punishment; they advocated "learning by doing"; they objected to training in the classics exclusively and urged the training of all the mental faculties — always with the metaphorical model before them that learning was simply the proper exercise of the muscles. (In connection with their belief that environment influenced mental behavior, they argued that infants should be exposed to as many "sensations" or

stimuli as possible. Recent studies in the cheerless wards of municipal hospitals have drawn much the same conclusions.)

In its role as a vehicle for cultural values, popular phrenology was intensely democratic, in the Jefferson-Jackson tradition. It confirmed every man's notion that he had individual talents that needed only to be discovered and exploited. These talents could be scientifically identified and a vocation chosen —they (and not, for example, social background) constituted a sufficient and legitimate entree to whatever career was indicated. That individual potential could be identified speedily and scientifically became an acceptable *fact*. Horace Greeley advocated editorially that phrenology be used in the selection of trainmen, as a way of reducing accidents. Want ads like this one, which appeared in the *New York Sun*, became fairly common:

> "Apprentice wanted.—A stout boy not over 15 years of age, of German or Scotch parents, to learn a good but difficult trade. N.B.—it will be necessary to bring a recommendation to his abilities from Messrs. Fowler and Wells, Phrenologists, Nassau Street. Apply corner of West and Franklin Streets."

Fowler and Wells did a booming business in such recommendations, and it is difficult to dismiss them as just another exhibit in the vast museum of suckerdom. Computerized matchmaking firms are doing a profitable business today, and their printed forms are remarkably similar in mode to the phrenological "test forms" with which stout boys trotted down to the corner of Franklin Street. It has become apparent that a goodly percentage of the aptitude and achievement tests widely adopted by school systems and by industry test only the ability to read or verbalize on certain middle-class wave lengths. The interesting thing here is not that it's easy to sling phrenological mud at modern psychometrics, but rather that *all* forms of psychometric assessment have been very generously received by American culture.

Even literature was informed by the phrenological movement. Poe based his entire theory of poetry on the faculty of Ideality, and his Roderick Usher

CHARLES DARWIN

types are cast in phrenological mold. Whitman salted his poetry and prose with phrenological names. He particularly loved Adhesiveness, because he was told that he had a large dose of that "comradely" virtue, and was so taken by the rating scale done for him by Fowler and Wells that he had it bound into the early editions of *Leaves of Grass*.

In its role as a discipline, phrenology performed importantly in the front lines of the virulent war between science and religion. Phrenology was bitterly attacked by conservative church groups for its radical implications for the life of society. It was regarded as inevitably leading to atheism and, because it made moral or immoral behavior dependent on the nature of the body, to immorality. Some observed with considerable outrage that things like soul, spirit and faith had to be squeezed into the organ of Reverence, just one among 37, and rather smaller than that of Amativeness, for instance. In short, there was a good deal of preliminary skirmishing, to be followed by the great battles between religion and science which were to be occasioned by the publication of *On the Origin of Species* in 1859.

In his introduction to that work, Darwin mentions a book called *Vestiges of the Natural History of Creation*. The *Vestiges* was published (anonymously) in 1844 and had gone through 10 editions and revisions by 1853. It had caused a frightful stink, having advanced a theory of the evolution of species which, however, lacked the theory of natural selection to be added by Darwin. The author of the *Vestiges* was Robert Chambers, a Scotsman and close friend of George Combe and his brother Andrew, physician to Queen Victoria and also a leading spokesman of the phrenological movement. Darwin praised the *Vestiges* in the following terms:

> "In my opinion it has done excellent service in this country in calling attention to the subject [evolution], in removing prejudice, and in thus preparing the ground for the reception of analogous views."

Cannot the same thing be said for phrenology as a whole? That it prepared the ground by introducing into the arena of public discussion many of the same issues and in many of the same terms? The phrenological movement displayed a perhaps inordinate optimism about the possibilities of change through education and modification of the environment, an optimism very like John B. Watson's. To mention an even more striking parallel, the "atmosphere" of phrenology is most congenial to many of the social and scientific assumptions that stand behind B. F. Skinner's *Walden Two* utopianism.

Man, and man's mind, could be studied objectively. Radical changes could be effected in the mind by altering the relationships among the various cerebral functions and by modifying the environment in which those relationships are formed. These radical changes in mental behavior were, for the most part, necessary and desirable. These are the conclusions that American functionalists drew from the Darwinian theories. And they are for the most part central to phrenological thought. The *Vestiges* drew heavily upon phrenological thought; phrenological thought got a thorough airing in the United States in the 1830s and '40s; and Darwin drew heavily on the *Vestiges*. That is to say, there seems to be a discernible underlying continuity or "tradition" of psychological theory and practice stretching from the early 1830s into the 20th Century, and it seems reasonable to suggest that the general terms in which phrenologists articulated their optimistic science sank into American culture and remained there, to be rearoused with the advent of the self-consciously scientific psychology of the late 19th and 20th Centuries.

ROBERT CHAMBERS

WILLIAM JAMES

JOHN DEWEY

Now is perhaps the time to underscore a point that must seem obvious; namely, that phrenology was a science of *individual differences*. It was grounded in the belief that every man had a different "cerebral musculature," and that conditions could and should be individually tailored to innate differences and with respect to the flexibility allowed by the analogy to the musculature. Gall and Spurzheim wanted to know *why* some men made good bankers or poets or murderers, and phrenology was the system they constructed as an "answer." Popular phrenology quickly appropriated this system and bent it to intensely practical uses—aptitude testing, vocational guidance, marriage counseling and patching up the sore spots of a man's life wherever they might lie.

'Ganz Amerikanisch'

Within psychology as a whole, there are two major approaches to psychological phenomena. One is the effort to obtain general propositions that hold for the generalized human organism. The other is a study of individual differences, the measurement and assessment of those individual capacities that enable a given person to adjust to and manipulate his environment. The study of individual differences lies at the cen-

ter of the functionalism that began with William James and with John Dewey and J. R. Angell. Historically, such functionalism exists in a prior or telegonic relationship with industrial psychology, with the social psychology of William McDougall, and with certain applications of behaviorist doctrines, all of which form a strand or cluster of emphasis felt to be characteristically American.

Psychology is usually considered to have been born as an independent discipline in the last quarter of the 19th Century. At this time, young American scholars went to Germany to learn the "new" psychology, largely from Wilhelm Wundt, who in 1879 had set up the first important laboratory for experimental psychology. His laboratory was designed to generate and test propositions that would be true for all persons, for a human mind assumed for the purposes of research to be generalized and non-unique. The American students returned to their colleges and universities to set up laboratories, do research and teach in the new ways they had acquired in Germany. However, almost immediately they began to use their new methods to study individual differences. They seemed to consider this radical change of target hardly worthy of comment, but Wundt referred to it as *ganz amerikanisch*—entirely and typically American.

Historians of psychology account for this seemingly instinctive shift of emphasis by speaking of pressures soundlessly exerted by the cultural environment, and they point to the confluence of Darwinian theories and the general competitiveness of American society as major sources of those pressures. But a case can be made, perhaps, for the following plot summary: the widespread familiarity with phrenological theories; the "repression" of these theories on the part of the scientific community both because of the failure of the doctrine of the skull and because of the excesses of popular vulgarized phrenology; the advent of the Darwinian argument, informed by many of the same theories; the enthusiastic and perhaps even uncritical reception by the scientific community of Darwin's theories; the ready seizure by American functionalists of certain Darwinian motifs, especially those relating to organic structure and function as the products of successful adaptation; the remarriage of these motifs with a bias toward individual differences that had been lurking in the context of scientific psychology since Spurzheim talked to the Boston doctors.

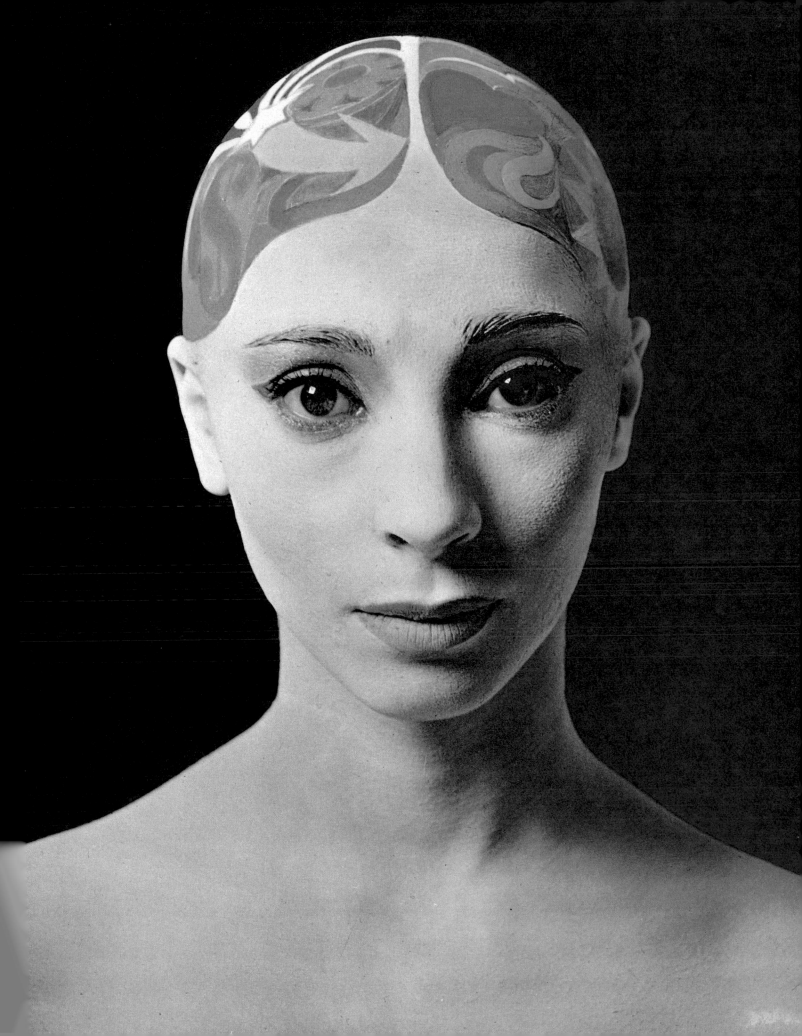

Are I.Q. TESTS Intelligent?

By Raymond Bernard Cattell

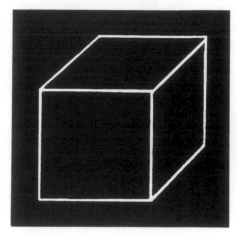

THE DILEMMA OF THE MENSA SOCIETY dramatizes the current upheaval in intelligence testing. Roughly three out of four of the prospective members selected on one kind of intelligence test failed to be selected by a second test, and three out of four of those chosen by the second type could not meet the standards of the first test. This international society, which limits entry to those at the 98th percentile or above in intelligence, was forced to make a policy decision on *which* kind of intelligence the society would consider.

Present controversy on the meaning of intelligence and of intelligence testing has erupted only in the past decade. It centers on whether there is a single factor of general intelligence and on the adequacy of present tests to measure it. My research indicates that there are two kinds of intelligence, fluid and crystallized, and that the former, which is independent of culture, can be measured as accurately as the latter.

To grasp what we now know of intelligence and the devices which attempt to measure it, one first must understand the background of the current dispute. In the first decade of this century, Charles Spearman brought to a field crowded with untutored, arbitrary, and generally naive definitions of intelligence, the theory of the "g" factor, a unitary, objectively defined, general-intelligence factor. For 50 years, Spearman's g factor has remained the only firm basis for the objective determination and measurement of intelligence.

This factor was defined by weights applied to different kinds of intellec-

tual performances, and its existence was proved by the peculiar form of correlation coefficients that appeared in correlations of ability measurement. If correlation coefficients show that four abilities, a, c, e, and g, are mutually positively related when measured over a group of 300 people, whereas the correlations are essentially zero on the abilities b, d, and f, we can assume some underlying unity behind a, c, e, and g.

There is no reason that there could not be two, three, or more such correlation clusters in a large group of abilities. But Spearman argued that the squared table of all possible correlations among a widely sampled set of abilities had a uniform slope which pointed to the existence of only one factor. To support this argument, he went beyond correlation clusters and developed factor analysis—a means of discovering the influences behind clusters.

Factor analysis is a method of calculating—from the various correlation coefficients of measured individual performances—the number and the general natures of the influences that account for observed relations. Through such an analysis, Spearman found the tests that bore most heavily on his general intelligence factor were those that had to do with reasoning and judgment. He therefore defined this factor as the capacity to educe relations and correlates.

Factor analysis also tells us how much of the individual variation in some particular performance is accounted for by each of the several factors that combine to produce that kind of behavior. Spearman concluded that g had about

a 9:1 ratio to special abilities in determining mathematical learning rate; about 7:1 in accounting for the size of one's properly used vocabulary; about 2:1 in determining musical ability; and about 1:4 in judging drawing ability.

Decades later, Louis Thurstone developed a multiple-factor analysis. This improvement over Spearman's methods led to Thurstone's discovery and definition of a dozen primary abilities, among them verbal comprehension, word fluency, number, space, and reasoning. Neither g nor the I.Q. were invalidated by Thurstone's work. On the contrary, advances in factor analysis rectified the only known statistical and structural flaw in Spearman's work. General intelligence now emerged from multiple-factor analysis as a single *second-order factor*, based on the intercorrelation among primary factors. The general intelligence concept was strengthened, for the pyramids of primary factors provided a far more reliable base than did the grains of innumerable small variables.

The question of how Thurstone's primary abilities grew out of Spearman's general ability remained unanswered, but researchers tended to neglect its importance. Instead of investigating the natural structure of abilities, the experts devised tests to fill the holes in a subjective framework. And so, for 30 years, there has been only trivial consolidation in this field, with a consequent hardening of attitudes and custom among professional intelligence testers.

As one who investigated with both Spearman and Thurstone, I at first was as much disturbed as intrigued when I

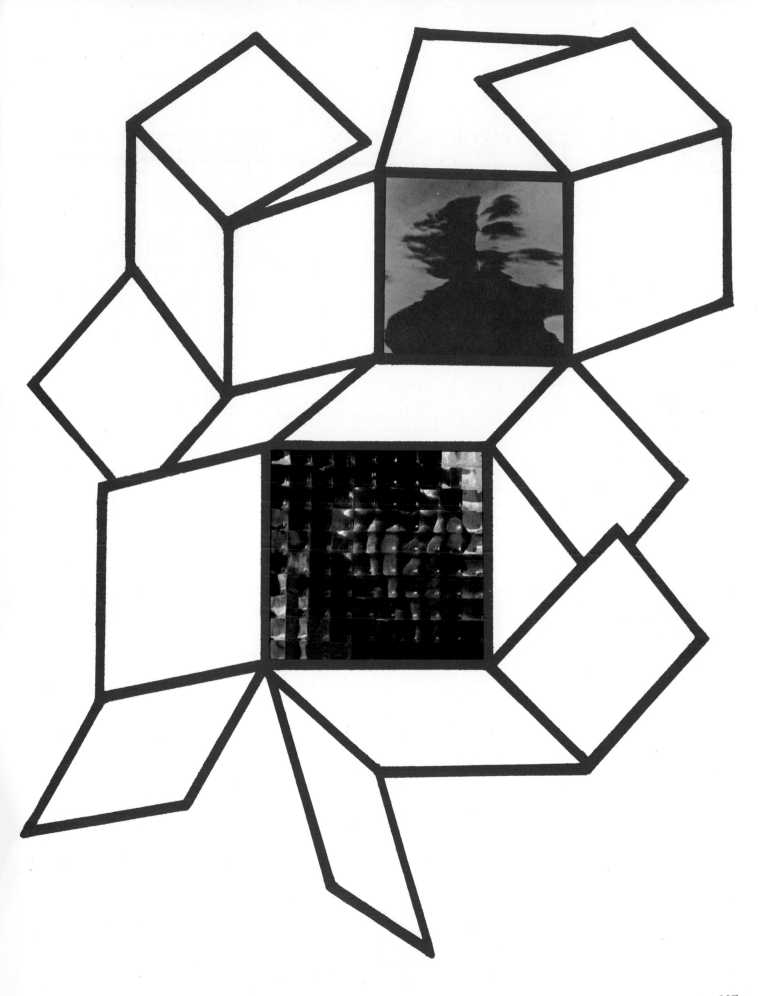

thought I saw flaws in their monolithic structure. The first signs appeared in data on the second-order analysis of primary abilities. There was evidence that *two* general factors rather than one were involved. On rather slender evidence, I put forward in 1940 the theory of two g's. Those original disquieting conceptions since have been strengthened by the accumulation of evidence.

The breadth of a factor and the number of factors depend upon what tests an experimenter uses to gather his data. From the 20 primary abilities surveyed by John French, John Horn obtained some four or five broad abilities, such as fluid intelligence, crystallized intelligence, speed, and visualization. But the broadest of all such abilities, and the ones with a semantic claim to the label "intelligence," are fluid and crystallized.

Crystallized general ability, "g_c," shows itself in judgmental skills that have been acquired by cultural experience: vocabulary, good use of synonyms, numerical skills, mechanical knowledge, a well-stocked memory, and even habits of logical reasoning. G_c is high on the subtests that traditionally have been built into intelligence tests: vocabulary size, analogies, and classifications involving cultural knowledge of objects in the problem. Crystallized ability stretches across the whole range of cultural acquisitions. Mechanical knowledge—which is negligible or even negative on fluid ability—has a measurable effect on crystallized ability.

Tests of fluid ability, "g_f," have little relation to a well-stocked memory. They are culture fair perceptual and performance tests and those specially developed tests of judgment and reasoning which have been considered relatively culture free. They involve solutions to tests of classifications, analogies, matrices, topology, and problems that do not involve much educational acquisition. Fluid ability does have a role in numerical reasoning and even in verbal skills. It is fairly powerful in spatial reasoning and very powerful in inductive reasoning. [*See illustration, upper right.*]

The difference between fluid and crystallized general abilities becomes apparent when the intellectual responses of two persons who contrast in them are described. To find a person high in fluid ability but low in crystallized, we should have to take someone who accidentally has missed schooling. I have measured deck-hands and farmers who scored much higher than average professors in fluid ability but who acquired no comparable level of crystallized ability because they had not systematically applied their fluid intelligence to what is usually called culture. Such men will astonish you in a game of chess, or by solving a wire puzzle with which you have struggled in vain, or in swift insights into men and motives. But their vocabularies may be arrested at a colloquial level, their knowledge of history negligible, and they never may have encountered algebra or geometry. These men often excel at the strategy of games, and one suspects they are naturally good soldiers. Lord Fisher, who designed the Dreadnought battleship, said, "In war

Primary Abilities of Specific Batteries	Research I: Boys (57) and Girls (5) of 6½ Years Old		Research II: Boys (151) and Girls (154) of 9, 10, & 11 Years Old		Research III: Boys and Girls (277) of 12 & 13 Years Old		Research IV: Men and Women (297) Adult Range	
	g_f	g_c	g_f	g_c	g_f	g_c	g_f	g_c
Verbal	−17	74	22	63	15	46	10	69
Spatial			73	03	32	14	30	−07
Reasoning	10	72			08	50	23	30
Number	43	49	47	35	05	59	24	29
Fluency					07	10	−03	25
Series: Culture Fair					35	23		
Classification: Culture Fair	58*	−11*	78*	09*	63	−02	48*	−08*
Matrices: Culture Fair					50	10		
Topology: Culture Fair					51	09		
Perceptual Speed							20	06
Flexibility							−03	03
Induction							55	12
Intellectual Speed							51	10
Mechanical Information							−15	48
Ego Strength	−07	−09					01	43
Self Sentiment							01	43
Super Ego								
Surgency								
Anxiety	10	−33	04	−04			−05	−26

Fluid and Crystallized General Ability Factors at Various Ages. Crystallized general ability shows itself in those judgmental skills dependent upon cultural experience, while fluid ability affects tests unrelated to well-stocked memory. Flexibility is distinct from either g_c or g_f. Note the consistent level of g_f scores throughout all the age groups.

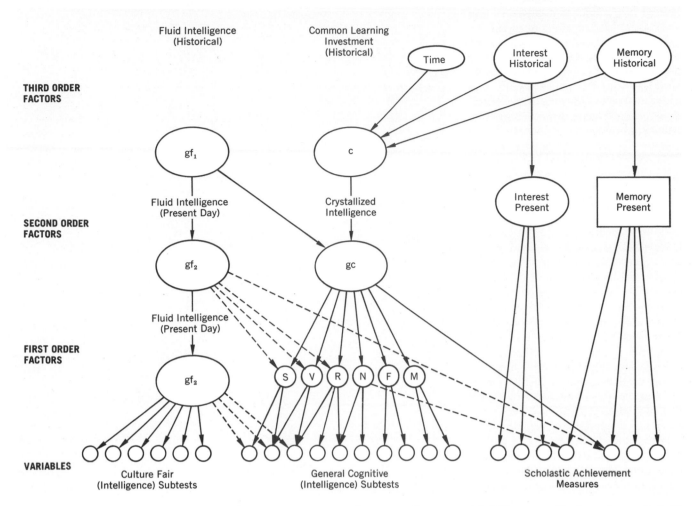

THIRD ORDER FACTORS

Fluid Intelligence (Historical)

Common Learning Investment (Historical)

Time

Interest Historical

Memory Historical

gf_1

c

SECOND ORDER FACTORS

Fluid Intelligence (Present Day)

Crystallized Intelligence

Interest Present

Memory Present

gf_2

gc

FIRST ORDER FACTORS

Fluid Intelligence (Present Day)

gf_2

S V R N F M

VARIABLES

Culture Fair (Intelligence) Subtests

General Cognitive (Intelligence) Subtests

Scholastic Achievement Measures

Causal Relations Between Fluid and Crystallized Ability Factors. Scores on the general intelligence subtests and on scholastic achievement measures are the result of time, interest, memory and both fluid and crystallized intelligence. Arrows indicate the direction of influence and solid arrows show major lines of influence. Note the lack of other influence on culture fair subtests.

you need surprise." Surprise bursts from situations in which crystallized intelligence is useless. Napoleon claimed that he would make his despairing opponents "burn their books on tactics." The characteristic of fluid intelligence is that it leads to perception of complex relationships in new environments.

The individual with a high level of crystallized intelligence has different capacities. He will have learned many intelligent responses to problem situations. He will recognize an engineering problem as requiring solution by differential calculus, and he will diagnose a defective sentence by pointing to a dangling participle. He could not have acquired these skills, however, unless he had the fluid ability to see them.

To illustrate a case where crystallized ability is clearly higher than fluid ability, we must take either a person in whom there has been some recession of fluid ability, as through aging or brain damage, or a person who has been over-educated for his ability—say, someone like Sheridan's Mrs. Malaprop, taught

a bigger vocabulary than natural judgment permits handling.

Crystallized and fluid intelligence abilities could not be isolated until technical progress in factor analytic experiments made their recognition possible. These two structures have been confirmed repeatedly by researchers over the whole age range, from five to 50.

Fluid and crystallized ability factors are positively correlated. According to the theory of two broad intelligences, fluid intelligence is a general relation-perceiving capacity, independent of sensory area, and it is determined by the individual's endowment in cortical, neurological-connection count development. It is a broad factor because such integrating power can be brought to bear in almost any perceptual or reasoning area. Crystallized ability, on the other hand, appears as a related circle of abilities—verbal, numerical, reasoning—that normally are taught at school. The extent to which an individual takes or leaves what he is taught depends on his fluid ability, on his years of formal education,

and on his motivation to learn. Thus, crystallized general ability reflects both the neurological integrative potential of the individual and his fortune in cultural experience.

Crystallized ability is not identical with scholastic achievement. Many scholastic skills depend largely on rote memory, whereas what factor analysis shows is crystallized ability in that section of school learning involving complex judgmental skills that have been acquired by the application of fluid ability. [*See illustration above.*]

Once these two general abilities are located and independently measured, further distinguishing characteristics appear. The age curve of growth for the two abilities turns out to be quite different. Fluid ability follows a biological growth curve and approaches a plateau at about 14 years, whereas crystallized ability shows an increase to 16, 18, and beyond. The evidence points to some steady decline in fluid intelligence after about 22 years of age, but crystallized intelligence keeps its level as far into later years as adequate samples have been taken. [*See illustration, right.*]

The standard deviation of the calculated I.Q.—mental age divided by actual age—is almost exactly 50 per cent greater for fluid than for crystallized ability, 24 points instead of 16 points. Socio-educational research might determine whether arranging brighter and duller streams of classroom instruction would permit more divergence of crystallized I.Q.

There are substantial indications that fluid and crystallized intelligence respond differently to brain damage. Localized injury may produce localized loss of skills, while leaving other abilities untouched. By the nature of fluid ability, an impairment in any cortical locality should produce some loss of general fluid-ability performance.

A pilot study on nature-nuture ratios suggests that heredity bears a greater relation to fluid than to crystallized intelligence. Tentative estimates of relative variance are 90 per cent for g_f and 70 per cent for g_c. An independent demonstration of the higher hereditary influence of fluid-ability levels has been given by John Loehlin, who compared the primary factor within pairs of both fraternal and identical twins. Verbal ability, fluency, and reasoning primaries naturally showed environmental influence, but a general genetic factor corresponding to fluid ability was apparent.

My own research and that of others indicates that day-to-day changes do occur in intelligence. Our subjective conviction that we are brighter on some days than we are on others is borne out by measures of g_f variability over time, as might be expected from the closer dependence of fluid intelligence upon total physiological efficiency.

Many of the puzzling phenomena in intelligence testing are explained if we consider that the traditional intelligence test actually is a mixture of fluid and crystallized factors. Discoveries of different ages for the end of intelligence growth, significant differences in the standard deviation of I.Q.'s, and different ratios of the weight of heredity and environment on the I.Q. all result from a confusion of the two factors in the usual intelligence test.

When I first called attention to the flaws in the general intelligence theory, I at once proceeded to investigate the correlations with the general fluid ability factor of a variety of "perceptual" tests. From my research came the culture fair intelligence test associated with present uses in cross-cultural studies and Head-

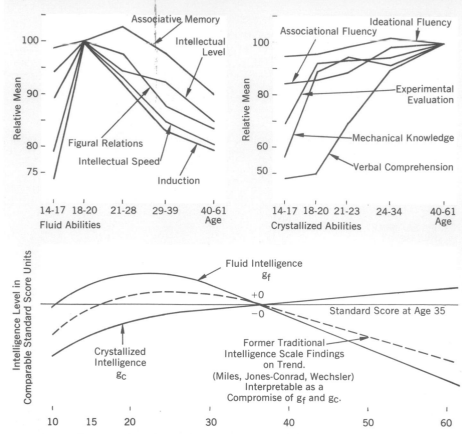

Age Curves Compared for Fluid and Crystallized General Ability and Traditional Tests.

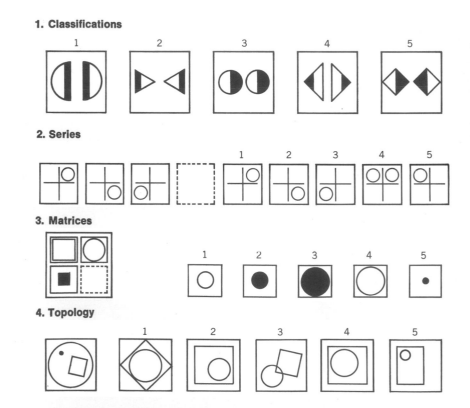

Sample Items from a Culture Fair Test.

1 **Which one of these is different from the remaining four? (No. 3)**
2 **Which of 5 figures on right would properly continue 3 on left, i.e., fill blank? (No. 5)**
3 **Which of figures on right should go into square on left to make it look right? (No. 2)**
4 **At left, dot is outside the square and inside the circle. In which of the figures on the right could you put a dot outside the square and inside the circle? (No. 3)**

1. Comparison of American and Chinese Children, 10 Years of Age, by IPAT Culture Fair Scale 2 (Rodd, 1960).

	American (1007)		Chinese (Hong Kong) (1007)	
	Mean	Stand. Dev.	Mean	Stand. Dev.
Culture Fair Form 2A	24.10	6.66	24.04	5.70

2. Comparison of American and Chinese College Students (Mean Age 18 yrs.) by IPAT Culture Fair Scale 3 (Rodd, 1960).

	American (1100)		Taiwanese (765)		Chinese Mainland Chinese (525)	
	Mean	Stand. Dev.	Mean	Stand. Dev.	Mean	Stand. Dev.
Culture Fair Form 3A	21.99	4.50	21.99	4.50	22.88	4.47
Culture Fair Form 3B	26.90	4.50	26.95	4.47	27.23	4.53

3. Correlation of Culture Fair and Traditional Tests with Social Status (McArthur and Elley, 1964).

1. Traditional Test (California Test of Mental Maturity)	+0.38
2. Traditional Test (Modified) (Lorge-Thorndike)	+0.27
3. Fluid Ability (IPAT Culture Fair) (On 271 12-and 13-Year-Olds)	+0.24

Cultural Differences and Culture Fair Scores. That culture is no barrier when a culture fair test is used shows in American and Chinese scores on the same test. The correlation between c_f and social status measures the relation of real ability to the status.

start programs. But whatever its present practical importance, the origin of these culture fair tests was in the first place the theoretical goal of defining the new form of intelligence.

In our first attempt at developing a fluid-ability test appropriate to all cultures, I took such common elements as parts of the human body, sun, moon, rain, and stars, as well as random blotches. But only the perceptual forms have been retained in later tests, for experiment has shown that these give accurate results. [*See illustration, lower right, page 340.*]

In choosing test elements, the effect on the score of cultural experience can be reduced by taking either what is over-learned in all cultures or what is absolutely strange to all. Anything in between these extremes is bound to show the influence of the culture in the test scores. To take overlearned items is more practicable, because valuable test time is wasted in getting responses on completely strange items.

To avoid pointless sociological arguments, we called fluid-ability measures culture *fair* rather than culture *free*. Objection from teachers to a culture-free concept arises from confusion between the cultural familiarity and test sophistication effects on test scores. *All* tests, culture fair tests included, are susceptible to test sophistication, and scores may continue to improve for some four to six retests. Scores increase due to familiarity with instructions, with layout, with timing, and with the tricks any good person being tested can learn. Studies by Sarason, Feingold, and me have shown that practice in the culture-fair type of spatial and analogies perception produced no real gain, unlike training in the verbal and numerical fields that dominate the traditional intelligence test. But with subjects unused to paper-and-pencil tests, and with subjects from other cultures, it would be ideal always to repeat testing several times and to throw away the results of the first three or four encounters.

The culture fair concept does not imply that no significant differences ever should be found between different populations living in different cultures or

	Correlation with School Total Achievement									Other Intelligence Tests		
	Validity General Factor	Marks by Teacher Amer.	Chin.	Stand. Ach. Test	English Amer.	Chin.	Reading	Math Amer.	Chin.	Calif. Test of Mental Maturity Verb.	Numer.	Wisc. I.Q.
Fluid Abil. (IPAT Cult. Fair Scale 2)	.79*	.34*		.35*			.52++					.72++
Fluid Abil. (IPAT Cult. Fair Scale 3)	.78°	.35**	.35**	.59 / .49	40	30+		64	47+	42	56	
Crystal. Abil. (Cal. Test Ment. Mat.)	.58*	.66*	0?	.65*			0?		0?			
Crystal. Abil. (Lorge-Thorndike)	.52*	.43*	0?	.35*			0?		0?			
Army Beta					25			34		27	58	
Henmon Nelson				.81								
Pintuer							.85++					.80++

* McArthur & Elley, 271, 12 and 13 year olds
** Domino, 94 college students
+ Rodd & Goodman (Atten. corrected on school test)
++ 79 children in Bridge Project School
° Bajard

Correlations of Fluid and Crystallized Intelligence Tests with other Measures. The validity in terms of general ability saturation is highest for the culture fair scales, but correlation with school grades is higher when the traditional intelligence test is used.

subcultures or social classes. The bright people in most societies tend to migrate to higher socio-economic levels. The correlation of .20 to .25 between fluid ability measures and social status presumably is a measure of the relation of real ability to status, but the correlation of .38 found with traditional intelligence tests represents also the scholastic gain of those with the luck to be born into more-educated families.

Where ulterior evidence suggests that peoples *are* equally gifted, a culture fair test must show absolutely no difference of score despite profound differences of culture. No differences have been demonstrated on the culture fair scales among American, British, German, French, and Italian samples. A more severe test was made by William Rodd, who compared Chinese (Taiwanese) and American school children and university students on identically printed culture fair tests. The raw scores are identical to three significant figures for Midwestern American and Taiwanese school children. American college students do not differ from the Taiwanese, but there is a significant difference between Taiwanese and mainland Chinese, which could be the result of differences in methods of student selection. [*See illustration, upper left, p. 341.*]

But testing does suggest that significant mean population differences *can* exist. Samples have shown higher means in the south than in the north of Japan, in the north than in the south of Italy, and in New Zealand migrants as compared with unselected British Isles stock. Further research might develop a world map of intelligence resources.

For school-age children, when intelligence tests are most used, the correlation between g_f and g_c scores is positive and substantial. It will probably become even higher if regular school attendance becomes universal and methods used in more efficient school systems become uniform. From this high correlation, casual administrators may argue that one kind of test—the old kind, of course —is enough. Indeed, hard-headed realism may assert that the traditional I.Q. test is preferable, because the g_c test predicts this or next year's scholastic performance slightly but systematically better than does the g_f test. [*See illustration, bottom, p. 341.*]

But if a maximum prediction of next year's academic achievement were all that one desired, one would not use an intelligence test at all! For a higher correlation can be obtained from *this* year's grades, or from a proper combination of intelligence, personality, and motivation measures, as our research has shown.

The purpose of an intelligence test is different. It should help us to understand the causes of a given person's good or poor grades or to predict what he will do in the future in radically changed circumstances. Over an interval of a year or so we can expect habits and situations and the momentum of interest to make scholastic performance *now* the best predictor of grades in the future. But when a person's life turns a corner, as when he goes from liberal education in the school to technical education in a career, the crystallized-ability measure may be quite misleading. A fluid-ability I.Q. from a culture fair test is likely to be a better predictor of performance.

The same principle holds if we compare children of fundamentally different backgrounds. The Binet in French, administered to a mixed group of 100 French, 100 American, and 100 Chinese children, would show a correlation of I.Q. with French language skills, but the Binet score would be no general predictor of language ability among the Americans and Chinese. In the same situation, a culture fair test would correlate with the native-language performance about equally in each of the three language groups.

During the school years, culture fair tests are both theoretically and practically useful, especially in localities with language or cultural differences. But the dual I.Q. becomes indispensable almost anywhere when testing adults. The two I.Q. values for a given person may be very different, and the kinds of prediction made from each will differ. Crystallized ability may remain steady or even climb, for it increases with age and experience, but fluid ability falls after age 22. A middle-aged man handles most situations in our culture more intelligently than he would have when he was 20, but if a younger and an older man were transferred to an absolutely new society, the probably higher fluid-intelligence level of the younger man would be likely to show itself. Where performance in radically different situations is involved, the man of 50 will perform very differently from what would be predicted for him on the basis of his g_c mental age. The g_f mental age would have predicted this difference.

Despite the tremendous accumulation of experience concerning intelligence testing between 10 and 20 years of age, there has been comparatively little over the 20- to 70-year range, and we know little about what happens to age trends, distribution, or sex differences of intelligence in that period.

Our society, which values high intelligence, must make some kind of policy decision on *which* kind of intelligence should be given emphasis in this period. A decision on culture fair and traditional test usage becomes even more imperative for the psychologist whose testing helps determine jobs and clinical outcomes. As men leave school and go into their special occupational fields, the statistical general factor begins to disintegrate, or to persist only as an historical relic. Vocabulary tests for the average man reveal a distinct falling off in ability after school. And if women in middle age are tested by intelligence tests (at least as mostly designed by men), they undergo an apparent drop in crystallized ability not shown by men.

To continue to regard the traditional intelligence tests as a general intelligence measure when applied after the age of 20 is pure illusion. If a g_c score predicts relation-perceiving capacity in new fields, it does so indirectly by harking back to the fact that scholastic ability at 18 was a measure of g_f intelligence. If that happens not to be true for a person, or if such things as brain damage have occurred since, the g_c prediction can be badly in error.

The need for a dual I.Q. score is rooted not only in what happens to the man but in what happens to the culture. A comparison that I made of all 11-year-olds in a city of 300,000 before World War II with 11-year-olds in the same city after the war and 13 years later showed no trace of any significant difference on a culture fair test. Yet Godfrey Thomson's comparisons on the British Binet at about the same period showed a very significant upward shift. Results in America by Frank Finch with various traditional crystallized-ability tests showed an even greater upward shift. The standardization of a traditional test becomes unanchored from the moment it is made, and it drifts in whatever direction the tide of educational investment happens to take. In this more prosperous age, the direction is upward. Since no such drift is demonstrable with culture fair, fluid-ability measures, error of prediction is less flagrant.

New answers to educational, political, and social questions may be reached through culture fair intelligence testing. Culture fair tests are not toys for anthropologists to take to remote cultures. They need to be used here and now to open equal educational opportunity to all our subcultures of class and race. ◪

Is Graphology Valid?

By Daniel S. Anthony

"The world desires to know what a man can do, not what he knows."
Booker T. Washington

ASK MOST PSYCHOLOGISTS ABOUT GRAPH- OLOGY—handwriting analysis—and they will say that it's as scientific as a shell game, a pastime for fools, a black art, or a combination of all three. Admittedly, I am partisan because I am a graph- ologist, but then I have more than a cas- ual acquaintance with the field *because* I have been a graphologist for 30 years. I am convinced that in the hands of a skilled practitioner graphology can assist corporations in the selection of produc- tive and reliable employees, can aid therapists in evaluating their patients, and can help youths choose their careers by pinpointing talents and personality traits. I believe that graphology could aid in difficult medical diagnoses.

On the Continent, graphology is wide- ly used. But here, so many amateurs and charlatans have invaded the field, and downgraded it, that only about 500 busi- ness firms respect and use handwriting analysis in personnel work, and only one college, The New School for Social Re-

search in New York, teaches it. I count just ten or twelve expert graphologists in the country today. In contrast, there are some 30,000 diploma-mill "grapho- analysis graduates" who peddle a two- dollar personality test which is based on how the *i*'s are dotted or how the *t*'s are crossed in one's script. (Five dollars brings you an "in-depth" analysis.) They advertise in all the pulp magazines, they are widely successful, and they even have begun to worm their way into scat- tered police stations and courts of law as "expert" witnesses on handwriting.

Legitimate graphology is, I maintain, a true subdiscipline of psychology. It sys- tematically scrutinizes the total impact of the writing on the page and all its interrelationships. It operates against a backdrop of psychological and grapho- logical investigation. It recognizes its limits and will expand its scope only on the basis of further controlled research. With my wife, Florence R. Anthony, I have evaluated 1,101 applicants for sales

positions with various life insurance companies during the last five years. We have an accuracy record of 93 percent. Out of the total group, we recommended 433 men, of whom 321 actually joined our client firms; and 295 of them per- formed as expected in the first year, with 274 measuring up to our predic- tions over the whole five-year period. Using graphology, our client agencies also reduced their employee turnover to well below the industry average of 80 percent every three years.

How does graphology work? Funda- mentally, it examines how the subject's handwriting deviates from the way he was taught. For most adults, this was by the Palmer Method, Zaner-Bloser, or one of the many other commercial types of cursive writing. Only the penmanship teachers themselves and a few account- ants and draftsmen ever were able to master careful cursive writing—and their handwriting accordingly is difficult to appraise. The rest of us lack the psycho-

343

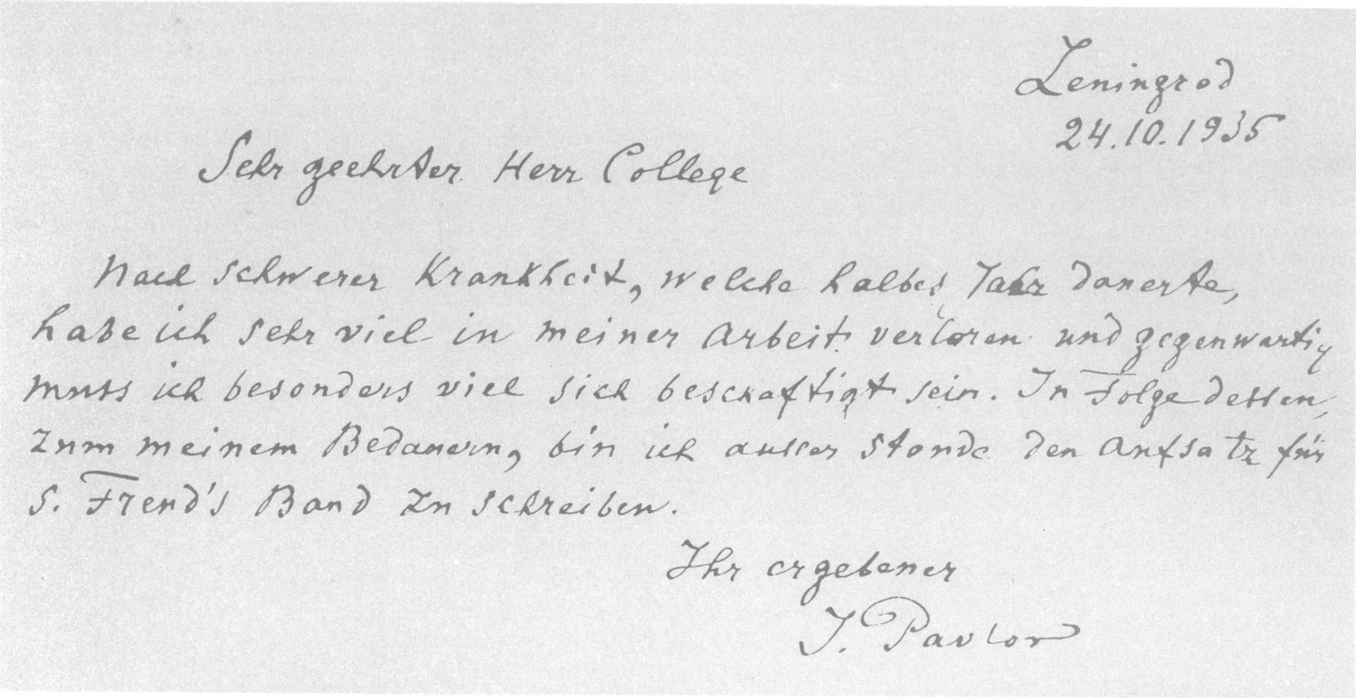

Leningrad
24.10.1935

Sehr geehrter Herr College

Nach schwerer Krankheit, welche halbes Jahr dauerte, habe ich sehr viel in meiner Arbeit verloren und gegenwärtig muss ich besonders viel sich beschäftigt sein. In Folge dessen, zum meinem Bedauern, bin ich außer Stande den Aufsatz für S. Freud's Band zu schreiben.

Ihr ergebener
J. Pavlov

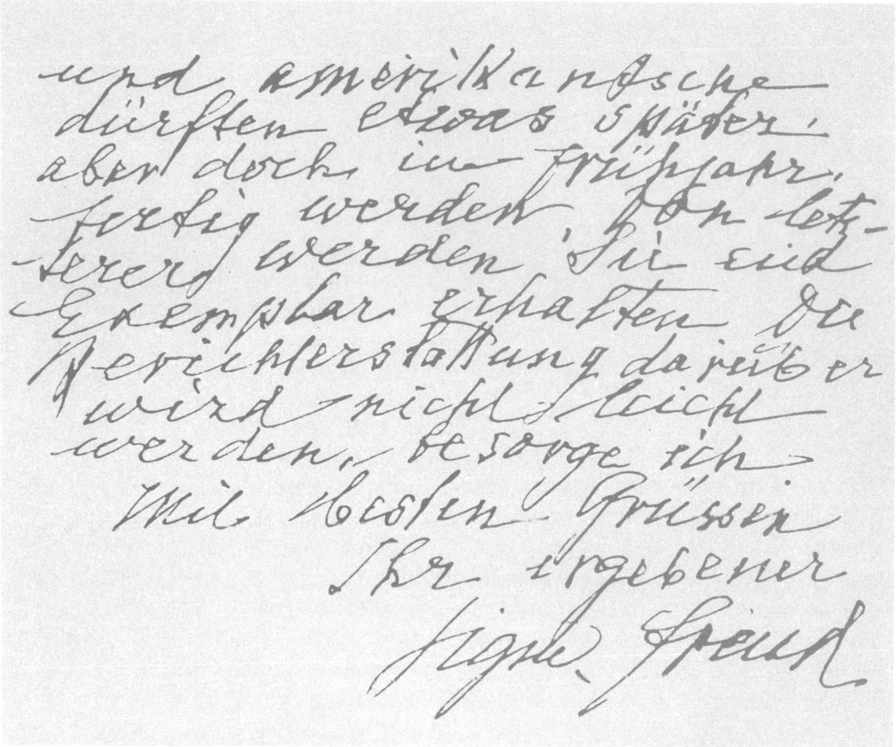

und amerikanische dürften etwas später, aber doch im Frühjahr fertig werden. Von letzterem werden Sie ein Exemplar erhalten. Die Berichterstattung darüber wird nicht leicht werden, besorge ich.
Mit besten Grüssen
Ihr ergebener
Sigm. Freud

motor control necessary for the flat forearm and rigid finger movements which produce such sterile symmetry and regularity, and so our personalities intrude upon our penmanship.

Today, the trend in private schools and many public schools is toward the teaching of print or printscript. This poses problems for the graphologist, but even here we detect individuality—in backhandedness, for example. I have analyzed many samples of printing, since so many job application forms are filled out this way. Whatever the style, the method by which the subject was taught of course must be determined if a study is to mean anything.

The theory of graphology is that each of us brings so much individuality to handwriting that it is impossible for anyone to duplicate the writing, and especially the signature, of someone else. Though you may waste an hour or two to prove me wrong, you cannot (even if you spend a lifetime saving signature samples) make any two of your own signatures look exactly alike. The very finest forgers also fail here. And yet our handwriting has such constancy and individuality that no one else can duplicate it perfectly. As an expert witness, I have testified at many a trial of men who weren't aware of this, and thus have languished long in prison. Signature and handwriting individuality were recognized legally for the first time in the Justinian Code of Rome, in 539 A.D. I long for the day of understanding that graphic configurations produced independently by different writers show the same patterns which can be related to their behavior and to all human behavior. Graphology also clearly shows differences in people. This is my belief.

To take two famous examples, Ivan Pavlov and Sigmund Freud certainly wrote distinctively [*see above*]. Pavlov's writing is stylized in a way that departs dramatically from the Cyrillic alphabet he was taught. Freud took far greater vertical liberties than his copybook dictated. Notice how the personality differences between the two men emerge. Freud, the iconoclast, showed a marked strength of stroke. Look at the impulsive penetration, the steady uphill drive of his acute configurations. He practically forced his ideograms onto the paper.

Pavlov showed a greater concern for form and organization. His precise regularity of spacing between words and lines paralleled the systematic, controlled experimentation that made him the father of stimulus-response psychology. In his neat, wide margins, Freud did show a certain deference to his reader's taste, but notice how little room for intrusion he left in the body of the letter. His Gothic German script indicates an almost uncontrollable self-assertion. Pavlov's is scrupulous and unassuming.

Although it takes years of study and experience to find and chart all of handwriting's subtle configurations, let us try to analyze a few aspects of the signature of a noted New York artist, Alexander Dobkin, to show some of the unusual factors of unconscious graphic occurrence and congruence, which I insist never could be controlled by conscious cerebral forces. [*See page 346.*] While many graphic variables—like letter size, slant, and form—are subject to conscious articulation, the marks of an original (or pedestrian) character and the flow of graphic elements and geometric designs are not.

To test this principle on your own writing, take these steps:

1. Check your favorite writing implement—pen or pencil—for good flow.

2. Get a piece of unlined white bond paper 8½"x11", a 12" translucent plastic ruler, and a very sharp ball-point pen or a No. 2 or No. 3 hard pencil that is well-sharpened.

3. Seat yourself in your favorite writing position with pen and paper ready.

4. With the greatest possible spontaneity and natural speed, write your full signature three or four times, sufficiently far apart so that no element of one signature touches any part of another.

5. If one of your signatures looks unnatural, if the pen stuck, or you don't like the spacing, do all three over again on a new sheet of paper.

6. Note opposite page. To determine the *Upper Zone,* draw line UZ connecting the tops of the two highest letters.

7. The *Base Line* is often harder to determine. It is that line which touches the bottom of the greatest number of large and small letters. If you have trouble drawing a single BL, mark several as I have done for Dobkin: He has no single consistent *Base Line.* Note how his vary from signature to signature, and within each signature.

8. The *Lower Zone* (LZ) joins the lowest projecting points. Usually this will be the bottom of letters, but I have marked an LZ to show Dobkin's differentiation on this score.

9. The MZ (*Middle Zone*) line will touch most of your small letters.

Now refer back to the cursive writing sample. Place your ruler over the tops of the upper-zone and middle-zone letters of *Booker T. Washington* [*see illustration, page 343*] and observe the regular-ized system of touch points, all almost exactly equidistant from the printed Base Line. This contrived condition is known as horizontal parallelism of letter sizes. "Proper" penmanship demands exactly equal elements in the upper, middle, and lower zones.

Looking back now at Dobkin's signature, examine line D of Signature 3. Its eight touch points demonstrate multiple congruences of unconscious alignment. To take another example, Line T, joining key points in all three signatures, shows an uncanny quality of graphic integration of form and figure on the paper.

See how many diagonal, vertical, and horizontal lines touch more than two top or bottom stroke elements, vertices or cross points (as in the A, B, C lines). As you follow the S, T, W, X, Y, and Z lines, going through the three signatures from top to bottom, you see how ingeniously his unconscious congruences are organized. Although the exact touch points of each line show significant originality from signature to signature, the overall configurational gestalt of each signature maintains an identity and uniqueness.

The positioning of Dobkin's three signatures shows a rare aesthetic organization and psycho-motor control. Observe, for instance, the red circle which is centered at the top of the capital D staff of Signature 2 (Point X). It marks almost exactly the central cross points of the main diagonal axis, X and Y. This demonstrates an unusual degree of unconscious balance, as the psyche automatically seeks equilibrium.

Note that the actual cross point of these diagonals is just midway between the beginning and end of Signature 2. And see how the circumference of the circle centered at Point X (Signature 2) touches exactly the same spot in the capital D of both Signatures 1 and 3. This shows a diagrammatic and mathematical perception that very few of us possess.

If your own signature comes closer to the copybook form, you probably have a tendency toward conformity. If you lean toward Dobkin's variation and versatility, you do not mind bucking the tide and you probably enjoy the arts and the pursuit of knowledge. Should your handwriting contain even half of Dobkin's touch points and coordinated intermeshing, you should be devoting part of your life to some form of mental gymnastics or creative activity.

This is my tentative scoring system, based on the analysis of the writing and drawing of more than 1,000 people:

1. *Touch points.* A high number of touch points on the diagonal and vertical extensions of any two key points shows creative productivity.

2. *Geometrical forms.* A profusion of equal interlocking units (like diameter, radius, or circumference in a single signature), plus variability of these units of measurement, indicates originality of expression and/or dynamic individuality.

3. *Overall composition.* The more ingenious the graphic design is, the richer is the state of psycho-social adjustment.

Supposing that you were an insurance company personnel manager and had to hire one of the two salesmen whose handwriting is shown here. [*See illustrations, p. 347.*] Which man would you choose? I am convinced that your perceptions and reactions to the men's handwriting will be somewhat similar to your feelings about the men themselves if you knew them on the job.

Each graphologist uses his own technique. Mine combines the "graphometrics" discussed above, with microscopic examination of stroke details and with charts. I also chart the "psychogram" profile, which was originated by Klara Roman and which I have revised. But my *feel* for the specimen is just as important. My first step in any analysis is a study of the overall gestalt impression of the layout and the arrangement of the "picture" on the page.

Gestalt theory and the psychology of expression are fundamental to a sound approach to handwriting, I believe. The study of art and an understanding of the growing thrust toward a psychology of art are vital. At the New School for Social Research, I require all my students to study Rudolf Arnheim's *Art and Visual Perception* to help them develop the capacity for the aesthetic perception of the interdependent relationship, which contributes to the unity that is handwriting. Successful handwriting analysis depends upon the analyst's perception of the immeasurable subjectivity of script as much as upon the objective elements.

Gestalt theory, then, has been the basis of all my work. To me, the diminishing status of Gestalt psychology on the American campus today is a regrettable manifestation of a surge toward measurable objectivity.

In 1948, Werner Wolff, then professor of psychology at Bard College, wrote what I consider the key work in American graphology, *Diagrams of the Unconscious.* It combined, in its approach to graphology, the best of Gestalt and expressive psychology with Wolff's own

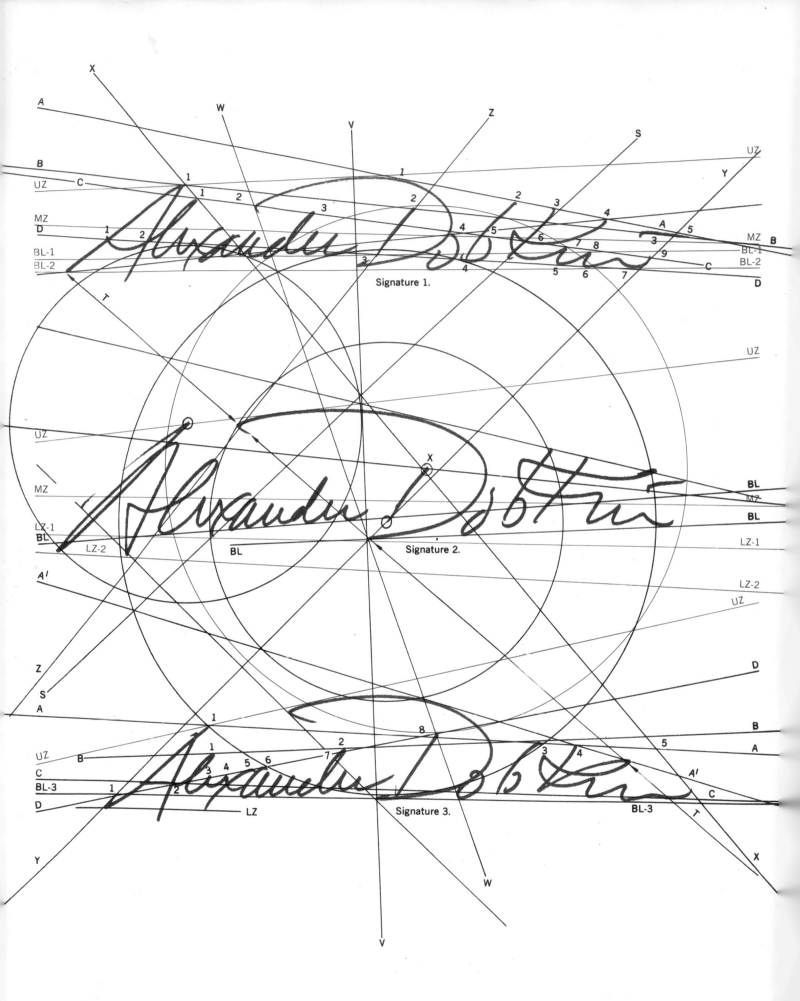

Signature 1.

Signature 2.

Signature 3.

346

depth psychology. In his book, he postulated that the unconscious forces which form handwriting style remain basically fixed, consistent and measurable—from our childhood scribbles to signing our last wills and testaments.

There are other important figures in the history of American graphology: June Downey, Thea Stein Lewinson, Rose Wolfson and Klara G. Roman, to name a few. Today, sadly, there is actually less activity in the field than yesterday. Alfred Kanfer is investigating cancer detection through signature analysis at the Strang Clinic in New York. But most new research in graphology is being carried out in Europe.

For example, the University of Moscow's Aleksandr R. Luria, a leading Soviet neurosurgeon, developed a simple bedside writing test which he says can pinpoint the location of brain lesions. Gerhard Gruenwald and Erica Zuberbier, at the University of Dusseldorf's Psychiatric Clinic of Medicine, have isolated the effect of stress and strain reactions on handwriting in both normal and brain-damaged persons. In 1960, Gruenwald noted the "disturbance and reorganization" of the writing act following shock treatment. Now he is looking into possible correlations between a subject's handwriting and his EKG, EEG, and myogram recordings. All this study is based on the neurobiological theory that handwriting reflects the mind-body condition of man. Graphology is taught at the graduate schools of the 12 major West German universities and at many French, Swedish, Swiss, and Dutch institutions of higher learning. These courses are required for licensing in

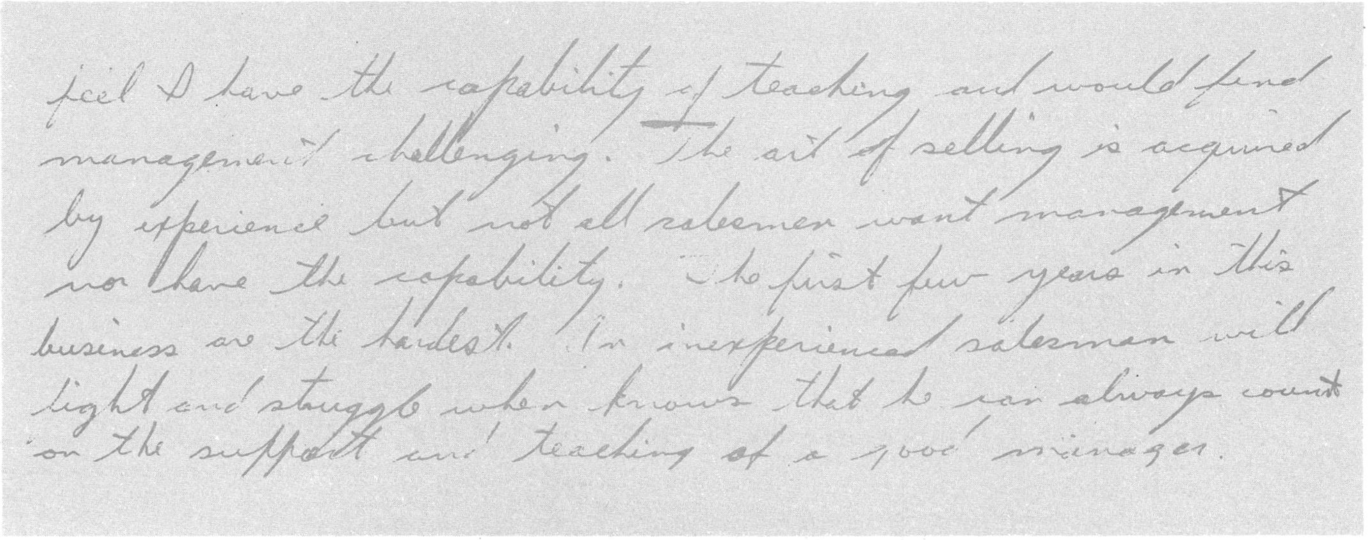

Which salesman would you hire? The author's graphology method selects the man whose writing appears below as the more aggressive, original and expressive.

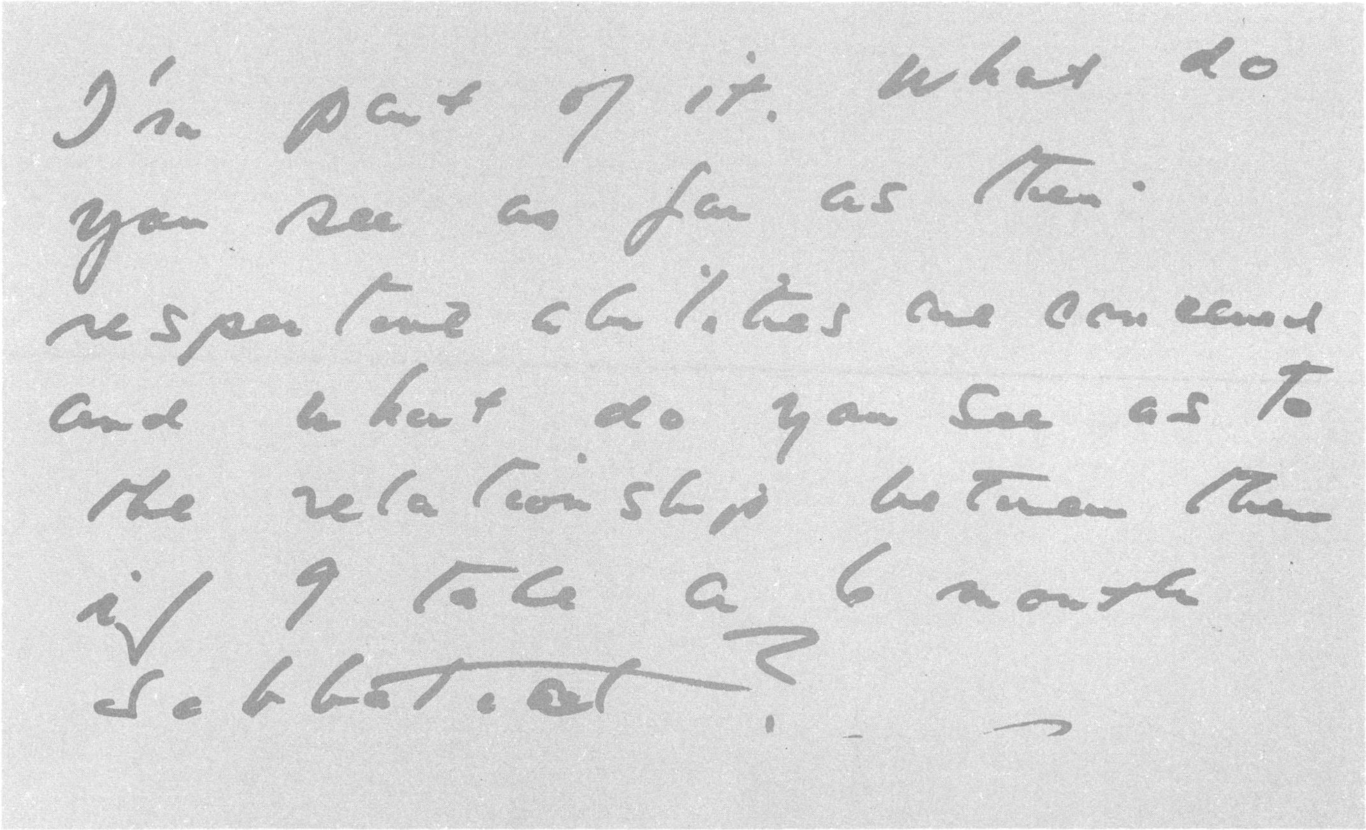

graphology. In America we have virtually no academic standing, no licensing system, and therefore no real research in a field that arouses considerable curiosity and controversy, and a field which just may have good research questions.

After I had testified as a handwriting expert in a check-forgery trial not long ago, the judge called me to his chambers and said: "I lost the use of my arms and legs through muscular dystrophy, and so I sign my name by holding my pen in my mouth. The most amazing thing is that my signature looks almost the same as when I could write with my good right hand." Is this judge simply a doggedly determined man who mastered an incredibly difficult task, or is he an example of the graphologists' theory that graphic pattern production originates in the brain and is transmitted through the central nervous system? Is handwriting perhaps *brain* writing, more than it is an act of our hands?

Itinerant magicians in the 16th century laid the earliest foundations for graphology, and during the Renaissance, writers, artists, and intellectuals fancied themselves proficient at evaluating certain aspects of behavior by studying samples of handwriting. The *medicine* of *bloodletting* and the *psychology* of *humors* fell before the advances of science. But graphology always has remained easy prey to untutored mystics, and it has been so popular in a silly way that it has been too often and too long ignored as the tool it well may be—one more handle to turn on one more door along the long corridor leading toward the understanding of man. Is graphology valid? Who can say me *nay*, for sure?

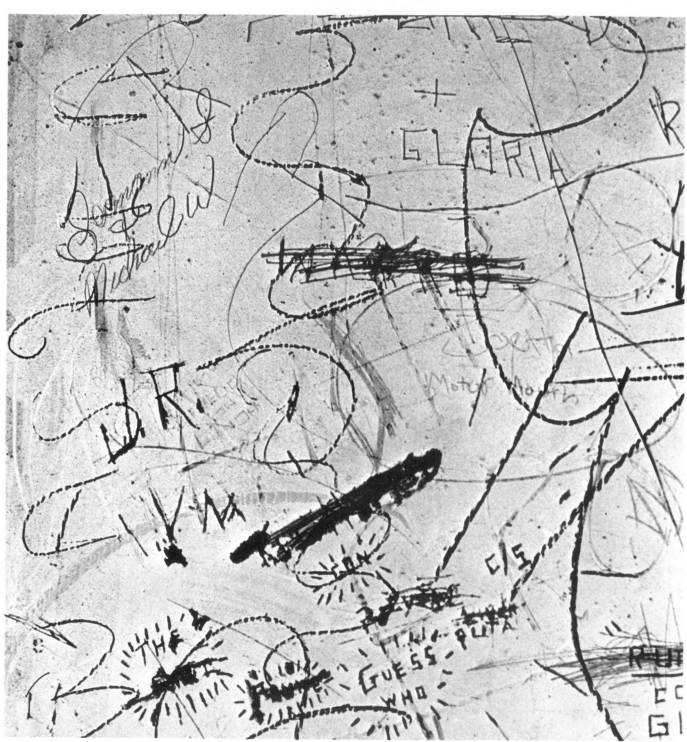

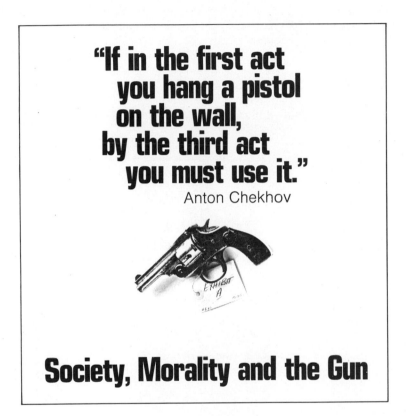

"If in the first act you hang a pistol on the wall, by the third act you must use it."
Anton Chekhov

Society, Morality and the Gun

What sets us up for violence? And what sets the stage for a better society? Let us look together at those big questions which may help us answer the biggest question of them all:

What do we hang on the wall of the future?

Impulse, Aggression and the Gun

By Leonard Berkowitz

In November of 1966, Robert Benjamin Smith, then 18 years old, entered a beauty shop in Mesa, Arizona, and shot seven strangers, killing five of them. He said he had been planning the murder for three months, ever since his parents gave him a 22-caliber pistol for target practice. His original inspiration, he went on, was the preceding summer's mass killings in Chicago and Austin, Texas.

Almost everyone in the United States read about the murder of the eight Chicago nurses and about the massacre from the University of Texas tower, and millions of Americans own guns. But we cannot disregard Smith's remarks simply because they do not completely explain his behavior.

Now, more than ever before, there is need to answer the question: what effect *do* available weapons and vicarious experience with violence have on a person who is "ready" to commit an aggressive act?

Two series of experiments that my colleagues and I have performed on impulsive aggression bear directly on these questions. The first series indicates that even so small a matter as the casual sight of a gun can sometimes stimulate aggressive behavior. The second suggests that, contrary to what the so-called catharsis theory predicts, the sight of violence can increase the chance that a viewer will express aggression himself.

In experiments to test the effect of the presence of guns on aggressiveness, we observed the behavior of 100 students at the University of Wisconsin under different sets of circumstances. Some students were angry and some were not, some saw the guns and some did not. (We did not reveal the study's real purpose, claiming instead to be measuring the students' physiological reaction to stress.)

The stress, we informed them, would be a series of one or more mild electric shocks. We asked each student to make a list of ideas a publicity agent could use to improve the record sales and public image of a popular singer. Then we gave each student a "partner," ostensibly another experimental subject but actually an ally of the experimenter. The pretend partner's task was to evaluate the student's publicity ideas. If the partner thought the student's ideas were very good, he would give him one electric shock; if he thought the student's work was bad, he would administer up to 10 shocks. Later, the student would be asked to evaluate a similar task of his partner's, and to convey his judgment in the same way.

By prearrangement with the experimenter, the partners gave one shock to half the students and seven shocks to the other half, regardless of the quality of the students' ideas. We assumed that the seven-shock students would feel physically uncomfortable and that they would feel humiliated as well. They were our angry group.

After each student had received the number of shocks allotted to him, the experimenter invited him to trade places with his partner and led him into the room containing the shock machine. The telegraph key that would send the shocks lay on a table at one end of the room. Sometimes the table was empty except for the key; at other times, badminton racquets and shuttlecocks (neutral objects) lay near the key. At still other times, the table held a 12-gauge shotgun and a snub-nosed .38 revolver.

The experimenter acted surprised at the sight of the guns and the racquets and explained that they had been "left over from another experiment." Matter-of-factly, he moved them aside. The students seemed to pay little or no attention to them. Later on, after the experiment was over, the experimenter asked each student what, if any, suspicions the student had felt. No doubts were voiced about the presence of the weapons.

Next, the experimenter showed the student his partner's "work" (actually prepared in advance and uniform for all partners). He reminded the student that he should use shocks to indicate his evaluation of his partner's work and he told the student that this was the last time shocks would be administered in the study.

As we suspected, the presence of the guns affected both the number of shocks the students gave their partners and how long they held the key down for each shock. Some differences between groups were less clear-cut than others; from a statistical point of view, our most significant finding was that the angry men who saw the guns gave more shocks than any other group.

Both common sense and personality theory tend to neglect the "weapons effect" that this study demonstrates. Instead, they stress motives and, perhaps, psychological and social dislocations. What is often overlooked, perhaps because it is a frightening idea, is that much violence is *impulsive*. It is not primarily planned, purposeful activity; neither is it the "inevitable" result of internal drives or maladjustments. These things set the stage and help carry the action forward, but in many cases it is also important that there be a stimulus or immediate cue to trigger aggression.

It is quite conceivable that many hostile acts which supposedly stem from unconscious motivation really arise because of the operation of aggressive cues. The aggression can even be thought of as a conditioned response to the stimulus. If a gun can be that stimulus, then it is a double-barreled threat—an immediate cue that also pre-

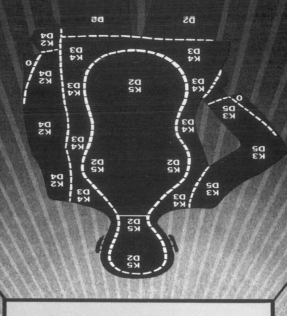
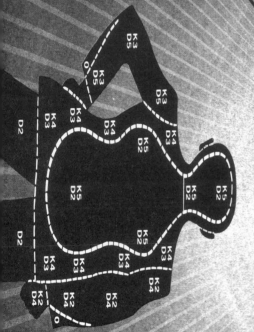
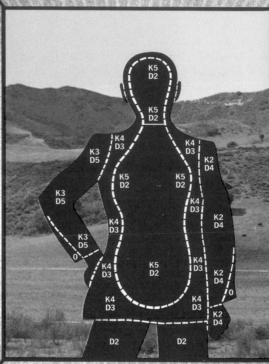
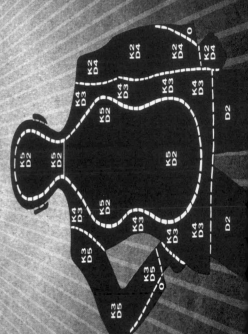
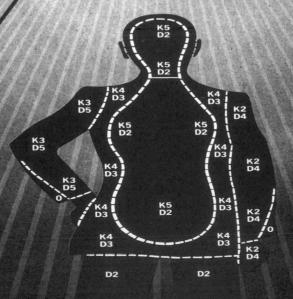

sents the aggressor with a deadly *means* of aggression.

With our subjects, the guns did not enhance aggression unless the students were angry to begin with. But studies conducted at the University of Indiana show that, at least with young children, anger is not necessarily a factor. In these experiments, youngsters played with an older child whom the psychologist in charge had asked to behave in a friendly, neutral way. There was no quarreling. Then some of the children were given toy guns to play with while others chatted quietly with adults conducting the experiment.

After this preparation, each child was told that the older youngster he had played with earlier had built a structure of blocks on a play table in another room. "If you push this button on my desk, you'll shake the table and his blocks will fall down," the experimenter said. *More of the children who had played with guns pushed the button.*

Neither group of children was angry, but the guns had an effect. Guns did more than lower the children's restraints against aggression; they seemed to pull out aggressive reactions that would not otherwise have occurred. Anger may not always be *necessary* in aggressive behavior, but it certainly facilitates it. And our society offers its citizens a wide array of anger-producing frustrations. It is not necessary to detail them here. It should be mentioned, though, that aggression is more likely to result from unrealized hopes than from deprivation alone. The deprived person who has no hope cannot really be said to be frustrated, because he does not really have a goal he is trying to move toward. A person works harder to get something—whether it is food, a sexual object, or a new car—if he thinks he has a chance. Similarly, his frustration is most severe when he is blocked from a satisfaction he thinks should and could be his.

In social terms, this concept of frustration reveals itself in "revolutions of rising expectations." Poverty-stricken groups are not frustrated merely because they have suffered severe deprivations; they are frustrated when they begin to hope. Privation is far less likely to cause violence than is the dashing of hopes. [See "Conflict, Crisis and Collision" by Ivo and Rosalind Feierabend, Section VIII.]

Even given high frustration and an immediate cue, violence will not erupt unless there is a third factor as well: low inhibitions. The "normal" level of inhibitions to violence in our society is not particularly high. We take a lenient attitude toward what is sometimes called defensive aggression. It is quite permissible, even admirable, for a man to defend with vigor not only himself but his family, his home and his country, and not only his physical safety but his principles of honor, law and democracy. Even defensive aggression that is quite violent and smacks more of revenge than defense tends to be seen as an act of courage, a mark of manhood.

The air that hovers over Hollywood and New York (not to mention Washington) smells of the frontier, and one can detect a breeze from the Crusades as well. Nowhere is violence in the cause of good more consistently and more enthusiastically touted than in movies and on TV.

Fictional representations of violence are often defended, by people in the industries that sell them and also by many consumers, on the grounds that they serve a cathartic purpose. The theory, loosely derived from Aristotle's view of the function of tragedy, contends that violence which is indulged in vicariously drains a reservoir of accumulated hostility and releases tensions that might otherwise explode into actual violent behavior.

This theory receives additional support from the ideas and writings of the eminent ethologist, Konrad Lorenz. Lorenz stresses the physiological rather than the psychological as a source of behavior: behavior results, he says, from the spontaneous accumulation of some excitation or substance in neural centers. He believes that "present-day civilized man suffers from insufficient discharge of his aggressive drive," and he recommends that society provide people with "safe" ways of venting their aggressive urge.

The question is, do vicarious or real-but-innocuous "outlets" in fact reduce the chances that aggressive behavior will occur? Although many psychologists continue to subscribe to the catharsis theory in some form, many others believe (and have demonstrated in experiments) that witnessed violence can stimulate actual violence and that a little aggression, like a snowball, can gather momentum and grow.

Let us examine the results of another series of studies. In this series, a group of students was made angry by ridicule and electric shock. Then, just before it was *their* turn to administer shocks, they were shown one of two movies. One was an exciting but nonviolent foot race between the first two men to run the mile in less than four minutes. The other was a violent scene from *Champion*, the Kirk Douglas movie in which the prize fighter played by Douglas absorbs a brutal beating in the ring.

The students who saw this movie had been given two different plot summaries to prepare them for the scene. Half were led to regard the beating as justified: Douglas was a heel who had it coming. The other half heard a summary that was much more sympathetic to Douglas: it was clear that he did not deserve what he got.

The filmed violence was not cathartic; in fact, it had an opposite effect, at least on the students who thought the beating was justified. When given a chance to administer shocks to the partners who earlier had delivered shocks to them, these students responded with more aggression than any other group. Rather than feeling purged of their hostility, the students seemed to feel freer to express it. It was as if the justified aggression on the screen justified as well their own aggression against their tormenters.

These findings have been confirmed in five independent experiments, the most recent of which was conducted by James Hoyt and Percy Tannenbaum, now at the University of Pennsylvania. Hoyt and Tannenbaum presented the prize fight to some of the angry students as a grudge-match. Douglas had behaved badly to his opponent, and now the opponent wanted revenge. These students gave more intense shocks than the other angry students, who had simply been reminded that violence was an inevitable part of prize fights.

Results like this present an awkward problem to TV and movie censorship agencies, and to producers who want to make violent films without encouraging real violence. The modern censorship agencies generally insist that crime and violence be used not just to entertain but to teach a lesson—"crime does not pay," for example. How the lesson should be taught is left vague; scriptwriters usually follow the maxim of "an eye for an eye."

But justified aggression is precisely the kind that seems likeliest to encourage the expression of aggression by members of the audience.

The effect is different if violence, though justified, seems excessive. If the punishment is badly out of proportion with the victim's crime, all aggression becomes less acceptable to the viewer, and his inhibitions rise. When some of the angry students who saw the boxing film were told that the fight had very serious results—Douglas was carried unconscious to his dressing room and died there—the scales that had been unbalanced by Douglas' villainy tipped the other way. These students gave fewer shocks to their experimental partners than those who were told the beating merely taught Douglas a lesson and induced him to reform.

In some ways, this is an encouraging finding. It means that viewed violence does not *necessarily* encourage actual violence. It can either lower inhibitions or raise them, depending on the viewer's interpretation of what he sees. Horror is an inhibiting emotion, and violence that strikes the viewer as disproportionate—as "too much" or "too real" —is likely to arouse horror. Many people who enjoyed *Champion* would not enjoy a front-row seat at a real prize fight in Madison Square Garden; many people who like war movies are extremely disturbed by photographs and news clips of the actual fighting in Vietnam.

However, the line between violence that is justified and unjustified, fictional and real, uninhibiting and inhibiting, is anything but clear. To take just one example, the television screen itself puts distance between the viewer and what he sees. Watching a riot on television may be horrifying, but it is less horrifying than being there. The emotional effect of a 90-minute documentary on riots is not so very different from the effect of a documentary-type movie about riots; the effect of a documentary-type movie is not so different from that of a "realistic drama"; and so it goes.

At some point on the continuum, viewed violence *stops* horrifying and *starts* exciting. Once this point has been reached, vicarious experience with aggressiveness begins to lower restraints against the real thing.

And it may begin to do something else as well. Like the guns in the experiment described earlier, witnessed violence can serve as a stimulus for the viewer, especially if he encounters someone he associates with the deserving victim in what he has just seen. At the beginning of the boxing film study, the partners of half the students were introduced as "Kirk" and the partners of the rest were called "Bob." The students who were led to believe that Kirk Douglas' beating was *justified* later gave more shocks to the "Kirks" than to the "Bobs."

In another experiment on this kind of mental association, students lost a chance to win a cash prize because (they thought) their partners had made a mistake. Soon afterwards, the students were asked to evaluate two job applicants, one of whom had the same first name as the partner. The students consistently saw more bad qualities in the applicant who bore the partner's name.

Thus associations help determine the target of an aggressive attack—or, to put it another way, the stimulus properties of a possible target can affect the probability that an attack will occur.

In some cases, however, stimulus and target are not related—all that is required is that both be present. In a study conducted at the University of Iowa, C. A. Loew had college students speak either aggressive or neutral words aloud in what the students thought was the first step of a learning task. Later, when these students were given an opportunity to shock their partners for errors, the ones who had said the aggressive words gave stronger shocks than the others.

As for the snowball effect, when experimental subjects are given a number of opportunities to attack, the intensity of their attacks more often than not builds up. By their own actions, the subjects—even if they are not emotionally aroused to begin with—provide their own aggressive stimuli and pull out further aggressive responses. Aggression stimulates more aggression.

The social implications of the research I have described are clear, though they are much easier to recite than to act on. A society that wants fewer violent outbursts should reduce frustration, leave inhibitions intact and remove immediate cues that can set off aggressive acts.

Reducing frustration in the United States, especially the frustration of social groups, is a long-term project that is receiving considerable attention. I will do no more here than recall the phrase "revolution of rising expectations" and mention that, for many people, expectations are likely to outstrip reality for a long time to come.

Leaving more of people's inhibitions against aggressiveness intact is, I think, a slightly less difficult matter. Is it really necessary to use violence as a major source of entertainment? The catharsis theory does not hold up very well, and the frontier tradition may not be as strong as we think. Perhaps people enjoy violent books and movies more because they are absorbing than because they are violent. Books and movies in which violence plays a small part, or no part at all, are also absorbing; we might be able to arrange to have more of these.

The third possibility, reducing the number of aggressive stimuli people encounter from day to day, is probably the easiest one to effect, and the fastest. This may seem a surprising statement—deciding to remove aggressive stimuli from American life is a little like setting out to clean the Augean stable. But the task seems more manageable when one realizes that most aggressive stimuli fall into only a few large categories, one of the largest of which bears the label "Guns." Guns not only permit violence, they can stimulate it as well. The finger pulls the trigger, but the trigger may also be pulling the finger.

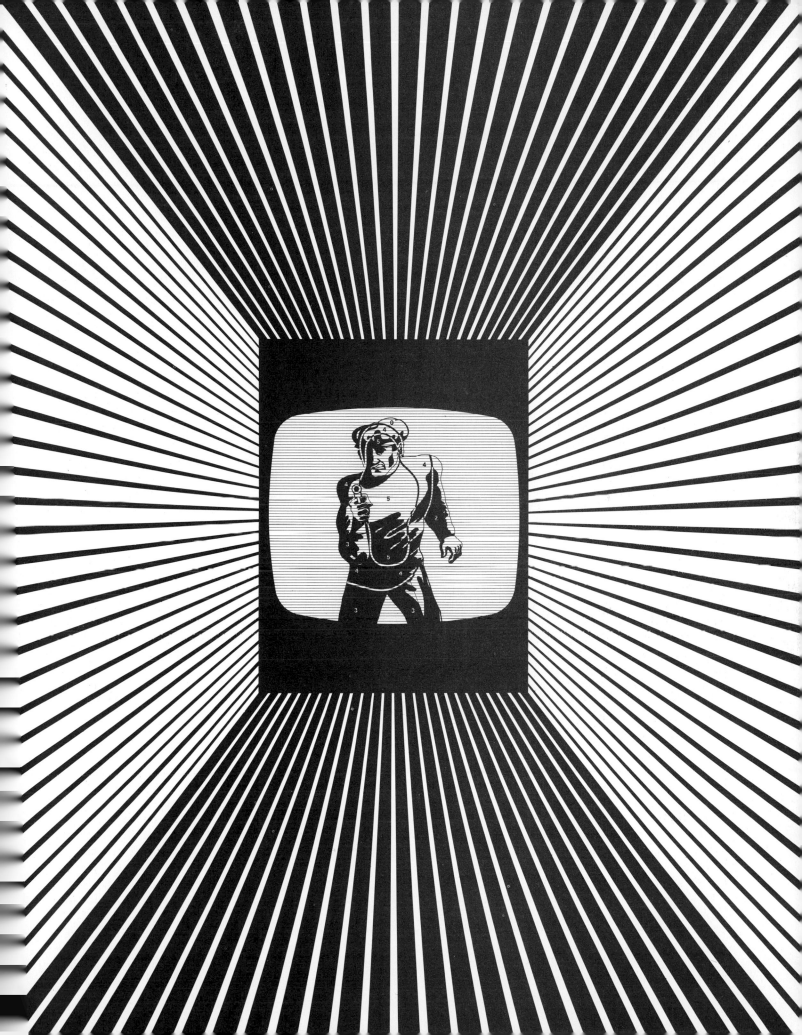

By Robert E. Kavanaugh

THE GRIM GENERATION

WHAT ARE THE CHANGES in today's college student? The public is conditioned to see the student in terms of revolt, dope, sex, or the image transmitted by the mass media. But I am a college counselor. I see unsmiling faces, peer into dreamless eyes, hear indictments of parents and country, am frightened by threats of anarchy, listen to pleas for instant friendship, react to demands for student power, and cringe at the nakedness of youth without hope.

There are drastic changes in the students, and they are more than passing whims of a few.

I dare write about the changing student only in light of the adage: "In the land of the blind, the one-eyed man is king." But I write after 17 years as university lecturer, administrator, campus pastor and counselor.

There is an absence of mirth on today's campus, a lack of humor. Long before the new student uprisings, even before the recent assassinations, life on campus had become intensely grim. Gone are the sick jokes, gone is the practical joke and the belly filled with goldfish. Humor magazines, planned buffoonery and silly laughter—long typical of college youth—are as rare as popularity for administrators. A Rowan and Martin "Laugh-In" can trigger giggly smiles, but the self-generated humor of the inner man, which normally helps the self gain perspective, is decidedly rare.

Perhaps the cause lies in the grimness of contemporary life or in the uncertainty of tomorrow. Perhaps it lies in the pressure for grades or in the frustration experienced as values crumble. No matter what the cause, life without laughter is pained and out of focus. Despite an alleged increase in sexual license and party atmosphere on campus, the cared-for student of today is not the carefree student of other years.

Our era of instant communication means instant feedback to the campus of mass media reports about student action. The scene is one of comic tragedy. Selective reporting provides easily memorized stage directions and

students—in search of an identity—seem to become what the commentators on our culture "direct" them to be.

The *malevolent dreamers* are the only students who drive me to say the prayer I read in the eyes of many administrators: "Oh, God, restore to us the apathy of the 1950s." No matter what their label — activists, leftists, radicals or anarchists—their cause is the overthrow of all authority and every institution with little regard for means and almost no regard for consequences. Their motivation ranges from philosophical theories of revolution to inner pain and frustrated hurt. A few choose gradualism and nonviolent change, but I see them in

astonishing numbers almost psychopathically wed to violence—now. Campus administrators still hopefully advocate dialogue, liberal professors still believe rational debate can direct this admirable energy along nonviolent channels; this stand is being tested hard and many academicians are retreating to the safe ground of the more precise *rule of law.*

Radical students debate mostly with each other or with faculty members of similar philosophy and administrators get little hearing. Radicals have deep respect for rational debate, but few activists venture to "fly without a flight plan" gained by prior group agreement. And the popular view that unkempt appearance is characteristic of an angry mob pushes the radical groups further away from all outsiders. And even further.

Other students protect the activists, for they share the activist concern for social and political betterment while lacking the activist daring to be heard. They also lack the ability to come up with alternate solutions. The continued stability of campus activism lies in this body of quiet sympathizers.

Black activists seem ambivalent. Sometimes they want to go it alone, sometimes they want the support of white brothers. They walk, speak and give orders with new confidence; they know that administrators are scurrying to put both more time and more money into minority-student recruitment and support. They know too that faculty planners are desperately arranging curricula in Afro-American studies, that professional schools will admit minority students who are "almost" qualified and that all academe blushes with shame.

The largest and least often identified type on campus can be called the *kept generation.* The dominant characteristics here are good reputation and moderation. Preoccupation with grades, noninvolvement in extracurricular affairs of a serious nature, and an overriding tone of cynicism are other characteristics. They make mock of

the hippy, debunk the activist, berate administrators, con the faculty and associate only with one another.

Their morality stems from habit and fear not from internalized conviction. They are adept at the dual standard, attending church only at home, writing letters as family peace and finances dictate, and cribbing on exams. They *ran* the family home and still *command* by phone or letter. In a sense they are what their parents designed.

If members of the kept generation accept an office, it is for personal benefit; if they take dope, it is out of curiosity or conformity; if they make love, contraceptives are more important than passion. They hate war because they must go. They abhor violence because it blights their plans. Though they loudly mock the student left, they fail to articulate the political right. Cynicism marks their typical humor: "Every time I eat a Hershey bar, I project a death wish." Their identity crisis is deferred, their umbilical cord strained but not severed.

The mark of the kept generation is on enough brows to determine the fate of this generation of students. Anarchists warn that if they sleepwalk back to suburbia they will find it in ruins. And should they awaken to involvement in social problems it is these kept kids who will tilt the balance of campus upheaval.

There are other students who are monastically hidden in the cells of their own personal concerns and who join the community only for the common prayer of the classroom. They are a taxpayers' delight because they use no campus services other than the academic. Their number is legion; they go uncounted because they are seldom noticed. The *monastic generation* includes the married student who works nights, the shy commuter, the virginal fat girl and the 4.0 student who studies incessantly. The monks have little to say on campus radicals, answer no polls, and seldom see a psychiatrist. Their views rarely are tinged with cynicism and only infrequently with self-pity. They are the potential drop-outs who refuse to drop out.

Benevolent dreamers are the young men and women

"Family authority is vested in 'daddy-son' or 'mommy-daughter.'"

who have passed through their identity crisis. They have "lost" their parents or "found" them in a new adult relationship. You see them tutoring in the inner city, raising funds to educate minority youth, leading campus governments, editing newspapers, and forming *ad hoc* committees. They are prominent in every legal and vital facet of campus or community life. They are willing to be measured. With high ideals and dreams for a better world, accompanied by the drive and ambition to make them effective, these students work mightily to avoid the basely utilitarian overtones they despise in their society. Especially is this true of the benevolent dreamers in the ranks of the non-violent New Left.

They feel threatened and wounded by draft demands, prospects of urban violence and the "immoral" approval of war, by racism, poverty and overpopulation. They feel strapped, stifled and betrayed by their elders. Such students are not unduly fearful of revolution but they opt for peaceful reform of American institutions. They are abrupt with tradition, suspicious of advice, impatient with authority and disdainful of duplicity.

Because their cause is seldom sensational and their tactics rarely flamboyant, they are not newsworthy. Some of them try drugs in their desperation for answers but if so they do not continue for—even if drugs help—they prefer the fight for legality to illegal involvement. They oversimplify life's complexities, switch heroes easily and, beneath their confident exterior, they are depressed, anxious and confused.

Small in number but important to the total picture are the *hippies*. Imitated by other students and often confused with nonacademic hippies, the authentic campus hippy is more than a court jester or a whipping boy. He frightens or disgusts those who measure men by garb and he confounds those who listen patiently to the rationale for his life style. He is trying, albeit naively, to downgrade material concerns.

The hippy hopes to find himself, to discover meaning and sanity in life. His experience with American life has been brief but distasteful. Usually from a home that is broken or breaking, the campus hippy resembles a soft-spoken Isaiah, decrying middle-class foibles. He preaches human love and worth in the face of campus scoffing and community snickers. Though he probably loves others no more than most of us, love is his shibboleth.

The campus hippy provides few answers. He prefers to raise questions. Unable to visualize life in any but simplistic terms of love and community, the hippy regularly locks-in to the dream world of his inner self, where felonies, personal inadequacies, selective service, economics and social shallowness cannot touch him. Most hippies are somewhat paranoid about police and community harrassment. They are a joy to counsel if handled respectfully in the framework of their own world.

Interestingly, though the hippy student professes little concern for grades, his marks tend to be above average.

And yet few campus hippies survive a full four years of college pressure. They drop out. But those who successfully negotiate the narrow path to graduation are potentially great people. They are willing to live in poverty, ready to share puff and pad, and they are able to follow their own convictions in the face of ridicule and scorn.

Campus hippies offer interesting predictions about their own future. Precious few forecast their own return to the Establishment when "their thing" is finished. The majority foresee the possibility of a permanent subculture, though they lack the concept of marriage or family that would allow such a continuance.

The saddest group in campus is one I see as the *graveyard generation:* the hippy who is on his way out and no longer can meet academic demands; the overextended student who holds on despite lack of talent or motivation until rescued by a face-saving transfer, by mononucleosis, or by wise counseling; the disillusioned youth, crushed by home problems, ineffective love affairs or financial duress; the late bloomer in his budding days of failure;

359

"Their morality stems from habit and fear, not from…conviction."

the student who punishes overanxious parents by his academic reluctance; and the one who is psychologically ill.

For this group, the gravestone always can be rolled away from the tomb by a meaningful love affair, by counseling, therapy or even by survival through development.

I see today's students move with sudden fluidity from group to group, or even reflect several strains at once. I see them belonging to one group while masking affiliation to another.

Many of the changes I see in today's students can be traced to our changed family structure. Crashed or crashing marriages at home intensify the student-identity crisis. The failure of the home, the school and the church to transmit a sound and solid value system further heightens the expected crisis. Today's student lacks a strong parental figure or a deeply indoctrinated sense of values to polarize his identity crisis. Yesterday's authoritarian father and overworked mother, community-backed teacher and "heaven-hell" church generated clearer paths for rebellion or acceptance. Polarization is hardly possible when family authority is vested in "daddy-son" or "mommy-daughter," when teachers are overly accepting, when churches impart vague platitudes. The student is torn between acceptance and rejection and confused by a diffusion of goals and values.

Because of its altered structure and increased mobility, the family creates personal isolation and insulation. At best today's family offers only limited opportunities for intimate relationships. When these are bungled by conflict or parental incapacity, the laboratory for friendship becomes the large high school, the shifting neighborhood, the dwindling extended family or a church.

The results show in the demise or changing structure of the fraternity-sorority system, faculty-student aloofness, the grasping and groping for instant friendship and the solidification of monogamous dating practices. Rare is the student who can cope simultaneously with several close relationships.

A new vision of the family is in the making. Rarely does the campus male animal fight for his woman. Children play an ever decreasing part in the college view of marriage. By admission—and even the reluctant permission—of the male, the wife dominates the married campus couple. And parental benefactors control the campus marriage with financial aid more often than the mendicant lovers realize.

Traditionally youth uses the future for dreaming, the past for bragging and the now for living. Yesterday there was little reluctance to permit the present to flow into the future. There was always the promise of a pleasant tomorrow. Some of today's students still enjoy the American dream: the ranch in suburbia, the niche in megapolis, the bench in St. Petersburg, the eternity box at the end. But a growing number believe they have tasted the "capitalistic dream" only to find it embittered by the prospect of war, jail or emigration. Activists lash out to increase their alternatives. Most students lock-in to the present and struggle to manufacture inarticulate dreams. They have no experience with the world they desire in their tomorrow.

Adoration of the present pervades the campus. The drug user readily admits his need to zero in on the present. Drugs add an intensity and reality to his dreams and fantasies which reality denies. The maximum decibel roar of the stereo provides the hard rock fan with a lesser lock-in. So do the total preoccupation with theoretical math, the endless hours in a lonesome lab, isolated hetero- and homosexual love affairs, attempts at oriental meditation, devotion to alcohol, addiction to cars, and insulated aloofness. Even concern for distant injustices, like the war in Vietnam and poverty in the inner city, makes the present tolerable.

This mania to make the present bearable results in an increased preoccupation with death, both in contemplated suicide and in folk music or other art forms. Violence that does not disturb the present (such as that depicted on movies or TV) is groovy, but fist fights (part of the en-

"Students speak out in terms of rights and rarely in terms of duties."

tertainment on yesterday's campus) are strangely absent.

The search for meaning and values *is* a major factor in student unrest. And the central campus value is this search for values. The framework for the search is one of mutual acceptance: each man has his own bag; don't interfere. (The unpracticed observer can read this non-intervention as a modern version of Cain and Abel, but it is more likely a stand *against* indoctrination and *for* individual freedom.) And the search intensifies as the excellence of the campus ascends from junior-college caliber to university level.

Organized religion plays a decreasing role on campus and possibly is saved from extinction only by the superior clergy assigned to most campuses. Scientific humanism attracts numerous students and continues as the "bag" for most faculty members. Political activism and expanding social concern provide new life for the departments of philosophy, political science, sociology and religion. Oriental cults attract fewer than the press, radio and TV imply.

Verbalized values are more negative than positive. Students speak out in terms of rights and rarely in terms of duties. There is almost no evidence of a right-wing viewpoint in social, political or moral matters, even though the confused students seem ripe for simplistic, solid answers.

The much-publicized growing sexual promiscuity is not general practice on the campus. Shyness, introversion, vestigial guilt, self-doubt and the fear of rejection keep students from the practice of their preaching, even with pills and intrauterine devices to reduce their fear of pregnancy. Actually, premarital pregnancies are on the wane, "sleeping around" is not admired and premarital sex is practiced most often in a semiresponsible and monogamous relationship.

Besides the vertical gap between this generation and the last there is a horizontal gap between students of the far left and their middle-of-the-road peers, between the science major and the artist, the engineer and the social scientist. As campus departments insulate themselves in their own concerns and jargon, upper division students share the isolation. A music student put it this way: "Dante could recreate the *Inferno* by putting me in eternity with two engineers."

Students are strangely willing—for the present—to grant the faculty immunity from the rebellious antiauthoritarianism they focus on the administration. This in spite of countless unintelligible or ill-prepared lectures, archaic and haphazard teaching methods, unjust and unscientific grading systems and sharply limited faculty office hours. *There are signals that this divine right is ending.*

The student of today studies much harder than any college student before him, even that post World War II generation of veterans. The standard of achievement is higher today and today's student worries more.

The 1968 college student already has conquered the American home, exchanging roles with his parents. He has been victorious over his high school where he found boredom instead of challenge. Now he is poised to lay siege to the American university.

The survival of the university seems to depend on whether faculty and administrators can provide a dream, a hope for tomorrow. Students want—they demand—that their dream include an end to injustice and to the suppression of truth and reality. They no longer want duplicity in morals. They demand a relevant curriculum and a concerned faculty. They want leaders who will take a stand on issues, who can provide meaning, a flame for their apathy, a respect for their right. They want leaders whose lives embody their dreams, leaders who listen. They want leaders who will work with them in the face of the nihilistic anguish of their hopeless present.

Academic arrogance will get us nowhere. These student demands are going to be hard to meet. I am just a counselor who listens. But I know the threat to every tree in the groves of academe if there is no change.

THE QUIET REVOLUTION

By Leonard and Elizabeth Uhr

DURING THE LAST EIGHT YEARS, and especially since 1963, a quiet revolution has been generating from college campuses throughout the United States. It is a strange revolution in which people are not trying to change society—just themselves. This is a revolution in which the individual chooses to go his own way, to make forays into the world of altered consciousness. And it is just this quiet revolution which is raising disquieting questions about society's role in protecting the individual against possible psychological damage.

The focus of this quiet revolution is a group of chemical compounds known as the psychedelic or "consciousness-expanding" drugs. Many people who try these drugs feel that they have undergone a profound, beautiful, self-revelatory experience. But there are clinical reports that the drug experience can produce anxiety, depression, and psychotic episodes. It is clear that the more powerful psychedelic drugs—LSD, psilocybin, mescaline, dimethyltryptamine, among others—are the agents for prodigious experience, and that their effects are far more pervasive than those of alcohol in freeing the individual from the usual controls of his conscious ego. No one knows how many Americans have used the psychedelics in the last few years, but for marijuana it must be millions, and for LSD, thousands, or hundreds of thousands.

Marijuana merits special attention because, though not strictly speaking a psychedelic drug, it occupies a central place in the quiet revolution. Marijuana is widely used throughout the country by people who are convinced that the effects are innocuous, the dangers nil, and the total impact good. However, marijuana is classified legally with heroin and other strong opiates because, it is claimed, its use leads to major crime, sex perversion, addiction, and mental illness. Punishment for sale or possession of marijuana is severe.

Because there has been almost no controlled experimentation with marijuana, it is difficult to make positive statements about the drug's effects. The consensus of scientists who have examined the literature, however, is that marijuana appears to be less psychologically addicting than alcohol, less likely to release aggressive and anti-social behavior, and far less likely to produce a hang-over. Marijuana seems to make people calmly happy, loving and friendly, and imbued with a feeling of goodness—in contrast to the anger, hostility, and maudlin behavior so often triggered by alcohol.

Responsible research should begin as soon as possible. If the facts show that marijuana is dangerous, effective and reasonable laws should be written to control its use. If it is not dangerous, the use and possession of marijuana should be removed from the list of criminal acts.

When Should a Drug Be Outlawed?

Most laws are instituted to protect society, or to protect the individual. Laws concerning drugs fit into this legal framework. For example, narcotics are outlawed because their continued use can cause physical and mental debilitation of the individual and lead to crime against society. Obviously, society must have laws governing the distribution and use of dangerous drugs, but are marijuana and the psychedelics really dangerous, or are they scapegoats in society's retaliation against the quiet revolution? Perhaps society is protecting itself against those who are using drugs as a weapon to expose the fraying fabric of a "phony society." On the other hand, society may be acting rationally in restricting the use of drugs about which too little is known. If the latter is true, is this cautiousness interfering with the basic right of the individual to pursue his happiness—in whatever form he views happiness—as long as he does not harm others? Can a society really legislate against psychological damage?

What if these drugs, despite their possible damaging effects, hold out a hope for enriching our lives? What kind of society would blindly suppress their use? And why should it limit scientific inquiry into their positive and negative effects? Legitimate research on marijuana has been cut off for years, and research on the psychedelic drugs has all but stopped, partly because of public caution and partly because scientists are reluctant to become involved in such a highly-charged subject.

Thus we find ourselves—the objective researchers—in the embarrassing position of knowing less than the students who are taking the drugs in their sub rosa activity. The student who is intrigued by the effects of LSD, who feels that it has given him a fresh view of the world, new understanding of himself, and a new warmth of compassion, is behaving much more in the great tradition of Western Civilization's search for the truth, the principles of the universe and the meaning of existence, than is the more passive, well-adjusted individual who accepts the non-truths of official culture. On the other hand, when students—as happened just recently at the University of California/Santa Barbara—search for spiritual meaning by lying on their backs marvelling at the sun and come out of an LSD trance with damaged retinas from the sun's rays, we must do something to help them. But instead we make ignorant and hypocritical statements which help no one.

Subjective Drug Effects

The variety of psychological effects produced by psychedelic drugs is legion, and subjective descriptions have been eloquently and ubiquitously expressed for years in books and in the press. Briefly, commonly occurring effects include: nausea, brilliantly colored visions of dancing lights, losses and variations in perceptual constancies, synesthesia (reaction to one sensory stimulus as though it were another—"seeing" bees buzz), loss of connection with one's body, increased sensitivity to other people, a deep feeling of oneness and empathy, profound philosophical and religious feelings, and swift flights of fancy. Any of these sensations may be accompanied by a profound emotional state, ranging from extreme anxiety or depression to an almost transcendent elation or euphoria.

Drug-takers believe that they see the

world in a new way, a true and valid way that deepens their understanding of sensuous reality. Often the freshness of early childhood becomes crystallized in a simple color tone or vibrant pattern. A homely object like a leaf, a crack in the ceiling, a grain of sand, anything—can be the departure point for journeys into new worlds of beauty and revelation. It is common to feel a calm and objective detachment from everyday anxieties, and to believe that life's true meanings are being understood from a higher and more mature plane. In these and many other ways, the drug experience has been described as profound, memorable, and enlightening.

The drug state is subtle, precarious, and easily manipulable. Probably the most important psychological component of psychedelic drugs is the freeing of the mind so that perceptions, thoughts, and emotions may wander unrestrained. The number of possible reactions is probably as large as the number of possible states of the normal human being, but each state is often enormously exaggerated. The effect of the drug experience seems to depend upon the total frame of mind of the taker, and upon all of his potentialities for experience. The effects further depend upon the subject's momentary mood, fears, and expectations—and upon conditions under which the drug is given, size of the dose, and physical and social environment.

Objective Drug Effects

There have been a number of attempts to explore the effects of the hallucinogenic drugs by controlling one or more variables, or by means of objective tests which measure the subject's intellectual or sensory functioning while under the influence of a drug. Unfortunately, scientific research has not been much more successful than "lay" research in pinning down the psychological effects of the psychedelics. More research is needed in which several groups of matched subjects are exposed to differences in setting, suggestion, drug dosage, and other relevant factors. Such studies are probably impossible until the current suppression of drug research is lifted and more rational attitudes prevail. Some important research has indicated, however, the crucial role which suggestion plays in the drug experience.

In Canada, psychotherapists who administered LSD to patients as part of a ritual involving white robes, burning candles, and crucifixions, reported a lot of Dante-esque religious content. The various groups centered on Aldous Huxley, Alan Watts, Timothy Leary, and Richard Alpert, have similarly stressed mystical-religious experience but with a Buddhist orientation—and have reported experiences resembling those described by Eastern mystics. In conventional psychiatric experiments conducted in hospitals or prisons, patients typically became extremely anxious when drugged, particularly if they were warned of the dangers of drug-taking.

This is not to say that "setting the stage" has been found to control drug effects completely; on the contrary, there are many other factors that might well determine an individual's reactions. To eliminate the effects of suggestion, J. Pollard and Leonard Uhr conducted an experiment in which drugs were administered in a bland and neutral setting. The aim was to eliminate any extraneous influences which an emotionally-charged setting might contribute to the drug's effects per se.

We had been struck by the reports that Mexican Indians and San Francisco beatniks were experiencing wonderful effects from these drugs, whereas experimental subjects participating in scientific investigations experienced extreme anxiety. Fortunately, in 1960 when we ran our experiment (as part of a large-scale continuing study of various psycho-active drugs), people had not yet been exposed to predisposing information or misinformation in the press, so it was possible to eliminate almost all of the suggestive factors surrounding drug-taking. Our results were in striking contrast to the previous scientific reports that the psychedelic drugs produced anxiety. Most of our subjects enjoyed the experience and found it interesting, but their reactions were far less profound, revelatory, and earth-shattering than those now reported in the press.

Objective studies of psychological functioning during the drug experience have produced solidly based and reproduceable results, but all too often they have examined aspects of behavior that are extraneous to our understanding of psychedelic phenomena. Moreover, confidence even in these results must be tempered, because reports convey the impression that when the experimenter intrudes into the drug-induced state, the subject regards what he is asked to do as being totally irrelevant and nonsensical—rather like being at a party, half-drunk, dancing with someone exciting, and having the host tap your shoulder and ask you to work out a series of problems in mental arithmetic.

In general, experiments on human subjects have shown that psychedelic drugs impair simple perceptual and cognitive functions, and that the impairment increases with the size of the dose. Performance scores go down in tests measuring ability in mental arithmetic, memorizing strings of numbers, word-naming, and verbal comprehension. Motor coordination may be less affected by psychedelic drugs than are sensory and mental functions.

There have been many subjective reports that psychedelic drugs greatly increase perceptual acuity, but objective tests suggest the opposite: Perceptual acuity is worse under the drug's influence. In a study of the effects of mescaline, LSD-25, and psilocybin, Hartman and Hollister found that color-perception, as judged by ability to discriminate between hues, decreased, and subjects responded more slowly to visual stimuli. These researchers concluded, "The experience appears to be more subjective than related to increased sensitivity."

A commonly reported drug effect is a conviction of attaining profound insight into the reality of things. But here again, objective studies have failed to demonstrate any increase in understanding. On the contrary, McKellar reports, "After administration of mescaline the subject's intellectual standards begin to exhibit deterioration. His thinking becomes more loose and slipshod. There is a weakening of the forces of control which direct his thought toward logic and evidence. . . ." Such observations may, of course, merely show a lack of communication between the drugged subject and the experimenter, or the subject may be captivated by thoughts and sensations quite alien to mundane intellectual procedures. During one of our experiments, an intelligent student-participant made the following sequence of statements: "I still feel like I'm being whizzed through outer space. Some high velocity. I wish I could listen to the Tiger game on the radio. . . . They might win. I don't know. I'm hungry." McKellar suggests that, "Mescaline and other hallucinogenic drugs may alert people to notice things that are going on all the time in normal mental life. Typical human thinking is less characterized either by realistic assessment of evidence, or by sustained acts of logical inference than is often supposed."

Psychedelic Psychotherapy

The most enthusiastic advocates of the psychedelic drugs are the handful of psychotherapists who make use of them in treatment. Unfortunately, there is little evidence that psychedelic drug therapy works. (But then again, there isn't any scientific evidence that psychotherapy of any kind—from psychoanalysis to shock treatment—works.)

In psychedelic psychotherapy, the administration of psilocybin has often been used as part of the diagnostic procedure, since some therapists hold that when the patient is drugged, "The outline of the underlying psychosis or neurosis is revealed or exaggerated as in a caricature by the induced psychological alterations, thus facilitating its identification." However, no firm conclusions can be drawn from such therapeutic studies because there is a lack of scientific rigor: no control groups, no valid criteria for improvement, and no adequate follow-up procedures.

Psychedelic drugs have been used alone or in conjunction with traditional psychotherapeutic sessions. Though some incredible successes have been reported, it should be borne in mind that clinical results are always hard to evaluate. Too often in the past, we have witnessed overenthusiasm for therapeutic methods whose value (if any) could not be demonstrated in scientific terms. Nevertheless, and in spite of negative or inconclusive reports, there seems to be more and more evidence that psychedelic drugs may have a place in treating a wide range of psychoneurotic, psychopathic, and near-psychotic disorders.

However, even in the most positively structured environment, psychedelic drugs may produce occasional bad effects ranging all the way from temporary anxiety, during the few hours under the drug's influence, to days or even months of psychosis. When such psychotic episodes do occur, one doesn't know whether they were triggered by the drug per se or whether they would have occurred anyway—without the drug's influence. The incidence of such episodes, as reported in the literature, range from three in 100 to one in 1000. Unfortunately, it is hard to know whether such rates are low or high. However, other studies have shown that people who volunteer to participate in drug experiments tend to be more unstable than the average and are therefore likely in the first place to be predisposed to such breaks. This is probably even more true of those who take drugs illicitly, in the face of social and legal pressures; thus, in addition to their irrational fears, they are subjected to rational fears that would exacerbate their anxiety.

What Must Be Done

Overenthusiastic and irresponsible proponents of expanded consciousness and mystico-religious experience have conducted their propaganda in such a way as to harden opinion against psychedelic drugs, and appreciably reduce the possibility that disinterested research can or will be conducted. Equally reprehensible has been the timidity of the academic and research establishment which has tended to prohibit socially-disapproved inquiry, to avoid controversy and publicity, and instead has turned quietly away to other, safer problems.

Good science and art are dedicated to the exploration of the unknown. There are far too many attempts, especially in psychology and the social sciences, to apply the results of scientific inquiry before there are any results, and to debase science into serving as propaganda for what society would like to believe. The fact is, the facts aren't there. We don't know enough about psychedelic drugs. We can learn only through free, enlightened, probing research.

But in the meantime psychedelic drugs are readily available, considered important by many, and widely used (and they are sure to be even more widely used in the future). If scientific experiments were to demonstrate that these drugs are dangerous, their use would drop precipitously, for it is not based upon addiction, and it is chiefly found among educated, scientifically-responsive people.

In the meantime, we must devise some effective way to control their present use. Further laws and increased legal restrictions will simply make matters worse (recall the days of Prohibition). Only a few users would be caught and they would be excessively punished. The number of responsible users might be reduced somewhat, but the number of thrill-seekers would increase.

However, until we have discovered and demonstrated that we can use them safely, we cannot let people buy these drugs over the counter. Control over their use should be put in the hands of people who understand and respect the drugs' possible potential for artistic creativity, self-fulfillment, and self-understanding, but who are *not* committed to any particular religious, medical, psychotherapeutic, or social dogma.

One possible way of accomplishing this—of institutionalizing the use of psychedelic drugs—would be to administer them to volunteers at research-study centers. People could then be screened psychologically and physically, and supported when necessary during the drug experience. Screening should be carried out by medical and psychological professionals who would be available to handle any untoward incidents. The research setting should be structured to offer a variety of pleasant surroundings and promote pleasant experiences. Such study centers should be run by responsible people—be they bankers, psychologists, journalists, lawyers, physicists, artists or neurologists—who wish to explore psychedelic phenomena.

Such centers could also serve the crucial scientific purpose of data collection. Valuable information about the incidence of anxiety, about psychotic episodes and other negative effects could easily be obtained if the centers were staffed properly. Such institutions would (a) restore to responsible citizenship the intelligent students and professional people who have become interested in these drugs; (b) make far less dangerous the drug experience; (c) change the general climate of ignorance, hostility, and titillation; and (d) initiate an era of calm, constructive research.

VII. disorder and therapy

all too often personalities go awry. The intricate balances between demands and counterdemands that characterize a stable, healthy, mature personality become unhinged. The healthy aggressive competitiveness characteristic of man is balanced by constructive restraint; when the balance fails, an apathetic vegetable or a mad killer may be let loose. Normal anxiety, which serves to keep risky behavior in bounds, is balanced by a firm grip on reality, which continually monitors the real dimensions of life's threats; when the balance fails, a fearless psychopath or an impotent, frightened neurotic may be released. Common interpersonal attraction is usually balanced by such social forces as the sanctity of the family; when this balance is overturned, unhappiness is the invariable result.

Mental illnesses range from the horribly crippling to the supernormal. Of course, it is impossible to give any single definition of normal, because normality depends on so many factors. What is normal for boys is abnormal for girls. What is normal today would have been abnormal twenty years ago. What is normal at eighteen is abnormal at fifty, and vice versa.

But there are clear deviations from normal that hinder the individual's dealing with the world. Likewise, there are deviations from normal that actually benefit the individual. The overaggressiveness of an insurance salesman, for example, is hardly normal but often makes him highly successful.

One group of tasks of the psychologist faced with mental illness is cataloguing and characterizing the diseases. In this collection, Brendan Maher characterizes the most salient feature of schizophrenia, nature's most severe and dehumanizing mental disease. Maher describes the shattered language of schizophrenia.

One purpose of a catalog of diseases is to group together similar disorders so that a common cause for each can be sought. The search for causes of mental illness is fundamental to psychology's success in dealing with them. Knowing the cause opens the way for prevention and cure. There are, perhaps unfortunately, as many theories of the causes of mental disease as there are schools of psychological theory. Ashley Montagu presents just one type of theory, the genetic. He points out that at least one type of behavioral abnormality may be traced to inherited genetic structure. Although this approach gets at a possible cause for mental disease deep within the biological structure of the organism, it unfortunately has little to say about effective methods for curing or caring for the individual.

Both Stoller and Murphy present discussions of methods of cure for certain types of personality imbalances. There is no question that many types of people are definitely helped by this brand of therapy, just as there is no question that all people are not. The task of fitting the therapy to the illness and the person is an abiding concern of the clinical psychologist.

Meanwhile, the theory of mental illness continues apace with these more ordinary but essential tasks. Calvin Hall and Bill Domhoff discuss dreams and dreaming in what is an interesting comment on theory. Moreover, criticism is never lacking. It is represented here by Frankel's discussion of some of the moral issues involved in psychological therapy.

It may seem strange that animals can help with our understanding of human mental illness. With animals one can intensively study simple and controlled situations that produce undesirable behavior bearing more than a superficial analogy to the disordered behavior of the mentally ill. Masserman, for example, was able to simulate neurotic behavior in a cat. His report makes for fascinating reading and at the same time holds out hope that effective techniques for the control and cure of simple neurosis may someday be found.

The problems that litter the road to an effective psychotherapy are legion and difficult. But the prize at the end of the road—complete success means an emptying of our bulging mental institutions and an end to crime and human disorder—is large enough to spur on generation after generation of investigators. Hans Eysenck discusses some new therapeutic ideas that have just come into prominence in the last decade or so.

Although it cannot be said that an effective therapy is yet at hand for more than a handful of mental disorders, these papers offer evidence that the battle against mental disease is being waged effectively on many fronts.

Chromosomes and Crime By Ashley Montagu

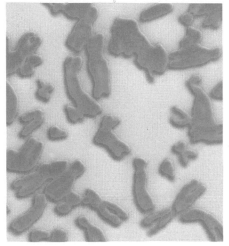

ARE some men "born criminals"? Is there a genetic basis for criminal behavior? The idea that criminals are degenerates because of "bad genes" has had wide appeal.

Johann Kaspar Spurzheim and Franz Joseph Gall, the inventors of phrenology early in the 19th Century, associated crime with various bumps on the head, reflecting the alleged structure of the particular region of the brain within. Later in the last century, Cesare Lombroso, an Italian criminologist, listed physical stigmata by which criminals might be recognized. Lombroso's marks of degeneration included lobeless and small ears, receding chins, low foreheads and crooked noses. These traits supposedly foretold of a biological predisposition to commit crimes.

In more recent years, Earnest A. Hooton of Harvard and William H. Sheldon of New York claimed to have found an association between body type and delinquent behavior. These claims, however, were shown to be quite unsound.

Of all the tales of "bad blood" and "bad genes," perhaps the two most famous are those of the "Jukes" and the "Kallikaks." The tale of the Jukes was first published in 1875 by Richard L. Dugdale, a New York prison inspector. In his report, "The Jukes: A Study in Crime, Pauperism, Disease, and Heredity," Dugdale covers seven generations, 540 blood relatives and 169 related by marriage or cohabitation. Although Dugdale did not invent the Jukes, he often fell back upon his imagination to bolster his theory of the hereditary causes of crime when the facts failed. When information about individuals was hard to come by, Dugdale resorted to characterizations as "supposed to have attempted rape," "reputed sheep-stealer, but never caught," "hardened character" and the like.

The Kallikaks were studied by Henry H. Goddard, director of a school for mentally retarded in New Jersey. In his report published in 1912, he followed the fortunes and misfortunes of two clans of Kallikaks. Both were descended from the same Revolutionary War

This illustration represents the popular misconception that criminality is "fated."

371

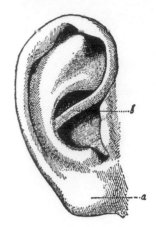

Criminal ear—one of Lombroso's marks of degeneration, from *Criminal Man* by Gina Lombroso Ferrero, Putnam's, 1911

soldier. The bad Kallikaks sprang from this soldier's union with a feeble-minded girl, who spawned a male so bad that he became known as "Old Horror."

"Old Horror" fathered 10 other horrors and they in turn became responsible for the hundreds of other horrible Kallikaks traced by Dr. Goddard. All of the good Kallikaks were descendants, of course, from the Revolutionary War soldier's marriage with a Quaker woman of good blood. Since none of the good Kallikaks seems to have inherited any "bad genes," something rather strange must have occurred in the lineage, for we know that a certain number of the good offspring should have shown some "degenerate" traits.

The Jukes and the Kallikaks are sometimes quoted as examples of what "good" and "bad" genes can do to human beings. While it is possible that a genetic defect may have been involved in some of these pedigrees, the disregard by the investigators of environmental effects renders their work valueless except for their quaint, anecdotal style of reporting.

The question of whether a man's genetic make-up may be responsible for his committing acts of violence has again come forward in the courts.

In France this year, Daniel Hugon was charged with the murder of a prostitute. Following his attempted suicide, he was found to be of XYY chromosomal constitution. Filled with remorse, Hugon had voluntarily surrendered to the police. His lawyers contended that he was unfit to stand trial because of his abnormality.

Richard Speck, the convicted murderer of eight nurses in Chicago in 1966, also is reported to be an XYY.

Tall, mentally dull, with an acne-marked face and a record of 40 arrests, Speck presents a characteristic example, both genotypically and phenotypically, of the XYY type. Whether he was "born to raise hell" as a consequence of his chromosomal constitution, or whether his impoverished social environment would have been a sufficient condition, or whether both were necessary for his fateful development, no one at the moment is in a position to say.

The possible link between an XYY chromosomal constitution and criminals first came to light three years ago in a study of prison hospital inmates. In December 1965, Patricia A. Jacobs and her colleagues at Western General Hospital in Edinburgh published their findings on 197 mentally abnormal inmates undergoing treatment in a special security institution in Scotland. All had dangerous, violent or criminal propensities.

Seven of these males were found to be of XYY chromosomal constitution, one was an XXYY, and another an XY/XXY mosaic. Since on theoretical grounds the occurrence of XYY males in the general population should be less frequent than the XXY type (the latter type occurs in some 1.3 out of 1,000 live births), the 3.5 per cent incidence of XYY males in a prison population was a highly significant finding.

There is still too little information available concerning the frequency of XYY males among the newly born or

adults, but there is little doubt that the frequency found by Jacobs and her colleagues is substantially higher than that in the general population. Few laboratories yet are able to do chromosome studies on a large scale, so information available is based on limited population samples from small areas. Current estimate of the frequency of XYY males at birth range from 0.5 to 3.5 per 1,000.

Jacobs also found that the XYY inmates were unusually tall, with a mean height of 6 feet 1.1 inches. Males in the institution with normal XY chromosomal constitution had a mean height of 5 feet 7 inches.

Since publication of the paper by Jacobs and her co-workers, about a dozen other reports have been published on XYY individuals, and all the reports confirm and enlarge upon the original findings. [*See illustration opposite.*] However, in many of these cases only inmates 6 feet or more in height were selected for study, so care must be taken in interpreting the findings.

In a sample of 3,395 prison and hospital inmates, 56 individuals were XYY, nine others had supernumerary Ys in one combination or another. Only eight of the inmates were XXY. Supernumerary Y chromosomes in any other combination are only one-fifth as frequent as the XYY—a significant fact that suggests it is the YY complement in the presence of a *single* X chromosome that constitutes the most frequent anomaly.

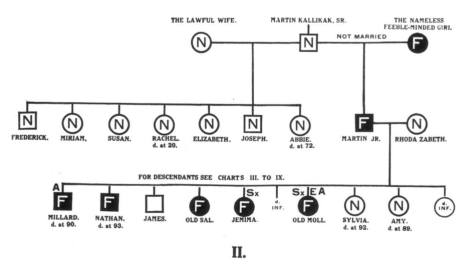

II.

CHART II.

N = Normal.   F = Feeble-minded.   Sx = Sexually immoral.   A = Alcoholic.   I = Insane.   Sy = Syphilitic.   C = Criminalistic.   D = Deaf.
d. inf. = died in infancy.   T = Tuberculous.

The good and the bad Kallikaks, from *The Kallikak Family* by Henry H. Goddard,
© Macmillan, 1912 (copyright renewed 1940 by Henry H. Goddard)

THE XYY SYNDROME

No.	Population	Status	Height Inches	Intelligence	Traits	XYY	XXYY	XY/XXY	XXY	XYY/XYYY	XYYY	Investigator
10,725	Maternity	Newborn				—	1	5	12	—	—	Maclean, N. et al. *Lancet*, i: 286-290, 1964.
2,607	Ordinary			Subnormal		—	2	—	—	—	—	Maclean, N. et al. *Lancet*, i: 293, 1962.
197	Security	Criminal	73.1	Subnormal		7	1	1	—	—	—	Jacobs, P. et al. *Nature*, Vol. 208: 1351, 1352, 1965.
942	Institutional	Criminal		Subnormal		12	7	2	—	—	—	Casey, M. et al. *Nature*, Vol. 209: 641, 642, 1966.
50	Institutional Mentally ill	Non-criminal				4	—	—	—	—	—	Casey, M. et al. *Lancet*, i: 859, 860, 1966.
24	Institutional	Criminal				2	—	—	—	—	—	Casey, M. et al. *Lancet*, i: 859, 860, 1966.
315	Security	Criminal	6 over 72	8 Subnormal 1 Schizophrenic		9	—	—	—	—	—	Price, W. et al. *Lancet*, i: 565, 566, 1966.
464	Institutional	Delinquent		Subnormal	Aggressive Grand mal	1	—	—	—	—	—	Welch, J. et al. *Nature*, Vol. 214: 500, 501, 1967.
19	Detention center	Criminal Sex crimes	74.1	I.Q. 83	Negro Acne	1	—	—	—	—	—	Telfer, M. et al. *Lancet*, i: 95, 1968.
129	Institutional	Criminal	+72			5	—	—	7	—	—	Telfer, M. et al. *Science*, Vol. 159: 1249, 1250, 1968.
34	Prison	Criminal	69-82½	2 Subnormal	Psychopathic	3	—	—	—	1	—	Wiener, S. et al. *Lancet*, i: 159, 1968.
1,021	Institutional Boys	Delinquent	Tall	I.Q. s 77, 78, 91	Property offenses	3	—	—	1	—	—	Hunter, H. *Lancet*, i: 816, 1968.
200	Institutional	Criminal	+72		Aggressive Sex offenders	9	—	—	—	—	—	Vanasek, F. et al., Atascadero State Hospital, Calif. (in press), 1968.
1	Ordinary	Embezzlement	78	I.Q. 118	Not overtly aggressive Depressed	1	—	—	—	—	—	Leff, J. and Scott, P. *Lancet*, i: 645, 1968.
1	Ordinary	8 yrs. 7 mo.	57	I.Q. 95	Aggressive	1	—	—	—	—	—	Cowie, J. and Kahn, J. *British Medical Journal*, Vol. 1: 748, 749, 1968.
1	Ordinary	5 yrs. 6 mo.	57	I.Q. 85	Undescended testes Simian creases	—	—	—	—	—	1	Townes, P. *Lancet*, i: 1041-1043, 1965.
1	Ordinary	44 yrs.	72	Average	Trouble keeping jobs	1	—	—	—	—	—	Hauschka, T. et al. *American Journal of Human Genetics*, Vol. 14: 22-30, 1962.
1	Ordinary	12 yrs.		Average	Undescended testes	1	—	—	—	—	—	Sandberg, A. et al. *New England Journal of Medicine*, Vol. 268: 585-589, 1963.

However, the presence of an extra Y chromosome, in any combination, appears to increase the chances of trouble. It also seems that the presence of an extra X chromosome, no matter what the number of extra Y chromosomes may be, in no way reduces the chance of trouble.

The Y chromosome, so to speak, seems to possess an elevated aggressiveness potential, whereas the X chromosome seems to possess a high gentleness component.

It appears probable that the ordinary quantum of aggressiveness of a normal XY male is derived from his Y chromosome, and that the addition of another Y chromosome presents a double dose of those potencies that may under certain conditions facilitate the development of aggressive behavior.

Of course, as with any chromosome, this does not mean that the genes are directly responsible for the end-effect. Rather, the genes on the sex chromosomes exercise their effects through a long chain of metabolic pathways. The final physiological or functional expression results from the interaction of the genes with their environments.

Genes do not determine anything. They simply influence the morphological and physiological expression of traits. Heredity, then, is the expression, not of what is given in one's genes at conception, but of the reciprocal interaction between the inherited genes and the environments to which they've been exposed.

Genes, chromosomes, or heredity are not to be interpreted, as so many people mistakenly do, as equivalent to fate or predestination. On the contrary, the genetic constitution, the genotype, is a labile system, capable of being influenced and changed to varying degrees.

Unchangeability and immutability are not characteristics of the genetic system. The genetic code for any trait contains a set of specific instructions. The manner in which those instructions will be carried out depends not only on those instructions but also upon the nature of their interaction with other sets of instructions as well as with their environments.

The phenotype, that is the visible product of the joint action of genes and the environment, is variable. The idea of genetic or hereditary preformation is as incorrect and unsound as is the doctrine of hereditary predestination. In discussing the behavioral traits so frequently associated with the XYY type, these facts must be especially borne in mind.

How does the XYY chromosomal aberration originate? Most probably the double Y complement is produced during formation of the sperm. During the process of meiosis, in which chromosomes divide and duplicate themselves, normal separation of the sex chromosomes leads to two kinds of sperm—those with an X chromosome, and those with a Y chromosome. If an X sperm fertilizes a normal X ovum, an XX individual (normal female) will result. If the Y sperm fertilizes the ovum, a normal XY male will result.

Failure of the sex chromosomes to separate normally is called nondisjunction. There are two divisions during meiosis. If nondisjunction occurs during the first meiotic division in the production of sperm, this leads to two kinds of sperm cells—those with both the X and Y chromosomes, and those with no sex chromosomes. If an XY sperm fertilizes a normal ovum, an XXY individual will be the result. The XXY individual is a male (Klinefelter's Syndrome), but is usually sterile, lacking functional testes. About 80 per cent of these males develop small breasts and at least 25 per cent are of limited intelligence.

If nondisjunction occurs at the second meiotic division of the paternal germ cells, three types of sperm are produced: XX, YY, and those containing no sex chromosomes. Offspring resulting from fertilization of a normal ovum will be, respectively, XXX, XYY, and XO.

An XYY individual also could be produced if the sex chromosomes fail to separate normally in the early stages of division (mitosis) of a normal, fertilized XY-ovum. However, in such an event, an individual with some type of mosaicism is more likely to occur.

Mosaicism refers to the existence of a different number of sex chromosomes in different tissues or parts of the body. For example, an individual may have only one X chromosome in some of his cells, and three chromosomes (XYY) in other cells. Such a mosaic would be designated XO/XYY. The O refers to the missing X or Y chromosome. If the single X chromosome is coupled with an isochromosome (I)—a chromosome with two identical arms—then the mosaic would be XI/XYY. Of course, other mosaics such as XY/XYY or XYY/XYYY occur.

Major physical abnormalities do not occur in XYY individuals for the reason that the Y chromosome carries relatively few genes. However, the physical abnormalities that do occur are interesting. As in most cases in which an extra sex chromosome is present, there is a high incidence of abnormal internal and external genitalia. Even in childhood, XYY individuals are usually strikingly tall, and as adults usually exceed six feet in height. Facial acne appears to be frequent in adolescence. Mentally, these individuals are usually rather dull, with I.Q.s between 80 and 95. Abnormal electroencephalographic recordings, and a relatively high incidence of epileptic and epileptiform conditions, suggest a wide spectrum of brain dysfunction. Disorders of the

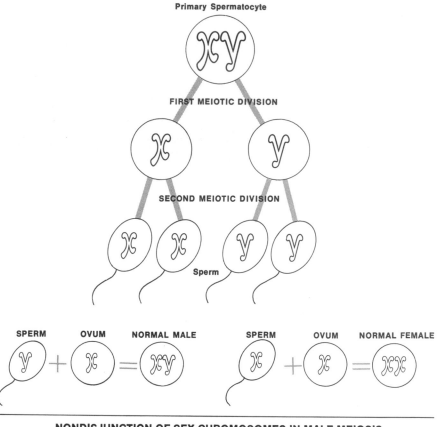

NORMAL MALE MEIOSIS
(Formation of the sperm)

Primary Spermatocyte

FIRST MEIOTIC DIVISION

SECOND MEIOTIC DIVISION

Sperm

| SPERM | OVUM | NORMAL MALE | SPERM | OVUM | NORMAL FEMALE |

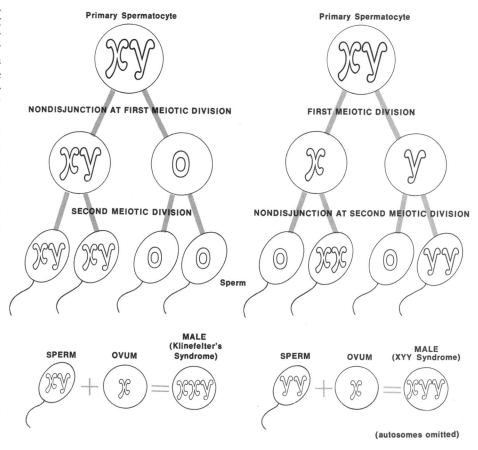

NONDISJUNCTION OF SEX CHROMOSOMES IN MALE MEIOSIS

Primary Spermatocyte

NONDISJUNCTION AT FIRST MEIOTIC DIVISION

SECOND MEIOTIC DIVISION

Sperm

MALE
(Klinefelter's Syndrome)

SPERM + OVUM =

Primary Spermatocyte

FIRST MEIOTIC DIVISION

NONDISJUNCTION AT SECOND MEIOTIC DIVISION

MALE
(XYY Syndrome)

SPERM + OVUM =

(autosomes omitted)

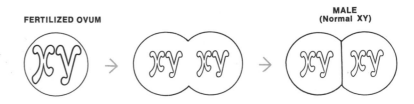

teeth, such as discolored enamel, malocclusion and arrested development, also have been noted.

Allowing for the fact that in many cases tall prison inmates were selected for study of the XYY syndrome, and while a number of known XYY individuals fall several inches short of 6 feet, it is nonetheless clear that tallness usually characterizes the XYY individual.

This may be a significant factor in influencing the individual's behavioral development. Among children his own age, an XYY boy may be teased and taunted because of his height, and impelled either to withdrawal or aggression. As a juvenile, adolescent or adult, he may find himself nurtured in environments that encourage physical aggression as a means of adaptation.

This should not be interpreted to mean that all tall men have an XYY constitution. Recently, Richard Goodman and his colleagues at Ohio State University examined the chromosomes of 36 basketball players ranging in height from 5 feet, 11 inches to 6 feet, 10 inches, and found no chromosomal abnormalities.

The resort to brawn rather than brain is not limited to individuals endowed with an extra Y chromosome. Most violent crimes are committed by chromosomally normal individuals. However, the high frequency with which individuals with XYY chromosomes commit crimes of violence leaves little doubt that in some cases the additional Y chromosome exerts a preponderantly powerful influence in the genesis of aggressive behavior.

In a maximum security prison in Melbourne, Australia, Saul Wiener and his colleagues found four XYY-type males in a study of 34 tall prisoners, all between 5 feet 9 inches and 6 feet 10.5 inches in height. A striking frequency of 11.8 per cent! Three of the inmates were XYY, one of whom was charged with attempted murder, the second had committed murder, and the third larceny. The fourth was an XYY/XYYY mosaic, and had committed murder.

An interesting fact is that the tallest of the XYY murderers, 6 feet 10.5 inches tall, had a sister who was even taller. The tallness of the sister indicates that even though the X chromosome is not usually associated with excessive height in families where the males are extremely tall, a trait for tallness may be also carried in the X chromosome.

As a consequence of the discovery of what may be called the XYY syndrome, there now can be very little doubt that genes do influence, to some extent, the development of behavior.

It also appears clear, that, with all other factors constant, genes of the same kind situated at the same locus on the chromosomes of different people may vary greatly both in their penetrance and their expressivity.

Penetrance refers to the regularity with which a gene produces its effect. When a gene regularly produces the same effect, it is said to have complete penetrance. When the trait is not manifested in some cases, the gene is said to have reduced penetrance.

Expressivity refers to the manifestation of a trait produced by a gene. When the manifestation differs from individual to individual, the gene is said to have variable expressivity. For example, the dominant gene for allergy may express itself as asthma, eczema, hay fever, urticarial rash, or angioneurotic edema.

Hence, it would be an error to identify the XYY constitution as *predisposed* to aggressive behavior.

Whatever genes are involved, they often fail to produce aggressive behavior, and even more often may be expressed in many different ways. In fact, the XYY phenotype, the product of the joint action of genes and environment, does vary from normal to various degrees of abnormality.

Some individuals, however, seem to be driven to their aggressive behavior as if they are possessed by a demon. The demon, it would seem, lies in the peculiar nature of the double-Y chromosome complement. That the combined power of several Y chromosomes can be so great, in some cases, as to cause a man to become unrestrainedly aggressive is dramatically borne out by a case reported by John Cowie and Jacob Kahn of East Ham Child Clinic, London, in March 1968.

The first-born, wanted child of a mother aged 23 and a father aged 25 was referred at the age of four and a half years to a psychiatrist because he was unmanageable at home, destructive, mischievous and defiant. He would smash his toys, rip the curtains, set fire to the room in his mother's absence, kick the cat and hit his eight-month-old brother. He was overadventurous and without fear. At two years of age, he began wandering away from home, and was brought back by the police on five occasions. He started school at five years and at once developed an interest in sharp-pointed objects. He would shoot drawing compasses across the schoolroom from an elastic band, and injured several children. In one incident, he rammed a screwdriver into a little girl's stomach.

At the age of eight years, seven months, he was 4 feet 9 inches tall, handsome, athletically proportioned, and of normal appearance. He is of

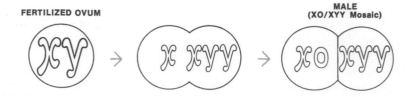

FERTILIZED OVUM

MALE
(XO/XYY Mosaic)

(autosomes omitted)

average intelligence, and often considerate and happy. His electroencephalogram is mildly abnormal. Both his parents and his brother have normal chromosomal complements, but the boy is of XYY constitution. His brother is a normally behaving child, and the parents are concerned, loving people.

As illustrated by this case, there is now an increasing amount of evidence that XYY individuals commence their aggressive and social behavior in early prepubertal years. In many cases, the offenses committed are against property rather than against persons. The XYY anomaly, therefore, should not be associated with one particular behavioral trait, but rather regarded as an aberration characterized by a wide spectrum of behavioral possibilities ranging from totally normal to persistent antisocial behavior. The degree of aggressiveness varies, and is only one component of the highly variable spectrum of behavioral contingencies.

We have shown how the XYY chromosomal aberration can originate in nondisjunction during meiosis or during mitosis. But does an XYY male transmit the abnormality to his offspring? To this question the answer is: probably not. One report on an Oregon XYY man indicates the double-Y chromosome complement may not be transmitted. The man has six sons, and all are of normal XY chromosomal constitution.

On the other hand, T. S. Hauschka of Roswell Park Memorial Institute and the Medical Foundation of Buffalo, and his colleagues, who discovered one of the first XYY individuals in 1961, suggest that there may be a hereditary predisposition to nondisjunction. The XYY individual they identified was a normal male who came to their attention because he had a daughter who suffered from Down's syndrome (mongolism). Since Down's syndrome, in most cases, also arises as a result of nondisjunction, this, coupled with other abnormalities in his offspring, suggested that he might be transmitting a hereditary tendency to nondisjunction.

The fact that the XYY complement is now known to be associated with persistent antisocial behavior in a large number of individuals raises a number of questions that the reasonable society, if not the Great Society, must consider seriously.

A first question, if not a first priority, is whether it would not now be desirable to type chromosomally all infants at birth or shortly after. At least one per cent of all babies born have a chromosomal abnormality of some sort, and about one-quarter of these involve sex chromosome abnormalities. Some of these will be XYY. Forearmed with such information, it might be possible to institute the proper preventive and other measures at an early age. These measures would be designed to help the individuals with the XYY chromosomal constitution to follow a less stormy development than they otherwise might.

A second question is how society should deal with individuals known to be of XYY constitution. Such individuals are genetically abnormal. They are not normal and, therefore, should not be treated as if they were. If the individual has the misfortune to have been endowed with an extra chromosome Number 21, he would have suffered from Down's syndrome (mongolism). He would not have been expected to behave as a normal individual. And why should the XYY individual be held any more responsible for his behavior than a mongoloid? Mongoloids are usually likeable, unaggressive individuals, and most sociable. The aggressive XYY individual is often the very opposite. Yet the unaggressive behavior of mongoloids is as much due to their genetic constitution as is the aggressive and antisocial behavior of the XYY individual.

Recognizing this fact, it becomes very necessary for us to consider how society and the law should deal with such individuals. We have learned how to identify and treat the hereditary defect of PKU (phenylketonuria), which can result in idiocy if not treated. Cannot we also develop measures to treat the XYY syndrome? Surgical intervention, such as sterilization, is totally inappropriate since it will not "cure" or alleviate the condition, nor will it reduce the frequency of XYY individuals in the general population. The XYY aberration, as far as we know, is not directly inherited, and quite probably arises primarily from nondisjunction of the sex chromosomes in completely normal parents.

Although we are in no position to control the genetic inheritance of an individual, we can do a great deal to change certain environmental conditions that may encourage the XYY individual to commit criminal acts.

A society does not properly acquit itself of its responsibilities if it places the entire burden of caring for abnormal individuals upon the parents. What we are talking about here is not a program of eugenic control, but a program of social therapy. There is every reason to believe that if we can successfully develop effective methods to help the aggressive XYY individual, then we will be moving in the right direction to control those social conditions that drive men to crime—regardless of their genotype.∎

the SHATTERED LANGUAGE of SCHIZOPHRENIA

SOMEWHERE IN A HOSPITAL WARD a patient writes: "**The subterfuge and the mistaken planned substitutions for that demanded American action can produce nothing but the general results of negative contention and the impractical results of careless applications, the natural results of misplacement, of mistaken purpose and unrighteous position, the impractical serviceabilities of unnecessary contradictions. For answers to this dilemma, consult Webster.**" The document is never sent to anyone; it is addressed to no one; and perhaps intended for no reader.

Another patient, miles away, writes: "**I am of I-Building in B . . State Hospital. With my nostrils clogged and Winter here, I chanced to be reading the magazine that Mentholatum advertised from. Kindly send it to me at the hospital. Send it to me Joseph Nemo in care of Joseph Nemo and me who answers by the name of Joseph Nemo and will care for it myself. Thanks everlasting and Merry New Year to Mentholatum Company for my nose for my nose for my nose for my nose for my nose.**"

A British patient writes: "**I hope to be home soon, very soon. I fancy chocolate eclairs, chocolate eclairs, Doenuts. I want some doenuts, I do want some golden syrup, a tin of golden syrup or treacle, jam . . . See the Committee about me coming home for Easter my twenty-fourth birthday. I hope all is well at home, how is Father getting on. Never mind there is hope, heaven will come, time heals all wounds, Rise again Glorious Greece and come to Hindoo Heavens, the Indian Heavens, The Dear old times will come back. We shall see Heaven and Glory yet, come everlasting life. I want a new writing pad of note paper . . .**" *

Yet another writes: "**Now to eat if one cannot the other can — and if we cant the girseau Q.C. Washpots prize-bloom capacities — turning out — replaced by the head patterns my own capacities — I was not very kind to them. Q.C. Washpots under-patterned against — bred to pattern. Animal sequestration capacities and animal sequestired capacities under leash — and animal secretions . . .**" *

*These quotations are taken from "The Neurology of Psychotic Speech" by McDonald Critchley

xperienced clinicians, when called upon to diagnose the writers of language like this, agree closely with each other (80 per cent of the time or more). The diagnosis: schizophrenia. Nearly every textbook on psychopathology presents similar examples, and nobody seems to have much difficulty in finding appropriate samples. It would seem obvious that there must be a well-established and explicit definition of what characteristics language must possess to be called schizophrenic. But when we ask clinicians to tell us exactly what specific features of an individual language sample led them to decide that the writer was schizophrenic, it turns out that they aren't exactly sure. Instead of explicit description, the expert comment is likely to be: "It has that schizophrenic flavor" or "It is the confusion of thought that convinces me."

Impressionistic descriptions abound. The language is described as *circumlocutious, repetitive, incoherent,* suffering from an *interpenetration of ideas, excessively concrete, regressed,* and the like. Doubtless, all of these descriptions have merit as clinical characterizations of the language. Unfortunately, they are quite imprecise, and they give us no adequate basis for developing theoretical accounts of the origin of schizophrenic language. This is, of course, hardly surprising. Quantitative studies of language have been notoriously laborious to undertake. However, two recent developments in behavioral sciences have combined to change the situation quite significantly. The first of these is the development of language-analysis programs for computer use, and the second is the increasing sophistication of psycholinguistics as a framework for the study of applied problems in the psychology of language.

Before turning to look at the consequences of these developments, we should glance at the kinds of hypotheses that have already been advanced to account for schizophrenic language. The first of these might be termed the *Cipher Hypothesis.* In its simplest form this says that the patient is trying to communicate something to a listener (actual or potential) but is afraid to say what he means in plain language. He is somewhat in the same straits as the normal individual faced with the problem of conveying, let us say, some very bad news to a listener. Rather than come right out and tell someone directly that a family member

is dying, the informant may become circumlocutious and perhaps so oblique that his message simply does not make sense at all.

In the case of the schizophrenic patient, however, it is assumed that the motives which drive him to disguise his message may be largely unconscious—that he could not put the message into plain language if he tried. Where the normal person is trying to spare the feelings of the listener by his distortions and evasions, the patient purportedly is sparing his own feelings by the use of similar techniques. This analogy can be stretched a little further. Just as the normal speaker is caught in a dilemma —the necessity to convey the message and the pressure to avoid conveying it too roughly—so the patient is caught in a conflict between the necessity of expressing himself on important personal topics and the imperative need to avoid being aware of his own real meanings. Thus, so the Cipher Hypothesis maintains, it is possible in principle to decipher the patient's message—provided one can crack the code. This hypothesis assumes, of course, that there really is a message.

Obviously, the Cipher Hypothesis owes its genesis to psychoanalytic theory. In essence, it is identical with Freud's interpretation of the relationship between manifest and latent dream content. Unfortunately, from a research point of view, this hypothesis suffers from the weakness of being very hard to disprove. No two patients are assumed to have the same code, and so the translation of schizophrenic language into a normal communication requires a detailed analysis of the case history of the individual writer. As the code that is discovered for any one case cannot be validated against any other case, the hypothesis rests its claim to acceptance upon its intrinsic plausibility *vis-à-vis* the facts of the life history of the patient. But plausible interpretations of a patient's language may reflect the creative (or empathetic) imagination of the clinician, rather than a valid discovery of an underlying process governing the patient's utterances.

One more or less necessary deduction from the Cipher Hypothesis is that language should become most disorganized when the topic under discussion is one of personal significance, and less disorganized when the topic is neutral. To date, no adequate test of this deduction has been reported. In the absence of this

By Brendan A. Maher

or other independent tests of the Cipher Hypothesis, it must be regarded for the time being as, at best, an interesting speculation.

A second explanation has been that the patient's communications are confusing and garbled precisely because he wishes to *avoid* communicating with other people. This hypothesis, which we shall call the *Avoidance Hypothesis,* interprets the disordered language as a response that is maintained and strengthened by its effectiveness in keeping other people away. Presumably, the normal listener becomes frustrated or bored with such a speaker and simply goes away, leaving the schizophrenic in the solitude he seeks. This theory rests, in turn, upon the assumption that the patient finds personal interactions threatening. We might expect that casual interactions—such as chatting about the weather—are relatively unthreatening and do not provoke avoidant disorder in language. The language disturbance should become more evident when the threat of personal involvement arises.

At this level, the Avoidance Hypothesis cannot be distinguished from the Cipher Hypothesis. The main difference between the two is that the Avoidance Hypothesis is concerned with a *dimension* of incomprehensibility and does not imply that the incomprehensible can be unscrambled. Both of these hypotheses have their attractions.

"For answers to this dilemma, consult Webster," wrote the first patient we have quoted. Is he just playing a word game with an imaginary reader or is there a meaning to his message? We might remark on the similarity of the prefix in many of the words he uses: *subterfuge, substitution; unrighteous, unnecessary; mistaken, misplacement; contention, contradiction.* His message might, indeed, sound like a random sampling from a dictionary.

Or did the dictionarylike nature of the "message" only occur to the patient himself toward the end—and hence the closing remark? In any event, the sample seems to fit plausibly into the notion that some kind of enciphering was going on between the patient's basic "message" and the language that he wrote.

Our fourth sample of schizophrenic language, on the other hand, seems to be absolutely incomprehensible. Fragments of phrases, neologisms ("girseau") and repetitions—*sequestration* and *sequestired*—combine into a jumble that seems to defy understanding. It is hard to believe that there might be a message

in disguise here, or even that the language was uttered with any wish to communicate.

Although both hypotheses can be made to seem plausible, they are intrinsically unsatisfying to the psychopathologist. They do not deal with the most fascinating problem of schizophrenic language: why does a particular patient utter the particular words that he does, rather than some other jumbled-up sequence?

ome beginnings of an answer to this question have begun to emerge. Years ago, Eugen Bleuler commented on the presence of *interfering associations* in schizophrenic language. He suggested that the difficulty for the patient was that ideas associated with the content of his message somehow intruded into the message and thus distorted it. A patient of his, whom he had seen walking around the hospital grounds with her father and son, was asked who her visitors were. "The father, son and Holy Ghost," she replied. These words have a strong mutual association as a single phrase and although the last item, "Holy Ghost," was probably not meant as part of her message, it intruded because of its strong associative links with other units in the message.

Bleuler also noticed the difficulty that patients seemed to have in *understanding* a pun, despite their tendency to talk in punning fashion. A patient asked about her relationships with people at home says, "I have many ties with my home! My father wears them around his collar." The pun on the word *tie* was unintentional, hence humorless.

Against the background of this general hypothesis of interfering associations, my students and I began investigations of schizophrenic language some years ago in Harvard's Laboratory of Social Relations. Our first concern was with the original question of definition. What must language contain to be labeled schizophrenic? Our work began with a plea to over 200 hospitals for examples of patients' writings—whether the patients were schizophrenic or not. Colleaguial response was rather overwhelming, and we amassed a very large number of letters, documents, diaries and simple messages written in almost every state of the Union. (Many of these were inappropriate to our purposes. A carton load of documents in Spanish from a Texas hospital, some brief obscenities scribbled on match-

covers and dropped daily onto the desk of a colleague in a St. Louis hospital and other similar items were eliminated, of course.)

From this mass, we selected a set of documents that were legible, long enough to include several consecutive sentences—and written in English. These texts were then read by a panel of clinicians. Each text was judged independently, and then was classified as *schizophrenic language* or *normal language.* (We obtained typical interjudge agreements of around 80 per cent.) At this juncture we did not know whether the writers of the letters had been diagnosed as schizophrenic or not. Our concern was with the characteristics of the language—and with the clinicians' reactions to it.

Our two sets of texts then were submitted for computer analysis with the aid of the *General Inquirer* program. This program codes and categorizes language in terms of content, and also provides a summary of grammatical features of the language. Out of this analysis, we developed some empirical rules (or a guide on how to write a document that a clinician will judge schizophrenic). Two of the most reliable rules were:

1. Write about politics, religion or science. Letters dealing with global social issues of this kind are highly likely to be regarded as schizophrenic by clinicians.
2. Write more *objects* than *subjects* in sentences. Typical sentences consist of enumerations of classes of objects in a form illustrated in our second and third examples above: "send it to me, Joseph Nemo, in care of Joseph Nemo and me who answers by the name of Joseph Nemo"; or "I fancy chocolate eclairs, chocolate eclairs, doenuts." Or in chains of associations at the end of a sentence. When, for example, a woman patient writes: "I like coffee, cream, cows, Elizabeth Taylor," the associational links between each word and the one following seem obvious.

This kind of associative chaining already had been described clinically by Bleuler; hence it was hardly surprising that the computer should find it to be a reliable discriminator in our document samples. What began to interest us, however, was the fact that these associations interfere most readily at the end of a sentence. Why not chains of subjects or chains of verbs, and why not at the beginning or middle of a sentence? Fur-

Vulnerable point ↓

Planned sentence: I have pains in my chest and wonder if there is something wrong

Associations:

aches ↓
doctor ↓

(weak) ↓ ↓ (strong)
ribs   BOX
lungs TRUNK
body   HOPE

right ↓
bad ↓
failure ↓

Utterance: "Doctor, I have pains in my chest and hope and wonder if my box

thermore, why is this kind of interference found clearly in some schizophrenic patients and yet never occurs at all in others?

For some time it has become increasingly apparent that, in schizophrenia, *attention* is greatly disrupted. It is hard for a patient to remain focused on any one stimulus for any length of time. He is unable to "tune out" or ignore other surrounding stimuli. These distract him; they enter consciousness at full strength and not in an attenuated fashion as they do with the normal person. Reports by the patients themselves make the point dramatically:

"Things are coming in too fast. I lose my grip of it and get lost. I am attending to everything at once and as a result I do not really attend to anything."[*]

"Everything seems to grip my attention, although I am not particularly interested in anything. I am speaking to you just now but I can hear noises going on next door and in the corridor. I find it difficult to concentrate on what I am saying to you."[*]

"I cannot seem to think or even put any plans together. I cannot see the picture. I get the book out and read the story but the activities and the story all just do not jar me into action."[*]

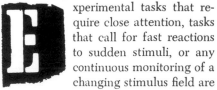xperimental tasks that require close attention, tasks that call for fast reactions to sudden stimuli, or any continuous monitoring of a changing stimulus field are almost invariably done poorly by schizophrenics. Sorting tasks, where the subject must organize objects or words into conceptual groups, are progressively more difficult for the schizophrenic if irrelevant or puzzling factors appear in the material.

We may regard the focusing of attention as a process whereby we effectively inhibit attention to everything but certain relevant stimuli in the environment. As attention lapses, we find ourselves being aware of various irrelevant stimuli —the inhibitory mechanism has failed temporarily.

It is possible that an analogous set of events takes place when we produce a complex sequence of language. Attention may be greater or lesser at some points in a language sequence than at others. The end of a sentence—the period point—may be particularly vulnerable to momentary attentional lapses: one thought has been successfully completed, but the next one may not yet have been formed into utterable shape. Within a single sentence itself, there may be other points of comparative vulnerability, though not perhaps as marked as at the sentence ending.

Uttering a sentence without disruption is an extremely skilled performance, but one that most of us acquire so early in life that we are unaware of its remarkable complexity. (However, we become more aware of how difficult it is to "make sense" when we are extremely tired, or ripped out of sleep by the telephone, or distraught, or drunk.)

Single words have strong associational bonds with other words—as the classic technique of word association indicates. We know that the word "black" will elicit the response "white" almost instantaneously from the majority of people. The associational bond between black and white is clearly very strong. Strong as it is, it will not be allowed to dominate consciousness when one is uttering a sentence such as "I am thinking about buying a black car." Our successful sentences come from the successful, sequential inhibition of all interfering associations that individual words in the sentence might generate. Just as successful visual attention involves tuning out irrelevant visual material, so successful utterance may involve tuning out irrelevant verbal static.

By the same token, disordered attention should lead to an increasing likelihood that this kind of interference will not be inhibited, but will actually intrude into language utterance. Its most probable point of intrusion is wherever attention is normally lowest.

"Portmanteau" words or puns provide unusually good occasions for disruptive

intrusions. Consider, for example, the word "stock." This word has several possible meanings, each of them with its own set of associations. Financial associations might be *Wall Street, bonds, dividend,* etc. Agricultural associations might include *cattle, barn* and *farm;* theatrical associations might be *summer, company* and the like. Webster's Third International Dictionary gives 42 different definitions of the word *stock,* many of them archaic or unusual, but many of them common. If one set of meanings intrudes into a sentence that is clearly built around another set of meanings, the effect is a pun, and an accompanying digression or cross-current in surface content. The sentences—"I have many ties with my home. My father wears them around his collar,"—seem to skip, like a stone on a lake, from *ties* (bonds) to *home* to *father* to *ties* (neckties). On the surface, this is a witty statement, but the speaker had no idea of what was really going on inside or underneath the form of words. The statement was therefore unwitting and hence unwitty.

oren Chapman and his associates, in work at Southern Illinois University, demonstrated that schizophrenics as a group are more open to interference from the most common meaning of a punning word. When we use a word like *stock* as a stimulus for word association, we discover that most normal respondents give financial associations first, and may find it difficult to respond when asked to "give associations to another meaning." Associations to the other meaning are weaker or less prepotent, and only emerge under special instructional sets. Chapman's work suggests that if the plan of a sentence calls for the use of a weaker meaning, the schizophrenic runs some risk that associational intrusions will interfere and actually produce a punning effect.

On the other hand, if the plan of a sentence involves the stronger meaning, then there may be no intrusion of associations. And if associations do intrude,

[*] *These quotations are taken from McGhie & Chapman's "Disorders of Attention in Schizophrenia"*

Vulnerable point

with my heart.

→ beat

soul → save → heaven

broken

A LOOK AT A SCHIZOPHRENIC UTTERANCE. Where a punning word occurs at a vulnerable point, the sequence becomes disrupted and disintegrates into associative chaining until it terminates. The emotional significance of what the schizophrenic plans to say may have little or no bearing on when an intrusion occurs or what it seems to mean.

is broken and heart is beaten for my soul and salvation and heaven, Amen."

these intrusions will appear relevant to the sentence and will not strike the listener as strange. Which meanings will be strong or weak will depend to some extent upon the culture from which the patient comes. (Personal experience may of course produce uniquely strong or weak associations in individual cases.) However, Chapman was able to predict correctly the direction of errors for schizophrenic patients as a group on the basis of estimates of strength obtained from normal respondents. Thus, some patients may have personal idiosyncracies, but the associations that interrupt the schizophrenic are generally the same as those that are strong for the population at large.

A parallel investigation I conducted at the University of Copenhagen included a study of the language of Danish schizophrenics. I observed the same general effect: patients were liable to interference from strong meanings of double-meaning words. English is a language, of course, that is unusually rich in puns, homonyms, cognates and indeed a whole lexicon of verbal trickery. But it seems plausible to suppose that in any language in which double-meaning words are to be found, this kind of schizophrenic disturbance may be found.

From these observations we can begin to piece together a picture of what happens when schizophrenic intrusions occur in a sentence that started out more or less normally. Where a punning word occurs at a vulnerable point, the sequence becomes disrupted and rapidly disintegrates into associative chaining until it terminates. [See illustration, above.]

We may look at schizophrenic utterances as the end result of a combination of two factors: the vulnerability of sentence structure to attentional lapses, and the inability of patients to inhibit associational intrusions, particularly at these lapse points. From this point of view, the problem of language is directly related to the other attentional difficulties which the schizophrenic has; he is handicapped in making language work clearly, just as

he is at any other task that requires sustained attention. The emotional significance of what the schizophrenic plans to say may have little or no bearing on when an intrusion occurs, or what it seems to mean. Any sentence with vulnerable points in its syntactic or semantic structure may result in confusion, whether the topic is of great psychological importance or has to do with a patient's harmless liking for chocolate eclairs and doughnuts.

Serious and sustained difficulties in the maintenance of attention suggest a biological defect. Peter Venables at the University of London has suggested swimming or unfocusable attention in schizophrenia may be connected with low thresholds of physiological arousal—stimuli can be very weak and yet trigger strong physiological reactions. This low arousal threshold is found mostly in acute, rather than chronic, schizophrenia.

Evidence from studies of a variety of attentional tasks supports this interpretation. Additional and intriguing evidence was obtained by one of my students, Dr. Joy Rice at the University of Wisconsin. Using electrochemical (galvanic) changes in the skin as a measure, she found that schizophrenic patients who were most responsive to noise stimulation were also the patients who showed the most difficulty in dealing with the meaning of punning sentences. The magnitude of galvanic skin response to external stimulation is presumably greatest in patients with low initial arousal levels (and hence the most receptivity to external stimulation). Rice's data may therefore support the notion that verbal associational interference is part and parcel of a total syndrome of which biological control of attention is a crucial central focus.

recent research into the effects of LSD has shown that it is people with low initial arousal systems who have the "good trips"; the most cursory glance at literary biography will reveal an extraordinary number of poets and writers who

were "sensitive," "neurasthenic," and so on. Which leads me to a sort of Parthian speculation.

Look again at the four samples quoted in the beginning of this article. What you see there, I think, is the literary imagination gone mad, if I may use so unclinical a term here. The first sample, had it come from the pen of someone whose brain we trusted, might almost be a crude parody of ponderous political tracts or socio-economo-political gobbledygook of one sort or another. In the second, the fragment, "With my nostrils clogged and Winter here," is really not bad, and one wouldn't be terribly surprised to find it occurring in, say, the *Cantos* of Ezra Pound. In the third quotation, there are unmistakable echoes from the New Testament, Lord Byron, and Ralph Waldo Emerson, or rather echoes from an entire chamber of the literary heritage. The kind of wordplay indulged in throughout the fourth quote is not essentially different technically from that employed by the later James Joyce, or by the John Lennon of *In his own write*.

What is lacking from these samples, so far as we can tell, is context and control and the critical, or pattern-imposing, intelligence. It would seem, therefore, that the mental substrata in which certain kinds of poetry are born probably are associative in a more or less schizophrenic way. (In the case of poets like Dylan Thomas or Hart Crane, of course, these substrata had to be blasted open by liquor.) The intelligence that shapes, cuts, edits, revises and erases is fed by many conscious sources, most of them cultural; but the wellsprings seem to be, as poets have been telling us for centuries, sort of divine and sort of mad.

By Jules H. Masserman

THE NEUROTIC CAT

The cat is ready to pounce. Well trained, healthy, and satisfied, he has worked a series of electric switches, waiting for the regular signal that food is in his box. A light goes on, a bell rings, and food is deposited in a box. In an instant, the cat is at the food box in his cage.

But now, a strong blast of air from a vent in the box strikes his face. Food forgotten, the startled cat leaps back quickly, crouches tensely at the far corner of his cage, and waits.

The next time a food signal is given, the cat may be slightly wary, but he will try again to behave "normally," going about the usual business of getting food. If *unpredictably* he then is hit by another blast of air, and by just a few irregularly spaced blasts on subsequent feeding attempts, his behavior will change. When the light flashes and the bell sounds, instead of responding eagerly and with confidence, the cat will crouch anxiously as far from the box as he can get. He will try to hide or to escape; he may tremble, show signs of anxiety, even of panic—indications of induced experimental "neurotic" behavior.

The Proper Study of Mankind Is . . .

When a scientist writes about animal behavior, using terms such as normal, neurotic, and psychotic, he is vulnerable to the accusation that he is anthropomorphizing. Do you really think, he is asked, that experiments with animals have results that apply to human behavior, which seems to be so infinitely more subjective and complex?

One answer is that all phenomena interpreted by men are "anthropomorphized." Another answer is that the behavioral differences between men and animals are more quantitative than qualitative. While men do behave with more versatility and sophistication than dogs, cats, or monkeys, we are not different in our needs nor in our *basic* patterns of adaptation to environment. As we look more closely at animal behavior in the laboratory, it seems disconcertingly reminiscent of the development and course of individual and social conduct in man. Animal neuroses and their treatment have a significant relationship to the same problems in humans. Perhaps the proper study of mankind is not only man, but the whole animal kingdom.

My experimental studies have convinced me that four main "biodynamic" principles underlie all animal activity, including that of man. First, behavior must gratify certain physiological needs present in the animal and it varies with the intensity, duration, and relationship of those needs. Second, organisms understand and interact with their environment not in terms of an absolute reality, but rather in accordance with their individual capacity, maturity, and experience. Third, in the higher animals, individual variations make many techniques of adaptation possible, so that stress and frustration can be met satisfactorily by trying new methods of coping with the problem or by altering current goals.

Finally, when two or more strong motivations are in such serious opposition to one another that they are mutually exclusive, the animal experiences a mounting tension (in human terms, "anxiety"). He develops inhibitions and aversions (phobias), certain ritualized activity (compulsions), various "psychosomatic" ailments, or self-isolation, paranoid suspiciousness, sexual aberrations, unusually strong aggressive or passive tendencies. These maladaptive actions might be called *neurotic;* other disorganized, regressive, and bizarrely symbolic animal activity (for example, fighting imaginary enemies) might be called a *psychotic* pattern of conduct. The unusual and unadjusted behavior may persist a long time, until the techniques described below are brought into play.

Any living organism can be used to study animal behavior. Amoebas have been used in the study of adaptation, and planaria have exhibited a sense of time and environment, individuality, "stubbornness," and aberrant conduct. Even these simple organisms act in a way—whether it is mental or physical in its derivation—which is undeniably *sentient;* that is, their behavior has a logical relation to their environment and motivations. Most of my experiments, however, have used higher animals, chiefly cats and monkeys.

Creating A Neurotic Cat

In order to study the cure of neurosis in the laboratory, one must first create it [*See illustrations on page 385.*] The initial step in doing this is to accustom an animal to a given experimental situation. For example, a cat that has been given no food for about 24 hours is placed in a glass-enclosed cage so that he can be observed from all angles at all times. At one end of the cage is a food box with a hinged lid. At first, food is dropped into the open box when a signal, such as a light-and-bell, is given. Within a few hours the cat learns that the light-and-bell combination means food is in the box. Then the lid of the box is half-closed when the food appears, and the cat has to pry it up to get his meal. Gradually, the cat learns to work switches that operate mechanisms for the signal and food, and so earns its own reward.

Teaching animals tasks like these indicates that, if sufficiently motivated, they can form quite complex symbolic associations. A cat will learn to count if he

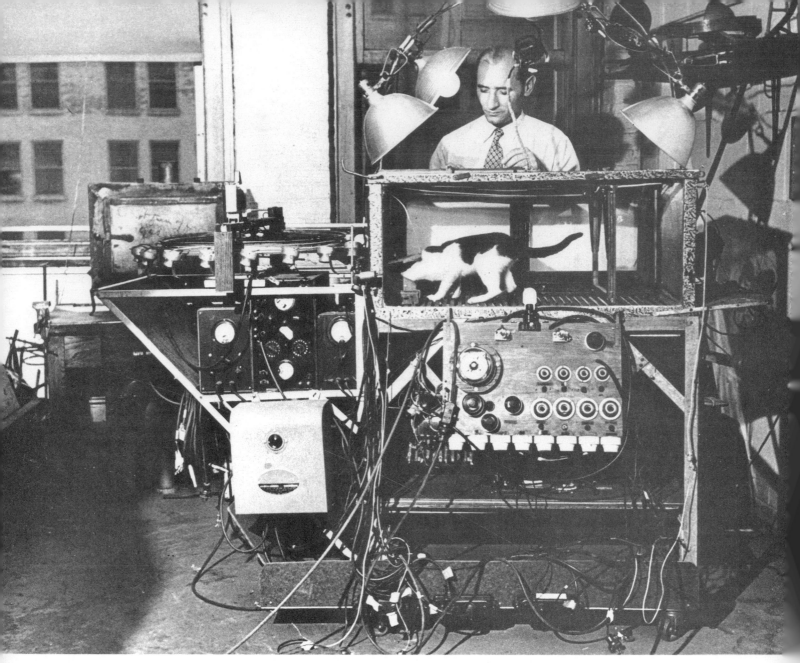

The author in the laboratory.

must press a series of switches in a required order a certain number of times before he gets food; he will learn to differentiate between signs lettered in German script reading *fressen* and *nicht fressen*, if food is available only when the *fressen* sign appears.

Yet if the cat's motivations are not strong enough, he will not exert the energy required to learn. If he is not hungry, he neglects the switches, signal, and food. Also, if the cat is required to make associations beyond his memory or ability to respond, he resists further learning, often resorting to aimless play, destructiveness, and attempts to escape from the cage.

If the training capitalizes on the animal's needs, however, and suits his capacities and temperament, he readily cooperates in the experimental situation, learning willingly and behaving in a friendly way toward the researcher. The well-adjusted cat lives happily and fairly contentedly, playing with other members of his group, waiting to be fed until the appropriate signal is given, confident that the signal will come and that he can manipulate the feeding device well enough to reach his meal.

Air Blasts and Electric Shock

After the cat has adjusted to the experimental routine, a neurosis may be induced by an impasse between opposite adaptations — for instance, by startling the cat with a strong blast of air just as he succeeds in raising the lid of the food box. At first the cat reacts by rushing to the other end of the cage and crouching there, tensely. After a time he moves back to the box again and opens it on cue, but he is more tentative, performing the familiar manipulations hesitantly, in a subtly different way.

The animal is allowed to feed normally a few times. Then he again is subjected to the traumatic, unsettling, even frightening stimulus. When he is forced to go through a number of these unpleasant experiences, a conflict naturally results between his desire for food and his fear of the new phenomenon. After several days, the cat responds to the feeding signal with anxiety: he is tense, and his blood pressure and pulse rate go up. He may develop abnormal physiologic reactions, breathing harshly or asthmatically and suffering from diarrhea or urinary problems. Previously quiet cats frequently pace restlessly back and forth with marked agitation. More excitable animals respond to the air blasts with passivity, lying wherever they are placed and moving lethargically.

For a while, the cat decides to do without food. He becomes increasingly self-occupied; he cleans and licks himself excessively and repeatedly invites petting and fondling. Or he may become almost vicious, ready to attack any potential victim.

Another method now under investigation for inducing neurosis is to teach a monkey to vocalize for a food reward and then to feed back his vocalizations to his own ears after a .2 second delay —a distortion of time sequence that also produces devastating effects in humans.

Parenthetically, some of our experiments have revealed social patterns in monkeys that are remarkably close to those in humans. For example, a monkey will "altruistically" refrain from working a switch for food if the operation administers electric shocks to a cage-mate. So also, individually submissive, weaker monkeys will ally themselves against a bully, and a female will seek superior status for herself and her progeny by mating with a dominant male of the colony.

In an investigation of patterns of masochism, cats were taught to press a switch for food and were given a mild electric shock when the switch was operated. The shock gradually was increased until it became quite severe and painful, yet always it was associated with getting food. These cats persisted in pressing the switch even when the reward of a meal was discontinued. Freudian observers who were unfamiliar with the cats' conditioning might say they indulged in self-punitive behavior related to the death instinct, but in reality, they were trying less to punish themselves than to win expected rewards.

In the experimental development of neurotic behavior, we have found that fear, in the form of dread of injury, is not necessary. It is possible to induce equally serious and lasting behavior problems by presenting the animal with difficult choices between two mutually exclusive satisfactions. For example, a female cat in heat was given a choice between food and a male cat; one attraction just about balanced the other. And a hungry new mother was presented with a litter needing milk and at the same time was given an opportunity to eat. Such mutually exclusive positive

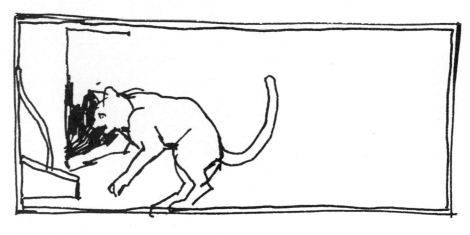

When a cat used to a food reward gets an air blast instead, he retreats in fear and hesitates when approaching the food box. Later, the cat may refuse to eat at all.

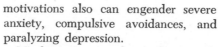

motivations also can engender severe anxiety, compulsive avoidances, and paralyzing depression.

Monkeys, too, can be made neurotic if their food-taking is interrupted with shocks or by the sudden appearance of toy snakes in the food box. (The toy snake evokes a strong response from monkeys in all cases, whether or not the monkey ever has seen one before.) Like the cats, neurotic monkeys display dramatically abnormal behavior. They are anxious, sometimes refuse to eat for days at a time, and stop exploring, grooming, and interacting with peers. They try to escape from anything that is even remotely connected with the conflict they are going through. For example, if the experimenter always wears a green coat, the monkey tries to avoid everything green. He responds to imaginary stimuli, brushing away insects that are not there or preferring imaginary pellets picked from the air to real food available in the feeding box. His erotic life is distorted, and he may seriously injure his sexual organs. He loses his place in the social structure of the monkey community and soon is willing to allow sexual aggression by monkeys of either sex.

Treatments for neurotic cats, like psychotherapy for neurotic human beings, utilize the transference, environmental manipulation, "working through," and social example.

What happens when neurotic monkeys and a control group of normal monkeys are faced with two equally attractive but mutually exclusive alternatives —when they must choose, for instance, between two favorite foods?

It is important to make the dilemma as difficult as possible: if a monkey likes peanuts better than cherries, fewer peanuts are made available, so that the competition between the two alternatives is equal. Under these circumstances, both normal and neurotic monkeys have trou-

ble making decisions. They hesitate, wavering back and forth between the two choices, and try to steal food from both compartments.

After about ten days, the neurotic monkeys' behavior is even more abnormal than it was. But the normal animals, too, begin to change under the strain.

They develop tics, are distractable, and engage in more unproductive activities such as avoidance of all food, vicious attacks, or immobile stupors. And the normal monkeys suffer the same setbacks that the neurotic monkeys already have undergone in their relations with the monkey community.

Finding A Cure

In almost every case in which neurotic patterns are induced in an animal, they not only rapidly extend to almost all his behavior; they also persist unless some sort of treatment is given. It is this therapy toward which the experiments described actually were directed. A few therapeutic procedures proved to be of value; significantly, they were parallel to techniques used successfully with human patients. [See illustrations this page.]

One treatment is to resolve the animal's conflict by satisfying one of his frustrated needs. If a cat that has refused food for two days is forcibly tube-fed to ease his hunger, his neurotic behavior gradually decreases. Or if a neurotic animal is removed from the laboratory for

from three to twelve months, to an environment that presents fewer stresses and problems, it nearly always shows less anxiety and more relaxed, less compulsive, less regressive behavior. But if the animal then is returned to the laboratory, the neurotic patterns reappear, even though the cat is not subjected to a repetition of the situation in which the conflict arose.

Another treatment is to force the animal to resolve the conflict himself. A hungry, neurotic cat, for example, is moved mechanically closer and closer to the food box and offered no way to resist or to escape from the cage. Finally, his head is almost in contact with a box of desirable food. Frequently, despite his fears, the cat will lunge at the food

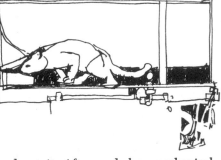

and eat it. Afterward, less mechanical force is needed, and the refusal to eat finally disappears completely. During this time, other neurotic manifestations also are eased.

Or, the animal can be shown new ways to use skills that his neurosis prevents him from utilizing in the usual way. A cat in the midst of a hunger strike can be induced to eat again if he is put into a different training situation, where a different series of manipulations is necessary for him to get food.

The neurotic animal also can learn by example. If a normal cagemate shows proper, nonneurotic behavior for a few weeks, the disturbed animal follows the other's lead and becomes more normal, at least in his overt behavior. But he never makes a complete recovery. Actually, the feeding phobia could be overcome even if a mechanical model of a cat, rather than a live, well-adjusted cat, demonstrated healthy behavior.

Another version of this sort of therapy calls upon the experimenter himself to

retrain the animal, using individual guidance and the animal's neurotic dependence on him for protection and care. All experimenters are not capable of achieving this rapport, however; those who are ill at ease with, or inconsiderate of, normal animals also have trouble helping neurotic ones by any method. If the animal's trust is not violated, he can be made to progress slowly toward nonneurotic behavior. First, he will take food from the man's hand and then, if the experimenter is there to reassure him, from the food box. After some time the animal will open the box in the way he was trained to do, while the man stands by protectively. If the experimenter has been careful not to demand too much and is always gentle and patient with the neurotic animal, the retraining can extend to an acceptance of the very stimuli that originally precipitated the conflict. Eventually the animal learns to accommodate himself to and even to welcome an air blast or an electric shock—although monkeys never learn to tolerate the toy snake—as an indication that food or some other sort of reward is imminent.

When we tried electroshock therapy, using the 60-cycle shock that is usual in treatment of humans, the shock did disintegrate complex and recently acquired patterns of behavior, both normal and neurotic. But it also resulted in permanent loss of efficiency of behavior. When weaker shocks were used, less lasting harm was done the animal, but there was a subsequent loss in therapeutic disorganization of the neurotic activity.

Brain operations, similar to those used on humans, also achieved the desired disorganization and "forgetting" of recently acquired behavior. But the effects of the same operation on different animals varied with the experiences and characteristics of the animal undergoing the surgery. In one case, the same operation on the thalamus was used on both normal and neurotic animals. The normal ones were left with impaired learning ability but were gentle and responsive to instruction; the neurotics came out of surgery irritable and vicious.

Drugs also were tested for their effects. When normal animals were given sedative and narcotic drugs, their response was a disorganization of complex behavior that increased with the degree of intoxication. Morphine, for example, seems to ease anxiety and inhibitions. Instead of retiring tensely to a far corner of the cage, at the feeding signal the animals managed to open the box and to feed somewhat groggily, as though able to forget their doubts and fears at least for the time being.

In one case, an animal was taught to open a food box and to respond to complex food signals by manipulating switches and running a very complicated maze. If given a small dose of morphine or alcohol, the animal would remember how to work the food switches but forget his way through the maze. Larger doses left him unable to work more than one switch. Finally, with still larger amounts of the narcotic, he was completely unable to reach the food. As he recovered from intoxication, the animal slowly retrieved his original learned responses in the order in which they had been taught.

alcoholic addicts [*see illustrations this page*] until their underlying neuroses were cured by one or more of the methods already outlined.

While drugs have a short-term effectiveness, none of them was able totally to erase neurotic behavior created by a long-term conflict. Moreover, their effectiveness was influenced by a number of circumstances. When animals were in their home cages, for example, the sedative and tranquilizing effects of the drugs were greater than when they were in an unfamiliar or stressful environment. The drugs were less useful when a mother was with her young, but their effectiveness was increased by the presence of a mate or a friendly companion.

Throughout this discussion of neurotic

Some neurotic cats, finding that a cocktail relieves tension, can become alcoholics.

In one experiment with neurotic cats, the animals were fed alcohol. Cats ordinarily refuse alcohol, but neurotic cats, when very thirsty, can be made to take it with their water. The effect was again to disorganize their complex fears, compulsions, and other neurotic symptoms, and so to release (disinhibit) more normal feeding and sex behavior. Later, when they were given a choice between alcoholic and nonalcoholic beverages, about half the neurotic animals preferred the spiked drinks and became animals and their treatment, no direct reference has been made to the corresponding phenomena in men. The resemblances are there, of course. Certainly, men are more complex, and many more variables affect the formation and existence of human character, neuroses, and psychoses. However, as with many areas of medicine, it is useful to take such problems into the laboratory, where their study can contribute substantially to the understanding and the eventual cure of human behavior disorders. ◗

The Dreams of Freud

When psychiatric research, normally content to draw on frailer men for its material, approaches one who is among the greatest of the human race, it is not doing so for the reasons so frequently assigned to it by laymen. 'To blacken the radiant and drag the sublime into the dust' is no part of its purpose, and there is no satisfaction for it in narrowing the gulf which separates the perfection of the great from the inadequacy of the objects that are its usual concern. But it cannot help finding worthy of understanding everything that can be recognized in these illustrious models, and it believes there is no one so great as to be disgraced by being subject to the laws which govern both normal and pathological activity with equal cogency.

["Leonardo Da Vinci and a Memory of His Childhood," by Sigmund Freud]

IT IS HARD TO IMAGINE two more "illustrious models" in the matter of dream analysis than Freud and Jung. Both men analyzed their own dreams—and, at times, each other's—so it is fitting to demonstrate the usefulness of a new analytic method by applying it to *their* dreams.

What follows is a comparative and quantitative study of the dreams of Freud and Jung as they reported them in their writings. Its main purpose is to demonstrate the value of quantitative content analysis of dreams and to relate the information conveyed by the dreams to known facts about the character and behavior of the two men.

Freud reported 28 dreams in two books, *The Interpretation of Dreams* and *On Dreams.* Jung reported 31, in his autobiographical study, *Memories, Dreams, Reflections.* Although we would like to have had more dreams to work with, previous studies that we have conducted show that as few as 20 dreams reveal significant aspects of a dreamer's personality. Moreover, the two men's choice of dreams to report might be prejudiced. For example, Freud might have selected dreams favorable to *his* theory, and Jung might have selected dreams favorable to *his* theory. It does seem evident that the two men's reasons for relating their dreams in the first place were quite different. Freud used his own dreams to illustrate various aspects of his dream theory; Jung's purpose was the more personal one of illuminating the nature of his inner life and development. This difference in purpose is evidenced by the books in which the dreams appear. Freud's are published in scientific treatises; Jung's are reported in his autobiography.

In spite of differing purposes, we expected that objective methods of dream analysis would reveal differences between the two men that were congruent with differences in their biographies.

We also expected to find many similarities in their dreams. There is, we think, a hard core of universality in the dreams of all human beings, no matter *when* they live, *where* they live, or *how*

and Jung

By Calvin S. Hall and Bill Domhoff

they live. Each dream was typed on a five by eight card. Freud's 28 dreams and Jung's 31 dreams were shuffled together before they were scored. One of us (Dr. Hall) did all the scoring, using content scales described in *The Content Analysis of Dreams* by Calvin Hall and Robert Van de Castle. In order to achieve greater accuracy, each dream was scored twice. The dreams were scored for the following variables: length, characters, objects, aggressive and friendly interactions, success and failure, good fortune and misfortune, oral incorporation and oral emphasis, and castration anxiety, castration wish, and penis envy.

To find out what was typical about Freud's and Jung's dreams, their scores were compared with the scores obtained for 500 dreams reported by 100 young American men and, in some cases, with other norms. Although the exact age at which each of Freud's and Jung's dreams occurred is known in only a few cases, it is believed that, with one exception, they were all dreamed during adult life. The exception is a dream Jung reports having had when he was three or four years old.

Here, then, are the results of our investigation into the dreams of Freud and Jung.

The total number of lines in Freud's 28 dream narratives is 286, just a shade more than 10 lines per dream. His longest dream is 34 lines, his shortest is one line. The total number of lines in Jung's 31 dreams is 458, just shy of 15 lines per dream. His longest dream is 51 lines, his shortest is four lines.

This fairly marked difference in average length of dream report is in keeping with the writing styles of the two men. Freud published as much if not more than Jung did, but Freud's style is compact and Jung's discursive. One cannot imagine Freud as the author of Jung's rambling *Memories, Dreams, Reflections,* nor Jung writing Freud's spare *Autobiographical Study.*

There are certain universal facts about the characters in all dreams. One of them, taken so much for granted that it is rarely commented upon, is that the dreamer is a character in virtually all his own dreams. Freud and Jung are no exceptions: they appear in all their own dreams. (In the Hall-Van de Castle system of content analysis, however, the dreamer is not counted as a character.)

Another universal is that men dream more about men than about women but women dream about equally of the two sexes. Freud and Jung abide by this general rule. They have almost identical sex ratios. The ratio of men to women in Freud's dreams is 2.56 to 1, and in Jung's dreams it is 2.50 to 1. These ratios are somewhat higher than the average ratio for American college men, which is about 2 to 1. It is known, however, that the sex ratio increases with age.

Still another universal is the proportion of single and plural characters. (A plural character is an undifferentiated group or crowd.) The typical proportion is .70 single characters to .30 plural characters. Jung's dreams show exactly that proportion, and Freud's a proportion that is only slightly different, .73 single characters to .27 plurals.

Dreams reported by adults are always peopled by many more adult characters than adolescents, children and babies. The proportion of adults in college men's dreams is .97. Freud's and Jung's proportions are .91 and .93, respectively, which are not significantly different from the norm.

Finally, there is a standard proportion of familiar and unfamiliar characters. A familiar character is a member of the dreamer's family, a relative, a friend or acquaintance, or a prominent person. An unfamiliar character is one who is not known to the dreamer in waking life. In typical dreams of men, .45 of the characters are familiar and .55 are unfamiliar. Freud's proportions are .53 for familiar characters and .47 for unfamiliar characters. Jung's proportions are .57 and .43. This difference between Freud and Jung is not significant, nor is the difference between their proportions and those of the normative group.

Up to this point, the results of the analysis of dream characters merely demonstrate that both Freud and Jung belonged to the male half of the human race. But there are also differences in the dream characters of the two men.

Freud has more characters in his dreams than Jung does, 85 to Jung's 70, although Jung reports more dreams and longer ones. The number of lines per character is 3.4 for Freud and 6.5 for Jung. The density coefficient of people in Freud's dreams is much higher than it is for Jung. Jung's dreams are filled with scenery, architecture and objects rather than with people.

This difference appears to be compatible with what is known about the two men. Freud was a sociable person. He had many close friends and disciples with whom he had very personal relationships. One imagines him surrounded by an entourage wherever he went. Jung was more solitary and kept would-be disciples at a distance. He spent much time in scholarly pursuits, poring over old manuscripts, and he was a lover of nature. Jung said of himself, "Today as then [in childhood] I am a solitary."

A difference in sociability between the two men is indicated by other evidence from their dreams and writings as well. Animals appear more frequently in Jung's dreams than in Freud's, which suggests that Jung identified more closely with the world of nature than with the world of men. He writes in *Memories, Dreams, Reflections*, "I loved all warmblooded animals . . . Animals were dear and faithful, unchanging and trustworthy. People I now distrusted more than ever." Mystical, fictional and historical figures turn up more often in Jung's dreams than in Freud's. This suggests that Jung lived more in the past whereas Freud lived more in the present. Indeed, Jung said that for years he felt more closely attuned to the past, especially to the Middle Ages and the 18th Century, than to the present.

Jung dreams more about members of his family; Freud dreams more about friends and acquaintances. This implies that Jung's sociability expressed itself within his immediate family, and Freud's

social life was centered more outside the family. It is interesting that, although Jung was an only child for nine years and then had only one sister, and Freud grew up in the midst of a large family, both men raised large families of their own. Freud had six children, and Jung had five. Nonetheless, Freud seems to have looked persistently for intimate and even paternal relations outside his family.

A letter written by Freud to Jung is characteristic of this search for intimacy. Here is a passage from the letter, which is reproduced in *Memories, Dreams, Reflections.* "It is remarkable that on the same evening that I formally adopted you as an eldest son, anointing you as my successor and crown prince etc. . . . I therefore don once more my hornrimmed paternal spectacles and warn my dear son to keep a cool head . . ." Given Jung's solitariness, his preference for nature and architecture, and his familial concerns, and also given his un-

satisfactory relationship with his own father, it is not difficult to imagine how repelled Jung was by Freud's adhesiveness or to believe how quickly the two men went their separate ways.

Here, we think, lies the real secret of their break. After all, Swiss intellectuals such as Oscar Pfister, a Protestant minister, and Ludwig Binswanger, who introduced existentialism and phenomenology into psychiatry, remained personal friends with Freud despite considerable intellectual differences. But Freud did not try to make sons out of Pfister and Binswanger; and Pfister and Binswanger, unlike Jung, did not have depressive, moody fathers who lost their faith and spent time in mental institutions.

There are 12 classes of objects and a miscellaneous class in the Hall-Van de Castle system of content analysis. Three of the classes—architecture, implements and body parts—have subclasses. There are many more objects in Jung's dreams than in Freud's, 297 versus 196. This suggests, as does the larger number of human characters in Freud's dreams, that Jung was more object-oriented and Freud was more person-oriented.

Further support is given to this statement by the kinds of objects each man dreamed about. Jung dreamed more about houses, buildings and architectural details—especially windows, doors and walls—and more about nature and landscape than either Freud or the norm group did. Freud, on the other hand, dreamed much more about parts of the body, particularly parts of the head, than either Jung or the norm group did.

It is interesting to speculate on the symbolic meaning of these differences. If architecture and nature are female symbols, for the most part, and if body parts, especially the head, are displacements of the male genitals, then it could be inferred that Jung was more oriented toward the female and Freud was more oriented toward the male. This inference ties in with other data to be presented below.

Jung's dreams contain no references to money, whereas Freud dreams of money about as often as the norm group.

Freud also refers more often than Jung to food, a fact which will be commented on later. Both men seldom mention implements, especially weapons and recreational equipment, which is probably not surprising considering that they were intellectuals and scholars.

In Freud's dreams, there are 16 aggressive and 16 friendly interactions; in Jung's dreams, 14 and 11, respectively. When these figures are divided by the number of characters, the proportions are much the same for Freud and Jung. Moreover, they are in close accord with the proportions for male dreamers between the ages of 30 and 80.

Other universal characteristics of Freud's and Jung's dreams are the large proportion of dreamer-involved aggression and friendliness as compared with witnessed aggression and friendliness, and the equal number of times that the dreamer is aggressor and victim.

With regard to the role of befriender and befriended, however, the two men are poles apart. Every time Jung is involved in a friendly interaction, he initiates the friendliness. Freud, on the other hand, is more often the recipient of friendliness (eight out of 11 times). The norm is midway between the figures for Freud and Jung. Does this signify that Freud wanted people to respond to him in a friendly manner and was sensitive about being rejected? It does seem that Freud was sensitive about being

slighted: for example, his feelings were hurt that Jung did not make an effort to visit him when Freud made a trip to Switzerland. And Freud's biographer, Ernest Jones, says that Freud became quite annoyed when friends to whom he had written did not reply at once.

Another indication of Jung's greater social autonomy is that, when we consider only the dreams in which aggression or friendliness occurs (and not the total number of aggressive and friendly encounters in all the dreams), Freud has almost twice as many "interactional"

dreams as Jung has. Freud's frequency agrees with the norm. In other words, Jung has fewer dreams in which he interacts in significant ways with other characters than does Freud.

By far the most interesting finding with respect to aggression and friendliness, however, is the striking difference in Freud's and Jung's aggressive and friendly encounters with male and female characters. The typical man has more aggressive interactions with men than with women, and more friendly interactions with women than with men. Jung's aggressive and friendly encounters with men and women are fairly typical. He has an aggressive interaction with about one out of four male characters in his dreams, and none at all with females. As for friendly encounters, Jung has about an equal number with men and women, which deviates slightly from the norm.

In Freud's dreams, the typical pattern is reversed. He has an aggressive encounter with one out of every four *female* characters, and almost none with males.

On the other hand, he has many more friendly encounters with men than with women. These results suggest that Freud had an inverted Oedipus complex. The Oedipus complex is characterized by hostility toward other men and friendliness or love toward women. In an inverted Oedipus complex, the tables are turned. There is a friendly attitude toward men and a hostile one toward women. (Freud's pattern of aggression and friendliness with men and women is not like that of the typical woman, who is both more aggressive and friendlier toward men than toward women. Nor is it like the pattern of a group of male patients in a mental hospital, who showed more aggression than friendliness toward both men and women.)

Is there any evidence from his biography that Freud had an inverted Oedipus complex? Many people have concluded after reading Freud that he was hostile toward women. Ernest Jones says that Freud's attitude toward women was "old fashioned": Freud considered that their main function was to serve as "ministering angels to the needs and comforts of men." He thought women "enigmatic" ("What do they want?" he asked Marie Bonaparte); he was attracted to masculine women; he was "quite peculiarly monogamous." Jones says that "the more passionate side of married life subsided with him [Freud] earlier than it does with many men." We assume this means

that Freud stopped having intercourse with his wife fairly early in their married life. That he was "quite peculiarly monogamous" suggests that he did not have affairs with other women.

As regards Freud's feelings for men, we know that he had a very intense relationship with Wilhelm Fliess. Freud spoke of overcoming his emotional homosexuality and admitted that alternations of love and hate affected his relationships with men. Jones also speaks of Freud's "mental bisexuality." By using the word "mental" as a qualifier, Jones implies that the bisexuality was never physically expressed. Freud wrote to his friend and colleague, Max Eitingon, "The affection of a group of courageous young men is the most precious gift that psychoanalysis has bestowed upon me." This remark is reminiscent of Michelangelo (whose art Freud greatly admired), who also found joy in being surrounded by young men.

It appears from his dreams, then, that Freud had an inverted Oedipus complex, and what biographical material is available supports this conclusion. Jung, on the other hand, seems to have had a fairly ordinary Oedipus complex, in the sense that hostility toward the father is inevitable. Nothing that is known of Jung's life changes the picture. He says in his autobiography that he felt much closer to his mother than he did to his father. When his father died he immediately assumed the role of father in the household, even to the point of moving into his father's room. Small wonder that Jung did not want to become a son again, least of all the son of a father with an inverted Oedipus complex.

Success and failure in dreams are almost always experienced by the dreamer himself, and this holds true for Freud and Jung. Most men have an equal amount of success and failure in their dreams. So does Jung, but Freud has much more success than failure. In fact, he succeeds six times and only fails once. This suggests that Freud was more strongly motivated to succeed than Jung was. Jones' remark that fame meant very little to Freud does not square with the fairly obvious fact that Freud aspired to greatness.

Jung, on the other hand, though he may have had the same aspiration, did not do many of the things that would

have helped him achieve fame. Unlike Freud, he did not found an international organization with its own journals and publishing house. He did not establish a chain of institutes throughout the world to promote his ideas. He did not encourage disciples. He preferred his stone tower to the bustle of the scientific market place. He did not seek worldly success, though he did not refuse it when it knocked at his door. Near the end of his life Jung wrote, "Today I can say it is truly astounding that I have had as much success as has been accorded me."

Good fortune in dreams is rare; misfortune is commonplace. Freud and Jung, true to this universal pattern, have more misfortune than good fortune in their dreams. In fact, Freud has no good fortune at all. Jung, however, has more good fortune than is to be expected. Good fortune is defined as something favorable that happens to a person without any effort on his part, and without a friendly intent upon another character's part. Freud's lack of good fortune, taken together with his large amount of success relative to failure, suggests that he saw success as the result of his own efforts, and not as luck. Jung was more likely to view the world, at least in his dreams, as a cornucopia of benefits. The impression one gets from Jung's

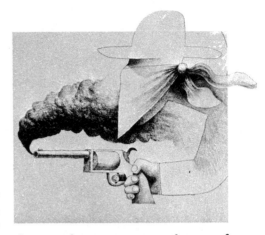

autobiography is that he was more fatalistic than Freud. He was inclined to let things happen to him, to let his life be lived rather than to live it. His life "developed naturally and by destiny"; he felt that it was ruled by forces over which he had no control, and which (though he spent much of his adult life trying) he did not completely understand. Freud was more rationalistic. By exercising reason, he felt that one could master the world.

It is customary in dreams for misfortune to befall the dreamer more often than other characters. This is the case in Jung's dreams, but the reverse is true for Freud. In his dreams, more misfortune comes to other characters than to himself. If misfortune to the dreamer is interpreted as an expression of self-punishment, then misfortune to others may be interpreted as a disguised expression of hostility. The dreamer intends harm to another person but he does not want to express it directly through an aggressive act. We have not been able to find any biographical substantiation for the high incidence of indirect hostility in Freud's dreams.

We do know from a previous study that having more misfortunes happen to characters other than the dreamer is less usual for men than for women. In this respect, then, Freud's dreams are more like those of women.

Oral incorporation is scored whenever there is mention of food, eating, drinking, cooking, restaurants and the like in the dream report. Oral emphasis consists of references to the mouth and to oral activities other than eating and drinking, as, for example, smoking, singing and so forth. On both scales, Freud scores higher than Jung, whose scores agree with the norms. Freud probably had a lot of orality in his makeup. We know he smoked a large number of ci-

gars. Jones informs us that Freud had a horror of ever having to be dependent upon others—a reaction formation against oral dependence. Freud's orality is also consistent with the fact that he received friendliness in his dreams more often than he initiated it. It is as if he wanted to be taken care of but fought this infantile wish. Orality is also consistent with the relatively high incidence of success and low incidence of good fortune in Freud's dreams. He wanted to achieve success through his own efforts partly in order to deny his underlying need to be dependent.

Orality does not appear to have played much of a role in Jung's life, nor does he seem to have had conflicts about being dependent upon others. On the contrary, Jung preferred to go it alone rather than be dependent on others.

The castration anxiety, castration wish, and penis envy scales reflect different aspects of the castration complex. Castration anxiety is shown in a dream by injury to part of the dreamer's body or damage to one of his possessions. Castration wish is shown when the same thing happens to another character in the dream. Penis envy reveals itself through the dreamer's acquisition of impressive phallic objects such as cars or guns. These three scales have been shown by Hall and Van de Castle to differentiate between male and female dreamers in a way consistent with Freudian theory.

There is little castration anxiety and no penis envy in either Freud's or Jung's dreams. Freud does express a wish to castrate others in a few of his dreams, but it does not exceed the norms. We may conclude that as far as their dreams tell us, neither of the men was unusually afflicted with this basic anxiety.

This completes our survey of some of the scorable features of the dreams of Freud and Jung. The results show, as we thought they would, that the dreams have universal characteristics as well as individual ones. In this instance, the individual traits are the more interesting because the subjects are Freud and Jung.

Our findings suggest that "scores," that is, frequencies and proportions, obtained from counting various elements in reported dreams bear a meaningful relationship to the personality and behavior of the dreamer. This fact not only demonstrates the value of the system of content analysis devised by Hall and Van de Castle. It also shows that there are important continuities between dreams and waking life: our evidence from the dreams of Freud and Jung supports the idea that their dream behavior is congruent with their behavior in waking life. And the dreams shed considerable light on the breakup of their friendship.

These findings are really not very astonishing when one considers that dreaming is as much a form of behavior as anything a person does in waking life. It would be surprising if dreams failed to reflect the same basic wishes and fears that govern waking behavior, since behavior—all behavior, in our opinion—is to a large degree a product of the timeless unconscious. It is the timeless unconscious (Freud's term) that confers a pattern upon a personality and that grinds out the same forms of behavior over and over again, in dreams as in waking life. To the old question, "Am I a butterfly who dreams he is an awake person or a sleeping person who dreams he is a butterfly?" we reply, "It makes no difference." The dream state merely reveals more clearly the wishes and fears that guide our actions in waking life.

Inside Psychotherapy

By David E. Orlinsky & Kenneth I. Howard

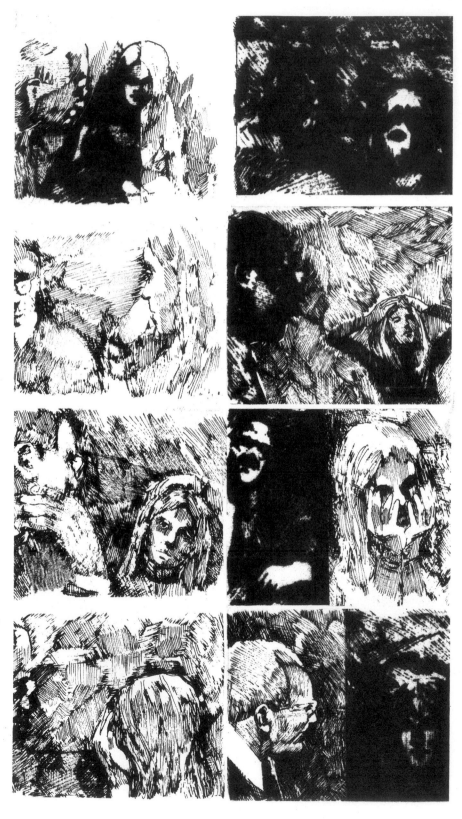

PSYCHOTHERAPY has been described by some as the confessional of the secular man, and as the weekday solace of the overeducated and underemployed suburban housewife. It has also been presented as the individual's best hope for attaining self-knowledge and personal authenticity in a confused and troubled society.

Because of its important place in our culture, psychotherapy has been put on frequent display in novels, films and plays—sometimes humorously and sometimes with serious intent. Yet with all this publicity, what do we actually know about psychotherapy? What takes place after patient and therapist disappear behind the closed office door? What is the experience of psychotherapy really like?

The theories and case histories of psychotherapists offer some answers, and so do the observations and evaluations of scientific researchers. But each of these sources has limitations. The clinical literature, though often suggestive and sometimes brilliant, is almost always impressionistic and purely qualitative. The research literature, though more systematic and quantitative, comprises chiefly objective observations by non-participants and after-the-fact evaluations. Such studies provide valuable knowledge, but they give no information about what the patients and therapists see, hear and feel during their sessions; about what they want from therapy, or about what they think of their psychotherapy.

Our desire to obtain reliable, precise information about psychotherapy as a subjective experience—to find out, in a precise, systematic and quantitative way, how the people who participate in psychotherapy see and feel it—led us to develop the Psychotherapy Session Project, based on reports from patients and therapists themselves.

For subjects, we turned to a group of patients and therapists at the Katharine Wright Mental Health Clinic in Chicago. During the first six months of the study, 60 patients filled out reports on a total of 890 sessions, and 17 therapists completed questionnaires on a total of 470 sessions. All patients were being seen in individual outpatient psychotherapy, and almost all had sessions once a week. All the patients were women between 20 and 60 years of age, but most were on the younger side—their average age was 28. In general, the patients were well educated: 90 per cent had finished high school, and a third had completed college or graduate studies. More than 80 per cent were employed, and 25 per cent were currently married.

The therapists who participated were both men and women. They had been trained in psychiatry, clinical psychology or psychiatric social work, with an average of six years' experience in the practice of psychotherapy. Most of them acknowledged some influence of Freud on their thinking and practice, but few would consider themselves psychoanalytically oriented in a strict sense. Like most clinicians, they draw upon a variety of approaches.

The reports were made independently by each patient and therapist as soon as possible after the session was over, while the experience was still fresh in their minds. We used two parallel questionnaires, one for patients and one for therapists, to survey various aspects of the therapy experience [see illustration, next page].

The questionnaires took only 10 or 15 minutes to complete, because they called for simple descriptions and evaluations rather than lengthy analyses. Before the first study, the questionnaires were trial-tested with a substantial number of therapists and patients, and modified where necessary. We tried to avoid the terminology of any special theoretical school or orientation but to include issues that are meaningful to most of them. The confidentiality of each person's answers was strictly assured so he could feel free to give his honest reactions to the questions.

The Typical Session

To gain a composite picture of the typical therapy experience, we tabulated the most frequently endorsed responses of patients and therapists to the items on the questionnaires [see illustration, page 397]. What patients seemed to want most in coming to therapy was to deepen their understanding of personal problems that they have difficulty talking about and, presumably, difficulty dealing with. This deepened understanding might be expected to alleviate the problems, or at least to help the patient deal with them more comfortably and more effectively. As they tried to move toward these goals, patients talked most frequently about themselves as they are in their present intimate social relations and vocational settings.

This contradicts the expectations based on clinical theory, which call for talk about relations with parents or siblings, memories of childhood experiences, and dreams or fantasies.

Though patients might find their sessions helpful, they did not, as a rule, find them pleasant. They tended to feel anxious and tense during interviews—understandably, perhaps, since they were trying to discuss and work out their most difficult personal problems. However, patients did appear to be actively and positively involved in the therapy relationship. This contrasts somewhat with their problematic concerns and felt distress. Patients come to a therapist for help but do not seem particularly helpless, at least in relating to him.

Inspection of the therapists' responses showed that patient and therapist generally worked toward the same goals, with some difference in nuance and detail. Patients, for example, were inclined to seek advice about their problems; therapists were less inclined to offer advice and wanted their patients to experience feelings rather than merely talk about them.

As one might expect, therapists generally felt comfortable with and positively responsive to their patients. (The joke that is told to beginning therapists, optimistically describing a therapist as the *less* anxious of the two persons in the room, seems to be borne out by the facts.) Our research showed that the popular image of the therapist as a reserved, neutral, unresponsive person seems to be a mistaken view. Therapists related to their patients the same way patients related to them: collaboratively, positively and feelingly.

Returning to the patients, what benefits did they find in their sessions? The most frequently reported satisfactions were a sense of honestly working together with the therapist, help in talking about important troubling matters, and better self-understanding. Thus patients typically did find what they sought in coming to therapy, and what their therapists hoped to give them. The process was often emotionally trying but, with their therapists' active support, the patients seemed to achieve helpful self-understanding.

The Ideal Session

Psychotherapy as it occurs in the typical session is undoubtedly a mixture of better and worse experiences. In order to deepen our understanding of essential therapeutic processes and to develop more effective practices, we felt it was desirable to isolate the better elements of the experience—to portray psychotherapy at its best [see illustration, page 397].A composite picture of the "ideal" experience—the aims, feelings and so forth that *distinguish* the ideal session—

was drawn from our data by noting the responses that correlated most highly with patients' and therapists' evaluations of the overall quality of their sessions.

Both the ideal and the average therapy experience included a desire on the patient's part for self-understanding and collaborative involvement with the therapist. The wish for insight and collaboration, present in the typical experience, was simply *more intense* in the ideal experience. And in the ideal experience, patients wanted to display their gains and successes to the therapist rather than to present their problems or solicit help and advice. The accent was on the positive, perhaps because some real gains were being made.

The better the session, the less emphasis patients placed on discussing immediate feelings about themselves. Instead, they stressed dreams or fantasies and memories of childhood experiences with family members, subjects that theoretically reflect underlying or unconscious patterns of motivation. The ideal session came closer than the typical one to clinical expectations of what it is most profitable to discuss in therapy.

The patients' feelings during the ideal session were quite different from those reported for the typical session. Instead of feeling anxious and tense, patients felt confident and pleased. On the other hand, the way patients acted towards their therapists was essentially the same in the ideal and the typical experiences. They were, presumably, *more* friendly, *more* interactive, and so forth in the ideal case than in the typical one. As might be expected, in the ideal session patients reported getting *all* the satisfactions listed on the questionnaire. This finding strengthens our confidence in the validity of their overall evaluations.

Therapists' goals in the ideal and typical sessions were essentially the same. These goals corresponded, in general, to what is prescribed by theories of psychotherapy. However, in the ideal session the therapists' goals also included support for the self-esteem of their patients. (The tendency to be rewarding or encouraging, like the patients' concern to show improvement, may be greater once real gains are at hand.)

In the ideal session, therapists felt more alert and effective, but also warmer and more personally involved, than in the typical session. Their way of relating to patients was essentially the same in the ideal as in the typical session, only more so. Patients and therapists approached each other in much the same

1. How do you feel about the therapy session which you have just completed? [*Alternatives from "one of the best" to "really poor session"*]

2. What did you talk about during this session? [*Checklist of 18 topics representing basic areas of life concerns*]

3. What did you want or hope to get out of this therapy session? [*Checklist of 20 potential patient goals*]

4. How did you act towards your therapist during this session? [*Checklist of 16 types of interpersonal behavior*]

5. How did you feel during this session? [*Checklist of 45 feelings*]

6. To what extent were you looking forward to coming to this session? [*Alternatives from "could hardly wait" to "had to make myself come"*]

7. How freely were you able to talk with your therapist during this session? [*Alternatives from "a great deal of difficulty" to "didn't have any difficulty in talking"*]

8. How clearly did you know what you wanted to talk about during this session? [*Alternatives from "knew clearly" to "my mind was blank"*]

9. How well did your therapist seem to understand how you were feeling and what was really on your mind during this session? [*Alternatives from "understood very well" to "misunderstood"*]

10. Do you feel that what your therapist said and did this session was helpful to you? [*Alternatives from "very helpful" to "made me worse off than I was"*]

11. Do you feel that you made progress in this session in dealing with the problems for which you are in therapy? [*Alternatives from "considerable progress" to "my problems got worse"*]

12. How well do you feel that you are getting along, emotionally and psychologically, at this time? [*Alternatives from "the way I would like" to "I can barely manage"*]

13. What do you feel that you got out of this session? [*Checklist of nine possible satisfactions*]

14. To what extent are you looking forward to your next session? [*Alternatives from "wish it were sooner" to "not so sure I will want to come"*]

15. How did your therapist act towards you during this session? [*Checklist of 16 types of interpersonal behavior*]

16. How did your therapist seem to feel during this session? [*Checklist of 34 feelings*]

A very similar revised version of this questionnaire is now in use with other patients and therapists.

WHAT THEY WERE ASKED. The only major difference between patient and therapist questionnaires was question 13. Therapists were asked "In what direction were you working with your patient during this session?" and chose from checklist of goals.

way, except that patients generally took more initiative in determining what was discussed in the session.

The typical session and the ideal session have many features in common, suggesting that by and large the average experience is a good one—or at least that the typical experience is considerably closer to the best than it is to the worst. But we must remember, too, that the ideal therapy experience is an abstraction, a composite of positive tendencies within the many real experiences of different patients and different therapists. It is not safe to assume that there is only one type of good therapy experience, or only one way to achieve it.

Indeed, we are warned against any such conclusion by other analyses of the questionnaires, which revealed at least three distinct positive patterns in the relationship between patient and therapist. Because these patterns emerge, independently or together, in any relationship, we have called them "therapeutic potentials." A brief description of what they are and how they were found should help illuminate the more complex connections between the typical and ideal patterns of therapy experience.

In the Psychotherapy Session Project,

we have been interested in how the experiences of individual patients and therapists differed from one another, as well as in average or composite patterns. To study these differences, and to define empirically the dimensions along which individual variation occurs, we applied the statistical technique of factor analysis. We analyzed the experiences of patients and of therapists separately, and then combined the results of these and analyzed the experiences of patient-therapist pairs together in order to determine the patterns of "conjoint experience" within the relationship. Three therapeutic potentials — "collaborative analytic progress," "healing magic," and "mutual personal openness" — emerged from this analysis.

"Collaborative analytic progress" is the type of good therapy relationship described in the psychoanalytic literature. It is marked by an effective "therapeutic alliance," or task-oriented collaboration, between patient and therapist; by an emotionally involving but basically cognitive ("analytic") exploration of the patient's significant problems and relationships; and by a sense of forward movement or progress in understanding. The role of the therapist in this pattern

of good therapy experience is that of a "head shrinker," or as younger and more hip patients sometimes say with affection, a "shrink." The image of head shrinking appears to refer both to the characteristic *reduction* of emotional problems through their verbal intellectual formulation, and to the *deflating* effect that recognition of one's less attractive unconscious desires has on the patient's ego.

"Healing magic," on the other hand, is marked by a very positive, enthusiastic, happy response on the part of the patient, who feels greatly helped by the effective power and benevolent acceptance of the therapist. In this type of good therapy experience it seems that it is not so much what the therapist does that counts as it is the personal qualities that the patient perceives in him. The therapist appears to enter the patient's experience as a "good parent" whose concern and acceptance are a balm to hurt feelings. This pattern, known in the psychoanalytic literature as "positive transference," has been likened to a kind of therapeutic honeymoon. Patients sometimes refer to their therapists in this type of positive experience as the "Wizard" (or simply as "Wiz") because of the power he seems to have to make them feel better. (Both the Wizard of Oz and Gandalf, the good wizard in Tolkien's *Lord of the Rings,* come to mind as possible prototypes.) One's tendency in this rationalistic age is to disbelieve in the potency of magic. But only those who have never experienced charismatic influence (or who have never been in love) can doubt that it has real effects in the realm of interpersonal relations.

"Mutual personal openness" is the type of good therapy experience that has been most fully described and advocated in existential, experiential, and recent client-centered writings on psychotherapy. In our sampling this pattern was marked by a sense of equality, trust and personal openness between patient and therapist. The therapist did not appear as a superior or as an impersonal being whose private reactions are hidden from view. Each participant had confidence in himself and confidence in the other, which permitted mutual sharing of "confidences" in a more intimate manner than had been the custom in a "professional" relationship. Mutual personal openness included, on the therapist's part, a willingness to be frankly evaluative and confronting with the patient: to let the patient know what was on his mind. This honest availability of the therapist's personal reactions to the patient was matched, on the patient's part, by a greater willingness or capacity to make inner feelings and fantasies known to the therapist. The patient and therapist appeared to esteem and to treat each other as adult persons who can "take it." Because of the personal nature of the encounter, the patient is frequently on a first-name basis with the therapist: the patient calls the therapist "Carl," for example, rather than "Doctor So-and-so."

Each of the three therapeutic potentials was reflected in the composite ideal therapy experience. The influence of "collaborative analytic progress" is seen from our research in the desire of both patient and therapist to work together to deepen the patient's insight and self-understanding. It can also be seen in the topical focus on dreams, and on memories of childhood experiences with important family members.

The influence of "healing magic," on the other hand, is found in the euphoric quality of the patients' feelings and in their reports that, in the ideal therapy experience, they received all the satisfactions listed on the questionnaire.

The effect of "mutual personal openness" can be traced in the sharing, give-and-take, emotionally responsive manner in which both patients and therapists related to each other, and in the heightened personal involvement shown in the therapists' reports of their own feelings.

Thus the evidence now available indicates at least three paths toward an experience that has therapeutic value. And this evidence may suggest a "three-factor theory" of therapeutic efficacy. The three types of experience are independent but not mutually exclusive, and they seem to be rooted in the potentials of the psychotherapy relationship as a helping and helpful experience. Further exploration along these lines may resolve some of the current differences between the various theoretical orientations to psychotherapy, each of which appears to stress one or another of these therapeutic potentials and to neglect the rest of them.

What we have learned from the Psychotherapy Session Project thus far is particularly exciting to us because it is based on a scientific analysis of the subjective experience of psychotherapy. It has given us an important glimpse "inside psychotherapy." As results come in from other studies now in progress, we hope this glimpse will become a much broader view. 𝄢

THE TYPICAL THERAPY EXPERIENCE

Patient wants to:	Get a better understanding of my feelings and behavior. Get help in talking about what is really troubling me. Work out a problem that I have. Work together with my therapist on a person-to-person basis. Get advice on how to deal with my life and with other people.
Patient talks about:	Feelings and attitudes toward myself. Social activities and relationships, friends and acquaintances. Relationship with spouse, boyfriend or girlfriend.
Patient feels:	Anxious Tense
Patient relates by:	Initiating topics. Engaging in a give-and-take relationship. Being friendly. Being emotional or stirred up.
Therapist tries to:	Increase my patient's insight and self-understanding. Move my patient closer to experiencing her real feelings, what she really is. Engage my patient in an honest person-to-person relationship, work together authentically.
Therapist feels:	Interested Calm Involved Alert Confident Sympathetic
Therapist relates by:	Interacting, working together. Engaging in give-and-take relationship. Being friendly. Being emotionally responsive, stirred.
Patient gets:	A sense of having an honest person-to-person relationship with my therapist, of working together. Help in being able to talk about what was troubling to me and really important. Better insight and self-understanding.

THE USUAL. Patient wants understanding and help, talks mostly about current feelings and activities, often feels anxious and tense; therapist tends to feel interested and calm.

THE IDEAL THERAPY EXPERIENCE

Patient wants to:	Get a better understanding of my feelings and behavior. Let my therapist see how I've improved. Work together with my therapist on a person-to-person basis.		
Patient talks about:	Relationship with spouse, boyfriend or girlfriend. Dreams, fantasies. Social activities and relationships, friends and acquaintances. Childhood experiences with family members and feelings about them.		
Patient feels:	Relieved Trusting Accepted Optimistic Alert	Interested Likeable Calm Relaxed Secure	Confident Satisfied Effective Energetic
Patient relates by:	Initiating topics. Interacting, working together. Engaging in give-and-take relationship. Being friendly. Being emotional.		
Therapist tries to:	Increase my patient's insight and self-understanding. Move my patient closer to experiencing her real feelings, what she really is. Support my patient's self-esteem.		
Therapist feels:	Optimistic Satisfied Close Involved Effective	Alert Pleased Interested Sympathetic	Confident Intimate Tender Attracted
Therapist relates by:	Interacting, working together. Engaging in give-and-take relationship. Being emotionally responsive, stirred.		
Patient gets:	All listed satisfactions.		

THE BEST. Now patient wants to demonstrate gains, talks more about fantasies and the past, usually feels relieved and trusting; therapist feels optimistic and satisfied.

PHILIP KIRKLAND

Morality in Psychotherapy

By Marvin Frankel

The year is 1930. The place, Berlin. You are a practicing psychoanalyst confronting an interesting new patient in your office. His name, Adolf Hitler. He is a professional politician regarded as one of the country's rising young men. □ Now he has come to you because he is troubled by persistent anxieties. He speaks confidently about his plans for Germany, yet he admits to fear of failure and therefore punishment by "lesser" beings. Lately, however, when he considers some of the harsh deeds demanded by his grandiose plans, he has been bothered by feelings of guilt. Nevertheless, he is convinced that the ends he has in mind fully justify the means. □ He is bothered only because his increasing anxieties and guilt feelings may impede him in the execution of his designs. Hitler asks you to put an end to these disturbing feelings. Can you help him?

FOR MANY, the answer would appear to be obvious—for certain actions, guilt necessarily is the result. Hitler must be convinced that his anxiety and guilt are altogether realistic in light of his harsh intentions; that such disturbing feelings occur not without reason, but come about directly from his grand designs because these designs are wrong. Hitler, one might say, feels guilty because his schemes violate his basic principles. As Hitler struggles with guilt, he is admitting, if only to himself, that he does indeed contemplate violating his every moral principle.

But he had come to the analyst to buy himself moral *carte blanche,* not to have his plans imposed upon. Given such a case today, we have reason to believe that many of our contemporary psychotherapists would be able to oblige an Adolf Hitler. This is because of the *kind* of values which they bring to bear upon the psychotherapeutic relationship. What are these values?

An inkling is provided by the recent book by Joseph Wolpe and Arnold Lazarus, *Behavior Therapy Techniques,* which devotes seven pages to "tactical principles." Using these "principles," we may theorize how they might have been applied to the neurotic German politician. Regarding the patient's fears, Wolpe and Lazarus undoubtedly would have invoked their third tactical principle, which says in effect that the patient should be made to realize that there is no "virtue" in confronting one's fear. Then, Hitler would have undergone the treatment the behaviorists call "desensitization," in which, with muscles relaxed, he would have learned to overcome his fear of certain authority figures. Thereafter, in any confrontation with authorities, although they well might fear this wild-eyed upstart, he no longer would need fear them; he could dismiss them from his life and from his dreams.

As for the patient's growing sense of guilt, Wolpe and Lazarus state explicitly on page 16 of their book that a patient has no choice in becoming what he is. Hence, blame and culpability are incongruous. Hitler, now fully confident and secure in the knowledge that he really shouldn't be blamed for the political tack he yearns to take, presumably would have given his mustache a touch, paid his bill, and trooped out of the office.

Mental treatment from Freudian analysis to behavior therapy has declared that it is wrong to censure the blameless patient—a patient without free-will, without responsibility, a patient whose acts are determined by his history.

The epistemological question of whether free-will really exists had best be left to philosophers. What is important for psychologists to realize is that people do, in fact, feel free. Every man makes choices every day. A hostess asks: "What will you have to drink?" The individual makes a decision not only on what to drink but whether he will take an alcoholic drink. Aside from the oft-reported social pressure to imbibe, he is under no compulsion to drink, or at least he would not recognize such a compulsion. He *feels* that he has made a free decision to have a drink.

This feeling becomes important to him when he recognizes that by his decision-making he can alter consequences. During the course of the evening, our guest may accept more drinks. Then comes the time when he thinks about his automobile and about the drive home. Here he faces alternatives: He can switch to coffee and drive home himself; he can have another drink and hand the car keys to a sober wife; or he can take another drink and drive home, anyway. Whether he drives home or not, in this instance he will know that he has affected consequences. If he ends up drunk and driving and then has an auto accident, his reaction—superficially at least—may be to blame the "other guy"; but if subsequently he is burdened with remorse, can it be said that he has no reason for his guilt?

I am not denying any of the usual symbolism—that the car represents his masculinity and to surrender the keys would be castration, or that by drinking and driving he is overcoming a feeling of inadequacy. But if this man should seek psychotherapy because of guilt over the accident, it seems primary to me that he jolly well knew the risks he was taking, that he took them, and lost. And *he,* not his masculinity, is responsible.

For contrast, let us consider another example. The same man dreams of being at a party, then drinking too much, and then crashing his car. He need feel no guilt, no responsibility for this nightmare. Before he goes to sleep, he cannot make a decision about what he will dream. Such a feat is beyond human control. Neither can he alter the events in his dream; obviously they too are beyond control. The preconditions for decision-making are not present in dreaming, either in fact or in the individual's feeling about them. Without the possibility of decision-making, there can be no responsibility and no freedom.

A person acts as though he possesses free-will to the extent that he engages in decision-making, and he experiences freedom to the degree that he feels responsible for the consequences. Decision-making takes place only when the individual, whether *rightfully* or not, decides that he can critically alter the outcome of an event. It is a clinical cliché, but nonetheless true, that some people assume responsibility for behavior that others would consider to be outside the margin of personal control. Clearly the boundaries of culpability are subjectively established, and this analysis also directly implies that free-will is not intrinsic to the nature of man. When an individual cannot make decisions with a sense of responsibility, he simply is not free. There are many people who cannot bear the feeling of responsibility and of possible guilt for their active decisions. And a person who will not pay the price of guilt cannot accept the cost of free-will. One can say that free-will is not an essential characteristic of the individual but resides instead in man's active capacity for registering his choices and preferences. A person can jail himself psychologically as easily as he can lock himself in a cell. A man may be quite capable of acting freely and yet at the same time suffer because the act of decision-making *necessarily* carries in its wake the responsibility for error and failure. Indeed, it may be argued that happiness often can be purchased at the expense of freedom.

Actually, patients in psychotherapy, and particularly in traditional psychoanalysis, may be said to be trading precisely in this kind of currency—often purchasing a form of security at the expense of freedom. Let us examine traditional psychoanalysis and the nature of the help it offers to the neurotic.

The patient who walks into the psychiatrist's office is a desperate man. As a neurotic, he exists in a rapidly diminishing life space in which he becomes more and more uncertain of his powers and of his responsibilities. He feels pushed or pulled by maternal sighs, wifely cries, employer ties. He sees himself as a creature enfeebled by circumstances—a victim. And he has come to the analyst when everything else has failed him.

Yet the very act of seeking help indicates that the neurotic still can make a decision and follow a course of action, that he still feels some sense of responsibility for his condition. He is uncertain about what is properly within and beyond his control. But does the analyst utilize and build on the remaining nodule of responsibility? No.

First, the patient is invited to free-associate. In doing so, he is asked to suspend his critical judgment, his powers such as they still may be to discriminate reality from fantasy. Then, of course, the patient's dreams are gone over in great detail, with emphasis on the meaningfulness of their content, despite the fact that they come without the patient's consent or control. His volitional, responsible communications thus are made subordinate to his involuntary productions. The patient initially was concerned with the extent of his responsibility for—and his increasing failure to exercise control over—his circumstances. In psychoanalysis, he is instructed that he best can understand his predicament through exhaustive examination of behavior generally regarded as outside his control.

Not only that, but the patient is invited to detail his woes while lying on a couch. Thus supine, with the analyst out of sight so that the patient will not be able to intuit approval or disapproval as indicated by facial expressions, he may "freely" associate. He will be free, that is, from noting the consequences of his behavior. Psychoanalysis is, of course, a private affair. And if an individual is having trouble coping with his life, what better place than the quiet, reflective atmosphere of the analyst's office? The patient immediately is instructed to postpone all major decisions. He gains the respectability of a prescription for what may be his trouble in the first place—inability to make a decision and to accept the consequences. And he

is cut off from the significant people in his life—for him, probably a big relief.

The contemporary analyst may object that the above techniques have been much modified today, and that in any case treatment hardly stops with free association and with dream analysis, used for insights into the patient's general life style. In answer, we might say that, while methodology today may be different, there still remains the basic assumption that the behavior of the neurotic is not motivated responsibly, but instead is the result of unconscious processes. When the patient leaves psychoanalysis, he is firmly assured that in all or almost all he personally is blameless.

At fault here, of course, is the general psychoanalytic conception of the origin of neurosis. Briefly, the neurotic is characterized as an individual unable to translate his instinctual impulses into proper social channels as a result of the overly restrictive and punitive child-rearing practices of his parents. According to such thinking, the patient's freedom to determine his own circumstances and life style was stunted before he could be held accountable for any action. The repressed sexual wishes of childhood haunt the man throughout his days, rendering him unable to cope adequately with his life.

If there is a strong element of pre-destination about my description of such thinking, let us consider from Freud's own writings just how much predetermination there is in his theories. In his analysis of a phobia in a five-year-old boy, Freud writes of Little Hans, who suffered a phobic fear of horses. Specifically, Hans was afraid that he would be bitten by a horse. Freud, taking his symbolic lens, viewed the phobia as the boy's terror of being punished (castrated) by his outraged father for sexually desiring his mother. Freud, of course, pointed out that Hans was quite unaware (unconscious) of his lust for his mother and of his fear of his father. Thus, neither in choice of symptom (the fear of horses) nor in its underlying

cause (the classic Oedipus situation) did Freud make any effort to show how Hans could have avoided his neurosis. Quite the contrary. Freud describes how he allayed Little Hans' anxiety by relating that, long before Hans came into the world, he, Freud, knew that a Little Hans would be born who would love his mother and fear his father's anger. Little Hans, having no responsibility for all that happened, was introduced to predestination and was absolved. Then Freud says that upon leaving the office the little boy looked up at his father and asked, "Does the professor talk to God?" If nothing else, one must admire the boy's powers of connecting concepts according to the evidence he was given.

Until 1945 psychotherapy and psychoanalysis were virtually synonomous terms. In the past few years, however, there has been a very healthy development of both theory and practice in the field of psychotherapy in particular, the approach of integrity therapy as expounded by O. H. Mowrer, of the University of Illinois, in a series of provocative articles. As its name implies, integrity therapy epitomizes a curative process which articulates how neurosis results from the patient's active decisions, decisions for which he alone can be held accountable. During therapy, the important distinction is drawn between behavior which simply is caused and behavior which indeed is motivated. The analytical and practical importance of distinguishing between a motive and a cause perhaps can be made clear with a brief example which is taken from clinical practice:

Mr. A, a psychotherapy patient, disclosed in the first interview that he unconsciously did many things which indicated that he wanted to fail. To illustrate, Mr. A told of having completed a write-up for a research design for which he needed the support of his two immediate supervisors. Mr. W, the first supervisor, rejected the proposal, Mr. A was somewhat dismayed, but he took his proposal to Mr. X, the second

"Integrity therapy tries to focus on the patient's free choices—his motives and decisions."

supervisor. And then, without even being asked, he volunteered to Mr. X the information that Mr. W had rejected his write-up. The following day, the second supervisor also turned down the proposal. Mr. A felt that he literally had doomed himself. Asked why he felt that way, he replied he once had been a successful salesman. "If there's one thing a salesman knows, it's that you don't tell the customer how unsuccessful you have been trying to sell the product," he said.

Of course, Mr. A did not chide himself with a motive for failure. Instead, he inferred an invidious operation, beyond his control, of unconscious motives (causes, really) which affected his behavior in self-defeating ways. He assumed that he was victimized by unconscious forces and thus avoided responsibility for his defeat.

I am not inclined to view the unconscious as a necessary adjunct to psychotherapy and so I simply commented to Mr. A that, since he was of the opinion that he wanted to fail, we had what amounted to a success story. He was nonplussed. "You have succeeded in failing," I said. "What is the problem?"

It soon became clear that Mr. A did everything he could to sustain his hope that he could succeed if only he didn't stand in his own way. Mr. A began to cry. It was evident that he was experiencing the full shame of his decision to avoid facing the truth about his abilities. Moreover, he knew that he still was *freely unwilling to change,* and hence the tears. Suddenly Mr. A, the same patient who moments before aloofly had related the unconscious causes for his failure, was crying bitterly. How much happier he would have been, I thought, had I been of traditional psychoanalytical persuasion and had joined with him to affirm his defense of unconscious victimhood. Instead, my therapeutic response was designed to make him face the possibility that he was being *motivated* to fail, rather than merely being the innocent victim of hidden causes.

Integrity therapy tries to focus on the

patient's "free" choices—his motives and decisions. Thus, although Mr. A assuredly had a history of former conflicts, we did not plunge into a distracting examination of them for their own sake. Within the framework of integrity therapy, the historical problem is viewed as contemporary in the most vital sense— the patient currently is behaving in a way which ensures the perpetuation of his neurosis. Mr. A, for instance, was motivated in his conduct neither by instinctual gratification nor by sex phantasy, but simply by the need to sustain hope for a success which he secretly feared was beyond him. Unable to accept this, he intruded his "inadvertent" mistakes which ruined things for him. Then he further intruded an imagined mental problem which he had no way of knowing nor of controlling.

The basic point is that a distinction between motives and causes has been ignored in the deterministic approach to therapy. In his stimulating monograph, "The Concept of Motivation," R. S. Peters, of the University of London, argues that, while we can say that all motives are causes, the converse, that all causes are motives, is not necessarily so. An ankle broken while a boy plays basketball is a *cause* of his being allowed to stay home from school to rest up and soak up both the service and sympathy of his family. But a reluctance to take up again the rigors of school work, coupled with a desire to continue as the recipient of the family's service and sympathy, well may be the *motive* for a suspiciously lingering convalescence.

Freud, acute observer of the human scene that he was, failed to make this distinction: motive involves responsibility on the part of the patient; cause, despite its psychic origins, does not necessarily relate to personal responsibility.

To Freud, the etiology of neurosis could be compared to a flu victim's being infected with virus. The flu victim fails to know what his symptoms mean simply because he is not a doctor and hence lacks necessary understanding. In

the same way, the neurotic, according to Freud, has a faulty understanding of his conflict; "unconsciously" he does not want to know what it is. In Freudian theory it follows that, because the neurotic's ignorance is unconsciously caused, he no more can be blamed than can the flu victim. Further, says Freud, the neurotic even carries on in his unconscious way and himself distorts the symptoms. Thus he will complain of feeling guilty because he has broken personal rules.

The Freudian psychiatrist "knows" that guilt is the result of unconscious wishes for which the patient is blameless. After all, did Little Hans really attempt to seduce his mother? If we ask why the neurotic stops short of acting upon his supposed wishes, we are brought back to the "unconscious." We are told that too-exacting practices in rearing the child produced a neurotic man full of fear and with an over-severe conscience. How then does one cure such an unconscious illness? By unconscious means, of course!

The neurotic, in the course of treatment, develops a "positive transference" and begins to attribute to the analyst celestial powers. The patient then attends to the interpretations of this "deified" analyst and purportedly gets well. The analyst, to whom he unconsciously has attributed celestial powers, absolves him from his unconscious conflict. And so the Freudian story of neurosis is one in which the neurotic unconsciously is victimized into health, just as he was victimized into illness. I can see no freedom here.

The psychoanalytic method of treatment has been challenged many times, but, until recently, Freud's basic theory has been endorsed almost wholeheartedly, *especially in its de-emphasis on free-will.* Fortunately, the past few years have brought a reinterpretation of the origin of neurosis, through the work of Mowrer. In Mowrer's terms, the neurotic is guilty for his wishful impulses. Naturally, the neurotic feels guilty. He also feels himself a social outcast because *privately* he fails to live up to the standards which he endorses *publicly*. The conflict inherent in his hypocritical behavior aggravates his neurosis.

Some evidence for this point of view comes from a University of Tennessee study in which the backgrounds of 25 women seeking therapy at the University of Tennessee were compared with the case histories of a control group. The women with the most troubling emotional problems were those who indulged in sexual practices they actually believed were wrong.

If Mowrer's view of neurosis continues to be upheld, the individual soon may be able to know the risks he takes with his mental health, just as he now knows some of the risks he takes with his bodily health. If he violates his "principles," his chances of falling victim to neurosis are increased significantly, just as his chances of coming down with pneumonia are increased if he walks bare-chested through Central Park in late December.

Recalling my Mr. A, who so wanted to be reassured that his failures were not his fault, I wonder if the more rigorous and more realistic practice of psychotherapy as outlined by Mowrer ever will be as popular as the Freudian school. A neurotic by the very nature of his illness is quite pleased to shuck off responsibility for whatever personality traits disturb him or upset those close to him. The psychoanalyzed neurotic has purchased an anaesthesia called peace of mind, which allows him to act out his life while at crucial moments refusing all responsibility for his actions and their consequences. Such a man is not free. But his situation brings us to a universal problem and to a question for the future of psychotherapy: Can a man live with the knowledge that he and he alone is responsible for his decisions?

According to sociologist Karl Mannheim, it is entirely unrealistic to expect that man can exist in the context of unlimited choice; a certain degree of conformity is necessary. Probably quite true, but what degree? And where should man exercise his freedom? These well may be areas for psychology to define. Psychology can play a vital role in securing an empirical basis which permits man to exercise his freedom effectively. To do so, psychological knowledge must free man from ignorance and warn him of some of the dangers implicit in his free choice of how he is to live his life. As a physician would warn a youth against heroin by giving information about addiction, so could the psychologist warn man of the addictive (and therefore enslaving) nature of certain mental stimuli. We all have heard, of course, of the big-lie technique, perfected by the man whom I introduced at the beginning of this article. The big lie, if repeated often enough, becomes a soporific on the critical powers of the mind. A subject who thus has been desensitized to reality ceases to be able to make free decisions, but rather he reacts involuntarily to the big lie.

An example of how psychological knowledge brings freedom is in the role it has played in effecting the freedom of women. Psychological knowledge has allowed women to admit to pleasure in sexual love and to make more of their own decisions about sexual love. Also, in hand with medical science, it has allowed women to determine how many children they will have.

Within the Freudian perspective, man cannot determine the strength and magnitude of his sexual motives; at best he only decides on their manner of expression. Freud construed man as having to express behaviorally some optimal quota of his sexuality, or suffer from psychic consequences. Thus Freudian man is the victim of his own uncontrolled and scarcely known sexual forces. Actually, there is evidence that, rather than circumscribing fixed needs, man's sexual constitution exhibits considerable malleability. Kenneth Hardy has advanced an appetititive theory of sexual motivation which argues that mere exercise of sexuality increases one's subsequent sexual appetite. Should the appetite theory of sexual motivation continue to be consistent with accumulating empirical evidence, psychology soon may advance to a point where decision-making and freedom of choice will affect an area long regarded as a closed system. That is, man will neither fear his sexual drives as somehow sinful, nor will he resign himself to a sexual life predestined for him from the cradle. Rather, he may decide for himself how, and how much, to use his sexual drive, somewhat as he decides how and how much to indulge his appetite for food. In all of this we have an increase of knowledge and of free choice, and hence of responsibility.

Since I seem to have employed Freud for a whipping boy in discussing free-will, I should explain that the choice hardly was arbitrary. Freud's heavy emphasis on the "irrational" factors governing human behavior has been the major influence in 20th-century psychology. In the *Psychopathology of Everyday Life*, published in 1904, Freud discusses the very issue of free-will. But the principal goal of that investigation was to show that even the seemingly trivial, unmotivated, "accidental" behaviors of everyday life were "determined" by unconscious "causes." In 1904, psychoanalysis seemed upon the threshold of predicting what had been regarded as unpredictable—accidents. Unfortunately, Freud's slim volume today remains the most definitive statement yet made on the subject. We have ventured little beyond the threshold.

But if psychology would investigate what makes men feel free, I am convinced the findings would not contradict the view that behavior is lawful and predictable. The motivational conditions which make men feel free clearly represent another line of study from scientific causality. The latter can reveal what man actually does, while the former dwells upon what he thinks he does. Certainly the realm of man's thought is truly the area of human life that should be peculiarly his own.

The Long Weekend

By Frederick H. Stoller

You're on camera. Closed-circuit television captures behavior . . .

A YOUNG MEXICAN-AMERICAN, imprisoned for drug addiction, inarticulate, fearful, and sullen, becomes a forceful dormitory leader.

A Greek-Jewish survivor of a Nazi concentration camp, having vegetated for seven silent and inactive years in a state mental hospital, suddenly decides he wants to leave, begins work in the hospital laboratory, and earns his discharge within a few months.

A clinical psychologist whose sole aim has been competence as a technician begins to function as a recognized innovator in his field.

The drug addict, the concentration camp survivor, and the psychologist are linked by a common bond. Each, within a relatively brief time, made use of personal resources whose existence had been totally unrecognized by himself and by others. And each participated in an intense group experience that changed his view of himself, his world,

Close your eyes and relax. The object of this game is to demonstrate the child's trust as members of his family pass him about.

Focused feedback. After a group session, Stoller frequently reviews significant sections of the video tape individually with group members.

on video tape for later feedback to the entire group or to individuals.

and his future.

These three people did not undergo traditional group therapy. They were members of a different kind of group, one of the new intense encounter groups whose goal was exploration rather than cure, and whose orientation was self-education rather than the amelioration of psychopathology. Many techniques of the new group are not dissimilar from traditional psychotherapy, but the assumption made about the members is that they are *not* sick. This is true even when some or all group members are disturbed. But it is not necessary to feel that one "needs therapy" to join a group, for it appears that everyone can benefit from experimentation with new ways of behavior and new social arrangements, and the most effective groups are made up of "chronic undifferentiated people."

These new groups are explosive, because they concentrate on immediate behavior within the group, not on explanations of past behavior—that tempting search for a scapegoat. They are also unpredictable, because each participant is encouraged to scrutinize himself and his relationship to the world without the shackles of normal role expectations.

When a person is labeled—neurotic, psychotic, executive, teacher, salesman, psychologist—either by himself or by others, he restricts his behavior to the role and even may rely upon the role for security. This diminishes the kind of ex-

What's inside? The family gathered around the box share their fears by attempting to guess the contents.

perience he is likely to have. Indeed, it is groups whose members have a shared label—be it schizophrenic or executive—which are hardest to help move into intimate contact.

The importance of avoiding labels is shown by the experience of a young bachelor, who was urged by myself and other group members to stop frittering away his time at the YMCA when he should be involved in the heterosexual world. By the last day of the marathon he walked like a tiger—his growth was impressive. Then I discovered he was a former mental patient. Had I known this earlier, I would have thought, "Your adjustment is pretty good, considering where you've been." I never would have responded to him so directly. And his marked behavioral change would have been blunted.

During group sessions, exclusive reliance on a narrow range of roles is broken down. The chronically hospitalized patient who helps another patient or the juvenile delinquent who persuades a boy not to run away sees himself in a new and liberating light. It is this opportunity to shift freely from the role of patient to that of therapist or observer which is the unique feature of group therapy.

Since the essence of the new group movement is flexibility and experimentation, new techniques and procedures constantly are being tried. Experiments with the length of sessions resulted in the marathon group; experiments with technological innovations resulted in the use of video tape to capture behavior; experiments with group composition resulted in the family workshop.

The 300-Year Weekend

As its name implies, the marathon group, which grew out of my experiences in a sensitivity-training laboratory in 1963, is a continuous session. My first attempt to use the marathon—with a group of psychotics—was both rewarding and exciting. The model finally developed by George Bach, one of the pioneers in group psychotherapy, and myself lasts from 24 to 30 hours, often without a break for sleep—a distinct departure from the precisely scheduled "50-minute hour" of traditional psychotherapy. The marathon group represents a radical alteration in the quality of the psychotherapeutic experience. It assumes that people are capable of coping with undiluted, intense experience and do not require carefully measured exposure to therapy; it has been called a "pressure cooker" because of the tension it builds up. And like a pressure cooker, it also can compress the amount of time required to do its work. The development is infinitely more rapid than under conventional therapy and the progress can be startling. The marathon uniquely maximizes and legitimizes people's readiness for change.

The marathon group is more than an exercise in massive confrontation and involvement. It is an educational experience primarily useful for what *follows* the conflict—crisis, anxiety, and reaching out for contact.

And in order for what follows to be meaningful, it is essential that group members neither avoid nor dilute their discomfort. The tension must rise. Members of the group are asked to react to

each other, immediately and spontaneously, at all times; these immediate reactions — the "feedback" — inform the recipient in unmistakable terms of just what impact he has on others in the group. Thus ground rules for the marathon specify that the group remain together throughout the session; they outlaw psychological or psychiatric jargon of any school; and they call for authentic, honest, and direct reactions.

The group leader's role is quite different from his role in traditional therapy. He deliberately refrains from gathering case histories about the marathon group participants. The leader must build up his impression of participants exactly as other members of the group do and he must share the impact of each participant. For, in a marathon group, it is *not* to be *understood* that is essential; the importance is in being *reacted* to. Being understood may be comfortable, but it is also an avoidance of responsibility which the marathon does not offer to its participants.

The group leader sets the experience in motion so that the pressure gauge will begin to rise. His position is clear and unmistakable, but he does not remain the traditional, aloof clinician—he is also a group member, a distinct human being. For this reason, I frequently hold marathon groups in my home, and my wife participates along with me.

Marathons run a fairly predictable course. In the first phase, participants tell their "stories." Basically, they present themselves as they wish the world to see them: they describe their frustrations or their life circumstances, with careful attention to the response they

THE FAMILY DRAWING: Each family draws together for five minutes without speaking.

AT RIGHT: The mother tended to hang back, seemingly unhappy about the lack of structure inherent in the exercise. The father made more attempts to participate but these were largely toward the edge of the paper. The older girl worked in a neat fashion but the young boy began to fill the paper with his scribbling. Finally, there was an attempt on the part of the parents to involve the children in a tick-tack-toe game, which ultimately was scribbled over by the boy (including the tear in the paper). The mother complained that the boy inhibited her by his hyperactivity but she could be seen as inviting him to fill space by her reluctance to act without structure.

BELOW AND RIGHT: The children in this family constructed a number of individual drawings which the mother attempted to connect throughout the exercise by moving from drawing to drawing, rather than engaging in any production of her own. In contrast, the father became involved in a design closely related to his work and he reported that he became so absorbed he largely ignored the presence of his family except as their drawings inspired his designs. The parents were very verbal about their goals and principles of family life, but the observations made the father wonder whether his behavior differed from his words.

hope to evoke. They may anticipate solutions to their problems or look for support of their actions or attitudes. Inevitably they encounter static from the group—unexpected reactions which they find difficult to accept. Thus they meet their first crisis: feedback which is different from what they intended or wanted, or expected. And learning begins early. One man said that he felt—for the first time—that someone knew him well enough to tell him more about himself than he already knew.

Most people have learned that the best way to handle a crisis is to run away. However, the marathon does not offer that option. For one thing, retreat is against the rules. For another, each group member contributes to the crises of the other participants at the same time as he is experiencing his own, so that he is drawn closer to the very people with whom he is in conflict. A counterpoint between the urge to retreat and the necessity to become more involved characterizes the second phase of the marathon.

Tears and Threats

During this middle phase the group members, not surprisingly, learn a considerable amount about each other. They also learn to react more directly and honestly. Their ways of moving through the world become more and more apparent. They sense that their approach to others is limited and tentative, and so their awareness of other possibilities grows. No clear-cut solutions emerge, but the struggles at this point are intense. It is the most explosive period of the session. Dramatic, frightening, moving interchanges are likely to occur. Tears and threats are not uncommon.

It was at this point that I once had an extreme confrontation with a young man whose religious fanaticism made it impossible for him to have a relationship with anyone who did not share his feelings. As the marathon progressed, I found his insistent intrusion of religious dogma abrasive and, after making it clear that I did not operate within a religious framework, demanded that he specify his reactions to me. He was thrown into conflict between his usual stance and his feeling for me. Suddenly he cried and talked about his concern for hypocrisy he saw within his church.

Another young man, who had been observing quietly, also began to cry. He was so deeply moved by the religious man's struggle that tears coursed down his cheeks. He said it was the first time

in his life that he had found himself touched by another human being. Now he realized how distantly he had conducted his life. And he wept. The change in this silent observer was as profound as that in the young man who was the temporary focus of the group. This "spectator therapy" is a group phenomenon that is accentuated by the marathon experience.

As the session nears its end, there is in any marathon group a new sense of intimacy among all the members, and positive feelings emerge in a spontaneous and deeply felt fashion. This phase has been called a "love feast," because participants reach out to one another with unguarded intimacy. They now permit themselves to experience more —more fear, more love, more empathy, and more excitement. A Negro youth from Mississippi said to me once: "It seemed to get me out of that fake shield that I had been hiding behind practically all of my life."

Solutions and alternatives begin to emerge, usually through the realization by the group member that he can reveal more of himself than he thought safe.

Taking part in a marathon is like watching oneself through the wrong end of a telescope: everything is sharp, concentrated, miniaturized. It becomes clear in this microcosm that one's life is, to a considerable degree, something one creates oneself and something for which one is responsible. Gradually, the inhabitants of the small world learn to act upon their environment as well as to be acted upon. It becomes apparent that the larger world can be altered in similar fashion. This is my deep belief.

Mirror, Mirror on the Wall

One function of a group is to show its members the effect they have upon one another. Responding to other people develops one's ability to communicate perceptions directly and honestly; receiving responses increases one's self-knowledge. But it is hard to sit still and listen to information about oneself which may be unpleasant, and it is hard to assimilate what one is told in mere words. This is why I turned to a new medium, which some therapists since have adopted and which others question.

Video-tape equipment makes it possible for group members to see themselves in action, which they find highly informative as well as fascinating. In one group, a wife had spent considerable time complaining bitterly that her husband "behaved like a child" with

her. On video tape, I was able to show her that she used many of the mannerisms of a scolding mother with him— she would glare, shake her finger, and, when pleased, pat his head. "I couldn't believe it," she said. "It was worth a thousand words."

Contrary to what one might expect, placing a television camera in the midst of a group does not seem to affect behavior. Television camera and videotape machine become part of the group circle. The camera may be manned by a co-therapist or even by the group members themselves. This arrangement gives them a chance to observe the group from an unusual and therefore useful point of view. Their choice of what appears on the tape is in itself a commentary—on the action and on the cameraman as well.

Unless responses are observed soon after behavior, they have little value. So when Lee Myerhoff and I began to use video tape during marathons, I decided to interrupt the group from time to time and replay the tape. This did not break the continuity of group interaction. Instead, group members would react to themselves on the television monitor, and other members would react to this reaction. Consequently, the viewing usually was followed by fuller concentration than before on immediate group behavior and events.

Focused Feedback

Video tape shares one unfortunate characteristic with life: It contains too much information. It is necessary to select what relates to the goals of the group and to focus the attention of the group members on it. A rationale for focused feedback can be found in the works of George Herbert Mead, who preceded the technical reality of video tape by many decades. Essentially a social psychologist, Mead developed a theory of personality development which stressed the social environment within which man becomes human. Among Mead's speculations was the theory that, preceding each act, people rehearse that act in their minds and anticipate the response others will give to it. On the basis of the anticipated response, the act is initiated; on the basis of the actual response, behavior is modified. An act consists of a range of gestures, some of which (such as speech) can be monitored by the initiator, and some of which (such as facial expressions) cannot.

Video tape shows the group member —sometimes all too clearly—the relationship between an anticipated and an actual response. Often the two correspond; at critical times they often do not. In either case, comparing them is extremely useful for the group member. Tape also makes clear the discrepancy between a person's inner state and what he communicates to others. Most people are surprised to discover how much effort they invest in hiding their true responses, as if life were a poker game.

The visual pictures on the video tape are added to the verbal pictures painted of each group member by himself and others. And on the screen, for the first time the participant confronts himself, instead of information filtered through the mind of another individual. He also sees himself, on tape, in each of the three major group roles: the patient role, when he is the focus of attention; the therapist role, when he attempts to extend help to others; and the observer role, when he is an inactive witness to the struggles of others.

Recent studies by Margaret Robinson, in her doctoral research at Camarillo State Hospital, tend to confirm my observation that after seeing himself on video tape, a group member often changes his behavior before incorporating the change into his self-concept. After four sessions of focused feedback, there was a marked drop in the incidence of specific behavior units, which were the objects of the feedback, but the self-concept—as measured on self-rating tests—remained unchanged. When behavior first changes, there is a period of awkwardness, then an improved level of behavior. The changed behavior elicits new responses from other people, perhaps initiating a chain reaction.

Experiences with focused feedback and with marathon groups suggest that much of standard therapeutic practice should be questioned. It seems to me that what often is considered axiomatic in psychotherapy is only a set of long-standing assumptions. Such assumptions become transformed into unexamined definitions, difficult to question because they seem apparent.

Games Families Play

In our family workshops, developed in collaboration with Ann Dreyfuss, of Western Behavioral Sciences Institute, three or four families remain together for several days, generally for a weekend. At first, the scene is chaotic—children are everywhere, in constant motion. Because of their short attention span, young children sometimes are segregated from the main group from time to time during the weekend, but a rule of the family workshop is that *all* members participate, and no one is talked about when he is not present.

Parents are quite devious with their children, and they teach their children to be devious with them — beginning when the children still are at the pre-verbal level. And this is complicated by the fact that the family as a unit puts on an act before outsiders.

Families come to the workshop with ready-made relationships, but they have not learned to talk about them. As initial shyness and family chauvinism wear off, the interplay begins. Even very young children pick up the emotional tone of the workshop and seem to be aware that a struggle is taking place.

There are rules: Regardless of which family they belong to, group members are expected to respond to each other directly, and to express their perceptions as clearly as possible. As families get to know one another, they become aware of the implicit contractual arrangements which determine their behavior. The workshop, like the marathon, is a microcosm of the difficulties that families encounter at home; experimenting with new and more fruitful ways of dealing with these problems is a major goal of the session.

Early in our sessions, each family in turn is given a large piece of paper and pastels. The family is asked to draw a design together for five minutes, without speaking. Mothers are more likely to be uncomfortable in this situation than are fathers. Interestingly, most families will fight for space; each member will try to use the whole sheet and to invade others' territory.

After the picture is completed, the family members discuss their reactions, and then the rest of the group talks about how they perceived the family. During the discussion, family members tend to draw parallels between the ways they behaved in this situation and the ways they behave at home.

The picture exercise takes the workshop out of the realm of words and removes the advantage from the parent and gives it to the child. The art game actually helps teach youngsters to give feedback, and they soon warm to the task. [*See illustration, page 407.*]

On other occasions, a box is placed in the center of a family group. They are told that something terrible is inside the box and asked to imagine what it might be. Typical guesses range from "a little dinosaur" to "a creeping hand" or "something soft and gooey and icky." This game represents an attempt by the family to share their fears.

Sometimes we ask the chosen family to pass sticks in a circle according to a specified pattern, or to perform rhythmical handclapping "dances." The purpose of these games, which usually come late in the workshop, is to give the family a chance to have fun together, to cooperate under the easy conditions of play without the restrictions of the usual family roles. In other words, a mother is invited for a moment to stop functioning as a mother and to become instead a playmate with responsibilities no greater than her child's. Some mothers do this well and enjoy it, others do not—in either case, the results are informative.

If parents complain, as they often do, that their children never listen to them at home, the family may be asked to talk together for 15 or 20 minutes, perhaps about their reasons for coming to the workshop. The rest of the group comments on this; their response is supplemented by a replay of video tape.

The family workshop has wider implications. The current American family is becoming increasingly unique in that it sees itself as an independent unit, operating without reliance on the extended family — grandparents, uncles, aunts, cousins. This is an impossible task. As families are brought up in isolation, social agencies move into the vacuum created by the dissolution of the extended family. And as the family influence diminishes, there is an accompanying growth in the strength of the adolescent culture.

The intimate relationships developed during the workshop can be the nucleus from which to explore and experiment with new social arrangements. An intimate network of families who had shared workshop experiences could be created. These families would provide the help and emotional support originally supplied by the clan or the extended family.

A powerful group experience permits the individual to explore his own resources, those of the people with whom he finds himself, and those of the world about him. Group experiments provide experiences, not intellectual exercises— and experiences have the power to reshape us. Perhaps we need to establish "colleges for growth." Just as a student is not stupid because he goes to college to learn, so a person is not sick because he seeks group therapy or encounter experience to help him grow.

ESALEN

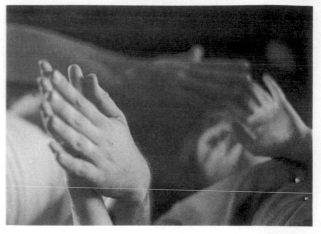

Big Sur, once the land of Henry Miller, is again the land of Esalen, but where at one time the Esalen Indians roamed the countryside, Esalen Institute now probes the boundaries of the human potential. And we are as controversial as Miller was, because we are willing to explore *any* approach which will extend the abilities of man. Esalen refuses to subscribe to any dogma—in philosophy, in psychology, or in religion—and for our seminars and encounter groups we bring in leaders from every field to contribute their own approach to the precarious condition of being human.

A weekend seminar with B. F. Skinner, the developer of operant conditioning, will be followed by a series of workshops with a Protestant theologian, an advocate of LSD, a Carmelite monk, an existential psychotherapist, the president of the American Psychological As-

DRUGS

Aldous Huxley (1894-1963), novelist and critic, who became interested in the effects of drugs and in Indian mysticism. His drug experiences were described in *The Doors of Perception.*

Humphrey Osmond invented the word "psychedelic"; introduced Aldous Huxley to mescaline.

Alan Watts, a popularizer of Zen Buddhism, who is working to unify science, philosophy, and religion. Advocates the use of LSD.

Timothy Leary, formerly of the Department of Psychology at Harvard University, has turned on and dropped out. Advocates the use of marijuana and LSD.

Hippies, members of a subculture in opposition to the dominant U.S. culture, characterized by dress, drugs, and communal living.

Freebies, the newest group on the scene; they are an extension of the hippies.

ESP (Extra-sensory Perception)

British Society for Psychical Research, founded in 1882 to conduct research into the fields of parapsychology.

American Society for Psychical Research, founded in 1888 and modeled after the British society.

Cross-correspondences, this attempt to communicate with the dead through mediums and by messages pre-arranged before death flourished especially from 1910-1930.

J. B. Rhine, the father of parapsychology, was connected with Duke University for many years. Since his retirement he has been director of The Foundation for Research on the Nature of Man and The Institute for Parapsychology.

Gardner Murphy, director of research at the Menninger Foundation, is the author of *Challenge of Psychical Research: a Primer of Parapsychology.*

Stanley Krippner, director of research, Dept. of Psychiatry, Moses Maimonides Hospital, New York. Conducts research on ESP during dream sleep.

Montague Ullman, on the staff at Moses Maimonides Hospital, New York. Conducts research on ESP during dream sleep.

Ian Stevenson, research psychiatrist, University of Virginia Medical School. Deals with cases suggestive of reincarnation.

J. G. Pratt, at University of Virginia Medical School. Has been a co-worker with J. B. Rhine in the field of parapsychology.

Charles Tart, at School of Medicine, University of Virginia. Interested in dreams, hypnosis, and personality.

HYPNOSIS

Franz Mesmer (1734-1815), Austrian physician, who developed the theory of animal magnetism, later known as Mesmerism.

Pierre Janet (1859-1947), French psychologist, a student — as was Sigmund Freud — of J. M. Charcot, who studied the disordered personality.

Sigmund Freud See below, PSYCHOANALYSIS.

Josef Breuer (1842-1925), Austrian physician and psychologist. A forerunner of psychoanalysis who used hypnosis in treating patients.

Bernard Aaronson, at School of Education, Rutgers University. Interested in verbal behavior, neural correlates of behavior, and psychotherapy.

Milton Erickson, a psychiatrist from Phoenix, whose fields are hypnotherapy, clinical psychotherapy, and training hypnosis.

Leslie LeCron, psychologist and hypnotherapist from Carmel, who does research in hypnosis and the alteration of consciousness.

MYSTICISM

William James (1842-1910), American psychologist and philosopher who delved into religion and mysticism in *The Varieties of Religious Experience.*

Gerald Heard, English writer now living in Southern California. His mystical philosophy greatly influenced Aldous Huxley.

Aldous Huxley See DRUGS.

D. T. Suzuki, the leading popularizer of Zen Buddhism in the United States.

Alan Watts See DRUGS.

First Zen Institute, founded in San Francisco. Now has a center in Big Sur near Esalen.

Arthur Dikeman, at the Austen Riggs Clinic, where he is engaged in meditation research sponsored by the National Institute of Mental Health.

The Beatles: George Harrison, Paul McCartney, Ringo Starr, and John Lennon; singing group in the vanguard of rock 'n roll, whose music has been influenced by Eastern music and who have been attracted by mystical thought.

Edward Maupin, a director of Esalen Institute, formerly on the staff of the Neuropsychiatric Institute at UCLA. His Ph.D. dissertation on meditation was probably the only one in America on that subject.

EVOLUTIONARY PHILOSOPHY

Julian Huxley, brother of Aldous Huxley; this English biologist related science to human social life and to religion.

Gerald Heard See above, MYSTICISM.

Pierre Teilhard de Chardin (1881-1955), French Jesuit paleontologist and thinker. He aimed at a metaphysic of evolution, holding that it was a process converging toward a final unity.

PSYCHOANALYSIS

Sigmund Freud (1856-1939), Austrian psychoanalyst and founder of psychoanalysis.

Otto Rank (1884-1939), Freud's pupil, who sought to modify Freud's theories to fit the needs of an industrial society.

Carl Jung (1875-1961), Swiss psychologist and psychiatrist, who founded analytic psychology. Former student of Freud.

Alfred Adler (1870-1937), Austrian psychoanalyst and student of Freud, who founded individual psychology.

David Rappaport, with Austen Riggs Clinic.

Robert Holt, George Klein: co-directors of Research Center for Mental Health, NYU, who are interested in the field of ego psychology.

Kurt Goldstein, psychiatrist and psychologist theorist, who invented the term "self-actualization."

Harry Harlow, professor of psychology at the University of Wisconsin and founder of the Primate Laboratory there.

Abraham Maslow, professor of psychology at Brandeis University. Noted for animal research and studies of human motivation; pioneering studies of psychological health.

Tony Suditch, editor of the *Journal of Humanistic Psychology.*

EXISTENTIALISM

Martin Buber, Jewish theologian and philosopher, who is the originator of the "I-Thou" concept.

Paul Tillich, Protestant theologian, who believed it was necessary to "demythicize" the Bible; author of *The Courage to Be* and *The Dynamics of Faith.*

Rollo May, psychotherapist and philosopher, who was a student of Alfred Adler. On the staff of both the William Alanson White Institute of Psychotherapy and New York University.

Victor Frankl, founder of logotherapy and author of *Man's Search for Meaning.*

Medard Boss, French psychiatrist.

Ludwig Binswanger, Swiss psychiatrist.

PSYCHOSIS

R. D. Laing, founder of the London Blowout Center at Tavistock Clinic.

Julius Silverman, connected with the National Institutes of Health, who is planning to work with the Esalen Blowout Center.

K. Dabrowski, Polish research psychiatrist and author of *Positive Disintegration.*

Mental Research Institute, Palo Alto, California.

"Garden of the Human Potential"

Shalal

Kairos

To Sonoma State College

Western Behavioral Institute Sciences

Gibb

To Esalen

Esalen

Satir

Argyris

Berlin

Human Development Institute

Gestalt therapy Perls

Bennis

Miles

Goodman

Kamiya

Stolle

Skinner Watson Pavlov

James

B

Wundt

Rogers

Bethel Mair

MAINSTREAM   **GESTALT PSYCHOLOGY**   **BEHAVIORISTIC**   **CLIENT-CENTERED THERAPY**

AKE a walk in the garden where the action is—the swinging, sensuous "Garden of the Human Potential," which grew in our artist's mind as Michael Murphy, president of Esalen Institute, talked about who he thinks is doing what and going where along the way toward the expansion of the mind of man.

times. Along with the trend toward life-long education has come a rise of popular interest in the existential philosophy of the here-and-now. We find more and more Americans who want to experience the present, to contact their feelings, to communicate intimately with others. At Esalen, as at Esalen-inspired institutes like Kairos in Southern California and Shalal in Vancouver, we try to expand human consciousness and help people "turn on" without drugs or alcohol.

The experiential methods used at Esalen have been developed primarily by our associates in residence, whose techniques demand the total involvement of participants and, like the experiences of an LSD trip, are intensely personal, and extremely difficult to describe in conventional language. To me, the experience of going through the workshops and observing the approaches used at Big Sur is like reading Lawrence Durrell's *Alexandria Quartet*.

On a walk around the grounds and through our redwood buildings clustered on a bluff high above the Pacific Ocean, one might see a blindfolded person led about silently in a group leader's effort to restore the individual's sense of touch and to give the experience of dependency. Or one might watch people "converse" with their bodies and eyes, cutting through society's excessive verbalism to authentic feelings, or one might find six or eight people lying side by side in a "sandwich" or rolling over one another to sense the presence of others, and to learn it's all right to touch each other.

Married couples, whose physical relationship has become mere repetition, are resensitized to each other. Eyes shut, they pat each other's faces and open their eyes to see a different person. They are taught new ways of body massage and brought into closer contact.

Our body-awareness workshops include a series of simple procedures to increase the sensitivity, to quiet the mind, and to achieve an optimal *tonus* between being too tense and being too relaxed. To these deceptively simple procedures is added a highly sensitive system of massage at the hot natural sulphur-water baths at our Big Sur center.

Frederick Perls, the 74-year-old founder of Gestalt therapy, works with a group structure in his institutes but leads each person individually to his impasse point and, hopefully, beyond. Nothing is too small to escape examination in his groups. He pays strict atten-

where it's at

By Michael Murphy

sociation, an historian, an authority on ESP, a Zen scholar, an architect, or a Hindu mystic. Skinner, Harvey Cox, Alan Watts, Father William McNamara, Rollo May, Abraham Maslow, Arnold Toynbee, Gardner Murphy, Shunryu Suzuki, Buckminster Fuller, and Hraidas Chaudhuri all have participated in the work of Esalen. Part of the excitement at Big Sur comes from the force of encountering the leading exponents of varied points of view.

Most of our workshops are experimental and experiential. They are conducted in an atmosphere with few institutional restrictions, where social scientists may "do their thing" and pioneer new methods of personal and interpersonal relations. Our primary concern is the affective domain—the senses and feelings, though we certainly are interested in the cognitive. We hope to educate people, if only for a weekend, in

what Aldous Huxley called the "non-verbal humanities"—long neglected in our culture because of the heavy emphasis which is placed on the verbal-rational aspect of man.

That man is capable of heightened functioning in *all* fields is proved every day. The wine tasters, the perfume smellers sharpen the senses; the skin diver, the mountain climber, the skydiver, the miler who keeps cutting seconds off his time—all push the limits of human functioning. And people in the fields of dance, the arts, and physical education are devising ways to extend the human potential.

Although most of our programs *could* be called therapies, we think of the thousands who come to Esalen not as sick people but as seekers of personal growth. They come from all walks of life, from business, universities, law offices, kitchens—and from Haight Asbury.

Esalen is, perhaps, a product of the

Tart

Pratt

Freebies

Stevenson

First Zen

Hippies

Leary

Watts

Krippner

Ullman

Erickson

Aaronson

LeCron

Osmond

Murphy

Huxley

Rhine

Freud

Breuer

Cross-correspondences,

Janet

American Society
for Psychical Research,

Soma 2000 B.C.

British Society
for Psychical Research,

Mesmer

DRUGS   **ESP**   **HYPNOSIS**

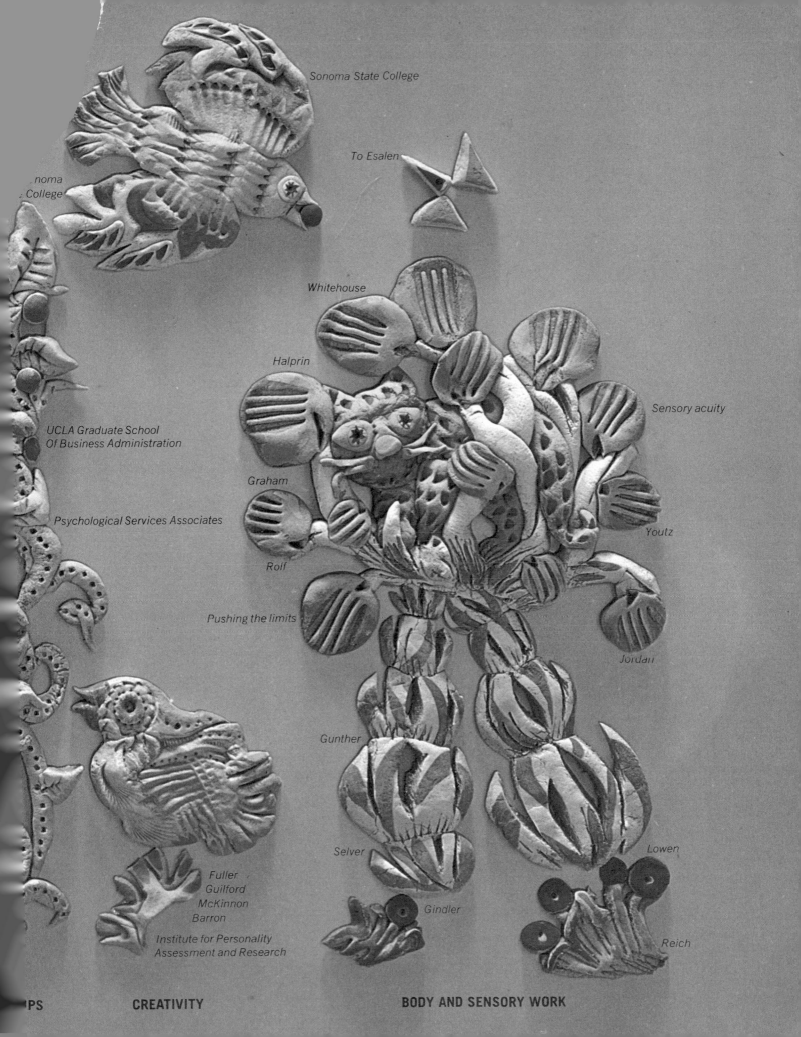

Sonoma State College

To Esalen

noma
College

Whitehouse

Halprin

Sensory acuity

UCLA Graduate School
Of Business Administration

Graham

Psychological Services Associates

Youtz

Rolf

Pushing the limits

Jordan

Gunther

Selver

Lowen

Fuller
Guilford
McKinnon
Barron

Gindler

Institute for Personality
Assessment and Research

Reich

PS   CREATIVITY   BODY AND SENSORY WORK

The breakthrough
in understanding
may come
through group
grope. Or
it may come
out of the
laboratory.
But, someday . . . .

through his self-defeating ego games. Not every person can break through his impasse, but in a Gestalt session, most do reach or approach an understanding of their own polarities.

Perls was influenced by Freud in Germany but abandoned traditional psychoanalysis in favor of his own gestalt technique many years ago. Today, his theories are similar to those of existential psychiatry, but he goes further in concentrating on sensory behavior and in declaiming the intellect as fantasy—"the rehearsal stage on which we prepare for the roles we want."

The basic theory of Gestalt therapy is that maturation is a continuous growth process in which environmental support is transformed into self-support. In healthy development, the infant mobilizes and learns to use his own resources. A neurosis develops in an environment which does not facilitate the maturation process. Development is perverted into patterns designed to control the environment by manipulation. At the core of the neurosis is an existential "impasse," a situation in which no environmental support is forthcoming, and the individual clings to the status quo, held back by a "catastrophic expectation" which prevents risk taking.

Virginia Satir, a founder of the Mental Research Institute in Palo Alto, California, conducts our family-therapy programs and workshops for couples. In her experiential sessions, she seeks four results from participants: heightened individual self-esteem; improved communication, particularly of a nonverbal nature, between couples and their children; an understanding of the couple or family as a system with a set of expectations; and a developed potential for new growth in any relationship.

A series of exercises—including "eye-alogues," where feelings are expressed to another solely with the eyes—art expression, encounter methods, and role-playing are used in their workshops to achieve what Virginia Satir considers a "creative marriage." In her conjoint family therapy, for example, she may ask family members to take each other's roles and thereby experience various points of view. She urges participants toward full understanding and expression of their feelings and a resolution of the conflict between intimacy and autonomy. She puts it like this: "In every marriage there is a 'me,' a 'you,' and an 'us.' Once people fully realize this, they can

tion to physical manifestations of inner conflicts, making the "patient" aware of the sound of his own voice, his breathing, and his posture.

A psychologist who also was trained by Max Reinhardt as a theatre director, Perls relies on props and on his uncanny sense of seeing a person's basic stance in the world. The props include a "hot seat" in which patients sit, a vacant chair which serves as a "screen" for the patient's projections and a focal point for his dialogue with other parts of his own body, and video-tape equipment for feedback. In a typical session, Perls may ask a patient to verbalize and to act out

a dream or fantasy, telling him to play all parts of the dream in the present tense. At one point, he may shift a dialogue between the patient and that part of his dream "sitting" in the vacant chair into a conversation between the patient's right and left hands.

Such dialogues call attention to basic polarities in the patient's personality and usually, after the patient has carried out his dialogue, bring him to the impasse point at which the dialogue ceases and he is in a panic-stricken whirl, unable to leave what Perls calls "the merry-go-round of compulsive repetition." Now the patient is stuck, unable to crack begin to think of totally new ways of self- and other-validation."

William Schutz, the director of the Group Process Section of the Albert Einstein School of Medicine before joining Esalen a couple of months ago, is a specialist in interpersonal behavior. His encounter groups cover many methods of exploring the human potential, including fantasy, body awareness, and psychodrama. In one exercise, for example, group members link arms in a circle and one person tries to break out of the ring, experiencing frustration and anger when he fails to do so. The group then may hold a person and throw him into the air to help him feel his passivity, or a pair may engage in an arm-wrestling contest. In another exercise, the members of a group lie on the floor in a circle, their heads together, to create a giant dandelion. Schutz gives them a situation, and they form a train of fantasy together. Afterwards they talk together about the fantasy and what it reveals. Schutz's goal is to amplify feelings and to help turn suspicious, hostile, or dull individuals into trusting and aware people capable of more meaningful lives.

We have grown a bit since our first tentative programs in the Fall of 1962; 4000 people come to the Institute at Big Sur every year now, and our new San Francisco center attracted 8000 people during its first three weeks of operation.

In September of last year, we began our first residential program, an attempt to combine elements of seminar programs into a unified nine months' curriculum. This Fall, 21 resident fellows—who include the curriculum expert from an Eastern state university, a Duke graduate student preparing a doctor thesis on meditation, and a theologian from a Jesuit college—began our second residential program in self-awareness under the direction of Schutz and Edward Maupin, formerly on the staff of the Neuropsychiatric Institute at UCLA.

It remains to be seen whether the moments of healing and moments of illumination which occur regularly in weekend workshops can be sustained on a long-term basis.

Richard Price, co-founder of Esalen, is working with R. D. Laing of London's Tavistock Clinic on a proposal to establish a Blowout Center at Big Sur, where a small, selected group of psychotics will be treated as persons on voyages of discovery and allowed to go through their psychoses. It appears that the nonpara-

At Esalen, it's "touch and go," with quiet contemplation, exercises to quicken sensory awareness and tone the body, in addition to seminars and encounter groups.

Resident seminars and workshops are becoming increasingly popular. Philosopher Abraham Kaplan (below), conducts a five-day intense-encounter workshop at Kairos, a new, Esalen-like center at Rancho Santa Fe, California.

doing, and some might agree with Abraham M. Maslow, who called Esalen "in *potential,* the most important educational institution in the world," many others consider us little more than kooks and cultists.

There are risks in an organization like Esalen, but we prefer risks to the status quo. Some of our approaches will hold up with passage of time; others will be discarded as foolish or useless. But no approach is too far out to be tried here. We intend to be on the cutting edge.

ꜰ

...oid, acute schizophrenic break is relatively short and is followed by a re-integrative process, so that the individual returns from his "trip" with a higher IQ than at the beginning. We hope to find new ways to make such breaks valuable, function-heightening experiences.

It is hard for us at Esalen to assess our impact on the scientific community. We are aware that Esalen is controversial. While many people respect what we are

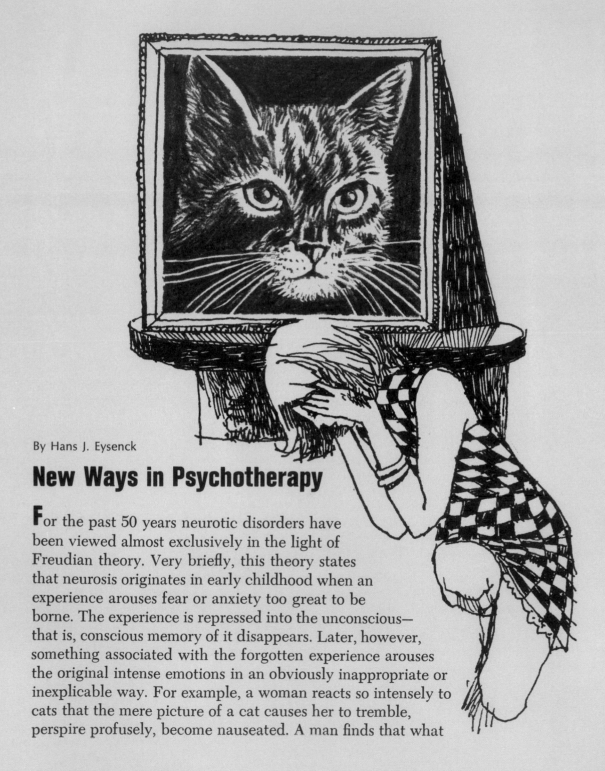

By Hans J. Eysenck

New Ways in Psychotherapy

For the past 50 years neurotic disorders have been viewed almost exclusively in the light of Freudian theory. Very briefly, this theory states that neurosis originates in early childhood when an experience arouses fear or anxiety too great to be borne. The experience is repressed into the unconscious—that is, conscious memory of it disappears. Later, however, something associated with the forgotten experience arouses the original intense emotions in an obviously inappropriate or inexplicable way. For example, a woman reacts so intensely to cats that the mere picture of a cat causes her to tremble, perspire profusely, become nauseated. A man finds that what he has regarded as a natural though unusual fastidiousness has gradually been transformed into an obsession that makes it impossible for him to touch anything handled by others—money, doorknobs, tableware, books.

According to prevailing Freudian theory, neurosis can be cured only through a therapy which, by painstaking probing in the course of many sessions, uncovers the repressed experience as well as the unconscious motives and conflicts associated with it. Now able to understand why the experience aroused such overwhelmingly painful emotions, the pa-

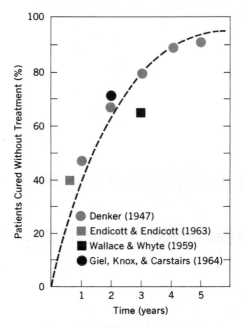

Spontaneous remission occurs when the symptoms of neurotic patients disappear of their own accord—without the "benefit" of psychotherapy. Here a curve of the spontaneous remission rate (dotted line) is fitted to the combined data of four independent studies of patients cured without treatment.

tient is cured. Without treatment, it is claimed, neurotic disorders will persist or get worse. Ridding the patient of the symptoms while ignoring the underlying causes will only complicate matters: There will be a relapse, or the underlying fears and anxieties will attach themselves to a different object, or a different set of symptoms will appear. The patient may, for example, be relieved of a neurotic fear of rats only to find himself even more seriously incapacitated by a fear of automobiles; the patient cured of his claustrophobia may be plunged into a deep depression.

It is generally believed that even though psychotherapeutic treatment may take years, it is thorough and will eventually lead to a permanent cure. These beliefs have seldom been con-

tested and there is virtually unanimous agreement—even among adherents of non-analytic psychotherapy—that neurotic disorders can best be understood and treated on the basis of Freudian or neo-Freudian theory.

The casual reader of modern textbooks of psychiatry or clinical psychology is scarcely aware that there is, in fact, no evidence to support Freudian theory, while there is considerable evidence that all the foregoing beliefs are actually false.

I wish to discuss only briefly some of the studies which disprove psychoanalytic dogma, and to focus on "behavior therapy," a new approach which offers an effective alternative, both in theory and in practice, to conventional "insight" or "dynamic" psychotherapy, and that promises at long last to bring scientific method to bear on a field until now ruled by faith and dogma.

Does Psychoanalysis Cure?

One of the most striking features of neurotic disorders is the fact that in the majority of cases they are subject to spontaneous remission—that is, in time the symptoms disappear without therapy. I have combined the results of four independent studies to show the percentage of severely neurotic patients whose symptoms disappeared without any psychiatric treatment whatsoever [*see illustration this page*].

In three of the studies, spontaneous remissions occurred in from 65 to 75 percent of the cases over the passage of two to three years; in the fourth, a long-term study, 90 percent of the patients were free of symptoms at the end of five years. There is much other evidence in the literature to substantiate the claim that neurotic symptoms sooner or later disappear spontaneously in a great number of cases.

This raises a serious question about the effectiveness of psychotherapy. To prove its worth, proponents of psychotherapy must show that the percentage of cures following treatment is significantly greater than the percentage of spontaneous remissions. In 1952 I analyzed a number of reports on the effects of psychotherapy and found that the figures for cures did not differ from those for spontaneous remissions. Statistically speaking, therefore, treatment had contributed nothing. Analyses of later studies on adults and children, including much more data, tended to support this conclusion.

It might nevertheless be argued that even though psychotherapy does not

produce more cures than does the passage of time alone, the cures it does achieve are more permanent—that is, there are fewer relapses. However, a 10-year follow-up study by Johannes Cremarius showed that this is not the case. Of more than 600 neurotic patients treated by various methods, including psychoanalysis, 73 percent were considered to be improved or cured when treatment ended. Eight to ten years later, only 25 percent of this group were still considered improved or cured. In other words, of those patients declared to have benefited from treatment, two out of three suffered a relapse.

To date, then, there is no real evidence for the effectiveness of psychotherapy—as is now admitted even by leading psychoanalysts and psychotherapists—though with further search such evidence might be uncovered.

Pavlov's Dogs

The theory and practice of behavior therapy are grounded on modern knowledge of learning and conditioning. Classical behaviorist theory holds (1) that behavior can be understood as a response to a stimulus, and (2) that most behavior is learned through a process called *conditioning* by which links are established between certain stimuli and responses.

To illuminate the meaning of these terms, let us recall Pavlov's salivating dogs. A hungry dog responds to food in its mouth (an unconditioned stimulus) by salivating (an unconditioned response). This is but one example of the many "built-in" responses or reflexes over which the organism has little or no control. Pavlov found that if an experimenter consistently rings a bell (a neutral stimulus) just before he puts the food into the dog's mouth, the dog will gradually associate the sound of the bell with the presence of the food. Eventually the sound of the bell (the conditioned stimulus) will alone be sufficient to cause the dog to salivate (now a conditioned response).

Much behavior is learned through conditioning of this sort; it is involuntary and may take place without the organism's being aware of it. But it must be *reinforced*; if it is not, the conditioned response will *extinguish*. In other words if, after the dog is conditioned to salivate at the sound of the bell, the bell is repeatedly rung but no food appears, the association between the conditioned and the unconditioned stimuli will extinguish and the dog will no longer salivate at the sound of the bell. These prin-

a conditioned salivary reflex

they were fed was made more and more similar to the original traumatic situation, by adding, one at a time, the stimuli associated with fear. Now, however, each stimulus became associated with gratification, and since gratification is incompatible with fear, Wolpe was able to extinguish the fear-response and restore the cats to apparent normality.

ciples of conditioning and extinction are fundamental to classical conditioning, the basis for much of behavior therapy.

"Unscaring" Scared Cats

Behavior therapy has its roots in the early studies of John B. Watson, Mary Jones, and other behaviorists, but it may be said to date from the end of the 1950's with the publication of Joseph Wolpe's book, *Psychotherapy by Reciprocal Inhibition,* and my paper, "Behavior Therapy." Since Wolpe's method is an important part—though only a part —of the general theory and practice of behavior therapy, it serves as an excellent starting point for discussion.

Increasingly dissatisfied by his lack of results with conventional psychotherapy, Wolpe set out to see if the behaviorist approach, so successful in changing the behavior of laboratory animals, could erase neurotic behavior in humans. In a series of exploratory experiments with cats, Wolpe gave them a mild electric shock at the same time he presented them with a variety of neutral stimuli such as a toy mouse, a rubber ball, flashing lights. Thus he was able to induce a "neurotic" fear of the previously neutral stimuli. He then conducted another series of experiments to see if he could erase their neurotic fear by reversing the conditioning process. He concluded that the most satisfactory treatment was to expose them to the fear-provoking stimuli under conditions which were incompatible with fear.

He began by feeding his cats in a "safe" environment in which there were no fear-provoking stimuli. Gradually, through a series of carefully worked-out stages, the safe environment in which

Just Relax

Wolpe next applied this approach, which he called *desensitization,* to problems of human neurosis. To start with, he looked for a practicable method of desensitizing his patients. He needed to find a response which would be incompatible with fear or anxiety. His search led him to the work of E. Jacobson who had developed a method for relaxing patients, and who recommended it as a treatment for neurotic disorders. Because it is impossible to be relaxed and anxious at the same time, Wolpe decided to use relaxation as the essential response which might damp down anxiety reactions in his patients.

At first he attempted to relax his patients in the presence of the objects which were producing their fear. But it was soon evident that this procedure would be both tedious and impractical. Not only would it involve gathering a large collection of objects to meet his patients' varied needs, but what of the patient who was terrified of horses, or was compelled to dive under a table at the sound of an airplane? Furthermore, in some patients the anxiety was not associated with an object but with an experience—for example, riding in an elevator or a subway.

Wolpe therefore began to experiment with the imaginary evocation of the anxiety-provoking stimuli, a method which was easy to manipulate in the consulting room and allowed a great deal of flexibility in planning treatment. In practice, Wolpe's desensitization tech-

nique works as follows. Before the desensitization treatment is begun, the therapist takes a general history of the patient and a complete history of the disorder. Next, he attempts to reduce or eliminate any conflicts or anxiety-producing situations in the patient's life which do not directly bear on his neurotic symptoms. Then he trains the patient in Jacobson's method of progressive relaxation where the subject is taught to relax first one muscle, then another, progressing from one part of the body to other parts. Finally, patient and therapist discuss all the stimuli and situations which might possibly produce anxiety, grading them in a hierarchy ranging from the most to the least disturbing.

a kitten playing with a ball of wool.. Pouncing on it

The Lady and the Cat

Now the patient is ready for desensitization. Let us illustrate this process through the story of a woman who suffers unbearable anxiety at the sight of a cat. In the course of discussions with her, the therapist has found that she is least disturbed at seeing a small kitten in the arms of a child. When treatment begins she is asked therefore to imagine this sight as clearly and vividly as she can. Though she feels some anxiety, it is bearable. Still keeping the picture firmly in mind, she is instructed to relax as she has been taught. She finds that when she is thoroughly relaxed her anxiety disappears. She repeats this exercise in subsequent sessions until she never experiences any anxiety while imagining a kitten in the arms of a child. Now the therapist asks her to imagine a slightly more disturbing situation—a kitten playing with a ball of wool, pouncing on it, biting it, and so on—while she relaxes. When this imaginary situation ceases to provoke anxiety, the therapist asks her to evoke a still more disturbing image, moving up the hierarchy which had been established prior to treatment. Eventually she is able to imagine with tranquility a big black tom cat stalking through the grass or curled up on her bed. And finally at the end of treatment, she is able to confront cats in real life as tranquilly as she can evoke their images in the consulting room.

Indeed, at each stage of treatment she finds she can transfer to real life her new ability to tolerate the stimulus. Thus when our hypothetical patient reaches the stage at which she can evoke the image of a playful kitten without anxiety in the therapist's office, she no longer experiences anxiety at the actual sight of a kitten frolicking in the neighbor's yard.

In behaviorist terms desensitization, as well as the other therapeutic procedures used by Wolpe, is based on a general principle which he states as follows: "If a response antagonistic to anxiety can be made to occur in the presence of anxiety-provoking stimuli so that it is accompanied by a complete or partial suppression of the anxiety responses, the bond between the stimuli and the anxiety responses will be weakened." In somewhat simpler terms, we can say that because relaxation suppresses, or inhibits anxiety, the lady was desensitized to cats by gradually conditioning herself to respond with relaxation. The "cat-anxiety" association has been replaced by a "cat-relaxation" association.

Does Behavior Therapy Work?

Wolpe claimed that desensitization was not only much more effective than psychotherapy, but was also quicker. In an unselected series of more than 300 cases he found that 90 percent were improved or cured after an average of 30 sessions. Reports by his students and followers on the whole corroborate his findings. None of these clinical studies, however, included the proper control groups—patients with similar disorders who were not treated, or patients treated by other methods. Thus questions about the superiority of desensitization to psychotherapy could not be effectively an-

swered in terms of percentages, treatment-times, and so on.

Recently, however, James Humphery carried out a study specifically designed to compare the results of behavior therapy with those of traditional psychotherapy. Formerly director of a child guidance clinic and a psychotherapist of many years' experience, Humphery was trained in behavior therapy specifically in order to conduct the investigation. His subjects were 71 children who

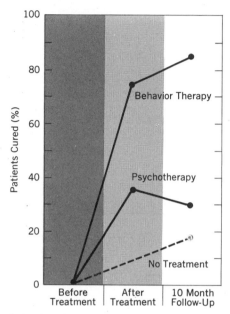

Behavior therapy is more effective than psychotherapy in curing psychiatric disorders. Follow-up diagnoses indicate that the cures produced by behavior therapy are more permanent than those produced by psychotherapy.

had been referred to London child guidance clinics for all types of disorders except brain damage and psychosis. The children were divided into matched groups: The 34 in the control group received no treatment of any kind; the 37 children in the treated group were then divided into two groups, one of which received behavior therapy and the other traditional psychotherapy. A five-point rating scale was used to establish the severity of each child's disorder (his clinical status) and to evaluate the success of the treatment. Each child was rated on this scale at the beginning of the study; the children in the treatment group were rated immediately after treatment, while those in the control group were rated 10 months after the start of the experiment. Experienced psychiatrists, who did not know to which group a child had been assigned, did the rating. The decision to end treatment was made in consultation between Humphery and the psychiatrist assigned to the case. A rise of two or more points

on the clinical rating scale was taken as an arbitrary criterion of "cure."

All children were again rated 10 months later. Seventy-five percent of the children who received behavior therapy were rated cured at the close of treatment, as compared with only 35 percent of those who received psychotherapy. At the 10-month follow-up, 85 percent of those who had received behavior therapy were rated as cured—an increase of 10 percentage points—but only 29 percent of those in the psychotherapy group were still considered cured. Of those who had received no treatment at all, 18 percent were found to be cured [see illustration this page].

These results are even more impressive when differences in the length of treatment are taken into account. The children receiving psychotherapy required 21 sessions spread over 31 weeks before it was thought that treatment could be terminated, but those receiving behavior therapy required only nine sessions during 18 weeks. Thus behavior therapy cured twice as many cases as did psychotherapy, and in less than half the number of sessions. By happenstance, moreover, the children assigned to the behavior therapy group were the more seriously ill, which would seem to militate against the success of behavior therapy. On the other hand, since the children given psychotherapy began treatment with a higher clinical-status rating they were less likely to achieve the two-point rise necessary to denote cure. These factors were undoubtedly important in accounting for the startling difference between the two groups. It should be noted, however, that the percentage of cures resulting from psychotherapy in this experiment did not differ from that usually obtained in the clinics involved in the study.

Interesting as the study may be, it can be criticized on various grounds. From the standpoint of this article, however, the most interesting focus for examination is the assumption that the crucial therapeutic element for the children treated with behavior therapy was the *combination* of desensitization and relaxation. This may not have been the case. At least three alternative hypotheses could be put forward. One, simple extinction might be involved. According to the laws of conditioning, if the anxiety-provoking stimulus is repeatedly evoked without any distressing consequences, the response should eventually be extinguished; thus we might conclude that desensitization—without relaxation—is sufficient to produce a cure. Two, since relaxation lowers the intensity of all responses (drive level), this in itself would reduce the intensity of the conditioned fear-response and might suffice to bring about a cure. Hence relaxation—without desensitization—might be the crucial therapeutic element. Three, it might be that the sympathetic attention of a person in authority is, by itself, all that is needed. Indeed, this view has often been expressed by those who claim that behavior therapy embodies important but standard psychotherapeutic procedures. For example, during the preliminary interviews the behavior therapist, despite his radically different approach to treatment, in fact employs such elements of psychotherapy as sympathy, acceptance of deviant behavior, and movement toward insight.

Clearly, questions such as these cannot be answered in the "clinical trial" type of investigation but must be dealt with in formal experimental studies. Fortunately, a number of such studies have been made in the last 10 years.

Neurosis in the Laboratory

Behavior therapists, taking these problems into the laboratory, have designed experimental studies previously thought impossible in so complex a field as human emotion and interaction. To compare the effects of differing treatments, it is essential that the pre- and post-treatment states of the patient be measured as accurately as possible. Studies have usually focused therefore on such relatively simple disorders as phobias for snakes and spiders.

Is it possible to measure fear with any degree of precision? To be sure, the patient confronted by a snake can be asked to rate his own fear on a numbered scale ranging from "intense" to "slight." But while his subjective feelings are certainly relevant, they are not objectively "observable" enough to meet scientific criteria. Objective measures of fear, based on involuntary physiological reactions, have therefore been devised. We are all aware that fear is accompanied by a temporary increase in heartbeat (our hearts "pound"), by a temporary restriction or collapse of capillary blood vessels (we "turn white"), by profuse sweating, a dry mouth, and other changes—all of which can be measured with suitable instruments. Indeed the polygraph, or so-called lie detector, does nothing more than measure several physiological concomitants of changes in emotional reaction.

In addition, it is possible to measure a patient's actual behavior vis-a-vis the

fear object—his *approach-avoidance* behavior. Fright is accompanied by an involuntary retreat from stimulus. How near will the patient approach the feared object? Will he touch it for a moment only? Will he handle it?

We can thus measure with some degree of accuracy the behavior we wish to modify and the degree of our success. This approach has enabled researchers to isolate specific components of behavior therapy and see which is the active ingredient. A study conducted by Stanley Rachman at Maudsley Hospital illustrates how this can be accomplished.

Rachman attempted to answer some of the questions posed by Wolpe's "reciprocal inhibition" theory, using as subjects a number of persons who feared spiders. He divided his subjects into four groups. One received behavior therapy (desensitization plus relaxation), a second desensitization only, a third relaxation only, and a fourth no treat-

ment at all. Rachman used two independent measures of anxiety: the subjects' own estimates of their fear and a scale based on the subjects' physical avoidance of spiders [*see illustrations on this page*].

The results show very clearly that only the *combination* of desensitization and relaxation significantly decreased the fear of spiders.

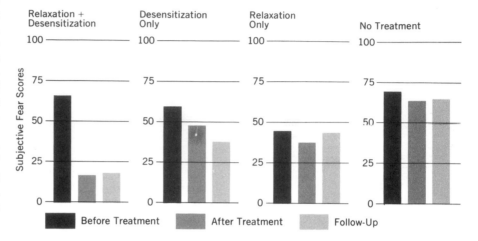

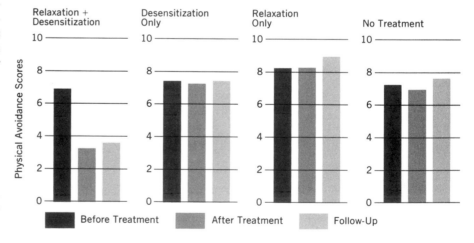

The importance of both desensitization and relaxation in behavior therapy is shown with patients suffering from an extreme fear of spiders. The effectiveness of desensitization + relaxation is compared with desensitization only, relaxation only, and no treatment at all (controls). Estimates of fear were obtained before treatment, after treatment, and in a follow-up evaluation. Two measures of fear were employed: the patients' own estimates of their fear (top) and a scale of the physical avoidance of spiders (bottom).

Behavior Therapy vs. Psychotherapy

In addition to testing out the effectiveness of different components of behavior therapy, recent laboratory experiments have enabled us to compare different treatments. The work of Gordon Paul at the University of Illinois is an example. Persons suffering from severe stage fright were divided into four groups: some received the desensitization-relaxation therapy, some received conventional psychotherapy, some received a placebo (in this case, non-therapy-oriented meetings between patient and

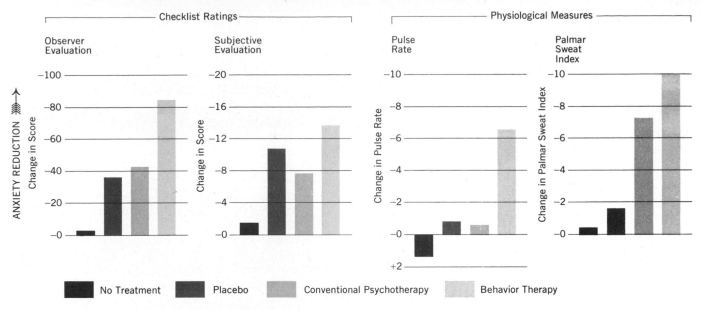

Observer
Evaluation

Subjective
Evaluation

Pulse
Rate

Palmar
Sweat
Index

No Treatment   Placebo   Conventional Psychotherapy   Behavior Therapy

Groups of patients suffering from anxiety caused by severe stage fright were given conventional psychotherapy, behavior therapy (desensitization + relaxation), placebo treatment (nontherapy oriented meetings with a therapist), or no treatment at all (controls). Anxiety was measured before and after treatment by observer and subjective checklist ratings and by pulse rate and palmar sweating physiological measures. (Scale values are not identical.) In all cases, behavior therapy produced the greatest amount of anxiety reduction.

therapist), and an untreated control group. Paul used four general measures of anxiety: (1) observable manifestations of anxiety during public speaking, as rated by trained observers; (2) the subjects' own ratings of their experienced anxiety; (3) pulse rate; and (4) palmar sweating.

Ratings made before and after treatment demonstrated that on all four criteria the group receiving behavior therapy showed the greatest average reduction of anxiety [see illustration above]. Indeed, only in this group was there a noticeable reduction in pulse rate after treatment, while pulse rate actually increased in the control group. Results with psychotherapy and the placebo were about the same, while the control group showed little change. It should be added that the behavior therapy was carried out by psychotherapists (specially trained in Wolpe's method for this experiment) who continued to prefer psychotherapy and its associated doctrines.

Gordon Paul and Donald Shannon later carried out a similar study in which they added a fifth experimental condition: Five patients were given behavior therapy as a group. This treatment was as effective as individual treatment. In addition, it was found that the academic performance of those given behavior therapy greatly improved, indicating that the specific reduction in anxiety achieved in the experiment may have generalized to other life situations.

Many more questions raised by behavior therapy are being studied in sim-ilar experiments, questions such as: Which is more effective, the presentation of the actual anxiety-producing stimulus or its imaginary evocation? Is it better to space the treatments or to compress them into short periods of time? How quickly does desensitization transfer to real-life situations?

These questions have not yet been definitively answered. Nor can it yet be claimed that the experiments I have described clearly show the superiority of behavior therapy. What may, I think, be claimed is that for the first time therapeutic methods are being tested in properly designed and controlled experiments, using objective criteria of known reliability. Vital questions which were until now discussed only in a subjective and anecdotal fashion are being brought under experimental control.

"Treatment Machines"

Psychoanalysts hold that an essential element in therapy is the transference—the interaction in which the patient transfers to the analyst his feelings toward significant persons in his life. Ex-perimental studies of Wolpe's method suggest, however, that since the important ingredient in behavior therapy is the combination of conditioned stimulus and relaxation, the presence of the therapist may not be necessary. Could learning machines be substituted for the therapist? Properly programmed, they might be used both to teach the patient how to relax and to carry him through the desensitization process, based as it is on the patient's visualization of the fear-provoking stimulus.

Machines may indeed replace the therapist. Peter Lang, at the University of Wisconsin, has shown not only that behavior therapy can be programmed, but that it can be as effective as person-

ally administered treatment. So far this has been demonstrated only with patients suffering from neuroses involving a single symptom, but an extension of this approach is inevitable. In the first place, there are very few trained behavior therapists and very many neurotics. Any method that shortens treatment and makes it possible to treat more patients is sure to be employed. In the second place, once patient and therapist have constructed the stimulus "hierarchies," the rest of the treatment is repetitive and mechanical. Most therapists would, it seems safe to say, gladly turn this part of their work over to a machine.

To be sure, much more study is needed before we can know whether, and to what extent, treatment by machine is feasible with the more complex neuroses, or with psychoses. It is possible, too, that the use of machines will be governed by the patient's personality-type or emotional needs. It might be that introverts would do well with programmed treatments while extroverts, or those particularly in need of personal support and human contact, would prefer to work only with the therapist.

Neurotic Symptoms or Bad Habits?

So far in this discussion we have dealt only with one type of neurotic disorder and with one type of behavior therapy. This is justifiable because most neurotic patients who seek psychiatric help are suffering from disorders which produce distressing symptoms—negative emotional states such as anxiety, phobic fear, depression, obsessional or compulsive reactions, and so on. In all these disorders —which I have called "disorders of the *first* kind"—behavior therapists hold that classical conditioning is implicated, either through a single traumatic experience or through a long series of subtraumatic events in which emotions of terror or anxiety are associated with some previously neutral stimulus.

Behavior therapists agree that neurotic symptoms are learned. That is, they are neither innate nor due to lesions in the nervous system. Consequently, any explanation of neurotic behavior ought to proceed from the firm basis of our knowledge, gained in the laboratory, of learning and conditioning. According to these theories, there is no "neurosis" or "complex," as such, which causes the symptoms. There are only symptoms. A patient's response of overwhelming anxiety to so neutral a stimulus as the picture of cat is, for example, in a real and literal sense *learned*. It is a "bad" (or maladaptive) habit, acquired through the processes of classical conditioning. The so-called symptom *is* the neurosis— I say "so-called" because the anxiety-response is not in fact symptomatic of anything. Behavior therapists are not pained, therefore, when psychoanalysts accuse them of curing only the symptoms. They answer that there is no disease other than the symptoms. And in any case, as someone has said, "It ill becomes those who cannot *even* cure the symptom to complain that others *only* cure the symptom."

Learning and conditioning theory can explain the otherwise puzzling fact of spontaneous remission. It has often been said that "time the great healer" is responsible for such cures. Clearly, however, it is not the mere passage of time which alone works the cure. It is the events which transpire during time. What are those events? If the symptom is in fact a conditioned response, then the response should gradually be extinguished if the sufferer, over a period of time, encounters the original fear-provoking stimulus without its being reinforced by a traumatic event. The woman who is terrified of cats will, from time to time, encounter cats, and if nothing happens to reinforce her fear it should gradually die away.

In many cases, however, this cannot come about because the patient refuses to encounter the conditioned stimulus. By taking great pains to avoid it he evades the possibility of testing reality. Furthermore, each time he avoids the stimulus he is consolidating the very behavior pattern which is the neurosis.

A striking example of this is the case of a woman we recently treated for a cat phobia so severe she was unable to leave her room. The phobia had developed when, as a very young girl, her father drowned her favorite kitten before her eyes. So traumatic was the experience that every time she saw a cat

she ran away. Doing so reduced her anxiety—and reinforced her avoidance behavior. The conditioned habit, feeding on itself, became so dominating that eventually she immured herself in her room. Behavior therapy, by gradually exposing her to the sight of cats while she was thoroughly relaxed, completely restored her to a normal life within a few weeks; there was no relapse, nor was there any indication that her anxiety had been transferred to some other object or had expressed itself in some other form.

what a pretty shoe

This freedom from relapse and symptom-substitution after behavior therapy has also been observed many times by other therapists, even by some who were unsympathetic to this approach. Nevertheless, long-term, follow-up studies are needed to put this point beyond argument.

Aversion Therapy

In addition to disorders of the first kind involving distressing symptoms such as anxiety, phobic fear, or depression, there are neurotic disorders of the *second* kind. They may arise when some socially desirable conditioning has failed to occur, as with psychopaths or sociopaths. Such people are characterized by an almost complete lack of social responsibility; they are the pathological liars, or those who steal or murder regardless of the fact that they will almost certainly be found out and punished.

Disorders of the second kind also arise when some socially undesirable or

unacceptable behavior has become associated with positive emotions such as pleasure, comfort, happiness, sexual arousal. The most obvious examples are associated with the sexual impulse—homosexuality, fetishism, transvestism, among others. For instance, an ordinarily neutral stimulus such as a shoe may accidentally become associated with sexual pleasure

and through subsequent reinforcement come to serve as a conditioned stimulus which calls forth a sexual response (shoe fetishism).

In cases of this kind the aim of the therapist is to break the association between the conditioned stimulus—a woman's shoe, for example—and the conditioned response—aberrant sexual satisfaction. The dissociation process is often called "aversion therapy," and is the opposite of desensitization. In desensitization therapy, the link between the conditioned stimulus (a cat) and the conditioned response (fear) is replaced by a new link between the conditioned stimulus and a pleasant response (relaxation). In aversion therapy, the link between the conditioned stimulus (a woman's shoe) and the pleasant sexual response is broken by linking the shoe-stimulus to an unpleasant experience.

The classic example of aversion therapy is the use of apomorphine to cure alcoholism. The patient takes the drug, which causes nausea and vomiting. Just before the onset of nausea, he is given a drink of liquor. The drink (conditioned stimulus) is now followed by a very distressing conditioned response—nausea. Behaviorist theory predicts that after many such repetitions, the mere sight of a drink will evoke the newly conditioned response.

In spite of its apparent crudity, aversion therapy works surprisingly well if properly carried out. However, research reports show that much useless effort has been expended by medical people with little knowledge of conditioning procedures. To take but one example: In treating alcoholism many would-be therapists have administered the drink *after* nausea has set in. Behaviorists know that conditioning will be effective only if the conditioned stimulus *precedes* the response to be conditioned; backward conditioning just does not occur.

Modern behavior therapists prefer to use electric shock rather than drugs in aversion therapy. The intensity of the unconditioned stimulus (the shock) can be much better controlled; it is less messy; and it can be administered at a precisely chosen moment. Where the patient urgently requests such treatment, electric shock has been used to cure certain sexual deviations, including homosexuality and transvestism.

Typically in such treatment, while the male homosexual is looking at pictures of nude males, he is given a moderately intense shock. The combination of the male picture (conditioned stimulus) with shock (unconditioned stimulus) should lead to an aversion to men as sex objects (conditioned response).

The treatment is not yet complete, however. The next step is to condition a positive response to women: the picture of the nude male is suddenly replaced by the picture of a nude female—and the shock is terminated. Since the cessation of shock is pleasurable, a favorable response to women is now established.

Techniques such as these offer a potentially powerful therapeutic approach. However, the effectiveness of these conditioning methods cannot as yet be judged because too few cases have been studied and there have not been enough long-term, follow-up studies.

"Operant" Conditioning

No article on behavior therapy would be complete without some discussion of *operant conditioning* as a technique for changing behavior. Because the theories of operant conditioning underlie such revolutionary new pedagogical methods as the use of teaching machines, as well as new approaches to therapy, I should like to describe this method briefly.

Operant conditioning was originally worked out by B. F. Skinner who succeeded in shaping the behavior of pigeons by reinforcing bits of behavior that were originally quite random. In one of Skinner's early experiments, he fed a hungry pigeon whenever it happened to stretch its neck above a predetermined point. Gradually it "caught on" and spent most of its time raising its head just as high as it could. This method of changing behavior is also called "instrumental conditioning," since the organism's behavior is instrumental itself in obtaining the "reward."

The notion that psychotics can learn to control their delusions or their unacceptable behavior is rejected by almost all knowledgeable people. Nevertheless, the technique of shaping behavior, originally worked out with pigeons, has been used with startling success to change the behavior of psychotic adults and disturbed children. Hardcore schizophrenics, considered hopeless, who had been vegetating for years in the back wards of mental hospitals, have been taught to relinquish the behavior which identified them as insane. An example is reported by Colin Blakemore of the Maudsley Hospital.

A middle-aged woman, suffering from severe paranoid delusions that communists were following her everywhere trying to kill her, was asked to wear earphones during her meetings with the therapist. Every time the woman mentioned her paranoid ideas, the therapist pressed a button which enabled him to deliver an unpleasant noise into the earphones. Whenever she talked normally, the therapist turned off the noise. Gradually the paranoid topic dropped out of her conversation completely—not only in the presence of the therapist, but in the ward as well.

As further proof of the efficacy of this technique, Blakemore reversed the process. He brought back her paranoid talk by punishing her whenever she spoke of normal topics; then he again taught her to leave communists and persecution out of her conversation. Thus he showed that by employing this technique he could bring her talk under complete experimental control.

This experiment, like many similar operant conditioning experiments with mental patients, raises more questions than it answers. Hopefully, these questions will be answered in the future with more experiments using many subjects and rigorous controls. In the meantime, however, operant conditioning has opened many new and undreamed-of avenues to the therapist.

Action Before Thought?

Some of the most important consequences of behavior therapy are its effects on theory. For example, it has long been held that thought precedes and controls action. Behavior therapy suggests that the contrary may often be true, so that changing a person's behavior through some form of conditioning process may actually change his thought or mental set.

For example, Teodoro Ayllon, at Anna State Hospital in Illinois, reports the case of a woman who was committed to a mental hospital because she would not eat for fear her husband would poison her. She refused to feed herself in the hospital and had to be fed by a nurse. Finding that she was very fastidious about her personal appearance and her clothing, Ayllon told the nurse to spill food on the woman's dress whenever she fed her, and to explain that it was very difficult to feed another person. Gradually the patient began to feed herself—and at the same time her delusions about being poisoned began to disappear. Her *actions* in feeding herself had changed her *thought* that she would be poisoned.

Of course, not too much should be read into isolated experiments of this sort. On the other hand, when we keep in mind that psychotherapists have had almost no success with cases such as these, it seems reasonable to suggest that behavior therapists are opening doors and windows, bringing fresh air into a room in which the atmosphere has grown very heavy, stale, and musty.

Science and Psychotherapy

The work of the behavior therapists has important implications for the treatment of neurotic and psychotic disorders, and has opened new paths toward understanding them. I would like to suggest, though, that their chief contribution has been to bring this hitherto mysterious realm under the discipline of scientific method. It is possible, though unlikely, that all the theories of conditioning discussed in this paper are wrong. But by insisting that both theory and practice be experimentally tested, behavior therapists are trying to insure that errors will be exposed, and that new evidence will be obtained on which new

and better theories can be based.

Behaviorist objections to psychoanalysis and its allied psychotherapeutic theory and practices are not based solely on opposition to Freudian *theory*. They are based on an opposition to the Freudian *approach* as well; it must be ruled out of court, as far as science is concerned, on two grounds. In the first place, Freudian theories are not stated in terms that permit them to be tested and verified; indeed it is almost impossible to think of experiments by which they could be either confirmed or disproved. In the second place, practitioners have made no effort to gather the kind of data, based on experience and observation with patients, that alone could give us a factual basis for evaluating their work. They demand belief, but they do not offer proof.

Behavior therapy is based on applying fundamental discoveries gained in the laboratory to practical problems—curing neurotic patients. The Freudian approach reversed this process. Freud's dynamic psychology was based on "discoveries" made in the course of treating patients. He and his followers universalized these ideas by applying them to all human beings. They manufactured new theories to bolster the original assumptions and attempted to fit all aspects of human behavior into their untested theoretical framework.

Behavior therapists hold that theories which attempt to explain behavior, neurotic or otherwise, should be based on fundamental scientific knowledge which is susceptible to experimental proof. They are attempting to test how well learning and conditioning theory can be applied to human problems, and they ask that judgment be suspended until the proof is conclusive. If their experiments are subject to criticism, better experiments will be designed in accordance with the criticism. If the theories do not stand up to experimental test, then better theories will be put forward to fit the established facts. As I see it, this is nothing more—nor less—than the long-delayed introduction of scientific method into the murky and emotion-ridden field of psychotherapy. In essence, psychotherapy involves changing those maladaptive emotional states and behavior patterns that interfere with adequate functioning. The new approaches and results I have described hold promise that, after 50 years in the twilight zone of unverified claims, unjustified beliefs, and passionately held dogma, psychotherapy will at last become truly scientific. ◊

VIII. social psychology

ocial psychology deals, as the name implies, with the psychology of an individual in a social context. Sometimes the social context is a single other human being with whom the subject forms a dyadic (two-person) group. In other studies the social context is two or more other people; and in still others the whole society or subculture is brought to bear as a social context upon the single individual. Occasionally, too, social psychologists deal not with single individuals but with groups of individuals who are held together by some common trait or characteristic. In these cases the behavior and characteristics of a group of individuals, such as teen-agers, are examined within the demands, benefits, stresses, and outlets provided by the social context in which the group is embedded.

More and more, the recent focus in social psychology has been upon particular problems, much as we saw in the area of personality (Part IV). The prize-winning work of Darley and Latané, for example, is a social psychological analysis of the helpfulness of individuals who find other individuals in crisis. Another example is Milgram's experimental study of the small-world problem. Here we do not have the simple problem of a dyadic group—Whom do you know?—but the question of extended and multiplied dyadic groups—Whom do your friends and your friends' friends know? As York points out in his letter reprinted in the Rebuttals, all of us have met someone who has met someone who has met former President Lyndon Johnson. He, in turn, has met Madame Chiang Kai-shek, who in turn has met such a range of Chinese that among them she could find one person who has met any single adult individual in the whole of China. In this sense, it is a tiny world, for purely on the basis of sequence of dyadic interactions each of us is linked to every single Chinese.

A different emphasis in contemporary psychology is exemplified by Leventhal's essay on changing attitudes toward smoking by fear. The area of attitude change (and methods of bringing it about) is probably the single most plowed field in social psychology today. Leventhal provides an introduction to its intricacies.

The suspected lawbreaker is faced, in Zimbardo's articles, with at least one inquisitorial policeman whose tasks, we are given to believe, include not only getting at the facts but also manipulating the suspect into a confession, if possible. The obvious ethical and moral implications are discussed, and Zimbardo also furnishes us with a hard look at the techniques employed—and he discusses some of the reasons why they are effective.

Propaganda is the art of swaying the opinions and attitudes of groups of people by selective communications to them. It is an abiding interest in social psychology and the subject of Jerome Frank's article on America's needs.

One of the techniques for promoting integration, an ultimate goal that clearly requires massive changes in attitude, is discussed by Cottle. Here the social psychologist stands apart from his subject matter in order to observe and interpret the effects of a situationally organized experience upon the behavior of individuals in a group.

Robert Rosenthal of Harvard University has long studied the effect on the outcome of scientific experiments of the expectations of the person performing the experiment. His sobering and well-documented conclusion is that what the scientist wants or expects to happen can influence what actually happens or what the scientist perceives as happening. The self-fulfilling prophecy obscures not only psychological science, which might be expected, but also the physical sciences.

Although social psychology has had fair success in analyzing, predicting, and controlling the behavior of individuals and groups, there has been relatively little work on predicting the behavior of groups as large as nations. The Feierabends write about progress in this area, and their studies have enabled them to make predictions about the stability and the behavior of nations. Although the correctness of these predictions may or may not stand the test of time, social psychology nevertheless has begun to have real success in its task of understanding the behavior of individuals and groups in a social context.

WHEN WILL PEOPLE HELP IN

by John M. Darley and Bibb Latané

Kitty Genovese is set upon by a maniac as she returns home from work at 3:00 a.m. Thirty-eight of her neighbors in Kew Gardens come to their windows when she cries out in terror; none come to her assistance even though her stalker takes over half an hour to murder her. No one even so much as calls the police. She dies.

Andrew Mormille is stabbed in the stomach as he rides the A train home to Manhattan. Eleven other riders watch the 17-year-old boy as he bleeds to death; none come to his assistance even though his attackers have left the car. He dies.

An 18-year-old switchboard operator, alone in her office in the Bronx, is raped and beaten. Escaping momentarily, she runs naked and bleeding to the street, screaming for help. A crowd of 40 passersby gathers and watches as, in broad daylight, the rapist tries to drag her back upstairs; no one interferes. Finally two policemen happen by and arrest her assailant.

Eleanor Bradley trips and breaks her leg while shopping on Fifth Avenue. Dazed and in shock, she calls for help, but the hurrying stream of executives and shoppers simply parts and flows past. After 40 minutes a taxi driver helps her to a doctor.

The shocking thing about these cases is that so many people failed to respond. If only one or two had ignored the victim, we might be able to understand their inaction. But when 38 people, or 11 people, or hundreds of people fail to help, we become disturbed. Actually, this fact that shocks us so much is itself the clue to understanding these cases. Although it seems obvious that the more people

428

A CRISIS?

who watch a victim in distress, the more likely someone will help, what really happens is exactly the opposite. If each member of a group of bystanders is aware that other people are also present, he will be less likely to notice the emergency, less likely to decide that it is an emergency, and less likely to act even if he thinks there is an emergency.

This is a surprising assertion—what we are saying is that the victim may actually be less likely to get help, the more people who watch his distress and are available to help. We shall discuss in detail the process through which an individual bystander must go in order to intervene, and we shall present the results of some experiments designed to show the effects of the number of onlookers on the likelihood of intervention.

Since we started research on bystander responses to emergencies, we have heard many explanations for the lack of intervention. "I would assign this to the effect of the megapolis in which we live, which makes closeness very difficult and leads to the alienation of the individual from the group," contributed a psychoanalyst. "A disaster syndrome," explained a sociologist, "that shook the sense of safety and sureness of the individuals involved and caused psychological withdrawal from the event by ignoring it." "Apathy," claimed others. "Indifference." "The gratification of unconscious sadistic impulses." "Lack of concern for our fellow men." "The Cold Society." All of these analyses of the person who fails to help share one characteristic; they set the indifferent witness apart from the rest of us as a different kind of person. Certainly not one of us who reads about these incidents in horror is apathetic, alienated or depersonalized. Certainly not one of us enjoys gratifying his sadistic impulses by watching others suffer. These terrifying cases in which people fail to help others certainly have no personal implications for us. That is, we might decide not to ride subways any more, or that New York isn't even "a nice place to visit," or "there ought to be a law" against apathy, but we needn't feel guilty, or re-examine ourselves, or anything like that.

Looking more closely at published descriptions of the behavior of witnesses to these incidents, the people involved begin to look a little less inhuman and a lot more like the rest of us. Although it is unquestionably true that the witnesses in the incidents above did nothing to save the victims, apathy, indifference and unconcern are not entirely accurate descriptions of their reactions. The 38 witnesses of Kitty Genovese's murder did not merely look at the scene once and then ignore it. They continued to stare out of their windows at what was going on. Caught, fascinated, distressed, unwilling to act but unable to turn away, their behavior was neither helpful nor heroic; but it was not indifferent or apathetic.

Actually, it was like crowd behavior in many other emergency situations. Car accidents, drownings, fires and attempted suicides all attract substantial numbers of people who watch the drama in helpless fascination without getting directly involved in the action. Are these people alienated and indifferent? Are the rest of us? Obviously not. Why, then, don't we act?

The bystander to an emergency has to make a series of decisions about what is happening and what he will do about it. The consequences of these decisions will determine his actions. There are three things he must do if he is to intervene: *notice* that something is happening, *interpret* that event as an emergency, and decide that he has *personal responsibility* for intervention. If he fails to notice the event, if he decides that it is not an emergency, or if he concludes that he is not personally responsible for acting, he will leave the victim unhelped. This state of affairs is shown graphically as a "decision tree" (*see illustration, right*). Only one path through this decision tree leads to intervention; all others lead to a failure to help. As we shall show, at each fork of the path in the decision tree, the presence of other bystanders may lead a person down the branch of not helping.

Noticing : The First Step

Suppose that an emergency is actually taking place; a middle-aged man has a heart attack. He stops short, clutches his chest, and staggers to the nearest building wall, where he slowly slumps to the sidewalk in a sitting position. What is the likelihood that a passerby will come to his assistance? First, the bystander has to *notice* that something is happening. The external event has to break into his thinking and intrude itself on his conscious mind. He must tear himself away from his private thoughts and pay attention to this unusual event.

But Americans consider it bad manners to look too closely at other people in public. We are taught to respect the privacy of others, and when among strangers, we do this by closing our ears and avoiding staring at others—we are embarrassed if caught doing otherwise. In a crowd, then, each person is less likely to notice the first sign of a potential emergency than when alone.

Experimental evidence corroborates this everyday observation. Darley and Latané asked college students to an interview about their reactions to urban living. As the students waited to see the interviewer, either by themselves or with two other students, they filled out a preliminary questionnaire. Solitary students often glanced idly about the room while filling out their questionnaires; those in groups, to avoid seeming rudely inquisitive, kept their eyes on their own papers.

As part of the study, we staged an emergency: smoke was released into the waiting room through a vent. Two-thirds of the subjects who were alone when the smoke appeared noticed it immediately, but only a quarter of the subjects waiting in groups saw it as quickly. Even after the room had completely filled with smoke one subject from a group of three finally looked up and exclaimed, "God! I must be smoking too much!" Although eventually all the subjects did become aware of the smoke, this study indicates that the more people present, the slower an individual may be to perceive that an emergency does exist and the more likely he is not to see it at all.

Once an event is noticed, an onlooker must decide whether or not it is truly an emergency. Emergencies

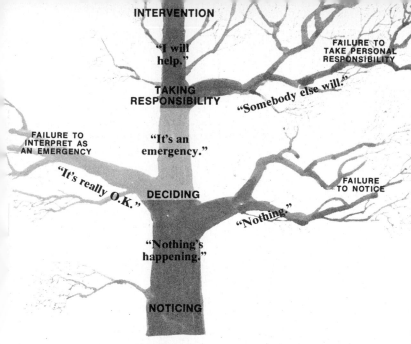

INTERVENTION

"I will help."

FAILURE TO TAKE PERSONAL RESPONSIBILITY

TAKING RESPONSIBILITY

"Somebody else will."

FAILURE TO INTERPRET AS AN EMERGENCY

"It's an emergency."

"It's really O.K."

DECIDING

FAILURE TO NOTICE

"Nothing."

"Nothing's happening."

NOTICING

THE DECISION TREE. In an emergency, a bystander must: 1) notice something is happening; 2) interpret it as an emergency; 3) decide that he has a personal responsibility for intervention.

are not always clearly labeled as such; smoke pouring from a building or into a waiting room may be caused by a fire, or it may merely indicate a leak in a steam pipe. Screams in the street may signal an assault or a family quarrel. A man lying in doorway may be having a coronary or be suffering from diabetic coma—he may simply be sleeping off a drunk. And in any unusual situation, Candid Camera may be watching.

A person trying to decide whether or not a given situation is an emergency often refers to the reactions of those around him; he looks at them to see how he should react himself. If everyone else is calm and indifferent, he will tend to remain calm and indifferent; if everyone else is reacting strongly, he will become aroused. This tendency is not merely slavish conformity; ordinarily we derive much valuable information about new situations from how others around us behave. It's a rare traveler who, in picking a roadside restaurant, chooses to stop at one with no other cars in the parking lot.

But occasionally the reactions of others provide false information. The studied nonchalance of patients in a dentist's waiting room is a poor indication of the pain awaiting them. In general, it is considered embarrassing to look overly concerned, to seem flustered, to "lose your cool" in public. When we are not alone, most of us try to seem less fearful and anxious than we really are.

In a potentially dangerous situation, then, everyone present will appear more unconcerned than they are in fact. Looking at the *apparent* impassivity and lack of reaction of the others, each person is led to believe that nothing really is wrong. Meanwhile the danger may be mounting, to the point where a single person, uninfluenced by the seeming calm of others, would react.

A crowd can thus force inaction on its members by implying, through its passivity and apparent indifference, that an event is not an emergency. Any individual in such

a crowd is uncomfortably aware that he'll look like a fool if he behaves as though it were—and in these circumstances, until someone acts, no one acts.

In the smoke-filled-room study, the smoke trickling from the wall constituted an ambiguous but potentially dangerous situation. How did the presence of other people affect a person's response to the situation? Typically, those who were in the waiting room by themselves noticed the smoke at once, gave a slight startle reaction, hesitated, got up and went over to investigate the smoke, hesitated again, and then left the room to find somebody to tell about the smoke. No one showed any signs of panic, but over three-quarters of these people were concerned enough to report the smoke.

Others went through an identical experience but in groups of three strangers. Their behavior was radically different. Typically, once someone noticed the smoke, he would look at the other people, see them doing nothing, shrug his shoulders, and then go back to his questionnaire, casting covert glances first at the smoke and then at the others. From these three-person groups, only three out of 24 people reported the smoke. The inhibiting effect of the group was so strong that the other 21 were willing to sit in a room filled with smoke rather than make themselves conspicuous by reacting with alarm and concern—this despite the fact that after three or four minutes the atmosphere in the waiting room grew most unpleasant. Even though they coughed, rubbed their eyes, tried to wave the smoke away, and opened the window, they apparently were unable to bring themselves to leave.

These dramatic differences between the behavior of people alone and those in a group indicate that the group imposed a definition of the situation upon its members which inhibited action.

"A leak in the air conditioning," said one person when we asked him what he thought caused the smoke. "Must be chemistry labs in the building." "Steam pipes." "Truth gas to make us give true answers on the questionnaire," reported the more imaginative. There were many explanations for the smoke, but they all had one thing in common: they did not mention the word fire. In defining the situation as a nonemergency, people explained to themselves why the other observers did not leave the room; they also removed any reason for action themselves. The other members of the group acted as nonresponsive models for each person—and as an audience for any "inappropriate" action he might consider. In such a situation it is all too easy to do nothing.

The results of this study clearly and strongly support the predictions. But are they general? Would the same effect show up with other emergencies, or is it limited to situations like the smoke study involving danger to the self as well as to others—or to situations in which there's no clearly defined "victim"? It may be that our college-age male subjects played "chicken" with one another to see who would lose face by first fleeing the room. It may be that groups were less likely to respond because no particular person was in danger. To see how generalizable these results are, Latané and Judith Rodin set up a second experiment, in which the emergency would cause no danger for the bystander, and in which a specific person was in trouble.

Subjects were paid $2 to participate in a survey of game and puzzle preferences conducted at Columbia by the Consumer Testing Bureau (CTB). An attractive young woman, the market-research representative, met them at the door and took them to the testing room. On the way, they passed the CTB office and through its open door they could see filing cabinets and a desk and bookcases piled high with papers. They entered the adjacent testing room, which contained a table and chairs and a variety of games, where they were given a preliminary background information and game preference questionnaire to fill out. The representative told subjects that she would be working next door in her office for about 10 minutes while they completed the questionnaires, and left by opening the collapsible curtain which divided the two rooms. She made sure the subjects knew that the curtain was unlocked, easily opened and a means of entry to her office. The representative stayed in her office, shuffling papers, opening drawers, and making enough noise to remind the subjects of her presence. Four minutes after leaving the testing area, she turned on a high fidelity stereophonic tape recorder.

If the subject listened carefully, he heard the representative climb up on a chair to reach for a stack of papers on the bookcase. Even if he were not listening carefully, he heard a loud crash and a scream as the chair collapsed and she fell to the floor. "Oh, my God, my foot....I...I...can't move it. Oh...my ankle," the representative moaned. "I...can't get this...thing...off me." She cried and moaned for about a minute longer, but the cries gradually got more subdued and controlled. Finally she muttered something about getting outside, knocked over the chair as she pulled herself up, and thumped to the door, closing it behind her as she left. This drama was of about two minutes' duration.

Some people were alone in the waiting room when the "accident" occurred. Seventy per cent of them offered to help the victim before she left the room. Many came through the curtain to offer their assistance, others simply called out to offer their help. Others faced the

emergency in pairs. Only 20 per cent of this group—eight out of 40—offered to help the victim. The other 32 remained unresponsive to her cries of distress. Again, the presence of other bystanders inhibited action.

And again, the noninterveners seemed to have decided the event was not an emergency. They were unsure what had happened but whatever it was, it was not too serious. "A mild sprain," some said. "I didn't want to embarrass her." In a "real" emergency, they assured us, they would be among the first to help the victim. Perhaps they would be, but in this situation they didn't help, because for them the event was not defined as an emergency.

Again, solitary people exposed to a potential emergency reacted more frequently than those exposed in groups. We found that the action-inhibiting effects of other bystanders works in two different situations, one of which involves risking danger to oneself and the other of which involves helping an injured woman. The result seems sufficiently general so that we may assume it operates to inhibit helping in real-life emergencies.

Diffused Responsibility

Even if a person has noticed an event and defined it as an emergency, the fact that he knows that other bystanders also witnessed it may still make him less likely to intervene. Others may inhibit intervention because they make a person feel that his responsibility is diffused and diluted. Each soldier in a firing squad feels less personally responsible for killing a man than he would if he alone pulled the trigger. Likewise, any person in a crowd of onlookers may feel less responsibility for saving a life than if he alone witnesses the emergency.

If your car breaks down on a busy highway, hundreds of drivers whiz by without anyone's stopping to help; if you are stuck on a nearly deserted country road, whoever passes you first is apt to stop. The personal responsibility that a passerby feels makes the difference. A driver on a lonely road knows that if he doesn't stop to help, the person will not get help; the same individual on the crowded highway feels he personally is no more responsible than any of a hundred other drivers. So even though an event clearly is an emergency, any person in a group who sees an emergency may feel less responsible, simply because any other bystander is equally responsible for helping.

This diffusion of responsibility might have occurred in the famous Kitty Genovese case, in which the observers were walled off from each other in separate apartments. From the silhouettes against windows, all that could be told was that others were also watching.

To test this line of thought, Darley and Latané simulated an emergency in a setting designed to resemble Kitty Genovese's murder. People overheard a victim calling for help. Some knew they were the only one to hear the victim's cries, the rest believed other people were aware of the victim's distress. As with the Genovese witnesses, subjects could not see each other or know what others were doing. The kind of direct group inhibition found in the smoke and fallen-woman studies could not operate.

For the simulation, we recruited male and female students at New York University to participate in a group discussion. Each student was put in an individual room equipped with a set of headphones and a microphone and told to listen for instructions over the headphones. The instructions informed the participant that the discussion was to consider personal problems of the normal college student in a high-pressure urban university. It was explained that, because participants might feel embarrassed about discussing personal problems publicly, several precautions had been taken to insure their anonymity: they would not meet the other people face to face, and the experimenter would not listen to the initial discussion but would only ask for their reactions later. Each person was to talk in turn. The first to talk reported that he found it difficult to adjust to New York and his studies. Then, very hesitantly and with obvious embarrassment, he mentioned that he was prone to nervous seizures, similar to but not really the same as epilepsy. These occurred particularly when he was under the stresses of studying and being graded.

Other people then discussed their own problems in turn. The number of other people in the discussion varied. But whatever the perceived size of the group —two, three or six people—only the subject was actually present; the others, as well as the instructions and the speeches of the victim-to-be, were present only on a pre-recorded tape.

When it again was the first person's turn to talk, after a few comments he launched into the following performance, getting increasingly louder with increasing speech difficulties:

"I can see a lot of er of er how other people's problems are similar to mine because er er I mean er it's er I mean some of the er same er kinds of things that I have and an er I'm sure that every everybody has and er er I mean er they're not er e-easy to handle sometimes and er I er er be upsetting like er er and er I er um I think I I need er if if could er er somebody er er er er er give me give me a little er give me a little help here because er I er I'm er h-h-having a a a a a real problem er right now and I er if somebody could help me out it would it would er er s-s-sure be sure be good be . . . because er there er er a cause I er *uh* I've got a a one of the er seiz—er er things coming *on* and and and I c-could really er use er some h-help s-so if somebody would er give me a little h-help uh er-er-er-er-er c-could somebody er er help er uh uh uh (choking sounds) . . . I'm gonna die er er I'm . . . gonna . . . die er help er er seiz-ure er er . . ." (chokes, then quiet).

While this was going on, the experimenter waited outside the student's door to see how soon he would emerge to cope with the emergency. Rather to our surprise, some people sat through the entire fit without helping; a disproportionately large percentage of these nonresponders were from the largest-size group. Eighty-five per cent of the people who believed themselves to be alone with the victim came out of their rooms to help, while 62 per cent of the people who believed there was one other bystander did so. Of those who believed there were four other bystanders, only 31 per cent reported the fit before the tape ended. The responsibility-diluting effect of other people was so strong that single individuals were more than twice as likely to report the emergency as those who thought other people also knew about it.

The Moral Dilemma Felt by Those Who Do Not Respond

People who failed to report the emergency showed few signs of apathy and indifference thought to characterize "unresponsive bystanders." When the experimenter entered the room to end the situation, the subject often asked if the victim was "all right." Many of these people showed physical signs of nervousness; they often had trembling hands and sweating palms. If anything, they seemed more emotionally aroused than did those who reported the emergency. Their emotional arousal was in sharp contrast to the behavior of the nonresponding subjects in the smoke and fallen-woman studies. Those subjects were calm and unconcerned when their experiments were over. Having interpreted the events as nonemergencies, there was no reason for them to be otherwise. It was only the subjects who did not respond in the face of the clear emergency represented by the fit, who felt the moral dilemma.

Why, then, didn't they respond? It is our impression that nonintervening subjects had not decided *not* to respond. Rather, they were still in a state of indecision and conflict concerning whether to respond or not. The emotional behavior of these nonresponding subjects was a sign of their continuing conflict; a conflict that other people resolved by responding. The distinction seems an academic one for the victim, since he gets no help in either case, but it is an extremely important one for arriving at an understanding of why bystanders fail to help.

The evidence is clear, then, that the presence of other bystanders and the various ways these other bystanders affect our decision processes, make a difference in how likely we are to give help in an emergency. The presence of strangers may keep us from noticing an emergency at all; group behavior may lead us to define the situation as one that does not require action; and when other people are there to share the burden of responsibility, we may feel less obligated to do something when action is required. Therefore, it will often be the case that the *more* people who witness his distress, the *less* likely it is that the victim of an emergency will get help.

Thus, the stereotype of the unconcerned, depersonalized *homo urbanis,* blandly watching the misfortunes of others, proves inaccurate. Instead, we find a bystander to an emergency is an anguished individual in genuine doubt, concerned to do the right thing but compelled to make complex decisions under pressure of stress and fear. His reactions are shaped by the actions of others—and all too frequently by their inaction.

And we are that bystander. Caught up by the apparent indifference of others, we may pass by an emergency without helping or even realizing that help is needed. Aware of the influence of those around us, however, we can resist it. We can choose to see distress and step forward to relieve it.

Fred Jones of Peoria, sitting in a sidewalk cafe in Tunis, and needing a light for his cigarette, asks the man at the next table for a match. They fall into conversation; the stranger is an Englishman who, it turns out, spent several months in Detroit studying the operation of an interchangeable-bottlecap-factory. "I know it's a foolish question," says Jones, "but did you ever by any chance run into a fellow named Ben Arkadian? He's an old friend of mine, manages a chain of supermarkets in Detroit . . ."

"Arkadian, Arkadian," the Englishman mutters. "Why, upon my soul, I believe I do! Small chap, very energetic, raised merry hell with the factory over a shipment of defective bottlecaps."

"No kidding!" Jones exclaims in amazement.

"Good lord, it's a small world, isn't it?"

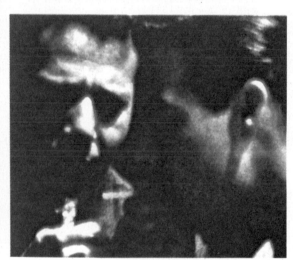

The Small-World Problem

By Stanley Milgram

Almost all of us have had the experience of encountering someone far from home, who, to our surprise, turns out to share a mutual acquaintance with us. This kind of experience occurs with sufficient frequency so that our language even provides a cliché to be uttered at the appropriate moment of recognizing mutual acquaintances.
We say, "My it's a small world."

Random dispersement of people in the small world.

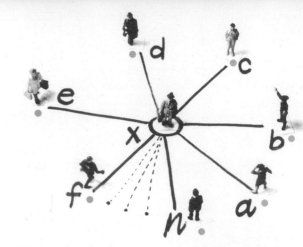

Each person's first-hand acquaintances are shown, A through N.

The simplest way of formulating the small-world problem is: Starting with any two people in the world, what is the probability that they will know each other? A somewhat more sophisticated formulation, however, takes account of the fact that while persons X and Z may not know each other directly, they may share a mutual acquaintance—that is, a person who knows both of them. One can then think of an acquaintance chain with X knowing Y and Y knowing Z. Moreover, one can imagine circumstances in which X is linked to Z not by a single link, but by a series of links, X-*a*-*b*-*c*-*d* . . . *y*-Z. That is to say, person X knows person *a* who in turn knows person *b*, who knows *c* . . . who knows *y*, who knows Z.

Therefore, another question one may ask is: Given any two people in the world, person X and person Z, how many intermediate acquaintance links are needed before X and Z are connected?

Concern with the small-world problem is not new, nor is it limited to social psychologists like myself. Historians, political scientists, and communication

specialists share an interest in the problem. Jane Jacobs, who is concerned with city planning, describes an acquaintance chain in terms of a children's game:

When my sister and I first came to New York from a small city, we used to amuse ourselves with a game we called Messages. I suppose we were trying, in a dim way, to get a grip on the great, bewildering world into which we had come from our cocoon. The idea was to pick two wildly dissimilar individuals—say a head hunter in the Solomon Islands and a cobbler in Rock Island, Illinois—and assume that one had to get a message to the other by word of mouth; then we would each silently figure out a plausible, or at least possible, chain of persons through which the message could go. The one who could make the shortest plausible chain of messengers won. The head hunter would speak to the head man of his village, who would speak to the trader who came to buy copra, who would speak to the Australian patrol officer when he came through, who would tell the man who was next slated to go to Melbourne on leave, etc. Down at the other end, the

cobbler would hear from his priest, who got it from the mayor, who got it from a state senator, who got it from the governor, etc. We soon had these close-to-home messengers down to a routine for almost everybody we could conjure up . . .

The importance of the problem does not lie in these entertaining aspects, but in the fact that it brings under discussion a certain mathematical structure in society, a structure that often plays a part, whether recognized or not, in many discussions of history, sociology, and other disciplines. For example, Henri Pirenne and George Duby, important historians, make the point that in the Dark Ages communication broke down between cities of western Europe. They became isolated and simply did not have contact with each other. The network of acquaintances of individuals became constricted. The disintegration of society was expressed in the growing isolation of communities, and the infrequent contact with those living outside a person's immediate place of residence.

There are two general philosophical views of the small-world problem. One

The network spreads, with complicated inter-connections.

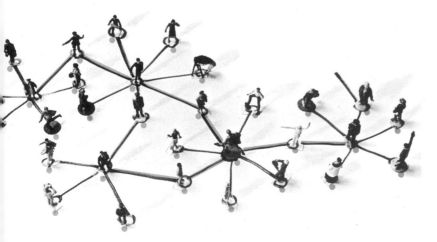

With group inbreeding, X's acquaintances feed back into his own circle, normally eliminating new contacts.

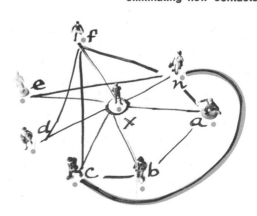

view holds that any two people in the world, no matter how remote from each other, can be linked in terms of intermediate acquaintances, and that the number of such intermediate links is relatively small. This view sees acquaintances in terms of an infinitely intersecting arrangement that permits movement from any social group to another through a series of connecting links.

The second view holds that there are unbridgeable gaps between various groups and that therefore, given any two people in the world, they will never link up because people have circles of acquaintances which do not necessarily intersect. A message will circulate in a particular group of acquaintances, but may never be able to make the jump to another circle. This view sees the world in terms of concentric circles of acquaintances, each within its own orbit.

The Underlying Structure

Sometimes it is useful to visualize the abstract properties of a scientific problem before studying it in detail; that is, we construct a model of the main features of the phenomenon as we understand them. Let us represent all the people in the United States by a number of blue points. Each point represents a person, while lines connecting two points show that the two persons are acquainted. [*See top illustration, opposite page.*] Each person has a certain number of first-hand acquaintances, which we shall represent by the letters $a, b, c, \ldots n$. Each acquaintance in turn has his own acquaintances, connected to still other points. The exact number of lines radiating from any point depends on the size of a person's circle of acquaintances. The entire structure takes on the form of a complex network of 200 million points, with complicated connections between them [*see bottom left illustration, opposite page*]. One way of restating the small-world problem in these terms is this: Given any two of these points chosen at random from this universe of 200 million points, through how many intermediate points would we pass before the chosen points could be connected by the shortest possible path?

Research at M.I.T.

There are many ways to go about the study of the small-world problem, and I shall soon present my own approach to it. But first, let us consider the important contributions of a group of workers at The Massachusetts Institute of Technology, under the leadership of Ithiel de Sola Pool. Working closely with Manfred Kochen of IBM, Pool decided to build a theoretical model of the small-world, a model which closely parallels the idea of points and lines shown. However, unlike my own model, which is purely pictorial, Pool and Kochen translate their thinking into strict mathematical terms.

To build such a model they needed certain information. First, they had to know how many acquaintances the average man has. Surprisingly, though this is a very basic question, no reliable answers could be found in the social science literature. So the information had to be obtained, a task which

The beginning of a typical chain (#111) in the Nebraska Study.

STARTING PERSON
Widowed clerk in Omaha, Nebraska

Michael Gurevitch, then a graduate student at M.I.T., undertook. Gurevitch asked a variety of men and women to keep a record of all the persons they came in contact with in the course of 100 days. It turned out that on the average, these people recorded names of roughly 500 persons, so that this figure could be used as the basis of the theoretical model. Now, if every person knows 500 other people, what are the chances that any two people will know each other? Making a set of rather simple assumptions, it turns out that there is only about one chance in 200,000 that any two Americans chosen at random will know each other. However, when you ask the chances of their having a mutual acquaintance, the odds drop sharply. And quite amazingly, there is better than a 50-50 chance that any two people can be linked up with two intermediate acquaintances. Or at least, that is what the Pool-Kochen theory indicates.

Of course, the investigators were aware that even if a man has 500 acquaintances, there may be a lot of in-breeding. That is, many of the 500 friends of my friend may be actually among the people I know anyway, so that they do not really contribute to a widening net of acquaintances; the acquaintances of X simply feed back into his own circle and fail to bring any new contacts into it [*see bottom right illustration, opposite page*]. It is a fairly straightforward job to check up on the amount of inbreeding if one uses only one or two circles of acquaintances, but it becomes almost impossible when the acquaintance chain stretches far and wide. So many people are involved that a count just isn't practical.

So the big obstacle one runs up against is the problem of social structure. Though poor people always have acquaintances, it would probably turn out that they tend to be among other poor people, and that the rich speak mostly to the rich. It is exceedingly difficult to assess the impact of social structure on a model of this sort. If you could

think of the American population as simply 200 million points, each with 500 random connections, the model would work. But the contours of social structure make this a perilous assumption, for society is not built on random connections among persons but tends to be fragmented into social classes and cliques.

A Harvard Approach

The Pool and Kochen mathematical model was interesting from a theoretical standpoint, but I wondered whether the problem might not be solved by a more direct experimental approach. The Laboratory of Social Relations at Harvard gave me $680 to prove that it could. I set out to find an experimental method whereby it would be possible to trace a line of acquaintances linking any two persons chosen at random.

Let us assume for the moment that the actual process of establishing the linkages between two persons runs only one way: from person A to person Z. Let us call person A the *starting* person, since he will initiate the process, and person Z the *target* person, since he is the person to be reached. All that would be necessary, therefore, would be to choose a starting person at random from the 200 million people who live in the United States, and then randomly choose a target person.

This is how the study was carried out. The general idea was to obtain a sample of men and women from all walks of life. Each of these persons would be given the name and address of the same target person, a person chosen at random, who lives somewhere in the United States. Each of the participants would be asked to move a message toward the target person, using only a chain of friends and acquaintances. Each person would be asked to transmit the message to the friend or acquaintance who he thought would be most likely to know the target person. Messages could move only to persons who knew each other on a first-name basis.

As a crude beginning, we thought it best to draw our starting persons from a distant city, so we chose Wichita, Kansas for our first study and Omaha, Nebraska for our second. (From Cambridge, these cities seem vaguely 'out there,' on the Great Plains or somewhere.) To obtain our sample, letters of solicitation were sent to residents in

1st REMOVE
Self-employed friend in Council Bluffs, Iowa

these cities asking them to participate in a study of social contact in American society. The target person in our first study lived in Cambridge and was the wife of a divinity school student. In the second study, carried out in collaboration with Jeffrey Travers, the target person was a stockbroker who worked in Boston and lived in Sharon, Massachusetts. To keep matters straight, I will refer to the first study as the Kansas Study, and the second as the Nebraska Study. These terms indicate merely where the starting persons were drawn from.

Each person who volunteered to serve as a starting person was sent a folder containing a document, which served as the main tool of the investigation. Briefly, the document contains:

1. The name of the target person as well as certain information about him. This orients the participants toward a specific individual.
2. A set of rules for reaching the target person. Perhaps the

most important rule is: *"If you do not know the target person on a personal basis, do not try to contact him directly. Instead, mail this folder . . . to a personal acquaintance who is more likely than you to know the target person . . . it must be someone you know on a first-name basis."* This rule sets the document into motion, moving it from one participant to the next, until it is sent to someone who knows the target person.
3. A roster on which each person in the chain writes his name. This tells the person who receives the folder exactly who sent it to him. The roster also has another practical effect; it prevents endless looping of the folder through participants who have already served as links in the chain, because each participant can see exactly what sequence of persons has led up to his own participation.

In addition to the document, the folder contains a stack of 15 business reply, or "tracer" cards. Each person receiving the folder takes out a card, fills it in, returns it to us, and sends the remaining cards along with the document to the next link.

Several other features of the procedure need to be emphasized. First, each

2nd REMOVE
Publisher in Belmont, Mass.

participant is supposed to send the folder on to one other person only. Thus the efficiency with which the chain is completed depends in part on the wisdom of his choice in this matter. Second, by means of the tracer card, we have continuous feedback on the progress of each chain. The cards are coded so we know which chain it comes from and which link in the chain has been completed. The card also provides us with relevant sociological characteristics of the senders of the cards. Thus, we know the characteristics of completed, as well as incomplete, chains. Third, the procedure permits experimental variation at many points.

In short, the device possesses some of the features of a chain letter, though it does not pyramid in any way; moreover

it is oriented toward a specific target, zeroes in on the target through the cooperation of a sequence of participants, and contains a tracer that allows us to keep track of its progress at all times.

Would It Work?

The question that plagued us most in undertaking this study was simply: Would the procedure work? Would any of the chains started in Kansas actually reach our target person in Massachusetts? Part of the excitement of experimental social psychology is that it is all so new we often have no way of knowing whether our techniques will work or simply turn out to be wispy pipe dreams.

The answer came fairly quickly. It will be recalled that our first target person

3rd REMOVE
Tanner in Sharon, Mass.

was the wife of a student living in Cambridge. Four days after the folders were sent to a group of starting persons in Kansas, an instructor at the Episcopal Theological Seminary approached our target person on the street. "Alice," he said, thrusting a brown folder toward her, "this is for you." At first she thought he was simply returning a folder

4th REMOVE
Sheet metal worker in Sharon, Mass.

that had gone astray and had never gotten out of Cambridge, but when we looked at the roster, we found to our pleased surprise that the document had started with a wheat farmer in Kansas. He had passed it on to an Episcopalian minister in his home town, who sent it

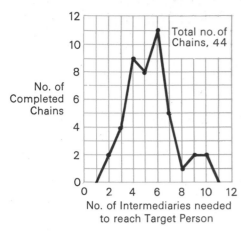

In the Nebraska Study the chains varied from two to 10 intermediate acquaintances with the median at five.

to the minister who taught in Cambridge, who gave it to the target person. Altogether the number of intermediate links between starting person and target person amounted to *two!*

How Many Intermediaries?

As it turned out, this was one of the shortest chains we were ever to receive, for as more tracers and folders came in, we learned that chains varied from two to 10 intermediate acquaintances, with the median at five [*see illustration above*]. A median of five intermediate persons is, in certain ways, impressive, considering the distances traversed. Recently, when I asked an intelligent friend of mine how many steps he thought it

5th REMOVE
Dentist in Sharon, Mass.

would take, he estimated that it would require 100 intermediate persons or more to move from Nebraska to Sharon. Many people make somewhat similar estimates, and are surprised to learn that only five intermediaries will—on the average—suffice. Somehow it does not accord with intuition. Later, I shall try to explain the basis of the discrepancy between intuition and fact.

On a purely theoretical basis, it is reasonable to assume that even fewer links are essential to complete the chains. First, since our participants can send the folder to only one of their 500 possible contacts, it is unlikely that even through careful selections, they will necessarily and at all times, select the contact best able to advance the chain to the target. On the whole they probably make pretty good guesses but surely, from time to time, they overlook some possibilities for short cuts. Thus, the chains obtained in our empirical study are less efficient than those generated theoretically.

Second, by working on a highly rational basis, each intermediary moves the folder toward the target person. That is, a certain amount of information about the target person—his place of employment, place of residence, schooling, and so forth—is given to the starting subject, and it is on the basis of this information alone that he selects the next recipient of the folder. Yet, in real life, we sometimes know a person because we chance to meet him on an ocean liner, or we spend a summer in camp together as teenagers, yet these haphazard bases of acquaintanceship cannot be fully exploited by the participants.

There is one factor, however, that could conceivably have worked in the opposite direction in our experiments, giving us the illusion that the chains are shorter than they really are. There is a certain decay in the number of active chains over each remove, even when they do not drop out because they reach the target person. Of 160 chains that started in Nebraska, 44 were completed and 126 dropped out. These chains die before completion because on each remove a certain proportion of participants simply do not cooperate and fail to send on the folder. Thus, the results we obtained on the distribution of chain lengths occurred within the general

6th REMOVE
Printer in Sharon, Mass.

drift of a decay curve. It is possible that some of the incomplete chains would have been longer than those that were completed. To account for this possibility, Harrison White of Harvard has constructed a mathematical model to show what the distribution of chain lengths would look like if all chains went through to completion. In terms of this model, there is a transformation of the data, yielding slightly longer chains.

Examining the Chains

Several features of the chains are worth examining, for they tell us something about the pattern of contact in American society. Consider, for example, the very pronounced tendency in our Kansas Study for females to send the folder on to females, and males to send it on to males. Of the 145 participants involved in the study, we find:

Female	⟫⟶	Female	56
Male	⟫⟶	Male	58
Female	⟫⟶	Male	18
Male	⟫⟶	Female	13

Thus participants were three times as likely to send the folder on to someone of the same sex as to someone of the opposite sex. Exactly why this is so is not easy to determine, but it suggests that certain kinds of communication are strongly conditioned by sex roles.

7th REMOVE
Clothing merchant in Sharon, Mass.

Participants indicated on the reply cards whether they were sending the folder on to a friend, a relative, or an acquaintance. In the Kansas Study, 123 sent the folder to friends and acquaintances, while only 22 sent it to relatives. Cross-cultural comparison would seem useful here. It is quite likely that in societies which possess extended kinship systems, relatives will be more heavily represented in the communication network than is true in the United States. In American society, where extended kinship links are not maintained, acquaintance and friendship links provide the preponderant basis for reaching the target person. I would guess, further, that within certain ethnic groups in the United States, a higher proportion of familial lines would be found in the data. Probably, for example, if the study were limited to persons of Italian extraction, one would get a higher proportion of relatives in the chain. This illustrates, I hope, how the small world technique may usefully illuminate varied aspects of social structure.

Spaced throughout the preceding text is a series of illustrations showing the kinds of people found in a typical chain (number 111) from the Nebraska Study.

Common Pathways

Each of us is embedded in a small-world structure. It is not true, however, that each of our acquaintances constitutes an equally important basis of contact with the larger social world. It is obvious that some of our acquaintances are more important than others in establishing contacts with broader social realms; some friends are relatively isolated, while others possess a wide circle of acquaintances, and contact with them brings us into a far-ranging network of additional persons.

Referring to our Nebraska Study, let us consider in detail the pattern of convergence crystallizing around the target person—the stockbroker living in Sharon, Massachusetts, and working in Boston [*see top illustration opposite page*]. A total of 64 chains reached him. (44 chains originated in Nebraska and 20 chains, from an auxiliary study, originated in the Boston area). Twenty-four of the chains reached him at his place of residence in the small town outside of Boston. Within Sharon, 16 were given to him by Mr. Jacobs, a clothing merchant in town. Thus, the clothing merchant served as the principal point of mediation between the broker and a larger world, a fact which came as a considerable surprise, and even something of a shock for the broker. At his place of work, in a Boston brokerage house, 10 of the chains passed through Mr. Jones, and five through Mr. Brown. Indeed, 48 percent of the chains to reach the broker were moved on to him by three persons: Jacobs, Jones, and Brown. Between Jacobs and Jones there is an interesting division of labor. Jacobs mediates the chains advancing to the broker by virtue of his residence. Jones performs a similar function in the occupational domain, and moves 10 chains enmeshed in the investment-brokerage network to the target person.

More detail thus fills in the picture of the small world. First, we learn that the target person is not surrounded by acquaintance points, each of which is equally likely to feed into an outside contact; rather, there appear to be highly popular channels for the transmission of the chain. Second, there is differentiation among these commonly used channels, so that certain of them provide the chief points of transmission in regard to residential contact, while others have specialized contact possibilities in the occupational domain. For each possible realm of activity in which the target person is involved, there is likely to emerge a sociometric star with specialized contact possibilities.

Geographic and Social Movement

The geographic movement of the folder from Nebraska to Massachusetts

TARGET PERSON
Mr. Jones, a Stock broker living in Sharon, Mass.

is striking. There is a progressive closing in on the target area as each new person is added to the chain. [*See bottom illustration, opposite page.*] In some cases, however, a chain moves all the way from Nebraska to the very neighborhood in which the target person resides, but then goes round and round, never quite making the necessary contact to complete the chain. Some chains died only a few hundred feet from the target person's house, after a successful journey of 1000 miles. Thus we see that social communication is sometimes restricted less by physical distance than by social distance.

The next step is to see what happens when we change the relationship between the starting person and the target person. That is, if the two are drawn from different class backgrounds, does this then decrease the probability of completing the chain? Does it increase the number of links?

In collaboration with Charles Korte, I am now applying the small-world method to the study of communications between subgroups in American society —Negro and white. We will have both Negro and white starting persons, but only Negro target persons, and try to trace the lines of communication between them. First, we want to ask: In what degree are the racial lines surmounted? Can any sizeable fraction of the communications get through the racial barrier? If the answer is yes, we then want to identify the typical locus of transmission. Does it occur at the neighborhood level, or at the place of work? We are particularly interested in the persons who serve as links between Negro and white groups. In what way do they differ from others in the chain? Do they tend to occupy particular professional categories, such as minister, teacher, and so forth? Is the communication flow between Negroes and whites easier in Northern or in Southern locales? Perhaps some new light can be cast on the structural relationships between Negro and white communities by probing with the small-world method.

Intuition and Fact

As we saw above, many people were surprised to learn that only five intermediaries will, on the average, suffice to link any two randomly chosen individuals, no matter where they happen to live in the United States. We ought to try to explain the discrepancy between intuition and fact.

The first point to remember is that although we deal directly with only five intermediaries, behind each of them stands a much larger group of from 500 to 2500 persons. That is, each participant has an acquaintance pool of 500 to 2500 persons from which he selects the person who, he thinks, is best able to advance the chain. Thus we are dealing only with the end product of a radical screening procedure.

The second thing to remember is that geometric progression is implicit in the search procedure, but nothing is more alien to mathematically untutored intuition than this form of thinking. As youngsters, many of us were asked the question: If you earned a penny a day and the sum were doubled each day, how much would you have earned by the end of a 30-day working period? Most frequently people give answers on the order of $1.87 or $6.45, when in fact the sum is more than $10 million for one 30-day working period, the last day alone yielding $5,368,709.12. Elements of geometric progression with an increase rate far more powerful than mere doubling underlie the small-world search procedure, and thus, with only a few

440

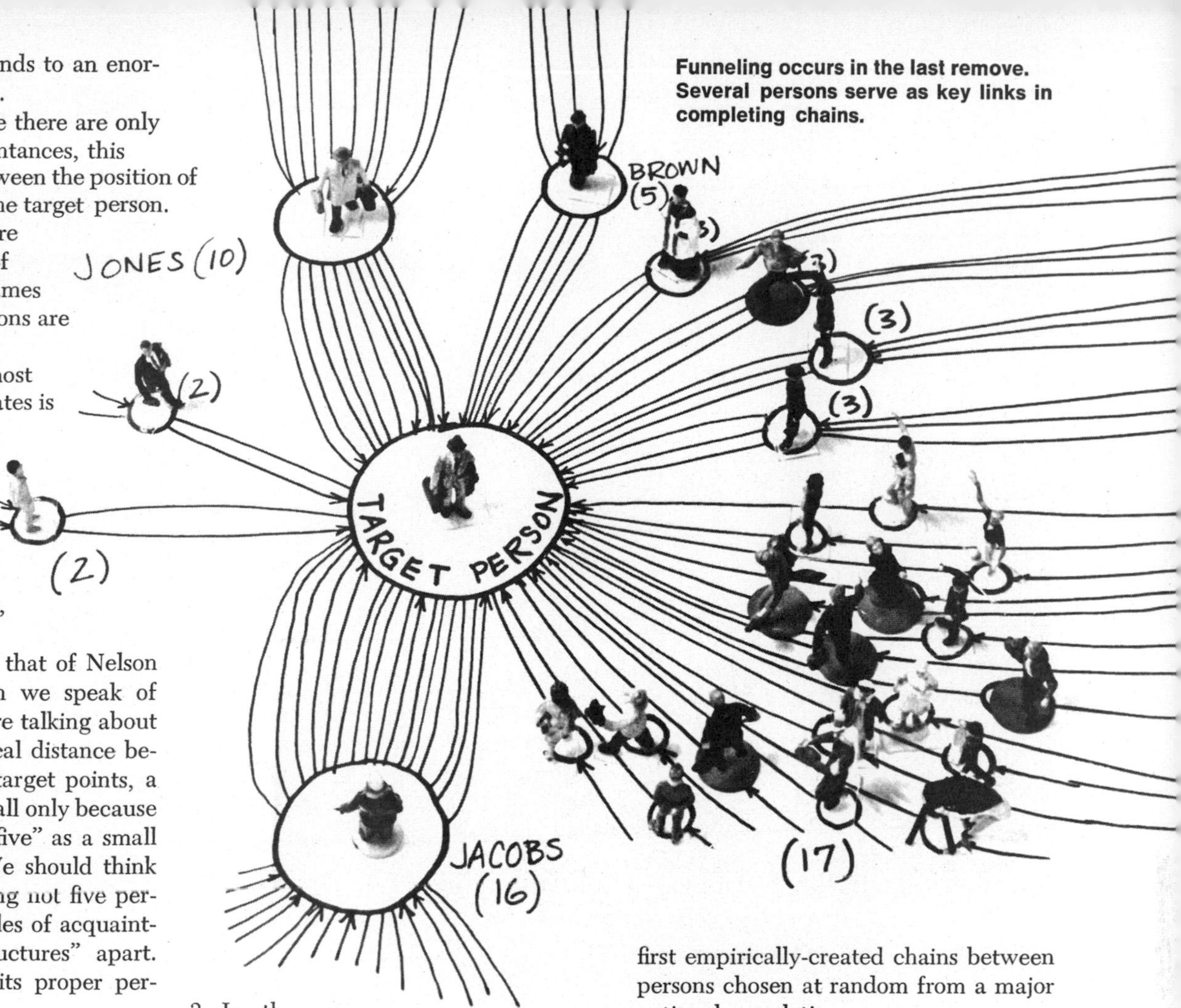

removes, the search extends to an enormous number of persons.

Finally, when we state there are only five intermediate acquaintances, this connotes a closeness between the position of the starting person and the target person. But this is in large measure misleading, a confusion of two entirely different frames of reference. If two persons are five removes apart, they are far apart indeed. Almost anyone in the United States is but a few removes from the President, or from Nelson Rockefeller, but this is true only in terms of a particular mathematical viewpoint and does not, in any practical sense, integrate our lives with that of Nelson Rockefeller. Thus, when we speak of five intermediaries, we are talking about an enormous psychological distance between the starting and target points, a distance which seems small only because we customarily regard "five" as a small manageable quantity. We should think of the two points as being not five persons apart, but "five circles of acquaintances" apart — five "structures" apart. This helps to set it in its proper perspective.

There is a very interesting theorem based on the model of the small world. It states that if two persons from two different populations cannot make contact, then no one within the entire population in which each is embedded can make contact with any person in the other population. In other words, if a particular person, a, embedded in population A (which consists of his circle of acquaintances), cannot make contact with a particular person, b, embedded in population B, then:

1. No other person in A can make contact with b.
2. No other person in A can make contact with any other person in B.

3. In other words, the two sub-populations are compeltely isolated from each other. Conceivably, this could happen if one of the populations were on an island never visited by the outside world. In principle, any person in the United States can be contacted by any other in relatively few steps, unless one of them is a complete and total hermit, and then he could not be contacted at all.

In sum, perhaps the most important accomplishment of the research described here is this: Although people have talked about the small-world problem, and have even theorized about it, this study achieved, as far as I know, the first empirically-created chains between persons chosen at random from a major national population.

Although the study started with a specific set of questions arising from the small-world problem, the procedure illuminates a far wider set of topics. It reveals a potential communication structure whose sociological characteristics have yet to be exposed. When we understand the structure of this potential communication net, we shall understand a good deal more about the integration of society in general. While many studies in social science show how the individual is alienated and cut off from the rest of society, this study demonstrates that, in some sense, we are all bound together in a tightly knit social fabric.

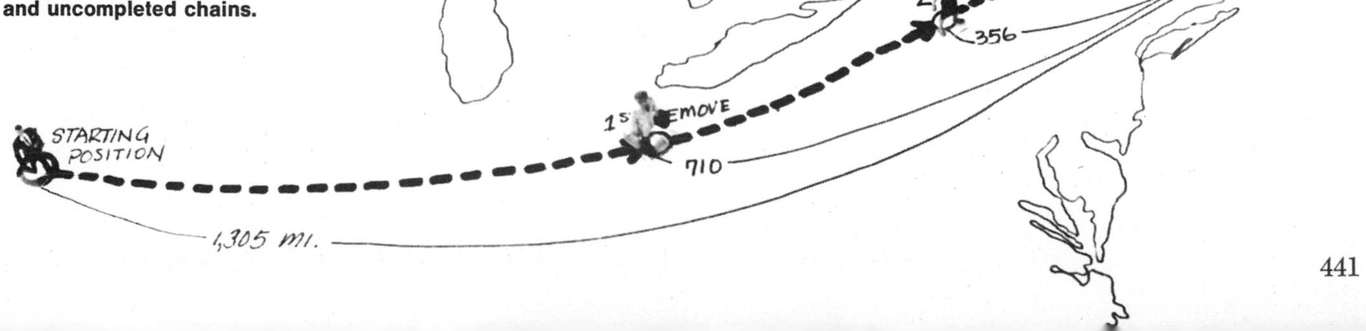

Funneling occurs in the last remove. Several persons serve as key links in completing chains.

JONES (10) · BROWN (5) · (3) · (3) · (3) · (3) · TARGET PERSON · JACOBS (16) · (2) · (2) · (17)

The chains progress from the starting position (Omaha) to the target area (Boston) with each remove. Diagram shows the number of miles from the target area, with the distance of each remove averaged over completed and uncompleted chains.

STARTING POSITION · 1,305 mi. · 1st REMOVE · 710 · 356 · 210 · 79 · 44 · 5th · 6th · TARGET AREA

441

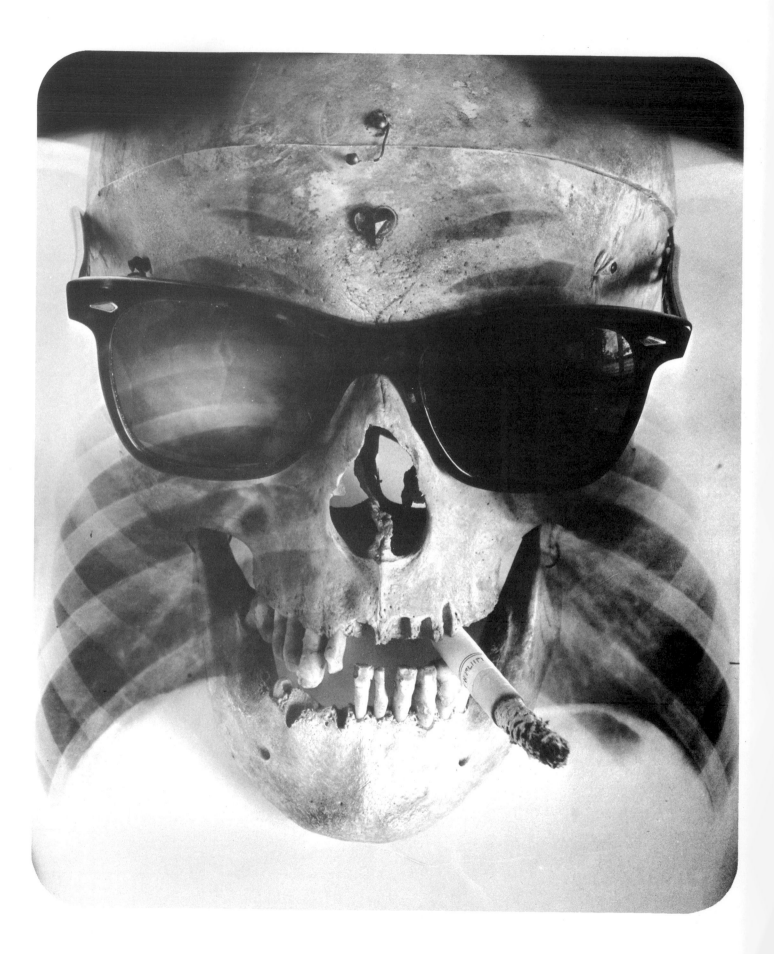

FEAR
-FOR YOUR HEALTH

By Howard Leventhal

MANY of our actions are based on a folk logic about fear. We think that the way to keep children from misbehaving is to instill in them a fear of punishment. We enforce traffic regulations in the belief that drivers fear the legal and natural consequences of disobedience, and we conduct fear campaigns to convince people that safety and health precautions are necessary and vital.

But can people be frightened into protecting themselves against disease and accidents? Observations in our daily lives leave this question still open. There

are many "scare programs" on smoking and automobile accidents—and how effective are they? Sales of cigarettes have not decreased. Even the printed warnings on the packages have been to no avail. Traffic accidents are on the rise in greater proportion than the increase in drivers.

Science has succeeded in controlling many infectious diseases, while deaths from chronic diseases and accidents are a growing public-health concern. Since these new dangers are related to–if not directly determined by—the victim's own behavior, medical science can do little to combat them. To avoid danger it becomes increasingly important to reach people to control their own actions. But educational efforts which simply give information on protective health practices have proved rather inadequate in changing people's beliefs and behavior.

Would we have better results if we combined information about protective-health practices with warnings on the dangers of not following such practices? Common sense makes contradictory recommendations about this prescription. It suggests that a good scare will get action and that a good scare will inhibit action. Given this ambiguity and the fact that fear is often aroused in situations of danger, it seemed important to investigate just how fear influences beliefs and actions. We conducted some experiments, we found some answers—and we raised a lot of new questions.

To see if a strong threat will motivate a person to change his behavior, our first experiments used communications containing different amounts of fear material, along with a common set of recommended procedures for health action. People were assigned at random to three different groups depending upon the amount of fear material used. For example, in one experiment in which we recommended that subjects stop smoking and take chest X-rays, the low-fear group was exposed only to the recommendation, with no other fear material presented. The moderate-fear group was given the recommendation and shown a movie depicting a young man who has taken a chest X-ray and been found to have lung cancer. The high-fear group was treated just like the moderate-fear group except that in addition they were shown a seven-minute color film of a lung-cancer operation which vividly portrayed the potential hazards confronting a smoker.

After these presentations, everyone in the three groups was asked a few questions: Do you believe that lung cancer is serious and that smoking is its cause? How undesirable is it to smoke? Do you intend to stop smoking? Will you take a chest X-ray? Later we checked to see whether the subject did in fact stop smoking or have an X-ray taken.

Several studies were conducted at state fairs. We rented theatres on the New York State fair grounds, for example, and put up posters advertising special health-education programs with movies. With the aid of a colorful barker we attracted large audiences. Once inside the theatre, they were "captured" by our "ushers"—experimental assistants armed with questionnaires who appealed to the people to lend a hand with an important project.

Fortunately, health authorities installed mobile X-ray units at the fair grounds and offered free X-rays to fairgoers. We could thus check whether our participants took an X-ray. Later we wrote and phoned people to ask if they had given up smoking. We then analyzed which message tone — low fear, moderate fear, or high fear — was most effective in getting our subjects to follow recommended health actions.

We were, in effect, testing the theory that fear activates a person's emotional "motor." Once activated by this motor, he is motivated to reduce or eliminate the disturbing emotional state. This he can do by stopping smoking and taking a chest X-ray, as suggested. Presumably, the stronger the threat is the greater will be his fear—and the stronger the drive to eliminate that fear. In our first study we were trying to test this straightforward theory. Indeed, we found that for each of the three fear messages, the people who were most frightened by the message were most eager to stop smoking and most likely to take X-rays. However, there did not seem to be a direct correlation between the degree of fear in the message and its effectiveness. The more frightening message was not necessarily more persuasive.

In two later studies we again found that those who were most frightened by *any* message were most eager to stop smoking. But these studies showed that the groups who saw the most frightening message were most interested in taking action to protect their health.

The Importance of Self-Esteem

Although most studies that have been conducted by a variety of investigators have shown that higher fear levels lead to greater acceptance, the findings are not always consistent. For instance, Doctors Janis and Feshbach reported in one study that their low-fear message was more persuasive than their high-fear message. They suggest that under certain conditions high fear stimulates psychological resistance. Is this contrary result an accident, or does it indicate that the relationship between fear responses and instrumental responses is far more complex than at first assumed?

Whereas the overall effect of raising the fear level was to increase persuasion, further research soon made it apparent that the effect was not the same for all people for all conditions.

What may be some of the mediating factors? To test the possible role of an individual's self-esteem upon his response to fear messages, James Dabbs and I first divided our subjects into two groups, one having high self-esteem and the other low self-esteem, based on their responses to an esteem-rating scale. The health recommendation in this study was to take tetanus inoculations, and volunteers in each of the esteem groups were exposed to different levels of fear messages.

We found that people who had a high opinion of themselves were more likely to agree with the recommendation when it was accompanied by a very threatening message. This was not true of subjects who were low in self-esteem.

However, these results held only for attitudes, not action. Regardless of their self-esteem, more and more subjects followed through by taking tetanus inoculations when they were exposed to the higher fear material. In general, however, the response to the recommendation was low throughout the experimental groups because the volunteers had to make their own arrangements to be inoculated.

In another study of esteem and fear level, Neil Kornzweig used three messages: a mild communication which simply recommended tetanus inoculation, a moderate message describing the recovery of a patient from the disease, and a high-threat message describing a painful death due to tetanus. Kornzweig found that high-esteem subjects were *more* likely to take shots when the communication was more threatening, whereas low-esteem subjects were *less* likely to act when the message was highly threatening.

Do it Now

Another interesting, although not entirely unexpected, finding was the degree to which immediate action was necessary, if there was to be any action at all. For example, when shots were immediately available in an inoculation clinic set up in the building where the experiment was conducted, 86 percent took shots. But when the participants had to bridge a one-day delay, only 28 percent took shots.

Some investigators have suggested that high fear is better than low fear only when action can be taken immediately. They argue that people will not tolerate prolonged states of fright. Instead, people exposed to a high-fear message will convince themselves that they cannot be hurt by the danger, particularly if they are low in self-esteem.

However, our test results failed to bear out this theory. In fact, our experiments showed exactly the opposite—only when immediate action was available did low-esteem subjects resist very fearful messages. After a delay, they behaved like high-esteem subjects and were more likely to follow recommendations given in high-fear messages than in low-fear messages.

We cannot be certain why raising the threat level has different effects depending on the subject's self-esteem. The results of one study suggest that persons with low self-esteem are less likely to be persuaded to act by high-threat levels —not because they are overly frightened but because they are generally less able to cope with the outer world.

In this study, using fear messages about automobile accidents, we first divided our subjects into highs, middles, and lows on the esteem scale. They were then shown one of two movies. The first was a startling film in which cars careened toward each other and crashed; the second showed gory scenes of dead and mutilated accident victims — a far more depressing and disgusting movie than the first. But to vary the impact of the two films, some subjects saw them on a huge (15' x 10') screen from a very close viewing distance while others sat far back and watched a small (3'x 2') image on the screen.

We found a definite interaction between image size and self-esteem. Subjects *low* in esteem were far more likely to accept protective recommendations when they were exposed to the *smaller* image. Their desire to take protective action dropped sharply when they were forced to view the large screen from close up.

High- and middle-esteem subjects more readily accepted the recommendations with the large, closely-viewed picture. Low-esteem subjects reported fatigue when they were exposed to the big picture and said they could not or did not want to think of themselves as accident victims. It seemed that they tried to cope with the danger by avoiding the issue altogether. The impression given by the huge images was one of unalterable reality, so low-esteem subjects saw little reason to take action to protect themselves.

Vulnerability as a Factor

Self-esteem is presumed to be a product of one's success and failure in handling and solving problems. It is logical for esteem to interact with reactions to threat. How this interaction occurs is not clear, for esteem is too general a characteristic to be revealing. A more specific factor, the subject's *perceived vulnerability to danger*, appears to interact with threat level, in the same way as self-esteem does.

One of our researchers, Patricia Niles, exposed three groups of college students to low-, moderate-, and high-fear messages about smoking and lung cancer. Each of the three groups was divided on the basis of their initial feeling of vulnerability to lung cancer. The findings were striking: Only those people expressing *low* susceptibility were increasingly persuaded to stop smoking and take X-rays as the messages became more threatening. *More* vulnerable people showed no difference in their expressed desire to stop smoking or to take X-rays as messages became more frightening.

Their answers to other questions suggested that the highly vulnerable subjects did not respond protectively because the high-threat messages convinced them they would get lung cancer even if they stopped smoking. Thus, they surrendered to the danger.

An important question is, are feelings of vulnerability a part of basic personality or are they affected by a person's behavior? Are there "high" and "low" vulnerables among people regardless of the issue in question, or are these labels easily changeable from one situation to the next?

Recently, Jean Watts and I explored this question in a study on smoking and lung cancer. The degree of vulnerability was varied by dividing a sample of New York fairgoers into smokers (vulnerable subjects) and nonsmokers (invulnerable subjects). Again, three levels of fear material were used.

As expected, we found that the messages had a strong impact on reported emotions: Fairgoers who saw the highly fearful message were much more frightened than those exposed to the other messages. But did they accept the protective recommendations? For nonsmokers, whose vulnerability to lung cancer from smoking is negligible, increasing the fearfulness of the message had no measurable effect—about 45 percent of the people in each group followed up the experiment by taking chest X-rays.

For smokers — the more vulnerable subjects—the results were quite different. There was a steady *decrease* in X-ray-taking going from the low-fear (53%) to moderate-fear (44%) to high-fear (6%) groups. Thus, when exposed to more fearful messages about contracting cancer, smokers were less willing to take X-rays and see if there might be cause for alarm.

Five months after the experiment, questionnaires were mailed to all who had participated, half of whom replied. They were asked if they had since taken X-rays, if they had tried to cut down on their smoking, and if they had succeeded in doing so. Comparing their answers by the levels of threat, we found that smokers exposed to the high-fear condition reported more success in reducing smoking. However, when it came to taking X-rays, high-fear subjects were less likely to follow the health recommendations than low-fear subjects.

This surprising result suggests that vulnerable subjects (smokers) avoid *both* X-rays and smoking. Their avoidance is a complex act. They want to avoid *detecting* cancer, and they want to avoid *getting* cancer. Their choices do make some sense, however. They felt that stopping smoking was a meaningful way to avoid cancer, whereas lung surgery seemed a doubtful cure. The subjects appeared to be selecting responses which to them seemed effective, yet did not involve them in any immediate serious danger.

Give Specific Instructions

A reasonable question at this point is what can be done to overcome the apparent inability of some persons to act to avoid danger. How can we help people feel more in control of their own personal health?

One method may be to enhance the effectiveness of the recommended action. If fear is important to the individual's motivation, then very effective responses would be more likely to reduce his fear —and he would be more likely to take immediate action.

Another method we tried was to make clear to the person just how he could carry out the recommended action. There was no attempt to convince him that the recommendation was a perfect preventative. Rather, we showed him that it was something *he* could do.

We explored ways of programming recommended behavior. Showing a person how to cope with danger seemed to be part of a more general goal: how to help him to convert his attitudes and intentions into *action*. A person is less likely to feel hopeless or paralyzed when he has, in addition to a specific goal, a clear idea of what he is to do and when he is to do it.

To test the effectiveness of this approach, we set up a study in which we used high- and low-fear messages along with a recommendation to take tetanus shots at a student-health service. Half the students at each fear level were given explicit instructions on how to get inoculations; the other half were not given the instructions.

The specific instructions helped. Combining results of both fear groups, 28 percent of those who received the instructions actually took shots, whereas only 3 percent of the students without specific instructions took the shots. Instructions had no effect on subjects' fear, intentions, or attitudes. In line with earlier results, people exposed to high-fear messages were more frightened, had more favorable attitudes toward tetanus inoculations, and were more willing to take shots. But fear itself had no apparent effect on behavior—on actually taking the shots.

Both specific instructions and fear information seemed to be necessary to motivate a person to take a tetanus shot. Since the subjects in this study were college seniors very familiar with the location of the health service, the specific instructions served only to link intentions with action.

To see if helpful instructions could eliminate an already existing response or habit, we tried a similar study with students on the issue of smoking. The specific instructions included a plan for stopping smoking and a large number of ancillary suggestions on how to avoid buying cigarettes, how to interfere with the impulse to smoke, and how to deal with social pressures for smoking.

Smokers were advised, for example, to purchase a book or magazine instead of cigarettes, to drink water or use some other device to deaden the impulse to smoke, and to have excuses ready when they were offered cigarettes at social functions. We emphasized preparing these acts in advance. Again, high- and low-fear messages were used in the experiment, both with and without the specific instructions.

The results paralleled those in the tetanus study; the high-fear message elicited more fear and stronger intentions to stop smoking. With regard to smoking behavior, we found that groups exposed to *any* fear communication smoked less than a control group receiving only specific instructions without fear information. Thus, a single persuasive fear communication was an effective deterrent to smoking for these college students.

What about the usefulness of specific instructions? We found that after three months, the students who had received specific instructions along with the fear messages were still smoking less, whereas those who had not received the specific instructions had begun to slip back into their old habits. These findings are like those of the tetanus experiment: Combining fear communications with specific instructions always produced the best results.

A New Model

All these studies raise important questions about the accuracy of our original theory or model that depicted fear as the activator of a person's emotional "motor," which in turn drives him to eliminate or reduce the emotional state via the suggested action.

We have seen that it is easier to create fear than it is to change beliefs and behavior. If fear is the mediator or "drive" which produces acceptance and change, one might expect the relationship between the two to be a bit more proportional. However, the connection between the "motor" and its consequences appears to be very loose. The fear-drive model also fails to predict those factors —esteem level, vulnerability, specific instructions—which we observed to interact with fear in stimulating attitude change and action.

Therefore, we propose a new model to describe the relationship between a communication and attitude changes and action. This model assumes a good deal of independence between response processes. It also recognizes that information can both create fear *and* change attitudes. The model does not exclude the possibility that fear reactions serve as mediators for other instrumental behaviors, but it does recognize the important role that cognitive factors may play in mediating responses.

We call our model the *parallel response paradigm*. It depicts the communication as consisting of various components which influence acceptance responses, emotional responses, or both. The responses are in parallel and do not necessarily influence one another. We are now beginning to explore the implications, applications, and wide varieties of problems opened by the new model. As we delve more deeply, we hope to find new relationships and to discover or conceive of new mediational concepts.

The Psychology of Police Confessions

by Philip G. Zimbardo

PART I

The fascination that the police have for the thief is manifested by the thief's temptation to confess when he is arrested. In the presence of the examining magistrate who questions him, he is seized with giddiness: the magistrate speaks gently to him, perhaps with kindness, explaining what is expected of him; practically nothing: an assent. If only once, just once, he did what was asked of him, if he uttered the "yes" that is requested, harmony of minds would be achieved. He would be told, "That's fine," perhaps he would be congratulated. It would be the end of hatred. The desire to confess is the mad dream of universal love; it is, as Genet himself says, the temptation of the human.

by Jean Paul Sartre from *St. Genet*, New York: George Braziller, 1963.

"MOST DEFENDANTS have, in effect, two trials. They are first tried by the police. If found guilty they are held for trial by the courts. If found innocent by the police, they are acquitted then and there. This procedure has no basis in law ... but we know from practical experience that far more cases are disposed of in this manner than ever reach our courts." So wrote W. R. Kidd 25 years ago. Now the question of police interrogation procedure has become one of the most controversial and basic legal issues ever to face the nation.

Many recent Supreme Court rulings have concentrated on guaranteeing the protection of suspects under police interrogation. Suspects now have the right to counsel during questioning, and must be apprised of their rights under the Fifth Amendment. These rulings are particularly important because, according to police statistics, more than 80 percent of all criminal cases are solved by confession. A defendant seldom is acquitted once his confession is admitted as evidence during his trial. Thus, for a majority of defendants, trial is but a mere formality.

By what methods do police obtain such an unbelievable percentage of confessions? Perhaps a goodly number of these confessions are false, elicited only by unfair, illegal, or reprehensible methods of interrogation. But even if all the confessions were in fact true, would the loss of individual rights and freedom be worth the gain in police efficiency?

These are basic issues with which every thoughtful citizen is deeply concerned.

We know from psychological studies of American prisoners of war in Communist interrogation camps in Korea that many good soldiers gave false confessions, incriminated themselves, and betrayed their fellow soldiers. In their study of Communist interrogation procedures, L. E. Hinkle and H. C. Wolfe reported that not only were men forced to confess to crimes they had not committed, but apparently they came "to believe in the truth of their confessions and to express sympathy and gratitude toward those who had imprisoned them." [See Bem, "When Saying Is Believing," *Psychology Today*, June 1967.] I am now convinced that the secret inquisitorial techniques of our police force are sometimes more highly developed, more psychologically sophisticated, and more effective than were those of the Chinese Communists.

What About the Supreme Court Rulings?

The new Supreme Court rulings do indeed represent an important safeguard of individual liberty and do, of course, clear up some of the legal inconsistencies and ambiguities surrounding police station confessions. But they leave a number of vital problems unsolved. First of all, there is no control over the way police tell a suspect what his rights are. "While a number of police departments have been issuing warnings," The New York Times said not long after the Supreme Court decisions, "the method probably has been cursory, with the words mumbled. Or, it has likely been done as a tactic to establish a rapport with the suspect."

A second unsolved problem involves the availability of legal advice. Some 60 percent of criminal suspects cannot afford to retain an attorney; some suspects distrust lawyers in general ("They are fast-talking shysters in it only for the money"); and some don't even know the name of a lawyer to call. Moreover, some police interrogators imply that requesting an attorney is a sign of guilt,

or that an attorney is a stranger who will interfere with the "man-to-man" conversation between the suspect and his "friends" in the police station. The right to silence is countered by a police argument: "If you have nothing to hide, why are you afraid to talk?"

Psychology, Not Law

Many more legal problems remain—and perhaps some of them can be solved only by psychologists. How can a court assess the amount of psychological coercion, tell whether a confession was truly voluntary, or measure a man's ability to resist pressure? Central in defining and analyzing these questions is a knowledge of personality, behavior deviations, performance under stress and deprivation, the "social demand" implicit in a situation, persuadability, and the conditions for attitude change.

We know, for example, that innocent men have confessed to crimes they did not commit. What conditions could exercise so much control over a man that he would confess falsely to murder and sign a confession? If a prisoner later denies his confession, there are only two real sources of information—the accused, and the accusor. And guess who usually wins. What we need are facts. Do judges really know what goes on in squad rooms? Does anyone?

Let us look at a frightening case in which a voluntary confession of murder was later proved false.

George Whitmore's Confession

In June, 1964, Patrolman Frank Isola came to the aid of Mrs. Elba Borrero as she was being sexually assaulted in the Brownsville section of Brooklyn. The attacker fled. Mrs. Borrero described her assailant as a Negro, 5-feet 9-inches tall, pock-marked, and weighing about 165 pounds. He had been wearing a raincoat from which she had torn a button as she fought him off. The button was the sole tangible piece of evidence in the attempted rape.

At 8 o'clock the next morning Patrolman Isola and Detective Richard Aidala picked up George Whitmore, Jr., in the

vicinity of the crime. He was a small man, just 5-feet 5-inches tall and he weighed only 140 pounds. But he *was* wearing a raincoat from which a button was missing, and he was a Negro. He was arrested because there was "a reasonable ground for suspicion supported by circumstances sufficiently strong in themselves."

Mrs. Borrero viewed him through a peephole and identified him as her attacker. By 10:30 that morning, Whitmore had confessed to the attempted rape of Mrs. Borrero. By noontime he had confessed to the knife-slaying of a Mrs. Edwards.

In looking over Whitmore's belongings, E. S. F. Bulger, a homicide detective who had been called in to witness the murder confession, saw a photograph of a white girl. For eight months Bulger and many others had been working on the tragic double murder of two unusually talented young career girls, Janice Wylie and Emily Hoffert, who were knifed in their Manhattan apartment. Bulger recognized the girl as Janice Wylie, and Whitmore's interrogation was resumed with far greater intensity.

By 4 a.m. Whitmore "broke" and confessed to having murdered the two girls—his third confession during 20 hours of continuous questioning. Chief of Detectives (now Chief Inspector) L. J. McKearney announced: "We've got the right guy, no question about it."

Manhattan Assistant District Attorney Peter Koste, who was called in to witness the confession, reported that Whitmore was "composed" and "alert" at the end of the interrogation. Detective Bulger, the principal interrogator, swore that he had obtained the confession without "feeding" Whitmore information about the murders.

The confession was persuasive and convincing, and so detailed that it was 61 typed pages long. It included drawings of the apartment where the girls had lived and died.

Two weeks later police discovered that the photograph was not a picture of Miss Wylie after all, and they turned their attentions toward proving that Whitmore had found it in the girls' apartment.

Meanwhile, Whitmore was tried and convicted of attempted rape. Brooklyn District Attorney S. A. Lichtman said in his summation to the jury: "We have nailed George Whitmore on the button, so to speak." (The prosecution suppressed the FBI laboratory report that the remaining buttons on Whitmore's coat were "different in size, design and construction" from the button Mrs. Borrero had torn off her attacker's coat.)

In October, a private citizen, Nathan Delaney, informed the police that his friend, Richard Robles, had admitted to murdering the two girls. Beginning to suspect the validity of the confession, the police began a new investigation.

Brilliantly, they matched the background of the photograph with a Wildwood, New Jersey, picnic area. They identified the girl in the photograph as Arlene Franco, who said she had thrown the picture away. Whitmore lived in Wildwood, and he had once said that he found the photograph there. After two witnesses swore that they had seen Whitmore in Wildwood the night the two girls were murdered in Manhattan, and after Robles confessed to the double slaying, George Whitmore finally was freed. An innocent man had spent eight months in jail. One police officer said: "It's an awful thing, but sooner or later things like this happen. I hate to say this but I'm sure that sometime in history we've sent innocent men to their deaths by unjust verdicts." And an assistant district attorney said: "If this had been what we so-called professionals call a run-of-the-mill murder, Whitmore might well have been slipped into the electric chair and killed for something he didn't do. Let's face it. We've had executions in the past based on nothing more than a dead body and a confession."

In New York State alone more than 500 appeals were made in 1965 by prisoners seeking to reopen cases based on confessions. One example of these appeals is the case of a Bronx factory worker who confessed to the murder of a woman and, after spending a year in jail, was found innocent by polygraph data which contradicted his confession. The accused, Santo Sanchez, a 40-year-old illiterate Puerto Rican father of six, went into the 41st Street Precinct in good physical condition, and after his indictment on December 21, 1964, was hospitalized for six weeks with cuts and bruises. (Incidentally, the major link to the crime was a photo of the accused which was found in the dead woman's apartment. But since they were relatives this does not seem so strange.)

Why did Whitmore confess? Why do any of them confess? "Call it what you want: brainwashing, hypnosis, fright. They made him give an untrue confession," said our assistant district attorney. Another said: "I am positive the police prepared the confession for Whitmore . . . I am also sure the police were the ones who gave Whitmore all the details of the killings that he recited to our office." Whitmore says he was beaten; the interrogator says he was not. The police claim his confession was voluntary, uncoerced, and freely given.

The squad room as portrayed in old movies—a dingy office, a light shining in the eyes of a suspect while a team of police shout questions and accusations —is long gone. Modern psychological methods have supplanted the old "third degree," because they are more effective. A popular police manual states that if the interrogator "has a layman's knowledge of practical psychology and uses the salesman's approach, he can . . . reach into a man's brain and pull out the facts he wants."

Police Interrogation Techniques

Though there is little direct evidence on what happens in the squad room, a secondary source of evidence comes from manuals used to train detectives and interrogators. Written chiefly by police officers, detectives, or former staff members of scientific crime laboratories, these manuals invariably include at least one chapter on interrogation techniques. The most recent manual, a 1962 revision of *Criminal Interrogation*, by F. E. Inbau and J. E. Reid, is devoted entirely to a discussion of the psychological tactics and techniques of effective interrogation of suspects.

Here is a sampling of many of the approaches suggested in police manuals. I am convinced that these methods are psychologically coercive; that they deprive the individual of his human dignity and fundamental rights; and that they debase the police who use them even though the police are trying to be fair as well as efficient. Let the reader judge my contention that they do not serve justice.

Inbau and Reid claim that none of the tactics they suggest are "apt to induce an innocent man to confess," but they present no evidence except personal opinion to support this key generalization. Questions at issue are: How voluntary are confessions obtained by such techniques? What degree of coercion and psychological force is implied? And to what extent are our basic constitutional and human rights violated?

Demand Characteristics of the Interrogation

Modern psychology has alerted the police to the potential significance of every detail in the stimulus situation which can be manipulated and controlled, but police do not understand the implications of where such control may lead. In police questioning, an environment is created which minimizes sensory stimulation, maximally exposes the suspect's vulnerability, and provides for complete control and domination by the interrogator.

Police manuals generally agree that the suspect should never be interrogated in an environment familiar to him nor in the presence of anyone he knows. The psychological support of a familiar environment should be withheld; the suspect must always feel that he is the "guest" of the police. Indeed, "By going to the police station the suspect has made the first act of yielding." (This and all quotations in the following section are taken from police manuals.) The

police interrogation room should never resemble a jail or police department office. It should be private and free from distractions or unplanned interruptions. Preferably it should have no windows. If there are windows and the usual bars, one manual suggests "Italian garden-gate" as a particularly suitable style for the ironwork. To keep attention properly focused on the business at hand, the room should be bare, with no pictures, only two chairs and perhaps a desk.

The suspect should be permitted no tension-relieving activities or objects (such as paper-clips or ash trays which "represent a tacit invitation to smoke"). If there is a phone, one manual suggests a fake one which the interrogator can ring surreptitiously if he needs an excuse to leave the room.

"Since the subject should be deprived of every psychological advantage," the atmosphere should suggest the invincibility of the law. The suspect should be placed in an armless, straight-backed chair so that he cannot become too comfortable, and so that all his bodily movements can be observed.

Intensive questioning should be conducted by a single interrogator, alone with the suspect and standing or sitting as close to him as he can. "When a person is close to another physically, he is closer psychologically." He should bring "the full weight of his personality . . . to bear on the emotional situation."

To "command the respect his position requires," he should wear a conservative suit and avoid loud ties. No guns or police symbols should be evident. He must have no distracting mannerisms, and he shouldn't distract the suspect by unpleasant breath, an item which should be checked by a fellow officer and remedied if necessary with mouthwash or "a chlorophyll mint." He must seize and maintain full control of the interview and never lose his composure. Small gestures which help establish his authority include directing the subject where to sit or telling him he cannot smoke.

The investigating officer is born, not made. "He must have a built-in psychology based on instinct and experience in which a man's weak points are exploited." Psychologist Hans Toch observed that citizens "meet police officers on an unequal basis, with punishment implicit in every encounter. Ultimately, the typical contact between police and public remains one in which there is essentially one-way communication against a backdrop of latent power." The suspect or potential witness is at a disadvantage which is intensified in every way possible. In this setting the interrogator "breaks a man by intelligence."

Perceptual and Judgmental Distortion

Confessions are often obtained by minimizing the seriousness of the offense, by allowing the suspect a face-saving "out," or by misrepresenting and exaggerating the seriousness of the crime.

The interrogator may say that he doesn't think the suspect's indiscretion was so serious, that he has seen thousands of others in the same situation. He may talk of extenuating circumstances, the environment, or human weaknesses—any of which might lead someone to do what the suspect did. He may suggest a morally acceptable motive like self-defense, or a crime of passion; he may even infer it was an accident or a mistake. One manual recommends that to "open up" a suspect, good "bait" is to lay the blame for the crime on someone else: an accomplice, a fence, loan sharks, even the victim.

Inbau and Reid offer provocative examples of how experts use bait. A 50-year-old man, accused of having taken "indecent liberties" with a 10-year-old girl is told: "This girl is well developed for her age. She probably learned a lot about sex from the boys . . . and from movies and TV; . . . she may have deliberately tried to excite you to see what you would do." Or, the manual notes, in forcible rape cases "where circumstances permit, the suggestion might be offered that the rape victim acted like she might be a prostitute . . . that the police knew she had been engaged in acts of prostitution. . . ." If the suspect is married, his wife may be blamed: "When a fellow like you doesn't get it at home, he seeks it elsewhere."

Another manual advises that once the suspect is in a state of emotional confusion, "he is unable to think logically and clearly, since his sense of values has been disturbed and his imagination is distorting his perspective." The investigator can "obtain admission or even a confession from the suspect by further misrepresenting the picture."

This can take several forms. The knowledge-bluff is one. The interrogator reveals a few known items and pretends to know more; he may lie, saying that a suspect's fingerprints or blood were found at the scene of the crime. A suspect may even be shown falsified samples and records. Sometimes in a murder case, interrogators are instructed by police manuals to say that the victim is still alive. Misrepresentation may be used to intensify fear. It is suggested that in statutory rape cases the suspect might be told that the victim "has testified to being forcibly raped." In theft and embezzlement, the reported loss—and thus the consequences—can be increased. "To make it look more authentic," according to Inbau and Reid, "a letter typed on company stationery can be prepared, reporting the larger loss to the police and the insurance company."

Such police perjury may take even more extreme forms. In the fixed line-up, the interrogation is interrupted so that alleged witnesses, who are really "ringers," can point out the suspect as the guilty man. The interrogator then resumes questioning with an air of increased confidence. In the reverse line-up, the suspect is falsely accused (by fake witnesses) of a real or fictitious crime more serious than the one for which he is held. Confessing to burglary may seem the easy way out for a man accused of murder, rape, or kidnapping.

Social-Psychological Distortions

Inbau and Reid urge the interrogator to role-play the position of the subject before the interrogation begins, and then respond to him "man to man, not as policeman to prisoner . . . It is a mistake to look upon the subject as an animal." The interrogator establishes a false relationship with the suspect by acting friendly, kind, sympathetic, understanding—by appearing as "a Dutch uncle," or an older brother. He can manipulate the suspect by bestowing social approval and status since "it is a basic human trait to seek and enjoy the approval of other persons."

Flattery is useful. The interrogator is advised to compliment a suspected getaway car driver on his maneuvering and cornering abilities. Teenagers are likened to a James Bond or a Willy Mays.

The white-collar first offender—the clerk, manager, cashier, or office worker—subscribes to orthodox ethical principles and moral standards, so the dignified approach of the physician is considered most effective. "The character of [such subjects] is weak and must be exploited fully," one manual says baldly.

To create rapport, the interrogator may pat the suspect on the shoulder, grip his hand, offer to get him a drink of water. "Gestures of this type . . . impart an attitude of understanding and sympathy better than words."

One of the most effective means by which the interrogator may gain a suspect's confidence is the *Mutt and Jeff* approach, reportedly used on George Whitmore. In this technique the arresting detective instills fear while the interrogating detective is being protective, supportive, and sympathetic. Records of Whitmore's case actually show that he believed Mutt was sincerely concerned about his welfare.

Jeff is typically big, cruel, relentless and Mutt is the kind-hearted family man whose brother perhaps was once in a similar scrape. He asks Jeff to leave the prisoner alone and get out of the room. Then he confesses that he, too, detests Mutt's tactics (which unfortunately will get worse). The suspect's only hope is to cooperate quickly with his friend Mutt by confessing.

Face-saving is a variation of this technique which is used primarily with prostitutes who refuse to inform on clients, agents, or underworld connections. Jeff calls her vile names. Mutt throws Jeff out and apologizes for his behavior. Mutt tells the girl Jeff could lose his job for such behavior and that he will see what he can do about having Jeff disciplined if she discusses freely the case at hand. Once she complies, of course, that is the end of the matter.

When there are two suspects, police are able to play one off against the other. Such tactics almost always succeed. Both may be locked in the same cell and the weaker of the two removed almost immediately for an hour during which nothing happens to him—he isn't even questioned. When he gets back to the cell, he says this but his story doesn't sound right. The interrogator calls for the other prisoner and tells him that his partner has squealed.

If the suspects are father and son, some manuals advise questioning the father first and persuading him, no matter what he has told the police, to send a note to his son saying: "I have told the truth, you should do the same."

In a third method, one suspect of a pair is taken into the squad room, with the other left to sit just outside. Screaming and thumping sounds (which are faked) come from the room and the man outside assumes his friend is getting the third degree and probably will talk. A similar tactic, *bluff-on-a-split-pair,* is quieter and considered more effective. One of the suspects is taken into the interrogation room and the other hears muffled voices as he waits outside. Eventually a secretary is called on the intercom and told to come into the interrogation room—with her notebook. Later, she returns to her desk and begins typing, stopping now and then to ask the waiting suspect things like how to spell his name. When it is the second prisoner's turn, the interrogator waves a typed "confession" and says that it puts all the blame on him. Resentment toward the "squealie" can result in a confession to even the score.

These tactics and deceptions support Hugo Munsterberg's classic analysis of false confessions in his book, *On the Witness Stand.* He writes that there are many motives that influence an accused person into making a voluntary false confession. Confronted with what seems overwhelmingly damaging circumstantial evidence, a man may make a false confession in the hope of receiving mercy. In a classic case, the brothers Boorn of Vermont confessed to murder in order to have the charge reduced from homicide to manslaughter—but the "corpse" turned up alive.

"Untrue confessions from hope or fear, through promises and threats, from cunning calculations and passive yielding shade off into others which are given with real conviction under the pressure of emotional excitement or under the spell of overpowering influences," Munsterberg says.

The Clinical-Psychological Approach

In Theodor Reik's brilliant analysis, *The Compulsion to Confess,* he focuses attention not only on the obviously mentally ill who flock to police stations with confessions after every major crime, but on all of us who harbor deep-seated guilt feelings for our real or imagined transgressions during childhood. Since guilt can be relieved only by confession, punishment, and absolution, Reik holds that to at least some degree the need to confess is present in us all.

Part of "sizing-up" a suspect includes assessing his personality and his strengths and weaknesses. Suspects who seem nervous are left alone to "sweat it out" for a long time. In handling "apparently guilty" subjects, the manuals say it may be necessary to offer justifications for their behavior before their guilt feelings are sufficiently reduced to enable them even to talk about their feelings and crimes.

When the suspect doesn't seem nervous, the interrogator is advised to point out that he is showing psychological and physiological symptoms of guilt. Calling attention to a part of the body or bodily process can cause the subject to react. Inbau and Reid suggest that attention should be directed to pulsation of the carotid artery in the neck, movement of the Adam's apple, dryness of the mouth, movement of the limbs, and a "peculiar feeling inside" caused by a troubled conscience. The authors urge the interrogator to be on the alert for "moments of indecision during which the suspect's struggle to avoid the consequences of his criminal act will be partially overcome by, or temporarily deadlocked with, his impulse to confess." This is the time to "move in."

If the suspect is a youngster, the interrogator may play on his feelings of guilt and shame by asking him how often he masturbates. This is so embarrassing to most youths that they will eagerly change the subject and can be led easily into talking about the crime of which they are accused. So says the manual. Basic innocence makes youth vulnerable to this tactic. But "intellectual type" men suspected of real sex offenses should be put off guard by reassuring reminders from the Kinsey reports: "Human and animal sex habits differ very little."

"Fear of the insane asylum" is discussed by W. R. Kidd. "We find some mentally affected persons who fear the asylum more than they do jail," he writes. "Threat of confinement in an asylum may secure a ready admission [of guilt]."

Police manuals remind interrogators to make use of all kinds of fears, including the common fear of lie detector tests. A suspect may be asked to take a lie detector test and told that refusal is an admission of guilt. Even nightmares are used. The interrogator may ask if a man ever dreamed of committing a crime like the one of which he is accused because "there is an obvious relationship between dreaming and acting out the crime."

Semantic and Verbal Distortion

Most manuals deal at length with the art of phrasing questions and of tailoring the vocabulary to fit each suspect. These recommendations help neophyte interrogators develop sensitivity to the power of language.

Some subjects can be classified readily, and for them the rules of procedure are specific. "Mother" is the magic word for most juveniles and the effect of the crime on her should be emphasized. The big-shot should be put down by using his first name, but the uneducated person should be flattered by being called "Mister." Inbau and Reid say that the culturally deprived "should be interrogated on a psychological level comparable to that usually employed in questioning a child." An adulteress should be called by her first name because the word "Mrs." may make her feel guilty. A homosexual should never be called a "pervert" or a "queer." That only causes resentment and lack of cooperation. And one manual insists that an elderly female suspect should never be called an "old whore." Even the interrogator's tone of voice is important. Inbau and Reid say: "Care must be exercised as to tone of voice, because a very soft voice seems to lull the subject into a state of tranquility."

Justice

Recent theory and research on public compliance and attitudes assuredly come into play with the suggestion that the interrogator should discourage a suspect's denial of guilt, since the more often any man repeats a lie the harder it becomes for him to tell the truth. Ω

TOWARD A MORE PERFECT JUSTICE

By Philip G. Zimbardo

PART II It is my professional opinion as a psychologist concerned with the experimental modification of attitudes and behavior that current police techniques represent a highly sophisticated application of psychological principles which for many people are more compelling and coercive than physical torture. These techniques involve confusing the suspect, lying, cheating, faking, distorting the facts, and manipulating a suspect's social values and personal needs.

Not only are police methods likely to make a guilty man incriminate himself against his will, but I am convinced that they also can lead to false confessions by the innocent and to voluntary and unintentional false testimony by witnesses. Any catalogue of current interrogation techniques would show a debasement of human nature and stands as a disgraceful slur on the American system of justice.

I am on the side of the individual; society's major function is safeguarding his rights—your rights. Such a position seems to conflict with today's police concepts of "efficiency" and "necessity." F. E. Inbau and J. E. Reid declare in their popular police manual that they "approve of such psychological tactics and techniques as trickery and deceit that are not only helpful but frequently necessary in order to secure incriminating information. . . ." These authors are not alone in their conviction. A former American Bar Association president, L. F. Powell, Jr., has said, "The pendulum may have swung too far in affording rights which are abused and misused by criminals." Many other experts are of the same opinion, and in fairness to their position, it must be noted that crime is increasing at a phenomenal rate in America, as in most countries. Since 1958, serious crime in the United States has increased by 60 percent, six times the population increase. The public is justifiably afraid, and police have responded to public pressure for action. Both the public and the police must remember, however, that the police are the enforcers of law. They do not make laws, nor should they be the judges of those who have broken the law.

Recently, many critics have questioned the need for police reliance on confessions. Certainly over-reliance on the effectiveness of interrogation lessens the use of other good crime detection methods. Back in 1872, the framers of the India Evidence Act said it for all time: "It is far easier to sit comfortably in the shade rubbing pepper into a poor devil's eyes than go out in the sun hunting up evidence." Confessions do absolve the individual of his guilt feelings, for both real and imaginary transgressions; in addition, they absolve police of the responsibility for court convictions which mean prison or death for

fellow human beings.

But do confessions really aid law enforcement as much as we have been led to believe? Washington, D.C. Police Chief Robert Murphy complained that new Supreme Court rulings reinforcing the rights of suspects "will result in a complete breakdown in law enforcement in the District of Columbia." Actually, Washington long has operated under Federal regulations which are protective of the individual. In comparable neighboring areas of Virginia and Maryland, there had been no such hampering of police efficiency. Felony crime rates in the nation's capital increased one percent from 1950 to 1960; in the surrounding areas, felony crime rose 69 percent during the same period. Protection of suspects' rights would seem, at least in this case, to serve the law well.

Chief Circuit Judge David L. Bazelon of the U.S. Court of Appeals has said: "We must deter not only crime but also the debasement of the individual." This imperative should include both the suspected criminal and the police interrogator. Tearing the cloak of secrecy from police interrogation, therefore, is of primary importance. Giving suspects the right to immediate arraignment would be one sure way to do this. With proper and workable procedure, suspects or witnesses could be brought at any hour to a central point where a magistrate, defense attorneys, and even interpreters for the non-English speaking would be available during questioning or arraignment. Such a centralized system would make video tape recordings feasible, and such records would be valuable safeguards for both the police and their suspects. (Detroit, which has come a long way toward effective and impeccable police work, is the first city to schedule video tapes for confession identification.)

Other effective ways to meet the challenge of justice in this era of misused

and misunderstood psychology might include: working with police academies to put to the empirical test many conclusions developed from the common-sense psychology of police manuals; serious study of the Supreme Court's criteria for invalidating a "coerced" confession; a study of public awareness of the legal rights of the individual; a before-and-after study of emotional and physiological responses of suspects during actual interrogations; and a large-scale study of various interrogation techniques on groups of subjects who vary in major personality traits, to see if there is a relationship between confession and character or personality. Central in determining the validity of confessions are the psychological criteria of coercion, free will, and the ability to resist. Psychologists have played no role in such determinations; they have not been involved professionally with this problem and do not save specific relevant empirical research findings to offer the courts.

Greater knowledge of the dangers involved in police attempts to coerce confessions is vital to our society. In our attempts to understand, the study of Carnegie Tech's Daryl Bem in inducing belief in false confessions is a landmark, as well as a model laboratory experiment (*Psychology Today,* June 1967). The self-persuasion factor in confessions is a major area of consideration if police interrogation is to serve justice well. Bem demonstrated that cues normally associated with telling the truth can cause us to recall the truth less accurately or to believe in our false confessions.

The United States is at a critical stage of development, and the rights of the individual to protest are being challenged all the way from Washington to Sacramento. Thus, responsible citizens must be alert, more than ever, to the malleability of man in order to safeguard his real freedom and human rights.

Enemies are real. They are not mere chimeras fabricated by clever propagandists. They exist. They kill. But do we really ever see our enemies clearly and truly? The very existence of a group that holds an ideology different from our own creates harsh anxiety in us. Why? Because the very fact that they maintain different beliefs implies that *ours might be wrong.* Often the enemy does possess the dangerous, hostile qualities we fear, but our mental image of him is shaped as much by our own inner psychological processes as by his reality. Once formed, this image is a filter in our perception of our enemy. We shape information to fit the enemy image. We screen out what may blur or change the picture—the face of the enemy—so vivid in our mind's eye. We are sadly, even tragically, unaware of this information filter—the process goes on outside of our consciousness.

The Face of the Enemy

By Jerome D. Frank

An ingenious experiment by J. W. Bagby of New York's Roosevelt Hospital illustrates the phenomenon of perceptual filtering. This psychologist asked American and Mexican school teachers to look into a device that showed simultaneously a different picture to each eye. One eye saw a picture of a baseball player and the other saw a bullfighter.

An overwhelming proportion of the Americans "saw" the baseball player; the overwhelming proportion of Mexicans "saw" the bullfighter. What these teachers saw, of course, *was* mostly determined by their cultural filter.

No psychiatrist or psychologist would be so rash as to claim that one can make solid inferences about the behavior of nations from that of individuals, but it is startling how often similarities between the man and his country emerge when one starts looking carefully.

One psychological principle certainly is highly relevant to international affairs: a person's beliefs and his expectations largely determine how he thinks and how he behaves. Since citizens of a nation tend to share the same beliefs and expectations, this principle is important if we are to understand how nations see each other and behave toward one another.

Characteristic of each nation's self-image is the belief in national sovereignty, territorial rights and national strength. Each nation believes in its right to pursue vital interests regardless of the effects on other nations.

The degree of fear in which one nation holds another nation depends upon perception of adversary ability and intent to harm. Whether the people of one nation perceive those of another as enemies depends primarily upon the nature of relations between the two countries. Thus it is when national interests clash and nations are in conflict that the enemy image begins to take its menacing shape. Because of the universal and innate distrust of strangers, a foreign power easily can arouse a sense of threat. Once the opinion-makers have singled out the threatening nation, this innate distrust is focused.

The Russian invasion of Czechoslovakia was portrayed by American mass media as an unprovoked rape of a country struggling toward freedom; the Russians justified it as necessary to forestall a takeover by anticommunist forces imperiling the security of the Warsaw Pact nations. With the U.S. invasion of the Dominican Republic, the shoe was on the other foot. To us, the action was necessary to remove a Communist threat to our security. To Russia, it was an unprovoked assault on the freedom of that little country.

Enemies create anxiety leading to a progressive simplification of their image in our eyes, and this results in formation of what has been called the mirror image of the enemy. These reciprocal images differ, of course, in the relative prominence of particular features. But to a surprising degree, enemies attribute the same virtues to themselves and the same vices to their opponents.

One excellent study of Russian and American self-images—as expressed in a selection of articles in both mass and elite publications of each nation—shows that virtually 100 per cent of the articles described the adversary's goal as international domination or expansion.

Each nation's press portrayed the other nation as aggressive and treacherous, and neither Americans nor Russians accepted the idea that the other was motivated by self-preservation.

Americans tended to be more realistic about their own motives for offering foreign aid, with 42 per cent of the articles in American periodicals indicating that the purpose of foreign aid was to strengthen their own side. But in Soviet Union publications, 95 per cent of the articles claimed that their own foreign-aid programs were just to be helpful, or else to make it possible for the countries to maintain neutrality. The press on both sides was virtually unanimous in claiming that the *other* side offered foreign aid not to help, but to strengthen a power position and to weaken that of their opponent.

The reciprocal images differed sharply in one respect

458

—foreign policy. Some 69 per cent of the Russian items regarded international events as predictable, while only seven per cent of the American items took this view. Strangely, this general view was contradicted by the way each side saw the other's specific behavior. The Russians described American foreign policy as a wild and unpredictable response to events, and the Americans tended to see Russian foreign policy as a masterful part of a deep-laid plot. Practically no articles in either American nor Russian publications stated that national military measures would bring about the other's downfall, and so there was reinforcement for the peaceful self-image of each nation.

In addition, the press of both nations indicated belief that internal weaknesses and contradictions in the other's system would lead to its eventual downfall. This finding is supported by Urie Bronfenbrenner of Cornell, a Russian-speaking psychologist, who did some informal but careful interviewing of people from different walks of life during a visit to the Soviet Union.

The Russians he interviewed believed that the people of the United States were being deluded and exploited, that they did not fully support the U. S. Government, that American leaders could not be trusted, and that U. S. foreign policy bordered on madness. (Many Americans reflect the flip side of the coin in their view of the Russians.)

Bronfenbrenner also found that nearly all of the Russians who came up to him and began a conversation expressed considerable discontent with life in the Soviet Union. On the other hand, more than 75 per cent of the Russians who did not speak until he had initiated the conversation identified fully with the Soviet way of life and the U. S. S. R. world view.

Another American scientist, Konrad Krauskopf of Stanford University, who visited the Soviet Union about the same time as Bronfenbrenner, had an opportunity for long, informal conversations with his Russian counterparts. He reported: "The Westerner regards the Russians as controlled for the most part without their knowledge, by an oligarchy of rapacious and malevolent men who seek constantly to foment world revolution. The Russian is equally convinced that the West (in Russian eyes, the West *is* the United States, and all other Western countries are American satellites) is victimized by a small group of profit-mad monopolists who pull the strings

that control the government and the communications media, and who try to instigate wars in order to sell munitions...it was impossible to resolve this difference in viewpoint. Each of us was repeating what he had read in his own newspapers, and each was suspicious of the other's sources."

A striking feature of the enemy mirror which Americans and Russians hold is the perception that it is *leaders* who are the real villains, and that the general population of the other country is either well disposed to one's own nation—or if they are not, it is because their leaders have misled them. Concomitant with this view is the belief that the masses in the other nation are discontented and would overthrow their leaders if only they could.

This combination is wonderfully consoling for citizens of both countries. It creates a positive image of one's own nation as a savior, and it simultaneously provides convenient, visualizable devils—the leaders—on whom to focus hostility and hate. This is illustrated by the Communists' monomania with "capitalists and monopolists" and with their intellectual concern for the "oppressed masses." And it is shown in the American tendency to focus on enemy leaders as targets—the Kaiser in World War I, Hitler in World War II, Stalin in the Cold War and more recently Castro, Mao, and Ho Chi Minh.

Contributing to the formation of the mirror image of the enemy is the need men have to reduce cognitive dissonance. When our perceptions of the enemy do not fit our preconceived image, anxiety is created and builds up. The effort to reduce this anxiety accounts for many phenomena in human thinking and behavior, and so there is continual effort to make our world view emotionally consistent, even if it is not logically consistent.

In order to survive, every person must organize the flood of experiences pouring in on him so that he can predict the effects of his behavior both upon people and upon other things. This organizing process starts as soon as he is born, and it is guided by his experiences with his family and with other people in his society.

In general, we filter and interpret incoming information to fit our preconceptions. Value systems are usually abstract enough so we can interpret events to fit beliefs, and also reinterpret our own behavior to make sure that it is consistent with those beliefs. The strain toward consistency tends, of course, to *reinforce* the enemy image.

But the same process also can help destroy the enemy

image when a former enemy becomes a needed ally. This is illustrated by a long series of public opinion polls on how Americans characterize people in other countries. In polls, respondents often are asked to choose from a list of adjectives the ones which best describe the people of another nation. In 1942, the first three adjectives chosen to characterize the Germans and the Japanese were: warlike, treacherous and cruel. Not one of these adjectives was among the top three describing the Russians, but by 1966, all three adjectives had disappeared from American descriptions of the Germans and Japanese, and the Russians were seen as warlike and treacherous. Predictably, the Communist Chinese by 1966 had become "warlike" and "treacherous" and "cruel." (Interestingly, the characterization "hardworking" rates high among descriptions of all these countries, whether friends or foes. A hardworking enemy is more to be feared, and a hardworking ally is a greater source of strength.)

A change in the American view of the Germans and Japanese followed their *total* defeat. The enemy ceased to be dangerous, and our demand for consistency required that the enemy image be altered. A factor supporting the change was the American belief that these former enemy nations were needed to help combat the spread of Communism.

Thus, in the eyes of many Americans the "warlike, treacherous, cruel, slant-eyed, buck-toothed little Japs" of World War II have become a highly cultivated, industrious, charming, and thoroughly attractive people. The American image of the German people is even more remarkable—it has flipped four times in less than half a century. Americans admired the Germans before World War I for their industry, their culture and their scientific know-how. Then, during the war, Germans became the hated "Huns." Next, the Germans of the Weimar Republic, a democracy, were regarded favorably. The Nazis changed that. Today Germans once more are staunch allies, even though many of the government officials are former Nazis.

By and large, the Germans today are the same people the Americans hated yesterday. Our change from hostility to friendliness has been made easier by the Germans' formal renunciation of Nazism. But, in retrospect, it may be observed that if these individuals were true Nazis, their change is suspect; and if most were not true Nazis, then they did not warrant our earlier hatred.

The strain to develop a consistent world view may lead nations with contrasting ideologies to exaggerate the differences in their behavior, and this raises the hopeful possibility that national value systems need not actually change much in order to permit acceptance of coexistence.

A study of American and Russian value systems by R. K. White of George Washington University shows that the American capitalist system which Soviet citizens have been taught to fear is not actually so very different from the "Good Society" that the Russians themselves would like to see develop in the U.S.S.R. Both systems are relatively modest variations on themes that seem to be among the common great aspirations of the human race.

In stressing how the group to which a person belongs determines his world view, I do not mean to imply that this view cannot be transcended by reflection and self-awareness. Today, human survival may depend on those individuals who can surmount a tribal outlook and appreciate the world views of people of other cultures.

A psychologically crucial part of the world view of any group is its ideology, and ideological differences contribute to the dehumanization of the enemy. Humans differ from other creatures primarily in the power to symbolize, so that we respond not only to physical violence but to psychological threats to our ideology or self-esteem.

Since nations cannot exist without ideologies, periodic "holy wars" may seem to be inevitable. But two factors mitigate this gloomy prospect. It is more satisfying psychologically to convert members of a rival belief system than to kill them. Conversion confirms superiority.

In addition, ideologies do not have to proclaim that they have exclusive possession of the truth. Some religions, such as Hinduism, declare that all religions have grasped some aspect of the Truth, and some secular ideologies, such as the American one, value diversity of of viewpoints in many areas. Adherents of world views like these can coexist with others indefinitely without resorting to armed conflict to protect their beliefs.

In the Vietnam war, ideological issues have become crucial. The North Vietnamese and the Viet Cong see themselves as fighting neocolonialism, as well as furthering the Communist ideology.

From a strictly materialistic viewpoint, Vietnam is of minor strategic importance to the United States.

461

"Leaders on each side fear that their own people are so naive that they easily can be misled by enemy propaganda."

The United States Government sees its action in Vietnam as part of a worldwide commitment to prevent the spread of Communism. And the U.S. also is motivated by a determination to show the world that we are steadfast, that we stand by our commitments.

The Vietnam war has assumed the ideological characteristics of a holy war. Throughout history, such holy wars usually end in mutual exhaustion after tremendous carnage, and with the survivors on both sides still clinging to their beliefs. Psychologically speaking, the notion that making people suffer causes them to abandon their beliefs is a hangover from the days of the Crusades.

Nations at war could be said to resemble children for whom punishment brings contrition only under certain conditions. As every parent knows, one can control behavior by punishment, but whether the punishment alters a basic attitude depends mainly on the child's belief that it was deserved.

There are studies that have attempted to relate personality attributes of individuals to their international attitudes, and most of these studies have dealt with an authoritarian character pattern whose dynamic core is the result of repressing strong hostility to parents and to other authority figures. The person with such a character pattern exaggerates the importance of power, of force, and of domination and submission in human affairs. He displaces his hostility to safer targets than the authority figures at home. He projects his internal psychological conflicts onto external enemies, and he expresses his bottled-up aggressive and sexual feelings indirectly by overconcern with the "immoral" behavior of foreigners and of the "out" groups in his own society.

People with authoritarian personalities score high on the "F-Scale," which consists of a series of statements like: "What youth needs most is strict discipline, rugged determination and the will to work and fight for family and country"; "Most of our social problems would be solved if we could somehow get rid of the immoral, crooked and feeble-minded people"; "People can be divided into two classes, the weak and the strong." The greater the number of such statements a person agrees with, the higher his score, and a high F-score correlates positively with extreme nationalism.

Within each country, individuals differ in the degrees that they see foreigners as enemies. At one extreme are those we might call xenophobic, those who hold a morbid dislike of foreigners and the other extreme are the xenophiles, who display an excessive acceptance of protestation of peaceful intent on the part of a foreign power, as well as holding hostility toward the leaders of their own country. Both extremists are likely to be hostile toward authority figures, but the xenophobe displaces his aggression to a foreign group and the xenophile focuses on his own leaders.

Since an enemy is seen as a threat to the survival of one's own nation, to change the enemy's image implies dropping one's guard. And the enemy's image has certain dynamic properties that make it resistant to change. First, an enemy mobilizes a nation's sense of solidarity and strength. He becomes a convenient scapegoat for internal problems. Second, the image that a nation holds of its enemy eventually will bring about behavior from the enemy that makes the image a reality.

The view that the actions of the other nation always are based on hostile motives may create a self-fulfilling prophecy. This term refers to the fact that a person's expectations come true. [See "Self-Fulfilling Prophecy," following.] A classic example is the international arms race. Each side anticipates that the other will add to its armament. In response to this expectation each increases its own arms, thereby fulfilling the expectations and convincing the other side that its fears are justified—which leads naturally to another round of arms increases.

Leaders on each side fear that their own people are so naive that they easily can be misled by enemy propaganda. The temptation to break off entirely or to restrict communication with the enemy is a strong one. Since the enemy is untrustworthy, if we communicate with him, he may trick us or learn something about us that we do not want him to know.

Another source of distortion of the enemy's characteristics is what G. Icheiser called the "mote-beam phenomenon." People who harbor unacceptable feelings may try to relieve their anxiety by projecting these traits to others, and then attacking them for possessing those traits. A person who tries to hide his own aggressiveness from himself is usually quick to spot aggression in others. In the same way, some Americans who turn a blind eye to the inequities in civil rights for Blacks are very concerned about the restrictions of freedom in the Soviet Union.

Bronfenbrenner showed some American fifth and sixth graders photographs of Russian roads lined with young trees. When he asked why the Russians had planted trees along the road, two of the answers were: "So that people won't be able to see what is going on beyond the road" and "It's to make work for the prisoners." When he asked why American roads have trees planted along the side, the children said "for shade" and "to keep the dust down."

The distorted image of the enemy acts, finally, to block acceptance of his genuine conciliatory moves. An apparently friendly gesture tends to be seen as either evidence of the enemy's weakening, or an effort to create dissension within one's own ranks. These responses are apparent in the Vietnam war. The Viet Cong interpret American gestures of peace as evidence of a weakening will to fight, while the American government sees the enemy's proposals as propaganda aimed at creating dissension in the United States.

An experiment done in a boys' camp by Muzafer Sherif of Pennsylvania State College some years ago suggests that activities requiring cooperation have a powerful effect in reducing antagonism between two hostile groups. When the boys arrived at camp, they were divided into two groups. Then the groups were made enemies through athletic competitions. In time, they became like two hostile nations. Members in each group chose friends only from among themselves, looked down on boys in the other group, and the two groups fought at every opportunity.

Once when a member of one group tried to act as a peacemaker, he was promptly ostracized by his fellows.

Then the camp director surreptitiously arranged events to force cooperation between the two groups. For example, he secretly arranged to have the camp water supply interrupted, and the whole camp had to work together to make necessary "repairs." A truck carrying food for an overnight hike "unaccountably" ran into a ditch. It took all the boys to pull it out with a tow-rope. A series of such events finally broke down hostility between the two groups, and friendly relations eventually were restored.

I would hesitate to generalize from boys in conflict to nations in conflict were it not for certain obvious parallels. In a sense, the nations of the world are in the same predicament today as the boys in that camp. Nations have to cooperate in order to survive, and the international scene contains many opportunities for cooperative activities, like those in the boys' camp, in yielding mutual benefits which one nation alone cannot attain. The International Geophysical Year is a good example.

The first step in contacting the enemy is psychologically the most difficult, and it takes considerable courage to make contact with a distrusted adversary, because this means exposure to dangers not only from the enemy but from one's own side. Here perhaps we can take advantage of what psychiatrists have learned about establishing communication with a frightened, angry and suspicious person. The first step, we have found, is simply to show persistent willingness to listen and to refuse to be discouraged by rebuffs. While you firmly defend yourself against physical attack, you ignore mere verbal abuse. It does not pay to be too friendly. The hostile person is convinced that you mean him no good, and so he is prone to interpret an overly friendly manner as an effort to deceive him. A firm and reserved, but not unfriendly manner, gets farther in reaching out to him.

Communication is only the first step. From a psychological standpoint, a central long-term task is learning how to foster cooperative projects among nations.

The chief danger of the distorted enemy image is that it makes false perceptions as hard to change as if they were true. Only by becoming highly aware of the psychological process that forms images can we hope to dispel the false aspects of an image. Otherwise, the difficulties in communicating with the enemy progressively harden our image of him. Fantasy fills the gaps left by insufficient information, and the face of the enemy reflects our own fears.

SETTING:
A psychologist is
seated at his desk.

There is a knock
on his office door.

PSYCHOLOGIST:
Come in.
(A male student enters)
Sit down, please.

**I am going to read you a set of
instructions. I am not permitted
to say anything which is not in the
instructions nor can I answer any
questions about this experiment.
OK? We are developing
a test of...**

After the student
has completed the
experiment, he leaves.
    There is another
knock at the door.

The only difference
between the two
episodes is the smile!
    Can a smile affect
results of an experiment?
It not only can,
but probably does.
In the laboratory.
In the classroom.
And everywhere in life.

PSYCHOLOGIST:
Come in.
(A female student enters)
Sit down, please.
(The psychologist smiles)
I am going to read you a set of instructions. I am not permitted to say anything which is not in the instructions nor can I answer any questions about this experiment. OK? We are developing a test of...

Self-Fulfilling Prophecy

By Robert Rosenthal

"I haven't pricked it yet," the Queen said, "but I soon shall — oh, oh, oh!"

ALICE THROUGH THE LOOKING GLASS

Can a child become brighter because a teacher's special smile shows that he is expected to be smarter than he thought he was?

Let us look at what happens when the behavioral scientist, *seeking* absolute objectivity and fairness, approaches an experiment in social research.

Much of our scientific knowledge is based upon careful observation and recording of events. That the observer himself may have a biasing effect on his observations has long been recognized. There are two basic types of experimenter effects. The first operates without affecting the event or subject being studied. It occurs in the eye, the hand and the brain of the researcher. The second type is the result of the *interaction* between the experimenter and the subject of the experiment. And when the research deals with humans and animals, as it does in the behavioral sciences, this interaction actually can alter the responses or data that are obtained.

Quite unconsciously, a psychologist interacts in subtle ways with the people he is studying so that he may get the response he expects to get. This happens even when the person cannot see the researcher. And, even more surprisingly, it occurs when the subject is not human but a rat.

If rats became brighter when expected to by their researcher, isn't it possible that children become brighter when their teachers expect them to be brighter?

Lenore Jacobson, of the South San Francisco Unified School District, and I set out to see if this is so. Every child in an elementary school was given an intelligence test, a test described by us as one that would predict "intellectual blooming."

The school was in a lower socioeconomic neighborhood on the West Coast. There were three classrooms for each grade—one for children of above average ability, one for average ability, and one for below average ability. About 20 per cent of the children in each classroom were chosen at random to form the experimental group. The teachers were given the names of this group and told that these children had scored high on the test for intellectual blooming and would show remarkable gains in intel-

lectual development during the next eight months.

In reality, the only difference between these children and their classmates was *in the minds* of their teachers.

At the end of the school year, all the children were again given the same I.Q. test. In the school as a whole, the children who had been designated as "bloomers" showed only a slightly greater gain in verbal I.Q. (two points) than their classmates. However, *in total* I.Q., the experimental group gained four points more on the average than their counterparts did, and in reasoning I.Q., the average gain was seven points more.

Usually, when educational theorists talk of improving scholastic achievement by improving teacher expectations, they are referring to children at the lower levels of achievement. It was interesting to find that teacher expectations affected children at the highest level of achievement as much as it did children at the lowest level.

At the end of the school year, we asked the teachers to describe the classroom behavior of all their pupils. The children in the group designated as the bloomers were seen as more interesting, more curious, and happier. The teachers also found "blooming" children slightly more appealing, better adjusted, and more affectionate, and with less need for social approval.

Many of the other children in the classes also gained in I.Q. during the year, but teachers reacted negatively to *unexpected* improvement. The more the undesignated children gained in I.Q. points, the more they were regarded as *less* well-adjusted, *less* interesting, and *less* affectionate. It appears that there may be hazards to unpredicted intellectual growth—at least in the eyes of the teacher. This is particularly true of children in the low-ability groups.

The effects of teacher expectation were most evident in reasoning I.Q.

gains. But only the girls in the group designated as "bloomers" showed greater gains than the rest of the class. The boys designated as bloomers actually gained less than their classmates. Partly to check this finding, Judy Evans and I repeated the experiment with schoolchildren in a small Midwestern town. The children here were from substantial middle-class families.

Again we found that teacher expectations affected reasoning I.Q. gains in pupils. However, this time it was the boys who tended to show greater gains than girls. These results underline the effects of teacher expectations, but they also indicate the complexity of these effects as a function of the pupil's sex, social status, and very likely other variables as well.

In another study, conducted by Lane K. Conn, Carl N. Edwards, Douglas Crowne and me, we selected an East Coast school with upper-middle-class pupils. This time we also measured the children's accuracy in judging the emotion conveyed in tone of voice. The children who were more accurate in judging the emotional tone of an adult female's voice benefited most from favorable teacher expectations. And in this school, both the boys and girls who were expected to bloom intellectually showed greater reasoning I.Q. gains than their classmates.

W. Victor Beez of Indiana University conducted an experiment in 1967 which sheds some light on the phenomenon of teacher expectancy. His pupils were 60 preschoolers from a summer Head-Start program. Each child had one teacher who taught him the meaning of a series of symbols. Half of the teachers were led to expect good symbol learning, and the other half were led to expect poor learning.

Nearly 77 per cent of the children designated as good intellectual prospects learned five or more symbols. Only 13 per cent of the children designated as poor prospects learned five or more symbols. A researcher from the outside who did not know what the teachers had been told about the children's intellectual prospects assessed the children's actual performance.

What happened in this study was that the teachers with favorable expectations tried to teach more symbols to their pupils than did teachers who had unfavorable expectations. This indicates that the teacher's expectations may not only be translated into subtle vocal and visual nuances, but also may cause dramatic alterations in teaching style. Surprisingly, however, even when the amount of teaching was held constant, the children who were expected to learn more did learn more.

Teacher expectancy effects are not limited to the teaching of intellectual tasks. Recent research reported by J. Randolph Burnham and Donald M. Hartsough of Purdue University indicates that the teaching of motor skills also may be affected by teacher expectations. At a camp for underprivileged children from the Philadelphia area, Burnham administered a test to nonswimmers that ostensibly would predict psychological readiness to swim. He then randomly selected children from various age groups and gave their names to the waterfront counselors as those who were "ready" to swim. He found that the children designated as "ready" tended to pass more of the tests in the Red Cross beginning swimmer's course than the average for their peer group.

If the expectancy effect occurs in the laboratory and in the classroom, then it

is not surprising to find it occurring in everyday life. Your expectation of how another person will behave often may become a self-fulfilling prophecy. We know that nonverbal and unintentional communication between people does take place. What we don't know is *how* such communication occurs. Further research on the interaction of the experimenter and the subject may eventually teach us more about dyadic interactions in general.

The interaction of experimenter and his subject is a major source of knowledge in the behavioral sciences. Until recently, however, this interaction has been an uncontrolled variable in psychological research. But the demonstration of experimenter effects does not necessarily invalidate a great deal of behavioral research. It does mean, however, that we must take extra precautions to reduce "expectancy" and other unintended effects of the experimenter.

Just what does a behavioral scientist unintentionally do in gathering his data so that he unwittingly influences his subjects' responses? This question must be answered satisfactorily if we want to have dependable knowledge in the behavioral sciences.

In our research, we have distinguished five categories of interactional effects between the experimenter and his subjects: the *Biosocial, Psychosocial, Situational, Modeling* and *Expectancy Effects*.

Biosocial Effects

The sex, age and race of investigators all have been found to affect the results of their research. It is tempting to assume that the subjects simply are responding to the biosocial attributes of the investigator. But the investigator himself, because of sex, age or race, may respond differently to male or female, young or old, white or Negro subjects. And even a slight change in behavior alters the experimental situation.

Our evidence suggests, for example, that male and female experimenters conduct the same experiment quite differently. The different results they obtain are not due to any error as such, but may well be due to the fact that they have unintentionally conducted different experiments.

In one study of the effect of the characteristics of subjects on the experimenter, the interaction between experimenters and subjects was recorded on sound film. Only 12 per cent of the investigators smiled even a little at male subjects, but 70 per cent smiled at female subjects. These smiles may well have affected the results of the experiment. It may be a heartening finding to know that chivalry is not dead, but as far as methodology is concerned it is a disconcerting finding. In general, the experimenter treated his male subjects and female subjects differently, so that, in a sense, men and women really were not in the same experiment at all.

Moreover, when we consider the sex of both the experimenter and the subject, other interaction effects emerge. In the study recorded on film, we found that the experimenters took more time to collect some of their data from subjects of the opposite sex than from subjects of the same sex.

The age of the investigator may also affect the subject's response. Studies suggest that young subjects are less likely to say "unacceptable" things to much older investigators, indicating that an "age-barrier" may exist in at least some behavioral studies.

The skin color of the investigator also may affect response, even when the response is physiological.

A number of studies have found that Negroes tend to control their hostility more when contacted by a white rather than a Negro experimenter and give more "proper" responses to white than black interviewers.

Psychosocial Effects

Experimenters are people, and so they differ in anxiety, in their need for approval, in personal hostility, authoritarianism, status and in personal warmth. Experimenters with different personalities tend to get different responses from their experimental subjects. For example, researchers higher in status—a professor as compared to a graduate student, or a captain as compared to a corporal—tend to obtain more responses that *conform* to the investigator's suggestions. And investigators who are warmer toward people tend to obtain more *pleasant* responses.

Situational Effects

Investigators experienced in conducting a given experiment usually obtain responses different from those of less experienced investigators. This may be because they behave differently. Also, experimenters who are acquainted with the people in the experimental group get results that differ from those obtained by researchers who have never met their subjects before.

What happens to the experimenter during the course of his experiment can influence his behavior, and changes in his behavior may lead to changes in the subjects' responses.

For instance, if the first few subjects respond as expected (*i.e.*, confirming the experimenter's hypothesis), the behavior of the researcher alters, and he influences subsequent subjects to respond in a way that supports his hypothesis.

Modeling Effects

Sometimes before an experimenter conducts a study, he first tries out the task he will have his research subjects perform. For example, if the task is to rate a series of 10 photos of faces according to how successful or unsuccessful the persons pictured appear to be, the experimenters may decide to rate the photos themselves before contacting their

subjects. Though evidence is not yet definite, it appears that at least sometimes the investigator's own ratings become a factor in the performance of his subjects. In particular, when the experimental stimuli, such as photos, are ambiguous, the subjects' interpretation may agree too often with the investigator's interpretation, even though the latter remains unspoken.

Some expectation of how the research might turn out is virtually a constant factor in all scientific experiments. In the behavioral sciences, this expectancy can lead the investigator to act unconsciously in such a way that he affects the responses of his subjects. When the investigator's expectancy influences the

responses in the direction of what the investigator expects to happen, we can appropriately regard his hypothesis as a *self-fulfilling prophecy*. One prophesies an event, and the expectation of the event then changes the behavior of the prophet in such a way as to make the prophesied event more likely.

In the history of psychology, the case of *Clever Hans* is a classic example of this phenomenon. Hans was a horse owned by a German mathematics instructor named Von Osten. Hans could perform difficult mathematical calculations, spell, read and solve problems of musical harmony by tapping his foot.

A panel of distinguished scientists and experts on animal behavior ruled that no fraud was involved. The horse was given no cues to tell him when to start or when to stop tapping his foot.

But, of course, there *were* cues. In a series of brilliant experiments reported in 1911, Oskar Pfungst showed that Hans could answer questions only when the questioner himself knew the answers and when the horse could see the questioner. Finally, Pfungst learned that a tiny forward movement of the experimenter's head was the signal for Hans to start tapping. A slight upward movement of the head, or even a raised eyebrow, was the signal for the horse to stop tapping.

Hans's questioners expected him to give the right answers, and their expectation was reflected in their unwitting signals to start and stop tapping. The horse had good eyesight, and he *was* a smart horse.

Self-fulfilling Prophecies

To demonstrate experimenter effects in behavioral research, we must have at least two groups of experimenters with different expectations. One approach is to take a survey of investigators in a certain area of research and ask those with opposite expectancies to conduct a standard experiment. But the differences in the results could be due to factors other than expectancy, and so a better strategy is required.

Rather than trying to find two groups of experimenters with different expectations, we could *create* such groups. In one experiment, we selected 10 advanced undergraduate and graduate students of psychology as our researchers. All were experienced in conducting research. Each was assigned a group of 20 participating students as his subjects. The experiment consisted of showing 10 photographs of people's faces one at a time to each subject. The participant was to rate the degree of success or failure reflected in the facial expression of the person in the photo. Each of the faces could be rated from −10 (extreme failure) to +10 (extreme success). The faces in the photos were actually quite neutral, and on the average the total ratings should have produced a numerical score of zero.

All 10 experimenters had identical instructions to read to their subjects, and they also had identical instructions on how to conduct the experiment. They were specifically cautioned not to deviate from these instructions.

Finally, we informed our researchers that the purpose of the experiment was to see how well they could duplicate results which were already well-established. We told half of the experimenters that the "well-established" finding was that people rated the faces in the photos as successful (+5). And we told the other half that people rated the faces in the photos as unsuccessful (−5). And thus informed, they began their research.

The results were clear-cut. Every researcher who was led to expect that the photographed people were successful obtained a higher average rating of success from his group than did any experimenter who expected low-success ratings.

We repeated this experiment twice with different groups with the same results. Research in other laboratories has shown much the same thing. Although not every experiment showed a significant effect, probability that results of all these experiments occurred by chance is less than one in a thousand billion.

Having found that what the experimenter expects to happen can affect the outcome of his research, we then began to look for some clues as to *how* the experimenter unwittingly communicates his expectancy to his subjects.

Through the use of accomplices who acted as subjects in an experiment, we learned how the responses of the first few subjects affected the experimenter's behavior to subsequent subjects. If the responses of the first few subjects confirmed the experimenter's hypothesis, his behavior to subsequent participants somehow influenced them also to confirm his hypothesis. But when the "planted" accomplices contradicted the expectations of the experimenter, the following subjects were affected by the experimenter's behavior so that they, too, tended to disconfirm his hypothesis. It seems, then, that the early returns of data in behavioral research can affect and possibly shape the final results.

Reverse Effects

In some of our experiments, when we offered too-obvious incentives or too-large rewards to investigators to bring in "good" data, the expectancy effect was reduced, and in some cases even reversed. Both the autonomy and the honesty of the researchers may have been challenged by the excessive rewards offered. It speaks well for the integrity of our student-researchers that they would not be bribed. In fact, they tended to bend over backwards to avoid the biasing effect of their expectation. But they often bent so far backward that the results of their experiments sometimes were the opposite of what they had been told to expect.

The process by which an experimenter unintentionally and covertly communicates instructions to his subjects is very subtle. For six years we have studied sound films of research interviews in an attempt to discover the cues that the experimenter unwittingly gives to the subject, and for six years we have failed, at least partly.

We know, however, that visual cues *are* important. Placing a screen between the investigator and the person he is interviewing reduces the investigator's influence on the results. But the expectancy effect is not eliminated completely, indicating that auditory cues are also important.

This was dramatically demonstrated by John G. Adair and Joyce Epstein of the University of Manitoba in their tape-recording experiment. They first duplicated the expectation effects study in which 10 photographs of people's faces are rated successful or unsuccessful. Half of the investigators were told to expect a success response and half a failure response. Adair and Epstein tape-recorded each of the sessions. The results matched those of the original studies.

Next, with a new group of subjects a second experiment was conducted. But instead of having live investigators, the subjects listened to the tape-recording of an investigator reading the standard instructions to the previous group. Again the results were much the same. Self-fulfilling prophecies, it seems, can come about as a result of the prophet's voice alone. Since in the experiment all prophets read standard instructions, self-fulfillment of prophecies may be brought about by the tone in which the prophet prophesies.

Early in our research on self-fulfilling prophecies, we thought that some form of operant conditioning might be the explanation. It could be that when the investigator obtained a response consistent with his expectations, he would look more pleasant, or smile, or glance

A dull rat

at the subject approvingly. The investigator could be entirely unaware of these reinforcing responses. We analyzed many experiments to see if this type of operant conditioning was present. If indeed it was, then the subject's responses should gradually become more like those expected by the investigator—there would be a "learning curve" for subjects.

But no learning curve was found. On the contrary, it turned out that the first responses of the subject were about as much affected by the investigator's expectations as the last responses.

Further analysis revealed that while there was no learning curve for the subjects, there seemed to be a learning curve for the investigators. As the investigator interviewed more and more subjects, the expectancy effect grew stronger. It appeared possible that the subject's response was the reinforcing event. The subjects, then, may quite unintentionally shape the investigator's behavior. So not only does the experimenter influence his subjects to respond in the expected manner, but the subjects may well influence the experimenter to behave in a way that leads to fulfillment of his prophecies.

Perhaps the most significant implication of this research is that human beings can engage in highly effective and influential unintended communication with one another—even under controlled laboratory conditions.

But do expectancy effects occur when the experimental subjects are not human? We designed a study to find out. Twelve experimenters were each given five rats that were to be taught to run a maze with the aid of visual cues. Six of the experimenters were told that their rats had been specially bred for maze-brightness; the other six were told that their rats had been bred for maze-dullness. Actually, there was no difference between the rats.

At the end of the experiment, researchers with "maze-bright" rats found superior learning in their rats compared to the researchers with maze-dull rats.

A second experiment made use of the special training setup designed by B. F. Skinner of Harvard. Half the researchers were led to believe that their rats were "Skinner box bright" and half were told that their rats were "Skinner box dull." Initially, there were not really such dif-

ferences in the rats, but at the end of the experiment the allegedly brighter animals *were* really brighter, and the alleged dullards *really* duller.

How can we reduce the expectancy effect in behavioral research?

One way is to design procedures that enable us to assess whether the expectancy effects have altered the results of an experiment. In addition, the experimenter could employ investigators who have not been told the purpose of the study, or automated data-collection systems could be used.

Perhaps a new profession of fulltime experimenters could be developed, who would perform others' experiments without becoming involved in setting up a hypothesis or interpreting the results. Precedents for such professionals are found in both medical research and public-opinion surveys.

Dependable Knowledge

Because of the general nature of expectancy and other experimenter effects, it would be desirable to use more experimenters for each study than we presently use. Having a larger number of returns we could assess the extent to which different experimenters obtained different results, and in any area of psychological research this is worth knowing.

Scientists have long employed control groups in their experiments. Usually the experimental group receives some kind

of treatment while the control group receives no treatment. To determine the extent of the expectancy effect, we could add two special "expectancy control" groups to the experiment. In one of these special groups, the investigator would be told that the group's subjects had received some treatment, when in fact it had not. The experimenter in the other group would be told the subjects had not received treatment when in fact it had. Such a research design would permit us to assess the magnitude of the effect of experimenter's expectancy.

To the extent that we hope for dependable knowledge in the behavioral sciences, we must have dependable knowledge about the psychological experiment and the interaction of experimenter and subject. We can no more hope to acquire accurate information for our disciplines without understanding the experimenter effect than astronomers or zoologists could hope to acquire accurate information without understanding the effects of their telescopes and microscopes. And behavioral scientists, being as scientifically self-conscious a group as they are, may one day produce a psychology of those psychologists who study psychologists.

Then, in the laboratory, in the classrooms, in every sector of our lives we will come closer to understanding the effect of a smile.

ENCOUNTER IN COLOR

BY THOMAS J. COTTLE

SCHOOL-BUSSING INTEGRATION PROGRAMS normally proceed along fairly predictable lines. Students of both races are told simply that a merger soon will occur; automatically, whites are designated as the home team, the Negroes are the visitors. The outnumbered transients—and Negroes feel like transients—then are plopped into the middle of a familiar and well-rehearsed drama, one in which they are totally uncomfortable. And throughout the entire process, teachers must assume responsibility for making the merger work.

The sadness of the drama is that it takes place with almost no psychological preparation and with no time devoted to the resolution of human and institutional complications. Yet as though by some magic, students are supposed to live together peaceably and to learn something. The drama's irony

is that where schools in the past have exulted in their socializing function, when integration becomes a reality they hurriedly retreat to their fundamental didactic activities. School boards try to combine the races in varying ratios—advantageous to the whites but justified by national or regional proportions—with the hope that somehow the kids will work it out. Afterwards social scientists are employed to diagnose the existing exigencies and to present the statistics on prior injustices and inequalities.

Social science methodology and sophistication hardly are required, however, to assess contemporary token integration programs, for anyone can observe the difficulties involved for students, teachers, and administrators. Anyone can vibrate to the currents of open and muffled prejudice and of hatreds. And of the inevitable despair.

Yet in the design of human environments social science can make one important contribution which provides a workable way in which integration and learning may evolve naturally.

For the past year, a group of us at Harvard have been engaged in a small project aimed at developing an experimental context which permits the observation of integration dynamics. At the same time we have offered an arena for the confrontation of adolescents who bring to this most complex encounter their conspicuous and well-rehearsed sentiments, and less well-understood, newly discovered fears and fantasies.

Our intention was to transport integration to a laboratory setting modeled after the real and often frightening world of contemporary high-school students. Our participants were lower- and middle-class Negro and white boys and girls, and their difficult task was to meet together and to speak directly upon the issues of race and social relations.

But these were not simple seminars. They were self-analytic groups. In self-analytic groups, an experienced leader "trains" group members to pursue the personal expressions and interpersonal processes which arise "spontaneously." Group members are encouraged to analyze their feelings and verbalize their attitudes, actions, and even fantasies. The emphasis in self-analytic groups rests on the meaning of group interactions, as well as on private revelations.

In such groups, the self-analytic procedures normally are not outlined fully to group members; rather they are insinuated by the leader into the ongoing

Whites are designated as the home team...

472

SCHOOL BUS

group processes. The leader guides the group towards more expansive observation and analysis, and the mood generated is one of constrained freedom. Anything can be said by anyone at any time, but the inferred rule is that expression and analysis must run contiguously.

This notion is borrowed from the psychoanalytic tradition which argues that the ego must be "split" if one is to perform two requisite therapeutic tasks. A second notion, taken from the same source, is that leaders (not unlike classical analysts), by participating minimally, create in the minds of group members a need to construct a viable social system with inherent institutional arrangements and necessary role allocations. (In fact, taciturn leaders, by creating social contracts which are seemingly devoid of normally evident sanctions, accentuate their own positions as the ultimate authority and render ever so complicated the nature of relationships between members.) The starkness of the self-analytic context, by compelling participants to develop for themselves a social order which they then must assess, brings to the laboratory a setting which some authors claim is suitable for studying the most primitive and complex forms of human behavior.

The greatness of such groups comes as they succeed in getting persons to confront both private and public issues normally avoided or not noticed.

The danger in the technique, as we employed it, was that innocent students inadvertently were transformed into cadres of miniature psychotherapists. And, untrained, they may have believed

mistakenly that manifest content had little value. The balance fell into the very human hands of the leader, who in the safety of his role and with his dappled moments of real understanding, had the power to drive the group to either end. In the process he came to be perceived, at least by people of his own race, as father, mother, teacher, older brother, therapist, and – if he played it wrong—as God himself.

Three points should be made here about our perspectives on the self-analytic technique. First, we did not consider the groups as psychotherapy. The assumption was *not* illness and the intention was *not* treatment. (This is not to say that people enlisting in self-analytic groups may not have been seeking the therapy context.)

Second, it was expected that when problems were so complex that they

could not be verbalized, groups would deal with them in fantasy terms, and thus provide both an outlet for their expression and a justification for direct interpretation. The open and direct line to their own fantasies held by adolescents actually increased the significance of this point.

Third, as in psychotherapy, every action of every moment was considered potentially significant. Thus, jokes, member absences, meeting time and place, physical appearance, and apparently casual topics assumed importance.

The application of self-analytic groups to racial integration barely has been explored. But we selected such groups for our program because we believe this format is ideal and offers stimulating experiences which also can be observed carefully. Furthermore, because of their flexibility, such groups

...The Negroes are the visitors.

473

The Negro girl nervously wandered through fantasy:

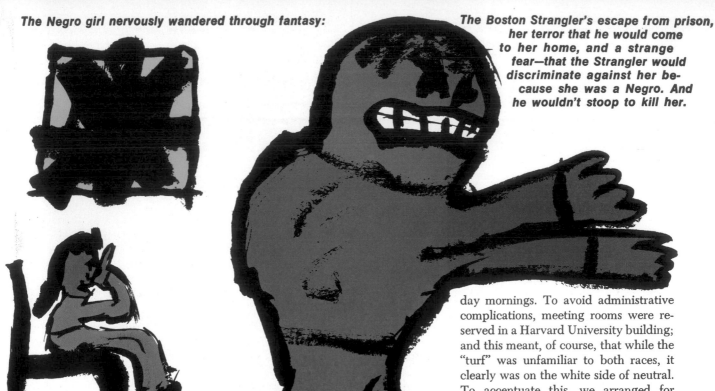

The Boston Strangler's escape from prison, her terror that he would come to her home, and a strange fear—that the Strangler would discriminate against her because she was a Negro. And he wouldn't stoop to kill her.

could be structured in at least two ways to simulate the paradigms for school-bussing operations.

The first school-bussing program, which may be called the "September plan," is the method by which reluctant administrators throw Negro and white students together in white schools, with instructions to get along. While the previous Summer has brought deep and searching thoughts and hopes for the impending merger, as well as pessimism and red hot antipathies, few professionals with the exception of men like Robert Coles, author of *Children of Crisis,* have concerned themselves with these, months before school integration, either in terms of research or as a time for support and guidance of the equally bewildered white and Negro students. Presumably a bit more humane, the "June plan" grants Negroes and whites a brief moment to discuss their fears and animosities in the privacy of their own academic and racial environments.

Accordingly, our groups were arranged to replicate these two alternative ways of handling school integration. Some of our groups consisted of Negroes and whites together from the start, with the size of groups limited to 10 or 12 students. Other groups of four to six youths each began in a segregated fashion and met thus for six sessions. After six meetings, we merged

the groups for six more weeks. For these groups, announcement of approaching integration came at the beginning of the first segregated session. Students were asked to participate in 12 group meetings, one per week, with each lasting a little more than an hour. Because of the students' busy school and work programs, the sessions all were scheduled in the early evenings or on Satur-

day mornings. To avoid administrative complications, meeting rooms were reserved in a Harvard University building; and this meant, of course, that while the "turf" was unfamiliar to both races, it clearly was on the white side of neutral. To accentuate this, we arranged for groups to meet after merger at the same time and in the same room as did white students during the segregated sessions. A community's university of course is hardly a neutral stimulus for lower-class adolescents. And the structure symbolized by the university, forbidding to Negroes, may be even more upsetting to white students for whom the university and the very idea of research represent familiar but unattainable objects.

Some 45 students were selected from local high schools, church groups, and neighborhood youth clubs for our self-analytic group experiment. They volunteered for a project advertised as an ex-

The eloquent Negro boy described local police (slow, dark, dirty) and highway police (sleek, neat, tall) but he said: "All of us are dark specks on a policeman's badge."

periment in human relations. Ironically, Negro participants had to be reimbursed for taxi fare necessary to transport them from their homes—both distant from and inconvenient to the university. There was no other reimbursement for members because we felt that only would complicate things. Termination of "salaried" students could be interpreted as the firing of inferior employees. (As an incentive and a gesture of nurture, however, students were given beverages and snacks during each meeting.)

Strict obeying of bussing statistics would urge white-dominated groups, but the natural anxieties attending self-analytic experiments of this type dictated instead a goal of population equality. Students of about the same age—sophomores and juniors—were assigned to groups in random fashion but with the stipulation that sexes and races should be distributed evenly. Definitely to be avoided in the project (and in schools as well!) was a group with one Negro or only one boy, and other such dramatic imbalances.

As it turned out, several of the students knew each other from school, and though prior acquaintanceship often interferes with group progress, actually it proved beneficial in some instances. In one group for example, a Negro boy listened intently to a white girl's discussion and then told of his prior distaste for her, and of his newly formed admiration. Her performance in the group demonstrated a courage and intelligence he had never seen in the classroom, he said. It was with obvious joy that he announced his change of heart.

Just as important as group composition was the selection of group leaders. If leaders were overly specialized, the possible general applicability of the project's results would be greatly decreased. Certainly our resources were limited by the availability of people possessing similar kinds of group experience so that relatively uniform group structures could be set up.

Available to us in almost superabundance, however, was a population of university students, both graduate and undergraduate, who not only had taken part in self-analytic groups but had spent additional months observing groups other than their own. This then became the delicate minimum for leader credentials: one year as a group member, plus at least one semester of observation.

Schoolroom realities suggested using female leaders—for us a sadly rare commodity. Hence, acknowledging both reality guideposts and the characteris-

tics of the university manpower pool, five white males — two graduate and three undergraduate students — were selected as group leaders. None of these young men had previous experience as leaders but each had been in groups and had worked in areas of race relations. It was through their mature insights and sensitivities, as well as through their natural apprehensions and reticence, that the project was conceived and launched.

It is always difficult to differentiate between rational calculations about what groups should be and the experimental designs drawn according to the less rational and invisible needs of those who direct them. The fact that the subtle

"In Viet Nam, it's the good whites against the bad colored."

expectancies of the experimenter influence the outcomes of research has been more than amply demonstrated by Robert Rosenthal in his book, *Experimental Effect in Behavioral Reserach.* Similarly, self-analytic groups all have expectations which drive members toward certain demarcated ends. Leaders—or therapists—do not create a vacuum with their ungainly silences and vocally bland penetrations; they build toward a discrete and peculiar atmosphere which often makes normal brain function difficult but putatively yields the desired and desirable ends.

We simply do not know the degree to which our own needs were met by project procedures. For example, our decision to substitute in-group observers and tape recorders for the frequently used one-way mirrors may be explained

in several ways: while public-private, formal-informal dimensions exist naturally in groups, there also are nebulous realms of insecurity, intimacy, competence, and potency. On the other hand, private, closed rooms protect leaders and members from outside evaluation.

The influence of leaders on groups, furthermore, varies from man to man, session to session, and probably from moment to moment. Leader strategies and reactions could not possibly be uniform, or even consistent, except perhaps in cases where single leaders ran both the Negro and white segregated groups prior to merging.

At best, leaders could but listen intensely and predicate their utterances upon a concern for their group members and upon what in a word is history, namely that only months before, as group members themselves, they too had struggled with similar problems in similar fashion.

Assessments of our results certainly must be made not only in light of integration factors and more characteristic adolescent social phenomena but also with consideration for the reaction of human beings to the novel, seductive, and perhaps terrifying system offered by group structure and purpose. The early phase of all our groups, for instance, was characterized by a grappling at so-called reality levels with the proposed (white) authority and intimacy, and on fantasy levels with the actual or promised racial merger. The groups sidled into the authority problem by verbal attacks on the University, inquiries into whether Harvard's president, the governor of Massachusetts, and even Senator Robert Kennedy would learn of the project. The groups wanted to know: Would it be written up? Were they guinea pigs? Was all this really confidential? What might result from the excessive freedom and exposure of one's inner self?

Contained within these natural queries, of course, was the students' hope that if they would open up to one another, the leader in turn would approve of their efforts, reveal his involvement with them, and even reward them ironically by declaring negative sanctions.

The major problem in our early meetings was to establish a social order involving trust but also taking account of authority hierarchies and qualities of interpersonal attachment. Sample conversations were: "We're just like the United Nations and he (the leader) is like a silent Secretary General." "What would happen if he weren't here?"

"There would be anarchy." "What would that mean?" "Probably free love for everyone." Every single group met and solved that problem: the transference of free minds and open discussions to free love and, to use a neologism often heard in groups, "orgification."

In his silence and manifest sureness, the self-analytic group leader perpetrates what at the beginning can be felt, if not perceived, as a legitimized seduction and human coalescence. If the coalescence is overly-sexual, group members must align their sex-role definitions and defenses in reaction to the aroused threats. If in his coalescing the leader appears overly paternalistic, an action not necessarily excluding Negroes, members must align their mutual associations in accordance with social codes appropriate in family and peer realms. Such alignments bring up unconscious interpretations of sexual prohibitions relating to patterns of incest, premarital intercourse, and ensuing illegitimate childbirth. "How many of us here are accidents?" one boy shouted as he attempted to discover a potentially uniting reality — and in so doing planted the seeds of an incestuous sibling rivalry.

No matter how he came across in our group, the leader was the unequivocal agent of integration and, in our segregated groups, he was also the sole person to share communications and histories of Negroes and whites alike. It became apparent that, whatever the source and strength of the leader-member tie might be, this bond necessarily transcended a pure racial identity. In fact, a form of "backlash" emerged as the neutrality of each group leader caused whites to see him often either as a turncoat or as a father abandoning

"If you see a strong Whitey,

you know he's been lifting weights."

Negroes see themselves as intruders, aliens from a different planet, soldiers from a different land.

his own children. Negroes began to perceive the leader as an inexplicably trustworthy person and perhaps even as a suitable stepfather. In the first session of one merged group, a Negro girl left her fellow Negroes and pulled her chair halfway around the room so that she might sit down next to (and a bit behind) the white leader.

Actual merger of the segregated groups naturally affected the quality of the transference to the leader. During segregated sessions, the approach of both whites and Negroes changed radically as the whites evidenced fear of abandonment and their disbelief that a member of their own race would lead them knowingly into such a predicament. Negroes tended to drift back to a more primitive self-perception and a stereotype ghetto behavior. Possibly because of this element in their shared group experience, the participants collectively returned to the leader during final sessions before merging in an almost childlike posture of dependence. We interpreted this as symbolizing their hopes that the leader would regulate their activities and thus bring the merger to its desired ending.

The transference, however, changed for a third time as group members gradually realized that they *alone* were the architects and inhabitants of this new community and that their prior real

and fantasy histories — both with and without the leader—had to be reconciled or even altered to accommodate a still newer environment. Although less clear, similar transformations occurred in integrated groups as well.

Given these many complexities, how does one interpret one white girl's explosive response to the proposition of racial merger and the presence of white male authority: "Let's talk about premarital sexuality!" And how do we explain the exquisite associations of a slight Negro girl as she nervously wandered through fantasy descriptions: gypsy marriages, desire for racial equality, student demonstrations in Florida, life in her own ghetto, the crimes committed by police, her pleasure at the Boston Strangler's escape from prison (an escape from another kind of ghetto), her terror that the Strangler would come to her home, and her subsequent and *real* preparations: boarding windows and doors and piling knives and scissors under her chair. Poignantly, she ended the verbal fantasy by revealing one more fear—that midst his seemingly uncontrollable psychosis, the Strangler still would discriminate against a Negro and reject her as a murder victim.

Our groups' remarks about premarital sexuality well may refer to what many participants saw as a "marriage" of the races, performed in the group by the integrating "ceremony" of the group leader who had "powers invested in him" and was equally associated with both white and Negro group members.

In one integrated group, an almost Quakerlike ceremony actually was performed as two boys, one Negro and the other white, gradually developed a closeness sufficiently strong and public to unite the entire group as a congregation. The presence of girls presumably kept the boys' intimacy from gaining the pejorative status.

In another experimental group composed of Negro and white gang boys, a similar intended marriage, if it can be called that, became aggressive and atavistic as each side designated one of its members as inferior and agreed to a contract of mutual denigration. Swelling with homosexual overtones, their project fizzled; a basketball game was proposed, with the leader acting as referee. The merger failed as the "bunch" of whites and "pile" of Negroes (their own description) never melded.

Much of the foregoing imagery seems to us related to the group's need for control, particularly in spheres of authority and morality. In our groups, authority assumed heightened significance in light of the racial merger, either scheduled or already enacted. It was not surprising therefore that participants made strong pleas for refereeing and social policing; someone must define not only psychospatial limits of the group but the "legal" extent of the merger's penetration.

In one of our integrated groups, an eloquent Negro boy was able to contrive a medium for expressing the vertical intimacies inherent in good authority arrangements. Speaking of the microcosm which was his group, he spelled out the disparities of local and highway police: the former—slow, dark, dirty, irresponsible, inconsistent in their punishment, unavailable when needed; the latter—sleek, neat, tall, strong, quick to attend. And his poetry continued: "All of us are dark specks on a policeman's badge." Soon afterwards, he turned these descriptions into a comparison of Negro and white fathers, and then he concluded by expressing his distaste for his own father in what seemed to the group to be his wish to be ministered to or even adopted by the leader, a man no more than three years his senior.

Comparable feelings were equally prevalent among white group members, but the undeniable existence of the white authority figure must not be overlooked, for it may have inspired what Eric Erickson calls negative identity elements in Negroes in the group and, at the same time, have made statements of

"The white people slide . . . we glide."

needs for parental-like gratifications more difficult for the whites.

In their attempt to sculpt a social identity it was expected our group members would turn to those aspects of family and peer-group subsystems which seemed sociologically appropriate and psychologically congenial. The group thus provided an unanticipated opportunity to engineer if not a miniature social-psychological Utopia, then at least a stage for rehearsing ideal psychosocial identity. Flexiblity and credulity in adolescent role playing made this rehearsal seem like the real thing, but the evolution of a Utopia was not without occasional racial and sexual clashes, replete with fantasies of violence, as the various interest groups bid to build their own special social structures.

One identity component which showed itself in our groups was the urge to become substantially more potent and to increase the felt sense of a free autonomy and naked power. Normal levels of potency and aggression just did not suffice when races and sexes saw themselves in public competition. But how often their concerns were swathed in terror. From white male students in one segregated group came: "What are they? Colored? Older? Girls?

They'll kill us. Make 'em younger . . . real small, pygmies with eyes like poison darts. Why are they coming? They'll want to fight! We'll talk and let them sit in the back of the room."

Then, with no apparent connecting thought: "Do you think there are people on the moon? No atmosphere . . . too low . . . too high . . . too many craters. No human could live there . . . We're not human as far as they're concerned."

From the Negro camp, though the groups were meeting separately, came the reciprocal posture of the aggressor. Negroes, too, spewed platitudes that revealed how deeply lodged the bigotry of ignorance was, and how clear the way in which their self-degradation was transformed into precarious esteem by the stereotyping of whites: "Whites aren't as good; you can't slick the slicker; you can't bullshit the bullshitter . . . The white people slide, we glide . . . We have natural-born rhythm. They can't dance. Can't sing soul . . . We're naturally strong. If you see a strong Whitey, you know he's been lifting weights . . . And we got better girls."

Clearly each side feared the devastation, and even total annihilation, of its own social fabric. In almost revolutionary terms, each group seemed to believe that one social order must be torn down before a new one could be installed. Evident throughout was the recurring disbelief of white students that a white leader could draft his own kind into such a battle; the Negroes, explicit acceptance of and preparation for battle; and in all the group participants, the primitive interweaving of both sexual and destructive fantasies.

The basic aggression and the uncertainty about the ultimately victorious and hence superior race came out in discussion about the war in Viet Nam, or school experiences involving teachers, which served as conversational starting points for almost every group. Typical talk went this way: "It's the good white against the bad colored... It's the pure and powerful stabilizers versus the vile and unclean troublemakers... It's racial violence... If the Negroes refused to fight, America would lose... Negroes are America's potency and the untapped potential for its continuing strength... Let's not confuse Negroes like us with the inferior types that come up from the South and in from Puerto Rico... You got to get immigration laws and keep the Puerto Ricans out... Who's better, Adam Clayton Powell or Edward Brooke? They're both no good. Powell doesn't help his own people and Brooke takes advantage of the white liberals and gets the rest of the vote by being a Republican. What's more they either marry white people or hire them as secretaries... You gotta crawl in and dig those Viet Cong out of their black tunnels... and either build a democracy for them or kill 'em!"

This concentration on defeat of the Viet Cong may have symbolized not only the eradication of Negroes, or racial integration. It also may have represented the Negroes' own destruction of existing stereotypes and their desire to be divorced from what they themselves labeled as "black trash."

Certainly Viet Nam represented aspects of white aggression, foreign invasion, and draft laws as both races encounter them. Like the war, conquest of the moon also provided a perfect medium for the embroidering of fantasies which ultimately were concerned with racial integration. "Aliens probably look like us," said one Negro boy, "Maybe they're a bit bigger with an extra finger... maybe just a glob of hair." Thus, intruders were Negroes from different communities, aliens from a different planet, or soldiers from a different country.

. . . And she left them on in the hall. Her point about skin color was forcibly communicated.

As important as the actual theme of fantasies was the fact that without suggestion, groups selected topics on which they could build elaborate fantasies serving the multifarious purposes and needs of *all* contributors. Perhaps the greatest impact of the self-analytic procedure is felt, not when the leader unraveled by interpretation the various intertwined fantasy threads and returned them to their originators, but when group members themselves recognized the various layers of implications as they were built up in the course of such embroidery sessions. Just such an experience was felt by one who tried to act out her unstated sense of a racial perspective by turning off the lights in the group room and leaving them on in the hall, and then reversing the procedure. Irrespective of the illumination or her own physical location, her point about skin-color permanence and the eye of the beholder was forcibly communicated. The more she went on with her fantasy, the more she realized what she was doing.

Typically, fantasy expression increased as experienced reality became more difficult to face head-on, but fantasies were not just alternatives to so-called reality considerations. Rather they were less threatening detours to them, or rehearsals for them. Often resembling free-form behavior trials, collective fantasies mirrored the fears, wishes, and defenses of participants as the group attempted to mold new sentiments and action strategies. Nowhere is this more true than during adolescence, a period condoning fantasy experimentation as a way of tasting those public morsels which someday may become reality.

One notion stemming from our project was that effecting change in adolescent fantasies may alter more real perceptions and hence change the eventual behavior. And so a question to be answered in our experiments was: how does the evolution of fantasy vary within basic group structures?

In the integrated groups, change came gradually from so-called internal dynamics, because from the start both races contended with a fixed structure.

In those Negro and white groups which were merged after six sessions, the physical merger seemed to render invalid the members' previously constructed fantasies. Even with preparation, the change may have been so disrupting that adaptability could not easily take place. One virtue of such a disruption is that prior belief systems

478

were seen to be inaccurate. Hence a second phase of adaption was required. A liability of the merger, of course, is that it may have communicated the necessity of relinquishing totally the familiar belief systems and a sense of competence within them.

In the long run as research continues, groups which merge after first meeting separately may prove the more effective paradigm, if only because actual social change becomes part of the process and history which lead to ongoing social engagements. Where the originally integrated groups should develop a sense of earlier-later, the merged groups might experience more of a sense of beforeness-afterness or even oldness—temporal feelings ideal for reinforcing the conception that something has, indeed, been accomplished.

Self-analytic groups do not provide *the* solution for all the tensions indigenous to school-integration programs, and the kinds of students volunteering for group membership and for leader roles in our project were not sufficiently representative to permit extensive generalization of any sort. Moreover, the self-analytic process, itself so idiosyncratic, cannot be alleged to work successfully in *all* school settings or in *all* community clubs. But the findings which came even from our small experiment are, to say the least, encouraging.

First, we have learned that the self-analytic technique can be fathomed and used by lower- and middle-class young adolescents. Second, we observed incredibly moving, deeply personal expressions and interpretations in groups which were led by nonprofessionals. The fact that leaders also were young and at times awkward may have helped to establish the trust so necessary for viable working groups.

The racial factor might have made the white leaders appear real and warm to white students while Negroes saw the leaders as the unfamiliar representatives of a hostile group. But our evidence did *not* show this at all.

Third, the procedure of keeping groups segregated at the start seemed to permit a direct and open confrontation of the realities and fantasies connected with integration, even—or especially—when the authority figure was white. While it is obvious that Negroes cannot grow to their full height in a society incessantly demanding that right be equated with white, the Negroes in our project may have been spared some of the tensions inherent in the existing social comparison.

For different reasons, our university buildings and leaders may have been just as foreign to the whites as to the Negroes. A study of racial integration cannot neglect, therefore, the discrete concerns of white students and the eminent force of social-class differentiations.

Fourth, the power of our self-analytic group to a limited extent came from an ability to cut through the barriers that are built into the "September plan," in which Negro and white students are herded together with neither group knowing what to expect nor how to act.

Perhaps the study's outstanding finding is that, even temporarily encountered, the social structure demanded solutions to problems which in their form and intensity tended to blur racial issues. As always in nondirective groups, the dilemmas of intimacy (with threats of homosexuality and heterosexuality) and the definitions of existing and potential power hierarchies had to be resolved, and unequivocal action taken.

Yet these facts also might indicate that the net effect of the self-analytic device was symptom *substitution* rather than *resolution*. Perhaps our efforts did little more than arouse new and different threats which were met with new and different defenses. Perhaps we did a disservice in fact by creating a structure which linked racial integration with authority, and with sexuality. But what else is the reality?

It cannot be denied that while our intention was to explore integration, our procedures at times deflected the emphasis away from race. By putting boys and girls together in a relatively free culture, we evoked that essence of human beings from which come social facts like interaction norms, incest taboos, prejudicial projections.

But, even if the integration-sexuality-authority linkage does represent a phenomenon underlying racial mergers, a potentially liberating experience still was provided by the group environment and significant bits of information still were exposed. School integration is not simply a coming together of people. It is a merger of boys and girls, and it is the convergence of their pre-established realities and fantasies. And, while leader strategies certainly pushed our groups in easily-definable directions, authorship of group fantasies, contents, and associations still belonged for the most part to the members.

To some people, integration well may symbolize intermarriage or even illegitimate intercourse, and white authority may signify the slave master, Uncle Tom,

or even white man (or strangler) looking for a Negro prostitute or victim. Though these images may seem absurd, no one can overlook the fantasies which are stimulated in high-school classrooms where teachers openly seduce some students, turn others into children or patients, and never bother at all with the rest. Talk in our groups pointed this up: "What about the little child just breaking out of her shell? (whom the teacher rejects in favor of some newcomer) . . . I'll do all in my power to hate that girl. She's gonna take all the love and care out of that room . . . No, she (the teacher) don't have to be my friend if she's gonna be that way . . . I don't like teachers who stick to one person."

We would invite the use of self-analytic techniques in schools, for not only could teachers and counselors learn to lead groups, but their participation as leaders could extricate them from restrictions normally placed on their expressive and integrating abilities.

Where groups seem to offer even greater natural implementations to the environment, however, is in the new concept of the educational park in which social scientists will have to prescribe ways to bring city and suburban populations together. In such environments the distinction between home team and visiting team will be lost, and the question about who is the aggressor or the intruder will be blurred. In the park plan, there will be no one to confront nor even to approach about the problems in bringing races together in schools. Thus, group encounters might well be built-in.

It may be that student-group encounters will offer direct roads to social and cultural problem areas. Such groups also can offer a radically new medium in which academic learning may take place. Social integration, after all, must be a part of all school activities, not just an hour a week of isolated research.

For the moment our own efforts are aimed at systematically assessing the value in both segregated and merged groups, as well as in evaluating the reactions to integration by sex, social class, and race. For us, the immediate future holds more groups with both female and Negro leaders and, hopefully, other groups in which parents will join their children in the self-analytic dialogue. Many participants in our first groups have expressed their desire to carry "the thing home." As one girl projected: "So maybe we can talk our problems out and they can go home and tell their parents, and we can go home and tell our parents . . ." ◗

CONFLICT, CRISIS & COLLISION A STUDY OF INTERNATIONAL STABILITY

By Ivo and Rosalind Feierabend

It is impossible to say that in May 1968 new revolution will break out in Bolivia or that Iraq, which supplied the Arab world with two brigades in the recent war with Israel, will be the scene of a *coup d'état* in early June. Nor can one predict that South Korea will provoke an incident across the 38th Parallel. But it is possible to say that all three nations belong to groups where some kind of aggression or political upheaval is not only possible but quite probable.

Neither internal nor external aggression appears to be a random occurrence. Both can be analyzed, measured and even scaled in empirical studies, as can a host of other political behaviors and socioeconomic conditions. If we can understand causes of aggression and identify specific underlying conditions, we may advance man's search for peace.

Hostile acts are easily recognized. When we charted an external aggression profile for 75 countries, based on their international actions from 1955-1960, the U.A.R., Israel and Jordan were among the 10 most aggressive nations. If we examine international affairs on the basis of this chart, neither the Israeli-Arab war of last year nor the recent Israeli attack upon Jordan is surprising. Indeed, after studying international behavior, one has an eerie feeling when the highly probable statistic becomes reality.

But attacking only symptoms can never put an end to aggression, nor can a compilation of warlike acts provide a precise forecast of revolutions and wars.

In our studies we try to recognize the conditions that make a country likely to overturn a government or attack a neighbor. If we begin to understand ourselves as nations in this broad sense, perhaps we can sometimes avert tragedy.

Aided by a team of researchers, we completed five studies in an attempt to isolate those conditions that increase the

GLOBAL INSTABILITY. Scale position of each nation depends on most unstable event of 1955-61. The last two digits show number of unstable events and determine rank within national group.

chances of violent behavior in a nation. Each study was based on actual incidents of instability and on general statistical data—such as gross national product or level of education—reported by the 84 countries we selected. Our first study determined the political stability of a country, the second related that stability to the social frustration of its people and to the nation's degree of modernity. In our third study, we examined our ability to predict changes in political stability over several years and compared these shifts to socioeconomic change, while our fourth study related the relative freedom or coercion of a country to its stability. Armed with this information,

we included international conflict, examining a nation's aggressive behavior, its frustration and its political stability. We discovered evidence of relationship among these measures.

Political Instability

For the purposes of our first study, we defined and measured political instability in terms of internally aggressive behavior. For this measurement, we developed a seven point rating system that ranged from 0 to 6, from extreme stability to extreme instability. Each point of the scale represents specific events. For example, a general election is rated 0; resignation or dismissal of a cabinet official or dissolution of legislature, 1; peaceful demonstrations, strikes or martial law, 2; riots or assassination of a significant political figure (but not a head of state), 3; large-scale arrests, plots or terrorism, 4; revolts or *coups d'état*, 5; revolution or civil war, 6. In all, we recognized some 30 different acts of instability within nations. Countries were assigned to groups on the basis of the most unstable event during a seven-year period, 1955-1961, their position within each group, on the other hand, was based on the number of disturbances that occurred [*see illustration below*].

0 STABILITY	1	2	3	4	5	6 INSTABILITY
N. Zealand 000	Norway 104		Tunisia 328	France 499	India 599	Indonesia 699
	Netherlands 104		Gr. Britain 325	U. of S. Africa 495	Argentina 599	Cuba 699
	Cambodia 104	W.Germany 217	Portugal 323	Haiti 478	Korea 596	Colombia 681
	Sweden 103	Czech. 212	Uruguay 318	Poland 465	Venezuela 584	Laos 652
	Saudi Arabia 103	Finland 211	Israel 317	Spain 463	Turkey 583	Hungary 652
	Iceland 103	Romania 206	Canada 317	Dominican Republic 463	Lebanon 581	
	Philippines 101	Ireland 202	U.S. 316	Iran 459	Iraq 579	
	Luxembourg 101	Costa Rica 202	Taiwan 314	Ceylon 454	Bolivia 556	
			Libya 309	Japan 453	Syria 554	
			Austria 309	Thailand 451	Peru 552	
			E. Germany 307	Mexico 451	Guatemala 546	
			Ethiopia 307	Ghana 451	Brazil 541	
			Denmark 306	Jordan 448	Honduras 535	
			Australia 306	Sudan 445	Cyprus 526	
			Switzerland 303	Morocco 443		
				Eygpt 438		
				Pakistan 437		
				Italy 433		
				Belgium 432		
				Paraguay 431		
				USSR 430		
				Nicaragua 430		
				Chile 427		
				Burma 427		
				Yugoslavia 422		
				Panama 422		
				Ecuador 422		
				China 422		
				El Salvador 421		
				Liberia 415		
				Malaya 413		
				Albania 412		
				Greece 409		
				Bulgaria 407		
				Afganistan 404		

480

Instability is far more prevalent than stability within the group of nations, and the cluster about point 4 on the scale indicates that disturbances on the level of wide-spread riots and arrests, or small-scale guerrilla uprisings with sabotage and terrorism, are common in today's world. The more modern nations hold the most stable positions, but a sprinkling of markedly underdeveloped countries (along with some of the nations from the Communist bloc) are relatively stable. Latin America, Asia and the Middle East provide examples of extremely unstable countries in our study.

Social Frustration

The greatest discrepancy between the goals of an underdeveloped society and their satisfaction—which translates itself as frustration—comes during the middle of the transitional phase between traditional societies and modernity. According to the basic frustration-aggression hypothesis, instability results from un-relieved social frustration. One form of systemic frustration occurs when there are wide gaps between the needs, expectations or demands of the population and their achievement. In the present century, the process of modernization creates new wants and aspirations and, in the long run, leads to their satisfaction. But there is an inevitable lag between an underdeveloped society's new awareness of modern patterns of behavior and organization and its achievement of modernization. Both traditional and modern societies are less frustrated—and tend to be more stable—than transitional societies. Truly traditional societies, such as isolated tribal communities, do not report data and have no way of being included in our study. Every nation that we have investigated, therefore, has been exposed in some way to modernity.

Since the frustration of any society arises from this discrepancy between the social wants of the people and the satisfaction of those wants, we calculated a frustration level for each society in our study. Gross national product and caloric intake per capita, physicians, telephones, newspapers and radios per unit of population were combined to give a rough indication of each country's socioeconomic satisfaction. Literacy and urbanization measure want formation, for they are the two most likely ways through which people can learn of the material benefits of modernization.

The Stable Country

A composite picture of the stable country comes from our research. It is a nation with a minimum of 90 per cent literacy; 65 radios, 120 newspapers and 20 telephones per 1,000 people; a diet of 2,525 calories per person per day, a physician for every 1,900 persons, a gross national product of $300 per person per year; and 45 per cent of the population living in urban centers. A majority of nations in our world fall below these threshold values.

By way of comparison, let us contrast these values for a highly developed and an underdeveloped state. The United States has a literacy rate of 98 per cent, 948 radios and 326 newspapers and 420 telephones per 1,000 people; the average diet is 3,100 calories per person per day; there is a physician for every 780 persons, a gross national product of $2,577 per person per year; and 52 per cent of the population live in urban centers. Comparable figures for Laos, a typical underdeveloped state, are 17.5 per cent literacy, 8 radios and .6 of one newspaper and 5 telephones per 1,000 people; a physician for every 100,000 people; 50 U.S. dollars per person per year, and 4 per cent of the people living in urban centers. The chasm between developmental levels seems beyond bridging.

Until the minimums of the stable country are reached, stability cannot be expected. Current events verify our studies. Based on figures of the period, 1955-1961, Greece rated as an unstable country with high systemic frustration, a combination that dramatically increases the likelihood of violence. Last April, the army suddenly seized power from King Constantine.

Predicting Changes in Stability

We also found, ironic and paradoxical as this may seem, that improving economic conditions does not necessarily increase stability. Rapid improvement in socioeconomic conditions, because it entails change, is essentially disruptive. The person in a transitional society is likely to be frustrated by his break with the past and by the fear and uncertainty of the present. When transition is too fast, it is even harder to adapt. Disruption, chaos and personal discomfort increase. Rapid change also opens new perspectives of modernity, thereby creating higher levels of aspiration and increasing the gap between wants and achievement.

The incidents of aggression collected for our first study clearly show that the world instability level increased sharply during the 15 years covered by the study, reaching its peak during the last six years. Hoping to assess changes in the rate of instability, we next collected information on a number of socioeconomic measures for the 28 years from 1935 to 1962. When we examined statistics for caloric intake, literacy, primary and postprimary education, national income, cost of living, infant mortality, urbanization and radios per thousand population, we found that nearly all countries in the group of 84 improved their position on all nine ratings. Countries undergoing a rapid rate of change in the nine indexes selected for study are the same countries that exhibit a highly erratic instability pattern. The higher the percentage rate of change, the greater the increase in instability.

Change in primary education is the best single predictor of instability over a long period of time, perhaps because it indicates an increased awareness of the

promises of modernity through widespread literacy. Surprisingly enough, change in literacy itself was the worst predictor of instability. We think this can be attributed to an inconsistency in the information collected on literacy over the 28-year period, for our first study showed a strong relationship between literacy and stability over a seven-year period.

Only when national income was considered did the modern countries show the highest rate of change. National income does not show marked improvement until a country is well on its way toward modernity and has a relatively high standard on measures like education, literacy, caloric intake and infant mortality. Because national income has no intrinsic ceiling, the modern nations continue to show gains. These countries

Government Coercion

Aggression is not always a nation's response to conflict and frustration. Restraints or inhibitions to aggression must be taken into account. When a relationship between frustration and aggression was first suggested by John Dollard and his colleagues in 1939, they postulated that the inhibition of any act of aggression varies directly with the strength of the anticipated punishment. Punishment, however, plays a dual role. It can inhibit the aggressive response or it can heighten frustration and thus instigate more aggression. Low levels of punishment inhibit neither a person nor a nation; only high levels of punishment are likely to cause anxiety and withdrawal. Moderate punishment acts as a frustrator and provokes further aggression — a sort

protected civil rights or occasional reprimand of the press, a rating of 2; occasional suspension of the press or a tolerated but ineffective political opposition, a rating of 3; manipulated elections or alternation of civilian and military governments, a rating of 4; perpetual governments or severe censorship of the press, a rating of 5; and total disregard of public opinion, a dictatorial head of government or no legal political opposition, a rating of 6.

We expected that both highly permissive and highly coercive governments would be stable, provided the countries with highly permissive governments were not highly frustrated. Political instability should be highest in the authoritarian systems of transitional states, where coercion, because it is not strong enough to prevent overt aggression, further stimulates frustration. (In an earlier test of this relationship between coercion and aggression, Robert LeVine, an anthropologist at the University of Chicago, found that the least amount of anti-European violence occurred in consistently repressive and consistently permissive African colonial systems.)

Political stability and coercion turned out to be related persuasively [see illustration, at left]. As expected, permissive countries are overwhelmingly stable, and coercive countries tend toward middle and high levels of instability: At the highest level of coercion (position 6), however, more countries are stable than unstable. Two-thirds of the countries at this scale position are stable, showing that coercion at this level is severe enough to inhibit aggression. In contrast, stability decreases as permissiveness increases among coercive governments, for only one-third of the countries at position 5 and only one-quarter of the countries at position 4 remain stable. This division may indicate the amount of political coercion necessary to maintain political stability in a highly frustrated country. All countries at scale position 1 are stable, which we attribute to the fact that these countries are the relatively satisfied modern democracies.

We divided the 84 countries into three groups — modern, transitional and traditional—and compared the coerciveness of their governments. The least modern countries tend to fall at mid-levels of coerciveness. Transitional states, the most unstable countries studied, are almost evenly divided between moderate and high levels of political coerciveness,

Among the stable countries, 68 per

Degree of Political Stability	LEVEL OF COERCION						Total
	Permissive (1-2)		Mid-Level Coercive (3-4)		Coercive (5-6)		
Stability	Australia Canada Costa Rica Denmark Finland Iceland Ireland Israel Luxembourg	Netherlands New Zealand Norway Sweden Switzerland Un. Kingdom Un. States Uruguay West Germany 18	Austria Cambodia Libya Philippines Tunisia	5	Czechoslovakia East Germany Ethiopia Portugal Romania Saudi Arabia Taiwan	7	30
Mid-Level Instability	Belgium Italy Mexico	3	Burma Ceylon Chile Ecuador El Salv. France Ghana Greece Iran	Japan Liberia Malaya Pakistan Panama Jordan Sudan Thailand 17	Afghan. Albania Bulgaria China Dom. Republic Egypt Haiti Morocco	Nicaragua Paraguay Poland Spain Un. S. Africa USSR Yugoslavia 15	35
Instability		0	Bolivia Brazil Colombia Cyprus Guatemala Honduras Indonesia	India Iraq Laos Lebanon Peru Syria Turkey 14	Argentina Cuba Hungary Korea Venezuela	5	19
Total		21		36		27	84

GOVERNMENT COERCION. Political stability and coercion are related persuasively. Permissive countries are overwhelmingly stable, but stability decreases as permissiveness increases among coercive governments. Only Hungary, among coercive unstable governments, falls at the highest level of coercion on the 6 point scale.

are relatively satisfied economically and relatively stable politically; therefore the remaining eight measures no longer change rapidly.

In contrast, the transitional nations are characterized by economic deprivation and by a high rate of change on many of the economic indicators, but by a low rate of growth on national income. The resulting frustration may be expressed in strikes, demonstrations, riots, *coups d'état* and even civil war. One compelling reason for the greater stability of modern countries is their greater ability to satisfy the wants of their citizens. Stability replaces instability only when a country is relatively satisfied.

of perpetual aggression-punishment-aggression sequence.

In order to relate punishment to frustration and political instability, it must be described in politically relevant terms. We equated punishment with governmental patterns of permissiveness and coerciveness, rating countries on a six-point scale, from most permissive (scale position 1) to most coercive (scale position 6). To establish the ratings, we used several standards relating to dictatorial, totalitarian governments or to democratic regimes. Full protection of the civil rights of the political opposition earned a nation a rating of 1; occasional attempts at infringement of legally cent show the high levels of economic satisfaction and governmental permissiveness typical of the modern industrial nation, while 75 per cent of the unstable nations suffer from moderate coerciveness and socioeconomic deprivation — both sources of frustration. No country in this highly unstable group is among the permissive nations of the world and only one, Argentina, is "satisfied" economically. The third group of countries, those showing moderate political instability, includes only one, Belgium, that is both permissive and satisfied. Belgium's lack of stability stems from ethnic group conflict between Flemish and Walloons. Italy and Mexico show moderate socioeconomic frustration and have permissive governments. Absolutely in contradiction to all prediction are Austria, Tunisia and the Philippines, which remain relatively stable despite a combination of moderate coercion and socioeconomic frustration.

Of the five countries (Argentina, Cuba, Hungary, Korea and Venezuela) that are both highly coercive and highly unstable politically—a combination that, according to our prediction, should not occur at all—only one, Hungary, is at position 6. Hungary could thus be considered a truly deviant country. (One should remember that aggression in this country was the result of a revolution following an ambiguously coercive government policy, itself the result of the de-Stalinization of the Soviet bloc.)

Contrary to our hypothesis, there is also a tendency toward a high level of coerciveness in satisfied countries. This suggests that some factor other than frustration as we have rated it is related to coerciveness. Of the five countries that combine coerciveness with socioeconomic satisfaction, three (Morocco, Argentina and the Union of South Africa) are subject to political instability, which may help explain the coerciveness of these governments.

These relationships between coercion and instability imply that the common response of governments to political unrest — repressive measures — may only heighten internal conflict. Nothing less than a truly totalitarian system appears to stabilize a country in turmoil.

INTERNATIONAL CONFLICT. Hostile acts against other nations are prevalent in today's world. External aggression rating for each nation is determined by act of highest intensity. Numbers indicate quantity of hostile acts by each nation during 1955-1960 period.

International Conflict

External aggression must be considered to assess the overall conflict level of each nation and to identify any relationship between warlike conduct and the findings of our previous studies. For this analysis, we defined international hostility as any hostile act perpetrated by members of one country against another, regardless of whether the action was provoked. This definition of external aggression includes not only warlike actions, but diplomatic notes of protest and even negative attitudes. Furthermore, any country that is party to a dispute, even if it only responds to an attack, is scored for its hostile behavior.

We combined our data with statistics from the collection on external conflict by political scientists Rudolph Rummel of the University of Hawaii and Raymond Tanter of the University of Michigan, who rated 75 nations over the six years from 1955-1960. Each of the 12 indicators used by Rummel and Tanter were placed on a scale according to the amount of violence attached to the act itself and an estimate of the probability of an aggressive response to the act. Protests, accusations, or threats (low intensity acts) were scale position 1; antiforeign demonstrations, the expulsion or recall of minor diplomatic officials or mobilizations, scale position 2; negative sanctions, the expulsion or recall of am-

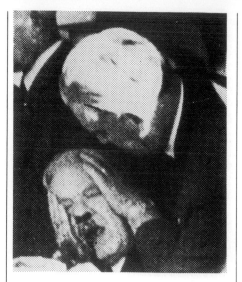

bassadors or troop movements, scale position 3; and the severance of diplomatic relations, military action short of war or war itself (high intensity acts) scale position 4.

On the basis of this scale, we charted an external aggression rating for each country [*see illustration below*]. Hostile acts were prevalent; 44 of the 75 nations committed at least one action rated as war or just short of war. Of all the countries in the sample, only Finland did not perpetrate a single aggressive act during the six years. This might be explained by her precarious geographical position. Ceylon, Liberia, Outer Mongolia and New Zealand,

					USSR 516
					U.S.A. 505
					U.A.R. 353
					Israel 245
					China 204
					India 185
					France 180
					Jordan 174
					United Kingdom 156
					Indonesia 099
					Cuba 096
					Pakistan 087
					South Korea 079
					Lebanon 076
					Iraq 068
					Argentina 067
					Hungary 065
					Formosa 063
					Turkey 054
					East Germany 051
					Nicaragua 050
					Guatemala 049
					Venezuela 045
					West Germany 043
					Mexico 040
					Yugoslavia 036
					Haiti 035
					Iran 035
			Irish Republic 137		Cambodia 030
			Poland 073		Honduras 030
			Italy 043		Chile 025
			Saudi Arabia 042		North Korea 022
			Dom. Republic 041		Paraguay 022
			Greece 039		U. of S. Africa 022
			Netherlands 035		Costa Rica 021
		Japan 064	Afghanistan 033		Albania 019
		Czechoslovakia 029	Thailand 021		Burma 017
		Sweden 023	Canada 020		Australia 015
		Switzerland 018	Brazil 016		Colombia 014
	Portugal 006	Panama 016	Bolivia 015		Equador 014
	New Zealand 003	Romania 016	El Salvador 014		Peru 013
	O. Mongolia 002	Norway 012	Belgium 012		Uruguay 011
	Liberia 002	Denmark 011	Nepal 011		Spain 011
Finland 000	Ceylon 002	Bulgaria 009	Philippines 011		Ethiopia 009
0	1	2	3		4
PEACE					WAR

486

guilty of only a few weak acts of aggression no more than a protest or an accusation, are either geographically isolated or noted for the relative weakness of their military establishments.

First- and second-rank powers of the cold war camps committed more acts of external aggression and acts of high intensity. The U.S.S.R. is the most aggressive country and the U.S. is second for this time period, while China is fifth, France, seventh, and the United Kingdom, ninth. On the other hand, if we measure the friendly behaviors of these nations toward other states, they also exceed those of most nations. A high external aggression score for these large powers is but one aspect of extensive participation in international affairs. Systemic frustration, therefore, is not the only factor underlying external aggression; power prominence in international relations is also important. Because an unusual degree of international power alters a country's condition to such an extent that the frustration-aggression sequence no longer has relevance, the five "super" powers were not considered further.

In order to determine whether systemic frustration is a primary factor in both internal instability and external aggression, we compared these measures. A consistent relationship emerges. Of 18 stable and peaceful countries, only four—Ecuador, El Salvador, Panama and Portugal—are highly frustrated according to our standard of socioeconomic deprivation, rate of change and coerciveness. At the other end of the scale, 13 countries are frustrated, politically unstable and externally aggressive. Six countries—Argentina, Chile, Cuba, Mexico, Pakistan and the Union of South Africa—are satisfied on two of the three frustration indexes, yet they are both unstable and aggressive.

We found that the relationship between systemic frustration and external aggression, when considered independently of internal unrest, is weak. Although the instigation to some form of internal aggression such as riot or civil war appears to be stronger in frustrated countries, the weak impulse to external aggression cannot be dismissed. Political instability is a guide to external aggression. Of 32 stable countries, almost 75 per cent are peaceful, while more than 65 per cent of the 35 unstable countries are aggressive.

By combining the findings of these studies, behavior syndromes can be identified in today's international arena. A potential non-aggression syndrome is displayed by the country with a permissive political regime, a low rate of change on economic indicators and only a small discrepancy between the formation of social wants and their satisfaction. [See illustration above.] These countries are stable and tend toward peaceful international relations. A possible external aggression syndrome consists of a coercive political regime, a high rate of change, great discrepancy between the formations of social wants and their satisfaction, internal turmoil and international hostility. Countries that are satisfied on two measures and frustrated on only one generally fit the non-aggression syndrome, while countries frustrated on two indexes and satisfied on only one follow the external aggression syndrome. There are three countries who deviate strongly from these patterns. Mexico and Pakistan, which should be peaceful, stable countries, are aggressive and unstable. El Salvador, frustrated, coercive and highly changeable, breaks the rule by being peaceful and stable. These exceptions emphasize the probabilistic nature of the research. The relationships we have discovered are only tendencies. Where they fail to predict, the fault may lie with the data or it may be due to other factors which we have as yet failed to measure. In spite of these limitations, the pattern is clear enough.

While the impulse to external aggression is less compelling than the impulse to internal instability, aggression is likely to occur if the country is also unstable. (Only one of the frustrated countries in the sample, Yugoslavia, is stable and externally aggressive.) If one considers internal and external aggression as two possible manifestations of the same impulse, then the relationship between social frustration and some form of political aggression is quite strong.

Neither external aggression nor non-aggression can be predicted with certainty. Nevertheless, when one knows a country's level of frustration and of political instability, the ability to predict

	Satisfied Permissive Low Change	Satisfied Permissive High Change	Satisfied Coercive Low Change	Frustrated Permissive Low Change	Satisfied Coercive High Change	Frustrated Permissive High Change	Frustrated Coercive Low Change	Frustrated Coercive High Change	Totals
Peaceful Stable	Canada Denmark Finland Ireland Netherlands New Zealand Norway Sweden Switzerland Uruguay		Bulgaria Czechoslovakia	Greece Philippines	Portugal	Panama	Ecuador	El Salvador	
	10	0	2	2	1	1	1	1	18
Aggressive Stable	Australia Israel West Germany	Costa Rica						Yugoslavia	
	3	1	0	0	0	0	0	1	5
Peaceful Unstable	Belgium Italy	Brazil	Spain		Colombia	Ceylon Japan		Bolivia Dom. Republic Peru Thailand	
	2	1	1	0	1	2	0	4	11
Aggressive Unstable	Mexico Pakistan		Argentina Cuba U. of S. Africa	Chile	Indonesia Iran Lebanon	India Turkey	Guatemala Paraguay	Egypt Haiti Iraq Nicaragua S. Korea Venezuela	
	2	0	3	1	3	2	2	6	19
Totals	17	2	6	3	5	5	3	12	53

EXTERNAL AGGRESSION. When ratings for frustration, rate of economic change and government coercion are compared with political stability and external aggression, consistent relationships emerge. A possible aggression syndrome consists of high economic change, frustration and government coercion, while peaceful nations show low rate of economic change, little frustration and highly permissive governments.

that country's international behavior is increased.

Empirical methods, when applied to national and cross-national behavior, are profitable. Events that appear to be isolated spring from identifiable factors. But these first studies do not include all influences on aggression.

We have begun to move in new directions. One is to concentrate on internal unrest caused by ethnic and racial friction. We plan to study minority group conflict within the systemic frustration framework. In other words, the minority within a nation will be rated for frustration and indications of unrest as were nations in our earlier studies.

We are broadening our studies of per-

mission and coercion to include a wider variety of government practices. To supplement our data on international conflict, we are studying conciliatory behavior and friendship patterns among nations.

When we finish, we hope to establish a source of comprehensive information on four kinds of aggression: popular unrest, minority group conflict, oppressive measures and international tension. Armed with this resource, though it covers but 20 years in the history of the world, perhaps we can achieve greater understanding. And with understanding comes the possibility of changing behavior.

rebuttals

I. INTRODUCTION

A *hallmark of psychological research and interpretation is disagreement. Disagreement, though not often over fact, occurs frequently over method and interpretation. The selected letters and comments that follow further illustrate the diversity of psychology today. They provide both positive and negative critical commentary as well as occasional intellectual extension of the articles included in this reader.*

Personality: Public or Private

In Floyd Ruch's article, "Personality: Public or Private," he concluded with the statement: "Why toss away one of society's useful modern tools?" The real question, which Ruch does not meet, is: *useful for what kind of society?* The issue is not the invasion of privacy but the destruction of individuality and the consequent neutralization of democracy.

. . . Test selection determines which types of personalities will "survive" in a competitive civilization (become incorporated into society, rise to the top, etc.). Testing fills the ranks of society with people made in the test's image.

The essence of a democratic society is the opportunity for comparison. When people in a democracy are forced to duplicate each other, democracy ceases to exist and the basis for comparison disappears. The ultimate effect of testing is the design of a culture, not matching employees to employers.

Alexis M. Nehemkis
Graduate Student
Department of Psychology
University of Oregon

The question concerning the future of psychological testing is a real problem in view of the increasing public alarm on the subject. The article by Floyd Ruch is therefore timely. Unfortunately the problem is not as limited as described in the article. Government legislation and policy is affecting a much wider segment of the psychological community than is represented by those people engaged in personnel selection. It is increasingly difficult to conduct research in many areas of personality and social psychology because of severe limitations imposed by regulations designed to protect the right for privacy and to safeguard the welfare of the research subject. . . .

While I agree with Ruch that the use of psychological tests can be defended by pointing out their usefulness, I must disagree with his conclusion that certain types of personality test, the so-called "objective self report inventories," do not represent an invasion of privacy because they are "straightforward." Objective tests are basically not any more straightforward than projective tests. Both involve a situation where a person is asked to say something the implication of which he cannot know. Personality tests, objective and projective, depend on this lack of knowledge by the person being tested. . . .

Even harder to understand is the misinformation Ruch spreads concerning so-called "projective tests." He reinforces the frequent and erroneous impression, probably the source for much of the opposition to testing, that projective tests are useless and devious. . . .

On the whole, I feel that Ruch's article has done the course of personality assessment more harm than good.

Rudolf Kalin
Assistant Professor
Psychology Department
Queen's University
Kingston, Ontario

Questions for the Global Conscience

Professor Dyck's remarks on suicide as a *moral* issue are irrelevant. The only way that withdrawal can be blameworthy is when the person remains in society and enjoys the benefits bestowed by the past and present. If a person commits suicide, he withdraws from his responsibilities and his benefits simultaneously, and the result is neutralization. Hence, the act is amoral.

Peter W. Williamson
Ipswich, Maine

III. PSYCHOLOGICAL DEVELOPMENT

Understanding Children's Art

The article on children's art by Rhoda Kellogg would have been excellent had she stayed within her own field and not presumed to pass judgment in another field of which she had very little knowledge.

How Miss Kellogg could pass judgment on *psychometrics* by having read works in the field of *psychoanalysis* is beyond me. Psychometrics is a field based upon statistical research so that a properly selected small sample can become representative of the whole, in much the same way a properly selected cup of sea water could be used to analyze the ocean.

In criticizing Dale Harris, Miss Kellogg shows that the most she has done with his book was to thumb through the last few pages. If she had looked in the front of the book, she would have found many pages of philosophical theory, much very similar to her own. She would have also found that Dr. Harris' sources reached from Alaska to Holland. In fact he is presently in the process of similar work among Indian tribes in South America.

Miss Kellogg's comments on the Bender-Gestalt revealed her lack of knowledge on this point, also. The Bender-Gestalt is one of the most widely used tests for doctoral work in psychometric comparisons. Various groups of children are assessed under controlled conditions over a period of time, using the Bender-Gestalt and many other measures.

Significant correlations are then run and the results are then analyzed by doctoral committees to see that the work was done scientifically rather than emotionally. Miss Kellogg's criticisms would imply that all such exacting efforts are nothing more than black magic with which to torture little children.

Lastly, I have used the Bender-Gestalt, the Draw-a-Person, and The Wechsler Intelligence Scale for Children, over a period of time in various school systems with children of differing social levels and differing races, and never cease to marvel at how close I can come to describing a teacher's daily experience with a child after only about an hour with the child.

I would like to stress again that Miss Kellogg's work was excellent as long as she stayed within her own realm of experience. If the persons working with her are using only one type of measurement to assess a child's intelligence, she should either suggest that they use a battery of tests or she should get psychologists who know how to use and *interpret* the battery. *A test is no better or worse than the mind that interprets it. A poor test with a good interpreter is better than a good test with a poor interpreter.*

Jim Woodward
School psychologist
Baytown, Texas

Editor's Note: San Francisco's Golden Gate Kindergarten Association, of which Miss Kellogg is director, is in the forefront of psychological testing methods. Miss Kellogg was discussing children's art.

The Autistic Child

Moosa V. P. Grant, president of the National Society for Autistic Children, Inc., writes of her efforts to find help for twin autistic daughters, "One eminent psychiatrist . . . said, on the cause of it all, 'Perhaps you have not radiated enough love to the children.' When we demurred, he said, 'Perhaps you have radiated too much love.' When we asked what was the right amount, he said every child was different." The struggles of [many parents of autistic children] are eloquent testimony to the need for deepened scientific inquiry into the cause, prevention and cure of infantile autism.

Kay T. Gilliland
Oakland, California

I found the article to be both enraging and frustrating. I am a teacher of emotionally disturbed children and an active board member of the National Society for Autistic Children. We have seen children who previously had violent tantrums and head-banging sessions able to discuss why these outbreaks occurred and do occur and most important, we have seen autistic children who communicated through extremely bizarre expressions, willing to hand over and share their mysterious speech recipes. Certainly this is "reaching out" on the part of the child and one can "reach in."

Linda Moyse
Albany, New York

I had the opportunity to visit Linwood Children's Center to which Mr. Ferster refers. I was amazed at the great success Miss Jeanne Simons was having using reinforcement therapy with autistic children.

Brad Herling
University of Massachusetts
Amherst, Massachusetts

To date, childhood autism was something to be ignored and looked down upon because of the little knowledge we possessed of it. Thanks to dedicated people like C. B. Ferster and Jeanne Simons and centers such as the Linwood Children's Center, these myths of childhood autism are finally disappearing. Ferster and other people like him are unquestionably the modern day Pinels.

Patrick C. Burns
Washington State University
Pullman, Washington

Can I Come to Summerhill? I Hate My School

Your article by A. S. Neill was a pleasant addition to your versatile coverage of the contemporary scene in psychology. Neill is a remarkable phenomenon—doing for half a century what James, Dewey, Skinner and others more often have spoken of and implied should be done. He would never admit kinship with Skinner, I suspect, and I am not sure that Skinner feels that Neill's handling of contingencies is as systematic as it could be. To some of us, it is a joy to see the increasing rapprochement of the learning laboratory and the human learning condition. As the lab relaxes (cautiously), our children may all yet gain.

You may be interested to know that the U.S.A.'s own Summerhill Society seems to be undergoing a spontaneous revival after existing quietly for several years. There appear to be nearly forty schools of varying Summerhillian adherence in the U.S.A. this year. There is a monthly bulletin of information exchange; regular forums and workshops are held on both the East and West Coasts. Addresses: 5 Beekman Street, New York City 10038; 6063 Hargis Street, Los Angeles 90034.

Lincoln F. Hanson
Department of Psychology
Rockland Community College
Suffern, New York

I have long been a staunch admirer and advocate of A. S. Neill's child-rearing philosophy. I would assert, however, that in the administration of his school he has not been anywhere nearly as courageous as he *could* be as far as providing for the overt expression of adolescent sexuality is concerned.

Several California group sex-sharing clubs for married couples have made "institutional" provision for direct satisfaction of their adolescent children's sex needs. Stable cliques of ten or twelve (even sex-ratio) adolescents have been organized by "swinging" parents in many communities; these teen groups typically meet at the same time as the parents' group, but at a different place. In addition to the plethora of "typical" adolescent party activities, these groups also engage in "swapping" and much overt copulatory behavior during the course of an evening.

As a citizen I firmly defend these new experiments in social living and hope that in time they can be effectively researched. For the good of mankind it is time we started taking seriously the biological fact that man reaches the apex of his sexual sensitivity between the ages of 16 and 20. The more accommodating a series of norms is to the fundamental nature of adolescent man, the greater the probability that those norms will be genuinely internalized and followed.

For the record, my own interest in this area is primarily that of a sociological researcher . . .

Brian G. Gilmartin
Graduate Research Assistant
Department of Sociology
University of Iowa

. . . Let me tell a story. When I first started teaching fifth grade, I was listening one day to three or four 10-year-olds talking to each other. In their talk, one of them said to the others and I can't convey in print the matter-of-factness with which he said this, "If I grow up. . . ." Every time I think of it I feel a large part of the appalled horror with which I first heard this innocent remark.

The reason we, the older generation, have lost our authority over kids has nothing to do with permissiveness. It is quite simply that we have destroyed, or allowed to be destroyed, the moral basis on which the authority of the old over the young has always been based—the fact that they could protect and were protecting the young, that they were holding and running a world into which the young people could

enter, in short, that they knew what they were doing. This is no longer the case. A world in which a 10-year-old child can face, and must face, as a perfectly commonplace sort of reality, the fact that he may never grow up, is not a world in which we can say to the young any longer that Daddy knows best.

. . . There is only one position that we adults have any right to take in dealing with children. "We didn't mean to get into this jam. We don't know how to get out. Don't abandon us. Help us." Only from this position can we have any meaningful dialogue with the young, and exert any reasonable and constructive influence over their lives.

John Holt
Boston, Massachusetts

Editor's Note: John Holt is the author of the well-known books *How Children Fail* and *How Children Learn*.

IV. THE SENSORY WORLD

Experiment in Perception

god damn. i tried and i tried and i tried.
here i am a writer, photographer, poet,
sketcher of objects,
reporter, reader, thinker and doer,
and by golly gee wow, I spent well over
an hour on your god damn dot patterns,
and I didn't see a thing.
That was the weirdest Rohrschac (misspelled no doubt) I've ever seen.

Yours for a better Living Environment,
Inside and Out,

Dennis D. Sandage
York, Pennsylvania

Sonic Booms

Mr. David M. Green's article "Sonic Booms" is excellent. But why does he shrink from the conclusion that a fleet of supersonic transport planes

flying over the U.S. would do $1,000,000 damage per day?

William A. Shurcliff, Ph.D.
Director
Citizens' League Against the
Sonic Boom
Cambridge, Massachusetts

Green foments a new rumor on sonic boom. The energy content is less than a pistol shot of what caliber—.22 or .38 magnum? Serious large-caliber shooters regularly use both fitted ear plugs and ear protectors such as are worn by jet-airplane ground-handlers.

Boom-time fashions may dictate that we all learn to communicate by hand-signal.

Bruce D. Marshall
Palo Alto, California

Chemical Perception in Newborn Snakes

I have had the opportunity . . . of reading your interesting article entitled "Chemical Perception in Newborn Snakes," in which Dr. Burghardt described snakes' use of their tongues and Jacobson's organs in the detection of their usual prey, and their resulting attacks on the vials or swabs containing traces of their natural prey.

Since most snakes have rather weak vision and are virtually without any ability to hear airborne sounds, their sense of smell either via their olfactory organs or the tongue-Jacobson's organ-route constitutes a most important avenue of prey detection and recognition. The pits of the pit vipers also constitute a reinforcement of the olfactory prey-detection avenue. The usual flicking of a snake's tongue, obvious evidence of an active sense, shows the importance of the dual route by which a snake seeks its prey. Dr. Burghardt's experiments have shown how important the tongue-Jacobson's organ-route is for the young garter snake when it is seeking and sensing its normal prey.

Certainly, his paper has done

much to explain and reinforce our knowledge of the accuracy whereby the tongue tips and the Jacobson's-organ route can, by chemical tracing, reinforce the snake's recognition of the presence of its prey.

Laurence M. Klauber
San Diego, California

Editor's Note: Mr. Klauber is a respected herpetologist and authority on the rattlesnake.

The Terrible Tenrec

. . . The tenrec is irresistible. I absolutely must comment upon it. Had the behavioral scientists (?) at Princeton approached their subject with any understanding of media systems they would have triumphed.

They were dealing with an obviously aural creature. Dentists have long known that aural creatures are easily anesthetized by use of high intensity white noise. Other less known examples of aural anesthesia are transistor radios and stereo hi-fi.

When our cultural whip, visual stimuli, is applied too heavily we turn up ye old volume. This aural narcotic is strongly evident in rock music. Psychedelic rock, through high wattage visual-aural output, serves to completely obliterate all social consciousness. Traditional guidelines to social intercourse, sermons and constitutional law are obliterated. We take a trip into a land of n-o-t-h-i-n-g-n-e-s-s by overwhelming our senses.

If Princeton should have a tenrec left they should subject it to a stereo recording of the Mothers. This recording should be played through a solid state amplifier driving 30-inch woofers, horn tweeters, electronic crossovers, and auxiliary amplifiers driving phantom transducers. The watts riot is a going thing, man. The tenrec will become almost human under this most common cultural phenom.

Gene Bennett
Richardson, Texas

V. HUMAN FUNCTION

The Importance of Daydreaming

As a professional fantasist (two novels and thirty or so short stories published so far) I read with great interest and general corroboration Jerome L. Singer's "The Importance of Daydreaming."

I was a bit staggered, though, to read: "In one experiment subjects seated in a small, dark, sensory-restriction chamber reported their thought content every 15 seconds. These signal detection and vigilance studies gave us a sample of thought that was independent of any stimulus and unrelated to any task."

Oh, come on! Any anxiety about a required report every 15 seconds surely constitutes stimulus, and the act of reporting is virtually pure "task."

Of necessity reasoning *ad hominem*, I can assure Dr. Singer that under his test conditions my responses would have been chiefly of ill-restrained hostility at having my lucubrations interrupted, probably resulting in a punch in somebody's snoot. Such hostility being unlike my pacific nature, I can only conclude that the test result would be flawed. Coleridge, you remember, was interrupted in his composition of "The Road to Xanadu" by some idiot from Porlock trying to sell him a new car or something, and the rest of the poem is forever lost.

Really, this is the purest example of the difficulty of micromensuration I've ever met—the altering of a dimension by the act of measuring it—and I just can't understand how Dr. Singer let it go by.

Joseph Whitehill
Chestertown, Maryland

VI. PERSONALITY

Is Graphology Valid?

As one of your charter subscribers, I was interested in Daniel Anthony's article "Is Graphology Valid?" having spent several decades in research and the practical applications of grapho-diagnosis—the scientific term for "graphology."

While I am in agreement with some of the author's statements, may I be permitted to make several comments and corrections. There are a number of additional reasons why handwriting analysis has not been more easily accepted in our country. Among them is a certain degree of reluctance on the part of duly accredited psychologists to become involved in a "taboo" topic. Not only have there been too many charlatans interested in exploiting graphology, but also many "well-meaning" graphologists are poorly or not sufficiently trained along academic psychological lines. Since graphologists are not subject to any registration or licensing laws, their professional ethics are subject to questioning. No wonder that the rank and file of academicians and clinicians look at graphology with a certain amount of distrust.

I don't share Mr. Anthony's pessimism concerning the future development of grapho-diagnosis in our country, as the results of the ongoing research become more widely known and accredited psychologists avail themselves of this splendid projective technique within the framework of test battery.

Herry O. Teltscher, Ph.D.
Morton Prince Clinic
for Hypnotherapy
New York, New York

The Grim Generation

Re: "The Grim Generation" by Robert E. Kavanaugh. Vietnam represents much more than a remote situation which is used by emotionally unstable people to force domestic change. I suggest respectfully that Mr. Kavanaugh read widely on Vietnam before making psychological statements on the beliefs of youth.

Carol Hannum
San Francisco, California

I have found my experience confirming Kavanaugh's observations concerning the categories into which he locates "The Grim Generation."

Rev. Richard Bowyer
Campus Minister
Wesley Foundation
Fairmont State College
Fairmont, West Virginia

Mr. R. E. Kavanaugh may only have joined the vast company of the Establishment, who, if they can think of no more effective criticism, charge the present generation with a lack of humor. The sense of humor of the younger generation may only have matured.

Franklin J. C. Hiller
Rochester, New York

I would suggest that, perhaps, grimness is more a matter of one man's perception and interpretation than a characteristic quality of a whole generation.

John W. Lounsbury
Portland, Oregon

I think if others from Mr. Kavanaugh's generation were to follow suit, our so-called generation gap would be severed if not completely closed.

Ray Lee
San Diego, California

The Quiet Revolution

The scare publicity about LSD and other psychedelic chemicals is reappearing so frequently that it has frightened some of our legislators into considering the passing of federal restrictions on its use and possession. . . . Like the mother who instinctively shields her young from strangers, our legislators are reacting emotionally to a new and threatening presence in their realm. Until that presence can clearly be shown to be harmless, the fear and hatred will remain. At present our society can best learn about these powerful chemicals *not* through the claims

and antics of our youth, but through the sensors of the society's research organs. . . .

If the promoters of psychedelics are correct, then the message will get through that the chemicals do little, if any, harm to the organism and that they may be of great benefit to it . . .

It cannot be denied that improper use of psychedelics *can* lead to gross personality distortions of uncertain duration, but it also appears that such incidents represent only a tiny fraction of psychedelic experiences. Research must be undertaken that not only quantifies the extent and characteristics by psychedelic experience, but that examines the conditions for positive use and that answers the questions about permanent damage and "genetic mutation."

Today's society is complex enough to have incubated, and to some extent incorporated, psychedelics (albeit illegally up to now); the question remains as to whether it is mature enough to overcome emotionalism and seriously investigate the possibility of beneficial use.

Edwin H. Elkin, Ph.D.
Washington, D.C.

VII. DISORDER AND THERAPY

Chromosomes and Crime

The tendency shown by Montagu and many others to devaluate the role played by genetics in human behavior very probably stems from a false pessimism—the idea that a genetic disorder is impossible to remedy, in contrast to a "psychological" disorder. Actually, the opposite is true. There are medical remedies for a rapidly growing list of behaviorally-relevant disorders of genetic determination (PKU being a widely known case in point), while the record for disorders of a supposedly "psychogenic" sort is dismal by comparison. A recent and as yet unpublished study shows even mongoloid individuals may be markedly im-

proved through biochemical treatment, if started early enough. . . .

Linus Pauling, father of the concept of "molecular medicine," has recently proposed a science of "orthomolecular psychiatry" (*Science,* April 19, 1968), based on the premise that much abnormal behavior may be treated by correcting errors in the body's own biochemical machinery. Based on available evidence, I would predict that much criminality—both by XYY and XY individuals—may be preventable within the next decade if the implications of this concept are actively pursued.

Bernard Rimland, Ph.D.
Director
Institute for Child Behavior
Research
San Diego, California

The Shattered Language of Schizophrenia

I found Brendan Maher's "The Shattered Language of Schizophrenia" to be most enlightening . . . if one is interested in changing the inference described, the schizophrenic must be brought to a new balance of attending to internal and external stimulation, respectively. This might be accomplished by exposing schizophrenics to novel, intense, and meaningful stimulation, all of which serve to raise the arousal level and promote attention to external stimuli. The theoretical basis for such treatment is not facilitated by the generally monotonous, attenuated and meaningless environment provided by many large custodial institutions.

Stephen J. Cummings
University of Colorado
Department of Psychology
Boulder, Colorado

The Neurotic Cat

Reaction to Skinner Box conditioning . . .

You starve a rat, and then you put him in one of those Skinner boxes where you build sick rats, and you give him a food pellet every time he pushes the little metal bar in the box . . . and he'll learn the bar-pressing pretty fast. He'll keep right on bar-pressing too . . . till he's not hungry anymore . . . till he's full. . . . You show fear to a kid, and then you show him how to build walls between his eyes and the things he's scared of . . . and he'll learn the wall-building behavior pretty fast. He'll keep on wall-building, too; keep on wall-building till the things he's scared of are gone . . . or till the walls shut out the light and the air and enclose his tomb.

These are the things we learn, aren't they? Don't we learn to do best the things that get us what we need to survive? Don't we learn to do best those things that get us full stomachs, full hearts, and steady, unscared eyes? And as long as doing the things we do keeps getting us the things we need, won't we keep doing the things we do? That's the stuff we're made of, isn't it? . . . a lot of bar-presses, a heck of a lot of liver and spinach . . . and walls?

Michael Bridge

St. John's College
Annapolis, Maryland

Morality in Psychotherapy

I would like to take issue with Marvin Frankel's "Morality in Psychotherapy." He seems to go out of his way to misrepresent the spirit of Freudian therapy in his overeagerness to praise the contributions of Mowrer. He charges Freud with bringing to the therapeutic situation a set of values that emphasize security, moral latitudinarianism, and predestination rather than freedom, responsibility, and I suppose, integrity.

He supports this thesis by quoting from Freud's "Analysis of a Phobia in a Five-Year-Old Boy." I find it a bit humorous that Frankel should support his view by quoting remarks Freud made to a patient whose

therapy he did not even conduct directly and who was but a five-year-old! A re-reading of the passage will make it clear that Freud's "predestination" comments are not to be taken seriously in this context. Moreover, I would like to ask, what efforts might Freud (or Mowrer) have made to show Little Hans he "could have avoided his neurosis?" And would these efforts have been of any therapeutic value?

. . . It becomes clear that the differences between Frankel (or Mowrer) and Freud are not simply differences with regard to the question how man ought to be treated in a therapeutic situation, but, even more so, differences concerning the question—what is the nature of man? Freud saw man as both agent and victim, as responsible and not responsible for his suffering and happiness. But insofar as man was victimized by his own motives (albeit, unconscious ones), there remained the possibility of enlarging his self-knowledge and hence his sphere of responsible behavior.

Michael J. Foster

Department of Philosophy
Union College
Schenectady, New York

Though I cannot whip up any enthusiastic interest over hungry flies, copulation of rats, and chemical perception of newborn snakes, I know the information has a place in life's puzzle . . .

Marvin Frankel's "Morality in Psychotherapy" gave me a tremendous lift because I'm one of your smart readers who reads a lot but who hasn't gotten to college yet (one husband and two sons in college are all we can manage right now). I like Mr. Frankel's choice of words and also his conclusions, which seem to agree with mine.

Lois Cronin, R.N.

Fairfield, Connecticut

I was delighted to read Marvin Frankel's article . . . It brought to

mind a terse verse I composed while still in college. To wit:

Psychiatry is the new national fad.
Psychoanalysis just must be bad—
For from the psychiatrist's magical vault
Man learns that his failings aren't really his fault.

I was happy to read an article which disagreed with the spoofed tenet.

Alice McKnight

Austin, Texas

New Ways in Psychotherapy

Hans Eysenck's "New Ways in Psychotherapy" was interesting, but illustrated clearly a tendency that from a patient's-eye-view should be stopped cold before it takes over completely. I mean the tendency to treat a patient as an interesting piece of machinery for the doctor to tinker with and test out his theories on.

. . . Today the doctor as healer is often in conflict with the doctor as scientist. The patient, to protect himself, should know which is which; and the doctor-as-scientist should confine himself to willing subjects who understand what the risks are and the nature of the study. Psychotics are helpless prisoners, just as much as the Jewish inmates of Ravensbrueck. If a doctor would hesitate to use a certain procedure on the temporarily deranged wife of the Chairman of Trustees of his own hospital, he has no business whatever using it on the friendless old lady from the back wards. To condition a patient to drop "insane" talk is to attempt healing, however superficial. To condition her to talk insanely in order to prove the doctor's theories is not healing, but the reverse; it should not be permitted. If this is science, then so was Ravensbrueck. People are not guinea pigs.

Dr. Eysenck rejoices in his success in extinguishing a patient's unjustified fear of cats or spiders. He has certainly reinforced my justified fear of scientist-doctors.

Sally Hornig

Lexington, Massachusetts

VIII. SOCIAL PSYCHOLOGY

The Small-World Problem

. . . Stanley Milgram's "The Small-World Problem" reminded me of something I read about 10 years ago. A bright youngster had invented the concept of "first met" and "second met"—in which a person you actually know is "first met" and someone known by a person you know is "second met." "First met" is less restrictive than "Small World" because you don't have to be on a first name basis with the person.

Every American has "second met" President Johnson, and since the President knows virtually all other heads of state—or former heads of state—by my method, everyone in the world has "fifth met" everyone else. One might suppose that in the case of Communist China another step would be needed. Actually you might even take off a step or two. Most people on the China mainland have "second met" Madame Chiang Kai-shek, and she has "second met" everyone in the outside world, so we have certainly "third met" or "fourth met" everyone in Communist China.

Herbert F. York
Member, President's
Science Advisory Committee

The Psychology of Police Confessions

. . . I must admit some serious trepidation as to "content" of Dr. Zimbardo's article and the somewhat narrow picture it paints of police tactics in the squad room. I have never been a member of any police organization and have no particular urge to defend the numerous misuses of police authority, but Dr. Zimbardo paints *all* police and most police methods as manipulative, psychological, brutal. Certainly this is hardly an impartial view of many dedicated and just police officials. His technique of quoting from certain police manuals smacks of "lifting from context" and certainly does

a great injustice to the work of Messrs. Inbau and Reid (*Criminal Interrogation*), a tome with which I am closely familiar, based upon research studies on polygraph examinations in which I participated. While Dr. Zimbardo's style is highly readable and his topic interestingly sensational, I do not feel that one-sided discourses which can mislead the lay public have a place in *Psychology Today*. If I am unduly harsh in what I freely admit is one psychologist's perception of this article, I apologize to both the author and the editor. However, I do reserve the right to speak out against what I feel is a disservice to our profession and to [your] readers . . .

Eugene C. Edel, Ph.D.
Senior Scientist
Mellonics Systems Development
Division
Litton Industries

The Face of the Enemy

"The Face of the Enemy," by Jerome D. Frank has implicitly cut materialistic considerations out of his notion of ideology. American ideology is more exactly the quite practical reasons for our anti-Communism and for our commitments. We seem to believe something about the market, upon which belief system we form policy, foreign and domestic.

Jon Weissman
Amherst College
Amherst, Massachusetts

I notice a reference to my concept, "mote-beam-mechanism." Actually Frank refers not to my new concept but to the old concept of "projection." In the case of projection, group A *attributes* to group B certain traits, i.e., "aggressiveness" which A does, but B, allegedly or seemingly, does not possess. In cases of the mote-beam-mechanism, we do not "attribute" to other people certain traits, which we possess but they do not, but are *perceiving* in

them what we *fail to perceive* in ourselves.

Gustav Ichheiser, Ph.D.
The University of Chicago
Chicago, Illinois

Mr. Frank owes us a sequel. He's told us how we build enemies out of nothing, how our judgment is ruled by our passions. Now we want him to tell us—how *do* we distinguish the real enemies, in time to keep them from giving us no alternative to peace?

Alfred B. Mason, M.D.
Crane, Indiana

Jerome D. Frank replies:

Enemies do not ordinarily emerge instantly as irreconcilable antagonists. The growth of mutual hostility is usually gradual, and often can be reversed before it is too late. Most nations, even when they are in conflict over some issues, also have other areas where their interests coincide. Russia and the United States, for example, have a common interest in securing a nuclear nonproliferation pact and in world stability in general, since unrest anywhere can drag them into a confrontation. They would also both stand to benefit from any number of cooperative international scientific ventures. The identification and exploitation of such mutual interests would counteract drift toward a position where each nation feels it has no alternative but war. . . .

Self-Fulfilling Prophecy

The credibility of the very impressive Rosenthal effect would be enhanced if the needed control experiment could be conducted. The basic problem, of course, is that the Rosenthal findings are predicted by the Rosenthal effect; i.e., Rosenthal *et al.* presumably have expected the results that they obtain, and, according to their own hypothesis, such results are somewhat suspect of experimenter bias.

The logical control experiment is

to have a "naive" graduate student (if one can be found) supervise the experimental efforts of some student colleagues, under the belief that he will find evidence for "the student research effect"—that apparent inability of student researchers to obtain results that are expected. From this point the procedure is *à la* Rosenthal, with two groups of student researchers led to expect opposite results. If our researcher reports that, contrary to his expectations, his student researchers obtained results in line with their expectations, this is support for the Rosenthal hypothesis. If, on the other hand, our researcher reports that, just as he had expected, his experimenters were unable to obtain the results they expected, then we have strong support for the Rosenthal hypothesis. Double Q.E.D.

Faced with this infinite regression of higher-order Rosenthal effects, perhaps we should simply concede that if Freud's theory can predict its own rejection, Rosenthal's hypothesis can predict its own confirmation.

Charles A. Perfetti
Assistant Professor of Psychology
University of Pittsburgh
Pittsburgh, Pennsylvania

biographies

Daniel S. Anthony ("Is Graphology Valid?") organized and directed the Rutgers University Workshops in Human Relations in the early 1950s, then served for 11 years as director of the Newark Human Rights Commission. In 1966 he received a Ford Foundation Fellowship for a year of study at Rutgers' newly founded Urban Studies Center.

Anthony was introduced to graphology by Louise Rice, founder of the American Graphological Society. He studied with Dr. Klara Roman at the New School for Social Research in New York City, and in 1959, when she retired, he took her place on the faculty.

Richard C. Atkinson ("The Computer Is a Tutor") joined the faculty of Stanford University in 1956, after receiving his Ph.B. from the University of Chicago and his doctorate from Indiana University. He is a professor of psychology and holds courtesy appointments in the Schools of Education and Engineering. Atkinson is coauthor of the fourth edition of Ernest Hilgard's textbook, *Introduction to Psychology* (1967), and a frequent contributor to scholarly and professional journals. His chief research interest is learning theory, particularly the formation and testing of mathematical models for human learning and memory.

Nathan Azrin ("Pain and Aggression") is director of research at the Anna State Hospital's Behavior Research Laboratory in Anna, Illinois, and is a professor at the Rehabilitation Institute at Southern Illinois University. In 1956 Azrin received his Ph.D. in psychology from Harvard University, where he studied under B. F. Skinner. Since then he has published widely in the field of behavioral research and has edited the *Journal of the Experimental Analysis of Behavior*. Though his initial training was in social psychology and personality at Boston University, he transferred to Harvard, not as the result of a change of interest, but rather because he felt that the problems of personality and social psychology could be handled most effectively within the behaviorist framework.

David Bakan ("Is Phrenology Foolish?") received his B.A. from Brooklyn College, his M.A. from Indiana University and his Ph.D. in 1948 from Ohio State University. Since 1961 he has been professor of psychology at the University of Chicago; before that time, he taught at Ohio State, the University of Missouri and Harvard. He is the author of many articles and several books, including *The Duality of Human Existence* and *On Method: Toward the Reconstruction of Psychological Investigation*.

Leonard Berkowitz ("Impulse, Aggression and the Gun") is a professor of psychology at the University of Wisconsin, where he has taught since 1955. Born in New York City, he did his undergraduate work at New York University and then moved on to the University of Michigan, where he received his doctorate in psychology in 1951.

His chief research interest is experimental social psychology, especially as it relates to aggression and altruism. He is the author of *Aggression: A Social-*

DANIEL S. ANTHONY   RICHARD C. ATKINSON   NATHAN AZRIN

GORDON BERMANT

LEONARD BERKOWITZ   DAVID BAKAN

Psychological Analysis (McGraw-Hill, 1962), editor of the three-volume *Advances in Experimental Social Psychology* (Academic Press) and associate editor of the *Journal of Personality and Social Psychology*.

Gordon Bermant ("Copulation in Rats"), professor of psychology at the University of California, Davis, is a Harvard Ph.D. who studied the behavior of chickens during his postdoctoral days at Harvard. A former student of Frank Beach, Bermant is critical of psychologists "who are so involved in looking at intrinsically uninteresting behavior in ecologically invalid surroundings, that the basic fact of the evolution of behavior to meet environmental demands escapes their attention." He sticks to the behavior of animals because he believes this approach maximizes the chances for results that will merge with the advances in knowledge in the biological sciences. His interests are the determinants of species-specific behavior, primarily reproductive behavior.

Sidney W. Bijou ("The Mentally Retarded Child") is professor of psychology and director of the Child Behavior Laboratory at the University of Illinois. Before joining the Illinois faculty, he taught psychology and served as director of the Developmental Psychology Laboratory at the University of Washington for almost 20 years.

Bijou received his B.S. from the University of Florida, his M.A. from Columbia and his Ph.D. from the University of Iowa. He has been editor of the *Journal of Experimental Child Psychology*, associate editor of the *International Review of Research in Mental Retardation* and a frequent contributor to professional journals. He is a member of the Research Advisory Board for the National Association for Retarded Children, the American Psychological Association, and the Society for Research in Child Development.

Henry David Block (coauthor, "The Psychology of Robots") did his undergraduate work at City College New York before receiving his Ph.D. in mathematics from Iowa State College. He currently is professor of applied mathematics at Cornell University and has published articles on topics ranging from eigenvalues and isoperimetric inequalities to learning in some simple nonbiological systems. "The original impetus for this article," he reports, "came from a demonstration at a friend's home where I tried to show their 12-year-old son how a simple machine made from paper cups could learn to beat us all at some games. From the discussion that followed, I became aware that many of the difficulties blocking the way to more sophisticated robots were closely related to current difficulties in theoretical psychology."

Jerome Brams ("From Freud to Fromm") completed his doctoral studies at the University of Missouri and for two years was a postdoctoral fellow at New York University. From 1965 to 1967, he was in Cuernavaca, Mexico, as Erich Fromm's research associate. Brams writes: "Since my return from Mexico, I've been impressed by the political and social activism of some college students. But at the same time, there seems to be a paradoxical sense of alienation from self among many of these and other students."

Jerome S. Bruner ("Up from Helplessness"), who helped found Harvard's Center for Cognitive Studies in 1960, is a graduate of Duke University. Bruner received his Ph.D. from Harvard in 1941. He joined the Harvard faculty in 1945 and has been professor of psychology there since 1952. He has published many books and articles on the nature of cognitive processes, including *On Knowing: Essays for the Left Hand* and *Toward a Theory of Instruction.*

Bruner has served on committees advising the White House, the State Department, the United Nations, the Department of Defense, the National Science Foundation and the National Institutes of

HENRY DAVID BLOCK

JEROME BRAMS

SIDNEY W. BIJOU

GORDON M. BURGHARDT

RAYMOND BERNARD CATTELL

Health; he is a founding member of the National Academy of Education and a past president of the American Psychological Association. In 1962, the APA awarded him its Distinguished Scientific Award.

Gordon M. Burghardt ("Chemical Perception in Newborn Snakes") is an assistant professor of psychology at the University of Tennessee. He began college as a chemistry major, but the lure of animal behavior became irresistible, especially after he studied with Eckhard Hess at Chicago.

Burghardt, who spent the summer of 1963 with

Konrad Lorenz and his associates at the Max Planck Institute in Seewiesen, West Germany, feels that the time is ripe for an experimental evolutionary and ethological approach to human behavior. He adds, "It is a tragic comment on man's irrationality that he looks at the present human condition and thinks seriously that rationality and intelligence are man's most characteristic attributes."

Raymond Bernard Cattell ("Are I.Q. Tests Intelligent?") is Distinguished Research Professor in the Department of Psychology, University of Illinois,

NOAM CHOMSKY

MICHAEL COLE

SHEILA COLE

THOMAS J. COTTLE

JEROME S. BRUNER

JOHN M. DARLEY

where he directs the Laboratory of Personality and Group Analysis. His study of intelligence began 40 years ago, when his Ph.D. research was done under the direction of Charles Spearman and Sir Cyril Burt at the University of London. He later received his D.Sc. from the same institution.

Cattell came to the United States at the invitation of E. L. Thorndike and has taught at Clark and Harvard Universities. He has published 265 articles, contrib-

uted 31 chapters to books, and written 28 books of his own.

Noam Chomsky ("Language and the Mind") holds the Ferrari P. Ward Professorship of Modern Languages and Linguistics at the Massachusetts Institute of Technology. He received his Ph.D. in linguistics at the University of Pennsylvania, where his dissertation was on transformational analysis.

He is the author of books and articles not only on linguistics but on philosophy, intellectual history and contemporary issues.

Michael Cole (coauthor, "Russian Nursery Schools") continues studying human learning by taking part in a new interdisciplinary program at the new Irvine campus of the University of California for the study of language and development. In this program anthropologists, linguists, psychologists, and other social scientists bring their skills to bear on the problem of cultural change and development.

Cole began his research on human learning during his doctoral program at Indiana University. Then, as a postdoctoral fellow in the Soviet-American Exchange Program, he studied at Moscow University under Alexander Luria. There he was introduced to cross-cultural research on the development of cognitive processes.

While at Stanford University, he became interested in a mathematics-learning project in Africa. He continues to study Kpelle culture and learning and commutes between California and Liberia.

Sheila Cole (coauthor, "Russian Nursery Schools") with her husband, Michael, spent the summer of 1966 in the Soviet Union, helping with preparations for the 18th International Congress of Psychologists and gathering material on Soviet nursery schools.

Mrs. Cole received her B.A. from Indiana University and her M.S. from the Columbia Graduate School of Journalism. She has worked on several newspapers, usually as an education writer, and is now a freelance journalist.

Thomas J. Cottle ("Encounter in Color") was graduated from Harvard University and received his Ph.D. from the University of Chicago. He is now lecturing in the Department of Social Relations at Harvard and doing research on racial integration and on the subjective definition of time.

John M. Darley (coauthor, "When Will People Help in a Crisis?") is a professor of psychology at Princeton University. While engaged in the research described in the study of bystander intervention, he was a member of the department of psychology at New York University.

Darley's undergraduate work was completed at Swarthmore and his M.A. and Ph.D. were obtained at Harvard, with a year's leave of absence for study at the University of Minnesota. He spent the summer of 1961 as a selection officer for the Peace Corps.

In addition to bystander intervention, Darley is studying determinants of conformity behavior and the relationship between subgroups and the majority. His research in the latter field includes work with experimentally created deviant subgroups.

Vincent Dethier ("The Hungry Fly") is professor of biology at Johns Hopkins University. He received his Ph.D. in biology in 1939 from Harvard and since that time has published widely in the field of physiology and behavior, "with side jaunts into ecology and classification"—and fiction. His *To Know a Fly,* a humorous, cartoon-illustrated paperback about the life of a scientist who studies flies, was described by *Science* magazine as a minor classic.

Dethier was in Africa during World War II and in 1951–1952 returned to the Belgian Congo on a Fulbright Scholarship to study sleeping sickness and how the tse-tse fly locates its host. Flies are excellent experimental animals, he says: "They have a simple nervous system, they are hardy, year-round, and rich in behavioral forms—all in all, our best bet."

J. Anthony Deutsch ("The Neural Basis of Memory") is professor of psychology at the University of California, San Diego, and an active researcher in the area of physiological psychology. His work has dealt mainly with the mechanism of thirst, intracranial self-stimulation and the physical basis of memory and learning. He did his undergraduate and doctoral studies at Oxford University, where he spent eight years on the faculty before coming to the Center for Advanced Study in the Behavioral Sciences at Stanford University in 1959. After spending some time on the faculty at Stanford and as a visiting associate professor at UCLA, he moved to New York University in 1964. He returned to California in 1966 to take up his present post at UCSD.

Deutsch's first book, *The Structural Basis of Behavior,* which dealt with his behavior theory, was published in 1960. More recently, he coauthored a textbook, *Physiological Psychology* (1966), with his wife, Diana.

Bill Domhoff (coauthor, "Dreams of Freud and Jung") is a cofounder, with Calvin S. Hall, of the Institute of Dream Research, established in Miami and located since 1966 in Santa Cruz, California, and

teaches psychology at the University of California, Santa Cruz.

Domhoff's doctorate is from the University of Miami, where he and Hall met. Before joining the psychology department at Santa Cruz in 1965, Domhoff taught psychology at California State College, Los Angeles, for several years. He is coeditor of *C. Wright Mills and the Power Elite* and author of *Who Rules America?* as well as several research articles on dreams.

J. ANTHONY DEUTSCH

BILL DOMHOFF

ARTHUR J. DYCK

VINCENT DETHIER

HANS J. EYSENCK

Arthur J. Dyck ("Questions for the Global Conscience") is assistant professor of social ethics at Harvard Divinity School and a member of the Harvard Center for Population Studies. He obtained his B.A. in sociology at Tabor College and followed it with two M.A.s—one in psychology and one in philosophy—from the University of Kansas. His Ph.D. in religious ethics is from Harvard.

He has been a teaching fellow and research assistant in psychology at the University of Kansas and special lecturer in philosophy at the University of Saskatchewan in his native Canada.

Hans J. Eysenck ("New Ways in Psychotherapy") is professor of psychology at the University of London and director of the Psychological Department at the Institute of Psychiatry, Maudsley and Bethlem Royal Hospitals. His experimental research in the field of personality has earned him international recognition. He has published more than 100 articles as well as eight books, including the *Structure of Human Per-*

EDMUND FANTINO   IVO AND ROSALIND FEIERABEND

C. B. FERSTER   JEROME D. FRANK

sonality, The Uses and Abuses of Psychology, and *The Psychology of Politics.* He takes this in stride but is proud of the fact he also has been published in *Punch* magazine.

Born in Berlin in 1916, Eysenck left Germany in 1934 to study French and English history and literature at the Universities of Dijon and Exeter, and received his Ph.D. in psychology in 1940 from the University of London.

Edmund Fantino ("Of Mice and Misers"), assistant professor of psychology at the University of California, San Diego, teaches courses in learning and motivation and in the control of behavior. For three

years before coming to UCSD, he was an assistant professor at Yale University.

A native of New York City, Fantino did his undergraduate work at Cornell, majoring in mathematics. He went to Harvard for his graduate work in psychology and received his Ph.D. in 1964.

His research at present concerns choice in the pigeon (supported by National Science Foundation grants), conditioned reinforcement, and escape and avoidance conditioning in the rat.

The five studies described by Ivo and **Rosalind Feierabend** ("Conflict, Crisis and Collision: A Study of International Stability") received the Socio-Psychological Prize of the American Association for the Advancement of Science, an annual award for socio-psychological inquiry that furthers the understanding of human behavior. *Political Aggression* is the full report of their findings.

Both members of this interdisciplinary team are on the staff of San Diego State College, where Ivo is an associate professor of political science and Rosalind is an assistant professor of psychology. They both completed their doctoral studies at Yale, where Ivo studied his native Czechoslovakia during the Second Republic and Rosalind explored the psychological meaning of words.

C. B. Ferster ("The Autistic Child") is professor of psychology at Georgetown University in Washington, D.C. For several years before joining the Georgetown faculty, he served as a director and as senior research associate at the Institute for Behavioral Research in Silver Spring, Maryland, working under a research career development award from NIH.

Ferster did his undergraduate work at Rutgers University and received his M.A. and Ph.D. from Columbia. After leaving Columbia, he spent five years as a research fellow at Harvard, then moved on for more research and teaching at the Yerkes Laboratory of Primate Biology in Florida, the Institute of Psychiatric Research at Indiana University and the University of Maryland.

He is the coauthor of *Behavior Principles* (with M. C. Perrott, 1968) and of *Schedules of Reinforcement* (with B. F. Skinner, 1957) and has written more than 50 articles for professional journals.

Jerome D. Frank ("The Face of the Enemy"), professor of psychiatry at Johns Hopkins University School of Medicine, is a member of the National Board, National Committee for a Sane Nuclear Policy, and a member of the Board of Directors, Council for a Livable World. In 1966 he testified by invitation before the Senate Foreign Relations Committee on the psychological aspects of international conflict. In 1967 he published *Sanity and Survival* (Random House), on the psychological aspects of disarmament.

After completing his undergraduate work at Harvard, Frank studied with Kurt Lewin at the University of Berlin. He returned to Harvard for his Ph.D. in psychology, then spent a postdoctoral year at Cornell with Lewin. Study for his M.D. at Harvard was followed by psychiatric training at the Henry Phipps Psychiatric Clinic at Johns Hopkins.

Frank is past president of both the Society for the Psychological Study of Social Issues and the American Psychopathological Association.

Marvin Frankel ("Morality in Psychotherapy") is an assistant professor of psychology at the University of Chicago.

Frankel's Ph.D. thesis was on childrearing practices, the need for achievement and risk-taking behavior in the Brahmin and Vaisha castes of northern India. He did his research during 1962 and 1963 while on a Murphy Fellowship in India. His psychotherapy internship was at the University of Chicago's counseling center.

Frank A. Geldard ("Body English") received his Ph.D. from Clark University in 1928; in that year he went to the University of Virginia, where he founded the Psychological Laboratory in 1929. In 1960 he became dean of the Graduate School of Arts and Sciences at Virginia; since 1962 he has been Stuart Professor of Psychology at Princeton University.

His books include *Fundamentals of Psychology* (Wiley, 1962) and *Communications Processes* (Pergamon Press, 1965).

Herbert Ginsburg (coauthor, "The Psychology of Robots") did undergraduate work at Harvard, then received his Ph.D. in 1965 from the University of North Carolina. His thesis was on Jean Piaget.

For the past several years, Ginsburg has been on the faculty of the Department of Child Development and Family Relations at Cornell University. His major research interest is in the cognitive development and education of children.

Israel Goldiamond ("Moral Behavior: A Functional Analysis") is a professor in the Department of Psychology and Psychiatry at the University of Chicago, where he received his Ph.D. in experimental psychology with an additional major in clinical psychology.

Until recently he was executive director of the Institute for Behavioral Research and a professor at Johns Hopkins University School of Medicine.

He has been actively engaged in the experimental analysis of perception and signal detection and of

problems of clinical, social and educational relevance. His research has included the development of specific programs to alter the behaviors studied.

Bert F. Green, Jr. ("The Computer Conquest of Psychology") learned to program a digital computer and to use computer simulations during the ten years he spent at MIT's Lincoln Laboratory after receiving his Ph.D. from Princeton in 1951.

Dr. Green is at the Carnegie-Mellon University as a

MARVIN FRANKEL

FRANK A. GELDARD

HERBERT GINSBURG

DAVID M. GREEN

ISRAEL GOLDIAMOND

professor in the psychology department. He is the author of *Digital Computers in Research* (1963) and of numerous articles on computer technology, quantitative methods and perception.

David M. Green ("Sonic Booms") is professor of psychology at the University of California, San Diego. He received his Ph.D. from the University of Michigan in 1959 and has been a member of the faculties of MIT and the University of Pennsylvania.

Green is actively engaged in research on psychoacoustics and detection of auditory signals. In 1966 he received the Biennial Award of the Acoustical Society of America for his work. He is the author of *Signal*

Detection Theory and Psychophysics (with J. A. Swets, Wiley, 1966).

In addition, he is chairman of a subpanel on psychoacoustic problems related to the sonic boom that reports to a sonic boom committee of the National Academy of Sciences–National Research Council.

Calvin S. Hall (coauthor, "Dreams of Freud and Jung") is a cofounder, with Bill Domhoff, of the Institute of Dream Research. Hall is director of the insti-

BERT F. GREEN, JR.   CALVIN S. HALL   WARD C. HALSTEAD

HARRY F. HARLOW

ELIOT HEARST

tute, which has one of the largest collections of dream reports in the world; and he also teaches psychology at the University of California, Santa Cruz.

Hall received his B.A. and Ph.D. in psychology from the University of California, Berkeley. A member of the faculty of Western Reserve University for 20 years, he has also taught at Berkeley, the University of Oregon, Syracuse University and the University of Miami and has served as a Fulbright Professor in the Netherlands. He is coauthor of *The Content Analysis of Dreams* and author of *The Primer of Freudian*

Psychology, The Meaning of Dreams and (with G. Lindzey) *Theories of Personality.*

Ward C. Halstead (coauthor, "Memory: A Molecular Maze") is credited with being one of the first to present a systematic model of how learning and memory might be stored in molecules such as proteins.

Born in Ohio, Halstead attended several colleges there before going to Northwestern University for his Ph.D. in physiological psychology, which he received in 1935. Since then he has taught at the University of Chicago.

Halstead is the author of many monographs and books, including *Brain and Intelligence* (a quantitative study of the frontal lobes) and *Brain Mechanisms and Behavior.* Both his battery of neuropsychological tests and his aphasia test are widely used in this country and abroad.

Harry F. Harlow and **Margaret Kuenne Harlow** ("The Young Monkeys") are famous for their work with surrogate mothers, both wire and cloth. During the last ten years the Harlows have discovered a variety of affection ties in monkeys. They have experimentally produced social and asocial monkeys, good and bad mothers, as well as sexually adjusted and maladjusted monkeys.

Dr. Harlow, a past president of the American Psychological Association, received his Ph.D. from Stanford and went to the University of Wisconsin in 1930 to "enrich the literature on rodents." When he arrived, he found that the university had demolished its animal laboratory to make room for a building finally erected 30 years later. In desperation, he turned to the Madison Zoo—and to the monkeys. "For better or worse," he says, "I became forever a monkey man."

Mrs. Harlow came to the university as a specialist in human development but soon broadened her interests to include other primates.

Eliot Hearst ("Psychology Across the Chessboard") is professor of psychology at the University of Missouri and a former captain of the U.S. Olympic Chess Team. After receiving his Ph.D. in psychology from Columbia University, he supervised research in experimental psychology at the National Institute of Mental Health's Clinical Neuropharmacology Research Center. Then he went to England to study pharmacology and do behavior research at the Royal College of Surgeons.

His chief professional interests are animal conditioning and learning (especially discrimination learning in pigeons, rats and monkeys), psychopharmacology, and theories of psychology. For five years, Hearst wrote a column on chess personalities for *Chess Life* magazine.

Paul N. Herman ("The Terrible Tenrec") is presently a member of the Department of Otolaryngology's Kresge Hearing Research Laboratory at the University of Oregon Medical School. Although primarily trained as a behavioral psychologist, his doctoral work at the University of Connecticut and subsequent work have been clustered in the areas of animal psychophysics and sensory physiology. He is now engaged in research with galagos, lemurs and human middle ear function.

Frederick Herzberg ("Motivation, Morale & Money"), a graduate of the City College of New York, received his doctorate from the University of Pittsburgh in 1950. He finished his studies at the Graduate School of Public Health, University of Pittsburgh.

Now professor of psychology at Case Western Reserve University in Cleveland, Herzberg is also a consultant to many industrial, educational and governmental organizations. He recently lectured on work motivation at the University of Leningrad and the Society for Engineers in Budapest, Hungary.

His publications include three books and numerous articles on job attitudes and man's motivation to work.

Robert D. Hess ("Political Attitudes in Children") did his undergraduate work at the University of California, Berkeley, then spent almost 20 years at the University of Chicago. In 1966 he went to Stanford as a fellow at the Center for Advanced Study in the Behavioral Sciences and is now Lee Jacks Professor of Child Education and professor of psychology at Stanford.

Hess received his Ph.D. in human development from Chicago in 1950. He was chairman of the Committee on Human Development from 1959 to 1964, then professor of human development and education, and, during his last few years on the Chicago faculty, director of the Urban Child Center and the Early Education Research Center.

Kenneth I. Howard (coauthor, "Inside Psychotherapy") is a staff therapist at the Katharine Wright Mental Health Clinic in Chicago.

Howard did his undergraduate work at the University of California, Berkeley, and received his Ph.D. from the University of Chicago. He has spent several years as research associate for the University of Chicago and for the Loyola University School of Medicine. At present he is with the Institute for Juvenile Research and is a professor of psychology at Northwestern University.

Irving L. Janis ("When Fear Is Healthy") is a social psychologist noted especially for his work on stress and persuasion. A graduate of the University of Chicago, Janis received his Ph.D. from Columbia University in 1948. Since 1947 he has been at Yale, where he is now professor of psychology.

He is an active member of the American Psychological Association and a consultant for the RAND Corporation. He has been consulting editor on the

MURRAY E. JARVIK

ROBERT D. HESS

PAUL N. HERMAN

KENNETH HOWARD

FREDERICK HERZBERG

IRVING L. JANIS

Journal of Abnormal and Social Psychology and the *Journal of Personality and Social Psychology*. Currently he is a member of the editorial board of the *Journal of Experimental Social Psychology*.

The paper on which Janis' article is based won the 1967 Socio-Psychological Prize of the American Association for the Advancement of Science.

Murray E. Jarvik ("The Psychopharmacological Revolution") is professor of pharmacology at the Albert

Einstein College of Medicine in New York City. He received his M.D. and his Ph.D. from the University of California, Berkeley. Jarvik's chief professional interests are the actions of drugs on behavior and the physiological basis of memory.

Bela Julesz ("Experiment in Perception") is head of the sensory and perceptual processes department at the Bell Telephone Laboratories in Murray Hill, New Jersey. He is noted for his research in visual perception using computer-generated patterns.

BELA JULESZ   JEROME KAGAN   JOE KAMIYA

ROBERT KAVANAUGH

RHODA KELLOGG   LAWRENCE KOHLBERG

Born in Budapest, he received his diploma in communication engineering from the Technical University there in 1950 and was graduated from the Hungarian Academy of Sciences in 1956. His doctoral thesis on the encoding of television signals presaged his later interest in analyzing and processing pictorial information.

Jerome Kagan ("The Many Faces of Response") is professor of developmental psychology at Harvard. Doctoral studies at Yale and a position at Ohio State University preceded his Army service, during which Kagan did a research study on attrition at West Point. He found that the poor risks were youths who were aware of a bad or hostile relationship with their fathers.

Later research at the Fels Research Institute, Antioch College, resulted in *Birth to Maturity,* 1963 winner of the Hofheimer Prize for research by the American Psychiatric Association.

Joe Kamiya ("Conscious Control of Brain Waves") is a lecturer in medical psychology at the Langley Porter Neuropsychiatric Institute of the University of California Medical Center in San Francisco.

His doctoral studies were completed at the Berkeley campus of the University of California, and he went on to teach social psychology at the University of Chicago. It was there that he became interested in sleep and dream research and made his first studies of alpha waves.

Robert ("Red") Kavanaugh ("The Grim Generation") is Revelle College Counselor, University of California, San Diego. In his work with students, he concentrates on the solution of problems that interfere with academic achievement or personal growth.

Kavanaugh has been a management consultant, a child-welfare worker and a member of the faculty at Michigan State University. He has been involved in marriage, family- and sex-education clinics and programs. His fields are both philosophy and the social sciences.

Rhoda Kellogg ("Understanding Children's Art") is the executive director of San Francisco's 80-year-old Golden Gate Kindergarten Association and administrator of the Phoebe A. Hearst Pre-School Learning Center, a model kindergarten operated by the association. With more than 40 years' experience in working with and observing children, Miss Kellogg has received widespread recognition for her work in preschool education. She is perhaps better known, however, as an international authority on preschool art. She hopes to show that certain children's reading difficulties can be prevented by analyzing the way they draw as preschoolers.

Lawrence Kohlberg ("The Child as a Moral Philosopher") received his Ph.D. in psychology at the University of Chicago. A postdoctoral residence at Children's Hospital, Boston, "confirmed my opinion that psychoanalysis had little to offer the systematic study of the development of moral ideals and feelings." Kohlberg then spent two years at Yale, studying psychosexual development and identification in early and mid-childhood. A year at the Center for Advanced

Study in the Behavioral Sciences was followed by five years at the University of Chicago. Kohlberg then spent a year at the Harvard Human Development Laboratory and has now settled at Harvard as professor of education and social psychology.

Bibb Latané (coauthor, "When Will People Help in a Crisis?") took his Ph.D. in psychology at the University of Minnesota and then taught for six years at the Department of Social Psychology at Columbia University. He is now associate professor of psychology at Ohio State University.

Latané's research efforts span the general area of social and emotional behavior. In the course of his research, he has worked with such diverse species as psychopathic criminals, albino rats, Navy enlisted men, gerbils, sky divers and college sophomores.

In addition to his research and teaching responsibilities, Latané is consulting editor of *Sociometry*. He is also editing a series of introductory paperbacks in social psychology.

Howard Leventhal ("Fear—for Your Health"), a professor of psychology at the University of Wisconsin, received his Ph.D. from the University of North Carolina in 1956 and was a Yale faculty member and a consultant to the Public Health Service. His interests also include biology and genetics.

Brendan Maher ("The Shattered Language of Schizophrenia") was born in England and did his undergraduate work at the University of Manchester. A Fulbright Scholarship brought him to Ohio State University, from which he received his Ph.D. in 1954.

After serving briefly as psychologist in Her Majesty's prison, Wakefield, England, Maher then taught at Northwestern University, Louisiana State University, Harvard and Wisconsin; currently, he is Riklis Professor of Behavioral Science at Brandeis.

Maher is the author of *Principles of Psychopathology* (McGraw-Hill, 1966) and *Introduction to Research in Abnormal Psychology*. He edits *Progress in Experimental Personality Research* (Academic Press) and has just finished editing a series of contributions of the late George Kelly.

Jules H. Masserman ("The Neurotic Cat") is a psychoanalyst and a neurophysiologist. Now professor of neurology and psychiatry at the Northwestern University Medical School, he is also scientific director of the National Foundation for Psychiatric Research, director of education at the Illinois State Psychiatric Institute, chief consultant at Downey Veterans Hospital, consultant at Great Lakes Naval Hospital and

member and past president of a number of professional organizations.

After emigrating to the United States from Poland, Dr. Masserman studied at Wayne State University, from which he received his M.D. degree in 1931. He is the author of numerous books and a frequent contributor to scholarly journals.

Frank B. McMahon, Jr. ("Psychological Testing—A Smoke Screen Against Logic") is an associate professor of psychology at Southern Illinois University. Previously he was a counselor and psychology teacher for

BIBB LATANÉ

HOWARD LEVENTHAL

FRANK B. MC MAHON, JR.

ALBERT MEHRABIAN

BRENDAN MAHER

J. MASSERMA

the St. Louis Junior College District, where he was named the teacher of the year in 1965.

For four years he worked as a therapist and counselor at the Washington University Counseling Center. He received his Ph.D. in clinical psychology from Washington University in 1965.

McMahon is currently working with Science Research Associates on the development of a perceptual vocational-interest test.

Albert Mehrabian ("Communication Without Words") was born in Tabriz, Iran, in 1939. He received his high school education in the preparatory section of the American University of Beirut, Lebanon, and then moved to the United States. He studied mechanical engineering at MIT, where he received his B.S. and M.S. degrees. He continued his graduate work at Clark University, which awarded him a Ph.D. in psychology in 1964. Since that time, he has been at UCLA.

ASHLEY MONTAGU

STANLEY MILGRAM

GARDNER MURPHY

MIKE MURPHY

ALEXANDER SUTHERLAND NEILL

Mehrabian is the author of *Language Within Language* (with Morton Wiener, Appleton-Century-Crofts, 1968) and *An Analysis of Personality Theories* (Prentice-Hall, 1968). His current research is proceeding along two paths: the subtleties of communicating feelings and the measurement and description of differences in the social behavior of individuals.

Stanley Milgram ("The Small-World Problem") is a professor at City College in New York. In 1960 he received his Ph.D. in social psychology from Harvard.

After spending three years at Yale University as assistant professor of psychology, Milgram returned to Harvard, where he taught experimental social psychology. His publications have been translated into French, German and Italian, and in 1964 the American Association for the Advancement of Science awarded him its prize for research in social psychology.

Noted anthropologist and social biologist **Ashley Montagu** ("Chromosomes and Crime") was born in England and came to the United States in 1930. He received his Ph.D. from Columbia University in 1937. He has written extensively on race, genetics and human evolution and was responsible for drafting the UNESCO statement on race. Among his 31 books are *The Human Revolution, Human Heredity* and *The Natural Superiority of Women.*

Gardner Murphy ("Parapsychology: New Neighbor or Unwelcome Guest?") divides his time between George Washington University and the Menninger Clinic in Topeka, where he holds the Henry March Pfeiffer Research-Training Chair in Psychiatry. He also oversees much of the parapsychological experimentation conducted at the American Society of Psychical Research, of which he is president.

After receiving his doctorate from Columbia in 1923, Murphy taught psychology there until 1940, when he moved to City College as chairman of the Psychology Department. While at CCNY, he published his chief systematic work, *Personality: A Biosocial Approach to Origins and Structures;* served as president of the American Psychological Association (1943–1944); and, at the invitation of the Indian government, participated in a 1950 UNESCO project concerning social tensions in India, particularly between Hindus and Muslims. In 1952, Murphy became director of research at the Menninger Foundation.

Mike Murphy ("Esalen: Where It's At"), did graduate work in philosophy, served in the Army, then went to an Ashram in India and studied meditation for a year and a half. In 1961, he and his brother, Dennis (film writer and author of the novel *The Sergeant*), inherited 150 acres of coastal land just south of Carmel, California—a mile-long strip complete with hot springs, cyprus trees, cabins and a lodge, just perfect for seminars.

In 1962, he and Dick Price, who was a classmate at Stanford, began programs at Esalen seeking to understand the limits of the human potential.

Alexander Sutherland Neill ("Can I Come to Summerhill? I Hate My School"), headmaster of Summerhill School, was born 85 years ago in Scotland. His ideas remain as controversial today as when they caused his resignation from the staff of King Alfred School in 1920. The forerunner of Summerhill was founded in 1921, when Neill set up an international school in Dresden, Germany. He moved this school first to the Austrian Tyrol and then, after seven months of harassment by the local peasants and the Austrian government, to England.

Neill, who holds the M.A. degree, is a graduate of Edinburgh University, where his major subject was English. He has written a number of books on education and child psychology.

David E. Orlinsky (coauthor, "Inside Psychotherapy") is a staff therapist at the Katharine Wright Mental Health Clinic in Chicago. He also serves as senior research associate at the Institute for Juvenile Research in Chicago and teaches at the University of Chicago, where he received his bachelor's degree and his doctorate as well.

Irvin Rock ("When the World Is Tilt") is a professor at the Institute for Cognitive Studies, Rutgers University. After completing his B.S. and M.A. at City College of New York, he received his Ph.D. from the New School for Social Research.

Robert Rosenthal ("Self-fulfilling Prophecy") is professor of social psychology at Harvard University. Born in Germany, which he left in 1938, Rosenthal received his Ph.D. from the University of California, Los Angeles, in 1956. He has extensive training and experience in the field of clinical psychology. In 1960, he was awarded the AAAS Socio-Psychological Prize (with Kermit Fode) for research on experimenter expectancy effects, and in 1967 he received with Lenore Jacobson the American Psychological Association's Cattell Fund Award for work on teacher expectancy effects in the classroom.

Rosenthal is the author of many articles and several books. His most recently published book is *Pygmalion in the Classroom,* coauthored by Lenore Jacobson.

His current research interests include methods to control experimenter effects, differences in the responses of volunteers and nonvolunteers in behavioral research and expectancy effects in everyday life.

Harris B. Rubin ("Rabbit Families and How They Grow"), who received his Ph.D. in psychology from the University of Chicago in 1965, is now a medical research associate at Anna State Hospital and an assistant professor at the Rehabilitation Institute of Southern Illinois University.

Floyd L. Ruch ("Personality: Public or Private") is founder and president of Psychological Services, Inc. He is professor of psychology at the University of Southern California. A pioneer in the field of aptitude and temperament testing, he developed the first "lie detector" for a personality test. Ruch is past president of both the California State Psychological Association and the Western Psychological Association and past

DAVID E. ORLINSKY ROBERT ROSENTHAL FLOYD L. RUCH

HARRIS B. RUBIN

WILLIAM B. RUCKER IRVIN ROCK

president of the Business and Industrial Division of the American Psychological Association. But he is best known to generations of college students as the author of *Psychology and Life,* one of the most widely used psychology texts in American colleges.

William B. Rucker (coauthor, "Memory: A Molecular Maze") obtained his Ph.D. in biopsychology from the University of Chicago in 1967 and is currently assistant professor of psychology at George Washington University. In addition to his molecular studies, Rucker maintains an interest in psycholinguistics.

James A. Simmons ("The Sonar Sight of Bats") studied under E. G. Wever at the Princeton Auditory Research Laboratories.

Much of his undergraduate work was in chemistry, and he hopes someday to study behavior from the point of view of chemical events in the central nervous system. He also is interested in studying the effects of certain chemicals on the mind, both from within and without.

FREDERICK H. STOLLER

JAMES A. SIMMONS

LEONARD UHR

JEROME L. SINGER

WILLIAM R. UTTAL

GEORGE TALLAND (deceased)

Jerome L. Singer ("The Importance of Daydreaming") has directed research programs on the psychology of daydreams and related fantasy processes for over ten years. He obtained his doctorate at the University of Pennsylvania. Later he attended the

William Alanson White Institute and received his certificate as a psychoanalyst.

Singer is professor of psychology and director of the Clinical Psychology Training Program, City College of the City University of New York. He also has a private practice in psychoanalysis. He is the author of *Daydreaming: An Introduction to the Experimental Study of Inner Experience.*

Frederick H. Stoller ("The Long Weekend"), after receiving his doctorate from UCLA, where he was trained in classical clinical psychology, served as a senior psychologist at Camarillo State Hospital. There he "obtained first-hand experience with people in trouble and learned not to be frightened of them—an important asset." He is now senior research associate at the Youth Studies Center of the University of Southern California. The center is operated under the auspices of the School of Public Administration, and Dr. Stoller finds his contact with an interdisciplinary group studying broader social structures a valuable supplement to his primary work on research and training in group methods.

The late **George A. Talland** ("Amnesia: A World Without Continuity") was associated with Massachusetts General Hospital as a psychologist and was assistant professor of psychology, Harvard Medical School. He was graduated with a degree in economics from Queen's College, Cambridge, in 1939, and earned his Ph.D. from the University of London's Institute of Psychiatry, Maudsley Hospital. In 1953 he came to Harvard University as a research fellow in the Laboratory of Social Relations. Talland published widely in the field of his chief professional interest, the experimental investigation of normal and impaired cognitive function. In 1961, the American Academy of Arts and Sciences awarded him its prize for the best monograph in the physical and biological sciences.

Leonard and Elizabeth Uhr ("The Quiet Revolution") are both prolific writers. Mrs. Uhr is a novelist, and her husband is the author of four books and more than 70 experimental and theoretical papers. Currently a professor in the Computer Sciences Department at the University of Wisconsin, Dr. Uhr is considered one of the most knowledgeable drug experts today. He graduated from Princeton and received his Ph.D. from the University of Michigan, where he remained until 1965 as research psychologist in the Mental Health Research Institute and an associate professor in the Department of Psychology. The objective behavioral measurement of the effects of psychoactive drugs has occupied much of his time.

William R. Uttal ("Teaching and Machines") is professor of psychology and was the coordinator of the Psychological Sciences group at the Mental Health Research Institute. Dr. Uttal became interested both in computers and in physiological psychology while in the Air Force. Before he joined the University of Michigan faculty, he had been a leader in the development of the teaching machine version of the IBM 650 and 1410 computers.

PHILIP G. ZIMBARDO

JOACHIM F. WOHLWILL

In 1965–1966, Uttal was a visiting professor at Japan's Kyoto Prefectural University of Medicine, a residence that gave him a chance to pursue his interest in Japanese culture. Two years ago, he published *Real Time Computers: Technique and Application in the Psychological Sciences* (Harper & Row).

Thom Verhave ("The Inspector General Is a Bird") was born in Amsterdam, the Netherlands, and immigrated to New York City in 1949. He received his Ph.D. in psychology from Columbia in 1956, after which he spent six years as a psychopharmacologist.

In 1963 he joined the faculty of Arizona State University.

Joachim F. Wohlwill ("The Mystery of the Prelogical Child") is a professor of psychology and director of the Graduate Training Program in Developmental Psychology at Clark University. Wohlwill worked with Jean Piaget at the Institut Rousseau in Geneva. Wohlwill graduated from Harvard in 1947 and received his Ph.D. in 1957 from the University of California, Berkeley. His main present interests are the development of perception and thinking in the child and formal instruction as opposed to spontaneous activity. This had led him to a related interest—people's responses to their physical environments, both natural and man-made.

Philip G. Zimbardo ("The Psychology of Police Confessions") received his Ph.D. in psychology from Yale University. He was an associate professor of psychology at New York University, where he received the Distinguished Teacher Award, and has been a visiting professor at Yale, Stanford and Barnard. He is now a professor at Stanford University.

THOM VERHAVE

bibliographies

I. INTRODUCTION

From Freud to Fromm

AN AUTOBIOGRAPHICAL STUDY. S. Freud. Norton, 1963.

ESCAPE FROM FREEDOM. E. Fromm. Rinehart, 1941.

THE FUTURE OF AN ILLUSION. S. Freud. Liveright, 1955.

THE HEART OF MAN. E. Fromm. Harper & Row, 1964.

MAN FOR HIMSELF. E. Fromm. Rinehart, 1947.

NEW INTRODUCTORY LECTURES ON PSYCHOANALYSIS. S. Freud. Norton, 1933.

AN OUTLINE OF PSYCHOANALYSIS. S. Freud. Norton, 1949.

THE SANE SOCIETY. E. Fromm. Holt, Rinehart and Winston, 1955.

Personality: Public or Private

THE AD HOC COMMITTEE ON SOCIAL IMPACT OF PSYCHOLOGICAL ASSESSMENT. R. F. Berdie in *American Psychologist*, Vol. 20, pp. 143–146, 1965.

THE BRAIN WATCHERS. M. L. Gross. Random House, 1962.

HOW EMPLOYEES FEEL ABOUT PERSONALITY TESTS. R. C. Winkler and T. W. Mathews in *Personnel Journal*, Vol. 46, pp. 490–492.

THE K FACTOR AS A (VALIDITY) SUPPRESSOR VARIABLE IN PREDICTING SUCCESS IN SELLING. F. L. Ruch and W. W. Ruch in *Journal of Applied Psychology*, Vol. 51, pp. 201–204, 1967.

PRIVACY AND BEHAVIORAL RESEARCH. O. M. Ruebhausen and O. G. Brim, Jr., in *American Psychologist*, Vol. 21, pp. 423–437, 1966.

PRIVACY AND FREEDOM. A. F. Westin. Atheneum, 1967.

PROBLEMS IN REVIEW: PUTTING EXECUTIVES TO THE TEST. L. B. Ward in *Harvard Business Review*, Vol. 38, p. 6, 1960.

PROJECTIVE METHODOLOGIES. G. G. Gleser in *Annual Review of Psychology*, Vol. 14, pp. 391–422, 1963.

SPECIAL ISSUE ON TESTING AND PUBLIC POLICY. *American Psychologist*, Vol. 20, No. 11, 1965.

Psychology Across the Chessboard

BOBBY FISCHER TEACHES CHESS: A PROGRAMMED TEXT. R. J. Fischer, S. Margulies. Basic Systems, Inc., 1966.

CHESS, OEDIPUS, AND THE MATER DOLOROSA. N. Reider in *International Journal of Psychoanalysis*, Vol. 40, pp. 1–14, 1959.

THE DEFENSE. V. Nabokov. Putnam, 1964.

MASTERS OF THE CHESSBOARD. R. Reti. McGraw-Hill, 1932.

MNEMONIC VIRTUOSITY: A STUDY OF CHESSPLAYERS. A. Binet. Translated by M. L. Simmel, S. B. Barron in *Genetic Psychology Monographs*, Vol. 74, pp. 127–162, 1966.

PSYCHOANALYTIC OBSERVATIONS ON CHESS AND CHESSMASTERS. R. Fine in *Psychoanalysis*, Vol. 4, No. 3, pp. 7–77, 1956.

THE PSYCHOLOGY OF BLINDFOLD CHESS: AN INTROSPECTIVE ACCOUNT. R. Fine in *Acta Psychologica*, Vol. 24, pp. 352–370, 1965.

THE ROYAL GAME. S. Zweig. Viking, 1944.

THIS MADE CHESS HISTORY; VON KEMPELEN'S AUTOMATON. K. H. Harkness, J. S. Battel in *Chess Review*, 1947.

THOUGHT AND CHOICE IN CHESS. A. D. De Groot. Basic Books, 1966.

The Computer Conquest of Psychology

THE ANALYSIS OF PROXIMITIES: MULTIDIMENSIONAL SCALING WITH AN UNKNOWN DISTANCE FUNCTION. R. N. Shepard in *Psychometrika*, Vol. 27, pp. 125–140 and 219–246, 1962.

COGNITION AND THOUGHT. W. R. Reitman. Wiley, 1965.

COMPUTERS AND THOUGHT. E. A. Feigenbaum, J. Feldman, eds. McGraw-Hill, 1963.

THE COMPUTER AS A PATTERN GENERATOR FOR PERCEPTUAL RESEARCH. Benjamin W. White in *Behavioral Science*, Vol. 6, pp. 252–259, 1961.

DIGITAL COMPUTERS IN RESEARCH. B. F. Green, Jr. McGraw-Hill, 1963.

TEACHING AND MACHINES. W. R. Uttal in *Psychology Today*, August, 1967.

Questions for the Global Conscience

THE CHALLENGE OF MAN'S FUTURE. Harrison Brown. Viking, 1954.

DOCTRINES AND ATTITUDES OF MAJOR RELIGIONS IN REGARD TO FERTILITY. Richard M. Fagley in *World Population Conference*, Vol. III, United Nations, 1967.

THE KHANNA STUDY. John B. Wyon and John E. Gordon in *Harvard Medical Alumni Bulletin*, No. 41, pp. 24–28, 1967.

POPULATION AND FOOD SUPPLIES: THE EDGE OF THE KNIFE. Roger Revelle in *Proceedings of the National Academy of Science*, Vol. LVI, No. 2, pp. 328–351, 1966.

POPULATION PROCESSES IN SOCIAL SYSTEMS. James M. Beshers. Free Press, 1967.

RELIGIOUS FACTORS IN THE POPULATION PROBLEM. Arthur J. Dyck in *The Religious Situation* (D. Cutler, ed.). Beacon Press, 1968.

The Psychology of Robots

BRAINS, MACHINES, AND MATHEMATICS. M. A. Arbib. McGraw-Hill, 1964.

CYBERNETICS. Norbert Wiener. Wiley, 1961.

CYBORG: EVOLUTION OF THE SUPERMAN. D. S. Halacy Jr. Harper & Row, 1965.

DESIGN FOR A BRAIN: THE ORIGIN OF ADAPTIVE BEHAVIOR. W. R. Ashby. Wiley, 1967.

LEARNING IN SOME SIMPLE NON-BIOLOGICAL SYSTEMS. H. D. Block in *American Scientist*, March, 1965.

511

SIMULATION OF STATISTICALLY COMPOSITE SYSTEMS—SELF-REPRODUCING MACHINES. H. D. Block in *Prospects for Simulation and Simulators of Dynamic Systems* (George Shapiro and Milton Rogers, eds.). Spartan Press, 1967.

THEORY OF SELF-REPRODUCING AUTOMATA. John Von Neumann. Edited and completed by A. W. Burks. University of Illinois Press, 1966.

Parapsychology: New Neighbor or Unwelcome Guest

CHALLENGE OF PSYCHICAL RESEARCH. Gardner Murphy. Harper & Row, 1961.

ESP AND PERSONALITY PATTERNS. G. R. Schmeidler and R. A. McConnell. Yale University Press, 1958.

ESP IN THE FRAMEWORK OF MODERN SCIENCE. Henry Margenau in *Journal of the American Society for Psychical Research*, Vol. 60, pp. 214–228, 1966.

AN EXPERIMENTAL APPROACH TO DREAMS AND TELEPATHY. Montague Ullman in *Archives of General Psychiatry*, Vol. 14, pp. 605–613, 1966.

THE INFLUENCE OF BELIEF AND DISBELIEF IN ESP UPON INDIVIDUAL SCORING LEVEL. Gertrude Schmeidler in *Journal of Experimental Psychology*, Vol. 36, pp. 271–276, 1946.

TELEPATHY AND EMOTIONAL STIMULI: A CONTROLLED EXPERIMENT. Thelma Moss and J. A. Gengerelli in *Journal of Abnormal Psychology*, Vol. 72, pp. 341–348, 1967.

II. LEARNING AND MOTIVATION

Motivation, Morale & Money

JOB ATTITUDES: RESEARCH AND OPINION. F. Herzberg, B. Mausner, R. Peterson, D. Capwell. Psychological Services of Pittsburgh, 1957.

MANAGEMENT ORGANIZATION AND JOB DESIGN. F. Herzberg in *Management in Perspective*. Houghton Mifflin, 1965.

THE MOTIVATION TO WORK. F. Herzberg, B. Mausner, B. Snyderman. Wiley, 1959.

WORK AND THE NATURE OF MAN. F. Herzberg. World, 1966.

Of Mice and Misers

FUNCTIONAL AUTONOMY OF MOTIVES AS AN EXTINCTION PHENOMENON. David C. McClelland in *Psychological Review*, Vol. 49, pp. 272–283, 1942.

THE MEASUREMENT OF NERVOUS HABITS IN NORMAL CHILDREN. Willard Olson. University of Minnesota Press, 1929.

MOTIVATION, PERFORMANCE AND EXTINCTION. Robert W. Earl in *Journal of Comparative and Physiological Psychology*, Vol. 50, pp. 248–251, 1957.

ON THE PERSISTENCE OF AN EAR-SCRATCHING RESPONSE IN THE RAT. William Datel, John P. Seward in *Journal of Abnormal and Social Psychology*, Vol. 47, pp. 58–61, 1952.

PATTERN AND GROWTH IN PERSONALITY. Gordon W. Allport. Holt, 1961.

PROBLEMS PRESENTED BY THE CONCEPT OF ACQUIRED DRIVES. J. S. Brown in *Current Theory and Research in Motivation: A Symposium*. University of Nebraska Press, 1953.

THE STRUCTURE OF FUNCTIONAL AUTONOMY. John P. Seward in *American Psychologist*, Vol. 18, pp. 703–710, 1963.

Beverly: The Computer Is a Tutor

COMPUTER-ASSISTED INSTRUCTION IN INITIAL READING: A PROGRESS REPORT ON Hansen in *Reading Research Quarterly*, Vol. 2, pp. 5–25, 1966.

COMPUTER-BASED INSTRUCTION IN INITIAL READING: A PROGRESS REPORT ON THE STANFORD PROJECT. H. A. Wilson, R. C. Atkinson in Technical Report 119, Institute for Mathematical Studies in the Social Sciences, Stanford University, 1967. (To be published in *Basic Studies in Reading*, H. Levin, J. Williams, eds. Harper & Row.)

HUMAN MEMORY: A PROPOSED SYSTEM AND ITS CONTROL PROCESSES. R. C. Atkinson and R. M. Shiffrin in *The Psychology of Learning and Motivation: Advances in Research and The-*

ory (K. W. Spence and J. T. Spence, eds.), Vol. 2. Academic Press, 1968.

INSTRUCTION IN INITIAL READING UNDER COMPUTER CONTROL: THE STANFORD PROJECT. R. C. Atkinson in *Journal of Educational Data Processing*, Vol. 4, 1967.

LINGUISTIC CONSIDERATIONS IN THE DESIGN OF THE STANFORD COMPUTER-BASED CURRICULUM IN INITIAL READING. T. S. Rodgers in Technical Report 111, Institute for Mathematical Studies in the Social Sciences, Stanford University, 1967.

MODELS FOR OPTIMIZING THE LEARNING PROCESS. G. J. Green, R. C. Atkinson in *Psychological Bulletin*, Vol. 66, pp. 309–320, 1966.

The Inspector General Is a Bird

THE COMPLEX DISCRIMINATED OPERANT: STUDIES OF MATCHING-TO-SAMPLE AND RELATED PROBLEMS. W. W. Cumming, R. Berryman in *Stimulus Generalization* (D. I. Mostofsky, ed.). Stanford University Press, 1965.

FROM GENERATION TO GENERATION. S. N. Eisenstadt. Free Press, 1956.

INTERMITTENT REINFORCEMENT OF MATCHING-TO-SAMPLE IN THE PIGEON. C. B. Ferster in *Journal of the Experimental Analysis of Behavior*, Vol. 3, pp. 259–272, 1960.

THE PIGEON AS A QUALITY-CONTROL INSPECTOR. T. Verhave in *American Psychologist*, Vol. 21, pp. 109–115, 1966.

SOCIAL ORGANIZATION. C. H. Cooley. Schocken Books, 1962.

SOME OBSERVATIONS ON EXTINCTION OF A COMPLEX DISCRIMINATED OPERANT. W. W. Cumming, R. Berryman, L. R. Cohen, R. N. Lanson in *Psychological Reports*, Vol. 20, pp. 1328–1330, 1967.

TRANSMISSION OF LEARNED BEHAVIOR BETWEEN RATS. Russell M. Church in *The Journal of Abnormal and Social Psychology*, Vol. 20, pp. 163–165, 1957.

WILL. R. J. Herrnstein in *Proceedings of the American Philosophical Society*, Vol. 108, No. 6, pp. 455–458, 1964.

Teaching
and Machines

THE AUTOMATIC GENERATION OF TEACHING MACHINE PROGRAMS. L. Uhr, August, 1965. Copies available from the author: Computer Sciences Department, University of Wisconsin.

CERTAIN MAJOR PSYCHOEDUCATIONAL ISSUES APPEARING IN THE CONFERENCE ON TEACHING MACHINES. S. L. Pressey in *Automatic Teaching: The State of the Art*, pp. 187–198. Wiley, 1959.

THE COMPILATION OF NATURAL LANGUAGE TEXT INTO TEACHING MACHINE PROGRAMS. L. Uhr in *AFPIS Conference Proceedings*, pp. 26 and 35–44, 1964.

COMPUTER-AIDED INSTRUCTION. J. A. Swets, W. Feurzeig in *Science*, Vol. 150, pp. 572–576, 1965.

"ELIZA"—A COMPUTER PROGRAM FOR THE STUDY OF NATURAL LANGUAGE COMMUNICATION BETWEEN MAN AND MACHINE. J. Weizenbaum in *Communications of the ACM*, Vol. 9, pp. 36–45, 1966.

ON CONVERSATIONAL INTERACTION. W. R. Uttal in *Programmed Learning and Computer-Based Instruction*, pp. 171–190. Wiley, 1962.

PRELIMINARY DISCUSSION OF THE LOGICAL DESIGN OF AN ELECTRONIC COMPUTING INSTRUMENT. A. W. Burks, H. H. Goldstien, J. von Neumann. Institute for Advanced Study, 1947. Part I, Vol. I.

PRELIMINARY EXPERIMENTS IN COMPUTER-AIDED TEACHING. J. C. R. Licklider in *Programmed Learning and Computer-Based Instruction*, pp. 217–239. Wiley, 1962.

Rabbit Families
and How They Grow

PATTERNS OF MAMMALIAN REPRODUCTION, 2nd ed. S. A. Asdell. Cornell University Press, 1964.

SEX AND BEHAVIOR. F. A. Beach, ed. Wiley, 1965.

SEX AND INTERNAL SECRETIONS. W. C. Young, ed. Williams & Wilkins, 1961.

A STUDY OF THE BIOLOGY OF THE WILD RABBIT *Orctolagus Cuniculus* IN CONFINED POPULATIONS. K. Myers, W. E. Poole in *Australian Journal of Zoology*, Vol. 10, pp. 225–267, 1962.

TEMPORAL PATTERNS OF SEXUAL BEHAVIOR IN RABBITS AS DETERMINED BY AN AUTOMATIC RECORDING TECHNIQUE. H. B. Rubin, N. H. Azrin in *Journal of Experimental Analysis of Behavior*, Vol. 10, pp. 219–231, March, 1967.

Copulation in Rats

CHARACTERISTICS OF MASCULINE "SEX DRIVE." F. A. Beach in *Nebraska Symposium on Motivation* (M. Jones, ed.), pp. 1–31. University of Nebraska Press, 1956.

CONDITIONING AND SEXUAL BEHAVIOR IN THE MALE ALBINO RAT. K. Larsson. Almqvist and Wiksell, 1956.

The Hungry Fly

INSECTS AND THE CONCEPT OF MOTIVATION. V. G. Dethier in the *Nebraska Symposium on Motivation*, pp. 105–136, 1966.

MICROSCOPIC BRAINS. V. G. Dethier in *Science*, Vol. 143, pp. 1138–1145, 1964.

TO KNOW A FLY. V. G. Dethier. Holden-Day, 1962.

Memory:
A Molecular Maze

THE EFFECTS OF POLARIZING CURRENTS ON THE CONSOLIDATION OF LEARNING. D. J. Albert in *Neuropsychologia*, Vol. 4, pp. 65–77, 1966.

MECHANISMS OF MEMORY. E. R. John. Academic Press, 1967.

MEMORY: ANTAGONISTIC TRANSFER EFFECTS. W. B. Rucker, W. C. Halstead in *Molecular Approaches to Learning and Memory* (William Byrne, ed.), Proceedings of the Symposium at AAAS annual meeting, New York City, 1967.

MEMORY IN MICE ANALYZED WITH ANTIBIOTICS. L. B. Flexner, J. B. Flexner, R. B. Roberts in *Science*, Vol. 155, pp. 1377–1383, 1967.

PROTEIN ORGANIZATION AND MENTAL FUNCTION. W. C. Halstead, J. J. Katz in *Comparative Psychology Monographs*, Vol. 20, pp. 1–38, 1950.

Neural Basis
of Memory

THE HUMAN BRAIN: ITS CAPACITIES AND FUNCTIONS. Isaac Asimov. Houghton Mifflin, 1964.

PHYSIOLOGICAL PSYCHOLOGY. J. A. Deutsch and D. Deutsch. Dorsey Press, 1966.

THE STRUCTURAL BASIS OF BEHAVIOR. J. A. Deutsch. University of Chicago Press, 1960.

Pain and Aggression

ATTACK, AVOIDANCE, AND ESCAPE REACTIONS TO AVERSIVE SHOCK. N. H. Azrin, R. R. Hutchinson, D. F. Hake in *Journal of the Experimental Analysis of Behavior*, Vol. 10, pp. 131–148, 1967.

EXTINCTION-INDUCED AGGRESSION. N. H. Azrin, R. R. Hutchinson, D. F. Hake in *Journal of the Experimental Analysis of Behavior*, Vol. 9, pp. 191–204, 1966.

REFLEXIVE FIGHTING IN RESPONSE TO AVERSIVE STIMULATION. R. E. Ulrich, N. H. Azrin in *Journal of the Experimental Analysis of Behavior*, Vol. 5, pp. 511–520, 1962.

III. PSYCHOLOGICAL DEVELOPMENT

Up From Helplessness

THE AUTOMATIC GRASPING RESPONSES OF INFANTS. T. E. Twitchell in *Journal of Neurophysiologia*, Vol. 3, pp. 247–259, 1965.

THE DEVELOPMENT OF LANGUAGE. D. McNeill in *Carmichael's Manual of Child Psychology* (P. A. Mussen, ed.). Wiley (in press).

PROCESSES OF GROWTH IN INFANCY. J. S. Bruner. Clark University Press and Barre Publishers, 1968.

STRUCTURAL ANTHROPOLOGY. Claude Leví-Strauss. Basic Books, 1963.

The Many Faces
of Response

BIRTH TO MATURITY: A STUDY IN PSYCHOLOGICAL DEVELOPMENT. J. Kagan, H. A. Moss. Wiley, 1962.

IMPULSIVE AND REFLECTIVE CHILDREN: SIGNIFICANCE OF CONCEPTUAL TEMPO. J. Kagan in *Learning and the Educational Process* (J. D. Krumboltz, ed.). Rand McNally, 1965.

INFANTS' DIFFERENTIAL REACTIONS TO FAMILIAR AND DISTORTED FACES. J. Kagan, B. A. Henker, A. Hen-Tov, J. Levine, M. Lewis in *Child Development*, Vol. 37, pp. 519–532, 1966.

ON THE NEED FOR RELATIVISM. J. Kagan in *American Psychologist*, Vol. 22, pp. 131–142, 1967.

PERSONALITY AND THE LEARNING PROCESS. J. Kagan in *Daedalus*, Vol. 94, pp. 553–563, 1965.

PERSONALITY, BEHAVIOR, AND TEMPERAMENT. J. Kagan in *Human Development* (Frank Falkner, ed.). Saunders, 1966.

STIMULUS-SCHEMA DISCREPANCY AND ATTENTION IN THE INFANT. R. B. McCall, J. Kagan in *Journal of Experimental Child Psychology*, Vol. 5, pp. 381–390, 1967.

Russian Nursery Schools

A HANDBOOK OF CONTEMPORARY SOVIET PSYCHOLOGY. Michael Cole, Irving Maltzman, eds. Basic Books, 1968.

PROGRAMMA VOSPITANIIA V DETSKOM SADU [The Program of Education in Nursery School]. M. V. Zaluzhskaia, ed. *Gosidarstvennoe Uchebno-Pedagogicheskoe Izdatel'stvo Ministerstua Prosveshcheniia* [Ministry of Education, RSFSR]. Moscow, 1962.

TEORIIA I PRAKTIKA SENSORNOVOV VOCPITANIIA V DETSKOM SADU [The Theory and Practice of Sensory Training in Nursery School]. A. P. Usovoi, N. P. Sakulinoi, eds. Proveshcheniia, Moscow, 1965.

The Young Monkeys

AFFECTION IN PRIMATES. M. K. Harlow, H. F. Harlow in *Discovery*, Vol. 27, pp. 11–17, 1966.

BEHAVIORAL ASPECTS OF REPRODUCTION IN PRIMATES. H. F. Harlow, W. Danforth Joslyn, M. G. Senko, A. Dopp in *Journal of Animal Science*, Vol. 25, pp. 49–67, 1966.

LEARNING TO LOVE. H. F. Harlow, M. K. Harlow in *American Scientist*, Vol. 54, pp. 244–272, 1966.

LOVE IN MONKEYS. H. F. Harlow in *Scientific American*, June, 1959.

MATERNAL BEHAVIOR OF RHESUS MONKEYS DEPRIVED OF MOTHERING AND PEER ASSOCIATION IN INFANCY. H. F. Harlow, M. K. Harlow, R. O. Dodsworth, G. L. Arling, in *Proceedings of the American Philosophical Society*, Vol. 110, pp. 329–335, 1967.

The Mystery of the Prelogical Child

THE CHILD'S CONCEPTION OF GEOMETRY. J. Piaget, B. Inhelder, A. Szaminska. Basic Books, 1960.

THE CHILD'S CONCEPTION OF NUMBER. J. Piaget. Norton, 1965.

CONCEPT GROWTH AND THE EDUCATION OF THE CHILD. J. G. Wallace. National Foundation for Educational Research in England and Wales, 1966.

COUNTING AND MEASURING. E. M. Churchill. University of Toronto Press, 1961.

THE DEVELOPMENTAL PSYCHOLOGY OF JEAN PIAGET. J. H. Flavell. Van Nostrand, 1963.

THE GROWTH OF BASIC MATHEMATICAL AND SCIENTIFIC CONCEPTS IN CHILDREN. K. Lovell. University of London Press, 1962.

INTELLIGENCE AND EXPERIENCE. McV. J. Hunt. Ronald Press, 1961.

Moral Behavior: A Functional Analysis

DISCRIMINATIVE PROPERTIES OF PUNISHMENT. William Holz, Nathan Azrin in *Journal of the Experimental Analysis of Behavior*, Vol. 4, pp. 225–232, 1961.

A FUNCTIONAL ANALYSIS OF BEHAVIOR. Israel Goldiamond, D. M. Thompson (in preparation).

MOTIVATIONAL ASPECTS OF ESCAPE FROM PUNISHMENT. Nathan Azrin, *et al.*, in *Journal of the Experimental Analysis of Behavior*, Vol. 8, pp. 31–44, 1965.

REINFORCEMENT THEORY. David Premack in *Nebraska Symposium on Motivation: 1965*. (Marshall Jones, ed.). University of Nebraska Press, 1965.

STIMULUS CONTROL. Herbert S. Terrace in *Operant Behavior: Areas of Research and Application* (Werner Honig, ed.). Appleton-Century-Crofts, 1966.

THE WISDOM OF THE BEHAVIOR: LEARNING, CONDITIONING, AND PSYCHOPATHOLOGY. Israel Goldiamond in *Neurobiological Aspects of Psychopathology* (Joseph Zubin, C. Shagass, eds.). Grune and Stratton, 1968.

Understanding Children's Art

CHILDREN'S DRAWINGS AS MEASURES OF INTELLECTUAL MATURITY. A REVISION AND EXTENSION OF THE GOODENOUGH DRAW-A-MAN TEST. Dale B. Harris. Harcourt, Brace & World, 1963.

THE ETERNAL PRESENT. S. Giedion. Pantheon Books, 1962.

EYE AND BRAIN. R. L. Gregory. McGraw-Hill, 1966.

FORM SIMILARITY BETWEEN PHOSPHENES OF ADULTS AND PRE-SCHOOL CHILDREN'S SCRIBBLING. R. Kellogg, M. Knoll, J. Kugler in *Nature*, Vol. 208, No. 5015, p. 1129, 1965.

RHODA KELLOGG CHILD ART COLLECTION. Rhoda Kellogg. Microfiche cards showing 7500 drawings of children aged 24–40 months. Microcard Editions, Inc., 1967.

UNFOLDING OF ARTISTIC ABILITY. Henry Schaefer-Simmern. New York City Press, 1950.

The Child as a Moral Philosopher

THE DEVELOPMENT OF CHILDREN'S ORIENTATIONS TOWARD A MORAL ORDER: 1. SEQUENCE IN THE DEVELOPMENT OF MORAL THOUGHT. Lawrence Kohlberg in *Vita Humana*, Vol. 6, pp. 11–33 (b), 1963.

DEVELOPMENT OF MORAL CHARACTER AND IDEOLOGY. Lawrence Kohlberg in *Review of Child Development Research* (M. L. Hoffman, ed.). Russell Sage, 1964.

EQUALITY. John Wilson. Hutchison, 1966.

THE LANGUAGE OF MORALS. R. M. Hare. Oxford University Press, 1952.

MORAL EDUCATION IN THE SCHOOLS; A DEVELOPMENTAL VIEW. Lawrence Kohlberg in *School Review*, Vol. 74, pp. 1–30, 1966.

MORALS IN EVOLUTION: A STUDY OF COMPARATIVE ETHICS. L. T. Hobhouse. London, 1951.

THE PSYCHOLOGY OF CHARACTER DEVELOPMENT. R. F. Peck, R. J. Havighurst. Wiley, 1960.

STAGES IN THE DEVELOPMENT OF MORAL THOUGHT AND ACTION. Lawrence Kohlberg. Holt, Rinehart, and Winston (in preparation).

The Autistic Child

ARBITRARY AND NATURAL REINFORCEMENT. C. B. Ferster in *The Psychological Record*, Vol. 17, No. 3, pp. 341–347, 1967.

AN EVALUATION OF BEHAVIOR THERAPY WITH CHILDREN. C. B. Ferster and Jeanne Simons in *The Psychological Record*, Vol. 16, No. 1, pp. 65–71, 1966.

INFANTILE AUTISM. Bernard Rimland. Appleton-Century-Crofts, 1964.

OPERANT REINFORCEMENT OF INFANTILE AUTISM. C. B. Ferster in *An Evaluation of the Results of the Psychotherapies* (S. Lesse, ed.). Charles C Thomas, 1968.

PERSPECTIVES IN PSYCHOLOGY: XXV, TRANSITION FROM ANIMAL LABORATORY TO CLINIC. C. B. Ferster in *The Psychological Record*, Vol. 17, No. 2, pp. 145–150, 1967.

POSITIVE REINFORCEMENT AND BEHAVIORAL DEFICITS OF AUTISTIC CHILDREN. C. B. Ferster in *Child Development*, Vol. 32, No. 3, pp. 437–456, 1961.

The Mentally Retarded Child

APPLICATION OF OPERANT CONDITIONING PROCEDURES TO THE BEHAVIOR PROBLEMS OF AN AUTISTIC CHILD. M. M. Wolf, T. R. Risley, H. L. Mees in *Behavior Research and Therapy*, Vol. 1, pp. 305–312, 1964.

CHILD DEVELOPMENT. S. W. Bijou, D. M. Baer. Appleton-Century-Crofts, 1961, 1965. Vols. 1 and 2.

A CONCEPTUAL APPROACH TO SOME PROBLEMS IN MENTAL RETARDATION. D. W. Zimmerman in *Psychological Record*, Vol. 15, pp. 175–183, 1965.

THE EFFECT OF SUPPLEMENTARY EXPERIENCES UPON THE BEHAVIORAL DEVELOPMENT OF INFANTS IN INSTITUTIONS. Yvonne Sayegh, Wayne Dennis in *Child Development*, Vol. 36, pp. 81–90, 1965.

FINAL NOTE ON A CASE OF EXTREME ISOLATION. Kingsley Davis in *American Journal of Sociology*, Vol. 57, pp. 432–457, 1947.

INFANT DEVELOPMENT UNDER ENVIRONMENTAL HANDICAP. Wayne Dennis, Pergouchi Najarian. *Psychological Monographs General and Applied*, Vol. 71, No. 7, Whole No. 436, 1957.

POSITIVE REINFORCEMENT AND BEHAVIOR DEFICITS OF AUTISTIC CHILDREN. C. B. Ferster in *Child Development*, Vol. 32, pp. 437–456, 1961.

REINFORCEMENT AND PUNISHMENT IN THE CONTROL OF HUMAN BEHAVIOR BY SOCIAL AGENCIES. C. B. Ferster in *Psychiatric Research Reports*, Vol. 10, pp. 101–118, 1958.

Can I Come to Summerhill? I Hate My School

FREEDOM, NOT LICENSE! A. S. Neill. Hart, 1966.

SUMMERHILL: A RADICAL APPROACH TO CHILD REARING. A. S. Neill. Hart, 1960.

Political Attitudes in Children

CHILDREN AND THE DEATH OF A PRESIDENT: MULTI-DISCIPLINARY STUDIES. Martha Wolfenstein and Gilbert Kliman. Doubleday, 1965.

CHILDREN AND POLITICS. Fred Greenstein. Yale University Press, 1965.

DEVELOPMENT OF POLITICAL ATTITUDES IN CHILDREN. Robert D. Hess and Judith V. Torney. Aldine, 1967.

POLITICAL LIFE: WHY PEOPLE GET INVOLVED IN POLITICS. Robert Lane. Free Press, 1959.

POLITICAL SOCIALIZATION: A STUDY IN THE PSYCHOLOGY OF POLITICAL BEHAVIOR. Herbert Hyman. Free Press, 1959.

IV. THE SENSORY WORLD

Experiment in Perception

BINOCULAR DEPTH PERCEPTION WITHOUT FAMILIARITY CUES. Bela Julesz in *Science*, Vol. 145, pp. 356–362, 1964.

EXTENSION OF PANUM'S FUSIONAL AREA IN BINOCULARLY STABILIZED VISION. Derek Fender, Bela Julesz in *Journal of the Optical Society of America*, Vol. 57, pp. 819–830, 1967.

THE SUPPRESSION OF MONOCULARLY PERCEIVABLE SYMMETRY DURING BINOCULAR FUSION. Bela Julesz in *Bell System Technical Journal*, Vol. 46, No. 6, pp. 1203–1221, July–August, 1967.

TEXTURE AND VISUAL PERCEPTION. Bela Julesz in *Scientific American*, Vol. 212, No. 2, pp. 38–48, February, 1965.

When the World Is Tilt

ADAPTATION, AFTEREFFECT, AND CONTRAST IN THE PERCEPTION OF CURVED LINES. J. J. Gibson in *Journal of Experimental Psychology*, Vol. 16, pp. 1–31, 1933.

THE FORMATION AND TRANSFORMATION OF THE PERCEPTUAL WORLD. Ivo Kohler in *Psychological Issues*, Vol. 3, No. 4, pp. 1–173, 1964.

GESTALT PSYCHOLOGY. Wolfgang Kohler. Liveright, 1947.

PLASTICITY IN SENSORY-MOTOR SYSTEMS. Richard Held in *Scientific American*, Vol. 213, No. 5, pp. 84–94, 1965.

VISION AND TOUCH. Irvin Rock, Charles Harris in *Scientific American*, Vol. 216, No. 5, pp. 96–104, 1967.

VISION WITHOUT INVERSION OF THE RETINAL IMAGE. George Stratton in *Psychological Review*, Vol. 4, pp. 341–360, 463–481, 1897.

Sonic Booms

REPORT ON HUMAN RESPONSE TO THE SONIC BOOM. National Academy of Sciences, National Research Council, June, 1968.

SENSORY PSYCHOLOGY. Conrad G. Mueller. Prentice-Hall, 1965.

SONIC BOOM EXPERIMENTS AT EDWARDS AIR FORCE BASE. Interim Report, National Sonic Boom Evaluation Office, Arlington, Va., July 28, 1967. Available from Clearinghouse for Federal Scientific & Technical Information, Springfield, Va.

SONIC BOOMS. Harvey H. Hubbard in *Physics Today*, February, 1968.

Body English

THE AMERICAN SCIENTIST: MAN OR SUPERMAN? Max Gunther in *Saturday Evening Post*, December 16, 1967.

CUTANEOUS CHANNELS OF COMMUNICATION. F. A. Geldard in *Sensory Communication* (W. A. Rosenblith, ed.). Wiley, 1961. Chap. 4.

CUTANEOUS CODING OF OPTICAL SIGNALS: THE OPTOHAPT. F. A. Geldard in *Perception and Psychophysics*, Vol. 1, pp. 377–381, 1966.

MULTIPLE CUTANEOUS STIMULATION: THE DISCRIMINATION OF VIBRATORY PATTERNS. F. A. Geldard and C. E. Sherrick in *Journal of the Acoustical Society*, Vol. 37, pp. 797–801, 1965.

PATTERN PERCEPTION BY THE SKIN. F. A. Geldard in *The Skin Senses* (D. Kenshalo, ed.). Charles C Thomas, 1968. Chap. 13.

SOME NEGLECTED POSSIBILITIES OF COMMUNICATION. F. A. Geldard in *Science*, Vol. 131, pp. 1583–1588, 1960.

Chemical Perception in Newborn Snakes

CHEMICAL CUE PREFERENCES OF INEXPERIENCED SNAKES: COMPARATIVE ASPECTS. G. M. Burghardt in *Science*, 1967.

ETHOLOGY: AN APPROACH TOWARD THE COMPLETE ANALYSIS OF BEHAVIOR. E. H. Hess in *New Directions in Psychology*, pp. 157–266. Holt, Rinehart, and Winston, 1962.

LIVING REPTILES OF THE WORLD. R. F. Inger, K. P. Schmidt. Doubleday, 1957.

THE NATURAL HISTORY OF NORTH AMERICAN AMPHIBIANS AND REPTILES. J. A. Oliver. Van Nostrand, 1955.

THE SCIENCE OF SMELL. R. H. Wright. Allen and Unwin, 1964.

STIMULUS CONTROL OF THE PREY ATTACK RESPONSE IN NAIVE GARTER SNAKES. G. M. Burghardt in *Psychonomic Science*, Vol. 4, pp. 37–38, 1966.

The Sonar Sight of Bats

ACOUSTIC SIGNALS FOR AUTO-INFORMATION OR ECHOLOCATION. F. Vincent in *Acoustic Behavior of Animals* (René Busnel, ed.). Elsevier, 1963.

ECHOLOCATION: AUDITORY CUES FOR RANGE PERCEPTION BY BATS. James Simmons in *Proceedings, 76th Annual Convention, American Psychological Association*.

LISTENING IN THE DARK. Donald Griffin. Yale University Press, 1958.

MECHANISMS OF ANIMAL BEHAVIOR. Peter Marler and W. J. Hamilton. Wiley, 1966.

The Terrible Tenrec

COLLEGE STUDENT STEREOTYPES OF THE PERSONALITY TRAITS OF RESEARCH SCIENTISTS. A. Bendig, P. Hountras in *Journal of Educational Psychology*, Vol. 49, pp. 309–314, 1958.

EVIDENCE FOR ECHOLOCATION IN THE TENRECIDAE OF MADAGASCAR. E. Gould in *Proceedings of the American Philosophical Society*, Vol. 109, pp. 352–360, 1965.

PUBLIC ATTITUDES TOWARD SCIENCE. L. Schlesinger in *Journal of Social Psychology*, Vol. 40, pp. 411–418, 1954.

STRIDULATION AND HEARING IN THE TENREC, HEMICENTETES SEMISPINOSUS. E. Wever, P. Herman in *Journal of Auditory Research* (in press).

V. HUMAN FUNCTION

Amnesia: A World Without Continuity

AMNESIA. O. L. Zangwill, C. W. M. Whitty, eds. Butterworth, 1967.

DERANGED MEMORY: A PSYCHONOMIC STUDY OF THE AMNESIC SYNDROME. G. A. Talland. Academic Press, 1965.

EMOTIONS AND MEMORY. D. Rapaport. Williams & Wilkins, 1942.

PLANS AND THE STRUCTURE OF BEHAVIOR. G. A. Miller, E. Galanter, K. H. Pribram. Holt, Rinehart and Winston, 1960.

REMEMBERING. F. C. Bartlett. Cambridge University Press, 1932.

Communication Without Words

THE COMMUNICATION OF EMOTIONAL MEANING. Joel Davitz, ed. McGraw-Hill, 1964.

EXPRESSION OF THE EMOTIONS IN MAN. Peter Knapp, ed. International University Press, 1963.

LANGUAGE WITHIN LANGUAGE: IMMEDIACY, A CHANNEL IN VERBAL COMMUNICATION. M. Wiener, Albert Mehrabian. Appleton-Century-Crofts, 1968.

THE SILENT LANGUAGE. Edward Hall. Doubleday, 1959 (in paperback, Fawcett, 1961).

Language and the Mind

ASPECTS OF THE THEORY OF SYNTAX. N. Chomsky. M.I.T. Press, 1965.

CARTESIAN LINGUISTICS. N. Chomsky. Harper & Row, 1966.

GRAMMATICAL STRUCTURE AND THE IMMEDIATE RECALL OF ENGLISH SENTENCES. H. Savin, E. Perchonock in *Journal of Verbal Learning and Verbal Behavior*, Vol. 4, pp. 348–353, 1965.

THE PHILOSOPHY OF LANGUAGE. J. Katz. Harper & Row, 1966.

THE PSYCHOLOGICAL REALITY OF LINGUISTIC SEGMENTS. J. Fodor, T. Bever in *Journal of Verbal Learning and Verbal Behavior*, Vol. 4, pp. 414–420, 1965.

SOUND PATTERN OF ENGLISH. N. Chomsky, M. Halle. Harper & Row, 1968.

STRUCTURE OF LANGUAGE: READINGS IN THE PHILOSOPHY OF LANGUAGE. J. Fodor, J. Katz, eds. Prentice-Hall, 1964.

The Importance
of Daydreaming

DAYDREAMING: AN INTRODUCTION TO THE EXPERIMENTAL STUDY OF INNER EXPERIENCE. J. Singer. Random House, 1966.

DAYDREAMING PATTERNS OF AMERICAN SUBCULTURAL GROUPS. J. Singer, V. McCraven in *International Journal of Social Psychiatry*, Vol. 8, pp. 272–282, 1962.

EYE MOVEMENTS ACCOMPANYING DAYDREAMING, VISUAL IMAGERY AND THOUGHT SUPPRESSION. J. Antrobus, J. S. Antrobus, J. Singer in *Journal of Abnormal and Social Psychology*, Vol. 69, pp. 244–252, 1964.

A FACTOR-ANALYTIC STUDY OF DAYDREAMING AND RELATED COGNITIVE AND PERSONALITY VARIABLES. J. Singer in *Perceptual and Motor Skills*, Monograph Supplement, Vol. 3, No. 17, 1963.

STUDIES IN THE STREAM OF CONSCIOUSNESS: EXPERIMENTAL ENHANCEMENT AND SUPPRESSION OF SPONTANEOUS COGNITIVE PROCESSES. J. S. Antrobus, J. Singer, S. Greenberg in *Perceptual and Motor Skills*, Vol. 23, pp. 399–417, 1966.

Conscious Control
of Brain Waves

EEG CORRELATES OF SLEEP: EVIDENCES FOR SEPARATE FOREBRAIN SUBSTRATES. M. Sterman, W. Wrywicka in *Brain Research*, Vol. 6, Pt. 1, pp. 143–163, 1967.

AN ELECTROENCEPHALOGRAPHIC STUDY ON THE ZEN MEDITATION (ZAZEN). A. Kasamatsu, T. Hirai in *Fol. Psychiat. Neurol. Japon.*, Vol. 20, pp. 315–336, 1966.

ELECTROPHYSIOLOGICAL CORRELATES OF SOME YOGI EXERCISES. B. K. Bagchi, M. A. Wenger in *EEG Clin. Neurophysiol.*, Supplement No. 7, pp. 132–149, 1957.

ELECTROPHYSIOLOGICAL STUDIES OF DREAMING AS THE PROTOTYPE OF A NEW STRATEGY IN THE STUDY OF CONSCIOUSNESS. J. Stoyva, J. Kamiya in *Psychological Review*.

TRAINED SELF-CONTROL OF THE EEG ALPHA RHYTHM. J. Kamiya in *Altered States of Consciousness* (C. Tart, ed.). Wiley (in press).

The
Psychopharmacological
Revolution

DRUGS AND ANIMAL BEHAVIOUR. Hannah Steinberg in *British Medical Bulletin*, Vol. 20, pp. 75–80, 1964.

DRUGS USED IN THE TREATMENT OF PSYCHIATRIC DISORDERS. M. E. Jarvik in *The Pharmacological Basis of Therapeutics* (L. S. Goodman, A. Gilman, eds.), 3rd ed., pp. 159–214, Macmillan, 1965.

THE HALLUCINOGENIC DRUGS. F. Barron, M. E. Jarvik, S. Bunnell, Jr. in *Scientific American*, Vol. 210, pp. 3–11; April, 1964.

THE INFLUENCE OF DRUGS UPON MEMORY. M. E. Jarvik in *Animal Behaviour and Drug Action* (Hannah Steinberg, A. V. S. de Reuck, Julie Knight, eds.). Churchill, 1964.

THE RELATION OF PSYCHIATRY TO PHARMACOLOGY. A. Wikler. Williams & Wilkins, 1957.

When Fear Is Healthy

EFFECTIVENESS OF EMOTIONAL ROLE-PLAYING IN MODIFYING SMOKING HABITS AND ATTITUDES. I. L. Janis, L. Mann in *Journal of Experimental Research in Personality*, Vol. 1, pp. 84–90, 1965.

THE EFFECTS OF EMOTIONAL ROLE-PLAYING ON DESIRE TO MODIFY SMOKING HABITS. L. Mann in *Journal of Experimental Social Psychology*, Vol. 3, pp. 334–348, 1967.

EFFECTS OF FEAR AROUSAL ON ATTITUDE CHANGE: RECENT DEVELOPMENTS IN THEORY AND EXPERIMENTAL RESEARCH. I. L. Janis in *Advances in Experimental Social Psychology* (L. Berkowitz, ed.), Vol. 3, pp. 166–224, 1967.

EFFECTS OF FEAR-AROUSING COMMUNICATIONS. I. L. Janis, S. Feshbach in *Journal of Abnormal and Social Psychology*, Vol. 48, pp. 78–92, 1953.

FEAR—FOR YOUR HEALTH. H. Leventhal in *Psychology Today*, September, 1967.

REDUCTION OF POSTOPERATIVE PAIN BY ENCOURAGEMENT AND INSTRUCTION OF PATIENTS. L. Egbert, G. Battit, C. Welch, M. Bartlett in *New England Journal of Medicine*, Vol. 270, pp. 825–827, 1964.

VI. PERSONALITY

Psychological Testing—
A Smoke Screen
Against Logic

CAN PERSONALITY BE MEASURED? H. J. Eysenck in *Sense and Nonsense in Psychology*. Penguin Books, 1964.

A CONTINGENT-ITEM METHOD FOR CONSTRUCTING A SHORT PERSONALITY QUESTIONNAIRE. F. B. McMahon in *Journal of Applied Psychology*, pp. 197–200, 1964.

THE FORTY-EIGHT ITEM TEST. Western Psychological Services, 1963.

GENERAL PROBLEMS IN PERSONALITY MEASUREMENT. L. J. Cronbach in *Essentials of Psychological Testing*. Harper, 1960.

AN INTRODUCTION TO PROJECTIVE TECHNIQUES. G. L. and H. H. Anderson, eds. Prentice-Hall, 1951.

PSYCHOLOGY: THE SCIENCE OF MENTAL LIFE. G. A. Miller. Harper & Row, 1962, pp. 315–327.

SELF-REPORT INVENTORIES. Anne Anastasi in *Psychological Testing*. Macmillan, 1961.

Is Phrenology
Foolish?

A HISTORY OF EXPERIMENTAL PSYCHOLOGY, 2nd ed. E. G. Boring. Appleton-Century-Crofts, 1950, pp. 50–60.

HUMAN NATURE IN AMERICAN THOUGHT; THE AGE OF REASON AND MORALITY, 1750–1860. M. Curti in *Political Science Quarterly*, Vol. 48, pp. 354–375, 1953.

THE INFLUENCE OF PHRENOLOGY ON AMERICAN PSYCHOLOGY. D. Bakan in *Journal of the History of the Behavioral Sciences*, Vol. 2, pp. 200–220, 1966.

PHRENOLOGY. J. G. Spurzheim. Lippincott, 1908.

PHRENOLOGY; FAD AND SCIENCE: A 19TH CENTURY AMERICAN CRUSADE. J. Davis, Yale University Press, 1955.

Are I.Q. Tests Intelligent?

THE ABILITIES OF MAN. C. Spearman. Macmillan, 1932.

CULTURE FAIR TESTING. A. Anastasi in *Educational Horizons*, Vol. 43, pp. 26–30, 1964.

A CULTURE FREE INTELLIGENCE TEST, I. R. Cattell in *Journal of Educational Psychology*, Vol. 31, pp. 161–179, 1940.

A CULTURE FREE INTELLIGENCE TEST, II. EVALUATION OF CULTURAL INFLUENCE ON TEST PERFORMANCE. R. Cattell, S. Feingold, S. Sarason in *Journal of Educational Psychology*, Vol. 32, pp. 81–100, 1941.

INTELLIGENCE AND CULTURAL DIFFERENCES. K. Eells, A. Davis, R. J. Havighurst, *et al.* University of Chicago Press, 1951.

INTELLIGENCE AND EXPERIENCE. J. McV. Hunt. Ronald Press, 1961.

THE IPAT CULTURE FAIR INTELLIGENCE TEST SCALES 1, 2, & 3. IPAT, Rev. 1960.

THE REDUCTION OF SOCIO-ECONOMIC BIAS IN INTELLIGENCE TESTING. R. T. McArthur, W. B. Elley, in *British Journal of Educational Psychology*, Vol. 33, pp. 107–119, 1963.

SOME THEORETICAL ISSUES IN ADULT INTELLIGENCE TESTING. R. Cattell in *Psychological Bulletin*, Vol. 38, p. 592, 1941.

THEORY OF FLUID AND CRYSTALLIZED INTELLIGENCE: A CRITICAL EXPERIMENT. R. Cattell in *Journal of Educational Psychology*, Vol. 54, pp. 1–22, 1963.

Is Graphology Valid?

GRAPHOLOGICAL PSYCHOGRAM—PSYCHOLOGICAL MEANING OF ITS SECTORS AND SYMBOLIC INTERPRETATION OF ITS INDICATORS. D. S. Anthony. 1964.

GRAPHOLOGY. Rose Wolfson in *An Introduction to Projective Techniques*. Prentice-Hall, 1951.

GRAPHOLOGY—SCIENCE WITH A FUTURE. D. S. Anthony in *Science Digest*, March, 1966.

HANDWRITING—A KEY TO PERSONALITY. Klara G. Roman. Pantheon Books, 1952.

AN INTRODUCTION TO PROJECTIVE TECHNIQUES. G. L. and H. H. Anderson, eds. Prentice-Hall, 1951.

STUDIES IN EXPRESSIVE MOVEMENT. G. W. Allport, P. E. Vernon. Macmillan, 1933.

A STUDY IN HANDWRITING ANALYSIS. Rose Wolfson. Edwards, 1949.

Impulse, Aggression and the Gun

AGGRESSION AND DEFENSE. C. D. Clemente, D. B. Lindsley, eds. University of California Press, 1967.

AGGRESSION: A SOCIAL-PSYCHOLOGICAL ANALYSIS. Leonard Berkowitz. McGraw-Hill, 1962.

PSYCHOLOGY OF AGGRESSION. A. H. Buss. Wiley, 1961.

ROOTS OF AGGRESSION: A RE-EXAMINATION OF THE FRUSTRATION-AGGRESSION HYPOTHESIS. Leonard Berkowitz, ed. Atherton, 1968.

URBAN VIOLENCE AND DISORDER. L. H. Masotti, ed. Special issue, *American Behavioral Scientist*, Vol. 2, No. 4, 1968. (To be published in book form by Sage Publications.)

The Grim Generation

THE AMERICAN COLLEGE. Nevitt Sanford. Wiley, 1962.

NO TIME FOR YOUTH: GROWTH AND CONSTRAINT IN COLLEGE STUDENTS. Joseph Katz, *et al.* Jossey-Bass, 1968.

THE STUDENT AND HIS STUDIES. Esther Raushenbush. Wesleyan University Press, 1964.

THE STUDENT IN HIGHER EDUCATION. Joseph Kaufmann, *et al.* Hazen Foundation, 1968.

THE UNCOMMITTED. Kenneth Keniston. Harcourt, Brace & World, 1965.

YOUNG RADICALS: NOTES ON COMMITTED YOUTH. Kenneth Keniston. Harcourt, Brace & World, 1968.

The Quiet Revolution

THE BEYOND WITHIN THE LSD STORY. S. Cohen. Atheneum, 1964.

DRUGS AND PHANTASY: THE EFFECTS OF LSD, PSILOCYBIN, AND SERNYL ON COLLEGE STUDENTS. J. C. Pollard, L. Uhr, E. Stern. Little, Brown, 1966.

THE HALLUCINOGENIC DRUGS. F. Barron, M. E. Jarvik, S. Bunnell, Jr. in *Scientific American*, Vol. 210, No. 4, 1964.

THE HALLUCINOGENIC DRUGS: A PERSPECTIVE WITH SPECIAL REFERENCE TO PEYOTE AND CANNABIS. W. McGlothlin. RAND Corporation, 1964.

UTOPIATES. R. Blum. Atherton Press, 1964.

VII. DISORDER AND THERAPY

Chromosomes and Crime

HUMAN HEREDITY. Ashley Montagu. World Publishing, 1964.

THE GENETIC CODE. Isaac Asimov. Grossman, 1963 (in paperback, Signet).

GENETICS. *Biology and Behavior Series*. David C. Glass, ed. Rockefeller University Press and Sage Foundation, 1968.

HUMAN POPULATION CYTOGENETICS. W. M. Court Brown. Wiley, 1967.

THE YY SYNDROME. *Lancet*, March 12, 1966.

The Shattered Language of Schizophrenia

THE NEUROLOGY OF PSYCHOTIC SPEECH. Macdonald Critchley in *British Journal of Psychiatry*, Vol. 110, pp. 353–364, 1964.

PATHOLOGICAL AND NORMAL LANGUAGE. Julius Laffal. Atherton Press, 1965.

SCHIZOPHRENIA: LANGUAGE AND THOUGHT. Brendan Maher in *Principles of Psychopathology*. McGraw-Hill, 1966. Chap. 15.

STUDIES IN PSYCHOTIC LANGUAGE. Brendan Maher, K. O. McKean and B.

McLaughlin in *The General Inquirer: A Computer Approach to Content Analysis* (P. J. Stone, D. C. Dunphy, M. S. Smith, D. M. Ogilvie, eds.). M.I.T. Press, 1966.

A THEORY OF VERBAL BEHAVIOR IN SCHIZOPHRENIA. L. J. Chapman, L. Chapman and G. A. Miller in *Progress in Experimental Personality Research*. Academic Press, 1964. Vol. 1.

The Neurotic Cat

CURRENT PSYCHIATRIC THERAPIES. J. H. Masserman. Grune & Stratton, annually from 1960. Vols. 1–7.

MODERN THERAPY OF PERSONALITY DISORDERS. J. H. Masserman. William C. Brown Co., 1966.

PRACTICE OF DYNAMIC PSYCHIATRY. J. B. Masserman. W. B. Saunders Co., 1955.

SCIENCE AND PSYCHOANALYSIS. Grune & Stratton, annually from 1956. Vols. 1–11.

The Dreams of Freud and Jung

AGGRESSION IN DREAMS. C. S. Hall, Bill Domhoff in *International Journal of Social Psychiatry*, Vol. 9, pp. 259–267, 1963.

THE CONTENT ANALYSIS OF DREAMS. C. S. Hall, R. L. Van de Castle. Appleton-Century-Crofts, 1966.

FRIENDLINESS IN DREAMS. C. S. Hall, Bill Domhoff in *Journal of Social Psychology*, Vol. 62, pp. 309–314, 1964.

THE INTERPRETATION OF DREAMS. Sigmund Freud. Hogarth Press, 1953. Vols. IV and V, Standard Edition.

THE LIFE AND WORK OF SIGMUND FREUD. Ernest Jones. Basic Books, 1955.

MEMORIES, DREAMS, REFLECTIONS. C. G. Jung. Pantheon, 1963.

ON DREAMS. Sigmund Freud. Hogarth Press, 1953. Vol. V, Standard Edition.

Inside Psychotherapy

COMMUNICATION RAPPORT AND PATIENT PROGRESS. D. E. Orlinsky, K. I. Howard in *Psychotherapy: Theory, Research and Practice*, 1968.

DIMENSIONS OF CONJOINT EXPERIENTIAL PROCESS IN PSYCHOTHERAPY RELATIONSHIPS. D. E. Orlinsky, K. I. Howard in *Proceedings, 75th Annual Meeting*, American Psychological Association, pp. 251–252, 1967.

THE GOOD THERAPY HOUR: EXPERIENTIAL CORRELATES OF PATIENTS' AND THERAPISTS' EVALUATIONS OF THERAPY SESSIONS. D. E. Orlinsky, K. I. Howard in *Archives of General Psychiatry*, Vol. 16, pp. 621–632, 1967.

THE PATIENT'S EXPERIENCE OF PSYCHOTHERAPY: SOME DIMENSIONS AND DETERMINANTS. K. I. Howard, D. E. Orlinsky, J. A. Hill in *Multivariate Behavioral Research*, 1968.

THE THERAPIST'S FEELINGS IN THE THERAPEUTIC PROCESS. K. I. Howard, D. E. Orlinsky, J. A. Hill in *Journal of Clinical Psychology*, 1968.

Morality in Psychotherapy

ANALYSIS OF A PHOBIA IN A FIVE-YEAR-OLD BOY. S. Freud in *The Complete Psychological Works of Sigmund Freud*. Hogarth Press, 1955. Vol. XIV.

AN APPETITIONAL THEORY OF SEXUAL MOTIVATION. K. R. Hardy in *Psychological Review*, pp. 1–18 and 71, 1964.

BEHAVIOR THERAPY TECHNIQUES. A. A. Lazarus, J. Wolpe. Pergamon Press, 1966.

THE CONCEPT OF MOTIVATION. R. S. Peters. Routledge & Kegan Paul, 1958.

A GENERAL INTRODUCTION TO PSYCHOANALYSIS. S. Freud. Liveright, 1920.

THE NEW GROUP THERAPY. O. H. Mowrer. Van Nostrand, 1964.

THE ORDEAL OF CHANGE. E. Hoffer. Harper & Row, 1964.

THE PSYCHOANALYTIC TECHNIQUE. A. Bernstein in *Handbook of Clinical Psychology*. McGraw-Hill, 1965.

THE PSYCHOPATHOLOGY OF EVERYDAY LIFE. S. Freud. Ernest Benn, 1904.

A STORY OF THREE DAYS. M. Wertheimer in *Documents of Gestalt Psychology*. University of California Press, 1961.

VALUE: BEHAVIORAL DECISION THEORY. G. M. Becker, C. G. McClintock in *Annual Review of Psychology*. Annual Reviews, Inc., 1967.

The Long Weekend

FACE TO FACE WITH THE DRUG ADDICT: AN ACCOUNT OF AN INTENSIVE GROUP EXPERIENCE. D. Kruschke and F. H. Stoller in *Federal Probation*, Vol. 31, No. 2, 1967, pp. 47–52.

FOCUSED FEEDBACK: EXTENDING GROUP FUNCTIONS WITH VIDEO TAPE and MARATHON GROUP THERAPY. Frederick H. Stoller in *Innovations in Group Therapy* (G. M. Gazda, ed.). Charles C Thomas, 1967.

GROUP PSYCHOTHERAPY ON TELEVISION: AN INNOVATION WITH HOSPITALIZED PATIENTS. F. H. Stoller in *American Psychologist*, Vol. 22, pp. 158–162, 1967.

THE LEMON EATERS. Jerry Sohl. Simon and Schuster, 1967.

THE MARATHON GROUP: INTENSIVE PRACTICE OF INTIMATE INTERACTION. G. R. Bach in *Psychological Reports*, Vol. 18, pp. 995–1002, 1966.

THE USE OF FOCUSED FEEDBACK VIA VIDEO TAPE IN SMALL GROUPS. F. H. Stoller in *Explorations in Human Relations Training and Research*, No. 1, National Training Laboratories, National Educational Association, 1966.

Esalen: Where It's At

CONJOINT FAMILY THERAPY. V. Satir. Science and Behavior Books, 1964.

EDUCATION AND ECSTASY. G. Leonard. Delacorte, in press.

GESTALT THERAPY. F. Perls, R. Hefferline, P. Goodman. Delta paperback. 1951.

JOY. W. Schutz. Grove Press, 1967.

TOWARD A PSYCHOLOGY OF BEING. A. Maslow. Van Nostrand, 1962.

New Ways in Psychotherapy

CAUSES AND CURES OF NEUROSIS. H. J. Eysenck, S. Rachman. Robert Knapp, 1965.

CASE STUDIES IN BEHAVIOR MODIFICATION. L. P. Ullman, L. Krasner. Holt, Rinehart and Winston, 1965.

CONDITIONING TECHNIQUES IN CLINICAL PRACTICE AND RESEARCH. C. Frank. Springer, 1964.

EXPERIMENTS IN BEHAVIOR THERAPY. H. J. Eysenck. Pergamon Press, 1963.

PSYCHOTHERAPY BY RECIPROCAL INHIBITION. J. Wolpe. Stanford University Press, 1958.

VIII. SOCIAL PSYCHOLOGY

When Will People Help in a Crisis?

BYSTANDER INTERVENTION IN EMERGENCIES: DIFFUSION OF RESPONSIBILITY. J. M. Darley and Bibb Latané in *Journal of Personality and Social Psychology*, Vol. 8, pp. 377–383, 1968.

GROUP INHIBITION OF BYSTANDER INTERVENTION IN EMERGENCIES. Bibb Latané and J. M. Darley in *Journal of Personality and Social Psychology* (in press).

A LADY IN DISTRESS: THE EFFECTS OF FRIENDS AND STRANGERS ON BYSTANDER INTERVENTION. Bibb Latané and Judy Rodin in *Journal of Experimental Social Psychology* (in press).

MURDER THEY HEARD. Stanley Migram and Paul Hollander in *The Nation*, Vol. 198, pp. 602–604, 1964.

RISK-TAKING AS A FUNCTION OF THE SITUATION, THE PERSON, AND THE GROUP. N. Kogan and M. Wallach in *New Directions in Psychology III*. Holt, Rinehart and Winston, 1967.

THIRTY-EIGHT WITNESSES. A. M. Rosenthal. McGraw-Hill, 1964.

THE THREAT OF IMPENDING DISASTER. George H. Grosser, Henry Wechsler and Milton Greenblatt, eds. M.I.T. Press, 1964.

The Small-World Problem

MATHEMATICAL MODELS IN THE SOCIAL SCIENCES. John G. Kemeny, J. Laurie Snell. Blaisdell, 1962.

MATHEMATICAL MODELS OF SOCIAL INTERACTION. Anatol Rapoport in *Handbook of Mathematical Psychology*, Vol. 2, Chap. 14 (D. Luce, Robert Bush, Eugene Galanter, eds.). Wiley, 1963.

STRUCTURAL MODELS: AN INTRODUCTION TO THE THEORY OF DIRECTED GRAPHS. Frank Harary, Robert Z. Norman, Dorwin Cartwright. Wiley, 1965.

Fear—for Your Health

EFFECTS OF FEAR AND SPECIFICITY OF RECOMMENDATIONS. H. Leventhal, R. P. Singer, Susan Jones in *Journal of Personality and Social Psychology*, Vol. 2, pp. 20–29, 1965.

AN EXPERIMENTAL STUDY OF PSYCHOLOGICAL RESISTANCES TO FEAR-AROUSING COMMUNICATIONS. I. L. Janis, R. Terwilliger in *Journal of Abnormal and Social Psychology*, Vol. 65, pp. 403–410, 1962.

FEAR COMMUNICATIONS IN THE ACCEPTANCE OF PREVENTIVE HEALTH PRACTICES. H. Leventhal in *Bulletin of the New York Academy of Medicine*, Vol. 41, pp. 1144–1168, 1965.

SOURCES OF RESISTANCE TO FEAR-AROUSING COMMUNICATIONS. H. Leventhal, Jean C. Watts in *Journal of Personality*, Vol. 34, pp. 155–175, 1966.

The Psychology of Police Confessions and Toward a More Perfect Justice

THE COMPULSION TO CONFESS. Theodor Reik. Farrar, Straus & Giroux, 1959.

COMMUNIST INTERROGATION AND INDOCTRINATION OF "ENEMIES OF THE STATE." L. E. Hinkle, H. C. Wolff in *Archives of Neurology and Psychiatry*, Vol. 76, pp. 115–174, August, 1956.

DISTINGUISHING CHARACTERISTICS OF COLLABORATORS AND RESISTERS AMONG AMERICAN PRISONERS OF WAR. E. H. Schein, W. E. Hill, H. L. Williams, A. Lubin in *Journal of Abnormal Social Psychology*, Vol. 55, pp. 197–201, 1957.

PSYCHOLINGUISTICS AND THE CONFESSION DILEMMA. R. Arens, A. Meadow in *Columbia Law Review*, Vol. 56, pp. 19–46, 1956.

THE PSYCHOLOGY OF CONFESSION. M. W. Horowitz in *Journal of Clinical and Experimental Psychopathology*, Vol. 18, pp. 381–382, 1957.

REACTION PATTERNS TO SEVERE, CHRONIC STRESS IN AMERICAN ARMY PRISONERS OF WAR OF THE CHINESE. E. H. Schein in *Journal of Social Issues*, Vol. 13, pp 21–30, 1957.

SOURCES OF DISTORTION AND DECEPTION IN PRISON INTERVIEWING. N. Johnson in *Federal Probation*, Vol. 20, pp. 43–48, 1956.

The Face of the Enemy

AN ALTERNATIVE TO WAR OR SURRENDER. C. E. Osgood. University of Illinois Press, 1962.

THE HUMAN DIMENSION IN INTERNATIONAL RELATIONS. Otto Klineberg. Holt, Rinehart and Winston, 1964.

IN COMMON PREDICAMENT: SOCIAL PSYCHOLOGY OF INTERGROUP CONFLICT AND COOPERATION. Muzafer Sherif and Carolyn Sherif. Houghton Mifflin, 1966.

INTERNATIONAL BEHAVIOR. Herbert Kelman, ed. Holt, Rinehart and Winston, 1965.

THE NATURE OF HUMAN CONFLICT. Elton McNeil, ed. Prentice-Hall, 1965.

PSYCHIATRIC ASPECTS OF THE PREVENTION OF NUCLEAR WAR. Committee on Social Issues, Group for the Advancement of Psychiatry, 1964.

SANITY AND SURVIVAL: PSYCHOLOGICAL ASPECTS OF WAR AND PEACE. Jerome Frank. Random House, 1967.

Self-Fulfilling Prophecy

CLEVER HANS, THE HORSE OF MR. VON OSTEN. Oskar Pfungst. Translated by C. L. Rahn. Holt, Rinehart and Winston, 1965.

EFFECT OF EXPERIMENTER'S EXPECTANCIES (THE "ROSENTHAL EFFECT") ON CHILDREN'S ABILITY TO LEARN TO SWIM. J. Randolph Burnham, Don M. Hartsough. Paper presented at the meeting of the Midwestern Psychological Association, Chicago, May, 1968.

EXPERIMENTER EFFECTS IN BEHAVIORAL RESEARCH. Robert Rosenthal. Appleton-Century-Crofts, 1966.

INFLUENCE OF BIASED PSYCHOLOGICAL REPORTS ON TEACHER BEHAVIOR AND PUPIL PERFORMANCE. W. Victor Beez in *Proceedings of the 76th Annual Convention of the American Psychological Association,* 1968.

PYGMALION IN THE CLASSROOM: TEACHER EXPECTATION AND PUPILS' INTELLECTUAL DEVELOPMENT. Robert Rosenthal, Lenore Jacobson. Holt, Rinehart and Winston, 1968.

Encounter in Color

CHILDREN OF CRISIS. R. Coles. Little, Brown, 1967.

EXPERIMENTAL EFFECTS IN BEHAVIORAL RESEARCH. R. Rosenthal. Appleton-Century-Crofts, 1966.

IDENTITY AND THE LIFE CYCLE. E. H. Erikson in *Psychological Issues,* Vol. 1, No. 1, 1959.

INTERPERSONAL STYLES AND GROUP DEVELOPMENT. R. Mann. Wiley, 1967.

MICROCOSM: STRUCTURAL, PSYCHOLOGICAL, AND RELIGIOUS EVALUATION IN GROUPS. P. E. Slater. Wiley, 1966.

Conflict, Crisis and Collision: A Study of International Stability

AGGRESSION: A SOCIAL PSYCHOLOGICAL ANALYSIS. Leonard Berkowitz. McGraw-Hill, 1962.

AGGRESSIVE BEHAVIORS WITHIN POLITIES, 1948–1962: A CROSS-NATIONAL STUDY. Ivo Feierabend, Rosalind Feierabend in *Journal of Conflict Resolution,* Vol. 10, No. 3, pp. 249–271, 1966.

ANTI-EUROPEAN VIOLENCE IN AFRICA: A COMPARATIVE ANALYSIS. Robert Le-Vine in *Journal of Conflict Resolution,* Vol. 3, No. 4, pp. 420–429, 1959.

DIMENSIONS OF CONFLICT BEHAVIOR WITHIN AND BETWEEN NATIONS. Rudolph Rummel in *General Systems Yearbook,* Vol. 8, pp. 1–50, 1963.

DIMENSIONS OF CONFLICT BEHAVIOR WITHIN AND BETWEEN NATIONS, 1958–60. Raymond Tanter in *Journal of Conflict Resolution,* Vol. 10, No. 1, pp. 41–65, 1966.

EXPLORING POLITICAL STABILITY: A NOTE ON THE COMPARATIVE METHOD. Ivo Feierabend in *Western Political Quarterly* (Supplement), Vol. 15, No. 3, pp. 18–19, 1962.

FRUSTRATION AND AGGRESSION. John Dollard, Leonard Doob, Neal Miller, O. Hobart Mowrer, Robert Sears. Yale University Press, 1939.

index

picture credits

I. Introduction. FROM FREUD TO FROMM: 4–7–photography, John Oldenkamp. PERSONALITY: PUBLIC OR PRIVATE: 10, 11–drawing, John Isely. PSYCHOLOGY ACROSS THE CHESSBOARD: 15, 20–photography, John Oldenkamp; 20–diagrams, THOUGHT AND CHOICE IN CHESS by Adriaan D. de Groot, © 1965 by Mouton & Co., Basic Books, Inc., New York, 1966. THE COMPUTER CONQUEST OF PSYCHOLOGY: 24, 27–photography, Bert F. Green, Jr.; 28, 29–photography, Benjamin W. White. QUESTIONS FOR THE GLOBAL CONSCIENCE: 30, 35–photography, John Oldenkamp; illustration, Karl Nicholason. THE PSYCHOLOGY OF ROBOTS: 36–38–illustrations, Robert Hostick; 41–illustrations, Darrell Millsap, Millsap & Kinyon; photography (top to bottom) courtesy of Henry Block and Stanford University/Bell Telephone Laboratories/Stanford University. PARAPSYCHOLOGY: NEW NEIGHBOR OR UNWELCOME GUEST: 42–photography, John Oldenkamp; coordination, Robert Hostick; 44–drawing courtesy of Gardner Murphy; 45–painting by Marc Chagall, courtesy of Montague Ullman.

II. Learning and Motivation. MOTIVATION, MORALE & MONEY: 51, 52–photography, John Oldenkamp. OF MICE AND MISERS: 56–photography, John Oldenkamp; illustration, Gerri Blake; 58–drawing, Karl Nicholason. BEVERLY: THE COMPUTER IS A TUTOR: 61, 62–photography, John Oldenkamp; 63–photography courtesy Richard C. Atkinson. THE INSPECTOR GENERAL IS A BIRD: 68–71, 73–photography, John Oldenkamp; 68–drawing, Gerri Blake; construction, Bob Fountain. TEACHING AND MACHINES: 74, 75–illustrations, Don Wright. RABBIT FAMILIES AND HOW THEY GROW: 78, 79–photography, John Oldenkamp; 80, 83–drawings, Gerri Blake. COPULATION IN RATS: 84–86–photography, John Oldenkamp. THE HUNGRY FLY: 93–photography, John Oldenkamp; 95, 97–100–courtesy of Vincent Dethier. MEMORY: A MOLECULAR MAZE: 102–construction, Tom Gould; photography, John Oldenkamp. NEURAL BASIS OF MEMORY: 108, 109–photography, John Oldenkamp; 111 (top)–depiction of nerve cell redrawn from Anthony Ravielli illustration in THE HUMAN BRAIN: ITS CAPACITIES AND FUNCTIONS by Isaac Asimov, Houghton Mifflin Co., 1964. PAIN AND AGGRESSION: 114–photography, John Oldenkamp; 116–121–courtesy of Nathan Azrin.

III. Psychological Development. UP FROM HELPLESSNESS: 126–art, Nat Antler, Maurice Woods; photography, John Oldenkamp; 128, 129–photography, Jerome Bruner. CHRISTOPHER: THE MANY FACES OF RESPONSE: 132, 133–photography, John Oldenkamp; 134–136–courtesy of Jerome Kagan. RUSSIAN NURSERY SCHOOLS: 139–photography, John Oldenkamp; 141–145–photography, Michael and Sheila Cole. THE YOUNG MONKEYS: 146, 147–photography, John Oldenkamp; 149–151, 153 courtesy of Harry and Margaret Harlow. THE MYSTERY OF THE PRELOGICAL CHILD: 154, 155, 162–164–photography, John Oldenkamp. MORAL BEHAVIOR: A FUNCTIONAL ANALYSIS: 165–photography, Stephen Wells. UNDERSTANDING CHILDREN'S ART: 170–179–courtesy Rhoda Kellogg Child Art Collection. THE CHILD AS A MORAL PHILOSOPHER: 180, 181, 184, 186–photography, John Oldenkamp; cookies, Joyce Fitzgerald. THE AUTISTIC CHILD: 188, 190, 191–photography, John Oldenkamp. THE MENTALLY RETARDED CHILD: 194–photography, John Oldenkamp. CAN I COME TO SUMMERHILL? I HATE MY SCHOOL: 197–202–photography, John Oldenkamp. POLITICAL ATTITUDES IN CHILDREN: 204, 205–photography, John Oldenkamp.

IV. The Sensory World. EXPERIMENT IN PERCEPTION: 213–221–experiments and illustrations courtesy of Bela Julesz. WHEN THE WORLD IS TILT: DISTORTION–HOW WE ADAPT: 223, 226–photography, John Oldenkamp; 224, 225, 227–229–drawings, Karl Nicholason; 225 (bottom)–photography, Paul Weller (prior publication in SCIENTIFIC AMERICAN). SONIC BOOMS: 230, 231–design, Tom Gould; illustration, Arline Thompson; 232–236–illustrations, Karl Nicholason. BODY ENGLISH: 237–241–photography, John Oldenkamp. CHEMICAL PERCEPTION IN NEWBORN SNAKES: 242, 246, 247–courtesy of Gordon M. Burghardt. THE SONAR SIGHT OF BATS: 252, 253, 256–illustrations, Robert Watts; 254–photography, James A. Simmons (left), Joseph Tobias (right); 255–photography, James A. Simmons (top), John V. Conover (bottom). THE TERRIBLE TENREC: 259, 261–264–drawings, Darrell Millsap, Millsap & Kinyon.

V. Human Function. AMNESIA: A WORLD WITHOUT CONTINUITY: 268–Russell Forester. COMMUNICATION WITHOUT WORDS: 276–design, Tom Gould; photography, Stephen Wells. LANGUAGE AND THE MIND: 281–photography, John Oldenkamp. THE IMPORTANCE OF DAYDREAMING: 288, 291, 292–295, 297–coordination, Robert Hostick; photography, John Oldenkamp. CONSCIOUS CONTROL OF BRAIN WAVES: 298–301–photography, John Waggaman. THE PSYCHOPHARMACOLOGICAL REVOLUTION: 303–305–illustrations, Mercury Archives; 304 (bottom)–Bettmann Archive; 306, 307–photography, John Oldenkamp; 308, 309–tables, Al Limpo. WHEN FEAR IS HEALTHY: 312–photography, John Oldenkamp.

VI. Personality. PSYCHOLOGICAL TESTING–A SMOKE SCREEN AGAINST LOGIC: 323–327–inkblots, Pam Morehouse; illustration, Karl Nicholason. IS PHRENOLOGY FOOLISH?: 328, 329, 335–photography, John Oldenkamp; 330–334–drawings, engravings, Mercury Archives; 330 (bottom)–Wolf-Heidegger, G.: Atlas of Systematic Human Anatomy, Vol. 3, Systema nervosum-Systema vasorum (Karger, Basel/New York 1962); 330, 331–drawings, courtesy of David Bakan. ARE I.Q. TESTS INTELLIGENT?: 337–photography, John Oldenkamp. IS GRAPHOLOGY VALID?: 348–photography, John Oldenkamp. IMPULSE, AGGRESSION AND THE GUN: 350, 352, 355–design, Don Wright; illustration, Pam Morehouse. THE GRIM GENERATION: 356, 357–cans by Karl Nicholason, Pam Morehouse, Henrik Christiansen; 356–361–photography, John Oldenkamp. THE QUIET REVOLUTION: 363–photographic props, John DeMarco; photography, John Oldenkamp.

VII. Disorder and Therapy. CHROMOSOMES AND CRIME: 370–photography, John Oldenkamp; 371–photography, D. K. Miller, Salk Institute of Biological Studies. THE SHATTERED LANGUAGE OF SCHIZOPHRENIA: 377–collage by Nat Antler. THE NEUROTIC CAT: 382–photography, John Oldenkamp; 384–photography, courtesy of Jules Masserman; 385 387–drawings, John Dawson. THE DREAMS OF FREUD AND JUNG: 388–393–illustrations, Philip Kirkland; 388, 389–photography, John Oldenkamp. INSIDE PSYCHOTHERAPY: 394–illustration, Karl Nicholason. MORALITY IN PSYCHOTHERAPY: 398–illustration, Philip Kirkland. THE LONG WEEKEND: 404–407–photography, John Oldenkamp. ESALEN: WHERE IT'S AT: 366, 410–415–photography, courtesy of Esalen Institute, photographer, Paul B. Herbert; foldout–bread dough construction painting, Joyce Fitzgerald. NEW WAYS IN PSYCHOTHERAPY: 416, 418, 421–423–drawings, John Dawson.

VIII. Social Psychology. WHEN WILL PEOPLE HELP IN A CRISIS?: 428, 429, 431–illustrations, Karl Nicholason. THE SMALL-WORLD PROBLEM: 434–436, 441–photography, John Oldenkamp; 437–440–illustrations, Don Wright. FEAR–FOR YOUR HEALTH: 442–photography, John Oldenkamp. THE PSYCHOLOGY OF POLICE CONFESSIONS, PART I: 447–photography, Cecil Caulfield; 451–photography, John Oldenkamp. TOWARD A MORE PERFECT JUSTICE: 455, 457–photography, Stephen Wells. THE FACE OF THE ENEMY: 459, 462–design, Tom Gould; photography, Stephen Wells. SELF-FULFILLING PROPHECY: 464–466, 468–471–illustrations, Karl Nicholason. ENCOUNTER IN COLOR: 472–478–drawings by Jan, Steve and Sheryl Wright. CONFLICT, CRISIS AND COLLISION: A STUDY OF INTERNATIONAL STABILITY: 480, 482, 486–488–photographs, United Press International Photo; 480–table, permission of JOURNAL OF CONFLICT RESOLUTION; 481, 483, 484–constructions, Robert Hostick; photography, John Oldenkamp; maps reprinted with permission of Rand McNally and Company; photographs from Wide World Photos and United Press International Photo.

CRM BOOKS

David A. Dushkin, *President and Publisher, CRM Books*

Richard L. Roe, *Vice-President, CRM Books, and Director, College Department*
Sales Manager, College Department, Richard M. Connelly
Fulfillment Manager, College Department, Nancy Le Clere
College Staff: Jacqueline McLoughlin, Elaine Kleiss, La Delle Willett, Vicki Hodge

Jean Smith, *Vice-President and Managing Editor, CRM Books*
Consultant, Dr. George S. Reynolds
Editors, Betsy H. Wyckoff, Arlyne Lazerson
Editorial Assistants, Jacquelyn Estrada, Donna L. Taylor

Jo Ann Gilberg, *Vice-President, CRM Books, and Director, Manufacturing and Production*
Production Manager, Eugene G. Schwartz
Production Supervisor, Dolly Mayer
Production Associate, Barbara Blum
Production Staff: Mona F. Drury, Georgene De Laune

Tom Suzuki, *Vice-President, CRM Books, and Director, Art and Design*
Designers, Reynold Hernandez, George Price
Assistant Designer, Donald Young
Art Assistants, Robert Fountain, Catherine Flanders
Art Staff: Joy S. Vorst

Paul Lapolla, *Vice-President, CRM Books, and Director, Psychology Today Book Club*
Assistant, Karen De Laria

Comptroller, Robert Geiserman

Office Manager, Lynn D. Crosby
Assistants, Phyllis J. Trout, Janie Fredericks, Drew Reeves

This book was printed and bound by American Book–Stratford Press, Inc., New York City, New York.